# As Old as the Industry

# 1898–1969

## DAVID G. STYLES

DALTON
WATSON

FINE BOOKS

# AS OLD AS THE INDUSTRY - RILEY

(winner of the Society of Automotive Historians 1983 Cugnot Award
for "The Best Book on Automotive History Published in 1982)
First published in 1982, Second Impression 1992, reprinted 2002

© David G Styles 1982, 1992, 2002

ISBN 1-85443-100-5

## By the same author:-

Riley 75
Sixty Years of Naval Eight/208
Sporting Rileys The Forgotten Champions *(Winner SAH Award of Distinction 1989)*
Alfa Romeo - The Legend Revived
Seventy Five Years On - The Flying Shuftis
Alfa Romeo The Spyder, Alfasud & Alfetta GT
Porsche The Road, Sports & Racing Cars (Editor/co-Author)
Aston Martin & Lagonda Vee-Engined Cars
MGA - The Complete Story *(Winner IAMC Moto Award 1996)*
Riley - A Centennial Celebration
Datsun Z Series - The Complete Story *(Winner IAMC Moto Award 1997)*
Riley - Beyond the Blue Diamond *(Winner IAMC Silver & Bronze Awards 1998)*
Alfa Romeo - Spirit of Milan *(Winner IAMC Silver Award 2000)*
Moto Guzzi - Forza in Movimento *(Winner IAMC Silver Award 2000)*
Volvo 1800 Series - The Complete Story

## British Cataloguing in Publication Data:

A CIP record for this publication is available from the British Library.

Published by Dalton Watson Fine Books Limited
1730 Christopher Drive
Deerfield
Illinois 60015
U. S. A.

TO MY WIFE, ANN.

« رَبِ زِدني علمًا »

قرآن كريم سورة طه الآية ١١٤

"MY LORD, INCREASE MY KNOWLEDGE"
HOLY QUR'AN, SURA TA HA : VERSE 114

This quotation is the motto of the University of Riyadh in Saudi Arabia and seems a fitting tribute to those un-named people in that Kingdom whose help has smoothed the progress of material for this book. It also seems so appropriate to the whole object of this book, whilst bridging, as it does, two very different cultures.

# Contents

## VOLUME I : 'AS MODERN AS THE HOUR' : 1898–1938

# VOLUME II : 'THE PHOENIX RISES' : 1939–1969

Footnote to Acknowledgements for the second impression:–

As this book rejoins its companion, "Sporting Rileys—The Forgotten Champions", I must not forget to acknowledge the powerful support of Riley enthusiasts worldwide, who have kindly bought copies of this book in its earlier form and then written to me with all kinds of snippets of information to help update or correct it. I am also particularly grateful for the continuing support of Keith Marvin, journalist, reviewer, past President of the Society of Automotive Historians and good friend. It was he who nominated "As Old As The Industry" for the S.A.H.'s most coveted prize, the Cugnot Award, which it won in 1983 for the best book on automotive history published in 1982.

DGS

# Acknowledgements

There are so many people to whom I am indebted for their help in my quest to make this book as comprehensive and accurate as possible, that I am hard pressed to list them all, but my thanks go equally to those whose names are not mentioned as to those whose are. All help was significant, but some merits individual mention for the time given over to the contribution of advice and material of various kinds.

This book might never have been published, even with all the material provided and researched, without the help of one man in particular and it is to him that my first acknowledgement must go. That man is Tony Bird, President of the Riley Register, Editor of the Riley Register Bulletin for many years, a Vice-President of the Riley Motor Club and formerly—now retired—Assistant Secretary of the Vintage Sports Car Club. Despite his retired status, he can still be seen marshalling at many motor-sporting events, and has never refused assistance or hesitated to give guidance to those who have asked. Tony's particular contribution to this text has been to undertake the laborious task of proof-reading the whole manuscript, giving good advice throughout, tinged with occasional applications of encouragement, and introducing the text to others for their advice where appropriate.

Arnold Farrar, Honorary Secretary, a director and Vice-President of the Riley Motor Club, a Vice-President of the Riley Register and former employee of Riley (Coventry) Limited is recognised as perhaps the foremost authority on Rileys of all ages. As the former Service Technical Manager of Riley Motors Limited, Arnold is used to dealing with ticklish questions, but some I bowled at him were verging on the ridiculous. Yet he never flinched, never refused and never failed to come up with a constructive answer. He, too, read the manuscript and gave considerable help in a regular flow of comment and advice.

Other people have done specialist research in their own particular sphere of interest in Riley lore and the fruits of their researches have been absorbed into this text. I am thinking in particular of Max Hoather, who gave much advice and material on the earliest of Rileys— the single and twin-cylinder engined vehicles and the earliest four-cylinder cars; Martin Lawrence, for his work on six-cylinder competition cars; David Johnson and David Miller for their researches on Sprite two seaters; Vernon Barker for his help with the later cars, in particular the Briggs-bodied saloons, and his contribution to Appendices 2 and 3. Robin Cameron looked over the drafts of those two appendices and threw in a few more items for good measure. Michael Plastow's research work on patents made Appendix 4 a very much simpler task than it otherwise would have been. My predecessor as Registrar/Historian to the Riley Register, Dr. Tony Birmingham, provided help with a number of illustrations for Volume I.

I must acknowledge, too, the kind permission of Her Majesty's Stationery Office for reproduction of just a few of the Riley patent abridgements. Harold Catt, the RAC's Librarian, and A. J. Mealey of Coventry City Libraries Department both gave invaluable help

in providing access to much early published material for my research. For many, communication has been less than easy, since much correspondence has run between Britain and the Kingdom of Saudi Arabia!

Talking of Saudi Arabia, a great deal of the later text of this book—and in particular the sorting of Appendices 2 and 3—was produced with the invaluable help of a number of people I met in that kingdom. David Crombie of Saudi Medcenter introduced me to John Spencer, Richard Denny and Bill Jones from that Company's AES Wordprocessor Division. Without their help, the use of their facilities in my leisure hours and the aid of Lena Davis, who taught my wife and me to use a wordprocessor (many a midnight hour has been passed working an AES since then), the sorting of those two appendices might have taken over a year—with it it took five days to process the first stage and only a few days more to complete. The page amendments and retypes were also completed by wordprocessor. That shortened the production time from first draft to finished manuscript by an incalculable amount. I shall always be grateful to my friends in AES—and to the President of Saudi Medcenter, Sheikh Mohammed Abdullah Kamel, for permitting the use of his facilities.

The heir to all that was Riley is BL Heritage Limited. The help I have received from that Company's Managing Director, Peter Mitchell, and it's Archivist, Anders Clausager, has been enormous. In particular, they have provided many valuable illustrations and a great deal of material for the text of Volume II.

Whilst all articles reproduced have been individually acknowledged, I would like to express here my gratitude to the editors of those periodicals from which material has been reproduced—and for their assistance in searching for articles I needed in some cases.

Much constructive help was given by the late Eddie Maher and the late Bill Muller from more conversations over many years than I care to count, answering tedious questions and searching for forgotten facts. Both were former senior members of the Riley Team and, until their deaths, were President and Vice-President respectively of the Riley Register. Without much of the information gleaned from them, an already formidable task would have been so daunting I may have given up years ago.

Finally, returning to those un-named people who have made no less significant contributions—and to the Riley Register itself for the inspiration—I must say a very sincere "Thank you".

David G. Styles,
*Riyadh,* 1982.

# Picture Acknowledgements

The author wishes to record his most sincere thanks to the following persons and organisations for supplying illustrative material, without which this volume could not have been produced. Where acknowledgement is not given, the illustration is from the author's collection.

*The Autocar,* pp. 76–77, 86, 120–123, 175–176, 229–230, 235–236, 253, 260, 384, 393 bottom, 400 bottom, 401–404, 440–446, 454–461, 473–476. *Automobile Engineer,* p. 49. BL Heritage, pp. 8, 14, 15, 18 bottom, 25 top and bottom, 31 top and bottom, 35 top and bottom, 37 top and bottom, 41 top and bottom, 43 top and centre, 48 bottom, 50 bottom, 51 top, 52 top, 82, 83 top, 87, 92 centre and bottom, 94 top and bottom, 95 top and bottom, 96 centre, 97 top, 99 top and bottom, 100 bottom, 102 top and bottom, 103, 104 bottom, 126, 127 top, centre and bottom, 128, 130 top, 139 bottom, 148 top and bottom, 150 top, centre and bottom, 151, 152, 168, 169, 180, 181 top and bottom, 183, 186, 188, 190 bottom, 191 top, 196, 197, 199 top, 200, 201 top, 208, 210 bottom, 212 top and bottom, 214 top and bottom, 218 top and bottom, 220 top, 223 top and bottom, 225, 227, 238, 239, 246, 249, 250, 359 all, 360 top, 378, 379 top and bottom, 382, 383, 385, 386 top and bottom, 388 top, 390 top and bottom, 391 top and bottom, 393 top, 394 top and bottom, 396, 397 top and bottom, 398 top and bottom, 399 top and bottom, 400 top, 406, 407, 408, 410 top and bottom, 412 top and bottom, 414 top and bottom, 415, 416 top and bottom, 418 top and bottom. Dr. A. T. Birmingham, pp. 43 bottom, 360 bottom. Chas. K. Bowers and Son, p. 240 top. A. Farrar, Esq., pp. 10, 39, top, centre and bottom, 48 top, 84 bottom, 124, 134–135, 170 top, 171 top and bottom, 189, 191 bottom. M. Gutteridge, Esq., p. 113 top. H. M. Hoather, Esq., pp. 18 top, 30 top and bottom, 33 top. P. Lane, Esq., p. 388 bottom. *The Light Car and Cyclecar,* pp. 50 top, 88–91, 116–119, 231–233, 279–280, 283–284, 289–291. *The Motor,* pp. 27–28, 45–46, 73–75, 78–79, 170 bottom, 177, 228, 255–256, 275–278, 285–288, 381, 438–439, 447–453, 462–472. *The Practical Motorist,* pp. 281–282. *The Riley Record,* pp. 234, 261–262. *Riley Register Bulletin* Editor's Collection, pp. 85, 241, 242, 247, 251. K. Schulz, Esq., p. 238. Air Marshal Sir Frederick Sowrey, p. 20 bottom. The late C. E. Wiles, Esq., pp. 96 bottom, 97 bottom, 104 top, 129 top and bottom, 130 bottom, 198, 244 top and bottom, 245, 254 top and bottom, 258 top.

# Preface

The purpose of this book is to provide a reference to the Riley enthusiast—whether that enthusiast be a long established owner, a newcomer to the breed, or simply a person with an appreciation of the products and respect for the company which probably contributed more to the development of the motor car in its first forty years of existence than any other British firm.

This book concentrates on the products, and some of the spin-offs, of the Riley companies. It makes no attempt to offer a history of the companies, the politics or the competition successes. Dr. Tony Birmingham has already written an excellent history of Riley's company and competition successes and failures, and the late Sidney Haddleton produced a first class maintenance manual for cars of the 1930 to 1956 period. There remains considerable scope for someone claiming greater expertise than I to produce a detailed competition history.

I do not claim this to be a 'complete' product history, neither can it be claimed to be '100% accurate', because much reliance has to be placed on press reports of the day, the sifting of fact as people remember it from 'faction or fiction', catalogues, other people's writings and simply hours of consultation with those one hopes remember. I do claim it to be as complete and accurate as I can make it with the facilities and material available to me. Nonetheless, inaccuracies will inevitably occur and I must rely on constructive comment and advice—and other people's specific knowledge—to minimise those inaccuracies. I cannot say whether there will be any future editions of this book, but the fruits of such constructive comment would of course be incorporated should revisions occur.

I never realised, when I embarked upon this task, just how much would be involved. Now, years on, I feel it was justified, even if only to put into print between one pair of covers the material which has been available, written and unwritten, from many sources over many years. Whilst those sources are diminishing with the years, the material must surely not.

D.G.S.

Footnote to the Preface for the second impression:–

It is ten years since I first published this book—a daunting task for a wholly amateur author/publisher, as I am reminded when reading again William Boddy's review of it in September 1982's issued of Motor Sport. As this book returns to print, now under the Dalton Watson imprint, I am also reminded of the awesome logistical problems of simply transmitting paper between Great Britain and the Kingdom of Saudi Arabia a decade ago, at a time when facsimile machines were not yet in common use and when, in order to maintain a level of awareness of the literary input to their country, the Saudis applied quite rigid controls on importing printed material. It was those problems of logistics which prevented the last sheet of errata being embodied into the original edition. However, they have now been embodied into this second impression, along with several other minor corrections discovered over the years, partly through my own researches but also very much through the kind help of many readers.

DGS

# VOLUME I

# AS MODERN AS THE HOUR
## 1898–1938

# Foreword

David Styles joined the Riley Register in 1961. During his early years of membership, he began to collect and collate all kinds of printed material on the subject of Rileys, simply because he felt there was a serious shortage of data and historical material about the cars that Riley built. Dr. Tony Birmingham's book "The Production and Competition History of Riley Motor Cars" did much to provide the kind of information that Riley owners needed, and was to be commended as the first historical book about Rileys. It gave an excellent social history of the pre-war Company, but David felt it left a number of gaps and that people still had to search for information about the cars. So, having accumulated a healthy personal library and many notes over the years, in March 1970 he became the Riley Register's Registrar/Historian upon the retirement from that office of Dr. Birmingham.

It was the responsibility of the Registrar/Historian to prepare and maintain a Register of Riley Cars. Within a few months of assuming office, David presented to the Committee of the Riley Register a proposal for such a register which was to entail the writing of a new Riley book. Now, at last, here it is, the culmination of years of painstaking research.

Having been privileged to read the draft of this book, I have no hesitation in commending it to all enthusiasts, incorporating as it does much new material which has come to light since the publication of Dr. Birmingham's well known volume. The inclusion of so many new and fascinating illustrations makes this book particularly attractive and I wish it every success.

TONY BIRD,
President, the Riley Register,
Vice-President, the Riley Motor Club.                    *Kingsclere, 1982.*

# Introduction

A glance at the contents page will tell the reader that this book is, as far as possible, laid out in chronological order. Each chapter covers a group of models which fit naturally together from a historical point of view.

Behind each chapter, because that seems to be the most logical place, is a group of data sheets and illustrations relating to the cars to which are referred. The aim is to provide one data sheet for each chassis type including a list of coachwork models offered on that chassis.

Riley models were, for the great majority, available over a number of years and many were available on more than one chassis type. The objective of the illustrations in this book is to provide the reader with a view of every Riley model built, though not necessarily related to particular years. To produce a year-by-year set of illustrations would result in considerable duplication, since the Company's policy was not to produce annual models.

This matter of Riley's model policy has led to a great deal of confusion in the past in the process of identifying the year of a car's design and production. For example, a car may well have been designated a 1936 model whilst having been built in the summer of 1935. This one year is perhaps the worst of the Company's model years, and for that reason merits mention. The first cars for the 1936 season were in fact built in July 1935, but were numbered with the prefix '26' (the first Sprite, for example, being S26S 2429). So a 1936 model can, from the point of view of its date of build and first registration date, be looked upon as a 1935 car, but it's year is really determined by the intentions of the manufacturer. Generally speaking, the model year ran from one annual Olympia Motor Show to the next, October to October, as was the case with most car manufacturers at the time.

For a number of perfectly logical reasons, many cars were built long before their first registration dates. Often the reason was no more complicated than that the car was being used for sales promotion, development or racing and, unless it had to be registered, it was run on general trade plates (plates used by the motor industry and trade for moving vehicles, carrying passengers or goods, from one point to another—this type of licence was withdrawn in the 1960s). In the case of Rileys, it has been suggested, for example, that all of the Brooklands Nine chassis were built before the end of 1930—highly unlikely, but even if they had been, the date of the car stems from the date it was built-up as a car—and the Brooklands was offered for sale well into 1932, with some registrations being as late as 1933.

It is possible that a dealer may have had a car in stock for a year or more after its manufacture and it may well have been manufactured in the middle of its model year. Also, a car may have been legally de-registered after being written off or exported, only to be re-registered after rebuild or re-import. All this must raise the question 'How does one date a car?'. And there is no easy answer!

Logically, if the information is available, the chassis number is the basis of a car's identity and so all should be simple. The second option is to use the registration number as the dating

basis; one which is taken by many to be absolute, until one remembers that most car manufacturers before the Second World War were rather loose with their use of number plates and
vehicle registrations. It was quite common for a registration number to be taken out on a
particular car, the number plates then being used like trade licence plates and switched
periodically from car to car, so that a 1928 car could easily end up with a 1930 registration
number—or worse, it was possible for a 1931 car to have a 1930 registration number, just
because the manufacturer had sold the car as used and with the registration number it had
been the last of a line to use, without being properly documented.

At the end of all that, one has to take into account what was the intention of the manufacturer at the time—because whilst a chassis may have been built in one year, it may not
have been assembled as a car until later and then detailed model improvements have to be
identified as part of the dating process.

Problems arise particularly for owners who are trying to establish eligibility of their cars
under specific date-related rules and definitions, such as the Vintage/Post Vintage Thoroughbred classifications of the Vintage Sports Car Club. In determining the eligibility of a car to be
included in a particular class, the V.S.C.C. is always sympathetic towards doubtful cases and
the benefit of genuine doubt usually falls to the owner. However, that does not mean, as the
foregoing text shows, that the owner of a car can present an appropriate catalogue and his
registration book and simply expect his car to be accepted as 'Vintage' or 'Post Vintage
Thoroughbred'. It could be as much as two years older or two years newer than he thought!

Appendix 1 seeks to take some of the dating doubt out of the situation as far as Rileys are
concerned, but is not absolute and can only be a guide.

Appendices 2 and 3 will give considerable reference value to the reader who seeks to
identify a particular car. They are not intended to be 'car-spotters guides', but they form a
register of known Rileys by listing the cars in two ways, by registration number in Appendix 2
and by chassis number in Appendix 3.

The remaining Appendices are aimed at giving the reader other useful information dealing
with Riley patents, car models available, the members of the Riley family with their companies and trade names, the Riley clubs and finally a list of some of the notable Riley competition successes.

Finally, to the title of this book. "As Old as the Industry" was the motto adopted in 1921
to describe the products of Riley (Coventry) Limited. Before that, the 17/30 and the four-
cylinder 10 h.p. cars were heralded with the motto "The King of Cars", a phrase which
continued in use after the Great War, but was then dropped in favour of what was clearly
seen as a more appropriate phrase. In 1925, the second half of the now well-known motto
was added: "As Modern as the Hour" (the title of the first volume). Other phrases were used
as descriptive bye-lines, such as "The Most Successful Car in the World" (the bold title of the
1934 catalogue) and "Magnificent Motoring" (a phrase not generally associated with the
pre-war Company), but only the one was ever adopted as part of the corporate badge and it
is that which was chosen as the title for a book which was to cover the whole product history
of Riley.

This then was the product which always was "As Old as the Industry—As Modern as the
Hour". Long may the memory live of "The Most Successful Car in the World".

D.G.S.

# CHAPTER ONE

# As Old as the Industry—
# the Riley Story in Brief

Weaving in the 1870s was heavily dependent upon cottage industry and child labour. When William Riley assumed the management responsibility of the family weaving business in 1870, one of the first things he had to consider was the effect of the Education Act upon that child labour. Further Education Acts up to 1880 created a situation where juvenile labour was virtually unavailable and the cost of adult labour began to have a telling effect on the economics of the weaving industry in Coventry.

As weaving began to decline, so Riley began to search for business alternatives and in 1890, having had some experience of things mechanical through his involvement with weaving machinery, he bought out the interests of Bonnick and Company. Bonnick was a cycle manufacturer and, under the careful management of William Riley, soon developed into a flourishing business—so much so that, on 23 May 1896, the Riley Cycle Company Limited was formed in King Street, Coventry. So began a period of just over 40 years in which the Riley family imprinted their name indelibly in the annals of motoring history.

Innovators from the start, Riley made the first constant-mesh gearbox, the first detachable wheels and numerous other 'firsts'. Riley wheels were fitted to Austro-Daimler, Hispano-Suiza, Mercedes, Napier, Rolls-Royce and many other fine cars, including the record-breaking 'Blitzen Benz'. Riley's own participation in motor sport began as early as 1899 with motor tricycles, progressing through the medium of motor bicycles and tricars to motor cars—ultimately the famous 9 h.p., six cylinder and $1\frac{1}{2}$ litre models. The most significant Riley victory must have been at Le Mans in 1934 when Rileys took 2nd, 3rd, 5th, 6th, 12th and 13th places overall—taking with them the 1500 cc. and 1100 cc. classes, the team prize and the Rudge-Whitworth Cup. Miss Dorothy Champney and Mrs Kay Petre also put up the fastest drive ever achieved by women drivers at Le....... As if to round off that phenomenal achievement, all six cars were then driv.......heir own power!

Victor, the eldest of William ............once observed that he remembered as a schoolboy, long before the first Ri.........built, seeing in his father's workshop what he described as a huge clockspring attached to a bicycle. The objective of this device was that, when wound, the spring would aid the rider of the cycle up hills, and subsequent descents would wind up the spring again. The value of mechanical propulsion was already realised!

Riley's first vehicles sold were motor bicycles, tricycles and quadricycles. The first publicly exhibited mechanically propelled Riley was a quadricycle, which was exhibited as the 'Royal Riley' quadricycle at the National Cycle Show in November 1899 at Crystal Palace. The vehicle had a fore-carriage in which the passenger rode and was powered by a $2\frac{1}{4}$ h.p. engine.

It is interesting to note that in 1899 Robert Crossley established the first track record with

*THAT FIRST RILEY CAR—1898.*

*Much has already been said and written about Percy Riley's first car—and even though this book deals with the products of the Riley companies, rather than private ventures, it would not be appropriate to leave it out, since it forms such a significant cornerstone to everything the Riley family did later.*

*Design on this first car started in 1893 and Percy started building it in 1896, completing the task in 1898. It says a great deal for the ingenuity and productive skill of the man himself that Percy Riley actually built the whole car in his own workshop. That much is now common knowledge.*

*The car was of the dog-cart concept and featured a front-mounted engine in a very sturdy frame. The engine was a single-cylinder type, of about 2¼ h.p. and was fitted with mechanically-operated valve gear   the first car ever to be so equipped.*

*Drive was transmitted to the rear wheels by means of a leather belt and the hand-operated throttle projected through the engine cover, as did the valve-lifter which was fitted to facilitate easier starting.*

*Suspension was orthodox dog-cart and the other creature comforts of this earliest of Rileys included seating for two, metal mudguards, two acetylene lamps fitted to the bulkhead and steering by wheel rather than tiller which was the favoured method by many of the early car-makers.*

*Tyres were initially solid on wheels which were not yet to be detachable   but that and many other features were all to be part of the ineradicable hallmark Riley was to put upon the British motor industry.*

*"As Old as the Industry—As Modern as the Hour"—Riley.*

a Riley motor tricycle. Later, in the early 1900s H. Rignold established a very healthy reputation for himself racing Riley motor-bicycles; and Allan Riley, Rignold and Burden collected many competition awards for the Company.

In 1903, Percy Riley set up the Riley Engine Company and produced a range of three engines of $2\frac{1}{4}$, 3 and $3\frac{1}{2}$ horsepower, the latter being available air or water cooled. All of these engines featured the Riley patent valve gear, incorporating a single cam and two rockers operating the inlet and exhaust valves, and providing valve overlap. Because public opinion was favouring motor bicycles at that time, Riley concentrated production in this direction, fitting their own engines instead of the Motor Manufacturing Company unit which had been used earlier.

Seeing the market expansion, the Company then widened its market appeal by adding the $3\frac{1}{2}$ h.p. fore-car, and later a $4\frac{1}{2}$ h.p. to the product range. The $4\frac{1}{2}$ h.p. model proved to be the last Riley to be built with the diamond shaped cycle frame, the next step being to produce the tricar range using lateral frames. Whilst the lateral frame marked the real change of fore-car to tricar some Riley publicity referred to the motor tricycle based fore-car as a tricar.

The 6 h.p. tricar brought with it the patent three-speed constant-mesh gearbox and was quickly followed by the 9 h.p. V-twin, which consisted of two $4\frac{1}{2}$ h.p. cylinders mounted on the 6 h.p. crankcase. The 9 h.p. model was so successful that it regularly swept the board in competition at the hands of Victor Riley, J. Browning and Stanley Riley. Its only real competition was considered to be the contemporary Lagonda and Singer machines, the latter being fitted with a Riley engine. With this success, Riley withdrew from the manufacture of motor-cycles and concentrated its energies on the production of tricars, supplementing the 6 h.p. and 9 h.p. models with a smaller and less costly 5 h.p. model designed by Stanley Riley. The 5 h.p. proved to be both a commercial and competition success, selling at £85 and winning many events in the hands of its designer.

The year 1906 brought the 9 h.p. V-twin four wheeled car, employing a duplex tubular frame. This was the first car in the world to be fitted with detachable wire wheels as standard equipment. It was developed from a design of 1905 and more than justified the Company's reputation with consistent competition successes.

Introduced in 1907 was an entirely new design of car, the 12/18 h.p. V-twin which, like its forebears, rapidly amassed a long list of successes including the winning of the Aston Hill Climb in 1908, a class win at the same event in 1909, class wins in the 1908 and 1909 Scot  n Trials, the 1909 Irish Trials and an outright win of the Ballinaslaughter Hill Climb in 1909.

By 1911, the Company had ceased making pedal cycles and was concentrating its efforts entirely on the production of motor cars. Competition successes continued to mount and production was concentrated on the 10 h.p. and 12/18 h.p. models. The 10 h.p. model was another of Stanley Riley's designs and his Speed Model, driven by himself, won its class in the Scottish Trials of 1909.

1913 brought with it the 17/30 h.p. four cylinder double sleeve valve design, which included among its features a gearbox with all helical gears. The sleeve-valve engine was replaced with a more orthodox side-valve engine before the car was put into production and only a few models were built before 1914, since that year brought with it the "War to end all wars".

Throughout the period of the 1914–18 War, Percy Riley devoted the whole resources of the Riley Engine Company to the manufacture of the tools of war, refusing to accept any profit in respect of contracts for the Ministry of Munitions. It was during this time that he

*Riley in its heyday—the 1932 Season's models on show at Olympia in October 1931. On the stand
can be seen: the 9 h.p. Coupe (to be called the Ascot in the next year), the 9 h.p. Tourer, the
Monaco, the Biarritz, the Gamecock (before acquiring the characteristic recessed running
boards), the Stelvio, the Alpine Tourer and the Alpine Saloon.*

designed a most ingenious aircraft engine, with the cylinders placed radially round the crankshaft, but lying in line with the crankshaft so as to reduce the frontal area of the engine, drag
being the plague of radial engines.

Production of the 17/30 h.p. continued, with a revised radiator and new bodywork
design, for a short period after the war, but for the 1919 Olympia Motor Show Riley introduced a new chassis, the Eleven, employing a side valve four cylinder engine of 10.8 h.p. and
introducing on it the now famous blue Riley diamond radiator badge.

The Sports Two Seater, introduced in 1922, was soon to re-establish the Company's
sporting reputation. Also in 1922, H. Anderson won a Gold Medal in the Scottish Trials in a
Riley Eleven, carrying the full complement of four people in the car and walking off (or
rather, driving off) with the Class Award.

In 1923, the Society of Motor Manufacturers and Traders (S.M.M. & T.) banned its
members from taking part in competitions, but Riley competition successes continued to be
amassed by private entrants. By the mid-1920's, the Riley range was based on two chassis—
the 10.8 h.p. Eleven Forty Sports models and the 11.9 h.p. Twelve models. Coachwork

options were varied, ranging from modestly priced saloons and touring cars to the elegant Coupe-de-Ville and Sedanca-de-Ville models; and from the Eleven-Forty Two Seat Sports Redwinger to the short-lived 11/50/65 supercharged sports introduced for 1927.

The success of these models laid the perfect foundation for what was perhaps Riley's greatest success—both in market popularity and competition achievements—the range that followed.

In 1926, the Company introduced a fabric-bodied four seat saloon powered by the now immortal 9 h.p. engine. That car was the first Monaco and was quickly joined in the range by the San Remo saloon and two open models. Almost as soon as these new models arrived on the scene, interest was shown in the engine by J. G. Parry-Thomas, who joined forces with Reid Railton to produce an 1100 cc. racing chassis which Railton drove to undreamed-of success at Brooklands. Later, after Thompson and Taylor had developed the chassis, Riley put into production the 9 h.p. Speed Model, which quickly became a legend as the Brooklands Nine. It was a Brooklands Nine which won the Rudge Whitworth Cup at Le Mans in 1934.

The 9 h.p. Monaco was the model produced in greatest numbers by Riley and it was soon joined by such attractive and advanced cars as the Kestrel, the Lynx, the Lincock. At the same time, proprietary coach-builders offered the products of their workmanship on Riley chassis; some, such as the Trinity by Meredith Coachcraft and the March Special by Kevill-Davies and March, being offered in the Riley catalogue through the Riley dealer network. Then came the six-cylinder engined models, available in 12 h.p. and 14 h.p. forms with a similar range of body designs to the Nines. The whole Riley range enjoyed a high reputation for reliability, performance and comfort. Competition successes were being amassed almost daily by such prominent names as Ashby, Dixon, Eyston, Gillow, Whitcroft and many more—by now driving 9 h.p. and six-cylinder engined cars.

For the 1935 Season, the 1½ Litre four-cylinder model was announced, with the introduction of newly-styled Falcon, Kestrel and Lynx models. The Nine continued with the Monaco, Kestrel, Lynx and Imp Two-Seater. The six-cylinder MPH continued until the introduction of the Sprite 1½ Litre, which was a new sports car design based upon an improvement of the same chassis. 1935 saw Freddie Dixon win the Ulster T.T. in a 1½ Litre Riley, a success he was to repeat in 1936. Also in 1936 Dixon won the B.R.D.C. '500' at Brooklands at the then phenomenal speed of 116.86 m.p.h., with a 2 litre six-cylinder Riley; he was followed into second place by the 4½ litre Bentley-engined Pacey-Hassan Special. Dixon's other Riley achievements included the 1934 B.R.D.C. Gold Star for track racing and a Brooklands 130 m.p.h. Badge achieved with a Riley in 1935.

The last three years, 1935–1938, of Riley (Coventry) Limited's existence brought many new innovations, including the Eight-Ninety V 8 model, the Big Four 2½ Litre and the use of a three-speed synchromesh gearbox with Borg-Warner dual overdrive. The wide range of Riley models available with the even wider variety of customer options was to be a major feature in the undoing of the Company. In September 1938, Riley (Coventry) Limited finally lost its battle for survival as an independent company and was sold to Lord Nuffield, it having made a financial loss from which recovery was not possible.

No review of Riley's history would be complete without mention of the late Raymond Mays and E.R.A., since Mays created that immortal racing breed out the famous "White Riley". The White Riley was a six-cylinder racing chassis—one of the Riley entry for the 1933 T.T.—fitted with a supercharger and was the development vehicle for the E.R.A. line of

enormously successful racing machines. The Riley Company made a direct contribution to that success, since English Racing Automobiles chose to use a much-modified version of the Riley six-cylinder engine.

Among the less well-known Riley products were railcars for South Africa and Tasmania, built between 1904 and 1907, engines for cross-country vehicles built in the same period, a series of electricity generators built in the early post World War I period and a highly successful range of 9 h.p. and six-cylinder marine engines in the early 1930s.

Through their forty years as a family business, the Riley companies worked tirelessly producing vehicles aimed at giving customer satisfaction. The factory sponsored competition successes were merely a means to that end, and the brothers Victor, Allan, Percy, Stanley and Cecil Riley will surely be remembered for their consistent achievement of success in manufacturing high quality moderately priced vehicles always 'As Old as the Industry—as Modern as the Hour'. To that achievement should be added one of the most colourful and consistent records of success in the many fields of motor sport ever established by the products of a single company in Britain or elsewhere.

# CHAPTER TWO

# The First Twenty Years—1898–1918

Riley's early products are a rather odd mixture of two, three and four wheeled vehicles.

Very little technical information now exists on Riley pedal cycles and despite attempts to obtain early literature, or locate an example, little has been unearthed. However the one illustration available suggests the Riley pedal cycle to have been quite a substantial machine and would have probably been completely at home alongside much later bicycles built even after the 1939/45 war.

Pedal cycles were not however enough for the innovative mind of Percy Riley and after he had built his first four wheeled motor car—only the second car in Coventry—he turned his attention to the development of motor bicycles.

The exercise of designing that motor car was far from wasted, despite the fact that William Riley would under no circumstances agree to its production, or the production of anything like it. It was firmly stressed that the Riley Cycle Company Limited was in the bicycle business and it was some years before William Riley did ultimately concede to the manufacture of motor cars in any form. But once Percy Riley had made his first engine, into which he designed the first ever mechanically operated inlet valve, he was determined to develop its application, seeing great advantages in motorised transport.

In 1903 Riley motor cycles were established in the market place and in that year the Riley Engine Company was established in Cook Street, Coventry under the management of Percy Riley. The initial product was a 3 h.p. single cylinder air cooled engine and it featured the mechanical inlet valve. The mechanically operated inlet valve was the subject of a patent application by the Benz Company in Germany, but Percy Riley's priority on the design foiled their application and probably saved the British motor industry millions of pounds in royalties and subsequent technical development.

In the early days of Riley motor bicycles, engines manufactured by Minerva, C.C.C. & the Motor Manufacturing Company were used, but these were quickly succeeded by Riley's own engine designs.

Numerous competition successes were achieved in those early days, resulting from which the product's reliability was continuously improved. It is worthy of note at this point that Percy Riley was really not very interested in competition, a view which he maintained throughout his life. His only real concern was the customer and the need to provide a reliable, safe and comfortable vehicle. As the prosperity of the Riley company grew, so Percy Riley was able to expand his thinking beyond motor bicycles and into the sphere of tricars. Throughout 1902 a series of experiments resulted in the first commercially successful tricar and by 1904 tricars had become the mainstay of the Company's production.

Motor cycle production continued however, and the Riley Engine Company was now making three sizes of engines—$2\frac{1}{4}$ h.p., 3 h.p. and $3\frac{1}{2}$ h.p. The larger engine was available in air or water cooled forms and was basically intended for use to power tricars.

**A.** *St. Nicholas Works (original works of William Riley & Son, also Riley Cycle Co.).
Note the 3 wide windows, top left, reminiscent of the old Trimming and Weaving
Trades of Coventry.* **B.** *The first Riley Car, 1898.* **C.** *The engine
of the first Riley car, 1898.* **D.** *Riley Motor Tricycle, 1899.*

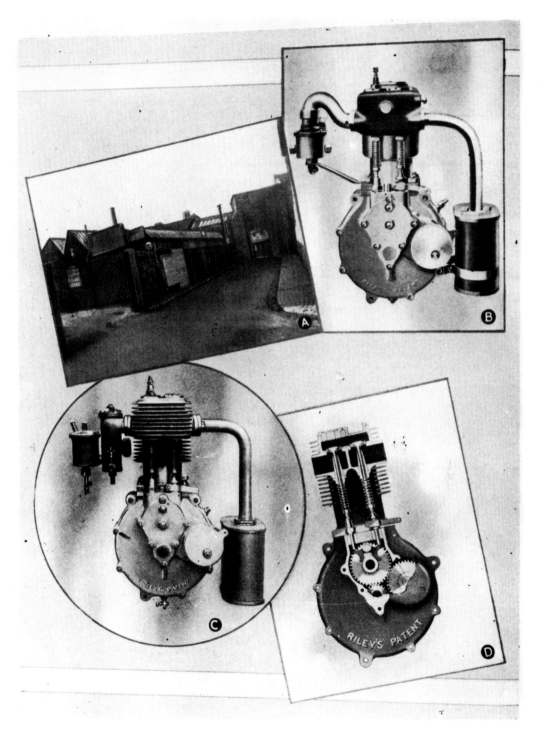

**A.** *Cook Street Works (original works of the Riley Engine Co.).* **B. C.** & **D.** *Illustrations of Riley engines (showing patent valve gear), 1903.*

As the tricar developed so did new engines and in 1904 a new 4½ h.p. single cylinder water cooled engine was produced, having a bore of 86 mm. and stroke of 89 mm. In 1905 there were 4 tricars offered to the market—the 4 h.p. air cooled version at 70 guineas; the 4½ h.p. water cooled engine model at 85 guineas; the 6 h.p. model at 120 guineas and the 9 h.p. at 130 guineas.

The 6 h.p. and 9 h.p. engines were of V-twin design, the 9 h.p. being simply two 4½ h.p. cylinder barrels mounted on a 6 h.p. crankcase. Drive was transmitted on these models through a three forward speed and 1 reverse gearbox with chain drive to the rear wheel.

The gearbox used in these tricars was the subject of one of Percy Riley's patents, in that it had constant-mesh gears—another Riley first.

In competitions Riley tricars fared well and as has already been said the only real rivals to Riley were Lagonda and Singer, the latter being fitted with a Riley engine. In the 1905 Auto Cycle Club tricar trials a 9 h.p. Riley was awarded a gold medal for travelling 125 miles on 2¾ gallons of petrol—over 45 miles per gallon. The same car also recorded fastest time in the Dashwood Hill Climb. Other A.C.C. successes included a first class award in the six-day trial and a silver medal in the penalty run. Riley successes were legion in trials, hill climbs and reliability runs between 1905 and 1907.

1907 was the year of the last word in Riley tricars. The model produced that year was a 9 h.p. machine with fully enclosed engine and much improved seating for both driver and passenger. The same year competition successes continued, among them being first place in the S.M.C. Reliability Trial and an outstanding lead in the Hertfordshire group M.C. Consumption Trial when a 9 h.p. tricar covered 50 miles on 7 pints of fuel.

While the Company was manufacturing motor bicycles and tricars, it also ventured into more commercial applications of its engine designs and of particular note are the inspection and maintenance trolleys built for the South African Railways. The trolleys were powered by 4½ h.p. single cylinder water cooled engines and used a 2 speed gearbox with the addition of a power take off drive used to power track laying tools. Two versions were built, one having an upholstered seat and being used for long range inspection, the other pulling a trailer which was fitted with a dynamo.

In the same period the Indian Government had bought a number of special vehicles for use in rough country which were built by the Singer Company—these too were equipped with Riley engines and gearboxes.

The durability of the Riley engine was acknowledged still further when South African Railways bought more trolleys, this time powered by the V-twin engine and fitted with a 3 speed gearbox. When Stanley Riley visited South Africa in 1912, the original Riley trolleys were still in regular use.

When finally the Riley Engine Company moved into larger works in the summer of 1906, they built a lorry in their own works, using Riley mechanical components, and transported loads of up to 2 tons into the new plant. Such was the quality of the product which established the Riley name in those early days.

In 1906, the new V-twin 9 h.p. car was announced, built on a duplex frame and introducing for the first time in the world detachable wire wheels as standard equipment. Also that year, the company brought another new model on to the market, the 12/18 h.p. V-twin which was a completely new design.

The 10 h.p., designed by Stanley Riley, and the 12/18 h.p. models were the basis of Riley production when pedal cycles were discontinued in 1911 to make way for more cars to be

built in the King Street works in Coventry. In March 1912 The Riley Cycle Company Ltd changed its name and was registered as Riley (Coventry) Limited.

1912 and 1913 saw the continuing success of the 10 h.p. and 12/18 h.p. models. With minor modifications, they continued in production though during 1913, Riley (Coventry) Ltd decided to discontinue making motor cars because detachable wheels were making more money. No less than 183 manufacturers were buying Riley detachable wheels, so the Riley brothers set up the Riley Motor Manufacturing Company to continue car production in a new factory at Aldbourne Road, Coventry, next to the works of the Riley Engine Company.

The last major design before the Great War was introduced at the 1913 Motor Show. It was the 17/30 h.p. and it represented a completely new concept of design. It was a larger car than Riley had produced before and it featured, for the first time in a Riley car, a four cylinder in-line engine. Unfortunately, the 17/30 h.p. was not produced for very long and no survivors are known to exist. This car was of 3 litres engine capacity and was first produced with a 3 speed gearbox, though the forerunner of the 'Silent Third' 4-speed gearbox was fitted by 1914.

With the onset of World War I, Riley production capacity turned to the tools of war. It was to be 1919 before more Riley cars were built. The first post-war cars were built from pre-war stock, resulting in further production of the 17/30 h.p., until the 1921 horsepower tax legislation made it more difficult to sell and eventually killed it off.

Stanley Riley also designed another 10 h.p. car, just after the introduction of the 17/30 h.p. It too had a four cylinder in-line engine, but of only 1096 cc., with three main bearings. It used a four speed gearbox, an enclosed propeller shaft and bevel gear final drive. Unfortunately it was introduced at a time when people were more concerned with the possible consequences of war than what car to buy for next year. It never had a chance to establish its own reputation, for it never went into serious production.

The whole of Riley production capacity during the Great War was devoted to war work for the Ministry of Munitions. The Company took no profit for this work, producing all it did at cost. The Riley brothers volunteered their services to the armed forces but Victor, Allan, Percy and Stanley were directed to remain at the works in Coventry, where their efforts were considered better channelled. Cecil, the youngest, did join the army however, initially as a despatch rider. Later, commissioned in the field, he joined the Royal Flying Corps, firstly as an observer and ultimately as a pilot.

Captain Riley returned from the Royal Air Force to the Drawing Office of the Riley Engine Company, then became Sales Manager of Riley (Coventry) Limited in 1920. He was later to take up the Company's export drive in West Africa.

Here, then, are the first products of a company which quickly proved its worth by being among the most fertile innovators in its industry.

*2¼ h.p. de Dion type engine of the 1899 Royal Riley Tricycle*

*The 1899 Royal Riley Quadricycle*

SPECIFICATIONS

| | |
|---|---|
| MODEL | **Royal Riley Quadricycle** *Year:* 1899 |

CHASSIS    Trapezoid frame with rear lateral A frame. Longitudinal parallel tubes, pivoted at rear, support forecarriage on $\frac{1}{2}$ elliptic springs.
*Frame Size:* 22 in.
*Track:* Front 2 ft. $11\frac{1}{4}$ in. Rear 2 ft $11\frac{1}{4}$ in.
*Type of Wheels:* Dunlop tangentially spoked wire.
*Tyres:* Front size 26 × 2 in. Rear size 26 × $2\frac{1}{2}$ in.
*Braking System:* Spoon brakes at front and band brake at rear, operated from handle-bar-mounted levers.

TRANSMISSION    *Clutch Type:* None—freewheel in pedal chainwheel.
*Gearbox Type:* Open spur and wheel in constant mesh.
*Gear Selecting Mechanism:* None—constant drive.
*Final Drive Type:* Pedal/chain drive assisting spur & wheel.
*Final Drive Ratio:* 8: 1 (10: 80)

ENGINE    *Engine Type:* Minerva de Dion Type.
*H.P. Rating:* 2.25
*Cubic Capacity:* 239.5 cc.
*Number of Cylinders:* 1
*Firing Order:* 1
*Bore:* 66 mm.
*Stroke:* 70 mm.
*Cylinder Type:* Air-cooled bolt-on with horizontal spark plug.
*Valve Gear:* Automatic inlet, mechanical exhaust.
*Number of Main Bearings:* 2
*Cooling System:* Air.
*Type of Ignition:* Coil and mechanical contact maker.
*Number, Make and Type of Carburetters:* None, direct feed via vapour tube from tank.
*Type of Inlet Manifold:* Direct feed tube.
*Type of Exhaust Manifold:* Fabricated bolt-on.
*Location of Fuel Tank:* Rear, attached to seat tube and A frame.
*Capacity of Fuel Tank:* $1\frac{1}{2}$ gallons.
*Method of Fuel Feed:* Gravity.

MODELS AVAILABLE    Royal Riley Quadricycle—frame sizes variable to order from 21 in. to 23 in.

| | |
|---|---|
| MODEL | **Royal Riley Tricycle** *Year:* 1899 |

CHASSIS    Trapezoid frame with rear lateral A frame supporting engine, fuel tank and rear drive.
*Wheelbase:* 3 ft. 7 in.
*Frame size:* 22 in.
*Track:* Rear 2 ft. $11\frac{1}{4}$ in.
*Type of Wheels:* Dunlop tangentially spoked wire.
*Tyres:* Front size 26 × $2\frac{1}{2}$ in. Rear size 26 × 3 in.
*Braking System:* Spoon brake at front and band brake at rear, operated from handle-bar-mounted levers.

TRANSMISSION    *Clutch Type:* None—freewheel in pedal chainwheel.
*Gearbox Type:* Open spur and wheel in constant mesh.
*Gear Selecting Mechanism:* None—constant drive.
*Final Drive Type:* Pedal/chain drive assisting spur & wheel.
*Final Drive Ratio:* 8: 1 (10: 80)

ENGINE    *Engine Type:* Minerva de Dion Type.
*H.P. rating:* 2.25
*Cubic Capacity:* 239.5 cc.
*Number of Cylinders:* 1
*Firing Order:* 1
*Bore:* 66 mm.

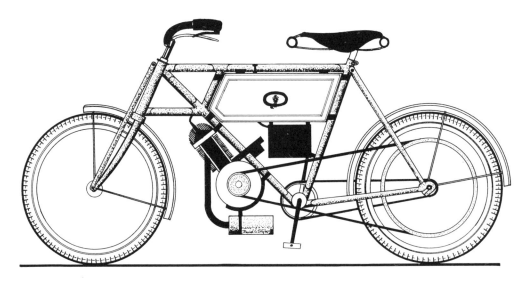

*1902/3 Riley 1½ h.p./3 h.p. Motor Bicycle*

*1903 3 h.p. air-cooled Tri-car with link-belt drive*

*Stroke:* 70 mm.
*Cylinder Type:* Air-cooled bolt-on with horizontal spark plug.
*Valve Gear:* Automatic inlet, mechanical exhaust.
*Number of Main Bearings:* 2
*Cooling System:* Air.
*Type of Ignition:* Trembler coil and mechanical contact maker.
*Number, Make and Type of Carburetters:* None, direct feed via vapour tube from tank.
*Type of Inlet Manifold:* Direct feed tube.
*Type of Exhaust Manifold:* Fabricated bolt-on.
*Location of Fuel Tank:* Rear, attached to seat tube and A frame.
*Capacity of Fuel Tank:* 1½ gallons.
*Method of Fuel Feed:* Gravity.

MODELS AVAILABLE　Royal Riley Tricycle—frame sizes variable to order from 21 in. to 23 in.

MODEL　　**Royal Riley Quadricycle**　　*Year:* 1901

CHASSIS　　Trapezoid frame with rear lateral A frame. Longitudinal parallel tubes, pivoted at rear, support forecarriage on ½ elliptic springs.
*Frame size:* 23 in.
*Track:* Front 3 ft. 0 in. Rear 2 ft. 11¼ in.
*Type of Wheels:* Dunlop tangentially spoked wire.
*Tyres:* Front Size 26 × 2½ in. Rear Size 26 × 3 in.
*Braking System:* Block brakes at front and band brake at rear, operated from handle-bar-mounted levers.

TRANSMISSION　　*Clutch Type:* Dog clutch, cable operated.
*Gearbox Type:* Sliding dog on spur wheel with freewheel on pedal chainwheel.
*Gear Selecting Mechanism:* Clutch lever on frame, cable operated.
*Final Drive Type:* Spur & wheel with pedal assistance.
*Final Drive Ratio:* 8 : 1 (10 : 80)

ENGINE　　*Engine Type:* C.C.C. 2¾ h.p.
*H.P. Rating:* 2.75
*Cubic Capacity:* 269.4 cc.
*Number of Cylinders:* 1
*Firing Order:* 1
*Bore:* 70 mm.
*Stroke:* 70 mm.
*Cylinder Type:* Air-cooled bolt-on with side-mounted spark plug.
*Valve Gear:* Automatic inlet, mechanical exhaust.
*Number of Main Bearings:* 2
*Cooling System:* Air.
*Type of Ignition:* Trembler coil and mechanical contact maker.
*Number, Make and Type of Carburetters:* Longuemare horizontal.
*Type of Inlet Manifold:* Fabricated copper tubular.
*Type of Exhaust Manifold:* Fabricated bolt-on.
*Location of Fuel Tank:* Rear, attached to seat tube and A frame.
*Capacity of Fuel Tank:* 1½ gallons.
*Method of Fuel Feed:* Gravity.

MODELS AVAILABLE　Royal Riley Quadricycle—frame sizes variable to order from 21 in. to 23 in.

MODEL　　**1½ H.P. Motor Bicycle ("Moto Bi")**　　*Year:* 1902–3

CHASSIS　　Trapezoid bicycle frame with engine attached to forward down-tube.
*Frame Size:* 22 in.
*Type of Wheels:* Dunlop tangentially spoked wire.
*Tyres:* Front Size: 26 × 2 in. Rear Size: 26 × 2 in.
*Braking System:* Block brake at front and band brake at rear, operated from handlebar-mounted levers.

TRANSMISSION          *Clutch Type:* None.
                      *Gearbox Type:* None—freewheel in rear hub for pedal drive.
                      *Gear Selecting Mechanism:* None.
                      *Final Drive Type:* Link-belt drive with pedal assistance.
                      *Final Drive Ratio:* 8:1

ENGINE                *Engine Type:* Minerva 1½ h.p.
                      *H.P. Rating:* 1.5
                      *Cubic Capacity:* 232.0 cc.
                      *Number of Cylinders:* 1
                      *Firing Order:* 1
                      *Bore:* 65 mm.
                      *Stroke:* 70 mm.
                      *Cylinder Type:* Air-cooled bolt-on with offset spark plug.
                      *Valve Gear:* Automatic inlet, mechanical exhaust.
                      *Number of Main Bearings:* 2
                      *Cooling System:* Air.
                      *Type of Ignition:* Trembler coil and mechanical contact maker.
                      *Number, Make and Type of Carburetters:* Longuemare horizontal.
                      *Type of Inlet Manifold:* Fabricated copper tubular.
                      *Type of Exhaust Manifold:* Fabricated bolt-on.
                      *Location of Fuel Tank:* Horizontally suspended under frame top tube.
                      *Capacity of Fuel Tank:* 2 gallons.
                      *Method of Fuel Feed:* Gravity.

MODELS AVAILABLE      Riley 1½ h.p. 'Moto Bi' Frame sizes variable to order from 21 in. to 23 in.


MODEL                 **2¼ H.P. Motor Bicycle ("Moto Bi")**                    *Year:* 1903–4

CHASSIS               Trapezoid bicycle frame with twin horizontal main tubes and twin support tubes
                      adjacent to steering tube. Engine attached to forward down-tube and bottom bracket.
                      *Frame Size:* 22 in.
                      *Type of Wheels:* Dunlop tangentially spoked wire.
                      *Tyres:* Front Size: 26 × 2 in. Rear Size: 26 × 2 in.
                      *Braking System:* Front rim and Riley-Bowden rear rim, operated from handlebar-
                      mounted levers.

TRANSMISSION          *Clutch Type:* Riley Motor Clutch Hub on later models (clutch mounted on engine
                      drive pulley).
                      *Gearbox Type:* None—freewheel in rear hub for pedal drive.
                      *Gear Selecting Mechanism:* None.
                      *Final Drive Type:* Lycett-Rawido link belt with pedal assistance.
                      *Final Drive Ratio:* 8:1

ENGINE                *Engine Type:* Riley 2¼ h.p.
                      *H.P. Rating:* 2.25
                      *Cubic Capacity:* 269.4 cc.
                      *Number of Cylinders:* 1
                      *Firing Order:* 1
                      *Bore:* 70 mm.
                      *Stroke:* 70 mm.
                      *Cylinder Type:* Air-cooled bolt-on with offset spark plug.
                      *Valve Gear:* Riley mechanical inlet and exhaust.
                      *Number of Main Bearings:* 2
                      *Cooling System:* Air.
                      *Type of Ignition:* Trembler coil with mechanical contact maker.
                      *Number, Make and Type of Carburetters:* Longuemare updraught.
                      *Type of Inlet Manifold:* Fabricated copper tubular.
                      *Type of Exhaust Manifold:* Fabricated bolt-on.
                      *Location of Fuel Tank:* Horizontally suspended under frame top tube.
                      *Capacity of Fuel Tank:* 2 gallons.
                      *Method of Fuel Feed:* Gravity.

MODELS AVAILABLE      Riley 2¼ h.p. 'Moto Bi' Frame sizes variable to order from 20 in. to 23 in.
                      Price, as described: 42 Guineas.

MODEL           **3 H.P. Motor Bicycle ("Moto Bi")**         *Year:* 1903–4

CHASSIS      Trapezoid bicycle frame with twin horizontal main tubes and twin support tubes adjacent to steering tube. Engine attached to forward down-tube and bottom bracket.
*Frame Size:* 23 in.
*Type of Wheels:* Dunlop tangentially spoked wire.
*Tyres:* Front Size: 28 × 2 in. Rear Size: 28 × 2 in.
*Braking System:* Front rim and Riley-Bowden rear rim, operated from handlebar-mounted levers.

TRANSMISSION    *Clutch Type:* Riley Motor Clutch Hub on later models (clutch mounted on engine drive pulley).
*Gearbox Type:* None—freewheel in rear hub for pedal drive.
*Gear Selecting Mechanism:* None.
*Final Drive Type:* Lycett-Rawido link belt with pedal assistance.
*Final Drive Ratio:* 8: 1

ENGINE        *Engine Type:* Riley 3 h.p.
*H.P. Rating:* 3.00
*Cubic Capacity:* 402.12 cc.
*Number of Cylinders:* 1
*Firing Order:* 1
*Bore:* 80 mm.
*Stroke:* 80 mm.
*Cylinder Type:* Air-cooled bolt-on with offset spark plug.
*Valve Gear:* Riley mechanical inlet and exhaust.
*Number of Main Bearings:* 2
*Cooling System:* Air.
*Type of Ignition:* Coil and mechanical contact maker.
*Number, Make and Type of Carburetters:* Longuemare updraught.
*Type of Inlet Manifold:* Fabricated copper tubular.
*Type of Exhaust Manifold:* Fabricated bolt-on.
*Location of Fuel Tank:* Horizontally suspended under frame top tube.
*Capacity of Fuel Tank:* 2 gallons.
*Method of Fuel Feed:* Gravity.

MODELS AVAILABLE  Riley 3 h.p. 'Moto Bi' Frame sizes variable to order from 21 in. to 23 in.
Price, as described: 46 Guineas.

MODEL           **3½ H.P. Motor Bicycle ("Moto Bi")**     *Year:* 1903–4

CHASSIS      Trapezoid bicycle frame with twin horizontal main tubes and twin support tubes adjacent to steering tube. Engine attached to forward down-tube and bottom bracket.
*Frame Size:* 23 in.
*Type of Wheels:* Dunlop tangentially spoked wire.
*Tyres:* Front Size 28 × 2½ in. Rear Size 28 × 2½ in.
*Braking System:* Front rim and Riley-Bowden rear rim, operated from handlebar-mounted levers.

TRANSMISSION    *Clutch Type:* Riley Motor Clutch Hub (clutch mounted on engine drive pulley) on later models.
*Gearbox Type:* None—freewheel in rear hub for pedal drive.
*Gear Selection Mechanism:* None.
*Final Drive Type:* Lycett-Rawido link belt with pedal assistance.
*Final Drive Ratio:* 8: 1

ENGINE        *Engine Type:* Riley 3½ h.p.
*H.P. Rating:* 3.50
*Cubic Capacity:* 517 cc.
*Number of Cylinders:* 1
*Firing Order:* 1
*Bore:* 86 mm.
*Stroke:* 89 mm.
*Cylinder Type:* Air-cooled bolt-on with offset spark plug.
*Valve Gear:* Riley mechanical inlet and exhaust side valves.
*Number of Main Bearings:* 2

*Cooling System:* Air.
*Type of Ignition:* Trembler coil and mechanical contact maker.
*Number, Make and Type of Carburetters:* Longuemare updraught.
*Type of Inlet Manifold:* Fabricated copper tubular.
*Type of Exhaust Manifold:* Fabricated bolt-on.
*Location of Fuel Tank:* Horizontally suspended under frame top tube.
*Capacity of Fuel Tank:* 2 gallons.
*Method of Fuel Feed:* Gravity.

MODELS AVAILABLE   Riley 3½ h.p. 'Moto Bi' Frame sizes variable to order from 21 in to 23 in.
Price, as described: 50 Guineas. Water-cooled engine also available.

MODEL             **3 H.P. Tricar (Fore-car)**                         *Year:* 1903–4

CHASSIS           Trapezoid cycle-type frame with A frame carrying front axle. Parallel tubes, anchored
at rear, support spring suspended forecarriage.
*Frame Size:* 23 in.
*Wheelbase:* 4 ft. 5 in.
*Front Track:* 3 ft. 3 in.
*Type of Wheels:* Dunlop tangentially spoked wire.
*Tyres:* Front Size 26 × 2 in. Rear Size 28 × 2¼ in.
*Braking System:* Foot-applied band brake to front wheels and pedal applied block
brake to rear driven pulley, with option of hand-applied rear brake to order.

TRANSMISSION      *Clutch Type:* Riley Motor Clutch Hub (clutch mounted on engine drive pulley) on
some later models.
*Gearbox Type:* None—freewheel on pedal-driven rear hub.
*Gear Selecting Mechanism:* None.
*Final Drive Type:* Lycett-Rawido link belt with pedal assistance.
*Final Drive Ratio:* 8 : 1

ENGINE            *Engine Type:* Riley 3 h.p.
*H.P. Rating:* 3.00
*Cubic Capacity:* 403.12 cc.
*Number of Cylinders:* 1
*Firing Order:* 1
*Bore:* 80 mm.
*Stroke:* 80 mm.
*Cylinder Type:* Air-cooled bolt-on with offset spark plug.
*Valve Gear:* Riley mechanical inlet and exhaust side valves.
*Number of Main Bearings:* 2
*Cooling System:* Air.
*Type of Ignition:* Trembler coil and mechanical contact maker.
*Number, Make and Type of Carburetters:* Longuemare updraught.
*Type of Inlet Manifold:* Fabricated copper tubular.
*Type of Exhaust Manifold:* Fabricated bolt-on.
*Location of Fuel Tank:* Horizontally suspended under frame top tube.
*Capacity of Fuel Tank:* 2 gallons.
*Method of Fuel Feed:* Gravity.

MODELS AVAILABLE   Riley 3 h.p. Tricar with art cane forecarriage and rug supplied. Coachbuilt forecarriage at extra cost of 4 Guineas.
Price, as described: 60 Guineas. Extra for 3½ h.p. engine: 4 Guineas. Extra for Riley
2-Speed gear with chain drive: 5 Guineas.

MODEL             **4½ H.P. Tricar (Fore-car)**                         *Year:* 1904

CHASSIS           Trapezoid cycle-type frame with A frame carrying front axle. Parallel tubes, anchored
at rear, with spring suspended forecarriage.
*Frame Size:* 23 in.
*Wheelbase:* 4 ft. 5 in.
*Front Track:* 3 ft. 3 in.
*Type of Wheels:* Dunlop tangentially spoked wire.

*1904 4½ h.p. water-cooled Tri-car*

*1905 4½ h.p. water-cooled Tri-car*

*Tyres:* Front Size 26 × 2 in. Rear Size 28 × 2¼ in.
*Braking System:* Foot-applied band brake to front wheels and pedal applied block
brake to rear driven pulley, with option of hand-applied rear brake to order.

TRANSMISSION       *Clutch Type:* Riley Motor Clutch Hub (clutch mounted on engine drive pulley).
*Gearbox Type:* None—freewheel in pedal-driven rear hub.
*Gear Selecting Mechanism:* None.
*Final Drive Type:* Lycett-Rawido link belt with pedal assistance.
*Final Drive Ratio:* 8:1

ENGINE             *Engine Type:* Riley 4½ h.p.
*H.P. Rating:* 4.50
*Cubic Capacity:* 517 cc.
*Number of Cylinders:* 1
*Firing Order:* 1
*Bore:* 86 mm.
*Stroke:* 89 mm.
*Cylinder Type:* Water-cooled bolt-on with offset spark plug.
*Valve Gear:* Riley mechanical inlet and exhaust side valves.
*Number of Main Bearings:* 2
*Cooling System:* Pump (5 g.p.m.)
*Type of Ignition:* Trembler coil and mechanical contact maker.
*Number, Make and Type of Carburetters:* Longuemare updraught.
*Type of Inlet Manifold:* Fabricated copper tubular.
*Type of Exhaust Manifold:* Fabricated bolt-on.
*Location of Fuel Tank:* Horizontally suspended under frame top tube.
*Capacity of Fuel Tank:* 2 gallons.
*Method of Fuel Feed:* Gravity.

MODELS AVAILABLE   Riley 4½ h.p. Tricar with coachbuilt forecarriage and rug supplied.
Price, as described: 80 Guineas. Extra for Riley Two Speed gear with chain drive:
5 Guineas.


MODEL              **4 & 4½ H.P. Tricar**                                    *Year:* 1905–07

CHASSIS            Trapezoid cycle-type frame with A frame carrying front axle. Parallel tubes, anchored
at rear, support spring suspended forecarriage.
*Frame Size:* 23 in.
*Wheelbase:* 4 ft. 5 in.
*Front Track:* 3 ft. 3 in.
*Type of Wheels:* Dunlop tangentially spoked wire.
*Tyres:* Front Size 26 × 2½ in. Rear Size 26 × 3 in.
*Braking System:* 7¼ in. band brakes to front wheels, hand-lever applied rear band brake.

TRANSMISSION       *Clutch Type:* Riley leather-faced cone type.
*Gearbox Type:* Riley patent 2-Speed constant mesh.
*Gearbox Ratios:* 1st—1.5:1, 2nd—1:1 (Optional 3rd speed 3.33:1)
*Gear Selecting Mechanism:* Sliding lever.
*Final Drive Type:* Chain drive from transverse engine to gearbox, with second chain
from gearbox to rear wheel.
*Final Drive Ratio:* 3.57:1 (50:14—also available with 54:14=3.86:1)

ENGINE             *Engine Type:* Riley 4 & 4½ h.p.
*H.P. Ratings:* 4 & 4.50
*Cubic Capacity:* 517 cc.
*Number of Cylinders:* 1
*Firing Order:* 1
*Bore:* 86 mm.
*Stroke:* 89 mm.
*Cylinder Type:* 4 h.p.—air cooled, 4½ h.p.—water cooled; both types bolt-on with off-
set spark plug & valves.
*Valve Gear:* Riley mechanical inlet and exhaust side valves.
*Number of Main Bearings:* 2
*Cooling System:* 4 h.p.—Air cooled, 4½ h.p.—pump (5 g.p.m.)
*Type of Ignition:* Trembler coil and mechanical contact maker.

268 THE MOTOR. *October 17th, 1905.*

# 1906 RILEY TRI-CARS.

The new tri-car models of the Riley Cycle Company are of two powers, 6h.p. and 9h.p., the specifications of which are similar except in the matter of engine dimensions. Both engines are of the two-cylinder V type, and the bores and strokes respectively are 80mm. by 80mm., and 86mm. by 89mm. The engines are specially made by the Riley Engine Company, and are of patented design. Perhaps the most novel feature of the new models is the change-speed gear. This also is built by the Riley Engine Company on car lines, and provides three speeds forward and a reverse, with a direct drive on the top gear. The design is such that the gears are always in mesh, and will be particularly attractive to the novice in that there can be no trouble at all in letting in the gear, a system of springs taking up the change automatically.

The clutch is of large size, leather to metal, and is quite efficient. It drives direct to the gear box from whence transmission is by a single chain. Ignition is by trembler coil and accumulator, and attention has been given to the feature of short and accessible wiring, whilst a three-way switch is fitted in a convenient position on the steering wheel. Water circulation is maintained by a gear-driven centrifugal pump, and the radiator and tank have a capacity of three gallons, the great length of the radiating tubes enabling the water to be kept cool under the most adverse conditions. The petrol tank is of large dimensions, having a capacity of four gallons, and the petrol consumption being about 40 miles per gallon, it will be seen that an average run can be undertaken without replenishing the fuel. One and a half gallons of lubricating oil can be carried, and the tanks are placed so as to form a smart-looking dash. The steering gear is of the rack and pinion type, and control is carried out by means of throttle, air and spark levers placed beneath the wheel. The left pedal operates the clutch, and the right pedal applies the band brakes to the front wheels. A double-acting band brake is fitted to the driving wheel, and is applied by a side lever, a second side lever operating the change-speed gear. The chassis is supported on semi-elliptical springs in front, and on helical springs at the rear. The rear springing device is well designed, and is such as to entirely prevent lateral sway. The front seat is suspended on springs, and being well upholstered will be found to be extremely comfortable. Ball bearings of substantial proportions are fitted to the wheels, and special precautions have been taken to ensure these being dust and mud proof. The mudguards are specially wide, and are constructed in a similar way to the car pattern. The tread is of ample width—being 4ft.—and this, together with low pitching, renders the vehicle a very stable one. Accessibility has been well considered in the design of the new Riley tri-cars, the body being hinged over the axle, and when raised every part is exposed, whilst for the sake of minor inspection purposes the rear seat itself is hinged, and can be swung over on releasing a small clutch.

## After Ten Years.

History is made very rapidly nowadays, but rarely, we should think, has history been made so quickly as in the case of the motorcar. When we survey the present position of automobilism it hardly seems possible that it was only ten years ago that Sir David Salomons proved the practical utility of motorcars by organising a show and demonstration at Tunbridge Wells. On that occasion six vehicles were exhibited on the Agricultural Show ground, and Sir David himself drove a Peugeot *vis-à-vis* car to display the ease with which it could be controlled. At the time we wrote of the event as follows :—" We are firmly convinced that the future is big with the promise of a startling revolution in road locomotion—a revolution which finds its parallel just over 70 years ago, when, on September 27th, 1825, George Stephenson proved the practical utility of the steam locomotive. Sir David Salomons has, in 1895, proved the practical use of road motors, and future generations will look back upon the event of last week at Tunbridge Wells as an epoch in the history of road locomotion." It will be seen that we were sanguine enough then, but even we would not have attempted to forecast that progress would have been as rapid and as startling as it has turned out to be. Ten years only have elapsed since the foregoing words were penned by the present writer, and in spite of the most persistent prejudice, in spite of the ingrained conservatism of the Britisher, the motor vehicle is the commonest object in our streets and on the country roads, and the motor industry is rapidly becoming one of the greatest in the country.

*1905 6 h.p. Tri-car Chassis*

2 Cylinder
Engine. . .

3 Speeds and
. . Reverse.

# 6 h.p. De Luxe Tri-car.

## —120 Guineas.—

**The Tri-car of Simplicity.**
Representing the most advanced features of Tri-car Manufacture.

**Other Models:**
4 h.p. Air-cooled, 70 Guineas.
4½ h.p. Water-cooled, 85 Guineas.

We are also supplying a similar machine embodying all the good points of the 6 h.p. Tri-car, but with a 9 h.p. Engine.

**PRICE 130 GUINEAS.**

Further Particulars can be obtained from

## THE RILEY CYCLE CO., LTD., City Works, Coventry.

London Depot :
15a, ELECTRIC AVENUE,
BRIXTON.

Leeds Depot :
11, BLENHEIM SQUARE,

Cardiff Depot :
1, WINDSOR PLACE.

B22       KINDLY MENTION "THE MOTOR" WHEN CORRESPONDING WITH ADVERTISERS.

*1905 6 h.p. Tri-car*

*Number, Make and Type of Carburetters:* Longuemare updraught.
*Type of Inlet Manifold:* Fabricated copper tubular.
*Type of Exhaust Manifold:* Fabricated bolt-on.
*Location of Fuel Tank:* Horizontally suspended under frame top tube.
*Capacity of Fuel Tank:* 2 gallons.
*Method of Fuel Feed:* Gravity.

MODELS AVAILABLE     Riley Tricar with coachbuilt forecarriage and rug supplied.
Riley 4 h.p. Tricar: £73.10s. Riley 4½ h.p. Tricar: £89.5s.

MODEL            **Tricar (6 & 9 H.P. Models)**                      *Year:* 1905–07

CHASSIS          Horizontal tubular 'A' frame with underslung reinforcing.
*Wheelbase:* 5 ft. 7 in.
*Front Track:* 4 ft. 0 in.
*Type of Wheels:* Dunlop tangentially spoked wire.
*Tyres:* Front Size: 26 × 3 in. Rear Size: 26 × 3 in.
*Braking System:* Foot-applied 7¼ in. band (early models) or 8 in. drum brakes to front
    wheels, with hand operated rear band brake (early models) or hand-ratchet
    applied metal-to-metal rear drum brake.

TRANSMISSION     *Clutch Type:* Riley leather-faced cone type.
*Gearbox Type:* Riley patent 3-Speed constant mesh with reverse.
*Gearbox Ratios:* 1st—3.33 : 1, 2nd—1.5 : 1, 3rd—1 : 1
    Also available with 1st—3.016 : 1, 2nd—1.74 : 1, 3rd—1 : 1.
*Gear Selecting Mechanism:* Right-hand sliding lever.
*Final Drive Type:* Chain drive from transverse engine/gearbox.
*Final Drive Ratio:* Choice of 3.57 : 1 (50 : 14), 3.86 : 1 (54 : 14) and 4.15 : 1 (54 : 13).

*Engine Types:* Riley 6 h.p. & 9 h.p. V-twin.
*H.P. Ratings:* 6.00, 9.00
*Cubic Capacities:* 804.25 cc., 1034 cc.
*Number of Cylinders:* 2
*Firing Order:* 1, 2
*Bore:* 6 h.p.—80 mm. 9 h.p.—86 mm.
*Stroke:* 6 h.p.—80 mm. 9 h.p.—89 mm.
*Cylinder Types:* Water-cooled, bolt-on, with offset spark plug.
*Valve Gear:* Riley mechanical inlet and exhaust side valves.
*Number of Main Bearings:* 2
*Cooling System:* Pump, rated 5 g.p.m.
*Type of Ignition:* Trembler coil and mechanical contact maker.
*Number, Make and Type of Carburetters:* Single Longuemare or Zenith.
*Type of Inlet Manifold:* Fabricated copper tube to aluminium cast manifold.
*Type of Exhaust Manifold:* Fabricated bolt-on.
*Location of Fuel Tank:* Dash-mounted.
*Capacity of Fuel Tank:* 4 gallons.
*Method of Fuel Feed:* Gravity.

MODELS AVAILABLE     Riley 6 h.p. Tricar: £126. 0s. Riley 9 h.p. Tricar: £136. 10s.

MODEL            **5 H.P. Tricar**                                   *Year:* 1907

CHASSIS          Horizontal 'A' frame with underslung tubular reinforcing.
*Wheelbase:* 5 ft. 7¼ in.
*Front Track:* 3 ft. 3 in.
*Type of Wheels:* Dunlop tangentially spoked wire.
*Tyres:* Front Size 26 × 2½ in. Rear Size 26 × 3 in.
*Braking System:* Foot-applied 8 in. band brakes to front wheels, hand-ratchet applied
    metal-to-metal rear band brake.

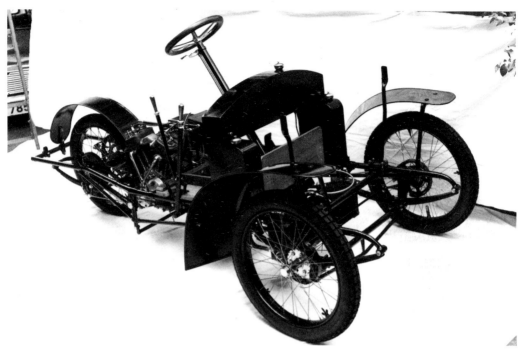

*Max Hoather's beautifully restored 1907 9 h.p. Tri-car chassis*

*Another view of the 1907 9 h.p. Tri-car chassis*

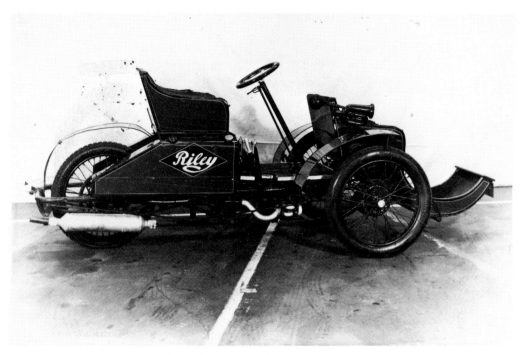

*1907 5 h.p. Tri-car (the Riley diamond was added many years later, as was the inelegant silencer)*

*Riley's first production 4-wheeled car, the 1907 9 h.p. V-Twin*

TRANSMISSION        *Clutch Type:* Riley leather-faced cone type.
                    *Gearbox Type:* Riley patent 2-Speed constant mesh.
                    *Gearbox Ratios:* 1st—3.33:1, 2nd—1.5:1
                    *Gear Selecting Mechanism:* Right-hand sliding lever.
                    *Final Drive Type:* Chain drive from transverse engine to gearbox with second chain
                        from gearbox to rear wheel.
                    *Final Drive Ratio:* 3.57:1 (50:14)

ENGINE              *Engine Type:* Riley 5 h.p.
                    *H.P. Rating:* 4.5
                    *Cubic Capacity:* 517 cc.
                    *Number of Cylinders:* 1
                    *Firing Order:* 1
                    *Bore:* 86 mm.
                    *Stroke:* 89 mm.
                    *Cylinder Type:* Water-cooled bolt-on with offset spark plug & valves.
                    *Valve Gear:* Riley mechanical inlet and exhaust side valves.
                    *Number of Main Bearings:* 2
                    *Cooling System:* Water pump (5 g.p.m.)
                    *Type of Ignition:* Trembler coil and mechanical contact maker.
                    *Number, Make and Type of Carburetters:* Single Longuemare or Zenith.
                    *Type of Inlet Manifold:* Fabricated copper tubular.
                    *Type of Exhaust Manifold:* Fabricated bolt-on.
                    *Location of Fuel Tank:* Beside driver's seat.
                    *Capacity of Fuel Tank:* 3 gallons.
                    *Method of Fuel Feed:* Gravity.

MODELS AVAILABLE    Riley 5 h.p. Tricar: £85.0.0


MODEL               **9 H.P. V-twin Car**                                    *Year:* 1906–07

CHASSIS             Duplex parallel tubular mainframe with front and rear crossmembers. Single parallel
                    tubular rear subframe, with tubular crossmember at rear.
                    *Wheelbase:* 6 ft. 8 in.
                    *Track:* Front 4 ft. 1 in. Rear 4 ft 1 in.
                    *Types of Wheels:* Dunlop tangentially spoked wire.
                    *Tyres:* Front Size 700×80 mm. grooved. Rear Size 700×80 mm. plain.
                    *Braking System:* Foot-applied 8 in. band brakes to rear wheels only, hand-ratchet
                        operation also.

TRANSMISSION        *Clutch Type:* Riley leather-faced cone type.
                    *Gearbox Type:* Riley patent 3-Speed constant mesh.
                    *Gearbox Ratios:* 1st—3.33:1, 2nd—1.5:1, 3rd—1:1
                    *Gear Selecting Mechanism:* Right-hand sliding lever.
                    *Final Drive Type:* Chain drive from transverse engine/gearbox
                    *Final Drive Ratio:* Quoted as 3.55:1, but with 50:14 chainwheel and sprocket, actual
                        ratio is 3.57:1

ENGINE              *Engine Type:* Riley 9 h.p.
                    *H.P. Rating:* 9.00
                    *Cubic Capacity:* 1034 cc.
                    *Number of Cylinders:* 2
                    *Firing Order:* 1, 2
                    *Bore:* 86 mm.
                    *Stroke:* 89 mm.
                    *Cylinder Type:* Water-cooled bolt-on with offset spark plug.
                    *Valve Gear:* Riley mechanical inlet and exhaust side valves.
                    *Number of Main Bearings:* 2
                    *Cooling System:* Water pump (5 g.p.m.)
                    *Type of Ignition:* Trembler coil and mechanical contact maker.
                    *Number, Make and Type of Carburetters:* Single Longuemare or Zenith.
                    *Type of Inlet Manifold:* Fabricated copper tube to aluminium cast manifold.
                    *Type of Exhaust Manifold:* Fabricated bolt-on.
                    *Location of Fuel Tank:* Dash-mounted.
                    *Capacity of Fuel Tank:* 5 gallons.
                    *Method of Fuel Feed:* Gravity.

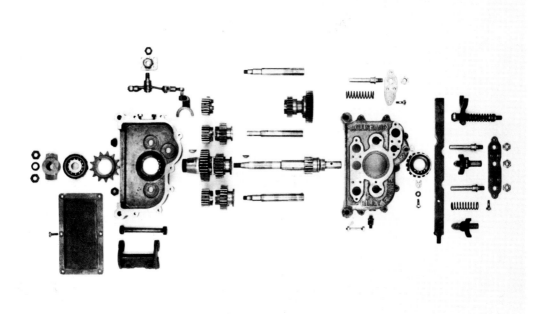

*The gearbox from Max Hoather's 1907 9 h.p. Tri-car*

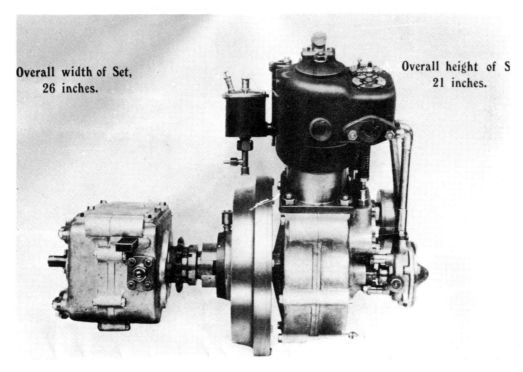

*A 9 h.p. V-twin engine and gearbox*

MODELS AVAILABLE  Riley 9 h.p. Car          : £168.os.
                  Riley Patent detachable
                  wheels (standard 1907)  : £2.1os.
                  Spare wheel & tyre       : £7.7s.
                  Pair of headlights       : £9.9s.
                  Electric tail-light set  : £2.5s.


MODEL             **12/18 H.P. Short Wheelbase**                                  *Year:* 1907–10

CHASSIS           Channel section parallel mainframe raised over rear axle.
                  *Wheelbase:* 8 ft. 0 in.
                  *Track:* Front 4 ft. 3 in. Rear 4 ft. 3 in.
                  *Type of Wheels:* Riley detachable wire.
                  *Tyres:* Front Size 750 × 85 mm. Rear Size 750 × 85 mm.
                  *Braking System:* Foot pedal to cardan brake, hand lever to rear wheel brakes.

TRANSMISSION      *Clutch Type:* Leather-faced cone.
                  *Gearbox Type:* Riley patent 3-speed.
                  *Gear Selecting Mechanism:* Right hand lever.
                  *Rear Axle Type:* Tubular with central differential.

ENGINE            *Engine Type:* 12/18 V-twin 90°
                  *RAC H.P. Rating:* 12.9
                  *Cubic Capacity:* 2039 cc.
                  *Number of Cylinders:* 2
                  *Firing Order:* 1, 2
                  *Bore:* 101.6 mm.
                  *Stroke:* 127 mm.
                  *Cylinder:* Water cooled with offset single spark plugs.
                  *Valve Gear:* Riley patent side valves.
                  *Number of Main Bearings:* 2
                  *Type of Oil Pump:* Pressure from tank.
                  *Cooling System:* Thermosyphon.
                  *Type of Ignition:* H.T. Distributor.
                  *Method of Advance/Retard:* Manual.
                  *Number, Make and Type of Carburetters:* Single Longuemare.
                  *Type of Inlet Manifold:* Cast bolt-on.
                  *Type of Exhaust Manifold:* Cast bolt-on.
                  *Location of Fuel Tank:* 1907  Rear mounted, 1908 Dash mounted, 1909–10 Beneath
                       seats.
                  *Capacity of Fuel Tank:* 7 gallons.
                  *Method of Fuel Feed:* Pressure.

MODELS & PRICES   1907/8—2 Seater: £236.5.0 (225 Guineas)
                  1907/8—5 Seater: £246.15.0 (235 Guineas)
                  1909  —2 Seater: £241.10.0 (230 Guineas)
                  1909  —5 Seater: £262.10.0 (250 Guineas)
                  1910  —2 Seater: £246.15.0 (235 Guineas)


MODEL             **12/18 H.P. Long Wheelbase**                                   *Year:* 1907–1910

CHASSIS           Channel section parallel mainframe raised over rear axle.
                  *Wheelbase:* 9 ft. 0 in.
                  *Track:* Front 4 ft. 2 in. Rear 4 ft. 2 in.
                  *Type of Wheels:* Riley detachable wire.
                  *Tyres:* Front Size 750 × 85 mm. Rear Size 750 × 85 mm.
                  *Braking System:* Pedal operated cardan brake, hand operated wheel brakes to rear
                  only—both types metal-to-metal.

TRANSMISSION      *Clutch Type:* Leather faced cone.
                  *Gearbox Type:* Riley constant mesh 3-speed.
                  *Gear Selecting Mechanism:* Right hand lever.
                  *Rear Axle Type:* Bevel crown wheel and pinion.

*1907/10 2 Seat SWB 12/18 h.p. Car*

*Victor Riley driving an early 1907 12/18 h.p. LWB 5 Seater*

ENGINE

*Engine Type:* V-twin 12/18.
*RAC H.P. Rating:* 12.9
*Cubic Capacity:* 2059 cc.
*Number of Cylinders:* 2
*Firing Order:* 1, 2
*Bore:* 101.6 mm.
*Stroke:* 127 mm.
*Cylinder:* Water cooled, offset single spark plug.
*Valve Gear:* Riley patent side valves.
*Number of Main Bearings:* 2
*Cooling System:* Thermosyphon.
*Type of Ignition:* H.T. Distributor.
*Method of Advance/Retard:* Manual.
*Number, Make and Type of Carburetters:* Single Longuemare.
*Type of Inlet Manifold:* Bolt-on cast.
*Type of Exhaust Manifold:* Cast bolt-on, separate to each cylinder.
*Location of Fuel Tank:* 1907 Rear mounted, 1908 dash mounted, 1909–10 Beneath
    driver's seat.
*Capacity of Fuel Tank:* 10 gallons.
*Method of Fuel Feed:* Air Pressure.

MODELS & PRICES

| | | |
|---|---|---|
| 1907—5 Seater: | £283.10.0 (270 Guineas) |
| 1908—5 Seater: | £294.0.0 (280 Guineas) |
| 1909—5 Seater: | £294.0.0 (280 Guineas) |
| 1909—Landaulette | £367.10.0 (350 Guineas) |
| 1910—5 Seater: | £309.15.0 (295 Guineas) |
| 1910—Landaulette | £367.10.0 (350 Guineas) |

MODEL                  **Bicycle**                          *Year:* 1911 (Final Production Year)

CHASSIS

Trapezoid cycle frame with parallel steering/seat tubes set at 72° from horizontal.
*Frame Size:* 22 in.
*Wheelbase:* 3 ft. 4½ in.
*Type of Wheels:* Tangentially spoked wire.
*Tyres:* Front Size Dunlop 28 × 2 in. Rear Size Dunlop 28 × 2 in.
*Braking System:* Caliper-operated block brakes controlled through handlebar-mounted
    levers and rod linkage.

TRANSMISSION

*Clutch Type:* None—freewheel on rear hub.
*Gearbox Type:* Single ratio chain drive by pedals, with 54 tooth chainwheel and 24
    tooth rear sprocket.
*Gear Ratios:* One ratio only—2.45 : 1

OTHER DATA

Frame available in other sizes between 20 in. and 23 in. to order. Lycett sprung saddle
standard mounted on adjustable tube, other types available to order. Handlebars of
horizontal upright type. Mudguards to front and rear wheels, 200° rear and 120°
front. Chainguard fitted—fully enclosed oil-bath type available at extra cost.

MODEL                  **10 H.P. Car**                          *Year:* 1909–1910

CHASSIS

Channel section parallel mainframe members raised over rear axle.
*Wheelbase:* 7 ft. 6 in.
*Track:* Front 4 ft. 2 in. Rear 4 ft. 2 in.
*Type of Wheels:* Artillery or Riley detachable.
*Tyres:* Front Size 750 × 85 mm. Plain. Rear Size 750 × 85 mm. grooved.
*Braking System:* Foot pedal to cardan brake, hand lever to rear wheels.

TRANSMISSION

*Clutch Type:* Leather faced cone.
*Gearbox Type:* Riley 3-speed.
*Gear Selecting Mechanism:* Right hand lever.
*Rear Axle Type:* Tubular, central differential, bevel gears.

*Stanley Riley driving a 1909 10 h.p. V-Twin in Army trials*

*A late production Pedal Bicycle of 1911*

ENGINE

*Engine Type:* 10 h.p. V-twin
*RAC H.P. Rating:* 11.4
*Cubic Capacity:* 1390 cc.
*Number of Cylinders:* 2
*Firing Order:* 1, 2
*Bore:* 96 mm.
*Stroke:* 96 mm.
*Cylinder:* Water cooled single offset spark plugs.
*Valve Gear:* Riley patent side valves.
*Number of Main Bearings:* 2
*Type of Oil Pump:* Pressure from tank.
*Cooling System:* Thermosyphon.
*Type of Ignition:* H.T. Distributor.
*Method of Advance/Retard:* Manual.
*Number, Make and Type of Carburetters:* Single Zenith.
*Type of Inlet Manifold:* Cast bolt-on.
*Type of Exhaust Manifold:* Cast bolt-on.
*Location of Fuel Tank:* Rear.
*Capacity of Fuel Tank:* 7 gallons.
*Method of Fuel Feed:* Air Pressure.

MODELS & PRICES

Chassis:      £188
2 Seater:     £200
Speed Model: £220

MODEL                **12/18 H.P. Short Wheelbase**                    *Year:* 1911–1914

CHASSIS

Channel section parallel mainframe raised over rear axle.
*Wheelbase:* 8 ft. 0 in.
*Track:* Front 4 ft. 3 in. (1913/14 4 ft. 6 in.) Rear 4 ft. 3 in. (1913/14 4 ft. 6 in.)
*Type of Wheels:* Riley detachable wire.
*Tyres:* Front Size 810×90 mm. Rear Size 810×90 mm.
*Braking System:* Foot pedal to cardan brake, hand lever to rear wheels.

TRANSMISSION

*Clutch Type:* Leather-faced cone.
*Gearbox Type:* Riley patent 3-speed.
*Gear Selecting Mechanism:* Right hand lever.
*Rear Axle Type:* Tubular to central differential housing, bevel gears.

ENGINE

*Engine Type:* 12/18 V-twin.
*RAC H.P. Rating:* 12.9
*Cubic Capacity:* 2039 cc.
*Number of Cylinders:* 2
*Firing Order:* 1, 2
*Bore:* 101.6
*Stroke:* 127
*Cylinder:* Water-cooled with offset single spark plugs.
*Valve Gear:* Riley mechanical side valves.
*Number of Main Bearings:* 2
*Type of Oil Pump:* Pressure feed from tank.
*Cooling System:* Fan and thermosyphon.
*Type of Ignition:* H.T. Magneto.
*Method of Advance/Retard:* Manual.
*Number, Make and Type of Carburetters:* 1911—single Riley, 1912–14 Single Zenith.
*Type of Inlet Manifold:* Cast bolt-on.
*Type of Exhaust Manifold:* Cast bolt-on.
*Location of Fuel Tank:* Rear.
*Capacity of Fuel Tank:* 7 gallons.
*Method of Fuel Feed:* Pressure.

MODELS & PRICES

1911/12—2 Seat Torpedo £283.10.0 (270 Guineas)
1913/14—2 Seat Torpedo £299.5.0 (285 Guineas)

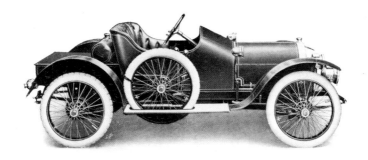

*1912 10 h.p. 2 Seat Torpedo*

*1912 12/18 h.p. Landaulette*

*1912 12/18 h.p. 2 Seat Torpedo*

| | | |
|---|---|---|
| MODEL | **12/18 H.P. Long Wheelbase** | *Year:* 1911–1914 |

CHASSIS
Channel section parallel mainframe raised over rear axle.
*Wheelbase:* 9 ft. 0 in.
*Track:* Front: 4 ft. 2 in. (1913/14 4 ft. 5 in.) Rear: 4 ft. 2 in. (1913/14 4 ft. 5 in.)
*Type of Wheels:* Riley detachable wire.
*Tyres:* Front Size: 810×90 mm. Rear Size: 810×90 mm.
*Braking System:* Foot pedal to cardan brake, hand lever to rear wheel brakes.

TRANSMISSION
*Clutch Type:* Leather faced cone.
*Gearbox Type:* Riley 3-speed.
*Gear Selecting Mechanism:* Right hand lever.
*Rear Axle Type:* Tubular with central differential, bevel gears.

ENGINE
*Engine Type:* 12/18 V-twin.
*RAC H.P. Rating:* 12.9
*Cubic Capacity:* 2059 cc.
*Number of Cylinders:* 2
*Firing Order:* 1, 2
*Bore:* 101.6
*Stroke:* 127
*Cylinder:* Water cooled with offset single spark plugs.
*Valve Gear:* Riley mechanical side valves.
*Number of Main Bearings:* 2
*Type of Oil Pump:* Pressure from tank.
*Cooling System:* Fan and thermosyphon.
*Type of Ignition:* Bosch magneto.
*Method of Advance/Retard:* Manual
*Number, Make and Type of Carburetters:* Single Riley 1911, Single Zenith 1912–14.
*Type of Inlet Manifold:* Cast bolt-on.
*Type of Exhaust Manifold:* Cast bolt-on.
*Location of Fuel Tank:* Rear mounted.
*Capacity of Fuel Tank:* 2 st—7 gallons, others 11 gallons.
*Method of Fuel Feed:* Pressure Feed.

MODELS & PRICES
1911    : 5 Seater £309.15.0 (295 Guineas), Landaulette £367.10.0 (350 Guineas)
        : 2 Seater £283.10.0 (270 Guineas).
1912    : 5 Seater £309.15.0 (295 Guineas), Landaulette £367.10.0 (350 Guineas)
        : 5 Seater £341.5.0 (325 Guineas), Torpedo 4 Seater £341.5.0 (325 Guineas)
        : 2 Seater £299.5.0 (295 Guineas), Landaulette £399.0.0 (380 Guineas),
        : Medico Special Coupe £388.10.0 (370 Guineas)

| | | |
|---|---|---|
| MODEL | **10 H.P. Car** | *Year:* 1911–1914 |

CHASSIS
Channel section parallel mainframe raised over rear axle.
*Wheelbase:* 8 ft. 0 in.
*Track:* Front 4 ft. 2 in. Rear 4 ft. 2 in.
*Type of Wheels:* Riley detachable wire.
*Tyres:* Front Size 800×85 mm. Plain. Rear 800×85 mm. Grooved.
*Braking System:* Foot pedal to cardan brake, hand lever to rear wheels.

TRANSMISSION
*Clutch Type:* Leather faced cone.
*Gearbox Type:* Riley patent 3-speed.
*Gear Selecting Mechanism:* Right hand lever.
*Rear Axle Type:* Tubular with central differential, bevel gears.

ENGINE
*Engine Type:* 10 h.p. V-twin.
*RAC H.P. Rating:* 11.4
*Cubic Capacity:* 1390 cc.
*Number of Cylinders:* 2
*Firing Order:* 1, 2
*Bore:* 96 mm.
*Stroke:* 96 mm.
*Cylinder:* Water cooled, single offset spark plugs.
*Valve Gear:* Riley mechanical side valves.

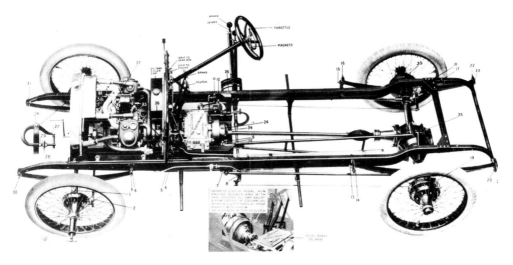

*1913 12/18 h.p. Chassis*

*1913 12/18 h.p. LWB 2 Seater at the Great Pyramid of Cheops in Egypt*

*Number of Main Bearings:* 2
*Type of Oil Pump:* Pressure from tank.
*Cooling System:* Thermosyphon.
*Type of Ignition:* H.T. Magneto (Bosch).
*Method of Advance/Retard:* Manual.
*Number, Make and Type of Carburetters:* 1911 Single Riley,
                             1912–14 Single Zenith.
*Type of Inlet Manifold:* Cast bolt-on.
*Type of Exhaust Manifold:* Fabricated bolt-on.
*Location of Fuel Tank:* Rear
*Capacity of Fuel Tank:* 7 gallons.
*Method of Fuel Feed:* Air Pressure.

MODELS & PRICES     1911/12 2 Seat Torpedo £220.10.0 (210 Guineas).
                                  1913/14 2 Seat Torpedo £231.0.0 (220 Guineas).

MODEL            **17/30 H.P. Car**                                                *Year:* 1913–22

CHASSIS         Channel mainframe members, narrow at front, widening at bulkhead, parallel to rear
end.
*Wheelbase:* 10 ft. 4 in.
*Track:* Front 4 ft. 9 in. Rear 4 ft. 9 in.
*Type of Wheels:* Riley detachable wire.
*Tyres:* Front Size 875 mm × 105 mm. Rear Size 875 × 105 mm.
*Braking System:* Foot brake—expanding shoes to rear wheels and cardan brake. Hand
lever operation to rear wheel brakes.

TRANSMISSION   *Clutch Type:* Leather faced cone 1913–14, fabric cone after 1914
*Gearbox Type:* 1913–14 models 3-speed, 1920–22 models 4-speed.
*Gear Selecting Mechanism:* Right hand gate and lever.
*Gear Ratios:* (4 spd) 1st—15.2:1, 2nd—9.2:1, 3rd—6.2:1, 4th—4.125:1, Reverse:
    15.2:1.
*Rear Axle Type:* Tubular type with Daimler worm drive.
*Final Drive Ratio:* 4.125:1.

ENGINE          *Engine Type:* Riley 17/30.
*RAC H.P. Rating:* 18.2
*Cubic Capacity:* 2951 cc.
*Number of Cylinders:* 4
*Firing Order:* 1243
*Bore:* 86 mm.
*Stroke:* 127 mm.
*Cylinder Head:* Water-cooled flat faced detachable with offset spark plugs.
*Valve Gear:* Side-located valves operated via tappets direct from single camshaft.
*Tappet Clearances Hot:* Inlet—0.002 in. Exhaust—0.003 in.
*Number of Main Bearings:* Five.
*Type of Oil Pump:* Plunger, operated by camshaft-driven eccentrics.
*Normal Oil Pressure (Hot):* 30—50 p.s.i.
*Cooling System:* Thermosyphon with fan assistance. Fan blades attached to rim of fly-
    wheel at rear of engine, drawing air through radiator & over engine.
*Type of Ignition:* Bosch magneto.
*Method of Advance/Retard:* Manual.
*Contact Breaker Gap:* 0.014 in.
*Plug Gap:* 0.018 in.
*Make of Type of Plug:* Champion 17.
*Number, Make and Type of Carburetters:* Single Zenith.
*Type of Inlet Manifold:* Cast alloy bolt-on.
*Type of Exhaust Manifold:* Cast iron bolt-on.
*Location of Fuel Tank:* Rear mounted.
*Fuel Capacity:* 12 gallons.
*Method of Fuel Feed:* Air pump driven from oil pump eccentric.

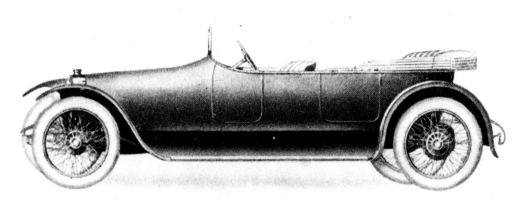

*1913 17/30 h.p. 5 Seater*

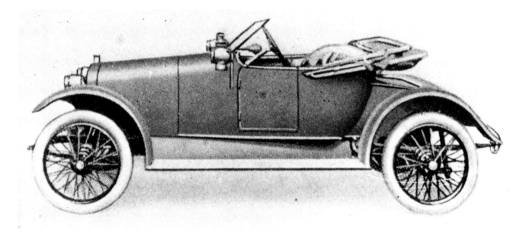

*1914 10 h.p. 4 Cylinder 2 Seater*

*1922 17/30 h.p. 5 Seat Tourer*

MODELS AVAILABLE   1913–14: 2 or 3 Seat              : £430
                   1913–14: 4 or 5 Seat Tourer : £450
                   1913–14: Chassis Only          : £335
                   4 Speed gearbox, extra        : £ 20
                   1920–22: 5 Seat Touring Car: £750
                   1920–22: Chassis only           : £500


MODEL                 **10 H.P. Car**                                                    *Year:* 1914

CHASSIS               Parallel mainframe channels raised over rear axle.
                      *Wheelbase:* 8 ft. 0 in.
                      *Track:* Front 4 ft. 0 in. Rear 4 ft. 0 in.
                      *Type of Wheels:* Riley detachable wire.
                      *Tyres:* Front Size 700 × 80 mm. Rear Size 700 × 80 mm.
                      *Braking System:* Expanding shoes to rear wheels only, pedal and hand lever operation.

TRANSMISSION          *Clutch Type:* Fabric Cone.
                      *Gearbox Type:* 4 Speed sliding gear type.
                      *Gear Selecting Mechanism:* Right hand gate and lever.
                      *Rear Axle Type:* Tubular with differential at centre. Bevel gears.

ENGINE                *Engine Type:* 10 h.p. 4
                      *RAC H.P. Rating:* 10
                      *Cubic Capacity:* 1096 cc.
                      *Number of Cylinders:* 4
                      *Firing Order:* 1, 2, 4, 3
                      *Bore:* 63 mm.
                      *Stroke:* 88 mm.
                      *Cylinder Head:* Flat water cooled, 1 spark plug per cylinder.
                      *Valve Gear:* Camshaft to fibre tipped tappets to side valves.
                      *Number of Main Bearings:* 3
                      *Type of Oil Pump:* Gear Driven Pump.
                      *Cooling System:* Thermosyphon.
                      *Type of Ignition:* H.T. Magneto (Bosch)
                      *Method of Advance/Retard:* Manual.
                      *Number, Make and Type of Carburetters:* Single Zenith.
                      *Type of Inlet Manifold:* Cast bolt-on.
                      *Type of Exhaust Manifold:* Cast bolt-on.
                      *Location of Fuel Tank:* Rear.
                      *Capacity of Fuel Tank:* 7 gallons.
                      *Method of Fuel Feed:* Air Pressure.

MODELS & PRICES       2 Seater: £195

OTHER DATA            This car might almost have been included in Chapter 9, since it was originally intended
                      that the Nero Engine Company should produce it. However, it was a Riley design and
                      only one car was built.

470 The Motor     ADVERTISEMENTS     NOVEMBER 14TH, 1907

# Stand No. 102, Olympia.

*The 12 h.p. Vibrationless*

## RILEY
(1908 Pattern).

| | | |
|---|---|---|
| 7 ft. 11 in. Wheelbase, 2-seat Body, 750 by 85 Tyres ... | 225 Guineas. | |
| 7 ft. 11 in. Wheelbase, 4 or 5-seat Body, Swinging Front Seat, 750 by 85 Tyres ... ... ... ... ... | 235 | ,, |
| 9 ft. 0 in. Wheelbase, 4 or 5-seat Body, Side Entrance, 810 by 90 Tyres ... ... ... ... ... ... | 270 | ,, |

9 h p. Model   -   -   -   160 Guineas.

Principal Features:
RILEY Detachable Wheel System.
RILEY Patent Spring Change Speed Gear.
RILEY Patent Metal-to-Metal Clutch (on 12 h.p. Model).

Further particulars free from

## THE RILEY CYCLE Co. *(Motor Dept.),*
## —— COVENTRY. ——

London Agents and Show-rooms—SIMPSON & Co., Dover Street, Piccadilly, W.    Sole Agents for Plymouth and 40-mile radius, also County of Cornwall—H. ANDREWS & Co., Athenaeum Place, Plymouth.

482 ——————————————— 𝕸𝖔𝖙𝖔𝖗 ——————————————— *November 14th, 1907.*

## Olympia Show, Contd.—Benz. Riley. Adler.

extra, independent-action band brake, with pedal control, is added, making four in all. Very interesting will be found the

MERCEDES PETROL-ELECTRIC CAR,

although this is not shown in chassis form. The electric motors, however, can be examined, as the components are shown. The engine, a four-cylinder 45h.p., drives a dynamo direct, which supplies current to the motors, which are built up with the rear wheels, these forming very large bosses or hubs. The motors are entirely enclosed and dust-proof, and there is one to each driving wheel. The field magnets are of the radial 12 pole type, mounted on the rear axle, and the armature which forms the outer shell or hub rotates round it. The dynamo and motors enable all intermediate transmission to be dispensed with, and the controller allows of a range of five forward speeds, three reverse speeds, and four electric brake points. This car is practically identical with any standard limousine, and it is only the unusual appearance of the rear wheels which makes it distinctive.

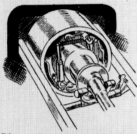

*Riley metal-to-metal expanding clutch.*

Riley, City Works, Coventry, show the 9h.p. V-engine, single chain drive model, and 12-18h.p., also fitted with two-cylinder V-engine, but mounted under bonnet. An expanding metal clutch is fitted to this model, but a leather clutch is used on the smaller. On the 12-18h.p. chassis the transmission is by live axle, three-speed gear of special design, wheels always in mesh, control by patented notched quadrant. Ignition by coil and accumulators with short wiring. Cooling is by simple

thermo system specially arranged. A new feature is the use of easily detachable wire wheels. The front axle is tubular, and frame is upswept at rear, and a transverse spring added. All brakes are internal expanding metal-to-metal. Cooling is fan assisted. Force pump oil circulation is

*The 12-18h.p. two-cylinder Riley car.*

used on the 12-18h.p. The detachable wheels (Riley patent) are very ingenious, as a spare wheel can be carried, which fits either front or back, and the rear brake action is not interfered with. An improved torque-rod system is fitted, both rods being in tension alternately. A feature that should be noted is that all the chassis is black stove-enamelled. A very strong method of fixing the running-board is adopted, special tubular brackets being hung from the frame. The silencer is of extra large proportions, this occupying about a third length of chassis. The control levers, throttle, and spark are on steering wheel. The carburetter is Longuemare automatic. The pinion ball bearing on the live axle is of extra length. The firing points are marked on the fly-

wheel and valve tappets are adjustable. Everything is readily accessible, there being ample clearance provided at all necessary points. This chassis strikes one as being highly original in many points of design

The Adler cars, shown by Messrs.

Morgan and Co., of Old Bond Street, are made in one of the largest factories in Germany, and it must be admitted by all who inspect them that the workmanship and design are of the very first order, whilst the quality of the metal can be gauged from the specimens which are shown, and which have seemingly been put to cruel tests. The 18h.p. chassis first attracts attention for its general completeness, gained

WITHOUT ANY SACRIFICE OF SIMPLICITY

or accessibility. The engine clutch and gearbox are mounted as a single component in an aluminium four-piece casing, making an exceedingly sound and rigid job. This block of engine and driving mechanism is then mounted on a sole plate riveted to the frame, and all dust is rigidly excluded by the enclosing of all spaces between engine and frame. The propeller shaft is cased, and springing from the forward end of the casing are two radius rods which proceed to the rear axles close to the wheels, and thus form a strong triangular brace which takes the thrust and the torsional strains, a strong coil spring being interposed between the collar at the apex of the triangle and the cross member of the frame. The universal joint at the forward end of the shaft is enclosed in a globe carried in a spherical bearing on the frame itself, so that the strains are taken by the frame and not by the driving mechanism. The 28h.p. limousine body is a fine specimen of Messrs. Morgan's carriage work, being beautifully finished and fitted inside, the upholstery being luxurious, and such fittings as window silencers (to prevent rattle, lockers, cupboards, tables, folding swivel seats, arm-rests, and electric lights being well arranged so as not to be in the way when not wanted.

Note.—The 9h.p. Adler car is described on page 506 of this issue.

*The 12-18h.p. Riley.*

E10

*The lower car of these two illustrated is a 9 h.p. not a 12/18.*

# CHAPTER THREE

# After the Peace—
# the Sidevalve Fours, 1919–1928

November 1918 brought the Great War to its end and innovative minds soon turned to thoughts of new car design and production. From the stock of components held since before the war, the Riley Engine Company began building a further batch of the 1913—designed 17/30 h.p. car, but this was really only a stop-gap measure, partly to use up materials and partly to employ manpower. The introduction of horsepower tax put a final end to the 17/30 h.p., the last example being sold in 1923.

However, by mid-1919 more re-organisation had taken place within the Riley companies. The Nero Engine Company was absorbed by Riley (Coventry) Ltd (to which the Riley Cycle Company had changed its name in 1912) and the reorganised company moved to Foleshill. The Riley Motor Manufacturing Company now changed its name to the Midland Motor Body Company, under the direction of Allan Riley.

By the time of the Olympia Motor Show of 1919, Riley introduced a completely new car design, developed to make production easier and less costly than before and to give the customer low maintenance cost and ease of operation. For example, there were merely six lubrication points on the chassis and these only required attention once every six months. Self lubricating bushes were widely used and of the design in general the *Automobile Engineer* was glowing in its praise.

The engine was a four cylinder in-line water cooled unit with the cylinder block detachable from the crankcase and the cylinder head removable from the block. The oil filter was removable without the use of special tools and a large cover plate on the nearside of the engine gave access to the valve gear.

The engine capacity was 1498 cc. and drive was transmitted via a cardan shaft to a separately mounted gearbox through an open propeller shaft to the rear axle.

These first post-war cars introduced the now-famous vee radiator and peaked shape of radiator shell (originally the tank itself) on which was mounted the equally famous Riley badge in the blue diamond-shaped surround.

Another feature of particular interest, and novelty, was that the chassis of this new model was built with all of its electrical wiring completely installed so that the body installation was a very simple matter of fitting it to the chassis. The bulkhead with instrument panel was part of the chassis, so the body was easily removable too. Originally two bodies were offered, both made by the Midland Motor Body Company, a Four Seater and a Three Seater—the Three Seater being the more expensive at £540, £50 more than the four seater.

At Olympia a chassis, a Four Seater and a coupé were exhibited. By early 1920 there were four Riley models available—the Four Seater at £550, the Family model at £550, the Two Seater at £520 and the Coupé at £600.

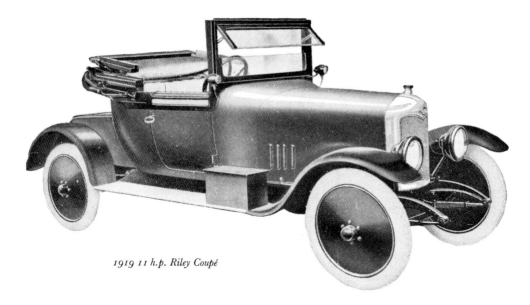

*1919 11 h.p. Riley Coupé*

*An attractive 1920 4 Seat Cabriolet. Note the laminated disc wheels, which were the subject of a 1919 patent by the*
*Coventry Disc Wheel Company, but abandoned by 1921.*

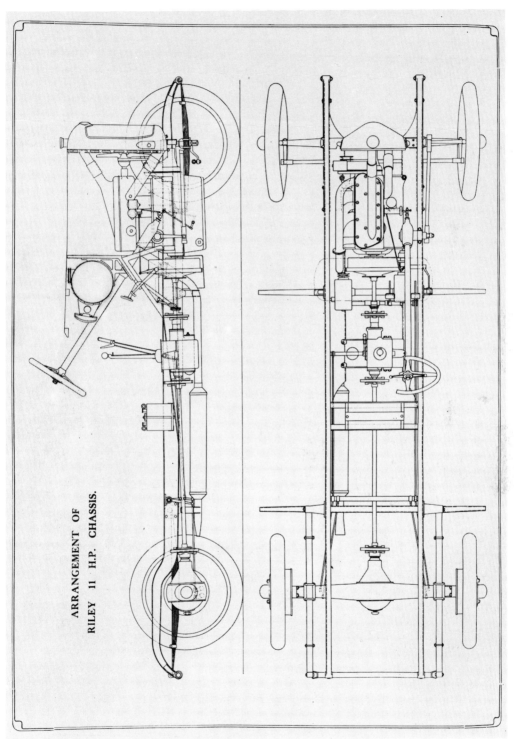

ARRANGEMENT OF
RILEY 11 H.P. CHASSIS.

*1921 11 h.p. Chassis general arrangement drawing*

The 1920 Olympia Motor Show was where the advertising by-line 'As Old as the Industry' was first used—the other half of Riley's famous motto coming into use at the 1925 Motor Show to make it 'As Old as the Industry—As Modern as the Hour'. That motto was to be kept in use until the Company collapsed in 1938. It was always appropriate.

That 1920 show brought price increases with it and one new model—the Saloon at £850. It was accompanied by the Two Seater at £630, the Four Seater at £650 and the Coupé at £700.

Early in 1921 another new model, an economy version of the 4 seater tourer was introduced at the price of £565. Here was the sign of a new trend, price reductions, which was to be followed in mid-year by the Coupé's price being reduced by £100. Of course, as production increased, so prices could be reduced, thereby widening the market still further (a factor which seems to have eluded the industry in much later years).

The 1921 Motor Show brought more price reductions and another new model—the Two Seater Sports at £520. The chassis was priced at £395, the Two Seat Tourer at £475, the Four Seater at £525, the Coupé at £595 and the Saloon at £795.

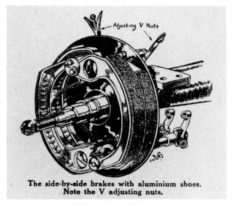

*1920 Illustration of Riley brakes*

*The 1920 11 h.p. Coupé—also featuring laminated disc wheels.*

*A pleasant view of the 1920 Standard 4 Seater*

Further price reductions came just before the 1922 Motor Show, reducing the All Season Four Seater (as it was now known) to £430, the Two Seater to £415, the Coupé to £495 and the Saloon to £695. A few minor improvements were also introduced at that time—notably the relocation of the magneto and starter motor, the introduction of optional right-hand or central gear change and the starter ring was no longer shrunk on to the flywheel, but cut integrally.

1923 was the year the 'Redwinger' Sports was born—in all but name that is. There was already a Sports Two Seater and now a Sports Four Seater was introduced: they were priced respectively at £495 and £450. Both were given guaranteed road speeds, the Two Seater 70 m.p.h. and the Four Seater 60 m.p.h. 1923 was also the last year in which the old 17/30 h.p. was still available, now priced at £500 for the chassis and £750 for the complete car.

By now, apart from the two Sports models and the occasional 17/30 h.p., Riley was offering a range of no less than six models, all on the one basic chassis, the 9 ft. wheelbase 11 h.p. They were: the All Season Two Seater at £415, the All Season Four Seater at £430, the All Season Four Seater Sporting Type (not to be confused with the Four Seat Sports) at £450, the Coupé at £495, the Saloon at £650 and the new Four Seat Coupé at £545. The chassis only was priced at £335, still including all electrics and the dash panel attached to the bulkhead. The range was added to still further in 1924 and now two wheelbases were available: 9 ft. and 9 ft. 6 in. Now the car was known as the Eleven-40, the power output having been

*1921 All-Season 4 Seater*

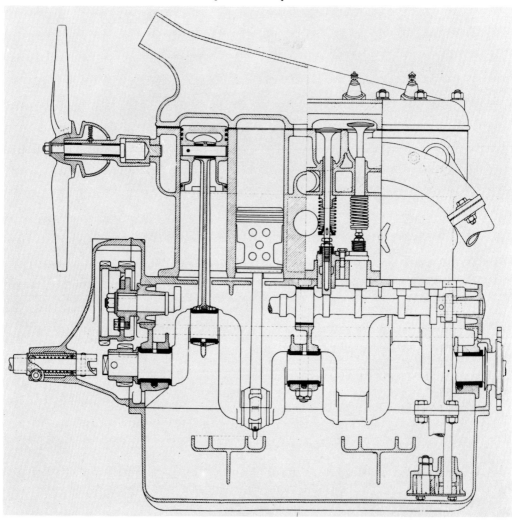

*Profile section of 1921 11 h.p. engine*

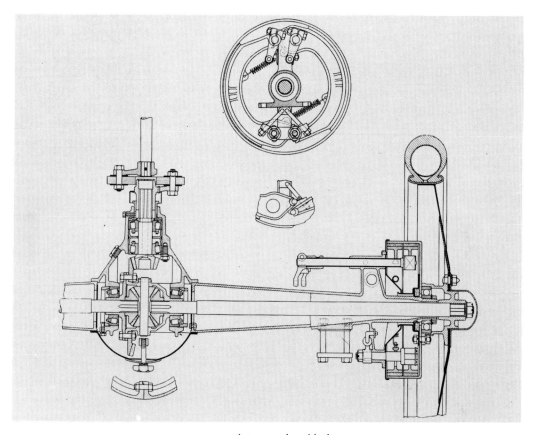

*1921 11 h.p. rear axle and brakes*

increased from 35 b.h.p. to 40 b.h.p. at 3600 r.p.m. That was quite a performance for its day, remembering that the 1½ litre of twelve years later—with all its improvements—was only delivering 45 b.h.p. in standard form.

On the 9 ft. 6 in. wheelbase chassis the models offered were: the Four Seater De Luxe at £460, the Four Door Four Seater at £395, the Two Seater at £395, the Saloon De Luxe at £620, the Saloon at £495, the Coupé at £465, the Four Seat Sports at £450, the Two/Three Seater at £390, the Four Seat Coupé at £635 and the Saloon Landaulette at £545. The 9 ft. wheelbase models included the Two Door Four Seater at £395, the Two Seater Sports at £495 and the Two/Three Seat Clover Leaf Model at £450. The Clover Leaf was really a three seat version of the Sports Two Seat body offered on the Standard 9 ft. chassis, but still with red wings and polished aluminium body like the Sports model. Thirteen models in all, plus the chassis only now priced at £315, were available in 1924—quite a range by anyone's standards.

Riley quality in 1924 was rewarded with a number of notable successes in competition that year. For example, eleven cars were entered in the London to Edinburgh trial and they achieved eleven first class awards: four cars were entered in the Lands End to John O'Groats and four first class awards were won. At the Brooklands Whitsun Meeting, a Standard Sports

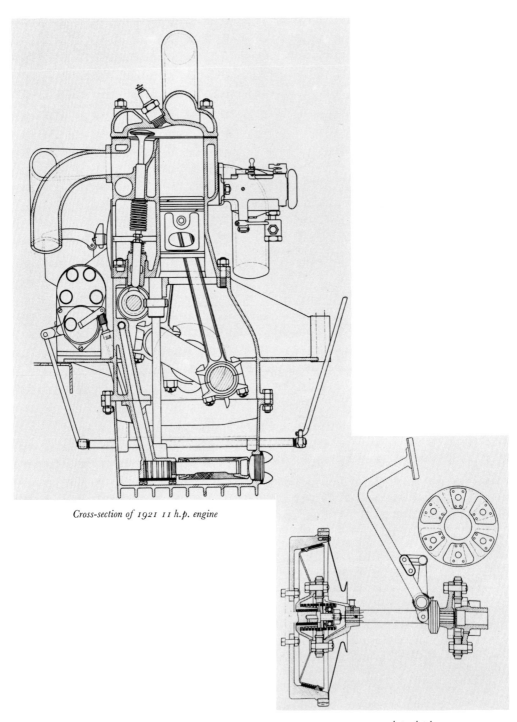

*Cross-section of 1921 11 h.p. engine*

*1921 11 h.p. clutch*

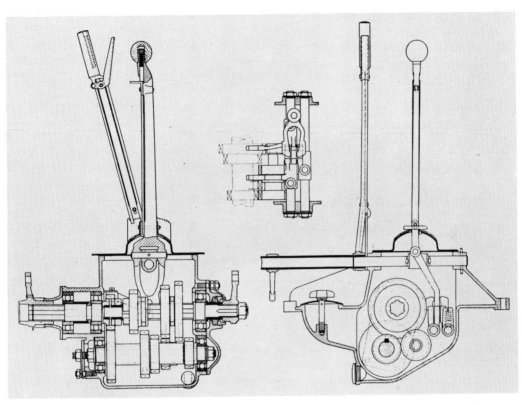

*1921 11 h.p. gearbox diagrams*

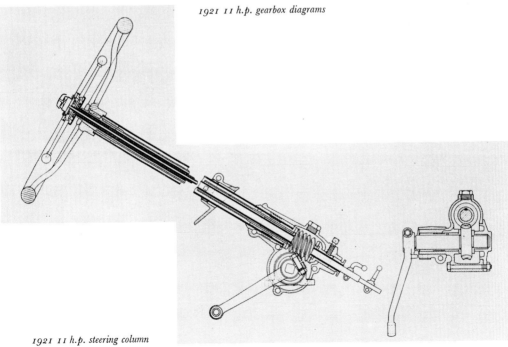

*1921 11 h.p. steering column*

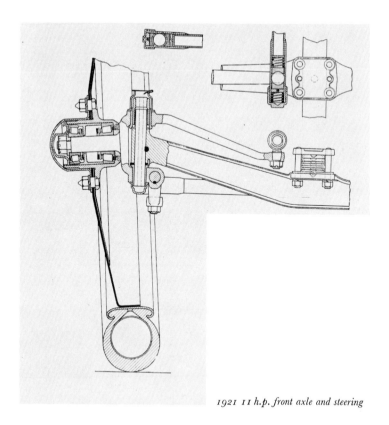

*1921 11 h.p. front axle and steering*

*1923 Saloon*

won the Light Car Handicap by ¾ of a mile—not bad for a 5¾ mile event. In the August meeting a Standard Sports again won the 90 m.p.h. Long Handicap and finished second in the 75 m.p.h. Short Handicap.

No wonder then that, by 1925, there were three sports models available from the Riley range. They were referred to in a special brochure as the Redwingers, the Two Seater being offered on the 9 ft. chassis at £495, the Four Seater at the same price on the 9 ft. chassis and a new, third, model on a specially short 8 ft. 6 in. wheelbase at a price which was 'on application'.

The remainder of the Riley range for 1925, the bread and butter models, were still offered on the 9 ft. 6 in. or 9 ft. chassis. By now, some rationalisation had taken place and, apart from the chassis only at £300, there were only eight models (plus the Sports cars) offered in the 1925 catalogue. These were: the 5 Seater De Luxe Tourer at £460, the Saloon at £495, the Saloon Landaulette at £525, the Saloon De Luxe at £595, the Coupé at £475, the Four/Five Seat Touring Car at £395 and the Two/Six Seater at £395. All of these models were on the 9 ft. 6 in. chassis. The Special Touring Car was the one remaining model and it was built on the 9 ft. chassis.

The engine for the 1925 range was still described as the Eleven 40, though in fact it was now a 12 h.p. engine, the bore having been increased to 69 mm. and the capacity to 1645 cc. The power output was now 42 b.h.p. The 10.8 h.p. 1498 cc. unit was still available and was still the standard engine for the Sports models.

The rationalised range of 1925 didn't stay rationalised for long—the sales handbook for the 1926 Season listed no fewer than seventeen models. The additions to the range were a Coupé with fixed roof at £480, a Coupé de Ville priced from £750, the Foleshill Tourer at £350, the Four Door Coach at £395, the Four/Five Seat Glass Enclosed Touring Car at £450, the Two Door Special Touring Car at £435, the Four Door Special Touring Car at £445 and a revived Two/Three Seater at £350. The Two and Four Seat Sports models continued as before with the smaller 10.8 h.p. engine. The chassis only was £310 with four wheel brakes, £300 with only rear wheel brakes. A very exciting new Sports Model was introduced in 1926 and was exhibited at the Motor Show that year. It was the 11/50/65 Sports on the 9 ft. 6 in. wheelbase chassis. The two principal features which made this car so exciting were the use of overhead valve gear and a supercharger. The engine was of 1498 cc. capacity and gave a reputed 65 b.h.p., which enabled Riley to guarantee its maximum speed to be at least 80 m.p.h. In chassis form, the 11/50/65 was £450: with two or four seat sports body the price was £550.

Exciting as the 11/50/65 was, its future was perhaps determined before it had any opportunity to prove its worth, because it was overshadowed by the introduction of a new and completely different Riley—the 9 h.p. Monaco, which made its first public appearance at Shelsley Walsh in the Summer of 1926. It may have been a blessing in disguise that the 9 h.p. overshadowed it. The supercharged car never went into production and was quickly withdrawn, because the design of the overhead valve gear was rather close to someone else's patent. More of the 9 h.p. in a later chapter, however. The Supercharged Sports model would undoubtedly have been a great success if the valve gear and supercharger had proved as reliable as the rest of the side valve models, because it was essentially a side-valve converted and supercharged. However, it was not to be and in any case two years later a much more exciting 80 m.p.h. sports two seater was to arrive.

For 1927 there were sixteen side valve cars in the range. The basic chassis was available

at £300 and in price sequence, the models were: the Foleshill at £330, Two/Three Seater at £350; the Four Door Coach, the Two/Six Seater and the Standard Tourer at £395; the Two/Six Glass Enclosed at £415 and the Special Two Door Tourer at £435; the Glass Enclosed Tourer at £450 and the De Luxe Tourer at £460; the Coupé at £475; the Four Door Saloon and the two Sports Models (Two and Four Seaters) at £495; the Saloon Landaulette at £525; the Saloon De Luxe at £595 and finally the Coupé de Ville starting at £750.

A number of prices were again reduced shortly before the 1927 Olympia Show and notable among these were the two Sports Models, the prices of which were reduced to £395 for the Two Seater and £398 for the Four Seater. They were joined in the range by a long Four Seater at £425, £27 more for an extra 6 in. of wheelbase.

During that year the Riley 9 h.p. commenced production at Aldbourne Road and was built jointly by the Riley Engine Company and Midland Motor Bodies. It was soon obvious, however, that production had to continue in the main works and during 1927 new bays were built on to the Body Mounting Shop. The Stores and Chassis Erecting Shop were moved and the Engine Shop took over the vacated space. Now production of the two types, the side valve and 9 h.p. models, ran side by side, though it was not to be long before production of the side valve was to cease, in 1928, to make way for the new 'Wonder Car'!

The 1928 side valve models, introduced at Olympia 1927, were much improved for what was to be their last year of production. In particular, the engine was now fitted with a cylinder head of Ricardo design and gave an extra 8 b.h.p. as a result, as well as improved fuel consumption.

The range of cars now offered by Riley was larger than it had ever been. There were six 9 h.p. models, with two chassis types available, and no less than fourteen side valves! For both 9 h.p. and side valve models, Standard and Colonial chassis were offered, the side valves being priced at £295 and £310 respectively.

The other side valve models in that year were the Lulworth at £350 and Lulworth Special at £365, the 12 h.p. Tourer at £365, the Four Door Coach at £375, the Two/Six Seat Glass Enclosed at £385, the Wentworth at £395, the Special Tourer at £398, the Chatsworth at £398, the Grangeworth at £398, the Midworth at £415, the Saloon De Luxe at £495 and the three sports models—the Two Seater at £395, the Four Seater short wheelbase at £398 and the Long Sports Four at £427.

The increasing popularity combined with much lower prices of the 9 h.p. models sounded the death-knell for the side valves. All good things must come to an end and so the end came for the cars which had done so well in establishing Riley's post-war reputation in the medium-priced car market. If the oncoming decade of the 9 h.p. was to be Riley's 'Golden Age', then surely the near-decade of the side valve must have been the 'Silver Era'. A car of true character, to some a work of art, had slipped into history leaving a tremendous record of sporting achievements and reliability as its heritage.

SPECIFICATIONS

| | | |
|---|---|---|
| MODEL | **Side-valve Eleven** | *Year:* 1919–1923 |

CHASSIS  Parallel channel swept up over rear axle 4 semi-elliptic springs, 5 cross members.
*Wheelbase:* 9 ft. 0 in.
*Track:* Front 4 ft. 2 in. Rear 4 ft. 2 in.
*Type of Wheels:* Disc, wire or artillery, 760×90, 4 stud mounting.
*Tyres:* Front Size 765×105 mm. Rear Size 765×105 mm.
*Braking System:* Rods to rear wheels, 4 shoes, 2 footbrake, 2 handbrake.

TRANSMISSION  *Clutch Type:* Dry fabric cone.
*Gearbox Type:* Riley 4 speed.
*Gear Selecting Mechanism:* Central; right hand optional.
*Gear Ratios:* 1st—15.5 or 16.7, 2nd—10.8 or 11.6, 3rd—6.9 or 7.4, 4th—4.4 or 4.7:1
    Reverse: 15.5 or 16.7
*Rear Axle Type:* Semi-floating spiral bevel.
*Rear Axle Ratio:* 4.4 or 4.7:1

ENGINE  *Engine Type:* 11–40
*RAC H.P. Rating:* 10.8
*Cubic Capacity:* 1498 cc.
*Number of Cylinders:* 4
*Firing Order:* 1, 2, 4, 3
*Bore:* 65.8 mm.
*Stroke:* 110 mm.
*Cylinder Head:* Detachable flat, with inclined spark plugs, water cooled.
*Valve Gear:* Side valve, located near side, 1 inlet +1 exhaust per cylinder, 1½ in.
    diameter.
*Valve Timing:* Inlet opens 10° ATDC.
*Number of Main Bearings:* 3 × 1⅜in.
*Sump Capacity:* 12 pints.
*Type of Oil Pump:* Gear driven, splash feed to big ends.
*Cooling System:* Thermosyphon.
*Type of Ignition:* Magneto.
*Method of Advance/Retard:* Manual.
*Contact Breaker Gap:* 0.012 in.
*Plug Gap:* 0.018 in.
*Number, Make and Type of Carburetters:* Single Zephyr.
*Type of Inlet Manifold:* Cast bolt-on.
*Type of Exhaust Manifold:* Cast bolt-on.
*Location of Fuel Tank:* Dash mounted under bonnet.
*Capacity of Fuel Tank:* 7 gallons.
*Method of Fuel Feed:* Gravity.

COACHWORK
MODELS  1919–20: 4 Seater £550, Family Tourer £550, 2 Seater £520, Coupé £600
1921    : 4 Seater £650, All Season Tourer £565, 2 Seater £630, Coupé £700,
    Saloon £850.
1922    : Chassis £395, 2 Seater £475, Sports 2 Seater £520, Touring £525, Coupé
    £595, Saloon £795.
1923    : Chassis £335, All Season 2 Seater £415, All Season 4 Seater £430, All
    Season 4 Seater (2 door) £450, Coupé £495, Saloon £650, 4 Seat
    Coupé £545, Sports 2 Seater £495.

| | | |
|---|---|---|
| MODEL | **Side-valve Eleven-40 (LWB)** | *Year:* 1924 |

CHASSIS  Channel section parallel frame, 5 cross members, frame swept up over rear axle.
*Wheelbase:* 9 ft. 6 in.
*Track:* Front 4 ft. 2 in. (Disc) 4 ft. 4 in. (Wire). Rear 4 ft. 2 in. (Disc) 4 ft. 4 in.
    (Wire/Art.)

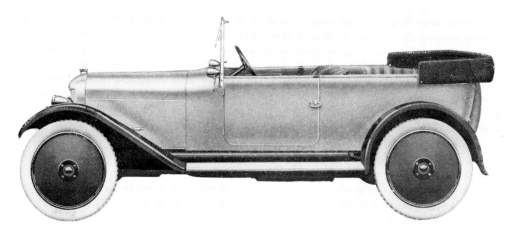

*1923 All-Season 4 Seater*

*1923 All-Season 2 Seater*

*1923 4 Seat Coupé*

*Type of Wheels:* Optional Disc (track 4 ft. 2 in., Artillery or wire 4 bolt fixing 760×90.
*Tyres:* Front Size 760×90 mm. (Saloon DeLuxe 30×5 in.) Rear Size 760×90 mm.
    (Saloon DeLuxe 30×5 in.)
*Braking System:* Self compensating rod brakes, 4 shoes rear wheels only, handbrake on
    2 shoes.

TRANSMISSION

*Clutch Type:* Dry Fabric Cone.
*Gearbox Type:* Riley 4 speed.
*Gear Selecting Mechanism:* Central, right hand optional extra £5.
*Gear Ratios:* 1st—16.7:1, 2nd—11.6:1, 3rd—7.4:1, Reverse 16.7:1
*Rear Axle Type:* Semi floating spiral bevel.
*Rear Axle Ratio:* 4.7:1

ENGINE

*Engine Type:* 11/40
*RAC H.P. Rating:* 10.8
*Cubic Capacity:* 1498 cc.
*Number of Cylinders:* 4
*Firing Order:* 1, 2, 4, 3
*Bore:* 65.8 mm.
*Stroke:* 110 mm.
*Cylinder Head:* Flat detachable with inclined spark plugs, water cooled.
*Valve Gear:* Side valves, located near side, 2 per cylinder, chain drive camshaft.
*Valve Timing:* Inlet opens 10° ATDC.
*Number of Main Bearings:* 3 × 1⅜ in.
*Sump Capacity:* 12 pints.
*Type of Oil Pump:* Gear driven, splash feed to big ends.
*Cooling System:* Thermosyphon.
*Type of Ignition:* Magneto.
*Method of Advance/Retard:* Manual.
*Contact Breaker Gap:* 0.012 in.
*Plug Gap:* 0.018 in.
*Number, Make and Type of Carburetters:* Single Cox-Atmos.
*Type of Inlet Manifold:* Cast, bolt-on.
*Type of Exhaust Manifold:* Cast, bolt-on.
*Location of Fuel Tank:* Dash mounted, cylindrical, under bonnet.
*Capacity of Fuel Tank:* 7 gallons.
*Method of Fuel Feed:* Gravity.

MODELS AVAILABLE

Four Seater De-Luxe £460, Four Door Four Seater £395, Two Seater £395, Saloon
De-Luxe £620, Saloon £495, Coupé £465, 2/3 Seater £390, Four Seat Coupé £635,
Saloon Laundaulette £545, Four Seat Sports £450.

MODEL            **Side-valve Eleven-40 (SWB)**                    *Year:* 1924

CHASSIS

Channel section parallel frame, swept up over rear axle, 5 cross members.
*Wheelbase:* 9 ft. 0 in.
*Track:* Front 4 ft. 2 in. or 4 ft. 4 in. Rear 4 ft. 2 in. or 4 ft. 4 in.
*Type of Wheels:* 760×90 mm. 4 stud disc (4 ft. 2 in. track) 760×90 mm. 4 stud wire
    (4 ft. 4 in. track).
*Tyres:* Front Size 760×90 mm. Rear Size 760×90 mm.
*Braking System:* Self compensating rod brakes 4 shoe, 2 footbrake, 2 handbrake.

TRANSMISSION

*Clutch Type:* Dry fabric cone.
*Gearbox Type:* Riley 4-speed.
*Gear Selecting Mechanism:* Central, right hand optional.
*Gear Ratios:* 1st—16.7:1, 2nd—11.6:1, 3rd—7.4:1, 4th—4.7:1, Reverse: 16.7:1
*Rear Axle Type:* Semi floating spiral bevel.
*Rear Axle Ratio:* 4.7:1

ENGINE

*Engine Type:* 11/40
*RAC H.P. Rating:* 10.8
*Cubic Capacity:* 1498 cc.
*Number of Cylinders:* 4
*Firing Order:* 1, 2, 4, 3
*Bore:* 65.8 mm.

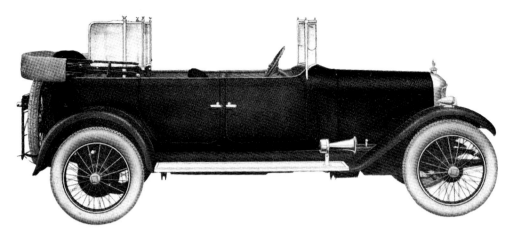

*1924 4 Seater de Luxe*

*1924 4 Door 4 Seater*

*1924 Two Seater*

*1924 2/3 Seat Clover-Leaf and 1924 2/3 Seater*

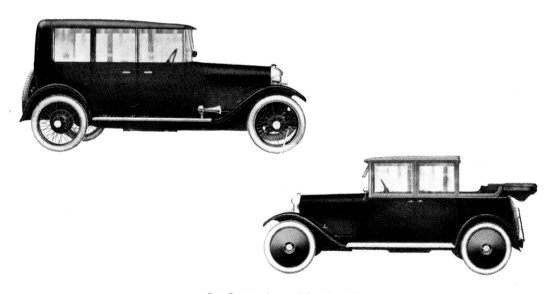

*1924 4 Seat Coupé and 1924 Saloon Landaulette*

*Stroke:* 110 mm.
*Cylinder Head:* Flat detachable with inclined spark plugs, water cooled.
*Valve Gear:* Chain drive camshaft to side valves on near side, 2 per cylinder of 1½ in.
    diameter.
*Valve Timing:* Inlet opens 10° ATDC.
*Number of Main Bearings:* 3 × 1⅜ in.
*Sump Capacity:* 12 pints.
*Type of Oil Pump:* Gear driven, big ends splash fed.
*Cooling System:* Thermosyphon.
*Type of Ignition:* Magneto.
*Method of Advance/Retard:* Manual.
*Contact Breaker Gap:* 0.012 in.
*Plug Gap:* 0.018 in.
*Number, Make and Type of Carburetters:* Single Cox-Atmos.
*Type of Inlet Manifold:* Cast, bolt-on.
*Type of Exhaust Manifold:* Cast, bolt-on.
*Location of Fuel Tank:* Dash mounted under bonnet.
*Capacity of Fuel Tank:* 7 gallons.
*Method of Fuel Feed:* Gravity.

MODELS AVAILABLE   Two Door Four Seater £395, Two Seat Sports £495, Two/Three Seat Clover Leaf
Model £450.

| | | |
|---|---|---|
| MODEL | **Side-valve Eleven-40** | *Year:* 1925–28 |

CHASSIS          Channel section parallel frame swept up over rear axle, 5 cross members.
*Wheelbase:* 9 ft. 0 in.
*Track:* Front 4 ft. 4 in. Rear 4 ft. 4 in.
*Type of Wheels:* Artillery or wire 19 × 3.0 in. 6 stud fixing.
*Tyres:* Front 29 × 4.95 in (Sports 27 × 4.40 in)
       Rear 29 × 4.95 in (Sports 27 × 4.40 in)
*Braking System:* Four wheel brakes, self compensating, 4 wheel footbrake, 2 handbrake.

TRANSMISSION   *Clutch Type:* Fabric cone in oilbath (1925/27) single.
*Gearbox Type:* Riley 4-speed.
*Gear Selecting Mechanism:* Dry plate type 1928. Central, right hand optional on non
    sports models.
*Gear Ratios:* 1st—18.2:1, 2nd—11.6:1, 3rd—7.4:1, 4th—4.7:1, Reverse: 18.2:1
*Rear Axle Type:* Riley semi-floating spiral bevel.
*Rear Axle Ratio:* 4.7:1

ENGINE          *Engine Type:* Eleven-40
*RAC H.P. Rating:* 10.8
*Cubic Capacity:* 1498 cc.
*Number of Cylinders:* 4
*Firing Order:* 1, 2, 4, 3
*Bore:* 65.8 mm.
*Stroke:* 110 mm.
*Cylinder Head:* Flat detachable water cooled with inclined spark plugs.
*Valve Gear:* Near side located chain drive camshaft to side valves, 2 per cylinder, 1½ in
    diameter.
*Valve Timing:* Inlet opens 10° ATDC.
*Number of Main Bearings:* 3 × 1⅝ in.
*Sump Capacity:* 12 pints.
*Type of Oil Pump:* Gear driven, splash fed big ends.
*Cooling System:* Thermosyphon with fan.
*Type of Ignition:* Magneto.
*Method of Advance/Retard:* Manual.
*Contact Breaker Gap:* 0.012 in.
*Plug Gap:* 0.018 in.
*Number, Make and Type of Carburetters:* Single Cox Atmos (1925) Zenith (1926–28)
*Type of Inlet Manifold:* Cast bolt-on.
*Type of Exhaust Manifold:* Cast bolt-on.

*Location of Fuel Tank:* Dash mounted under bonnet.
*Capacity of Fuel Tank:* 7 gallons
*Method of Fuel Feed:* Gravity.

MODELS AVAILABLE   1925: Special Touring Car (2 door 4 seater) £435, 2 Seat Sports £495, 4 Seat Sports £495.
1926: 2 Door Special Tourer £435, Sports 2 Seater £495, Sports 4 Seater £495.
1927: 2 Door Special Tourer £435, Sports 2 Seater £495, Sports 4 Seater £495.
1928: 2 Seat Sports £395, 4 Seat Sports £398, Long Sports Four (9 ft. 6 in. wheelbase) £427.

*1924 Saloon de Luxe*

*1924 Coupé*

| MODEL | **Side-valve Twelve** | *Year:* 1925–28 |

CHASSIS Channel section parallel frame with reinforcing central subframe. 5 cross members.
*Wheelbase:* 9 ft. 6 in. (9 ft. 9 in. Saloon Landaulette).
*Track:* Front 4 ft. 4 in. (4 ft. 8 in. Colonial) Rear 4 ft. 4 in. (4 ft. 8 in. Colonial)
*Type of Wheels:* Artillery or wire 19 × 3.0 in. 6 stud fixing.
*Tyres:* Front Size 29 × 4.95 in. Rear Size 29 × 4.95 in.
*Braking System:* 4 wheel footbrake, self compensating. 2 wheel handbrake.

TRANSMISSION *Clutch Type:* Fabric cone, oilbath type (1925–27 Single) Dry. Plate Type 1928.
*Gearbox Type:* Riley 4 speed.
*Gear Selecting Mechanism:* Central, right hand optional.
*Gear Ratios:* 1st—1925–27 18.2:1, (1928 19.4:1) 2nd—1925–27 11.6, (1928 12.1)
3rd—1925–27 7.4, (1928 7.8), 4th—1925–27 4.7 (1828 5) Reverse 1925–27
18.2:1 (1928 24.6:1)
*Rear Axle Type:* Riley semi-floating spiral bevel (4.7:1 for 1925–27, 5:1 for 1928).
*Rear Axle Ratio:* 1925–27 4.7:1 (1928 5:1)

ENGINE *Engine Type:* 1925 11/40, 1926/8 12 h.p.
*RAC H.P. Rating:* 11.9
*Cubic Capacity:* 1645 cc.
*Number of Cylinders:* 4
*Firing Order:* 1, 2, 4, 3
*Bore:* 69 mm.
*Stroke:* 110 mm.
*Cylinder Head:* Flat detachable water cooled with inclined spark plugs. 1928 Ricardo
head with vertical spark plugs.
*Valve Gear:* Near side located chain driven camshaft operating side valves, 2 per
cylinder, 1½ in. diameter.
*Valve Timing:* Inlet opens 10° ATDC.
*Number of Main Bearings:* 3 × 1⅝ in.
*Sump Capacity:* 12 pints.
*Type of Oil Pump:* Gear drive, splash fed big ends.
*Cooling System:* Thermosyphon with fan.
*Type of Ignition:* Magneto.
*Method of Advance/Retard:* Manual.
*Contact Breaker Gap:* 0.012 in.
*Plug Gap:* 0.018 in.
*Number, Make and Type of Carburetters:* 1925—Single Cox-Atmos 1926–28 Single
Zenith.
*Type of Inlet Manifold:* Cast bolt-on.
*Type of Exhaust Manifold:* Cast bolt-on.
*Location of Fuel Tank:* Dash mounted under bonnet.
*Capacity of Fuel Tank:* 7 gallons.
*Method of Fuel Feed:* Gravity.

MODELS AVAILABLE 1925: 5 Seat Deluxe Tourer £460, Saloon £495, Saloon Deluxe £595, Coupé £475
4/5 Seat Tourer £395, 2/6 Seater £395, Saloon Landaulette (9 ft. 9 in. WB)
£525, Chassis only £300.
1926: Chassis with rear wheel brakes only £300, with FWB £310, Coupé £475,
Coupé with fixed top £480, Coupé De Ville from £750, De Luxe Touring £460,
Foleshill Tourer £350, Four Door coach £395, Glass enclosed Tourer £450,
Saloon £495, Saloon Landaulette (9 ft. 9 in. WB) £525, Saloon De Luxe £595,
4 Door Special Touring £445, 4/5 Seat 'Tourer £395, 2/6 Seat Glass Enclosed
£395, 2/3 Seater £350.
1927: Chassis Only £300, Foleshill Tourer £330, 2/3 Seater £350, Four Door Coach
£395, 2/6 Seater £395, Standard Tourer £395, 2/6 Seat Glass Enclosed £415,
Glass Enclosed Tourer £450, De Luxe Touring £460, Coupé £475, 4 Door
Saloon £495, Saloon Landaulette (9 ft. 9 in. WB) £525, Saloon De Luxe £595.
1928: Lulworth Saloon £350, Lulworth Special £365, Standard Tourer £365,
4 Door Coach £375, 2/6 Seat Glass Enclosed £385, Wentworth £395, Special
Tourer £398, Chatsworth £398, Grangeworth £398, Midworth £415, Saloon
De Luxe £495.

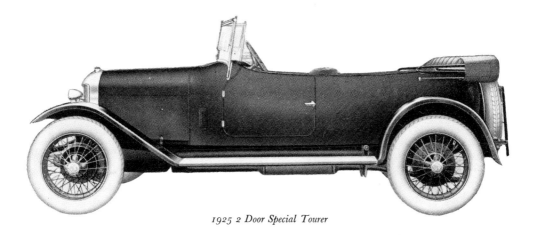

*1925 2 Door Special Tourer*

*1925 2/6 Seater*

*1925 5 Seat Tourer de Luxe*

*1926/27 Saloon Landaulette*

*1926/27 Twelve Chassis*

*1927 Coupé de Ville*

*1927 Glass Enclosed Tourer*

*1927 Foleshill Tourer*

*1927 2/3 Seater*

*1927 Four Door Coach*

*1927 2/6 Seat Glass Enclosed*

*1928 Lulworth Saloon*

*1928 Wentworth Coupé*

*1928 Grangeworth Saloon*

*1928 Chatsworth Saloon*

December 24, 1919.    989    The **Motor**

# THE NEW RILEY.

## 11 h.p. Detachable-head Engine. Four-speed Gearbox. Air-cooled Brakes. Six Parts Only to Lubricate Half-yearly.

*The standard four-seater Riley.*

THAT critical and much-neglected person, the owner-driver, will have no quarrel with the designer of the 11 h.p. Riley, because in this most interesting production his requirements have received an unusual and welcome measure of consideration.

One of the aims of the designer has been to save the owner-driver trouble, to reduce the bugbear of periodical lubrication to a minimum, and to ensure that when necessary it can be accomplished with convenience and ease. Apart from the engine, the lubrication points are six only and require attention but once in six months; moreover they are very accessible. There are no greasers, and where oil is not required as in the case of all spring shackle bolts and oscillating shafts, self-lubricating bushes of compressed asbestos impregnated with graphite are employed. That is but one of the many admirable features. Seldom have we seen a design in which such careful attention has been given to ease of production, without the sacrifice of any feature which is likely to make for efficiency in performance.

*The camshaft and magneto driving chains. Two are employed instead of the single chain "triangular" drive which is more usual.*

So far as can be gathered, the aim has been so to design the car that it shall be as ideal to make in the factory as to use upon the road, and towards this achievement a big step forward has been taken. Throughout the chassis use has been made of all those manufacturing processes which are known to make for economy in production, whilst contributing largely to lightness of construction. Pressed steel is used extensively, and over 60 steel stampings can be counted. The engine, gearbox and axle filler caps—too often made as clumsy castings—are of light pressed steel, so is the gearbox lid, the cone clutch and its cover, and many other parts. There is evidence throughout of an expert appreciation of the economics of design, as well as the mechanics of the subject, and the balance is well struck. The result is a chassis which positively bristles with good points from every aspect.

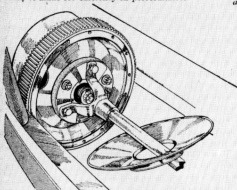

*The clutch is of the pressed steel cone type, fabric lined. The cover of clutch—also a pressing—is shown removed in this sketch to expose the flexible joint, of which there are two between the engine and gearbox. The toothed ring for the starter is of steel shrunk on the flywheel.*

c17

The Motor                    990                    December 24, 1919.

## THE 11 h.p. RILEY.—Contd.

The engine has a bore of 65.8 mm. and a stroke of 110 mm., and the four cylinders form a monobloc casting separate from the crankcase, and fitted with a detachable head—a form of construction which differs from and possesses certain advantages over the combined cylinder and crankcase type of casting.

### The Power Unit.

The valves are on the near side, are inclined and are actuated by an unusual form of square section

*The twin rear brakes with the brake drum, hub and axle shaft removed. Note the air scoops on the drum and the novel design of the aluminium shoes. The wing nuts for the ingenious brake adjustment can be seen just above the spring.*

tappet from a camshaft running in three die-cast bearings and driven by a Renold silent chain. Light subsidiary springs hold the tappets constantly against the valve stems to ensure silence in operation, and a neat pressed steel cover encloses the whole. The carburetter—a Zephyr—bolts direct to the off side of the cylinder casting, and the mixture is drawn through ports cast in the block. The magneto is on the near side and is driven by a silent chain from the large timing wheel. Two chains are thus employed instead of the more usual " triangular " type of drive with a single chain, the object being to remove all possibilities of trouble on account of chain stretch.

Aluminium pistons are used, and the fixing of the gudgeon pin by a particularly simple though absolutely efficacious method must be given prominence. The crankshaft runs in three die-cast bearings, which receive their lubrication from galleries cast in the upper half of the crankcase and supplied by a separate lead from the oiling system. The gear

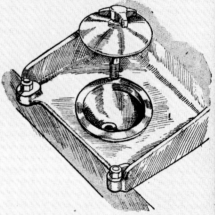

*The large gearbox filler and its quickly detachable cover. Oil is employed as a lubricant for the gears, as there is no grease used on the Riley chassis.*

pump, driven by a vertical shaft from the camshaft, also delivers oil to troughs cast in the lower half of the crankcase, from which the big ends take their lubrication by means of dippers. The oil filter arrangement is extremely well thought out, and its removal can be effected by simply unscrewing a special plug by means of a jack handle which it is shaped to receive. The oil-filling orifice is commendably large and accessibly placed, and is covered by a neat pressed steel spring lid. A well-designed oil level indicator rod is provided, and the bottom of the sump is ribbed for oil cooling purposes. A two-bladed cast-aluminium fan, the bearings of which are so designed as to retain lubrication for a long period, assists the thermo-syphon cooling system.

*Three-quarter view of the Riley chassis. Note the neat arrangement of the petrol tank and instrument board, the novel lamp brackets, and the running board supports which extend right across the frame.*

c18

December 24, 1919.          991          The **Motor**

## THE 11 h.p RILEY.—*Contd.*

### The Use of Pressed Steel.

The fan pulley is made of two saucer-shaped pressings placed back to back, and the dynamo driving pulley is simply spun on the pressed-steel cover plate which encloses the clutch. This is typical of the designers' resource in employing pressed steel wherever possible and saving weight and manufacturing costs thereby. The clutch is of the cone type made of pressed steel and fabric lined. Carried on the cone, and enclosed by the cover plate already mentioned, is a fabric disc type of universal joint from which the drive is taken by a short shaft to a similar joint at the front of the gearbox, which is separately mounted. Four speeds and reverse are provided, the reverse pinions being at rest when not in use, and the change-speed and brake levers are centrally mounted upon the pressed-steel cover of the box. A special feature of the brake lever is that the pawl engages several of the quadrant notches at the same time, thus giving unusual security.

From the gearbox an open propeller shaft, provided with fabric disc universal joints at either end, takes the drive to the bevel-driven rear axle. The axle casing is of cast steel, made in two halves, and the tubular portion of the casing is elliptical in section, the largest diameter being vertical, so that the axle is particularly strong. The centre portion is provided with a large-diameter rear cover plate through which the differential and all its details can be removed when the axle shafts have been withdrawn, as they very easily can be.

*The large oil filler with its pressed steel lid. Note the hemispherical casing at the back of the fan pulley. This holds the oil which lubricates the fan bearing for a long period. There is no chance of oil leakage as the lubricant is thrown by centrifugal force to the periphery of the casing whence a small quantity constantly finds its way to the bearing through a pipe.*

### Originality in Brake Design.

One of the most striking features is the design of the twin rear brakes. The shoes are of aluminium, fabric faced, and they work side by side in large-diameter drums which are air-cooled by a novel method. Each drum has a number of cowled openings through which, when the car is in motion, air is "scooped" into the interior of the drum, passing out through apertures formed in the inside steel cover after it has cooled the shoes. It might be thought

that mud and dust would also enter in the same way, but we are informed that such does not occur in practice.

The brake adjustment is distinctly clever, as wear is taken up by altering the position of the brake shoe pivots so that the actuating cams are undisturbed, and are always in the most efficient working position. Large accessible wing nuts enable the adjustment to be made.

The ingenuity which has been applied to the brake design extends all through the axle features. Oil leakage has been most carefully considered and is impossible except at certain points where it is allowed to "leak" in order to lubricate some part such as the brake operating cam-shaft. Adjustable Timken bearings support the differential and the bevel pinion, and the rear hubs have a single large ball bearing each. As this is practically on the centre line of the wheels there is almost a complete absence of overhang.

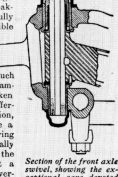

*Section of the front axle swivel, showing the exceptional care devoted to oil retention. There is literally no possibility of leakage.*

### A Car with a Future.

Without personal inspection of this car it is difficult for an adequate idea of the attractiveness of the design to be conveyed. It was seen by many persons at the Show, of course, but the car must be examined in the making for its good points really to be appreciated. On the road in the course of a short run, our experiences were such as to lead us to expect great things from it in the way of performance. It is remarkably lively, with great powers of acceleration.

In it are combined all those features which should make for success. There seems to have been the closest liaison between the designing and producing departments of the factory behind it, and put into large-scale production this, the latest product of the Riley Co., should achieve an enviable position amongst the cars of its class.

The prices are as follow:—Two-seater body, £465; four-seater body, £490; coupé body, £545. Makers:—Riley Motor Co., Coventry.

*The Riley standard coupe. The polished aluminium bonnet is fitted as standard.*

THE AUTOCAR, October 27th, 1922.     801

# THE 17 H.P. RILEY.

**Sturdy Construction the Feature of a Carefully Designed Three-litre Four-speed Touring Car.**

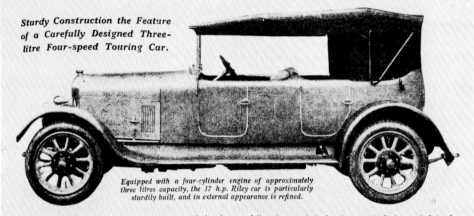

*Equipped with a four-cylinder engine of approximately three litres capacity, the 17 h.p. Riley car is particularly sturdily built, and in external appearance is refined.*

INSPECTION of this car reveals a chassis obviously built for durability, for the construction is very robust. The complete five-seater touring car weighs 28 cwt., but since the engine develops on the brake some 58 h.p. at 2,500 r.p.m., and as a four-speed gear box is fitted, the road performance should be good. It may be mentioned incidentally that the car is a product of the Riley Engine Co., Castle Works, Coventry, whose name was familiar to motorists before the war in connection with a very sturdy 12-18 h.p. car fitted with a two-cylinder water-cooled V engine.

### Accessible Unit Details.

Though the latest four-cylinder 17 h.p. car in general follows standard practice, there are in its construction a number of special points. In the engine, for example, the crankshaft is carried in five bearings, and there are in the side of the top half of the aluminium crank case a series of large inspection doors, one of which carries the slide-valve plunger pump of the lubrication system, the latter being fully forced. The oil level in the base chamber is indicated by a float, and the strainer is so arranged that it can be removed without emptying out the oil. This is a convenience if the strainer needs cleaning

For the cylinder a block casting is used, the head being integral and water spaces being allowed between individual barrels. The valves are in line on the left side, whilst to the right side of the block a Zenith triple diffuser carburetter is attached.

---

**SPECIFICATION.**

**ENGINE:** 17 h.p., four cylinders, 85·7 × 127 mm. (2,932 c.c.). Rating 18·2 h.p. Tax £19.
**TRANSMISSION:** Cone clutch, unit four-speed gear box, worm final drive.
**SPRINGING:** Half-elliptic front and threequarter-elliptic rear.
**WHEELS:** Detachable spoke with 820 × 120 mm. tyres.
**WHEELBASE:** 10 ft. 6 in. Track 4 ft. 8in.
**PRICE:** Five-seater, £750.

---

Like the crankshaft, the camshaft is carried in five bearings and driven through helical toothed gearing; while across the front of the engine is a transverse shaft, actuating on one side a centrifugal pump for the water circulation, and on the other the magneto. To assist cooling, a link belt-driven fan is provided, a second link belt from the fan spindle pulley in turn driving the lighting dynamo. C.A.V. electrical equipment with a five-lamp set is used, and the starting motor situated on the left side of the clutch pit drives through a toothed ring cut on the rim of the flywheel.

### A Silent Indirect Speed.

Unit construction is employed for the engine and gear box, and is attached at three points, the rear end being supported on a massive tubular cross member. The aluminium casing which joins the engine to the gear box is left open at the top to enable the leather cone clutch to be reached when necessary; the latter is split for removal, and is fitted with adjustable springs and with flat first intention springs up under the leather.

Coming now to the transmission we find that, giving absolute ratios of, bottom 15.2, second 9.6, third 6.2, and top 4.1 to 1, the gear box is interesting for several reasons, foremost amongst which is that both third and fourth speeds are meshed through sliding dogs, the constant mesh wheels and the third speed gear wheels having helically cut teeth, so that both top and third speeds are quiet running. The gear change is operated through a lever carried on the right side of the car,

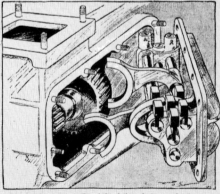

*By removing ten nuts the whole of the selector mechanism can be removed for Inspection.*

3        c 21

*802*                                          *THE AUTOCAR, October 27th, 1922.*

*The 17 h.p. Riley.*

but mounted independently of the frame on an extension of the gear box, whilst in the lid of the latter is a gear drive for the speedometer cable. At the back of the gear box is a contracting shoe foot brake which is entirely encased, but easily adjustable, the reason of the casing being that the gear box assembly terminates in a spherical housing for the hollow ball of the torque tube. In construction the rear axle casing consists of an aluminium centre with large taper, steel tubes, on the outside of which the hub bearings are mounted, the shafts being made to carry none of the load, but only take the driver. The propeller-shaft is enclosed by the torque tube, and the final drive is by worm.

Swept inwards at the front and upwards at the back, the frame is of deep section, and is attached to

*Details of the air and oil pumps shown detached from the crank case.*

the axles by semi-elliptic front and threequarter-elliptic underslung rear springs. A worm and worm wheel carried on ball bearings is used for the steering gear. At the back of the frame the petrol tank is fitted and feeds the carburetter either through a vacuum tank or through an air-pressure system, as preferred.

In appearance the lines of the car are well balanced, the body being of the streamline variety and fitted with three doors. The seats are well placed as to angle, and the upholstery is comfortable. An adjustable double panel windscreen is fitted, and there are easily detachable celluloid side panels opening and closing with the doors for use in conjunction with the black hood. Besides the standard five-seater body a feature is made of supplying any desired coachwork. The chassis is priced at £500.

The Motor                 616                 *May 13, 1924.*

# A Car to Fit Anybody.

## Adjustable Seats and Novel Features on the Riley de Luxe Model.

The seating is upholstered in best-quality leather, which can be obtained in art shades harmonizing with the paintwork, in which there is a wide choice of colours. The seats are of generous proportions, but, far more important, they are adjustable, so that driver and passengers of varying dimensions can all be seated in equal comfort. This adjustment is provided in an ingenious manner, as shown in the accompanying sketches; the angle of both seat cushions and back squabs can be altered. The sides at the rear are padded and provided with arm rests, and the luxurious appear-

WITH the very first glance at the four-seater de luxe touring model of the 11-40 h.p. Riley, one would exclaim: "What a handsome car!" If the hood and side curtains were erected, one would take it for a specially built all-weather model with metal head. Closer examination will show many unusual features and, in short, a really luxurious equipment of a touring car at a very moderate price. The radiator, bonnet, scuttle and body lines give it at once an imposing and a graceful appearance, accentuated by a narrow angle V-screen and a black, highly glazed, flexible leather-cloth hood.

Let us describe the interior fittings of this car in detail. The extremely handsome facia board, which is divided into three panels, would first attract attention. The centre panel takes a neat group of instruments with the lighting switchboard and ammeter in the centre, and a clock and speedometer on each side, illuminated from above by a revolving type of dash lamp. In the panel on the right is a smoker's companion with ash tray, and on the left a dull silver-finished cap which, when pulled out, discloses a mirror in the lid and a powder puff.

The upper panel of the screen is adjustable and divided, so that the screen in front of the passenger may be closed at times when it is necessary to open the other side to provide better vision for the driver. A hand-operated screen wiper is fitted.

*Showing the maximum adjustment of the front seats. The angle of the rear squab is determined by a strap which is neatly covered with art leather.*

ance of the upholstery is accentuated by metal beadings covered with leather.

Still further to suit the car to drivers short or tall, the angle of the steering column and the reach of

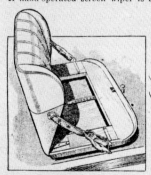

*The adjustable seats both front and rear on the Riley de luxe model. The fore and aft position of the front seat and the angle of the rear squab can be altered to suit persons of different stature with a similar adjustment of the rear seat which is fixed in position by two wing nuts. (Right) The headlamp supports, which permit of the lamps being swivelled round to show a light on the kerb when driving in fog.*

*May 13, 1924.*     617     The **Motor**

### A CAR TO FIT ANYBODY.—Contd.

the pedals are adjustable, while the position of the front seats can also be varied.

When the hood is erected—which can be done with a minimum of effort—and the side panels are in place, the appearance of a closed saloon is given. The side panels are of celluloid with metal frames and large lights, there being three on each side, and are so fitted as to make the car completely weatherproof. When used as an open touring car, these

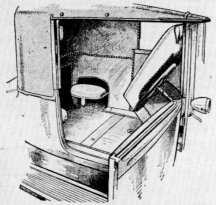

*An interior view, showing the occasional seats behind the tipping front seats on the Riley coupe.*

panels can be left erected or stowed away, while the hood is enclosed in a leather cloth envelope. The rear passengers are then protected by an adjustable rear screen, which is also included in the very complete equipment.

Other interesting details are a double type of steel springing in each seat cushion, neat panelling along the top rail of the body, which is turned over the edges of the woodwork and fastened internally, white-metal door handles, solid nickel body furniture, a real wool carpet fitted to the floors, round the back of the front seats, and the sides of the body, and rubber step mats fitted to the running boards opposite each of the four doors.

The chassis is slightly altered from the standard model, inasmuch that wire wheels (or artillery wheels at choice) with large-section low-pressure tyres are fitted, while a luggage grid is included.

Amongst the details of the equipment is a Boyce radiator thermometer. The headlamps have a novel form of attachment, arranged so that they can be swivelled round to direct a beam of light on to the kerb—a useful provision when driving in fog.

The price of the four-seater de luxe Riley is £460, and that of the standard model, which is also a very handsome car, £395.

#### A New Open and Closed Two-seater.

A comparatively new model is a two-seater which can be used as a six-seater, and this is made both as an open touring car at the price of £395, or as a coupé, with glass windows in large doors, at £465. Behind the adjustable seats of both these models are two tip-up seats which will easily carry two children. When folded away, there is a useful space for luggage. In addition, there is a sunken double dickey seat.

The accompanying illustrations will give an idea of the appearance of these special models, which are only a few of the range of all types of bodies fitted to the single Riley chassis.

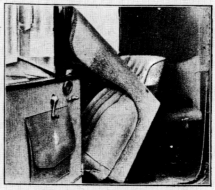

*Another view of the coupe interior. Note the convenient position of the door handle.*

The Riley power unit is a four-cylinder monobloc engine with detachable head and large inclined side valves having a bore of 65.8 mm. and a stroke of 110 mm., which, with a cubic capacity of 1,498 c.c., develops, at 3,500 r.p.m., no less than 40 b.h.p. The crankshaft and camshaft are carried on three large gunmetal bearings lined with white metal.

Transmission is through a fabric cone clutch with a four-speed-and-reverse gearbox with central change-speed lever (thus providing for a door on the driver's side but right-hand change can be fitted at £5 extra), and thence by an open propeller shaft to a semi-floating spiral bevel rear axle drive. Steering is by worm and complete wheel, with the magneto and carburetter controls conveniently arranged in the centre of the steering wheel, while the swivel pin bearings are of large diameter arranged for central pivoting. Suspension is by semi-elliptic springs,

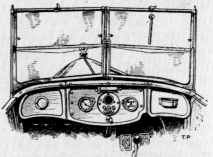

*The symmetrical handsome facia board. On the left is a ladies' puff-case and mirror, and on the right an ash-tray.*

with a large number of thin leaves enclosed in gaiters. Petrol supply is from a seven-gallon tank mounted under the bonnet and having an exceptionally wide filler cap. Both brakes operate in large ribbed drums on the rear wheels and are enclosed, so protecting them from dust and moisture, while the brake shoes are asbestos-lined aluminium, with the object of dispersing heat. The chassis has a very excellent performance and reputation and, with the handsome, well-finished bodywork of the de luxe models, provides an ideal family car.

Riley cars are produced by Riley (Coventry), Ltd., Coventry, with London showrooms at 42, North Audley Street, W.1.

# CHAPTER FOUR

# 'The Wonder Car'— 9 hp Models, 1926–1938

It is said that the bodywork design for the first Riley Nine, the Monaco Saloon, was the result of an idea conceived by Stanley Riley whilst he was still a schoolboy. It was he who designed the Monaco and it was this car which turned many heads at that Shelsley Walsh meeting in July 1926. It is certain that the Riley brothers could not have foreseen the tremendous success their car was to achieve—and more particularly the engine design concept. Who, in 1926, would have had the courage to forecast that an engine bearing the Riley name, and of the same design concept, would be in production still 30 years later? That was eighteeen years after the Riley Company had been sold to Nuffield—such was the contribution made by Riley to the industry!

The designs of the Nine were completed in 1925 and after a thorough road-testing programme which covered England, Scotland, Wales, Ireland and the Alps, the car was announced to the world. Within a year, it had earned the reputation 'The Wonder Car'.

New design features included Percy Riley's 'PR' cylinder head, with its hemispherical combustion chambers and overhead valves inclined at 45° operated by camshafts located high in the cylinder block/crankcase, so that the pushrods were as short as possible to give the running efficiency of an overhead camshaft engine with the serviceability of a pushrod design. The Silent Third gearbox was a joy to use, because, as ever, Riley had concentrated— as they had always done—on making the gearchange as easy as possible for even the most inexperienced driver: it was just as significant that the gearbox really was quiet in operation.

The hot-spot induction system introduced on the new model featured exhaust gas heating of the induction manifold to ensure the most efficient gas flow into the combustion chambers. This was achieved by running a pipe across the back of the cylinder head connecting the exhaust manifold to the inlet manifold.

In plan view the chassis was narrow at the front, widening from behind the front wheels to a point roughly in line with the handbrake lever and then running parallel to the rear. In profile, the mainframe was downswept at the front ends of the front springs and rising in a gentle curve to a flat top which arched slightly over the rear wheels.

The engine and gearbox were mounted into the frame in unit in a very novel way. A cross-shaft ran through the crankcase and was mounted into the engine on conical rubber mountings held in place by cast aluminium cones which served to keep the mounting rubbers in mild compression. The aluminium cones were kept in place by large nuts on the threaded portion of the cross-shaft, the ends of which, and thus the engine, were located in special mounting brackets each secured by two bolts into lugs on the chassis frame itself.

The third mounting point for the engine and gearbox was at the point where the gearbox connected to the torque tube enclosing the front universal joint and propeller shaft. A cross-

*The 9 h.p. Monaco prototype—announced at*
*Shelsley Walsh in July 1926.*

member in the chassis frame at that location supported the rear end of the gearbox—or
more correctly, the front half of the universal joint housing between the gearbox rear face and
the torque tube front face—and so supported the front end of the torque tube as well. The
gearbox rear mounting was also on rubber, so the driveline and chassis were isolated from
each other's shocks but in sufficiently rigid a combination to contribute usefully to the car's
undoubted handling qualities.

The gearbox was of four-speed type, originally with a right-hand located gate and selector
lever and the handbrake was located at the right on the early cars too, though later both gear
and handbrake levers were located in the centre with an optional right-hand location available
at £5 extra cost. The pedals were arranged with the accelerator on the right (many contemporary cars were still putting it between the clutch and brake pedals), the brake in the centre
and the delightfully light clutch pedal on the left. All were well designed in terms of reach and
angle of operation and helped to make the car a very easy driving experience.

The original Monaco which attracted such interest at Shelsley Walsh was slightly modified for production and then offered to the market at the price of £285. It was accompanied
by a Four Seat Tourer at £235. The Monaco had wire wheels, and whilst the prototype had
four bolt fixings to the wheels, the production models had five. The tourer was offered on steel
artillery wheels, but wire wheels were available at an extra cost of 6 guineas.

By 1928, the range of bodywork was wider and there were two chassis variations now
available. The frame was identical in both cases, but the Colonial chassis offered greater
ground clearance with a standard track and reinforced lamp brackets to sustain the more
rigorous environment in the Colonies! The two chassis were priced at £200 and £210.

The models available now included the Monaco, the San Remo (a more orthodox saloon)
the Two Seat Tourer, the Four Seat Tourer, the Sports Four and, a little later, the Speed
Model.

The chassis of the Speed Model (the Brooklands, as it came to be known) was totally
different from the standard range of cars. It was the result of some keen-eyed awareness of the
Riley Nine's potential on the part of J. G. Parry-Thomas and Reid Railton, who took a pro-

*The Mk. I production Monaco Saloon for the 1928 Season.*
*Note the differences between this and the prototype*
*(this is a mock-up, identified by the four-stud wheels).*

*1928 9 h.p. Four Seater*

*1928 San Remo Saloon*

*1928 9 h.p. Two Seater*

*1929 Biarritz Silent Saloon*

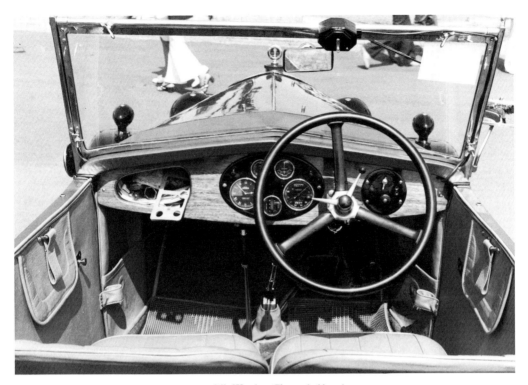

*1929 Mk IV 9 h.p. Tourer dashboard*

duction 9 h.p. chassis and changed its shape such that it became an extremely low-built, boat tailed two-seat racing machine. Railton was extremely successful with his early competition outings in the car—so much so that Thomson and Taylor Ltd developed the design and built a few cars, after which Riley themselves put the model into production. It was originally offered in 1928, at £395 and by the time the 'Plus' series model was available in 1931 it was £420 for the Standard car and £475 for the 'Plus' model with its four Amal carburetters. The Sports Four or Special Tourer was simply a Four Seat Tourer with two carburetters and its price was £298.

Optional extras on these early Nines included a bulb horn for £2.10.0; a Motometer on the radiator cap for £1.10.0 and an extra spare wheel, without tyre, and twin spare wheel carrier for £4.10.0. The usual paint options were offered and wire wheels were available where artillery wheels were standard equipment. Black finish was available on those parts which were normally nickel plated at a price of £3 and, perhaps most important of all (because it demonstrated that Riley had a concern for safety which was only equalled by other manufacturers many years later) the option of Triplex Safety Glass in the windscreen. Triplex laminated glass was to become standard the next year on all Riley cars.

For 1929, all models were offered on wire wheels and the San Remo was dropped in favour of a new, more luxurious saloon to be known as the Biarritz Silent Saloon. Riley's own words upon its introduction were: 'We are confident that there is a restricted but willing demand for this model and that the motorist of experience will readily realise the advance it represents in body construction and design'. The Biarritz was, again in Riley's words,

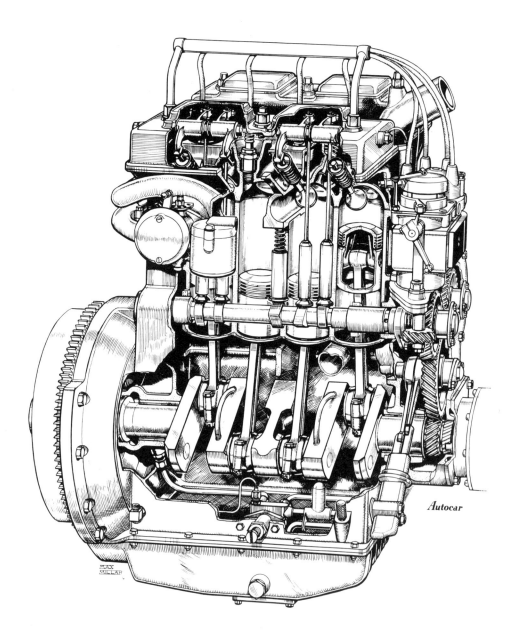

*Autocar*

### A PRODUCTION RILEY NINE ENGINE

*This is an early 9 type h.p. engine of pre-Engine No 28000. Noteworthy features in this cutaway are the external oil feed to the front of the rocker shafts—the valve gear, with the pushrods operating inboard of each pair of valves, the valves being inclined at 45°(opposed to each other at 90°)—the lag tappet at the centre of the camshaft. The oil pressure relief valve can be seen in line above the sump drain plug and the oil pump is also of interest—this view shows the eccentric drive at the rear of the intermediate timing gear and the two plungers can be seen in the pump body. The unusually long main journals are also of interest. A taper at the rear end of the crankshaft carries the flywheel, located by a Woodruff key and retained by a single large nut, whilst at the front end of the crankshaft, the crankshaft timing wheel extends to a drive dog for the front mounted dynamo. The rocker shafts are carried in the rocker boxes, not mounted separately to the cylinder head.*

*1930 Monaco Plus Series Saloon*

developed from the Weymann principles employed in the earlier Monaco and San Remo designs, but intended to be better and quieter. Its price was £325.

The other models of that year were the Two Seater, the Four Seat Tourer, the Special Tourer and the Monaco on the 8 ft. 10 in. chassis—plus the Brooklands Speed Model on its own special chassis.

The range continued into 1930, with an improved Monaco which now had a full-width boot, the Four Seater which was fabric bodied, the Two Seater which had metal panelling, the Special Tourer and the Biarritz. The Brooklands Speed Model was also to continue in production.

1931 brought the 'Plus' Series, shown for the first time at the 1930 Motor Show, and whilst they used the same basic chassis a number of improvements had taken place. The catalogue introducing the new cars detailed 15 improvements:

1. Wider, more durable and lighter coachwork.
2. Radiator of improved design.
3. Radiator shell and bright parts in Firth's stainless 'Staybrite' steel.
4. Petrol tank at rear with increased capacity, to $7\frac{1}{2}$ gallons, and fitted with electric petrol gauge.
5. Improved tool locker underneath the bonnet.
6. Grouped lubrication points.
7. Finger tip controls on the steering column for lamps, dipper, ignition, horn and mixture with independent hand throttle.
8. Improved, illuminated instrument board, with cubby holes.
9. Spring steering wheel.
10. Jacking points on front and rear axles at the same height.
11. Batteries at rear instantly accessible from hinged rear seat.
12. Hinged rear seat giving access to rear shock absorbers.
13. Leveroll seat slides with more comfortable front seats.
14. Better and more comfortable suspension with 'Silentbloc' bushes.
15. Flanged exhaust joints which entirely prevent leakage of exhaust gases.

The Monaco continued in production, together with the Biarritz (which was now a half-panelled saloon), the Sunshine Saloon version of either Monaco or Biarritz, the Fabric 4 seat

THE Lion Car
AND Cyclecar

314

FEBRUARY 1

TUNING AND MAINTENANCE

# THE 9 H.P. RILEY

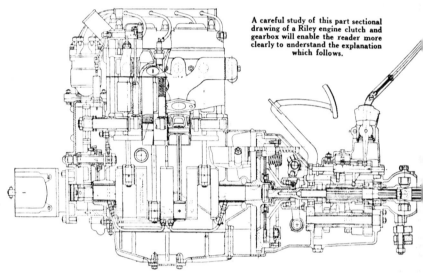

A careful study of this part sectional drawing of a Riley engine clutch and gearbox will enable the reader more clearly to understand the explanation which follows.

Written by a Member of the Staff, who is at Present Driving a 1930 Mona Model, this Series has been Prepared with the Hearty Co-operation of Ri (Coventry), Ltd., and Contains the Very Latest Information

THE Riley Nine was recognized at its inception as a car which clearly revealed an effort on the part of its designers, Riley (Coventry), Ltd., Dunbar Av., Foleshill, Coventry, to break away from convention—not so much in broad principle as in detail. For this reason it is an extremely interesting production, and for this reason also it calls for a greater degree of understanding by those who are owners or prospective owners.

The Mark V chassis, with which we propose to deal at length in this series of articles, differs little from the models immediately preceding it, and as the Mark V has already made its appearance in large numbers, we propose to confine our remarks exclusively to it. Owners of older models, however, should find little difficulty in detecting points which are not directly applicable and in seeing how they should be applied.

For the guidance of prospective owners we should add that the Mark V is distinguished from the front by an apron between the dumbirons and from the back by the large luggage carrier, the sides of which merge gracefully into those of the body.

### Characteristics of the Chassis.

It is desirable that a man who intends to drive and maintain a car properly should understand it from a mechanical point of view; he should know what this does and what that does and why they have to do it. As the article proceeds, therefore, the various parts of the chassis will be described with as much attention to detail as space permits, and immediately following this, tuning and maintenance points will be outlined.

The general characteristics of the Mark V chassis clearly show at a glance that the car was designed

to have a superior road performance and up to the gruelling of prolonged hard drivin has been taken, for example, to introduce the r " stiffening-up " process all round ; twin cross with a stout sheet-metal connecting used fore and aft (in addition to other sturmembers), the frame members are deep and paratively heavy section, the engine mount an unusual and very sturdy kind, the brake d

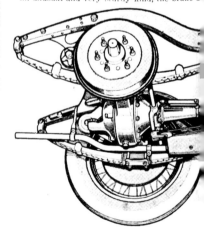

RUARY 14, 1930.

315

THE Light Car AND Cyclecar

ge diameter and the road springs are of the multi-
l semi-elliptic type.

certain respects the specification of the car is
r to that ordained by convention; that is to say,
udes a four-cylinder engine, plate clutch, four-
gearbox, torque tube, and so on, but it will be
at as we proceed that each of these components
ceived special treatment and that in some ways
re unique in the light car world.

much for a general introduction to the car; we
ow get down to business beginning with that
portant part of the make-up, the engine. This,
have previously pointed out, has four cylinders,
re being 60.3 mm., the stroke 95.2 mm., the cubic
ty 1,087 c.c., the R.A.C. treasury rating 9.01,
e tax £9.

s mounted at three points, two being at the front,
ll having a rubber buffer between the bearer
nd the mounting. The front mounting takes
rm of a steel bar running through a tunnel
tegral with the crankcase and so arranged that
nnecting-rods in cylinders No. 1 and 2 (viewed
the front) work on each side of this cast-iron

### How to Tighten the Engine Mounting.

ernally, the tunnel takes the form of an enlarged
which may be likened to the outer member of a
lutch. Mounted on the steel bar which passes
one frame member through the tunnel to the
frame member is the equivalent of the inner
h" cone. This cone is made of aluminium, and
en it and the boss there is a rubber gland. Each of
o inner cones is free to move on the supporting
the latter is screwed at each end so that
ans of large nuts the cones can be pressed tightly
ngagement with the interior of the bosses, the
forming a shock-proof joint between.

n this it will be observed that it is possible to
up the engine mounting, but care should be
to tighten each nut the same amount, other-
he engine will be thrown out of line.

At the rear the engine-gearbox unit is suspended
from the adjacent cross-member by means of a bolt
screwed into the torque ball cover at one end and at
the lower end to a plate sandwiched between two
rubber pads. The anchorage bolt should not be pulled
up tight, and there should be play between the bolt
fixed to the torque ball cover and the hole in the cross-
member through which it passes.

The main engine block consists of three main sections,
namely, the detachable head, the combined cylinder
block and crankcase and the ribbed aluminium sump.
The timing case at the front is completely detachable,
and carries the front main bearing of the crankshaft.
The rear bearing of the crankshaft is formed integral
with the wall of the crankcase. Neither of these
bearings, by the way, is split, whilst the latter is
pressed into position. The con. rods are of H section,
and high-efficiency pistons with four rings are employed.

In erecting the crankshaft it is first of all entered
into the rear bearing, then the bearing carried by the
timing case is threaded over the front journal.

For the timing arrangements a train of helical-tooth
gears takes the place of the chain more commonly
employed. No adjustment is needed for the former
construction, and all the wheels are of steel. This
principle has yet another advantage, for the teeth
of the wheels can be appropriately marked so that
retiming is reduced to the simplest possible formula.
An accompanying sketch shows the relationship of the
wheels to each other and the manner in which they
are marked.

Here, perhaps, it should be explained that the engine
has twin camshafts, each one being driven by a
separate gearwheel running in mesh with an intermediate wheel which, in turn, is driven by a pinion
on the end of the crankshaft. The o.h. valves are
operated by push-rods.

### Magneto Driven by Skew Gear.

By means of skew gears the magneto is driven from
the off-side cam wheel, and the teeth are marked so
that the magneto can be meshed correctly following,
say, an overhaul. The magneto itself rests on a platform and is secured by three bolts, all of which pass
through slotted holes. By slacking off all three nuts
the instrument can be pivoted so as to give a variation of 15 degrees in the timing. Before attempting to
move the magneto, however, the clamp ring round

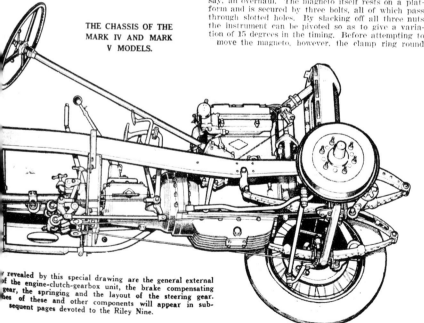

THE CHASSIS OF THE
MARK IV AND MARK
V MODELS.

revealed by this special drawing are the general external
of the engine-clutch-gearbox unit, the brake compensating
gear, the springing and the layout of the steering gear.
hes of these and other components will appear in subsequent pages devoted to the Riley Nine.

THE Light Car
• Cyclecar                              316                          FEBRUARY 14, 1930.

the contact breaker must be slacked off so as to allow for the necessary adjustment.

The magneto, complete with its mounting bracket, is secured to the side of the crankcase by four bolts, and if the nuts thereof be removed the whole unit

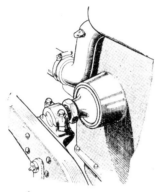

One of the front "cushion" bearer arms of the engine. It consists of a rubber "gland" tightly sandwiched between an inner sliding cone and an outer cone forming part of the engine block. By tightening the nut on each bearer arm evenly any slackness which develops can be taken up.

can be withdrawn. On the top of the timing case there is a tube, which at first sight looks as though it were merely a protection for an oil pipe which emerges from it. Actually, it is a breather tube, and the pipe is carried up within it for the sake of convenience. This brings us to the question of lubrication.

The oil pump is bolted to the front of the crankcase. It is literally of the force-feed type, for twin tubes worked by eccentrics off the intermediate timing wheel reciprocate within the pump, one tube acting as a slide valve and the other as a pump plunger. By undoing the setscrews which secure the pump to the body of the crankcase the former can be drawn away, leaving the tubes and their eccentrics in situ.

There are two oil delivery systems, the one being a high and the other a low-pressure delivery. The high-pressure delivery pipe feeds the main bearings and the big-ends—through the drilled crankshaft—and the spindle of the intermediate timing wheel (whence the oil finds its way on to the gears). The low-pressure

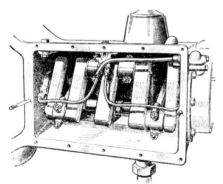

With sump removed The high-pressure pipe from the pump (right) to the relief valve has been disconnected, but the suction pipe is clearly visible. Small-bore pipes are led from the top of the relief valve to the o.h. gear and pressure gauge respectively.

pipe is connected with the overhead rocker shafts via a pipe passing up through the breather, surplus oil gravitating down the push-rod tunnels and feeding the cams and unusually long and robust tappets.

B22

On some cars the needle of the facia-board gauge oscillates violently. This is generally due to an air bubble, and as a rule it can be cured by disconnecting the pipe, clearing it out and reconnecting it.

The engine is replenished by removing the quickly detachable valve rocker covers, a little oil being poured through each of the four orifices so that the valve gear itself receives a refresher from time to time. Cork washers are employed under these tappet covers, whilst beneath the tappet box and the cylinder head proper a brown paper washer is used.

Riley owners sometimes complain that the sparking plug cavities become filled with oil. This does not matter a great deal, for the obvious reason that the

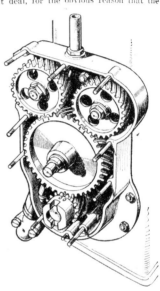

The timing gear as seen with its cover and the magneto platform removed. The assembly consists of the crankshaft pinion (with its dynamo driving dog), an intermediate wheel and two cam wheels. Note how the teeth are marked so as to simplify re-timing operations. This sketch also shows the oil pump in position and the breather tube.

oil comes in contact only with "earthed" parts of the ignition circuit. Such accumulation, however, can be prevented if care is taken to see that the cork and the paper washers are all in good order. There are also fibre washers under the dome nuts securing the box to the cylinder head, and these may be a cause of leakage.

The sump is drained in the ordinary way by undoing the plug on the off side and just below the oil-release valve, which, by the way, should be left severely alone by inexperienced owners. The drain plug mentioned will not entirely drain the sump, and this can be effected only by taking off the square flange underneath the sump itself. This drain flange has a cork washer which should be treated carefully.

### Overfilling the Sump.

When refilling the sump a gallon of oil will be found to be slightly too much, but this is a good rather than a bad fault, and no trouble should be experienced with plugs if the sump is overfilled by pouring in a whole gallon. The oil, it will be observed, has to pass down the push-rod tunnels, and after doing so it has to percolate through a sump gauze of an area nearly as great as that of the sump and which, in fact, forms a dividing wall between the sump and the crankcase. The gauze is held in place by four screws, and about every 3,000 miles it pays to lower the sump so that both sump and gauze can be thoroughly cleansed.

For the best performance the sump should be drained about every 1,500 miles. This may cause some surprise, even to Riley owners, but it should be understood that the engine seldom needs replenishing and

FEBRUARY 14, 1930.    317    THE Light Car AND Cyclecar

that with a unit of this kind, able to give a high performance, perfectly reliable oil is essential. The money expended on new oil and the trouble involved in draining the sump should not, therefore, be grudged.

With new oil the pressure registered by the facia-board gauge will be slightly higher than that shown when the oil has lost some of its viscosity. As a guide, however, a pressure of from 45-50 lb. per square inch should be registered when the car is travelling at 30 m.p.h. in top gear.

How the two tubes of the oil pump—one forming a valve and the other a plunger—are driven by eccentrics off the intermediate timing wheel. The suction and delivery ports are on the centre line of the pump. The remaining two holes are for anchorage bolts.

Other details of interest concerning the engine are as follow. The dynamo is held in place by four bolts and, being driven by dogs, can be dismounted without difficulty and re-erected with equal ease. The starter motor is held in place by a strap secured with two bolts and can be slipped off when the nuts have been slackened. When replacing the instrument it should be slid along within the strap until it comes up against a shoulder which automatically governs the correct position. The firing order is 1, 2, 4, 3, and with the ignition lever fully advanced the points of the contact breaker should be just separating when the t.d.c. mark on the flywheel is actually 2¼ ins. before t.d.c.

### Timing Details.

As already mentioned, a slight variation of the timing can be obtained by swivelling the magneto itself. The marks on the timing wheels definitely identify the valve-timing arrangements, but as a general guide it may be said that the exhaust opens 55 degrees before bottom dead centre. The carburetter settings are as follow :—Single-port model, Zenith, 85 main, 85 compensator, 17 choke ; twin-port model, Zenith, 75 main, 75 compensator, 18 choke. Where an S.U. carburetter is employed a variable mixture control is provided and no attempt should be made to alter the setting of the jet needle. The standard needle is D4. Incidentally the twin-port model has no hot spot assembly.

The oil recommended by the manufacturers is Castrol XL, and the following plugs have been approved :—Single-port model, Lodge H1 ; twin-port model, K.L.G. 483. The engine will give every satisfaction if used with ordinary petrol ; benzole mixture may also be used. The dynamo should cut in at from 18 m.p.h. to 20 m.p.h., and should give a full charge rate of 8 amps. at about 30 m.p.h. in top gear.

Various points in connection with engine controls call for lubrication. These, however, should be self-evident, and we do not think it necessary to go into details here.

Finally, it might be of interest to note that at 2,000 r.p.m. the engine develops 14.75 b.h.p., whilst the curve peaks at 4,000 r.p.m. with a brake-horse-power of 27.7.

*(To be continued.)*

*1930 Biarritz Saloon*

*1930 9 h.p. WD Tourer*

*An artist's impression of the new 1932/3 prototype Gamecock—note the running boards are not the recessed design of the production model.*

*1932 Plus Ultra Monaco*

Tourer and the Brooklands. All of the cars were now on six stud wheels of 27 × 4.40 size and Special Series models, with twin carburetters, Duplex Hartford shock absorbers and a guaranteed road speed of 65 m.p.h., were available at £27 extra. This did not apply of course to the Brooklands, which had its own guaranteed road speed of 80 m.p.h.

The 'Plus Ultra' series of 1932 brought yet another change in the appearance of Riley models with the introduction of the dropped chassis frame. Since the introduction of the 9 h.p. car in 1926, Riley had laid great stress on the benefits of keeping the occupants of the car inside the wheelbase and extra leg and foot space for the rear seat passengers was provided by the use of rear footwells, which had enabled the roofline of the car to be lower than most of its contemporaries. Now the Company was giving the customer the same interaxle seating, substantial legroom in the rear and low roofline, but was increasing the capacity of the body-work and improving the ease of access for entry and exit with dignity.

*The Autocar,* in its Motor Show Review of October 16th 1931 said of the 9 h.p. range: 'First of the superlative type of 9 h.p. car, firmly established, regularly improved, and as yet scarcely challenged in its class, the Riley Nine has a very definite appeal to those who can appreciate performance, safety, comfort and an appearance out of the ruck'. Praise indeed!

The 9 h.p. cars on show that year were, according to *The Autocar,* a Monaco with half-pannelled Weymann saloon body, as well as a fabric body, which had both pairs of doors hinged at their rear edges; the full-panelled Two Seat Coupé; and the new Gamecock shown for the first time. All were offered at £298. The Army type overseas Four Seat Tourer painted War Office Green was priced at £310, whilst the Biarritz half-panelled Silent Saloon was £325. A chassis was also on display.

At the end of 1932, Riley published its new catalogue to introduce the 1933 models— and what a range! This was a return to the kind of diversity which had been available in the late twenties on the side-valve chassis. Eleven different coachwork types, some being offered

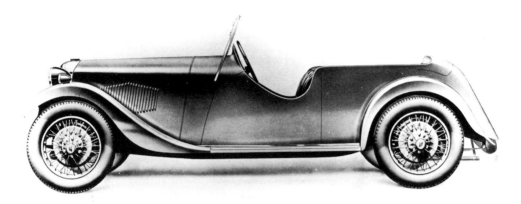

*Artist's impression of the prototype 1933 Lynx 9 h.p. 2 Door.*

*1933 Monaco 9 h.p. Saloon (bumpers were not standard)*

on 12 h.p. and 14 h.p. six-cylinder chassis as well as the 9 h.p., making a total of nineteen model variations from which the customer had the choice.

In the 9 h.p. models, the catalogue offered the Monaco, the Lincock (a new closed coupé of very attractive lines, fitted—like the Falcon 9—with the Riley patent roof-door to allow easy entry and exit in a car of such low roof-line), the Ascot Coupé, the Falcon Saloon, the Kestrel Saloon and the Lynx Two Door Four Seat Tourer. The Lynx, the Lincock and the Ascot were also available on the six-cylinder chassis with both 12 h.p. and 14 h.p. engine

*1933 Trinity 9 h.p. Coupé with hood erect*

*1933 Trinity 9 h.p. Coupé with hood lowered*

options. All models were now available with Special Series engines at extra cost—though the road speed guarantee had by now been quietly dropped. The Trinity Coupé was also available in 1933, but was not actually made by Riley. It was built by Meredith Coachcraft Limited and offered as a Riley model. The name Trinity was chosen because the car was able, with the use of an ingenious sliding panel and disappearing hood, to be converted from an open Two Seater to an open Four Seater to a Closed Coupé—a three-in-one car.

The March Special was the only sporting car available in the range for that year. The design was the work of the then Earl of March (later to inherit the family title of Duke of Richmond and Gordon) and the bodies were built by John Charles & Sons of Kew. The model was fitted with matching 5 in. speedometer and revolution counter and was offered on the Special Series chassis in 9 h.p. and 12 h.p. six-cylinder versions to comply with the 1100 cc. and 1500 cc. competition classes. Almost all of the cars built were on the 9 h.p. chassis, which was priced at £335. More information on this model appears in Chapter Eight—'The Sporting Rileys'.

All of the 9 h.p. cars on offer with Standard Series engines were priced at £298, except the Falcon and Kestrel Saloons which were priced at £315 and £308 respectively, and the Trinity which was priced at £325. The Special Series models now featured a two-carburetter engine and cost only £17 extra.

*1933 Kestrel 9 Saloon*

*1933 Lincock 9 h.p. Fixed-Head Coupé*

*1933 Riley roof-door used
on Falcon/Lincock*

*1933 Falcon 9 h.p. Saloon prototype*

*1933 Falcon 9 h.p. Saloon production model*

The 1934 catalogue was published as a beautifully bound book entitled "The Most Successful Car in the World". Its opening paragraphs read: 'The title of this book is a bold, perhaps a boastful, one. But it will be forgiven the manufacturers, who claim their product to be no less than the most successful car in the world, if they in their turn can convince the future owners of their cars that the title is justified.

What, then, constitutes success in the Motoring World? Surely, in the first place, ability to stay, and to progress, in the industry itself. The young, modern motorist will scarcely remember names, famous in their day, of Motor-cars long since forgotten. Yet at one time they were contemporary and competitive with Riley.

That so many have failed to stay the course in what is admittedly one of the most exacting and fiercely competitive of industries is perhaps not surprising. What is possibly more note-worthy is that, amid the many meteoric rises to fame—and as many rapid falls into oblivion—of numerous cars and their makers, the Riley Company has held, consolidated and advanced its status through thirty five years of automobile engineering in such a way as to express the very spirit of motoring.

For the Riley Car has made "motorists" in the best sense of the word. It is characteristic of the Company's products that they have never been cheap mass-produced cars; nor yet have they been expensive "only-for-the-few" models; but they have always been—and never to a greater degree than at the present time—"popular" cars.'

Proud words. And in hindsight they were true words. Who, then, would choose now to argue with the contention that Riley was 'The Most Successful Car in the World'? After all, they were not claiming to be the 'Best Car in the World', or the 'Fastest Car in the World'— just the most successful. It may be that the Riley family would have cause to reflect on these words just four years or so later, but in 1934—and indeed in the later years—they had just cause to reflect on their past and current successes and contemplate the right to their claim. In view of the tremendous contribution of innovation and development proved by competitive success after success, were they not as entitled to their claim, perhaps more so, as another certain manufacturer who arrived on the scene rather later than Riley, made few innovative contributions to the industry at large, for a time used Riley wheels and laid claim to making the 'Best Car in the World'?

Who can say? For opinion in such matters is always the victim of subjective points of view.

In that 1934 catalogue were more new features. Preselectagear was now available, centre-lock wire wheels were fitted, a one-shot lubrication system was fitted and chassis frames were now employing box-section construction for greater rigidity in areas of high stress. The catalogue tells us that a single 12 volt battery of greater capacity was now being fitted (and shows a Kestrel with just such a battery)—though cars were still being fitted with dual 6 volt units—and, of course, Triplex glass was fitted as a standard feature on all Rileys.

Two low-line saloons were offered, both on the Special Series chassis. They were the Kestrel, which had been introduced earlier in 1933, and the Falcon. The catalogue shows this Falcon Saloon to have been quite different from its 1932/33 forebear in that it had acquired a boot—making it look rather like a lowered Monaco. The Monaco continued of course, now as a fully coachbuilt saloon, together with the Lincock, the Lynx (now with four doors) and the six-cylinder cars. The Kestrel 9 and Falcon were both priced at £325 with the all-helical gearbox and at £352 with Preselectagear. The Standard Series Lynx, Lincock and Monaco were all £298—in Special Series they were £315 and with Preselectagear were £325.

The first Preselectagear was an E.N.V. epicyclic preselector gearbox connected to the

*1934 Falcon 9 h.p. Saloon (note the increase in overall height and the addition of a luggage boot)*

*1934 9 h.p. Chassis*

*1934 Ascot 9 h.p. Drop-Head Coupé*

*1934 Lynx 9 h.p. Tourer with unusual flat-topped front doors.*

*The 1934/5 Lynx 9 h.p. Tourer, now without disappearing
hood and with centre-lock wheels.*

torque tube enclosed propeller shaft and driven via a Newton centrifugal clutch. The change selector lever was located on the steering column on Rileys (other manufacturers put them elsewhere) and what had previously been the clutch pedal was now the change actuating pedal. With proper use, and not too many revs on the engine, it was intended that the driver could be sitting in a stationary car with first gear engaged in the gearbox (but not driving because the clutch had not engaged) and second gear selected on the change quadrant.

Once again, Riley had succeeded in making the action of gear changing, and so driving, easier for the inexperienced—and a great deal more fun for the experienced, with extremely fast getaways from standstill for those disposed to use the facility.

Also introduced for 1934 was a new sports car. Riley had been without a two seater sports car for 1933, choosing to offer the March Special Two/Four Seater instead. Obviously the company was in a bit of a quandary over the new Imp model because whilst the wheelbase of the March Special was rather long, they obviously felt it worthwhile hanging on to the two/four seat concept because the prototype Imp—shown at Olympia—was a two/four seater with a very clear Riley identity, showing its relationship through the shape of the wings. The body itself was quite like the March Special in profile although a little shorter—the wheelbase was 7 ft. 6 in.

However, all this was not to be. Whilst the Grebe was dropped from the 1933 six cylinder range before more than one car had been built, so it was with the Imp Two/Four Seater. The stylish and very different (some say 'borrowed' from Alfa Romeo—but that was the privilege of another Coventry—based car maker) MPH sports car had such impact it was decided to offer a 9 h.p. version of the same car, appropriately scaled down of course. Thus was born one of the prettiest two seat Rileys ever—the Imp Sports Two Seater. The 1934 Scottish Rally was the Imp's competition debut in which it acquitted itself well.

In 1934 the Riley Nine reached its competition zenith, by winning the Rudge-Whitworth Cup at Le Mans, in addition to being placed 5th, 6th, 12th and 13th overall, securing the 1100 cc. class win and a special Ladies prize.

1935 saw the Nine being rather overshadowed, perhaps the beginning of its eclipse, by the appearance of a four cylinder $1\frac{1}{2}$ litre engine. This was the first new engine since 1928 but bore a remarkable similarity to the Nine. This engine was to power the majority of Riley models from now on. The ubiquitous Monaco continued for another year, in company with the Kestrel as the two saloon models—they were now offered as Special models with Preselecta-gear as standard. The Lynx continued in production too, accompanied only by the Imp as the remaining model in the 9 h.p. range.

A number of improvements had been made to the Nine between 1934 and 1935. The gearbox was now the Armstrong Siddeley preselector in place of the E.N.V. type. The clutch was the newer, twin plate, centrifugal unit. By 1936 the engine had changed too. It now had round rocker box filler lids, instead of square, with improved fastening and the oil pipes to the rocker shafts were external again instead of internal drillings.

But there were only four 9 h.p. models in 1935 and by 1936 there were to be only two: the new Merlin and an updated Kestrel. The Merlin had adopted the shape of the $1\frac{1}{2}$ litre Falcon, but was made in all-steel for cost effectiveness. The Kestrel was the shape of the 1935 $1\frac{1}{2}$ litre Kestrel and in the eyes of some was the most attractive of the 9 h.p. Kestrels.

Again the engine underwent a number of changes. The big-end bearings were increased from $1\frac{11}{16}$ in. to $1\frac{7}{8}$ in. in diameter and the connecting rods were a shorter length from the earlier types. An oil filter was fitted which used replaceable elements and the oil pump was

*1934/5 Monaco 9 h.p. Saloon—now with centre-lock wheels.*

*Profile of the 1934/5 Kestrel 9 h.p. Saloon*

of single-plunger design. For 1936, there was no Monaco, hitherto the flagship of the Riley Nine range; it seemed the very cornerstone of the Riley Nine legend had gone.

Almost as if by public demand, the Monaco returned for 1937, with a new, quite attractive body style which, whilst looking rather like a scaled-down Adelphi, looked quite sleek and lacked the bulbousness of the Adelphi's rear quarters. The engine in this new Monaco Saloon was the Special Series two carburetter version of the Merlin series 9 h.p. unit and the price of the car was £298.

The Merlin Nine continued in production, at the price of £269, and was little changed for the new season, although during 1937 it was joined by another model which was very similar in appearance. It was in fact a 'Merlin with a boot' and was known as the 9 h.p. Touring Saloon. It was offered with the preselector gearbox or a new 3 speed overdrive gearbox with synchromesh on second and top gears. The price of the car was £290 but it was short-lived, being available after September 1937 in 1½ litre form only.

In the Company's last year of business before being taken over by Lord Nuffield, there was only one 9 h.p. model, the Victor. It was the end of the road for the car which had been made famous in the hands of such great names as Ashby, Dixon, Eldridge, Eyston, Gardiner, Gillow, the Maclures, Whitcroft, Mrs Petre, Mrs Wisdom and many more.

The Riley Nine Victor was a 9 h.p. version of what was basically intended to be a 1½ litre engined car and it did not enjoy the success of its illustrious forbears. Some say it was a bold attempt to combine Riley quality with volume production techniques—others believe it was a contributor to the downfall of the Company because it forsook its heritage. Whichever you choose to believe, it was a Riley, competitively priced at £299 with either engine and featuring many of the innovations Riley had introduced in its recent models. However, the Victor was vanquished—it was the end of a line, of the Company as it had been and of an era. Riley was next to submit to a period of mediocrity before recovering under Nuffield with the RM series.

*An excellent rear quarter view of the 1934/5 Kestrel*
*9 h.p. Saloon with the optional spare wheel cover.*

*1936 Merlin 9 h.p. Saloon*

*The new 1937 Monaco 9 h.p. Saloon*

SPECIFICATIONS

| | |
|---|---|
| MODEL | **9 H.P. (Chassis nos. 600001—604293) MKS I—III** *Year:* 1926-29 |
| CHASSIS | Channel section side members, 4 cross members, narrow at front, arched over rear axle. |

*Wheelbase:* 8 ft. 10½ in.
*Track:* Front 3 ft. 11 in. Rear 3 ft. 11 in.
*Type of Wheels:* Five stud mounted wire or artillery, 5 stud, 19 × 2.50 in.
*Tyres:* Front 27 × 4.40 in. Rear 27 × 4.40 in.
*Braking System:* Four wheel footbrake, handbrake rear only, rod operation. 10⅛ in. brake drums.

TRANSMISSION

*Clutch Type:* Fabric Cone (Single Dry Plate Mk II From No 601001.)
*Gearbox Type:* 4 speed silent third.
*Gear Selecting Mechanism:* Right hand 1926/27, centre change available 1928.
*Gear Ratios:* 1st—20.37, 2nd—13.125, 3rd—7.66, 4th—5.25, Reverse—20.37 : 1
*Rear Axle Type:* Semi-floating banjo type with spiral bevel drive.
*Rear Axle Ratio:* 5.25:1

ENGINE

*Engine Type:* 4 cylinder 9 h.p.
*RAC H.P. Rating:* 9.01
*Cubic Capacity:* 1087 cc.
*Number of Cylinders:* 4
*Firing Order:* 1, 2, 4, 3
*Bore:* 60.3 mm.
*Stroke:* 95.2 mm.
*Cylinder Head:* P.R. head with overhead valves at 45° and hemispherical combustion chambers, 10 stud fixing.
*Valve Gear:* Operated by 2 camshafts high in the block via short pushrods.
*Valve Timing:* Inlet opens 0° before TDC, closes 50° after BDC.
    Exhaust opens 55° before BDC, closes 30° after TDC.
*Number of Main Bearings:* 2
*Diameter of Main Bearings:* 1½ in Front and Rear.
*Diameter of Big-End Bearings:* $1\frac{9}{16}$ in.
*Sump Capacity:* 7 pints.
*Type of Oil Pump:* Double Plunger.
*Normal Oil Pressure:* (Hot: 40–60 p.s.i.
*Cooling System:* Thermosyphon.
*Type of Ignition:* Magneto.
*Method of Advance/Retard:* Manual.
*Contact Breaker Gap:* 0.012 in.
*Plug Gap:* 0.018 in.
*Number, Make and Type of Carburetters:* Standard Series: Single Zenith Solex or SU-Sports: Twin Solex or SU.
*Type of Inlet Manifold:* Bolt on cast aluminium.
*Type of Exhaust Manifold:* Bolt on cast iron.
*Location of Fuel Tank:* Dash mounted under bonnet.
*Capacity of Fuel Tank:* 5½ gallons.
*Method of Feed:* Gravity.

MODELS AVAILABLE

1926–27: Monaco Saloon £285, 4 Seat Tourer £235.
1928 : Chassis £200, Colonial Chassis £210, 2 Seater £235, 4 Seater £235, San Remo Saloon £265, Monaco Saloon £285, Sports Four £298.
1929 : Monaco Fabric Saloon £298 (with Sports engine & 2 carburetters £325), Biarritz Silent Saloon £325 (with Sports engine & 2 carburetters £352), 2 Seater £265 (with Sports engine & 2 carburetters £292), Open Four Seater £265 (with Sports engine & 2 carburetters £292), Special 4 Seat Tourer £298 (including Sports engine & 2 carburetters).

| | |
|---|---|
| MODEL | **9 H.P. MK IV (Chassis nos. 604294—6011012)** *Year:* 1929/1930 |
| CHASSIS | Channel section side members, 4 cross members, narrow at front, arched over rear axle. |

*Wheelbase:* 8 ft. 10½ in.
*Track:* Front 3 ft. 11¾ in. Rear 3 ft. 11¾ in.
*Type of Wheels:* Six-stud mounted wire 19 × 3.0 in.
*Tyres:* Front 4.50 × 19 in. Rear 4.50 × 19 in.
*Braking System:* Riley continuous cable fully compensating 4 wheel cam operated shoes in 13 in. drums.

**TRANSMISSION**

*Clutch Type:* Single Dry Plate.
*Gearbox Type:* Silent 3rd 4 speed.
*Gear Selecting Mechanism:* Central lever and gate, reverse lockout.
*Gear Ratios:* 1st—20.37:1, 2nd—13.13:1, 3rd—7.67:1, 4th—5.25:1, Reverse—20.37
*Gearbox Oil Capacity:* 3 pints.
*Rear Axle Oil Capacity:* 3½ pints.
*Rear Axle Type:* Semi-floating banjo type, spiral bevel gears.
*Rear Axle Ratio:* 5.25

**ENGINE**

*Engine Type:* Riley Nine.
*RAC H.P. Rating:* 9.01
*Cubic Capacity:* 1087 cc.
*Number of Cylinders:* 4
*Firing Order:* 1, 2, 4, 3
*Bore:* 60.3 mm.
*Stroke:* 95.2 mm.
*Cylinder Head:* P.R. detachable 10 stud, with 45° valves and hemispherical combustion chambers.
*Valve Gear:* 2 Camshafts high in cylinder block operate valves via tappets and short pushrods.
*Diameters of Valve Heads:* Inlet 1⅜ in. Exhaust 1⅜ in.
*Tappet Clearance (Hot):* Inlet 0.002 in. Exhaust 0..003 in.
*Valve Timing:* Inlet opens 0° before TDC, closes 50° after BDC
Exhaust opens 55° before BDC, closes 30° after TDC
*Number of Main Bearings:* 2
*Diameter of Main Bearings:* 1½ in. front and rear.
*Diameter of Big End Bearings:* 1-9/16 in.
*Sump Capacity:* 7 pints.
*Type of Oil Pump:* Eccentric drive double plunger.
*Normal Oil Pressure (Hot):* 40 p.s.i.
*Cooling System:* Thermosyphon.
*Type of Ignition:* Magneto.
*Method of Advance/Retard:* Manual.
*Contact Breaker Gap:* 0.014 in.
*Plug Gap:* 0.018 in.
*Number, Make and Type of Carburetters:* Standard series: single SU, Solex or Zenith—Special series: Twin.
*Type of Inlet Manifold:* Cast Aluminium alloy with hot spot fed from exhaust via rear of block.
*Type of Exhaust Manifold:* Cast iron bolt-on.
*Location of Fuel Tank:* Scuttle mounted under bonnet.
*Capacity of Fuel Tank:* 7½ gallons.
*Method of Fuel Feed:* Gravity.

**MODELS AVAILABLE**

Monaco Saloon £298
Biarritz Saloon £325
Four Seat Fabric Tourer £265
Two Seat Coachbuilt Tourer £265
4 Seat Special (Coachbuilt Tourer £298

Special Series £27 extra

**MODEL**

**9 H.P. Plus Series (Chassis nos. 6011013—6014999)**          *Year:* 1930/31

**CHASSIS**

Channel mainframe members laid narrow at front, widening to bulkhead mounting, lowered centre section. Ground clearance on Army Tourer 11½ in.
*Wheelbase:* 8 ft. 10½ in.
*Track:* Front 3 ft. 11¾ in. Rear 3 ft. 11¾ in.
*Type of Wheels:* Six stud mounting 3.0 × 19 in. wire (Army Tourer 3 × 21 in.)
*Tyres:* Front: 4.50 × 19 in. (Army Tourer 5.25 × 21 in.)
Rear 4.50 × 19 in. (Army Tourer 5.25 × 21 in.)
*Braking System:* Riley continuous cable; cam operated shoes, 13 in. drums.

| | |
|---|---|
| TRANSMISSION | *Clutch Type:* Single dry plate.<br>*Gearbox Type:* Silent third 4 speed.<br>*Gear Selecting Mechanism:* Central lever with selector gate.<br>*Gear Ratios:* 1st—20.37:1, 2nd—13.13:1, 3rd—7.67:1, 4th—5.25:1, Reverse—20.37:1<br>*Gearbox Oil Capacity:* 3 pints.<br>*Rear Axle Oil Capacity:* $3\frac{1}{2}$ pints.<br>*Rear Axle Type:* Semi-floating banjo with spiral bevel gears connected to torque tube.<br>    (Long Pinion from C/N 6013186)<br>*Rear Axle Ratio:* 5.25 |
| ENGINE | *Engine Type:* Riley 9<br>*RAC H.P. Rating:* 9.01<br>*Cubic Capacity:* 1087 cc.<br>*Number of Cylinders:* 4<br>*Firing Order:* 1, 2, 4, 3<br>*Bore:* 60.3 mm.<br>*Stroke:* 95.2 mm.<br>*Cylinder Head:* P.R. detachable 10 stud with hemispherical combustion chambers.<br>*Valve Gear:* Overhead 45° valves operated by high camshafts through tappets and<br>    short pushrods. *N.B.* Internal oil feed to rocker shafts from C/N 6012013 (Engine<br>    28000).<br>*Diameter of Valve Heads:* Inlet $1\frac{3}{8}$ in. Exhaust $1\frac{3}{8}$ in.<br>*Tappet Clearance (Hot):* Inlet 0.002 in. Exhaust 0.003 in.<br>*Valve Timing:* Inlet opens 0° before TDC, closes 50° after BDC<br>    Exhaust opens 55° before BDC, closes 30° after TDC<br>*Number of Main Bearings:* 2<br>*Diameter of Main Bearings:* $1\frac{1}{2}$ in front and rear.<br>*Diameter of Big-end Bearings:* $1\frac{9}{16}$ in.<br>*Sump Capacity:* 7 pints.<br>*Type of Oil Pump:* Eccentric drive double plunger.<br>*Normal Oil Pressure (Hot):* 40 p.s.i.<br>*Cooling System:* Thermosyphon.<br>*Type of Ignition:* Magneto<br>*Method of Advance/Retard:* Manual.<br>*Contact Breaker Gap:* 0.012 in.<br>*Plug Gap:* 0.018 in.<br>*Make and Type of Plug:* Champion 16.<br>*Number, Make and Type of Carburetters:* Standard series: Single solex or SU HV2.<br>    Special Series: Twin Solex or SU HV1.<br>*Type of Inlet Manifold:* Cast alloy bolt-on with gas hot spot.<br>*Type of Exhaust Manifold:* Cast iron bolt-on.<br>*Location of Fuel Tank:* Rear Mounted.<br>*Capacity of Fuel Tank:* $7\frac{1}{2}$ gallons.<br>*Method of Fuel Feed:* Autovac. |
| MODELS AVAILABLE | Monaco Saloon £298<br>Biarritz Half-Panelled Saloon £325 } Sunshine Roof £7.10.0 extra.<br>Four Seat Fabric Tourer £298, Two Seat Coupé £298<br>Army Tourer £310<br>Special Series £27 extra on all models. |
| MODEL | **9 H.P. Plus Ultra Series (Chassis nos. 6015000—6018999)**    *Year:* 1931/2 |
| CHASSIS | Channel mainframe members being narrow at front, widening to bulkhead mounting<br>and lowered between axles. (Army Tourer $11\frac{1}{2}$ in. ground clearance).<br>*Wheelbase:* 8 ft. $10\frac{1}{2}$ in.<br>*Track:* Front 3 ft. $11\frac{3}{4}$ in. Rear 3 ft. $11\frac{3}{4}$ in.<br>*Type of Wheels:* Six stud mounting $3.0 \times 19$ in. wire (Army Tourer $3.5 \times 21$ in.)<br>*Tyres:* Front $4.50 \times 19$ in. (Army Tourer $5.25 \times 21$ in.)<br>    Rear $4.50 \times 19$ in. (Army Tourer $5.25 \times 21$ in.)<br>*Braking System:* Riley continuous cable with cam operated shoes in 13 in drums. |
| TRANSMISSION | *Clutch Type:* Single dry plate.<br>*Gearbox Type:* Silent 3rd 4 speed.<br>*Gear Selecting Mechanism:* Central lever with selector gate.<br>*Gear Ratios:* 1st—20.37:1, 2nd—13.13:1, 3rd—7.67:1, 4th—5.25:1, Reverse—20.37:1 |

*Gearbox Oil Capacity:* 3 pints.
*Rear Axle Oil Capacity:* 3½ pints.
*Rear Axle Type:* Semi-floating banjo connected to torque tube with spiral bevel gears
*Rear Axle Ratio:* 5.25:1

ENGINE

*Engine Type:* Riley 9
*RAC H.P. Rating:* 9.01
*Cubic Capacity:* 1087 cc.
*Number of Cylinders:* 4
*Firing Order:* 1, 2, 4, 3
*Bore:* 60.3 mm.
*Stroke:* 95.2 mm.
*Cylinder Head:* P.R. detachable 10 stud with hemispherical combustion chambers.
*Valve Gear:* Overhead at 45° operated from high camshafts via tappets and short
    pushrods.
*Diameter of Valve Heads:* Inlet 1⅜ in. Exhaust 1⅜ in.
*Tappet Clearances (Hot):* Inlet 0.002 in. Exhaust 0.003 in.
*Valve Timing:* Inlet opens 0° before TDC, closes 50° after BDC
    Exhaust opens 55° before BDC, closes 30° after TDC
*Number of Main Bearings:* 2
*Diameter of Main Bearings:* 1½in. front and rear.
*Diameter of Big End Bearings:* 1 9/16 in.
*Sump Capacity:* 7 pints.
*Type of Oil Pump:* Eccentric drive double plunger.
*Normal Oil Pressure (Hot):* 40 p.s.i.
*Cooling System:* Thermosyphon.
*Type of Ignition:* Magneto.
*Method of Advance/Retard:* Manual.
*Contact Breaker Gap:* 0.012 in.
*Plug Gap:* 0.018 in.
*Make and Type of Plug:* Champion 16.
*Number, Make and Type of Carburetters:* Standard series: Single solex or SU Special
    series; Twin solex or SU.
*Type of Inlet Manifold:* Cast alloy bolt-on with gas hot spot from rear.
*Type of Exhaust Manifold:* Cast iron bolt-on.
*Location of Fuel Tank:* Rear mounted.
*Capacity of Fuel Tank:* 7½ gallons.
*Method of Fuel Feed:* Autovac.

MODELS AVAILABLE

Monaco Fabric Saloon £298, Monaco Half-Panelled Saloon £298, Biarritz Silent
Saloon £325, 2 Seat Drophead Coupé £298, Army Tourer £310, Gamecock 2 Seater
£298
Special series on all models £27 extra.

MODEL

**9 H.P. (Chassis nos. 6019000—6019799)**          *Year:* 1932 (1933 SEASON)

CHASSIS

Channel section mainframe members narrow at front and widening to scuttle; lowered
centre section.
*Wheelbase:* 8 ft. 10½ in.
*Track:* Front 3 ft. 11¾ in. Rear 3 ft. 11¾ in.
*Type of Wheels:* Six stud mounting 3.0 × 19 in. wire.
*Tyres:* Front 4.50 × 19 in. Rear 4.50 × 19 in.
*Braking System:* Riley continuous cable, cam-operated shoes, 13 in. drums.

TRANSMISSION

*Clutch Type:* Single Dry Plate.
*Gearbox Type:* Silent third 4 speed.
*Gear Selecting Mechanism:* Central lever in gate selector.
*Gear Ratios:* 1st—20.37:1, 2nd—13.13:1, 3rd—7.67:1, 4th—5.25:1, Reverse—20.37:1
*Gearbox Oil Capacity:* 3 pints.
*Rear Axle Oil Capacity:* 3½ pints.
*Rear Axle Type:* Semi-floating banjo connected to torque tube: spiral bevel gears.
*Rear Axle Ratio:* 5.25:1

ENGINE

*Engine Type:* Riley 9
*RAC H.P. Rating:* 9.01
*Cubic Capacity:* 1087 cc.

*Number of Cylinders:* 4
*Firing Order:* 1, 2, 4, 3
*Bore:* 60.3 mm.
*Stroke:* 95.2 mm.
*Cylinder Head:* P.R. detachable 10 stud with hemispherical combustion chambers.
*Valve Gear:* Overhead 45° operated from high camshafts via tappets and short pushrods.
*Diameters of Valve Heads:* Inlet 1⅜ in. Exhaust 1⅜ in.
*Tappet Clearances (Hot):* Inlet 0.002 in. Exhaust 0.003 in.
*Valve Timing:* Inlet opens 0° before TDC, closes 50° after BDC
    Exhaust opens 55° before BDC, closes 30° after TDC
*Number of Main Bearings:* 2
*Diamter of Main Bearings:* 1½ in.
*Diameter of Big End Bearings:* 1⁹⁄₁₆ in.
*Sump Capacity:* 7 pints.
*Type of Oil Pump:* Eccentric drive double plunger.
*Normal Oil Pressure (Hot):* 40 p.s.i.
*Cooling System:* Thermosyphon.
*Type of Ignition:* Magneto.
*Method of Advance/Retard:* Manual.
*Contact Breaker Gap:* 0.012 in.
*Plug Gap:* 0.018 in.
*Make and Type of Plug:* Champion 16
*Number, Make and Type of Carburetters:* Standard series: single Solex, SU or Zenith.
    Special Series: Twin Solex or SU.
*Type of Inlet Manifold:* Cast alloy bolt-on with gas hot spot from rear.
*Type of Exhaust Manifold:* Cast Iron bolt-on.
*Location of Fuel Tank:* Rear mounted.
*Capacity of Fuel Tank:* 7½ gallons.
*Method of Fuel Feed:* Electric Pump.

MODELS AVAILABLE   Monaco Coachbuilt Saloon £298, Lincock Fixed Head Coupé £298.
    Ascot Drophead Coupé £298, Gamecock 2 Seater £298
    Lynx 2 Door 4 Seat Tourer £298, Falcon Saloon £315
    Kestrel Saloon £308, March Special 2/4 Seater £335
    Trinity 2/4 Seat Coupé £325.

MODEL    **9 H.P. (Chassis nos. 6019800—6022600)**    *Year:* 1933

CHASSIS    Channel section mainframe members set narrow at the front and widening to the bulkhead mounting. Lowered centre section between axles.
*Wheelbase:* 8 ft. 10½ in.
*Track:* Front 3 ft. 11¾ in. Rear 3 ft. 11¾ in.
*Type of Wheels:* Six stud mounting 3.0 × 19 in. wire.
*Tyres:* Front 4.50 × 19 in. Rear 4.50 × 19 in.
*Braking System:* Riley continuous cable with cam-operated shoes in 13 in. drums.

TRANSMISSION    *Clutch Type:* Single Dry plate.
*Gearbox Type:* All helical 4 speed.
*Gear Selecting Mechanism:* Central lever selector gate.
*Gear Ratios:* 1st—20.37: 1, 2nd—13.13: 1, 3rd—7.67: 1, 4th—5.25: 1, Reverse—20.37: 1
*Gearbox Oil Capacity:* 3 pints.
*Rear Axle Oil Capacity:* 3½ pints.
*Rear Axle Type:* Semi-floating banjo type connected to enclose drive torque tube.
    Spiral bevel gears.
*Rear Axle Ratio:* 5.25: 1

ENGINE    *Engine Type:* Riley 9
*RAC H.P. Rating:* 9.01
*Cubic Capacity:* 1087 cc.
*Number of Cylinders:* 4
*Firing Order:* 1, 2, 4, 3
*Bore:* 60.3 mm.
*Stroke:* 95.2 mm.
*Cylinder Head:* P.R. detachable 10 stud with hemispherical combustion chambers.
*Valve Gear:* Overhead 45° operated from high camshafts via tappets and short pushrods.

*Diameters of Valve Heads:* Inlet 1⅜ in. Exhaust 1⅜ in.
*Tappet Clearances (Hot):* Inlet 0.002 in. Exhaust 0.003 in.
*Valve Timing:* Inlet opens 0° before TDC, closes 50° after BDC
       Exhaust opens 55° before BDC, closes 30° after TDC
*Number of Main Bearings:* 2
*Diameter of Main Bearings:* 1½ in.
*Diameter of Big End Bearings:* 1 11/16 in.
*Sump Capacity:* 7 pints
*Type of Oil Pump:* Eccentric drive double plunger.
*Normal Oil Pressure (Hot):* 40 p.s.i.
*Cooling System:* Thermosyphon.
*Type of Ignition:* Coil & Distributor (Magneto on March Special).
*Method of Advance/Retard:* Manual & centrifugal.
*Contact Breaker Gap:* 0.012–0.016 in.
*Plug Gap:* 0.018 in.
*Make and Type of Plug:* Champion 16 or 17.
*Number, Make and Type of Carburetters:* Standard series: Single Solex or SU Special
    Series: Twin Solex or SU.
*Type of Inlet Manifold:* Cast alloy bolt-on with gas heated hot spot from rear.
*Type of Exhaust Manifold:* Cast iron bolt-on.
*Location of Fuel Tank:* Rear mounted.
*Capacity of Fuel Tank:* 7½ gallons.
*Method of Fuel Feed:* Electric Pump.

MODELS AVAILABLE   Monaco Coachbuilt Saloon £298, Lincock Fixed Head Coupé £298
Falcon Coachbuilt Saloon £315, Kestrel Saloon £308
Ascot Drophead Coupé £298
Lynx 2 Door 4 Seat Tourer £298, March Special 2/4 Seater £335
Trinity 2/4 Seat Coupé £325.

| | | |
|---|---|---|
| MODEL | **9 H.P. (Chassis nos. 6022601—6027000)** | *Year:* 1933/34 |

CHASSIS      Channel section mainframe members, boxed for strengthening, set narrow at front and
widening to bulkhead mounting. Lowered centre section.
*Wheelbase:* 8 ft. 10½ in.
*Track:* Front 3 ft. 11¾ in. Rear 3 ft. 11¾ in.
*Type of Wheels:* Centre-lock 3.0 × 19 in. wire.
*Tyres:* Front 4.50 × 19 in. Rear 4.50 × 19 in
*Braking System:* Riley continuous cable with cam-operated shoes in 13 in. drums.

TRANSMISSION  *Clutch Type:* Single dry plate or 1st type centrifugal 4 plate. 2nd type 2 plate from
    C/N 6025048.
*Gearbox Type:* All-helical or E.N.V. preselector 4 speed.
*Gear Selecting Mechanism:* Central lever in selector gate or preselector quadrant on
    steering column.
*Gear Ratios:* 1st—20.86 (21.45): 1, 2nd—13.50 (12.26): 1, 3rd—8.06 (8.06): 1, 4th—
    5.5 (5.5): 1, Reverse—19.36 (33.82): 1
*Gearbox Oil Capacity:* All helical 3 pints, preselector 4½ pints.
*Rear Axle Oil Capacity:* 3½ pints.
*Rear Axle Type:* Semi-floating banjo from enclosed drive torque tube. Spiral bevel
    gears.
*Rear Axle Ratio:* 5.5: 1

ENGINE      *Engine Type:* Riley 9
*RAC H.P. Rating:* 9.01
*Cubic Capacity:* 1087 cc.
*Number of Cylinders:* 4
*Firing Order:* 1, 2, 4, 3
*Bore:* 60.3 mm.
*Stroke:* 95.2 mm.
*Cylinder Head:* P.R. detachable 10 stud with hemispherical combustion chambers.
*Valve Gear:* Overhead 45° operated from high camshafts via tappets and short push-
    rods.
*Diameters of Valve Heads:* Inlet 1⅜ in. Exhaust 1⅜ in.
*Tappet Clearance (Hot):* Inlet 0.002 in. Exhaust 0.003 in.
*Valve Timing:* Inlet opens 0° before TDC, closes 50° after BDC
    Exhaust opens 55° before BDC, closes 30° after TDC

*Number of Main Bearings:* 2
*Diameter of Main Bearings:* 1½ in.
*Diameter of Big End Bearings:* 1 11/16 in.
*Sump Capacity:* 7 pints.
*Type of Oil Pump:* Eccentric drive double plunger.
*Normal Oil Pressure (Hot):* 40 p.s.i.
*Cooling System:* Thermosyphon.
*Type of Ignition:* Coil & Distributor.
*Method of Advance/Retard:* Manual & centrifugal.
*Contact Breaker Gap:* 0.012—0.016 in.
*Plug Gap:* 0.018 in.
*Make and Type of Plug:* Champion 16 or 17.
*Number, Make and Type of Carburetters:* Standard series: Single solex or SU Special
　　Series: Twin solex or SU.
*Type of Inlet Manifold:* Cast alloy bolt-on with gas hot spot from rear.
*Type of Exhaust Manifold:* Cast iron bolt-on.
*Location of Fuel Tank:* Rear mounted.
*Capacity of Fuel Tank:* 7½ gallons.
*Method of Fuel Feed:* Electric Pump.

MODELS AVAILABLE　Monaco Saloon £298, Falcon Saloon £325 (Special Series only),
Kestrel Saloon £325 (Special Series only), Lincock Coupé £298,
Ascot Drophead Coupé £298, Lynx 4 seat 4 Door Tourer £298.
Special Series £17 extra, Preselectagear £27 Extra.

MODEL　　　**9 H.P. (Chassis nos. 6027001—6027900)**　　　*Year:* 1934/35

CHASSIS　　Channel section main members.
*Wheelbase:* 8 ft. 10½ in.
*Track:* Front 3 ft. 11¾ in. Rear 3 ft. 11¾ in.
*Type of Wheels:* Centre-lock wire 3 × 19 in.
*Tyres:* Front 4.50 × 19 in. Rear 4.50 × 19 in.
*Braking System:* Riley continuous cable, fully compensating, internally adjustable.

TRANSMISSION　*Clutch Type:* Newton dry 2 plate centrifugal (2nd type).
*Gearbox Type:* E.N.V. preselector to C/N 6027030, then Armstrong Siddeley pre-
　　selector.
*Gear Selecting Mechanism:* Quadrant on steering column.
*Gear Ratios:* 1st—21.45: 1, 2nd—12.26: 1, 3rd—8.06: 1, 4th—5.5: 1, Reverse—33.82: 1
*Gearbox Oil Capacity:* 4½ pints E.N.V., 5 pints Armstrong Siddeley.
*Rear Axle Oil Capacity:* 3½ pints.
*Rear Axle Type:* Spiral bevel banjo, semi-floating.
*Rear Axle Ratio:* 5.5: 1

ENGINE　　*Engine Type:* Riley 9
*RAC H.P. Rating:* 9.01
*Cubic Capacity:* 1087 cc.
*Number of Cylinders:* 4
*Firing Order:* 1, 2, 4, 3
*Bore:* 60.3 mm.
*Stroke:* 95.2 mm.
*Cylinder Head:* P.R. cast iron 10 stud with hemispherical combustion chambers.
*Valve Gear:* Overhead valves at 45° operated by high cams via tappets and short
　　pushrods.
*Diameter of Valve Heads:* Inlet 1⅜ in. Exhaust 1⅜ in.
*Tappet Clearance (Hot):* Inlet 0.003 in. Exhaust 0.004 in.
*Valve Timing:* Inlet opens 0° before TDC, closes 50° after BDC
　　Exhaust opens 55° before BDC, closes 30° after TDC
*Number of Main Bearings:* 2
*Diameter of Main Bearings:* 1½ in. front and rear.
*Diameter of Big End Bearings:* 1 11/16 in.
*Sump Capacity:* 7 pints.
*Type of Oil Pump:* Eccentric drive double plunger.
*Normal Oil Pressure (Hot):* 40 p.s.i.
*Cooling System:* Thermosyphon.
*Type of Ignition:* Coil & Distributor.

*Method of Advance/Retard:* Manual and centrifugal.
*Contact Breaker Gap:* 0.012 in.
*Plug Gap:* 0.025 in.
*Number, Make and Type of Carburetters:* Special series 2 solex 26 mm. or SU HV1
*Type of Inlet Manifold:* Cast alloy with hot spot from exhaust manifold at rear.
*Type of Exhaust Manifold:* Cast iron bolt-on.
*Location of Fuel Tank:* Rear between mainframe.
*Capacity of Fuel Tank:* $7\frac{1}{2}$ gallons.
*Method of Fuel Feed:* Electric Pump.

MODELS AVAILABLE    Monaco Coachbuilt Saloon £298
Kestrel Coachbuilt Saloon £325
Lynx 4 Door 4 seat Tourer £298

MODEL      **9 H.P. (Chassis no. prefix 66)**      *Year:* 1936

CHASSIS      Channel section boxed and drilled mainframe with tubular cross members and X-form cable bracing. Profile arched over front and rear axles.
*Wheelbase:* 8 ft. 10 in.
*Track:* Front 4 ft. 0 in. Rear 4 ft. 0 in.
*Type of Wheels:* Centre lock Dunlop $2.50 \times 19$ in. wire.
*Tyres:* Front $4.50 \times 19$ in. Rear $4.50 \times 19$ in.
*Braking System:* Girling mechanical rod with wedge operated shoes in 11 in. drums.

TRANSMISSION      *Clutch Type:* 3rd type single plate centrifugal.
*Gearbox Type:* Armstrong Siddeley 4 speed preselector.
*Gear Selecting Mechanism:* Steering column mounted quadrant.
*Gear Ratios:* 1st—M:23.46, K:20.09:1, 2nd—M:13.35, K:11.64:1, 3rd—M:8.68, K:7.84:1, 4th—M:5.75, K:5.5:1, Reverse M:31.5:1, K:25.19:1
*Gearbox Oil Capacity:* 5 pints.
*Rear Axle Oil Capacity:* 3 pints.
*Rear Axle Type:* Semi-floating banjo with spiral bevel gears and open propeller shaft.
*Rear Axle Ratio:* M—5.75, K—5.5

ENGINE      *Engine Type:* Riley 9
*RAC H.P. Rating:* 9.01
*Cubic Capacity:* 1087 cc.
*Number of Cylinders:* 4
*Firing Order:* 1, 2, 4, 3
*Bore:* 60.3 mm.
*Stroke:* 95.2 mm.
*Cylinder Head:* P.R. detachable 10 stud, hemispherical combustion chambers, external rocker oil feed.
*Valve Gear:* Overhead 45° operated from high camshafts via tappets and short pushrods.
*Diameter of Valve Heads:* Inlet $1\frac{3}{8}$ in. Exhuast $1\frac{3}{8}$ in.
*Tappet Clearances (Hot):* Inlet 0.002 in. Exhaust 0.003 in.
*Valve Timing:* Inlet opens 0° before TDC, closes 50° after BDC
     Exhaust opens 55° before BDC, closes 30° after TDC.
*Number of Main Bearings:* 2
*Diameter of Main Bearings:* F—$1\frac{1}{2}$ in., R—$1\frac{5}{8}$ in.
*Diameter of Big End Bearings:* $1\frac{7}{8}$ in.
*Sump Capacity:* 7 pints.
*Type of Oil Pump:* Eccentric drive single plunger.
*Normal Oil Pressure (Hot):* 40 p.s.i.
*Cooling System:* Thermosyphon.
*Type of Ignition:* Coil and distributor.
*Method of Advance/Retard:* Manual and centrifugal.
*Contact Breaker Gap:* 0.012—0.016 in.
*Plug Gap:* 0.018 in.
*Number, Make and Type of Carburetters:* Standard Series: Single Zenith. Special Series: Single Zenith.
*Type of Inlet Manifold:* Cast alloy with gas heated hot spot.
*Type of Exhaust Manifold:* Cast iron bolt-on.
*Location of Fuel Tank:* Rear Mounted.
*Capacity of Fuel Tank:* $9\frac{1}{2}$ gallons.
*Method of Fuel Feed:* Electric pump.

*1937 Experimental 9 h.p. Saloon*

*1938 Victor 9 h.p. Saloon. Also available as a 1½ litre model.*

MODELS AVAILABLE  (66M) Merlin Saloon Standare Series £269 Special Series (S66M) £279 (S66K) Kestrel Saloon Special Series £295.

| | |
|---|---|
| MODEL | **9 H.P. (Chassis no. Prefix 67)**                    *Year:* 1937. |

CHASSIS

Channel section boxed and drilled mainframe with 5 crossmembers and cable bracing
*Wheelbase:* 8 ft. 10 in.
*Track:* Front 3 ft. 11¾ in. Rear 3 ft. 11¾ in.
*Type of Wheels:* Dunlop centre lock wire 2.50 × 19 in.
*Tyres:* Front 4.50 × 19 in. Rear 4.50 × 19 in.
*Braking System:* Girling Mechanical rod type with wedge operated shoes in 11 in. drums.

TRANSMISSION

*Clutch Type:* S67ZX & S67CX Single dry plate 8 in, all others Newton centrifugal 3rd type single plate.
*Gearbox Type:* S67ZX & S67CX 3 speed dual overdrive, all others Armstrong Siddeley preselector 4 speed.
*Gear Selecting Mechanism:* Steering column located quadrant—overdrive models central lever.
*Gear Ratios: S67Z*—1st—22.44: 1, 2nd—12.79: 1, 3rd—8.32: 1, 4th—5.5: 1, Reverse—27.40: 1. *67M & S67M* 1st—23.46: 1, 2nd—13.38: 1, 3rd—8.69: 1, 4th—5.75: 1, Reverse—31.52: 1. *Overdrive gearbox ratios* 1st—17.35: 1, 2nd—10.46: 1, O/D 2nd—7.55: 1, 3rd—6.75: 1, O/D 3rd—4.87: 1.
*Gearbox Oil Capacity:* 5 pints.
*Rear Axle Oil Capacity:* 3 pints.
*Rear Axle Type:* Semi-floating banjo type spiral bevel, open propeller shaft.
*Rear Axle Ratio:* (S) 67M 5.75: 1, S67Z 5.5: 1, S67ZX/CX 6.75: 1

ENGINE

*Engine Type:* Riley 9
*RAC H.P. Rating:* 9.01
*Cubic Capacity:* 1087 cc.
*Number of Cylinders:* 4
*Firing Order:* 1, 2, 4, 3
*Bore:* 60.3 mm.
*Stroke:* 95.2 mm.
*Cylinder Head:* P.R. type cast iron 10 stud hemispherical combustion chambers, external rocker oil feed.
*Valve Gear:* Overhead at 45° via twin high camshafts, tappets & pushrods.
*Diameter of Valve Heads:* Inlet 1⅜ in. Exhaust 1⅜ in.
*Tappet Clearances (Hot):* Inlet 0.002 in. Exhaust 0.003 in.
*Valve Timing:* Inlet opens 0° before TDC, closes 50° after BDC
Exhaust opens 55° before BDC, closes 30° after TDC
*Number of Main Bearings:* 2
*Diameter of Main Bearings:* F—1½ in. R—1⅝ in.
*Diameter of Big End Bearings:* 1⅞ in.
*Sump Capacity:* 7 pints.
*Type of Oil Pump:* Eccentric drive single plunger.
*Normal Oil Pressure (Hot):* 40 p.s.i.
*Cooling System:* Thermosyphon.
*Type of Ignition:* Coil and distributor.
*Method of Advance/Retard:* Manual and centrifugal.
*Contact Breaker Gap:* 0.012 in.
*Plug Gap:* 0.018 in.
*Number, Make and Type of Carburetters:* Standard series: single Solex or Zenith. Special series: 2 Solex 26 mm. horizontal or Zenith.
*Type of Inlet Manifold:* Cast alloy bolt-on with hot spot to rear from exhaust.
*Type of Exhaust Manifold:* Cast iron bolt-on.
*Location of Fuel Tank:* Rear between mainframe.
*Capacity of Fuel Tank:* 9½ gallons.
*Method of Fuel Feed:* SU Electric pump.

MODELS AVAILABLE  67M—Standard Series Merlin £275, S67M—Special Series Merlin £285
S67Z—Special Series Monaco £298, S67ZX—Special Series Monaco Overdrive £298
S67CX—Touring Saloon Overdrive £290, S67C—Touring Saloon Preselectagear £290

| | | |
|---|---|---|
| MODEL | **9 H.P. (Chassis no. Prefix 68)** | *Year:* 1938 |

CHASSIS       Channel section boxed and drilled mainframe with tubular crossmembers and X-form cable bracing. Raised over front and rear axles.
*Wheelbase:* 8 ft. 10 in.
*Track:* Front 4 ft. 0 in. Rear 4 ft. 0 in.
*Type of Wheels:* Dunlop centre lock 2.50 × 19 in. wire.
*Tyres:* Front 4.50 × 19 in. Rear 4.50 × 19 in.
*Braking System:* Girling mechanical rod system with wedge operated shoes in 11 in. drums.

TRANSMISSION       *Clutch Type:* 3rd type centrifugal single plate.
*Gearbox Type:* Armstrong Siddeley 4 speed preselector.
*Gear Selecting Mechanism:* Steering column mounted quadrant.
*Gear Ratios:* 1st—18.79: 1, 2nd—10.91: 1, 3rd—7.39: 1, 4th—5.22: 1, Reverse: 23.33: 1.
*Gearbox Oil Capacity:* 5 pints.
*Rear Axle Oil Capacity:* 3½ pints.
*Rear Axle Type:* Semi-floating banjo type with spiral bevel gears connected to enclosed torque tube drive.
*Rear Axle Ratio:* 5.22: 1

ENGINE       *Engine Type:* Riley 9
*RAC H.P. Rating:* 9.01
*Cubic Capacity:* 1087 cc.
*Number of Cylinders:* 4
*Firing Order:* 1, 2, 4, 3
*Bore:* 60.3 mm.
*Stroke:* 95.2 mm.
*Cylinder Head:* P.R. detachable 10 stud, hemispherical combustion chambers, external rocker oil feed.
*Valve Gear:* 45° overhead with high camshafts operating through tappets and short pushrods.
*Diameter of Valve Heads:* Inlet 1⅜ in. Exhaust 1⅜ in.
*Tappet Clearances (Hot):* Inlet 0.002 in. Exhaust 0.003 in.
*Valve Timing:* Inlet opens 0° before TDC, closes 50° after BDC
      Exhaust opens 55° before BDC, closes 30° after TDC
*Number of Main Bearings:* 3
*Diameter of Main Bearings:* F—1½ in, R—1⅝ in.
*Diameter of Big End Bearings:* 1⅞ in.
*Sump Capacity:* 7 pints.
*Type of Oil Pump:* Eccentric drive single plunger.
*Normal Oil Pressure (Hot):* 40 p.s.i.
*Cooling System:* Thermosyphon.
*Type of Ignition:* Coil and distributor.
*Method of Advance/Retard:* Manual and centrifugal.
*Contact Breaker Gap:* 0.012–0.016 in.
*Plug Gap:* 0.018 in.
*Make and Type of Plug:* Champion 17.
*Number, Make and Type of Carburetters:* Single Zenith.
*Type of Inlet Manifold:* Cast alloy bolt-on with gas-heated hot spot.
*Type of Exhaust Manifold:* Cast Iron bolt-on.
*Location of Fuel Tank:* Rear mounted.
*Capacity of Fuel Tank:* 9½ gallons.
*Method of Fuel Feed:* Electric Pump.

MODELS AVAILABLE    Victor Saloon £299.

The Light Car                    40                    JUNE 2, 1933.

# HILL HUNTING IN WALES

## with a

# RILEY LYNX

### An Energetic Two-day Trip from the Midlands in Search of Observed Sections for the Riley Club's "Twenty-four"

"IT occurs to me that if you would lend me a car for a day or two, it would be possible to find two or three suitable hills . . ." I replied thus to a letter from the Riley Motor Club's hon. trials secretary, Capt. Cecil Riley, for had he not informed me that for the third Riley "Twenty-four" "there is rather too much main road"? He had. Did he not ask for "information about trials hills adjacent to this section"? He did. Was I not in urgent need of a couple of days in Wales? I was. Very well, then.

So it came to pass that one fine afternoon saw me leaving the Riley works in a beautiful black and cream Lynx Nine. Of the journey from the Midlands to Wales on the following morning I will say nothing, because these lines will probably be read by one who is only too ready to accuse me of furious driving. It's a hard world!

According to the daily papers, about 80,000 extra people were in employment at the time of my little trip. Perhaps that accounts for the fact that all my friends were too busy to come with me. Anyhow, I had to go alone and that is always a mistake, because a passenger is frequently useful for opening gates and as stage property in a photograph.

For those who doubt the solitariness of my journey in view of the photographs (supposing the Editor sees fit to publish them, of course!), I must explain that I own a very useful little clockwork affair which presses the camera button when all is ready. If only it would open gates as well, it would be almost priceless.

The fact is, that in each and every photograph I took, the car was stationary, and as several of them were taken in distinctly tricky places—photos never

do give a proper idea of gradient—it says a good deal for the Riley that one was able to put it in the required position. This often meant moving the car a few inches at a time, after the camera was set up,

*(Above) Hush! Hush! Descending a hill which must be nameless, but may figure in the Riley "Twenty-four." (Below) A pause for breath on Nantmoor, the Pass of Many Gates, whilst the self-exposing camera does its work.*

(Above) *Typical of Wild Wales—the Riley on one of the countless hairpin bends on which it was able to demonstrate its excellent lock. (Below) A corner on Color Manor hill, one of the many "finds."*

so there should be no ground for complaints that the hills found are too severe.

One might imagine that there would be no difficulty in finding hills in Wales, particularly in the neighbourhood of Snowdon. Actually, the hills are there all right, but the Welsh people are all against making roads up them.

This accounts for the fact that just 98½ per cent. of the likely looking tracks are less than half a mile long and end in a farmyard just before the real gradient starts. Most of the remaining 1½ per cent. are cunningly arranged so that just when they ought to be getting interesting they wriggle round to one side and along some quite inoffensive little nant, bwlch, or pass.

For example, there is quite a probable sort of track leading off the Nant Gwynant, which goes nicely upwards for a few hundred yards, but before you can say Heath Robinson, or whatever the proper exclamation is, it turns away and wanders down Nantmor, which is a place where they breed gates and sheep, but mostly gates. If that Lynx had been the least little bit difficult to get in and out of, I doubt if I should have survived the surfeit of exercise.

Another very valuable feature of a car for this sort of job is that it shall be capable of running slowly as well as quickly. The only way to find these hills is to prowl along and to explore every turning which goes towards high ground—and that means every turning there is.

Still another important point is general manœuvrability. Of course, there isn't the very slightest excuse for a man who takes a car *down* a steep, strange hill without first ascertaining that there is either a way out or room to turn at the bottom.

I know that very well, and repeated it to myself many times when turning the Lynx on a 6-ft. road with a bog on one side and a bank on the other. I think that is what the old lady at a near-by cottage was saying, too, but I don't understand Welsh. Anyhow, we got round *and* up the hill. Believe me, it was no mean achievement.

## A "Bag" of Three Hills.

In spite of these little difficulties, we—the Lynx and I—managed to find three quite reasonable hills, including one which is definitely good. Whether they will actually appear on the route card I do not know, but I expect to see competitors on two of them on June 24, so perhaps I ought not to say very much about them at present.

If the Riley Club does go that way, it will be remembered locally for many a long day, for this is a part of the world where nothing happens, or so the inhabitants say. One such, of whom I made inquiries concerning a possible hill, openly envied my city life with its many interests and entertainments. I, on the other hand, was equally envious of his country life with its glorious fresh air and his half-crown rent. Curious how we always want the other fellow's lot! But we both agreed about the desirability of the Lynx.

How pleasant, after doddering about in narrow lanes, to get back on to the Holyhead Road and let the Riley have its head again. Two good days, yet not two days, for the whole 350-mile trip occupied a bare 32½ hours, including a good, long night in bed. Still, for practical purposes, two good days, thoroughly enjoyable, even though one is glad to be home once more.

Yes, my Welsh friend was right. There is something to be said for 'change. Main roads are good and lanes are good. England is fine and so is Wales. Yet the more you have of any one of them the more you appreciate the other.

Certainly, though, if you are in the mood for sport and a little rough-stuff, then Wales has it every time. For that it is perfect—given the right car.   W.
**B17**

That slogan, " it's such fun to drive," was not of our origination, but was given us by one of the leading Motoring Correspondents of to-day.

Before he gave expression to that opinion, he had put the Riley through its pacings — he had driven it for miles — no doubt he had anticipated many of the shortcomings of the light car of usual design —

But he found none of them, and in his enthusiasm, after enumerating its many virtues — its smoothness — its easy controllability — its wonderful road-holding qualities — its exceptional acceleration — its remarkable silent third, etc. — he summed up the case with these words — " and it's such fun to drive."

And no small part of the " fun " was to be attributed to the comfort of the driver's seat.

Here that feature is emphasized, and we say just once again that as a result of the Riley's unique body design, there is not an ounce of fatigue in a whole day's run !

And that is only one point where the Riley scores, but it is a point of infinite importance and can only be efficiently demonstrated by actual experience.

We are always ready to prove this — let us arrange a demonstration.

Write us and we'll do so gladly.

*" it's such fun to drive"*

**RILEY (Coventry)**    *Riley*    **LIMITED, COVENTRY,**
and 42 North Audley St.,     LONDON, W.1.

*Our illustration is of the PLUS-  ULTRA MONACO Saloon £298*
with Dunlop Tyres and Triplex Glass standard.

OCTOBER 13, 1933.

The Light Car & Cyclecar 49

# Judging a car TO·DAY means:

## Judging its PEAK performance!

# "9"

The 9 h.p. Riley from £298. Dunlop Tyres and Triplex Glass. New model details from Riley (Coventry) Ltd., Coventry, & 42 North Audley Street, London, W.1.

EVERY car "performs." What car, then, reaches PEAK performance? With a Riley "Nine" you have bought a 9 h.p. car only in as far as OFFICIALLY RATED horse-power is concerned. In all other respects PEAK performance lifts it far out of the 9 h.p. class; gives it speed, comfort, safety; protects you against the rapid depreciation of the ordinary car; makes, in short, a real "motorist" of you.

The new features of the new Nine: new frame, new engine mounting, new lines, new one-shot lubrication and PRESELECTAGEAR all help in maintaining PEAK performance.

Why envy the Riley owner its possession? Be one yourself.

OLYMPIA

STAND 114

## *Riley*

AS OLD AS THE INDUSTRY — AS MODERN AS THE HOUR

## *most successful car in the world*

RILEY (COVENTRY) LIMITED, COVENTRY, & 42 NORTH AUDLEY ST., LONDON, W.

MENTION of "*The Light Car and Cyclecar*" *when corresponding with advertisers assists the cause of economical motoring.* B61

542                    The Autocar                    September 27th, 1935.

# Now a Merlin Riley

## Very Interesting New Cars Brought Into Being by a Policy of Wider Appeal

ALTHOUGH the complete programme of the Riley organisation for 1936 is not yet made public, it is possible to announce the advent of a new series, the Merlin, and to forecast that the current series will mostly be continued, although with additions and on quite fresh lines of appeal to the car purchaser. Bearing in mind the shape of the familiar Riley badge, this new range of appeal might aptly be termed the Quadrilateral Plan.

Each side of the quadrilateral represents a separate group of chassis with engines of different sizes, bearing certain styles of coachwork. Group 1 meets the needs of people who put comfort, safety, and ease of driving first. Group 2 offers the same, or more compact, coachwork accommodation, with more engine power and a higher performance. Group 3 offers the maximum power and performance for normal Riley closed cars, with increased equipment, and Group 4 comprises racing and competition cars. It will be seen that this range caters very effectively for the individualist. Exactly how the various models in these groups will be arranged will be explained in the future, and at the moment we are concerned only with the new Merlin series, examples of which fall into three of the four groups. In a sense the Merlin is the famous Riley Nine, redesigned.

### Entirely New Frame

The engine is practically unaltered, as also the four-speed pre-selecta gear, but the power unit is mounted in an entirely new frame, with new final transmission and new brakes. This chassis is built to accommodate a very good-looking, pressed-steel saloon body of a characteristic semi-streamline shape—perhaps the best-looking Riley body up to date. It has the clever and commodious seating arrangement evolved by the Riley people years ago, and now so extensively copied.

This body is slightly larger than the Nine saloon of 1935, but is definitely not so large as the Falcon 1½-litre, and does not supersede that series. The Merlin Nine is an obviously strongly built car,

and therefore is not light, but for all that it has a fair, if unhurried, performance. It is the quiet driver's car, and is priced at £269. It can be had, if desired, with a special series two-carburetter high-compression engine to give an increased performance, for £279.

The next class should meet similar requirements even better, for it is the same car fitted with the powerful and sweet-running 1½-litre four-cylinder engine, and with certain extra equip-

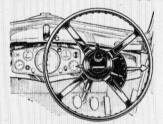

*Of interest to the driver: the new instrument panel, and gear control on the steering column.*

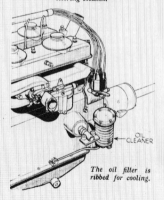

*The oil filter is ribbed for cooling.*

ment is priced at £308. It should be a good performer. Even so, there is a more vivid Merlin still to be obtained, the 1½-litre Merlin Special Series, that is, with a twin-carburetter high-compression specially tuned engine, the price being £335.

This gives a broad outline of the Merlin range, but before going into details the temptation to write a few words about Merlins generally cannot be resisted. The merlin is the smallest bird in the hawk family, and was, and is, used for falconry. It is very courageous and will attack birds of much greater size. If it is chased, as birds of prey sometimes are, by a flock of indignant small birds, it will turn round and attack them, which is unusual. It flies low and fast.

There was also another Merlin in the past, a man of subtle charms and enchantments, who was discovered, according to rumour, by a Yankee at the Court of King Arthur.

### Body Details

Now as to details. The pressed-steel body, to be dealt with first, is wide, with a low floor level, and has four wide doors which are hinged from the centre pillar. Its general appearance is typically Riley, and is similar to that of the Falcon. The roof sweeps down into a streamline type of tail, and in this there is a large locker for luggage, whilst recessed into the lid of the locker is a space to carry the spare wheel, which is concealed by a detachable circular cover. A separate small compartment at the base of the luggage locker is devised so that room is provided for carrying a second spare wheel on a special bracket if required. The locker lid has twin screw-locking handles, and is easily opened, but when closed can be clamped up so as to be rattleproof.

The exterior of the body is very graceful; the tail narrows as it sweeps downwards, and blends into the rear wings. Incidentally, the number plate and tail lamp are neatly recessed into the spare wheel cover. Within the body there is plenty of room, for the seating accommodation is arranged on the Riley

c 16

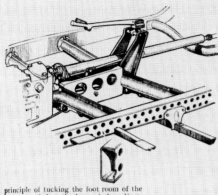

*(Left) New frame construction of the Merlin.*

**Now a Merlin Riley**

*(Right) Rear of the chassis showing the open propeller shaft.*

principle of tucking the foot room of the rear seats below the base of the adjustable front seats, which are broad and high backed. The rear seats have plenty of width and leg room, for deep and long foot wells are used. Pneumatic seat cushions are employed. Behind the top of the squab of the rear seat is a convenient shelf for odd parcels.

One of the features is the width of the doors, which gives plenty of foot room for getting in or out, a point made more valuable by the fact that the hand-brake lever is centrally placed between the front seats and is of the pull-up type, whilst the gear control is a finger-tip type of lever, mounted beneath the steering wheel. Hence the driving seat can be entered with equal facility from right or left forward door.

**Controls**

Well-arranged controls are a particular feature of the car, and everything is placed just where it should be for easy and convenient handling. Above the centre of the spring steering wheel are switches for the traffic indicators, horn, lighting circuits, dipping head lamp switch, and a spark advance lever, whilst below the wheel are the "pre-selecta-gear" finger-tip lever, and a slow-running setting control. The steering column can be adjusted for angle of rake.

In front of the driver is a neat group of plain and visible instruments, with a large-dial speedometer in the centre, whilst the instrument panel is flanked by cubby shelves. For the windscreen control there is a central winding handle, dual wiper blades are driven by a Berkshire electric motor, and in the

roof, which slides, is a balanced anti-glare blind. The interior woodwork is of a dark colour, and is tastefully simple in design.

In the design of the well-proven Riley Nine engine there are no material changes. It is perhaps one of the most universally successful 9 h.p. engines ever produced, for it has stood up to the needs of hard wear in the hands of private owners, besides performing with repeated and conspicuous triumph in racing. Rated at 9.01 h.p. and taxed at £6 15s., it has four cylinders, 60.3 by 95.2 mm. (1,089 c.c.), and appears to be able to develop anything from 45 to 70 brake-horse-power according to the way

in which it is specialised and tuned. Cylinder block and crank case are in one rigid casting, carrying the stiff crankshaft in two large bearings. The cylinder head is detachable, and has hemispherical combustion chambers with 90 degree inclined overhead valves and central sparking plugs. The valve ports are on opposite sides, and like the combustion chambers are machined true and clean, so that there is every aid to high efficiency.

The valves are cleverly operated through overhead rockers and short, light push-rods from a pair of camshafts, one on each side of the cylinder block. Each camshaft has a stabilising cam to eliminate chatter, and the shafts themselves are driven by helical-toothed timing gears. On the Merlin engine the pressure feed engine oiling system is provided with a large oil cleaner, and the

*From front and rear the new Riley is pleasing in appearance.*

single carburetter is fitted with an air cleaner and silencer.

In unit with the engine is a four-speed preselective gear box of the epicyclic type, whilst the clutch is automatically controlled on the centrifugal principle, and disengages if the engine speed drops below 500–600 r.p.m. The gear ratios of the Merlin Nine are: first 23.46, second 13.35, third 8.68, and top 5.75 to 1, whilst those of the 1½-litre Merlin are first 19.07, second 11.05, third 7.44, and top 5.22 to 1.

D 3

544                    *The Autocar*                    September 27th, 1935.

One particularly interesting feature of the design is the frame, which is exceptionally rigid. The side-members are of a built-up welded box section from end to end, and the cross-members are many and of built-up tubular section, whilst the centre portion between the axles is further tied with cross cable bracing underneath. At the front the wing supports are triangulated to the centre of the forward cross-member, and are exceedingly stiff. At the rear of the frame is a 9½-gallon fuel tank. At the front of the steel body shell is a stout curved bulkhead, in which are tool lockers accessible from beneath the bonnet.

Girling four-wheel brakes are fitted on the Merlin series. The tyre size for the Nine is 4.5 by 19in. The 1½-litre Merlin has 4.75 by 18in. tyres, also brake drums of larger size, thermostat engine temperature control, a combined petrol and oil sump gauge, extra large chromium-plated lamps, and a fog lamp.

Already with a string of successes to its credit, the Riley 1½-litre engine is

*Bulkhead dash with inspection cover for access to instruments: note the two lockers for tools.*

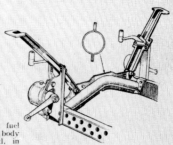

*Front cross-member of the new frame and wing supports.*

somewhat similar in general layout to the Nine, but has a three-bearing crankshaft. It is rated at 11.9 h.p., tax £9, and has four cylinders, 69 by 100 mm. (1,496 c.c.). The wheelbase of the Merlin chassis is 8ft. 10in. and the track 4ft., whilst the overall dimensions of the complete car are: length 13ft. 10½in., height 5ft. 2in., and width 4ft. 10in.

# THE RUMOUR THAT'S BECOME A ROAR !

# There's a new Riley "Nine"

Tea-change gear must hands need never leave the wheel.

Pre-selectagear literally gives finger-tip control!

We abolish floorboard levers. No longer need the driver step into the traffic stream.

"We never realised there was so much room." The passengers always say that.

Pioneers of the built-in luggage container: bikes & gadgets have installed themselves in this one-theme.

IN 1933-4 the Riley "Nine" with Pre-selectagear Transmission cost £325. To-day you can own this NEW Riley "Nine" for £269

THE first Riley "Nine" was built in 1927. So far ahead was it in design that for seven years it underwent comparatively little modification. No need to change for changing's sake! Now, with the perfecting of the all-steel body, the definitely exclusive experience gained by participating—successfully—each year in racing and competitions, the general acceptance of Pre-selectagear as the easiest and most efficient form of gear-change and transmission. . . .

. . . re-designed, re-priced—the NEW Riley "Nine" with giant stride outstrips its contemporaries as did the original model of 1927.

Need we tell you about performance? What is there that matters left for Riley to win? Need we tell you about appearance, comfort? Here are pictures showing amazing beauty of line, surprising roominess. The Riley is the most copied car in the world, but the masterpiece remains unrivalled.

And the Riley "Nine" is only ONE of the finest, widest range of cars the Riley Company has ever built

Other Riley models, in addition to the famous "Nine" at £269 (Tax £7 10s.), are: The famous 1½ LITRE 4-cylinder chassis (11.9 h.p., Tax £9) equipped with Lynx touring body and three types of saloon coachwork at prices from £298 to £375. All these models obtainable with Special Series engines at £27 extra. The much powerful 15 h.p. SIX CYLINDER chassis (Tax £11 5s.) equipped with Lynx touring body and three types of saloon coachwork at prices from £365 to £480. And appearing at Olympia, the new "EIGHT-NINETY," an attractive eight-cylinder model with amazing performance. Prices from £490. Dunlop Tyres and Triplex Glass.
Ask your nearest Riley dealer for full particulars.

Consider but a few of its features: aero-line body, all steel, of amazing strength—inter-axle seating, first introduced by Riley, and without which perfect passenger comfort is unattainable—clear front floor, from which all levers have been banished, so that the driver need not step out of the offside door into a traffic stream—Pre-selectagear, uncrashable, easiest of all gear-change systems and incidentally the most costly to manufacture — capacious luggage locker under cover, making grids, platforms, and buried spare wheels things of the past—easy jacking, automatic chassis lubrication, concealed direction indicators, chromium bumpers—every worth-while accessory and trouble-saving device.

The NEW Riley "Nine" is in production. You can have a demonstration NOW. You can order knowing that not only will this car be exhibited at Olympia, but that it will remain a "new" car, in the best sense of the word, for many years to come. OWN A RILEY AND DRIVE WITH CONFIDENCE.

Riley

THE MOST SUCCESSFUL CAR IN THE WORLD

Riley (Coventry) Limited, Coventry

---

# The New 9 h.p. Riley

The 1936 edition of a popular car brought up to date with cruciform frame, built up of box members, drilled for lightness.

The body is considerably wider and, consequently, more roomy.

The spare wheel is recessed into the lid of the capacious luggage locker.

Although considerably altered and improved at many points, the new car is essentially a Riley.

The pictures in top centre convey some idea of its comfort.

# $A$nother "Wonder" Car

"Certain characteristics, as original as they are concisely practical, have caused the Riley "9" to be regarded as the most advanced design of British built small cars on the market — Now the makers have completed the task of giving the "9" a larger brother and are placing on the market a five seater of similar characteristics, but with a six cylinder engine."

So writes the leading British Automobile Authority — "The Autocar" — and in a few words they have concisely expressed our intention and purpose.

The advance in British Motor Car design, as represented by the Riley "9" has never been questioned by those who really "know" and are the best judges, not only of Motor Car construction but of the needs and requirements of the Public, and it is because we are convinced that in both the "9" chassis and body we have achieved not only something exceptional, but something that fills a long felt need among buyers of the individualistic car, that we have embodied in the design and construction of the 14 h.p. Six all the characteristics which are primarily responsible for that advancement.

In a word, the Riley "Six" among six cyclinder cars represents definitely as great a step forward as did the "9" at the time of its introduction. The latter may be said to have created an entirely new vogue and the "Six" in our belief will have the same effect among larger cars.

Certainly its reception encourages that belief and we are convinced that its many merits will be confirmed by demonstration.

## Riley (Coventry) Ltd
## Foleshill Coventry

'Phone : Coventry 8051          Telegrams : "Kite, Coventry"

LONDON OFFICE & SHOWROOMS :

42, NORTH AUDLEY STREET, W. 1

'Phone : Mayfair 3674          Telegrams : "Kitecoll, Audley, London"

# CHAPTER FIVE

# 'The Wonder Car Plus Two'
# —the Sixes, 1929–1938

At first sight, the six-cylinder Riley engine was a 'Nine-Plus-Two', in that it had identical bore and stroke with the 9 h.p. but two extra cylinders, giving 1633 cc. It was introduced in late 1928 as the 14/50 h.p. Six and was named the Stelvio Weymann Saloon. After the Nine, this new car was rather large—it had a 10 ft. wheelbase and 4 ft. 8 in. track and looked rather like a scaled-up Biarritz.

The engine featured pump assisted water circulation for cooling, with the water pump being driven from the front end of the exhaust camshaft. The front end of the inlet camshaft was used to drive the distributor, for these early sixes used coil and distributor ignition. Carburation was by a single SU carburettor with a hot-spot of the same configuration as the 9 h.p. engine. The three-phase crankshaft had a large damper at its front end to smooth its rotation and in front of that was the dynamo.

The mountings of the Six engine were identical with the Nine and the rocker covers were of the same shape, though obviously larger, with larger rectangular oil filler covers. The early engines had three plain main bearings, the centre one being of $3\frac{3}{4}$ in. diameter which clearly gave rise to considerations of the need to cool it and so later (1933/4) engines had a water jacket in the centre main bearing housing, but it was not successful and as cylinder blocks were damaged and replaced their owners were offered the uncooled variety in place of the original.

The water-cooled centre main bearing was a very good idea in principle and originated with the Brooklands Six of 1932. The problem was that anti-freeze was neither in general use at that time nor was it very good anyway. Added to that was the fact that the centre main bearing had its own drain tap and owners frequently forgot to open it on frosty nights, with the inevitable result that the water jacket split as the water inside froze, causing the need for replacement. A number of owners, both at the time and later, chose to 'solve' the problem by filling the water jacket with cement—in some cases that proved even more disastrous because water ran into the porous filling and instead of just causing a split, which might have been repairable, it pushed a chunk out of the crankcase instead!

The gearbox used on the early six-cylinder cars was the Silent Third four-speed unit already in use on the Nine and drive was similarly transmitted through an enclosed torque tube to the rear axle.

A new innovation on this car was the braking system. It was the fore-runner of the Riley continuous cable system (though the single cable was to come later) and was adjustable from the inside of the car whilst it was in motion. This new cable system provided fully compensated brakes front to rear and was very effective

The first cars offered on this new chassis were the Stelvio Fabric Saloon at £495, the

*1929/30 Deauville 14 h.p. Saloon*

Deauville Coachbuilt Saloon at £525 and the Special 5 Seat Tourer at £455. The Deauville and the Special Tourer were built by Hancock and Warman Limited, coachbuilders of some quality who, conveniently, were located in Coventry and who had established a high reputation for themselves with Riley for the earlier side-valve Lulworth and Special Tourer models as well as the early 9 h.p. Fabric Tourer.

Some refinement was found to be necessary in these early six-cylinder cars and it was to follow with the introduction of the Light Six in October 1929 for the 1930 Season. The later engine acquired fins on the crankcase and the vertical surfaces of the sump, which held 16 pints of oil. The water pump position was re-located to the off-side of the cylinder block and this much improved pump was driven from the inlet camshaft, as was the ignition distributor.

The new Light Six chassis was of 9 ft. 6 in. wheelbase and 3 ft. 11¾ in, track, employing many parts in common with the 9 h.p. range. For example axles, gearboxes, wheels and steering gear were some of the items with common usage between the models. After all, the Six was almost a 'Nine-Plus-Two' in more ways than just the engine—the eight inches extra wheelbase meant that, from the scuttle back, the cars could be near identical.

There were, however, two chassis on offer for the Six and they became known as the Six (Long) and the Six (Short). The long models continued with the Stelvio and the Deauville; later the Edinburgh and the Winchester models came on the scene. The Six (Short) featured the Alpine Fabric and Half-Panelled Saloons and the Alpine Tourer—all three were priced in 1931 at £365.

In 1931 then, there were the two chassis models—Long (10 ft.) and Short (9 ft. 6 in.)—and the models offered were the Stelvio II Saloon at £398 and the Sportsman's Fabric Coupé at £465 on the Long chassis with the three Alpine models on the Short chassis. The Deauville

*1931 Alpine 14 h.p. Fabric Saloon*

*1931 Alpine 14 h.p. Half-Panelled Saloon*

*1931 Alpine 14 h.p. Tourer*

was no longer offered, because its coachbuilder, Hancock and Warman, had ceased trading after a disastrous fire had destroyed their Stoke works.

The 1932 range of six-cylinder cars continued as for 1931, though the small modification of a thermostat was introduced to the engine. Mid-1932 saw the introduction of the water-cooled centre main bearing, co-incident with the announcement of a six-cylinder Brooklands Speed Model. This new car fore-ran the 6/12 version of the engine and had a reduced bore (57.5 mm.) to comply with the International class F engine capacity of 1500 cc. The resultant capacity was 1486 cc. (The capacity of the production 6/12 engine was 1458 cc., the bore having been·reduced to 57 mm). The Brooklands Six—which won the 1500 cc. class of the 1932 T.T. in only its second competition outing—was priced at £595 and looked to be potentially very successful, but for reasons best known to Riley it did not go into production.

Late in 1932, the 1933 range of cars was catalogued introducing a considerable extension to the number of models available. There were now the Ascot Coupé, the Alpine Saloon (now just a 6/14 version of the Mentone), the Edinburgh Saloon, the Kestrel Saloon, the Lincock Fixed Head Coupé, the Lynx Tourer, the Mentone Saloon, the Stelvio Saloon, the Winchester Saloon and the Winchester Limousine. The Ascot, Kestrel, Lincock and Lynx models were available in either 12 or 14 h.p. versions; the Mentone only in 12 h.p. and all the others were only fitted with the 14 h.p. engine.

The Gamecock is not mentioned in the catalogue, nor was it featured at Olympia in the Motor Show, but it just crept into 1933 before being dropped altogether from production. Six special cars were fitted with Gamecock bodies—three for the 1933 and three for the 1934 Alpine Rallies.

Six-cylinder sporting taste was not very well provided for in 1933, since the Gamecock (which was not really a sports car as far as Riley was concerned anyway) did not sell, the March Special was offered as a Six at £375, but had a very long wheelbase as a Two/Four Seater, and, like the Brooklands Six before it, the Grebe was announced to the world and just as quickly forgotten.

It was to be early 1934 before a real 1½ litre sporting Riley was available again—the last one being the Redwinger which was discontinued in 1928—when the very elegant MPH came on to the scene. Before that, however, the Grebe was built on a chassis of 8 ft. 6 in.

*1933 Edinburgh 14 h.p. Saloon*

*1933 Winchester 14 h.p. Limousine*

*1933 Mentone Six-Twelve Saloon*

*1933 Stelvio 14 h.p. Saloon*

*1933 Kestrel Six Saloon*

*Peter Cattell's superb restoration of a Special Series 1933 Lynx Six-Fourteen*

wheelbase and offered at the price of £595. The engine, like the Brooklands Six before it, was of 1486 cc. capacity and the car was offered as a competitive machine under Class F of the International Sporting Code. It seems, though, that the MPH design, which was now well under way, was to put the Grebe into the realms of fantasy, like its predecessor, because it was obviously felt that the prettier appearance of the newer design would have a wider market appeal. In fact, only a few MPHs were built anyway.

An interesting feature of the 1933 catalogue is that it offered, at an extra cost of £30 on the 9 h.p. and £50 on the Sixes, the Riley Fluid Clutch and Free Selection Transmission—the Salerni Patent Fluid Flywheel system later known as 'Flexoil'. This employed a fluid flywheel instead of the ordinary clutch in front of the gearbox, which was of normal Riley type, and a freewheel device behind it. This meant that the driver could have silent gearchanges through-out the range, none of the complications of other types of transmission and a smooth takeoff from standstill. The catalogue quotes: "The novice can change gear as efficiently as the most expert racing driver and always without noise". Note that no comment was made in reference to the speed of that gearchange, however!

By 1934, the Preselectagear had overtaken the Flexoil transmission, except for the Edin-burgh Saloon or Limousine which still used the Flexoil installation. All of the other models were now offered with standard or preselector gearboxes. The 1934 Sixes now consisted of the Six Twelve (which were all on the 9 ft. 6 in. wheelbase chassis), the Six Fourteen Short on the 9 ft. 6 in. chassis and the Six Fourteen Long on the 10 ft. chassis.

The Short chassis models were the Ascot Coupé, the Kestrel Saloon, the Lynx Tourer and the Lincock Coupé—all of which were available with 12 h.p. or 14 h.p. engines. The Mentone Saloon was a 12 h.p. car and became the Alpine when fitted with the 14 h.p. engine.

The Long Chassis models were the Stelvio Saloon, the Winchester Saloon, the Edinburgh Saloon and the Edinburgh Limousine. In addition to these cars was the MPH Two Seat Sports which, whilst it had a chassis number running in the same series as the Six Twelve and Six Fourteen Short chassis models (prefixed 44T), had a totally different, shorter and lower, chassis frame.

Following the lessons with the four six-cylinder cars which took part in the 1933 Ulster Tourist Trophy Race, the 1934 Season's production cars all featured centre-lock wheels with knock-on hub nuts.

In October 1934 the new $1\frac{1}{2}$ litre models were announced with a four cylinder engine, based upon the original 9 h.p. design, but with a number of feature changes, and at the same time a new Six was announced. Not just a new car but a new engine. This new engine, known as the 6/15, bore an obvious similarity to its predecessor, but it had rounded rocker box lids like the $1\frac{1}{2}$ litre, it had a gear driven oil pump and was mated to the Armstrong Siddeley preselector gearbox. The MPH and Stelvio however continued with the existing engine, until they went out of production, retaining the plunger type oil pump and square rocker covers.

The 6/15 engine was fitted into a new car, the Falcon Saloon. The engine had an increased bore of 62 mm, giving a swept volume of 1726 cc., since the stroke remained 95.2 mm. An option on the Falcon, peculiarly, was the 12 h.p. 6 cylinder engine—basically the new engine but with the old bore of 57 mm. and 1458 cc. capacity.

The engines fitted to the MPH and Stelvio models were, as has already been said, of the early type, but they were offered as 15 h.p. engines too, being bored to 62 mm.

The Stelvio for 1935 was an improved version of this now rather long-in-the-tooth big saloon and it certainly benefitted from a little extra engine capacity. But 1935 was to be its last year of production, high hopes being placed in the Falcon Saloon as the new large saloon of the range.

The Falcon was an aero-line saloon in the same image as the Kestrel, but was built with a higher roofline to give more interior headroom. The chassis was entirely new and had box section main members with tubular cross members, except for the gearbox support member which was channel section. In addition, the chassis was cable braced with the cables laid in an X between the mainframe members and being adjustable for correct tension. Its wheelbase was 9 ft. $4\frac{1}{2}$ in. The engine was mounted in the now-traditional Riley 3 point manner and power was transmitted to the rear axle via the usual enclosed propeller shaft.

The MPH continued to be offered in 1935, unchanged from 1934 except that it was now offered with the 6/15 engine instead of the 6/14. The 12 h.p. engine also continued to be offered in the MPH for those people interested in having a car which could compete as a $1\frac{1}{2}$ litre in International Class F.

The Falcon continued into 1936 as a 6/15, still with the option offered of a 12 h.p. engine at no variation in price. Now, it was to be joined by a larger, six light, saloon to be known as the Adelphi (this was the real replacement for the Stelvio) and a very elegant sportman's saloon, the six-light Kestrel. The Kestrel and Adelphi saloons were $1\frac{3}{4}$ in. wider overall than the Falcon and had 4 ft. 3 in. track axles. The Falcon was also available as a Special Series Model that year at an extra cost of £48.

Two open six-cylinder cars were listed as available in 1936—the Lynx Tourer, offered in

Standard Series form at £375 and in Special Series at £423, and the Sprite Two Seater. A six-cylinder Sprite was offered for competition use and featured a 2 litre engine for the ex-works price of £550—the same price as its predecessor, the MPH, upon which chassis the Sprite design was based. Whether any Sprite Sixes were sold as such is very doubtful, especially since the TT Sprite was an out-and-out competition car and there would have been little saving for the potential customer in a fully prepared 2 litre version of the road-going car.

For 1937, apart from a few minor cosmetic changes, the range continued as the previous year, with the Falcon, Adelphi and Kestrel as the saloons and the Lynx as the six-cylinder tourer. Among the cosmetic changes made was one of title. Previously, the Sixes had been identified by the word 'Six' and then the R.A.C. horsepower rating. The change meant that all but one of the Riley engine types would be identified by horsepower rating followed by the number of cylinders. This had already happened with the 12/4, though the 8–90 was to remain odd-man-out. So the Six-Fifteen was now to be known as the Fifteen-Six, probably for no better reason than that someone thought the latter was easier to say and remember. Being much more powerful—and probably quite a bit less expensive to produce—it took over where the less developed Six left off.

The Riley Six was perhaps never really developed as a production engine quite as far as it might, or perhaps should, have been. The smoothness of a six-cylinder engine and the power available from the Riley-built racing sixes were beyond dispute, as the reliability. These points were amply proved by English Racing Automobiles in their exploits with the supercharged engines, which were not so greatly different from the basic Riley Six, apart from the alloy cylinder head and the blower.

Ah, what might have been! Despite whatever shortcomings it might have had in the everyday use of owners, the Riley Six engine is still something to behold. And it still has something, more than just two extra cylinders, which other Riley engines do not.

The "STELVIO"
Fabric Saloon

14 H.P.

The model illustrated above represents a distinct advance in scientific body construction.

As the Riley "9" did, it will set a vogue, a vogue, moreover, which will be lasting, because of its exceedingly graceful lines and the great convenience and comfort which it offers to both driver and passengers.

Wide doors give exceptionally easy access to the interior. The body has been designed from the inside rather than the out; in other words, comfort and roominess have been our first consideration, yet these attributes to ideal motoring have been so happily combined that while they have been attained in maximum degree, no sacrifice of external beauty has been needed.

The upholstery throughout is of the finest furniture hide, and deep pneumatic cushions give a luxuriousness seldom experienced in any but the largest and most costly vehicles.

The equipment includes 5 Wire Wheels and Dunlop Tyres, Automatic Windscreen Wiper, Clock, Dashboard Lamp and Locker, Electric Horn, Tool Box, License Holder, Speedometer, 5 Lamps, Number plates, Driving Mirror and Shock Absorbers, and the standard colourings are Blue, Brown, Maroon, Black and Red — wings, wheels and chassis painted to choice.

The price of the "Stelvio" Fabric
Saloon with Triplex Glass and Dunlop          **£495**
Tyres delivered at Coventry Works is

and other models in the range, which will be illustrated later, are
THE "DEAUVILLE" COACHBUILT SALOON, £525, and the SPECIAL TOURER SIX, £455

Chassis Riley Six

SPECIFICATIONS

| | |
|---|---|
| MODEL | **Riley Six (Chassis Prefix 14/14S)** *Year:* 1928/30 |

CHASSIS

Channel section frame members widening from the front and then parallel to rear.
*Wheelbase:* 10 ft. 0 in.
*Track:* Front 4 ft. 8 in. Rear 4 ft. 8 in.
*Type of Wheels:* Wire 6 stud fixing 3.50 × 20 in.
*Tyres:* Front 5.00 × 20 in. Rear 5.00 × 20 in.
*Braking System:* Cable and rod fully compensating—footbrake 4 wheels, handbrake rear.

TRANSMISSION

*Clutch Type:* Single dry plate.
*Gearbox Type:* Riley silent third 4 speed.
*Gear Selecting Mechanism:* Centre lever and gate.
*Gear Ratios:* 1st—22.31:1, 2nd—14.37:1, 3rd—8.39:1, 4th—5.75:1, Reverse—22.31:1
*Gearbox Oil Capacity:* 3 pints.
*Rear Axle Oil Capacity:* 3½ pints.
*Rear Axle Type:* Banjo, semi-floating; spiral bevel gears.
*Rear Axle Ratio:* 5.75:1

ENGINE

*Engine Type:* Riley 6/14 (14/50 h.p.)
*RAC H.P. Rating:* 13.5
*Cubic Capacity:* 1633 cc.
*Number of Cylinders:* 6
*Firing Order:* 1, 5, 3, 6, 2, 4
*Bore:* 60.3 mm.
*Stroke:* 95.2 mm.
*Cylinder Head:* P.R. detachable; hemispherical combustion chambers 14 stud fixing.
*Valve Gear:* 2 per cylinder, overhead via tappets & short pushrods.
*Tappet Clearances (Hot):* Inlet 0.002 in. Exhaust 0.003 in.
*Valve Timing:* Inlet opens 0° before TDC, closes 50° after BDC
     Exhaust opens 55° before BDC, closes 30° after TDC.
*Number of Main Bearings:* 3
*Diameter of Main Bearings:* F—1⅝ in. C—3¾ in. R—1¾ in.
*Diameter of Big End Bearings:* 1¹¹⁄₁₆ in.
*Sump Capacity:* 16 pints.
*Type of Oil Pump:* Eccentric drive double plunger.
*Normal Oil Pressure (Hot):* 40—60 p.s.i.
*Cooling System:* Thermosyphon & Pump.
*Type of Ignition:* Coil and distributor.
*Method of Advance/Retard:* Manual.
*Contact Breaker Gap:* .012 in—.016 in.
*Plug Gap:* 000.018 in.
*Number, Make and Type of Carburetters:* Single SU 1¼ in HV3.
*Type of Inlet Manifold:* Cast aluminium.
*Type of Exhaust Manifold:* Cast iron.
*Location of Fuel Tank:* Rear.
*Capacity of Fuel Tank:* 11 gallons
*Method of Fuel Feed:* Autovac.

MODELS AVAILABLE

(14S) Stelvio I Fabric Saloon £495
(14) Deauville Saloon £525
(14) 5 Seat Special Tourer £455

Remarks: Internal oil feed to rockers from chassis number 14/14S–369

| | |
|---|---|
| MODEL | **Light Six (Chassis Prefix 14L)** *Year:* 1929–1932 |

CHASSIS

Channel main frame widening from front and parallel to rear, raised over axle.
*Wheelbase:* 9 ft. 6 in.
*Track:* Front 3 ft. 11¾ in. Rear 3 ft. 11¾ in.
*Type of Wheels:* Riley wire 6 stud fixing 3.0 × 19 in.
*Tyres:* Front 5.00 × 19 in. Rear 5.00 × 19 in.

*Braking System:* Riley single continuous cable 4 wheel brakes, fully compensating, 13 in. drums.

TRANSMISSION

*Clutch Type:* Single dry 10 in. plate.
*Gearbox Type:* Silent third.
*Gear Selecting Mechanism:* Central lever and gate, reverse lockout.
*Gear Ratios:* 1st—22.31:1, 2nd—14.37:1, 3rd—8.39:1, 4th—5.75:1, Reverse— 22.31:1
*Gearbox Oil Capacity:* 3 pints.
*Rear Axle Oil Capacity:* 3½ pints.
*Rear Axle Type:* Semi-floating banjo spiral bevel.
*Rear Axle Ratio:* 5.75:1

ENGINE

*Engine Type:* 14/50 Six
*RAC H.P. Rating:* 13.5
*Cubic Capacity:* 1633 cc.
*Number of Cylinders:* 6
*Firing Order:* 1, 5, 3, 6, 2, 4
*Bore:* 60.3 mm.
*Stroke:* 95.2 mm.
*Cylinder Head:* P.R. detachable; hemispherical combustion chambers: 14 stud fixing.
*Valve Gear:* Overhead operated by twin high camshafts at 45° via tappets and short pushrods.*
*Diameter of Valve Heads:* Inlet 1⅜ in. Exhaust 1¾ in.
*Tappet Clearances (Hot):* Inlet 0.002 in. Exhaust 0.003 in.
*Valve Timing:* Inlet opens 0° before TDC, closes 50° after BDC.
   Exhaust opens 55° before BDC, closes 30° after TDC.
*Number of Main Bearings:* 3
*Diameter of Main Bearings:* F—1⅝ in. C—3¾ in. R—1¾ in.
*Diameter of Big End Bearings:* 1¹¹⁄₁₆ in.
*Sump Capacity:* 16 pints.
*Type of Oil Pump:* Eccentric drive double plunger.
*Normal Oil Pressure (Hot):* 40 p.s.i.
*Cooling System:* Pump and thermostat.
*Type of Ignition:* Coil and distributor.
*Method of Advance/Retard:* Manual.
*Contact Breaker Gap:* 0.012 in.—0.016 in.
*Plug Gap:* 0.018 in.
*Number, Make and Type of Carburetters:* One SU 1¼ in. HV3.
*Type of Inlet Manifold:* Cast aluminium alloy with rear-fed hot spot from exhaust.
*Type of Exhaust Manifold:* Cast iron bolt-on.
*Location of Fuel Tank:* Rear between mainframe.
*Capacity of Fuel Tank:* 11 gallons.
*Method of Fuel Feed:* Autovac.

MODELS AVAILABLE

1929/30 (14L) Light Six Saloon £395.
1931/32 (14L) Alpine Saloon (Fabric or half panelled) £365
            Alpine Tourer £365.
*Internal oil feed to rocker shafts from 14L-567

MODEL

**Long Six (Chassis no. prefixes 14S, 88E, 15S)**   *Year:* 1931-35

CHASSIS

Channel section mainframe widening from front dumbirons and parallel from mountings to rear. Arched over rear axle.
*Wheelbase:* 10 ft. 0 in.
*Track:* Front 4 ft. 8 in. Rear 4 ft. 8 in.
*Type of Wheels:* Six stud mountings 3.0 × 20 in. wire.
*Tyres:* Front 5.00 × 20 in. Rear 5.00 × 20 in.
*Braking System:* Riley continuous cable with cam-operated shoes in 13 in. drums.

TRANSMISSION

*Clutch Type:* Single dry plate 10 in.
*Gearbox Type:* Silent 3rd or all-helical 4 speed.
*Gear Selecting Mechanism:* Central lever in selector gate.

*Gear Ratios: Silent Third* 1st—22.31:1, 2nd—14.37:1, 3rd—8.39:1, 4th—5.75:1,
Reverse 22.31:1, *All-Helical* 1st—20.86:1, 2nd—13.5:1, 3rd—8.06:1, 4th—5.1:1,
Reverse—19.36:1, The 14S Stelvio of 1934 was fitted as an option with preselecta-
gear. The 15S Stelvio of 1936 was fitted with preselectagear as standard. Ratios
were: 1st—20.09:1, 2nd—11.64:1, 3rd—7.84:1, 4th—5.5:1, Reverse 25.19:1
*Gearbox Oil Capacity:* 3 pints.
*Rear Axle Oil Capacity:* 3½ pints.
*Rear Axle Type:* Semi-floating banjo type with enclosed torque tube drive to spiral
bevel gears.
*Rear Axle Ratio:* 5.75:1, 5.5:1

ENGINE

*Engine Type:* 6/14 or 6/15
*RAC H.P. Rating:* 13.5 or 14.3
*Cubic Capacity:* 1633 cc./1726 cc.
*Number of Cylinders:* 6
*Firing Order:* 1, 5, 3, 6, 2, 4
*Bore:* 60.3 mm./62 mm.
*Stroke:* 95.2 mm.
*Cylinder Head:* P.R. detachable 14 stud with hemispherical combustion chambers.
*Valve Gear:* 45° overhead operated from high camshafts via tappets and short pushrods.
*Diameters of Valve Heads:* Inlet 1⅜ in. Exhaust 1⅛ in.
*Tappet Clearance (Hot):* Inlet 14 h.p. 0.002 in. Exhaust 14 h.p. 0.003 in.
   Inlet 15 h.p. 0.003 in. Exhaust 15 h.p. 0.004 in.
*Valve Timing: 14 h.p.* Inlet opens 0° before TDC, closes 50° after BDC.
   Exhaust opens 55° before BDC, closes 30° after TDC.
   *15 h.p.* Inlet opens 0° before TDC, closes 55° after BDC
   Exhaust opens 50° before BDC, closes 21° after TDC.
*Number of Main Bearings:* 3
*Diameter of Main Bearings:* F—1⅝ in. C—3¾ in. R—6/14 Models—1¾ in.
   6/15 Models—2 in.
*Diameter of Big End Bearings:* 1¹¹⁄₁₆ in. (6/15 Models—1⅞ in.)
*Sump Capacity:* 16 pints.
*Type of Oil Pump:* 14 h.p.—eccentric double plunger.
*Normal Oil Pressure (Hot):* 40—60 p.s.i.
*Cooling System:* Pump and thermostat.
*Type of Ignition:* Coil and distributor
*Method of Advance/Retard:* Manual (and centrifugal from 1932).
*Contact Breaker Gap:* 0.012—0.016 in.
*Plug Gap:* 0.018 in.
*Number, Make and Type of Carburetters:* Single SU HV3
*Type of Inlet Manifold:* Cast alloy bolt-on with hot spot.
*Type of Exhaust Manifold:* Cast iron bolt-on.
*Location of Fuel Tank:* Rear mounted.
*Capacity of Fuel Tank:* 12 gallons.
*Method of Fuel Feed:* Autovac or electric pump.

MODELS AVAILABLE

1931–34: 14S Stelvio Saloon £398.
1933–34: 88E Winchester Saloon £448, Winchester Limousine £460 (1933 only)
1933–34: 88E Edinburgh Saloon £498, Edinburgh Limousine £510
1935    : 15S Stelvio Saloon £425
Special Series £60 extra. Preselectagear £27 extra in 1934.

MODEL

**Short Six (44T Series)**                                    *Year:* 1933–34

CHASSIS

Channel section mainframe (boxed in 1934) joined by tubular cross members,
narrow at front and widening to scuttle mountings. Arched over rear axle.
*Wheelbase:* 9 ft. 2⁵⁄₁₆ in, 9 ft. 5½ in.
*Track:* Front 3 ft. 11¾ in. Rear 3 ft. 11¾ in.
*Type of Wheels:* Six stud mounting 3.0 × 19 in (1933) Centre lock
   3.0 × 18 in. (1934) wire.
*Tyres:* Front (1933) 4.75 × 19 in. (1934) 4.75 × 18 in.
   Rear (1933) 4.75 × 19 in. (1934) 4.75 × 18 in.
*Braking System:* Riley continuous cable with cam operated shoes in 13 in. drums.

TRANSMISSION

*Clutch Type:* Single 10 in. dry plate.
*Gearbox Type:* All helical 4 speed.

*1934 Six-Cylinder Chassis*

*1935 Falcon Six-Fifteen Saloon*

*Gear Selecting Mechanism:* Central lever in selector gate.
*Gear Ratios:* 5.25 & 5.5:1 final drives available.
    *Hi:* 1st—19.91:1, 2nd—12.88:1, 3rd—7.69:1, 4th—5.25:1, Reverse—18.48:1.
    or: 20.09:1, 11.64:1, 7.84:1, and 5.5:1 *Lo:* 1st—20.86:1, 2nd—13.5:1,
    3rd—8.06:1, 4th—5.5:1, Reverse—19.36:1
*Gearbox Oil Capacity:* 3 pints.
*Rear Axle Oil Capacity:* 3½ pints.
*Rear Axle Type:* Semi-floating banjo with enclosed torque tube drive to spiral bevel
    gears.
*Rear Axle Ratio:* 5.5/5.25:1

ENGINE

*Engine Type:* 6/12 or 6/14
*RAC H.P. Rating:* 12.01 or 13.5
*Cubic Capacity:* 1458 cc./1633 cc.
*Number of Cylinders:* 6
*Firing Order:* 1, 5, 3, 6, 2, 4
*Bore:* 57 mm./60.3 mm.
*Stroke:* 95.2 mm.
*Cylinder Head:* P.R. detachable 14 stud with hemispherical combustion chambers.
*Valve Gear:* 45° overhead operated from high camshafts via tappets and short pushrods.
*Diameters of Valve Heads:* Inlet 1⅜ in. Exhaust 1⅜ in.
*Tappet Clearances (Hot):* Inlet 0.002 in. Exhaust 0.003 in.
*Valve Timing:* Inlet opens 0° before TDC, closes 50° after BDC
    Exhaust opens 55° before BDC, closes 30° after TDC
*Number of Main Bearings:* 3
*Diameter of Main Bearings:* F—1⅝ in. C—3¾ in. R—6/12 Models—1¾ in.
    6/14 Models—2 in.
*Diameter of Big End Bearings:* 1 11/16 in. *Sump Capacity:* 16 pints.
*Type of Oil Pump:* Eccentric drive double plunger.
*Normal Oil Pressure (Hot):* 40—60 p.s.i.
*Cooling System:* Pump and thermostat.
*Type of Ignition:* Magneto or distributor and coil.
*Method of Advance/Retard:* Manual/manual and centrifugal.
*Contact Breaker Gap:* Mag: 0.014 in. Coil: 0.012–6 in.
*Plug Gap:* 0.018 in.
*Make and Type of Plug:* Champion 16
*Number, Make and Type of Carburetters:* Standard series 1933/4—single SU. Special
    series 1933/4—3SU.
*Type of Inlet Manifold:* 1933/4 cast alloy bolt-on.
*Type of Exhaust Manifold:* Cast iron bolt-on.
*Location of Fuel Tank:* Rear mounted.
*Capacity of Fuel Tank:* 11 gallons.
*Method of Fuel Feed:* Electric pump.

MODELS AVAILABLE

1933: Lincock 6/12 Coupé £338, 6/14 £365: Lynx 2 door 4 seater Tourer 6/12 £338,
    6/14 £366, Ascot D/H 6/12 Coupé £338, 6/14 £365: Mentone 6/12 £338.
1933: Alpine 6/14 £365: Kestrel 6/12 Saloon £348, 6/14 £375: 6/12 March Special
    (Special Series) £375.
1934: Kestrel Saloon £358, Lynx 4 Door 4 Seat Tourer £348, Lincock F/H Coupé
    £348, Ascot D/H Coupé £348—14 h.p. Engine £27 extra. Mentone Saloon 6/12
    £348, Alpine 6/14 Saloon £375.
    Special series engine £60 extra, Preselectagear (1934) £27 extra.
    Preselctagear Ratios: 20.09:1, 11.64:1, 7.84:1 & 5.5:1, Reverse 25.19:1

MODEL

**6/15 Short (Chassis prefix 44T)**                            *Year:* 1935

CHASSIS

Channel section mainframes with tubular cross members and X-form cable bracing.
Arched over rear axle.
*Wheelbase:* 9 ft. 4½ in.
*Track:* Front 4 ft. 0 in. Rear 4 ft. 0 in.
*Type of Wheels:* Dunlop centre-lock 3.0 × 18 in. wire.
*Tyres:* Front 4.75 × 18 in. Rear 4.75 × 18 in.
*Braking System:* Girling mechanical rod with wedge operated shoes in 13 in. drums.

TRANSMISSION

*Clutch Type:* 2nd type 2 plate centrifugal.
*Gearbox Type:* Armstrong Siddeley preselector 4 speed.
*Gear Selecting Mechanism:* Selector quadrant on steering column.

*Gear Ratios:* 1st—20.09: 1, 2nd—11.64: 1, 3rd—7.84: 1, 4th—5.5: 1, Reverse—25.19: 1
*Gearbox Oil Capacity:* 5 pints.
*Rear Axle Oil Capacity:* 3½ pints.
*Rear Axle Type:* Semi-floating banjo; enclosed torque tube driving spiral bevel gears.
*Rear Axle Ratio:* 5.5: 1

ENGINE

*Engine Type:* Riley 6/15
*RAC H.P. Rating:* 14.3
*Cubic Capacity:* 1726 cc.
*Number of Cylinders:* 6
*Firing Order:* 1, 5, 3, 6, 2, 4
*Bore:* 62 mm.
*Stroke:* 95.2 mm.
*Cylinder Head:* P.R. detachable 14 stud with hemispherical combustion chambers.
*Valve Gear:* 45° overhead operated from high camshafts via tappets and short pushrods.
*Diameters of Valve Heads:* Inlet 1⅜ in. Exhaust 1⅜ in.
*Tappet Clearances (Hot):* Inlet 0.002 in. Exhaust 0.003 in.
*Valve Timing:* Inlet opens 0° before TDC, closes 55° after BDC
　　　Exhaust opens 50° before BDC, closes 21° after TDC.
*Number of Main Bearings:* 3
*Diameter of Main Bearings:* F—1⅝ in. C—3¾ in. R—2 in.
*Diameter of Main Bearings:* 1⅞ in.
*Sump Capacity:* 16 pints.
*Type of Oil Pump:* Gear driven from inlet camshaft.
*Normal Oil Pressure (Hot):* 40—60 p.s.i.
*Cooling System:* Pump, thermostat and fan.
*Type of Ignition:* Coil and distributor.
*Method of Advance/Retard:* Manual & Centrifugal.
*Contact Breaker Gap:* 0.012—0.014 in.
*Plug Gap:* 0.018 in.
*Make and Type of Plug:* Champion 16 or L10.
*Number, Make and Type of Carburetters:* Single Zenith.
*Type of Inlet Manifold:* 3 piece cast alloy bolt-on.
*Type of Exhaust Manifold:* Cast iron bolt-on.
*Location of Fuel Tank:* Rear Mounted.
*Capacity of Fuel Tank:* 10 gallons.
*Method of Fuel Feed:* Electric Pump.

MODELS AVAILABLE　44T—Falcon Saloon £365
44T—Kestrel Saloon £380
12 H.P. Six cylinder engine available at no extra cost; specification as above except bore 57 mm. and capacity 1458 cc.

MODEL　　**6/15 Narrow Track-Short (Chassis prefixes 46F & L)**　　*Year:* 1936

CHASSIS　　Boxed channel section mainframes with tubular cross members and X-form cable bracing. Arched over rear axle.
*Wheelbase:* 9 ft. 4½ in.
*Track:* Front 4 ft. 0 in. Rear 4 ft. 0 in.
*Type of Wheels:* Dunlop centre lock 3.0 × 18 in. wire.
*Tyres:* Front 4.75 × 18 in. Rear: 4.75 × 18 in.
*Braking System:* Girling mechanical rod with wedge operated shoes in 13 in. drums.

TRANSMISSION　*Clutch Type:* 2nd type Newton centrifugal 2 plate.
*Gearbox Type:* Armstrong Siddeley preselector 4 speed.
*Gear Selecting Mechanism:* Selector quadrant on steering column.
*Gear Ratios:* 1st—20.09: 1, 2nd—11.64: 1, 3rd—7.84: 1, 4th—5.5: 1, Reverse—25.19: 1
*Gearbox Oil Capacity:* 5 pints
*Rear Axle Oil Capacity:* 3½ pints.
*Rear Axle Type:* Semi-floating banjo, enclosed torque tube driving spiral bevel gears.
*Rear Axle Ratio:* 5.5: 1

ENGINE　　*Engine Type:* Riley 6/15
*RAC H.P. Rating:* 14.3
*Cubic Capacity:* 1726 cc.
*Number of Cylinders:* 6
*Firing Order:* 1, 5, 3, 6, 2, 4,

*The three ages of the Riley Six engine*

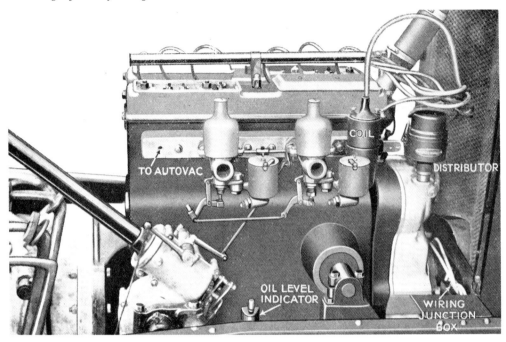

*1929 14 h.p. engine*

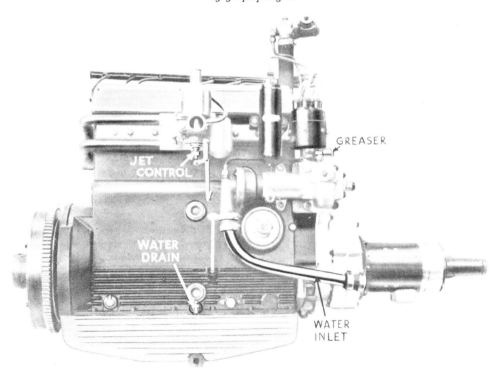

*1933 Six-Twelve engine*

GEARBOX
FILLER

CHASSIS
LUBRICATION
SUCTION UNION

CHAMBER ENCLOSING
OIL PUMP
VERTICAL
SHAFT

DISTRIBUTOR
CLAMP BOLT

GEARBOX OPERATING
LEVER

OIL SUMP
DRAIN PLUG

OIL
DIPSTICK

SLACKEN COVER TO INSPECT
DYNAMO BRUSHES

*1936 Six-Fifteen engine*

*Bore:* 62 mm.
*Stroke:* 95.2 mm.
*Cylinder Head:* P.R. detachable 14 stud with hemispherical combustion chambers.
*Valve Gear:* 45° overhead with high camshafts operating tappets and short pushrods.
*Diameters of Valve Heads:* Inlet $1\frac{3}{8}$ in. Exhaust: $1\frac{3}{8}$ in.
*Tappet Clearances (Hot):* Inlet 0.003 in. Exhaust 0.004 in.
*Valve Timing:* Inlet opens 0° before TDC, closes 55° after BDC.
        Exhaust opens 50° before BDC, closes 21° after TDC.
*Number of Main Bearings:* 3
*Diameter of Main Bearings:* F—$1\frac{5}{8}$ in. C—$3\frac{3}{4}$ in. R—2 in.
*Diameter of Big End Bearings:* $1\frac{7}{8}$ in.
*Sump Capacity:* 16 pints.
*Type of Oil Pump:* Gear driven from inlet camshaft.
*Normal Oil Pressure (Hot):* 40—60 p.s.i.
*Cooling System:* Pump, Thermostat and fan.
*Type of Ignition:* Coil and distributor.
*Method of Advance/Retard:* Manual and centrifugal.
*Contact Breaker Gap:* 0.012—0.014 in.
*Plug Gap:* 0.018 in.
*Make and Type of Plug:* Champion 16 or L10.
*Number, Make and Type of Carburetters:* Single Zenith.
*Type of Inlet Manifold:* 3 piece cast alloy bolt-on.
*Type of Exhaust Manifold:* Cast iron bolt-on.
*Location of Fuel Tank:* Rear mounted.
*Capacity of Fuel Tank:* 10 gallons
*Method of Fuel Feed:* Electric pump.

MODELS AVAILABLE    46F—Falcon Saloon £365
46L—Lynx 4 Seat Tourer £375. Chassis only £305.
Special Series 3 carburetter engine £48 extra.
12 h.p. Six cylinder engine available at no extra cost: specification.
as above except bore=57 mm. and capacity=1458 cc.

| | |
|---|---|
| MODEL | **6/15 Wide Track Short (Chassis Prefixes 46A & K)**          *Year:* 1936 |
| CHASSIS | Boxed channel mainframes with tubular cross members and X-form cable bracing. |
| | *Wheelbase:* 9 ft. 4½ in. |
| | *Track:* Front 4 ft. 3 in. Rear 4 ft. 3 in. |
| | *Type of Wheels:* Dunlop 3.0 × 18 in. centre lock wire. |
| | *Tyres:* Front 4.75 × 18 in. Rear 4.75 × 18 in. |
| | *Braking System:* Girling mechanical rod with wedge operated shoes in 13 in. drums. |
| TRANSMISSION | *Clutch Type:* 2nd Type Newton centrifugal 2 plate. |
| | *Gearbox Type:* Armstrong Siddeley preselector 4 speed. |
| | *Gear Selecting Mechanism:* Steering column located preselector quadrant. |
| | *Gear Ratios:* 1st—20.09:1, 2nd—11.64:1, 3rd—7.84:1, 4th—5.5:1, Reverse—25.19:1 |
| | *Gearbox Oil Capacity:* 5 pints. |
| | *Rear Axle Oil Capacity:* 3½ pints. |
| | *Rear Axle Type:* Banjo semi-floating. Torque tube drive to spiral bevel gears. |
| | *Rear Axle Ratio:* 5.5:1 |
| ENGINE | *Engine Type:* Riley 6/15 |
| | *RAC H.P. Rating:* 14.3 |
| | *Cubic Capacity:* 1726 cc. |
| | *Number of Cylinders:* 6 |
| | *Firing Order:* 1, 5, 3, 6, 2, 4 |
| | *Bore:* 62 mm. |
| | *Stroke:* 95.2 mm. |
| | *Cylinder Head:* P.R. detachable 14 stud with hemispherical combustion chambers. |
| | *Valve Gear:* 45° overhead with high camshafts operating tappets and short pushrods. |
| | *Diameters of Valve Heads:* Inlet 1½ in. Exhaust 1½ in. |
| | *Tappet clearance (Hot):* Inlet 0.003 in. Exhaust 0.004 in. |
| | *Valve Timing:* Inlet opens 0° before TDC, closes 55° after BDC. |
| | Exhaust opens 50° before BDC, closes 21° after TDC. |
| | *Number of Main Bearings:* 3 |
| | *Diameter of Main Bearings:* F—1⅝ in. C3—¾ in. R—2 in. |
| | *Diameter of Big End Bearings:* 1 7/8 in. |
| | *Sump Capacity:* 16 pints. |
| | *Type of Oil Pump:* Gear Driven. |
| | *Normal Oil Pressure (Hot):* 40—60 p.s.i. |
| | *Cooling System:* Pump, thermostat and fan. |
| | *Type of Ignition:* Coil and distributor. |
| | *Method of Advance/Retard:* Manual and centrifugal. |
| | *Contact Breaker Gap.* 0.012—0.014 in. |
| | *Plug Gap:* 0.018 in. |
| | *Make and Type of Plug:* Champion 16 or L10. |
| | *Number, Make and Type of Carburetters:* Single Zenith. |
| | *Type of Inlet Manifold:* 3 piece cast alloy bolt-on. |
| | *Type of Exhaust Manifold:* Cast iron bolt-on. |
| | *Location of Fuel Tank:* Rear mounted. |
| | *Capacity of Fuel Tank:* 11½ gallons. |
| | *Method of Fuel Feed:* Electric Pump. |
| MODELS AVAILABLE | 46A—Adelphi Saloon £380 |
| | 46K—Kestrel Saloon £380 |
| | Chassis Only £310 |
| | Special series 2 carburetter engine £48 extra. |
| MODEL | **15/6 Wide Track Long (Chassis no. Prefix 47/48)**          *Year:* 1937–38 |
| CHASSIS | Boxed channel mainframe, tubular cross members and cable bracing. |
| | *Wheelbase:* 9 ft. 8½ in. |
| | *Track:* Front 4ft. 3 in. Rear 4 ft. 3 in. |
| | *Type of Wheels:* Dunlop 3.0 × 18 in. centre lock wire. |
| | *Tyres:* Front 4.75 × 18 in. Rear 4.75 × 18 in. |
| | *Braking System:* Girling mechanical rod with wedge operated shoes in 13 in. drums. |
| TRANSMISSION | *Clutch Type:* 3rd type Newton centrifugal single plate. |
| | *Gearbox Type:* Armstrong Siddeley PSG 4 speed. |

*Gear Selecting Mechanism:* Steering column located preselector quadrant.
*Gear Ratios:* 1st—18.79:1, 2nd—10.91:1, 3rd—7.39:1, 4th—5.22:1, Reverse—23.33:1
*Gearbox Oil Capacity:* 5 pints.
*Rear Axle Oil Capacity:* 3½ pints.
*Rear Axle Type:* Semi-floating banjo, torque tube drive to spiral bevel gears.
*Rear Axle Ratio:* 5.22:1

ENGINE

*Engine Type:* Riley 15/6
*RAC H.P. Rating:* 14.3
*Cubic Capacity:* 1726 cc.
*Number of Cylinders:* 6
*Firing Order:* 1, 5, 3, 6, 2, 4
*Bore:* 62 mm.
*Stroke:* 95.2 mm.
*Cylinder Head:* P.R. detachable 14 stud with hemispherical combustion chambers.
*Valve Gear:* 45° overhead operated from high camshafts via tappets and short pushrods.
*Diameters of Valve Heads:* Inlet 1½ in. Exhaust 1½ in.
*Tappet Clearances (Hot):* Inlet 1½ in. Exhaust 1½ in.
*Valve Timing:* Inlet opens 0° before TDC, closes 55° after BDC
    Exhaust opens 50° before BDC, closes 21° after TDC.
*Number of Main Bearings:* 3
*Diameters of Main Bearings:* F—1⅝ in. C–3¾ in. R—2 in.
*Diameter of Big End Bearings:* 1⅞ in.
*Sump Capacity:* 16 pints.
*Type of Oil Pump:* Vertical gear driven.
*Normal Oil Pressure (Hot):* 40—60 p.s.i.
*Cooling System:* Pump, thermostat and fan.
*Type of Ignition:* Coil and distributor.
*Method of Advance/Retard:* Manual and centrifugal.
*Contact Breaker Gap:* 0.012 in—0.016 in.
*Plug Gap:* 0.018 in.
*Make and Type of Plug:* Champion L10
*Number, Make and Type of Carburetters:* Standard series—single Zenith. Special series—
    twin Zenith.
*Type of Inlet Manifold:* 3 piece cast alloy bolt-on.
*Type of Exhaust Manifold:* Cast iron bolt-on.
*Location of Fuel Tank:* Rear mounted.
*Capacity of Fuel Tank:* 11½ gallons.
*Method of Fuel Feed:* Mechanical pump.

MODELS AVAILABLE    1937: Chassis only £310, 47K Kestrel Saloon £385, 47A Adelphi Saloon £385.
1938: Chassis only £335, 48A Adelphi Saloon £405, 48K Kestrel Saloon £415.
Special series engine available 1937 at £48 extra.

*1938 Adelphi 15 h.p. Saloon*

*1938 Kestrel 15/6 Saloon*

CHAPTER SIX

# The New Age—the 1½ Litres, 1935–1938

September 1934 heralded the introduction of a new 1½ litre range of cars from the Riley stable, rather a case of "Something Old—Something New" in a way. Two features made it something old: it was a revival of the four-cylinder 1½ litre engine format—extinct as far as Riley were concerned since 1928—and it incorporated most of the design features of the now-famous Nine. Two features also made it something new: it was a completely new range of cars with an engine designed by a newcomer to the Riley design team—Hugh Rose.

It has been said that differing design opinions split those responsible and that, as a result, Victor Riley diverted Mr. Rose from his work on transmissions to design a new four-cylinder 1½ litre engine to be based upon the Nine concept. It seems that Victor and Stanley Riley wanted to produce such an engine as the 1½ Litre became, whilst it seems Percy Riley was anxious to develop the Six. There are some who might think that latter would have been the best development route, since it could perhaps have been made available in various sizes and might have saved the design costs of both the V8 and Big Four engines. Whatever the reasons and politics, we can now only contemplate what might have been and reflect upon what was. And whatever else it might have been or was, the new engine was a success.

This new design featured a bore and stroke of 69 mm. × 100 mm., giving a capacity of 1496 cc., and reviews of the day commented that the new model was being talked of as capable of 70 m.p.h. with ease! History has proved that talk to be correct.

The hemispherical combustion chambers were retained, as were the three point mounting system and the twin high camshafts. The hot-spot system was changed—some say for the worse—to feature two gas pipes running through the cylinder block between the exhaust manifold and an elbow connecting them to the inlet manifold. It was thought to be more efficient, but it is interesting to note that the Riley Service Department had to devise a special tool to remove the elbow on the inlet side! Suffice it to say that the hot-spot worked quite satisfactorily whilst undisturbed, but possessed all the faults of mating aluminium alloy with steel when it was disturbed. A certain maintenance manual is known to have recommended cutting the pipes at the alloy elbow to facilitate easy removal.

The first 233 engines of this new design had chain and sprocket camshaft drive for valve timing (from Chassis number 22T101 to 22T333). It was discovered that chain thrash occurred at certain engine speeds, causing premature wear, whereupon second thoughts clearly registered themselves and the already tried and tested, but expensive to manufacture, gear timing was revived.

The crankshaft, like the Nine and Six, was threaded into the crankcase from one end (in this case the rear) and was of the balanced web type. Like the Six, it had three main bearings, though the centre one was of rather less generous proportions—2¾ in. diameter instead of 3¾

*1935 1½ Litre 4 Light Kestrel Saloon (the same basic body design was used for the 1935 Six-Fifteen and 1936 9 h.p. Kestrels).*

in.—allowing for a little less concern over the surface speed of the bearing at high engine speeds.

Carburation was initially by means of a single Zenith, though later a Special Series engine was offered and was available with two Zenith or SU instruments. A cast iron exhaust manifold was fitted and the power output of the Standard Series engine was 45/46 b.h.p., the Special Series 52 b.h.p., and the Sprite Series engine of 1936/38 gave 59/61 b.h.p. This, of course, sounded the death knell for the 12/6 engine, although it continued to be offered into 1936 (there is no evidence of any being sold as late as that, however), since, in standard form it was less powerful—and was much heavier. The Sprite Series engine which was offered in all but the Two-Seater featured the "cross-flow" cylinder head with water heated inlet manifold, instead of gas hot-spots, and two SU carburetters. This type of manifold was fitted to some Special Series cars too.

The Armstrong Siddeley four speed preselector gearbox was coupled to the new engine via the Second Type, two plate, Newton centrifugal clutch and the whole was connected to the rear axle by means of the well-established Riley practice—an enclosed propeller shaft in a torque tube.

*A 1935/6 Falcon 1½ Litre Saloon (note less louvres in the bonnet sides than the later models—this car was built July 1935).*

Around all of this new machinery was put a new range of coachwork on a new design of chassis frame. The frame was of box-channel section with strong crossmembers and cable bracing laid in X-form, connecting at the crossover of the cables with a crossmember. This made the chassis very rigid and very strong. The profile of the frame was swept up over the front axle in a gentle curve, running down to the front shackle point of the rear springs and then arching generously over the rear axle to the rear shackles.

The Kestrel Saloon and the Lynx Four Door Tourer were already well known to the Riley market and so it made a lot of sense to remodel them to adapt to the new chassis, making them a little more elegant in the process. Both became very well accepted. They were joined by a completely new car, the Falcon Saloon, which exploited the then fashionable 'Aero-Line' styling (it should be appreciated that Riley pioneered the long sloping rear quarter style which, forty years later, became known as 'Fast-back'!). This new Falcon Saloon was the only Riley on show at Olympia without a preselector gearbox. It featured an entirely new synchromesh gearbox which had synchro on all four forward speeds. That could well have been an interesting development but, for reasons best known to the decision-makers at Coventry, it joined the ranks of seemingly good but abandoned Riley projects.

The Falcon was a taller car than the Kestrel and was intended to appeal to the motorist who sought greater headroom in the front and rear seats of the car. This it provided well— and at the very reasonable price of £335 compared with the Lynx tourer at the same price and the Kestrel at £10 more, £345.

Wheels and tyres were Dunlop, Riley having made their own wheels for a period, using Dunlop made hubs, but cars were now well and truly their business. And Dunlop had established itself as a wheelmaker of high quality as well as the premier tyre maker of the day, so it was Dunlop 3.00 × 18 in. centre-lock wire wheels with Dunlop tyres which were standard equipment on the Riley 1½ Litre range.

The braking system on these new cars was another departure from what had come to be accepted as 'standard Riley'. Now the Girling mechanical system was adopted, with rod linkage connecting the footbrake pedal and handbrake lever to the wheels. The shoes were in 13 in. drums and now were wedge-operated instead of using cams. Wedge brakes had the single advantage of being economically priced because they took less material and effort to manufacture. The cam-brake was undoubtedly more efficient in principle, but production costing won the day—and of course the wedge brake was easier to maintain and cheaper to replace if anything went wrong.

Much has been said about the relative merits of cam-versus-wedge brakes and it is a certain fact that the Girling wedge brake, operated through rods, gave better everyday braking performances on the road than did the cable-operated cam brake of earlier models, simply because there were no cable-stretch problems with the Girling design. However, to compare like with like, one has to examine the two with the same method of actuation, for example truck brakes of modern times use air operation instead of cables or rods. An air-actuated cam brake will always give better performance than an air-actuated wedge brake. There were car-makers who used rod operation of cam brakes in the 1930s and their cars gave exceptional braking performances—but most gave way in the end to the lower-cost wedge brake, simply as a means of holding down production costs and car prices in difficult times, so Riley was far from shamed by its decision to abandon the cam brake.

These cars made quite an impact on the motoring press of the day, as will be seen from Chapter eleven, but clearly they did not satisfy the Riley company, for within a year more

*1936 Falcon 1½ Litre Saloon (a factory illustration depicting the new radiator grille projected for that year, but not adopted).*

*1936 Adelphi 1½ Litre Saloon*

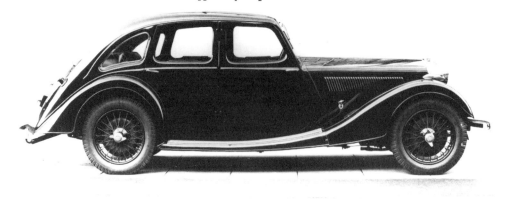

*1936/7 Kestrel Six-Light 1½ Litre Saloon*

*1936/7 Lynx 1½ Litre Special Series Concours Model*

new models were to appear and improvements were made to the chassis. It may be true to say that this period of the Company's history was its most fertile for new designs and different models.

1936 brought improvements in the Falcon and the Lynx models. It also brought the Adelphi Saloon (the successor, as a large spacious saloon, to the Stelvio which was now decidedly long in the tooth), and the low-cost all-steel Merlin Saloon which was not, as is often supposed, just a steel bodied Falcon (it was on a chassis 3 in. shorter in wheelbase than the Falcon.)

A new sports model, based on the MPH. chassis, was introduced too. It was a very elegant, streamlined two seater which, after the prototype models, did not have the now traditional Riley radiator, but a streamlined radiator cowl. It was, of course, the 1½ litre Sprite and its price was £425 upon introduction. The first brochure of this new model showed it with the traditional radiator, which was available upon demand, but by the 1935 Motor Show, the car displayed had the new cowl fitted.

Last but not least was the new six light Kestrel Saloon, which must be the pinnacle of Riley styling. This was a truly beautiful car which had that rare mixture of elegance, fashion and practicality possessed by only a handful of cars in any era (perhaps in a century of motor cars!). Very few cars are elegant and pleasing to look at from any angle (most have a bad spot from which the appearance is marred) but the Riley Six Light Kestrel was such a car. Small wonder then that it turned heads in the 1930's—and was as sought after in the last quarter of the century as in its own time.

The 1½ litre Riley was now another success story, not quite the innovation that the Riley Nine had been the decade before, but it could hardly have been expected to be since its engine was based upon the Nine design. But it was a true case of success begetting success— and deservedly. The art of driving was made available for many more people than might have been so, simply by the use of a preselector gearbox. What is more, those people who benefitted

from the installation of a preselector instead of the contemporary orthodox gearboxes were made safer drivers by Riley's constant efforts to keep things easy to use.

As if this new range of coachwork was not enough, Riley now had three different chassis in the $1\frac{1}{2}$ litre range—an 8 ft. 10 in. wheelbase, a 9 ft. 1 in. wheelbase and the long 9 ft. $4\frac{1}{2}$ in. wheelbase. The 8 ft. 10 in. was of course a Merlin Nine with a bigger engine, but the 9 ft. 1 in. and the 9 ft. $4\frac{1}{2}$ in. each carried two variations of coachwork. The shorter was the Falcon and Lynx chassis and the long version was for the Adelphi and Kestrel models.

In addition, the 9 ft. $4\frac{1}{2}$ in. frame was adapted to carry the Six-fifteen in 1936 and the newly announced 8/90 V8 engine. In mid 1936 there were four different engine sizes available from Riley and twenty two model variations

The $1\frac{1}{2}$ litre range consisted, by mid 1936, of the Adelphi and Kestrel Saloons at £350 each, the Falcon Saloon at £335 and the Lynx Tourer at £345 in the Standard Series. Special Series models were available at £27 extra and the Kestrel and Lynx were available with the Sprite series engine, both being £450 when introduced, but rather quickly reduced to £398, making very good value. The Sprite Two seater was available in two versions, one the production model with $1\frac{1}{2}$ litre engine and the other a competition version with a six cylinder engine for the price of £550.

Lastly came the Lynx Special Series Concours Model at the price of £398. At that time Concours d'Elegance were quite popular and so this version of the Lynx was offered with just about every conceivable extra. It had fitted suitcases in the boot, tools in special trays under the luggage compartment, a set of gaskets on a panel inside the bootlid—the panel doubling as a picnic tray—a pair of chromium plated horns on the front bumper and a centrally located fog light. Other features which completed the Concours specification included lamp stoneguards, a fire extinguisher, an automatic reversing light and a Ski-Lady mascot on the radiator filler cap. It really was quite a Special car.

For 1937, the range continued with a few minor changes. All the 1937 models were fitted with water pumps and mechanical fuel pumps. The built-in jacks were no longer fitted. One significant engineering change was the introduction of the Third Type Newton-design centrifugal clutch which was in effect a single plate type. Two friction plates were used in fact, but each was faced on only one side and they were rivetted together, making a single plate.

*A derivative of the Lynx $1\frac{1}{2}$ Litre, the 1936 $1\frac{1}{2}$ Litre*
*Army Tourer never went into production.*

*1937 1½ Litre Touring Sprite Saloon (this car first belonged to Reginald Dixon, the Blackpool organist, and later to the author).*

The Falcon was rebodied, using an all-steel version of the Briggs body, enabling a reduction of £20 to be made in its price. At the same time, an extension of the range came by the simple expedient of making the Sprite engine available in all of the 1½ Litre models, so popular had it become. This meant, of course, that Rileys had that edge over other 1½ litre cars which the Nine had enjoyed over other 1100 cc. cars ten years before.

One new model joined the Riley ranks for 1937, in the very pretty shape of the Touring Saloon, which became known unofficially as the Continental Touring Saloon. Rumour has it that Riley intended that to be the car's name, but a certain other manufacturer, claiming to make the best car in the world (not the "Most Successful", you will note) made known their priority on the name, so its use was prevented. And the car became known at first as the Touring Saloon, later the Close-Coupled Touring Saloon—names which did little credit to its quite attractive lines.

Like the other cars in the range, the Touring Saloon was offered with Standard Series engine at £350, or with the Special Series engine at £377 and the Sprite engined version was £398. A most intriguing feature of the design was the boot lid, which was in two sections— one top hinged and the other bottom hinged, carrying the spare wheel. The objective was to enable large suitcases or small trunks to fit, but it proved not very practical. However, the Touring Saloon design was clearly the inspiration for the post-war Nuffield Rileys and all round was a very pleasant car.

The 1937 Motor Show at Olympia brought with it the new season's cars (they had actually been released to the press some little time before) and it also brought a few revisions and price increases.

The most significant revision was actually announced in mid-1937 and was the option of a three speed dual overdrive gearbox instead of preselector. It gave a very useful five gearbox

*The engine of the Touring Sprite Saloon, showing the water return pipe
from the inlet manifold on the cross-flow cooled cylinder head. The
water provides manifold heating as it returns to the radiator.*

speeds instead of four, closing the gap between the ratios but demanding a little more skill
and understanding to enable the driver to extract the best performance from gearbox and car.

Also introduced earlier in the year had been the 'Hi-charge' induction system. The idea
behind the introduction of this revised manifolding was to improve the volumetric efficiency
of the engine, it being assumed that the normal volumetric efficiency of an engine running at a
speed of 1,000 r.p.m. was 80%. By lengthening the inlet manifold pipes and putting them in the
vertical plane, it was believed that it was possible to increase that volumetric efficiency by the
engine accepting a higher percentage of the available fuel charge. The increased pipe length
would raise the speed of gas flow, creating an improvement in the effective compression ratio
and raising the power output of the engine because of its improved operating efficiency.
Notwithstanding all of this fine theory, the 'Hi-charge' system was modified to horizontal
pipes by the time of the Motor Show and eventually was abandoned.

The new cars for 1938 were the Victor Saloon and the Touring Saloon. The Victor was
an all-steel saloon very much along the lines of the Merlin of two years earlier. Indeed, it was
basically the same chassis, being of 8 ft. 10 in. wheelbase and 4 ft. track. It was originally
offered at the Motor Show with the options of 1½ litre engine and dual overdrive gearbox or
9 h.p. engine and preselector gearbox. It was fitted with 4.75 × 18 in. tyres, used 11 in. diameter brakes and was still upholstered in leather and trimmed with wooden door cappings
and dashboard. The price of the Victor, in 1½ litre or 9 h.p. form, was originally set at £299—

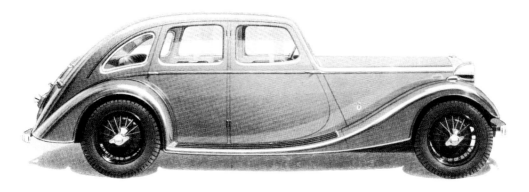

*1938 Kestrel 1½ Litre Saloon*

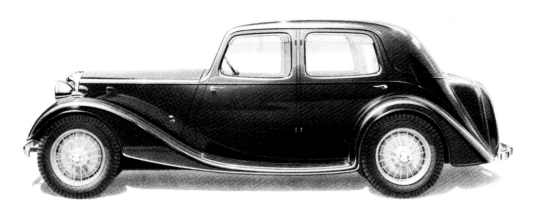

*1938 1½ Litre Touring Saloon*

excellent value at the time and a markedly lower price than the other Riley cars of that year.

The 1938 Touring Saloon was built, like the Falcons, Merlins and Victors, by Briggs Motor Bodies Limited. It was a new model introduced on the 4 ft. track short chassis of 9 ft. 1 in. wheelbase which had previously accommodated the Falcon and was still in use for the Lynx. Basically, the new car was a Falcon with a boot—a rather awkward boot it was too, being accessible through a top-mounted lid rather than having a hinged rear panel. The spare wheel was mounted on the rear panel and was enclosed inside a metal cover. Despite its awkwardness of access, the boot made the car look rather longer and lower than was the fact and so it looked really quite sleek. Though it was no match in appearance for its predecessor, the Close Coupled Touring Saloon, it represented very reasonable value at £345.

The Adelphi, Kestrel and Lynx models all continued in production into 1938 little changed, though two significant recognition features of these and all the 1938 models was the elimination of the bonnet-side louvres used in previous years and the use of vertical chrome-plated slats in the radiator shells, replacing the earlier dummy honeycomb. The price of the

Adelphi in standard form was now £375, with the Kestrel and Lynx both priced at £385. Special Series versions were still available at the remarkably consistent extra cost of £27 and the Sprite engine option was still a £48 option on top of the standard price. All of these models were available with a choice of preselector or dual-overdrive gearboxes at no difference in price.

The Sprite Two seater was still very much alive too, though its price had now been increased by £25, putting it up to £450. The customer still had the choice of the standard preselector gearbox or the optional manual unit, though the manual version was still not a 'modern' synchromesh type and so it is perhaps hardly surprising that most (probably all in 1938) customers bought their Sprites with preselectors.

The sad state of the Company's finances was now frighteningly close to becoming common knowledge and at the beginning of November 1937 an ordinary general meeting was called for November 10th. That meeting was postponed to November 29th with the announcement that the accounts for an eighteen month period ending 31st July 1937 would be made available and that they would reflect a trading loss. It had been hoped that the profits placed in reserve in previous years would cover that loss, but matters grew steadily worse.

On 24th February 1938, Sir W. H. Peat K.B.E. was appointed Receiver and Manager of Riley (Coventry) Limited and continued to run the affairs of the Company until its sale to Lord Nuffield in September of that year. Attempts had been made to merge Riley with another Coventry car maker, Triumph, but to no avail.

In the meantime cars continued to be produced and the Victor, which had been the last new model offered, was now priced at £325 and was available with preselector gearbox now in both variants, $1\frac{1}{2}$ litre and 9 h.p. The wheel size was changed too. The car was now on 3.00 × 17 in. wheels with 5.00 × 17 in. tyres. However it failed the test of survival and Riley (Coventry) Limited was doomed to become Riley (Coventry) Successors Limited under the Nuffield banner. Many feared the demise of the Riley character with the death of the family firm, but assurances were given by Lord Nuffield that the characteristics of the car would be retained and that every effort would be given to ensure that 'the company may add to the great reputation it has so deservedly won'.

Lord Nuffield sold Riley to Morris Motors Limited for the handsome sum of £1 (so it was rumoured) and the company's new parent set about showing the world how it would add to the reputation that Riley had so deservedly won by announcing the 1939 models, a six light saloon and a two door four seat drophead with only the $1\frac{1}{2}$ and $2\frac{1}{2}$ litre engines available.

Mediocrity and Riley had never come together before and in 1939, they were ill bed-fellows. Interesting to note, though, that a pre-war model—the Close Coupled Touring Saloon—should have so much influence over the styling of the car which was to follow those 1939/40 models after the Second World War.

*1938 Lynx 1½ Litre Tourer*

*1938 1½ Litre engine with overdrive gearbox*

SPECIFICATIONS


MODEL                 **1½ Litre (Chassis Prefix 22T)**                                    *Year:* 1935

CHASSIS               Boxed channel mainframe, X-form cable braced, arched over rear axle.
                      *Wheelbase:* 9 ft. 1 in.
                      *Track:* Front 4 ft. o in. Rear 4 ft. o in.
                      *Type of Wheels:* Dunlop 3 × 18 in. centre lock wire.
                      *Tyres:* Front 4.75 × 18 in. Rear 4.75 × 18 in.
                      *Braking System:* Girling mechanical rod with wedge-operated shoes in 13 in. drums.

TRANSMISSION          *Clutch Type:* 2nd type Newton centrifugal 2 plate.
                      *Gearbox Type:* Armstrong Siddeley PSG 4 speed.
                      *Gear Selecting Mechanism:* Preselector quadrant on steering column.
                      *Gear Ratios:* 1st—20.09: 1, 2nd—11.64: 1, 3rd—7.84: 1, 4th—5.5: 1, Reverse 25.19: 1
                      *Gearbox Oil Capacity:* 5 pints.
                      *Rear Axle Oil Capacity:* 3½ pints.
                      *Rear Axle Type:* Semi-floating banjo with torque tube drive to spiral gears.
                      *Rear Axle Ratio:* 5.5: 1

ENGINE                *Engine Type:* 1½ litre 12/4
                      *RAC H.P. Rating:* 11.9
                      *Cubic Capacity:* 1496 cc.
                      *Number of Cylinders:* 4
                      *Firing Order:* 1, 2, 4, 3
                      *Bore:* 69 mm.
                      *Stroke:* 100 mm.
                      *Cylinder Head:* P.R. detachable 12 stud with hemispherical combustion chambers.
                      *Valve Gear:* 45° overhead operated by high camshafts via tappets and short pushrods.
                      Chain driven valve gear from 22T101 to 22T333, gear driven thereafter.
                      *Diameters of Valve Heads:* Inlet 1⅜ in. Exhaust 1⅜ in.
                      *Tappet Clearances (Hot):* Inlet 0.003 in. Exhaust 0.004 in.
                      *Valve Timing:* Inlet opens 0° before TDC, closes 55° after BDC.
                      Exhaust opens 50° before BDC, closes 20° after TDC.
                      *Number of Main Bearings:* 3
                      *Diameter of Main Bearings:* F—1¾ in. C—2¾ in. R—1¾ in.
                      *Diameter of Big End Bearings:* 1⅞ in.
                      *Sump Capacity:* 8½ pints*.
                      *Type of Oil Pump:* Vertical driven gear from inlet camshaft.
                      *Normal Oil Pressure (Hot):* 30—50 p.s.i.
                      *Cooling System:* Thermosyphon.
                      *Type of Ignition:* Coil and Distributor.
                      *Method of Advance/Retard:* Manual and centrifugal.
                      *Contact Breaker Gap:* 0.012 in—0.016 in.
                      *Plug Gap:* 0.018 in.
                      *Make and Type of Plug:* Champion L10S.
                      *Number, Make and Type of Carburetters:* Standard series—single Zenith. Special series—
                      Twin SU or Zenith.
                      *Type of Inlet Manifold:* Cast alloy bolt-on with central hot-spot.
                      *Type of Exhaust Manifold:* Cast iron bolt-on.
                      *Location of Fuel Tank:* Rear mounted.
                      *Capacity of Fuel Tank:* 10 gallons.
                      *Method of Fuel Feed:* Electric Pump.

MODELS AVAILABLE      Chassis Only £275
                      Kestrel Saloon £345, Falcon Saloon £335
                      Lynx 4 Seat Tourer £335
                      Special series engine available at £27 extra.



*Engines up to number 1580 had sump capacity of 11 pints.

| | |
|---|---|
| MODEL | **1½ Litre (Chassis Prefix 26M)** *Year:* 1936. |
| CHASSIS | Boxed channel mainframe, lightened and cable braced, arched over rear axle.<br>*Wheelbase:* 8 ft. 10 in.<br>*Track:* Front 4 ft. 0 in. Rear 4 ft. 0 in.<br>*Type of Wheels:* Dunlop 3.00 × 18 in. centre lock wire.<br>*Tyres:* Front 4.75 × 18 in. Rear 4.75 × 18 in.<br>*Braking System:* Girling mechanical rod with wedge operated shoes in 13 in. drums. |
| TRANSMISSION | *Clutch Type:* 2nd type Newton centrifugal 2 plate.<br>*Gearbox Type:* Armstrong Siddeley PSG 4 speed.<br>*Gear Selecting Mechanism:* Preselector quadrant on steering column..<br>*Gear Ratios:* 1st—19.07:1, 2nd—11.05:1, 3rd—7.44:1, 4th—5.22:1, Reverse—23.91 : 1<br>*Gearbox Oil Capacity:* 5 pints.<br>*Rear Axle Oil Capacity:* 3½ pints.<br>*Rear Axle Type:* Semi-floating banjo with torque tube drive to spiral bevel.<br>*Rear Axle Ratio:* 5.22:1 |
| ENGINE | *Engine Type:* 1½ litre 12/4<br>*RAC H.P. Rating:* 11.9<br>*Cubic Capacity:* 1496 cc.<br>*Number of Cylinders:* 4<br>*Firing Order:* 1, 2, 4, 3<br>*Bore:* 69 mm.<br>*Stroke:* 100 mm.<br>*Cylinder Head:* P. R. detachable 12 stud with hemispherical combustion chambers.<br>*Valve Gear:* 45° overhead operated by high camshafts via tappets and short pushrods<br>*Diameters of Valve Heads:* Inlet 1 $\frac{7}{16}$ in. Exhaust 1 $\frac{7}{16}$ in.<br>*Tappet Clearances (Hot):* Inlet 0.003 in. Exhaust 0.004 in.<br>*Valve Timing:* Inlet opens 0° before TDC, closes 55° after BDC.<br>   Exhaust opens 50° before BDC, closes 20° after TDC.<br>*Number of Main Bearings:* 3<br>*Diameter of Main Bearings:* F & R—1$\frac{3}{4}$ in. C—2$\frac{3}{4}$ in.<br>*Diameter of Big End Bearings:* 1$\frac{7}{8}$ in.<br>*Sump Capacity:* 8½ pints.<br>*Type of Oil Pump:* Gear driven.<br>*Normal Oil Pressure (Hot):* 30—50 p.s.i.<br>*Cooling System:* Thermosyphon.<br>*Type of Ignition:* Coil & Distributor.<br>*Method of Advance/Retard:* Manual & Centrifugal.<br>*Contact Breaker Gap:* 0.012—0.016 in.<br>*Plug Gap:* 0.018 in.<br>*Make and Type of Plug:* Champion L10S.<br>*Number, Make and Type of Carburetters:* Standard series—single Zenith. Special series—twin Zenith.<br>*Type of Inlet Manifold:* Cast alloy bolt-on with central hot-spot.<br>*Type of Exhaust Manifold:* Cast iron bolt-on.<br>*Location of Fuel Tank:* Rear mounted.<br>*Capacity of Fuel Tank:* 9½ gallons.<br>*Method of Fuel Feed:* Electric pump. |
| MODELS AVAILABLE | 26M—Merlin Saloon £308<br>S26M—Special Series Merlin Saloon £335<br>26M—Chassis only £256 (Special Series £27 extra) |
| MODEL | **1½ Litre 12/4 Short (Chassis Prefixes 26F, L: 27F, L: 28C, F, L.)** *Year:* 1936–38 |
| CHASSIS | Boxed channel mainframe with cable bracing and tubular crossmembers.<br>*Wheelbase:* 9 ft. 1 in.<br>*Track:* Front: 4 ft. 0 in. Rear: 4 ft. 0 in.<br>*Type of Wheels:* Dunlop 3.00 × 18 in. centre lock wire.<br>*Tyres:* Front: 4.75 × 18 in. Rear: 4.75 × 18 in.<br>*Braking System:* Girling mechanical rod with wedge operated shoes in 13 in. drums. |
| TRANSMISSION | *Clutch Type:* (26 series—2nd type 2 plate Newton) 3rd type Newton centrifugal single plate. |

*Gearbox Type:* Armstrong Siddeley PSG 4 speed.
*Gear Selecting Mechanism:* Preselector quadrant on steering column.
*Gear Ratios:* 1st—18.79:1, 2nd—10.91:1, 3rd—7.39:1, 4th—5.22:1, Reverse—
   23.33:1. *27F/28C* 1st—18:1, 2nd—10.45:1, 3rd—7.08:1, 4th..5:1, Reverse—
   22.35:1. Dual overdrive gearbox available on 28 series (Standard on 28C, with
   PSG optional) 1st—17.35:1, 2nd—10.46:1, O.D. 2nd—7.55:1 3rd—6.75:1,
   O.D. 3rd—4.87:1. (Rear axle ratio 6.75:1)
*Gearbox Oil Capacity:* 5 pints.
*Rear Axle Oil Capacity:* $3\frac{1}{2}$ pints.
*Rear Axle Type:* Semi-floating banjo. Torque tube drive to spiral bevel gears.
*Rear Axle Ratio:* 5.22:1—27F/28C/28F=5.0:1. 28 Series also fitted with 5.22 and
   5.5:1.

ENGINE

*Engine Type:* $1\frac{1}{2}$ litre 12/4
*RAC H.P. Rating:* 11.9
*Cubic Capacity:* 1496 cc.
*Number of Cylinders:* 4
*Firing Order:* 1, 2, 4, 3
*Bore:* 69 mm.
*Stroke:* 100 mm.
*Cylinders Head:* P.R. detachable 12 stud with hemispherical combustion chambers.
*Valve Gear:* 45° overhead operated from high camshafts via tappets and short pushrods.
*Diameter of Valve Heads:* Inlet $1\frac{7}{16}$ in. Exhaust $1\frac{7}{16}$ in.
   1938=$1\frac{9}{16}$ in. Inlet diameter.
*Tappet Clearances (Hot):* Inlet 0.003 in. Exhaust 0.004 in.
*Valve Timing:* Inlet opens 0° (SS—20°) before TDC, closes 55° (SS—50°) after BDC.
   Exhaust opens 50° before BDC, closes 20° after TDC.
*Number of Main Bearings:* 3
*Diameter of Main Bearings:* F & R—$1\frac{3}{4}$ in. C—$2\frac{3}{4}$ in.
*Diameter of Big End Bearings:* $1\frac{7}{8}$ in.
*Sump Capacity:* $8\frac{1}{2}$ pints.
*Type of Pump:* Gear driven vertical.
*Normal Oil Pressure (Hot):* 30—50 p.s.i.
*Cooling System:* 26 series Thermosyphon 27/28 series Pump and fan.
*Type of Ignition:* Coil and distributor (SS—Scintilla magneto).
*Method of Advance/Retard:* Manual and centrifugal.
*Contact Breaker Gap:* 0.012—0.016 in. (SS—0.094 in.)
*Plug Gap:* 0.018 in.
*Make and Type of Plug:* Champion L10. (SS—J10)
*Number, Make and Type of Carburetters:* Standard series—single Zenith. Special series—
   2 Zenith. Sprite series—2SU.
*Type of Inlet Manifold:* Cast alloy bolt-on (water heated hot spot some Sprite series).
*Type of Exhaust Manifold:* Cast iron bolt-on.
*Location of Fuel Tank:* Rear mounted.
*Capacity of Fuel Tank:* 10 gallons.
*Method of Fuel Feed:* Electric pump 26 series, mechanical pump 27/28 series

MODELS AVAILABLE

Standard Series 1936: 26F—Falcon Saloon £335, 26L—Lynx Tourer £345, Chassis
only £275. S26L—Lynx Special Series Concours £398.
Standard Series 1937: 27F—Falcon Saloon £315, 27L—Lynx Tourer £345, Chassis
only £275. S27L—Lynx Special Series Concours model £398 (Chassis £317).
Standard Series 1938: 28FX—Touring Saloon O/D £345, 28L—Lynx Tourer £385,
Chassis £295.
Special series models: S26L, S27L, S27F, S28L, S28F, £27 extra.
Sprite series models: SS26L, SS27L, SS27F, SS28L £48 extra to standard. Sprite
series not offered for Lynx concours model.

MODEL

**$1\frac{1}{2}$ Litre 12/4 Long (Chassis Prefixes 26A, K: 27A, K, C: 28A, K)** *Year:* 1936–38

CHASSIS

Boxed channel mainframe with tubular crossmembers and cable bracing.
*Wheelbase:* 9 ft. $4\frac{1}{2}$ in.
*Track:* Front 4 ft. 3 in. Rear: 4 ft. 3 in.
*Type of Wheels:* Dunlop 3.00 × 18 in. centre lock wire.
*Tyres:* Front 4.75 × 18 in. Rear 4.75 × 18 in.
*Braking System:* Girling mechanical rod with wedge operated shoes in 13 in. drums.

| TRANSMISSION | *Clutch Type:* (26 series—2nd type Newton twin plate) 3rd type Newton centrifugal single plate. |
|---|---|

*Clutch Type:* (26 series—2nd type Newton twin plate)
   3rd type Newton centrifugal single plate.
*Gearbox Type:* Armstrong Siddeley PSG 4 speed.
*Gear Selecting Mechanism:* Steering column mounted preselector quadrant.
*Gear Ratios:* 1st—18.79:1,  2nd—10.91:1,  3rd—7.39:1,  3th—5.22:1,  Reverse—23.91:1. 26 series 1st—19.07:1, 2nd—11.05:1, 3rd—7.44:1, 4th—5.22:1 1938 models available with dual overdrive option at no extra cost. 1st—17.35:1 2nd—10.46:1, O.D. 2nd—7.55:1, 3rd—6.75:1, O.D. 3rd—4.87:1 (Rear axle ratio 6.75:1)
*Gearbox Oil Capacity:* 5 pints.
*Rear Axle Oil Capacity:* 3½ pints.
*Rear Axle Type:* Semi-floating banjo. Torque tube drive to spiral bevel gears.
*Rear Axle Ratio:* 5.22:1

**ENGINE**

*Engine Type:* 1½ litre 12/4
*RAC H.P. Rating:* 11.9
*Cubic Capacity:* 1496 cc.
*Number of Cylinders:* 4
*Firing Order:* 1, 2, 4, 3
*Bore:* 69 mm.
*Stroke:* 100 mm.
*Cylinder Head:* P.R. detachable 12 stud with hemispherical combustion chambers.
*Valve Gear:* 45° overhead from high camshaft via tappets and short pushrods.
*Diameter of Valve Heads:* Inlet 1 7/16 in. (1938—1 9/16 in) Exhaust 1 7/16 in.
*Tappet Clearance (Hot):* Inlet 0.003 in. Exhaust 0.004 in.
*Valve Timing:* Inlet opens 0° (SS—20°) before TDC, closes 55° (SS—50°) after BDC. Exhaust opens 50° before BDC, closes 20° after TDC.
*Number of Main Bearings:* 3
*Diameter of Main Bearings:* F & R—1¾ in. C—2¾ in.
*Diameter of Big End Bearings:* 1⅞ in.
*Sump Capacity:* 8½ pints.
*Type of Oil Pump:* Vertical gear driven.
*Normal Oil Pressure (Hot):* 30—50 p.s.i.
*Cooling System:* 26 series—thermosyphon. 27/28 series—Pump and fan.
*Type of Ignition:* Standard—Coil and distributor. Sprite Series—Scintilla Magneto.
*Method of Advance/Retard:* Manual and centrifugal.
*Contact Breaker Gap:* 0.012—0.016 in. (Sprite 0.014 in.)
*Plug Gap:* 0.018 in.
*Make and Type of Plug:* Champion L10 or J10.
*Number, Make and Type of Carburetters:* Standard series—single Zenith or Solex. Special series—Twin Zenith or Solex. Sprite series—Twin SU.
*Type of Inlet Manifold:* cast alloy bolt-on with central hot spot (some Sprite series—water heated).
*Type of Exhaust Manifold:* Cast iron bolt-on.
*Location of Fuel Tank:* Rear mounted.
*Capacity of Fuel Tank:* 11½ gallons.
*Method of Fuel Feed:* 26 series electric pump, 27 series mechanical pump.

**MODELS AVAILABLE:**
**STANDARD SERIES**

1936  : 26A—Adelphi Saloon £350, 26K—Kestrel Saloon £350, Chassis £280
1937  : 27A—Adelphi Saloon £350, 27C—Close Coupled Touring Saloon £350, 27K—Kestrel Saloon £350, Chassis Only £280.
1938: 28A—Adelphi Saloon £375, 28K—Kestrel Saloon £385, chassis only £305
1936–38: Special series models S26A, S26K, S27A, S27C, S27K, S28A, S28K £27 extra.
1936–38: Sprite series models SS26K, SS27A, SS27C, SS27K, SS28K—£48 extra.

**MODEL**          **1½ Litre 12/4 (Chassis Prefix 28V)**                    *Year:* 1938

**CHASSIS**

Channel section boxed and drilled mainframe with tubular crossmembers and X-form cable bracing.
*Wheelbase:* 8 ft. 10 in.
*Track:* Front 4 ft. 0 in. Rear 4 ft. 0 in.
*Type of Wheels:* Dunlop centre lock 3.00 × 18 in. (3.0 × 17 in. from early 1938).
*Tyres:* Front 4.75 × 18 in. (5.00 × 17 in. mid 1938).
   Rear 4.75 × 18 in. (5.00 × 17 in. mid 1938).
*Braking System:* Girling mechanical rod with wedge operated shoes in 11 in. drums.

TRANSMISSION
*Clutch Type:* Overdrive—Single Dry 8 in. plate.
      P.S.G.—Single plate 3rd type centrifugal.
*Gearbox Type:* 3 speed dual overdrive or Armstrong Siddeley 4 speed preselector.
*Gear Selecting Mechanism:* Overdrive: central floor mounted lever
      P.S.G: Steering column quadrant.
*Gear Ratios:* P.S.G. 1st—18.79:1, 2nd—10.91:1, 3rd—7.39:1, 4th—5.22:1,
      Reverse—23.33 : 1
      Overdrive 1st—17.35:1, 2nd—10.46:1, 3rd—6.75:1, O/D 2nd—7.55:1
      O/D 3rd—4.87:1
*Gearbox Oil Capacity:* Overdrive—3 pints, P.S.G.—5 pints.
*Rear Axle Oil Capacity:* $3\frac{1}{2}$ pints.
*Rear Axle Type:* Semi-floating banjo type with enclosed torque tube drive.
*Rear Axle Ratio:* Overdrive—6.75:1. P.S.G.—5.22:1

ENGINE
*Engine Type:* $1\frac{1}{2}$ litre.
*RAC H.P. Rating:* 11.9
*Cubic Capacity:* 1496 cc.
*Number of Cylinders:* 4
*Firing Order:* 1, 2, 4, 3
*Bore:* 69 mm.
*Stroke:* 100 mm.
*Cylinder Head:* P.R. detachable 12 stud with hemispherical combustion chambers.
*Valve Gear:* $45°$ overhead with high camshafts operating tappets and short pushrods.
*Diameters of Valve Heads:* Inlet—$1\frac{9}{16}$ in. Exhaust—$1\frac{7}{16}$ in.
*Tappet Clearance (Hot):* Inlet 0.003 in. Exhaust 0.004 in.
*Valve Timing:* Inlet opens $0°$ before TDC, closes $55°$ after BDC.
      Exhaust opens $50°$ before BDC, closes $20°$ after TDC.
*Number of Main Bearings:* 3
*Diameter of Main Bearings:* F & R—$1\frac{3}{4}$ in. C—$2\frac{3}{4}$ in.
*Diameter of Big End Bearings:* $1\frac{7}{8}$ in.
*Sump Capacity:* 8 pints.
*Type of Oil Pump:* Gear driven from inlet camshafts.
*Normal Oil Pressure (Hot):* 30—50 p.s.i.
*Cooling System:* Pump.
*Type of Ignition:* Coil and distributor.
*Method of Advance/Retard:* Manual and centrifugal.
*Contact Breaker Gap:* 0.012—0.016 in.
*Plug Gap:* 0.018 in.
*Make and Type of Plug:* Champion L10.
*Number, Make and Type of Carburetters:* Single Zenith.
*Type of Inlet Manifold:* Cast alloy bolt-on with central hot spot.
*Type of Exhaust Manifold:* Cast iron bolt-on.
*Location of Fuel Tank:* Rear mounted.
*Capacity of Fuel Tank:* $9\frac{1}{2}$ gallons.
*Method of Fuel Feed:* Mechanical Pump.

MODELS AVAILABLE   28V—Victor Saloon £299 (1937–early 1938) £325 1938, with preselector g/b optional
      £325.0s.

This drawing, specially prepared by a staff artist, gives an excellent idea of the 1½-litre Riley chassis. Apparently conventional, this chassis will be seen on closer examination to have many unusual features, amongst which may be mentioned the cable chassis bracing, the special cylinder-head layout, the unconventional engine mounting, the automatic clutch, and the self-changing gearbox.

The Light Car

444

FEBRUARY 26, 1937.

## Under the Microscope (1)

# THE 1½-LITRE RILEY CHASSIS

# CHAPTER SEVEN

# The Final Fling—the V8 and Big Four, 1935–1938

The last two engine designs from Riley were really quite adventurous, each in their own way. The V8 8–90 was a new departure for Riley. They had built V engines before of course, with the Tri-car and early four wheeled cars, but they were V-twins and a V8 was a rather different proposition. It was the largest engine they had ever produced and was certainly the most complicated. On the other hand, the Big Four was really an enlarged and improved $1\frac{1}{2}$.

The 8–90 model was first introduced in October 1935 and was offered on the 9 ft. $4\frac{1}{2}$ in. chassis with Adelphi or Kestrel coachwork. The engine consisted basically of two 9 h.p. cylinder blocks on a common crankcase. Naturally the design was updated in many respects to bring it into line with $1\frac{1}{2}$ litre practice. For example, the oil pump was gear driven, the valve rocker gear was mounted to the cylinder heads instead of being carried in the rocker boxes and the rocker covers resembled those of the $1\frac{1}{2}$ litre. Carburation was by two down-draught Zeniths which originally were mounted on to separate inlet manifolds, one carburetter feeding each bank of cylinders.

The two plane crankshaft of the V8 carried two connecting rods per crankpin and had three main bearings of generous proportions. The front and centre mains were the same diameters as the rear and centre bearings of the six-cylinder engine, 2 in. and $3\frac{3}{4}$ in., and the rear main was $2\frac{7}{8}$ in. across.

There were three gear-driven camshafts, one centrally located inlet and two exhaust. The offside exhaust camshaft drove the oil pump and the inlet drove the distributor from the rear end. The water pump was also gear driven, from an auxiliary shaft off the inlet timing wheel and the drive pulley for the cooling fan was mounted on the front end of the inlet camshaft. Drive was conveyed to the fan by belt.

Other features of the 8–90 included the continued use of hot-spots running through the cylinder block from the exhaust manifolds to the inlet manifolds, external oil feed to the rocker shafts and a new five-point mounting for the engine.

The engine was coupled to an Armstrong Siddeley four speed preselector gearbox which drove a higher final drive ratio of 4.55 : 1 via the usual enclosed propeller shaft. This gearbox was physically larger than the normal version used by Rileys and had an oil capacity of 7 pints.

An interesting feature about the 8–90 chassis is that it appears to have been adapted from the 6/15 chassis, being of the same overall dimensions, for 1936–37 and then the Big Four chassis seems to have carried the 1938 V8s. Chassis numbers for the 1936 models were prefixed 86A or K and for 1937 the prefix was 87. This 87 continued, unusually for Riley, into 1938, probably because so few cars were built and of course the 88 prefix had already been used six years earlier with the Edinburgh and Winchester six-cylinder models.

*1937 V8 8-90 Adelphi Saloon*

The saviour from confusion over chassis numbers between 1937 and 1938, remembering that they were different in many ways, was no doubt the fact that so few were built—probably not more than a few dozen in all—and the chances are they were built in three batches.

Most of the cars built were Adelphis, though it is said that two Kestrels were sold to one of the Swiss Riley distributors of the day. This seems to have been, so the story goes, because orders were placed which the Company did not really want to fulfil, but it was obliged to do so because the dealer faced a threat of legal action since the 8-90 Kestrel had been offered in Riley's initial sales literature. However, if they were supplied—and it is open to conjecture whether they were or not—they seem to have disappeared without trace. All the known 8-90s are therefore Adelphis—that is until some enterprising enthusiast takes a holiday in Switzerland and returns with a Kestrel 8-90!

The cars offered in the 1936 season had, according to the Riley Sales Data Book of that year, 4 ft. 3 in. track axles fitted with 13 in. brakes and were in the 86 chassis Series. The 1937, 87 Series, models, according to the same source for that year, featured 14 in. brakes. However, the 1938 brochure shows us that 16 in. brakes were fitted to that season's cars, the same size as the Big Four models—again in the 87 Series.

Magna multi-stud wire wheels were used on the 1937/38 models instead of the centre-lock type. The earlier models featured 18 in. wheels shod with 5.25 × 18 in. tyres, whereas the 1937 cars were fitted with 5.25 × 17 in. This was changed back to 18 in. for 1938—probably to achieve standardisation with the Big Four.

For 1936 and 1937, prices of the complete cars were the same at £450 and in 1938 the Adelphi only was offered at £475. It has been said that the 8-90 was not a financial success (and that is probably a very modest understatement in view of the numbers built): nonetheless it remained on offer for three trading seasons. It would probably have sold better if it had been offered in Kestrel and Lynx variants, but, like so many things Riley, who can say?

*The crankshaft of the 8-90 engine*

*The three camshafts of the 8-90 engine.*

Despite, or probably because of, the financial pressures upon the Company in 1937, it proceeded to offer one last new type before its sad collapse, the 16 h.p. Big Four range.

The Big Four engine was of 2½ litres capacity, having a bore of 80.5 mm., a stroke of 120 mm., and an R.A.C. horsepower rating of 16.07. It was very much a Riley engine, having a number of details in common with the 1½ Litre, but at the same time incorporated a number of new features.

The great advantages of the Big Four from the sales point of view were that it was less expensive to manufacture, it was easier to maintain and there was a family resemblance between this and other Riley engines. Though it did look different in a number of ways, it was a four cylinder engine. Would-be owners were therefore not frightened off by the rumoured complications (which prevail today) of V8 engines. Many specification features were familiar: for example, it had the well-tried Riley hemispherical combustion chambers and a gear-driven oil pump and a certain "Riley look" about it.

Interesting departures from then-traditional Riley practice included mounting the engine

*An attractive rear quarter view of the 1938 Big Four
(or Blue Streak) 16 h.p. Kestrel Saloon*

differently, no longer employing a bar through the cylinder block. Now, there were two large rubber mountings at the front of the engine, in a cradle, and a small cradle at the rear end of the gearbox with two smaller rubber mountings, effectively maintaining the principle of a three-point engine support. There were also two torque reaction rods attached to the clutch housing and restraint cables placed between the sump/crankcase flanges and the chassis main members. All this was intended to eliminate engine wobble at low speed or under acceleration.

Another major departure from previous practice was the way in which the crankshaft was fitted to the engine. It was no longer threaded into the crankcase from the rear end but was fitted from underneath and held in place by the main bearing caps, reducing a number of problems from the service and production points of view. The main bearings were all of the same diameter, though the rear journal was considerably longer than the other two to support the flywheel.

The front end of the crankcase no longer carried the dynamo which was of the orthodox belt-drive type and mounted on adjustable brackets at the inlet side of the engine. The sump was of 12 pints capacity and was filled through a separate orifice next to the exhaust manifold.

The rocker boxes on the $2\frac{1}{2}$ litre engine were unlike their predecessors. In fact the cylinder head overall was quite different. The rocker boxes were integral with the cylinder head and the covers were now only cover plates. The inlet ports were cast into the cylinder head and the inlet manifold was mounted on the exhaust side of the engine above the exhaust manifold (one way to dispense with 'Hi-charge *and* hotspots all in one go!').

The Big Four chassis was of 9 ft. $8\frac{1}{2}$ in. wheelbase, like the late 8–90, and its track was 4 ft. 3 in. As was now usual, the brakes were of Girling mechanical rod type with wedge operated shoes in 16 in. drums. Like the 8–90, the wheels were Magna wire of 3.25 in. × 18 in. dimensions with 5.25 × 18 in. tyres.

The gearbox was a Borg Warner dual overdrive, similar to that now being offered on the $1\frac{1}{2}$ litre models. It had three direct speeds and overdrive on second and top giving five ratios

*The only 1938 16 h.p. Big Four Lynx Tourer—with wartime headlight shields and white-edged running boards.*

in all. Drive was transmitted to an enclosed propeller shaft in torque tube to the rear axle, the ratio of which was 5.5 : 1.

Five coachwork models were offered on the 'Blue Streak' as it was to be known (the 8–90 was the 'Silver Streak'). They were the Adelphi at £405 and the Kestrel at £415 plus two Touring Saloons (yes, two) and the Lynx Tourer. The Lynx never went beyond the one-off stage and Hector Dobbs (a famous name in Riley racing circles and a Riley dealer) bought that.

The Touring Saloons however were an interesting dichotomy, one the 1937 Close Coupled (Continental) design and the other the 1938 design scaled up from the 'Falcon-with-a-boot' type. They were actually given different names for presentation to the public, but would-be Big Four car buyers must have been very curious to see two models of different design serving the same purpose. However, the Close Coupled Saloon was offered at £415 and the Touring Saloon was priced at £385—quite a modest price in comparison with the other Big Fours.

The Touring Saloon was designed to make use of the body manufactured for Riley by Briggs Motor Bodies Limited, who also had made the bodies for the $1\frac{1}{2}$ litre and six-cylinder Falcon, the Merlin, the 9 h.p. and $1\frac{1}{2}$ litre Touring Saloons and the Victor—all derived from the same basic design. It was intended, it seems, that the same body as was used on the $1\frac{1}{2}$ litre Touring Saloon be fitted to the Big Four chassis, but apparently the problems of fitting to a longer and wider chassis were so great that the project was abandoned. It has been said that none of this model were built, but a prototype was certainly attempted, it is also said that up to half a dozen were laid down for production before the model was abandoned. And sightings of a Big Four Touring Saloon have certainly been claimed.

An interesting feature of these cars is the way in which they were identified. Riley had almost run out of two-digit numbers in which the first did not coincide with the year of build,

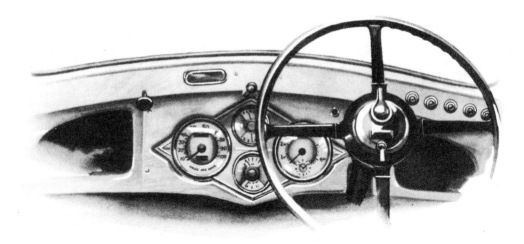

*1938 Big Four dashboard layout*

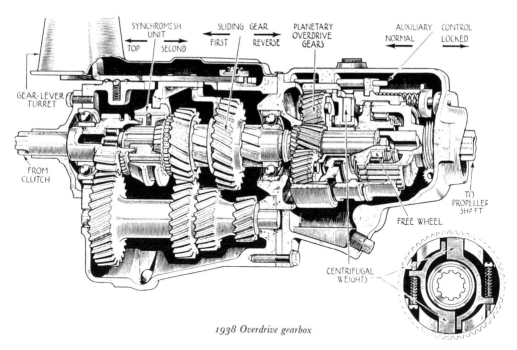

*1938 Overdrive gearbox*

but in which the second did. For example, the $1\frac{1}{2}$ litre cars ran in a number sequence in the 20s, the six-cylinder cars in the 40s, the Nine in the 60s and the 8–90 in the 80s. So they settled for the first time for a number sequence which did coincide with the year and so the chassis number prefix for the Big Fours was 38. All of the cars were fitted with the dual overdrive gearbox and so all were identified as 38–X; the Adelphi being 38AX, the Kestrel being 38KX, the Lynx was allotted 38LX and the Touring Saloons of both types were allotted 38BX, though at least one Close Coupled Saloon escaped with 38CX as its prefix.

*1938 16 h.p. Touring Saloon*

*1938 16 h.p. Close-Coupled Saloon*

All in all, the 16 h.p. 'Blue Streak' models were very fine cars. Their only fault was the timing of their arrival on ⋅the market—in that they came too late to save the Company. Reflecting on what might have been, the Big Four showed all the signs of being able to sell well with a little more time and had the Company conceived this model at the time (or possibly even instead) of the 8–90, it might just have recovered. Contemplating what was, it is interesting to note that in late 1939, the now Nuffield-owned Company was pressed, and succumbed to the pressure to re-introduce the Big Four Kestrel. It was quite a relief after the cheese-pairing six-light Rileys of that year to see the Kestrel resurrected and continue in production into 1940. It was followed after the war by a design very closely related to the Close Coupled Saloon.

So ended four decades of a family business which had been born at the dawn of the industry—and which had always striven to take⋅ and maintain a lead in that industry— an endeavour in which they had been more successful than most—though at a great price ultimately.

The $2\frac{1}{2}$ litre Riley engine was to continue in production, with modifications, until 1957, but only in the shadow of its—and its proprietors'—former glory. It was perhaps not of his own doing, but Lord Nuffield's promise had been broken and the Company lost the greatness of reputation it had so deservedly won in earlier years.

SPECIFICATIONS

| | |
|---|---|
| MODEL | **8-90 18 H.P. V8 Short (Chassis no. Prefix 86, 87)**          *Year:* 1936–37. |
| CHASSIS | Boxed section mainframe, cable braced with tubular cross members. |
| | *Wheelbase:* 9 ft. 4½ in. |
| | *Track:* Front 4 ft. 3 in. Rear 4 ft. 3 in. |
| | *Type of Wheels:* Dunlop 3.25 × 18 in. centre lock wire (86 series). |
| | Magna 3.25 × 17 in. wire (87 series). |
| | *Tyres:* Front (86) 5.25 × 18 in. (87—5.25 × 17 in). |
| | Rear (86) 5.25 × 18 in. (87—5.25 × 17 in.) |
| | *Braking System:* Girling mechanical rod with wedge operated shoes in 13 in. drums (86 series). 14 in. drums (87 series). |
| TRANSMISSION | *Clutch Type:* 86 series—2nd type, 87 series—3rd type centrifugal. |
| | *Gearbox Type:* Armstrong Siddeley PSG 4 speed. |
| | *Gear Selecting Mechanism:* Steering column located preselector quadrant. |
| | *Gear Ratios:* 1st—18.2 : 1, 2nd—10.3 : 1, 3rd—6.71 : 1, 4th—4.55 : 1, Reverse—20.33 : 1 |
| | *Gearbox Oil Capacity:* 7 pints. |
| | *Rear Axle Oil Capacity:* 3½ pints. |
| | *Rear Axle Type:* Semi-floating banjo. Enclosed torque tube drive to spiral bevel gears. |
| | *Rear Axle Ratio:* 4.55 : 1 |
| ENGINE | *Engine Type:* Riley 8—90 |
| | *RAC H.P. Rating:* 18.05 |
| | *Cubic Capacity:* 2178 cc. |
| | *Number of Cylinders:* 8 |
| | *Firing Order:* 1, 5, 4, 8, 6, 3, 7, 2 |
| | *Bore:* 60.3 mm. |
| | *Stroke:* 95.2 mm. |
| | *Cylinder Head:* Two P.R. detachable 10 stud with hemispherical combustion chambers. |
| | *Valve Gear:* 45° overhead from 3 camshafts via tappets and short pushrods to rockers. |
| | *Tappet Clearances (Hot):* Inlet 0.003 in. Exhaust 0.004 in. |
| | *Valve Timing:* Inlet opens 5° before TDC, closes 50° after BDC |
| | Exhaust opens 50° before BDC, closes 20° after TDC. |
| | *Number of Main Bearings:* 3 |
| | *Diameter of Main Bearings:* F—2 in. C—3¾ in. R—2⅞ in. |
| | *Diameter of Big End Bearings:* 1⅛ in. |
| | *Sump Capacity:* 16 pints. |
| | *Type of Oil Pump:* Gear driven from RH exhaust camshaft. |
| | *Normal Oil Pressure (Hot):* 30—50 p.s.i. |
| | *Cooling System:* Pump and Fan. |
| | *Type of Ignition:* Coil & Distributor. |
| | *Method of Advance/Retard:* Manual & Centrifugal. |
| | *Contact Breaker Gap:* 0.016 in. |
| | *Plug Gap:* 0.018 in. |
| | *Make and Type of Plug:* Champion L10S |
| | *Number, Make and Type of Carburetters:* 2 Zenith downdraught. |
| | *Type of Inlet Manifold:* 2 cast alloy bolt-on with exhaust-fed hotspots (1937: Hi-charge design). |
| | *Type of Exhaust Manifold:* 2 cast iron bolt-on. |
| | *Location of Fuel Tank:* Rear mounted. |
| | *Capacity of Fuel Tank:* 11½ gallons. |
| | *Method of Fuel Feed:* Twin electric pumps. |
| MODELS AVAILABLE | 1936: 86A—Adelphi Saloon £450, 86K—Kestrel Saloon £450 Chassis only £375. |
| | 1937: 87A—Adelphi Saloon £450, Chassis only £375. |
| MODEL | **8-90 18H.P. V8 Long (Chassis Prefix 87A)**          *Year:* 1938. |
| CHASSIS | Boxed section mainframe, cable braced, with 7 cross members. |
| | *Wheelbase:* 9 ft. 8½ in. |
| | *Track:* Front 4 ft. 3 in. Rear 4 ft. 3 in. |
| | *Type of Wheels:* Magna wire 3.25 × 18 in. |

*Tyres:* Front 5.25 × 18 in. Rear 5.25 × 18 in.
*Braking System:* Girling mechanical rod with wedge operated shoes in 16 in. drums.

TRANSMISSION

*Clutch Type:* 3rd type Newton centrifugal single plate.
*Gearbox Type:* Armstrong Siddeley PSG 4 speed.
*Gear Selecting Mechanism:* Preselector quadrant on steering column.
*Gear Ratios:* 1st—18.2: 1, 2nd—10.4: 1, 3rd—6.71: 1, 4th—4,55: 1, Reverse—20.33: 1
*Gearbox Oil Capacity:* 7 pints.
*Rear Axle Oil Capacity:* 3½ pints.
*Rear Axle Type:* Semi-floating banjo. Enclosed torque tube drive to spiral bevel gears.
*Rear Axle Ratio:* 4.55: 1

ENGINE

*Engine Type:* Riley 8—90
*RAC H.P. Rating:* 18.05
*Cubic Capacity:* 2178 cc.
*Number of Cylinders:* 8
*Firing Order:* 1, 5, 4, 8, 6, 3, 7, 2
*Bore:* 60.3 mm.
*Stroke* 95.2 mm.
*Cylinder Head:* Two P.R. detachable 10 stud with hemispherical combustion chambers
*Valve Gear:* 45° overhead from 3 camshafts (1 inlet, 2 exhaust) via tappets and short
　　pushrods.
*Tappet Clearances (Hot):* Inlet 0.003 in. Exhaust 0.004 in.
*Valve Timing:* Inlet opens 5° before TDC, closes 50° after BDC
　　Exhaust opens 50° before BDC, closes 20° after TDC.
*Number of Main Bearings:* 3
*Diameter of Main Bearings:* F—2 in. C—3¾ in. R—2⅞ in.
*Diameter of Big End Bearings:* 1⅞ in.
*Sump Capacity:* 16 pints.
*Type of Oil Pump:* Gear driven from R.H. exhaust camshaft.
*Normal Oil Pressure (Hot):* 30–50 p.s.i.
*Cooling System:* Pump & Fan.
*Type of Ignition:* Coil and distributor.
*Method of Advance/Retard:* Manual and centrifugal.
*Contact Breaker Gap:* 0.016 in.
*Plug Gap:* 0.018 in.
*Make and Type of Plug:* Champion L10S
*Number Make and Type of Carburetters:* 2 Zenith downdraught.
*Type of Inlet Manifold:* 2 cast alloy bolt-on.
*Type of Exhaust Manifold:* 2 cast iron bolt-on.
*Location of Fuel Tank:* Rear mounted.
*Capacity of Fuel Tank:* 11½ gallons.
*Method of Fuel Feed:* Twin electric pumps.

MODEL AVAILABLE　87A—Adelphi Saloon £475, Chassis only £400

MODEL　　**16 H.P. Big Four**　　*Year:* 1938

CHASSIS

Boxed section mainframe, cable braced, 7 crossmembers, upswept at front, arched over
rear axle.
*Wheelbase:* 9 ft. 8½ in.
*Track:* Front: 4 ft. 3 in. Rear: 4 ft. 3 in.
*Type of Wheels:* Magna wire 3.25 × 18 in.
*Tyres:* Front 5.25 × 18 in. Rear 5.25 × 18 in.
*Braking System:* Girling mechanical rod with wedge-operated shoes in 16 in. drums.

TRANSMISSION

*Clutch Type:* Single dry plate.
*Gearbox Type:* 3 speed dual overdrive.
*Gear Selecting Mechanism:* Floor-mounted central lever.
*Gear Ratios:* 1st—14.3: 1, 2nd—8.25: 1, 2nd O/D—6.15: 1, 3rd—5.5: 1,
　　3rd O/D—3.97: 1, Reverse—17.87: 1
*Gearbox Oil Capacity:* 3 pints.
*Rear Axle Oil Capacity:* 3½ pints.
*Rear Axle Type:* Semi-floating banjo. Enclosed torque tube drive to spiral bevel gears.
*Rear Axle Ratio:* 5.5: 1

ENGINE

*Engine Type:* 2½ Litre Big 4
*RAC H.P. Rating:* 16.07
*Cubic Capacity:* 2443 cc.
*Number of Cylinders:* 4
*Firing Order:* 1, 2, 4, 3
*Bore:* 80.5 mm.
*Stroke:* 120 mm.
*Cylinder Head:* P.R. detachable 12 stud with hemispherical combustion chambers.
*Valve Gear:* 45° overhead from high camshafts via tappets and short pushrods to rockers.
*Tappet Clearances (Hot):* Inlet 0.003 in. Exhaust 0.003 in.
*Valve Timing:* Inlet opens 7° before TDC, closes 50° after BDC
    Exhaust opens 50° before BDC, closes 17° after TDC.
*Number of Main Bearings:* 3
*Diameter of Main Bearings:* 2$\frac{35}{64}$ in.
*Diameter of Big End Bearings:* 2$\frac{21}{64}$ in.
*Sump Capacity:* 12 pints.
*Type of Oil Pump:* Gear driven from inlet camshaft.
*Normal Oil Pressure (Hot):* 30—50 p.s.i.
*Cooling System:* Pump & Fan.
*Type of Ignition:* Coil & Distributor.
*Method of Advance/Retard:* Manual and centrifugal.
*Contact Breaker Gap:* 0.016 in.
*Plug Gap:* 0.018 in.
*Make and Type of Plug:* Champion L10S Lodge C14.
*Number, Make and Type of Carburetters:* Single Zenith 36V12 downdraught.
*Type of Inlet Manifold:* Cast alloy bolt-on located exhaust side with ports through cylinder head.
*Type of Exhaust Manifold:* Cast iron bolt-on.
*Location of Fuel Tank:* Rear mounted.
*Capacity of Fuel Tank:* 11½ gallons.
*Method of Fuel Feed:* Mechanical Pump.

MODELS AVAILABLE  38AX—Adelphi Saloon £405, 38LX—Lynx Tourer £405 (38LX 1181 only one built)
38BX—Touring Saloon £385, 38BX (CX)—Close Coupled Saloon £415
38KX—Kestrel Saloon £415

668        *October 11th, 1935.*

# New Riley V-Eight

### Full Particulars of a Most Interesting New 18 h.p. Engine Available in Two Car Models

FOR a long time past—a year or more —there has been much speculation about the existence of a new Riley eight-cylinder engine, and last week the fact was divulged, although no details were given. *The Autocar* is now able to reveal the full particulars, and very interesting they are.

The new engine is rated at 18.05 h.p., eight cylinders, 60.32 by 95.25 mm. (2,178 c.c.), tax £13 10s. From the bore and stroke it is obvious that the design is based on the use of two four-cylinder blocks of the famous and well-tried Riley Nine engine, and this, indeed, is broadly the case.

Incidentally, the move is a wise one, for so many Riley Nines have been built and have been in regular service for so long that the reliability is proven and the best servicing methods are well understood. It is not perhaps absolutely correct to say that this V-eight consists of two 9 h.p. cylinder blocks, for there are differences in detail if not in principle.

In the new engine two banks of four cylinders are set at 90 degrees angle, and are cast monobloc with the crank case. The banks are slightly staggered, that is to say, the centre lines of opposing cylinders are not in the same plane. This is to allow for a pair of big-ends on each crankpin, whereby simple connecting rods without special articulation can be used. The crankshaft is of the two-plane type and is fitted with balance weights, and is carried in three large main bearings. This design gives excellent dynamic balance and is free from torsional vibration periods over its full speed range.

Naturally, the special Riley type of efficient valve arrangement is embodied,

and the valves are overhead, being set at 90 degrees in hemispherical combustion chambers, with the sparking plugs in the centre. These combusion chambers are machined to regular size, as also are the valve ports. The valves are operated by pressure lubricated overhead rockers complete with accessible adjustments and contained in neat oil-tight covers, the rockers being reciprocated by short, light push-rods from camshafts mounted fairly high in the cylinder block sides, a design which combines the efficiency of overhead valves with unusual accessibility.

Three camshafts are used in the new engine—one in the centre of the cylinder banks, which serves the inlet valves of both banks, whilst the two remaining camshafts are placed one on each outer side of the banks. Valve ports which run straight out on opposite sides of the cylinder head are always used on Riley engines, and thus it will be seen that on the V-eight the inlet ports face inwards and the exhaust ports outward.

This arrangement has two advantages.

The exhaust manifolds and pipes are low down and well away from the engine, so that it is possible to allow plenty of air to pass over them, and thus avoid the undue heat under the bonnet which is likely to arise from the mass of metal in a powerful engine. Secondly, the difficulty of arranging efficient carburation for eight cylinders is also avoided, for in this case each bank of cylinders has its own four-cylinder inlet manifolds and its own downdraught carburetter.

Each inlet manifold is provided with a central hot-spot by a port passing from the exhaust manifold through the cylinder block to the inlet side. The silencing system is, of course, in duplicate, with an exhaust pipe and silencer on each side of the car. Helical-toothed gears are used for the distribution, and in the centre is an auxiliary shaft which drives the water pump, and a pulley for a large belt-driven fan.

Lubrication is of the fully forced type and is supplied by a gear-type pump driven from the centre of the offside exhaust camshaft. An accessible pressure-type oil filter is provided, and in this the release valve is concealed. The distribution head of the ignition system is placed in a high and accessible position above the centre of the cylinder banks and towards the rear.

Riley enthusiasts will naturally be very interested to know what is the power output of the new engine. The designers, however,

*Views which show the general arrangement of the Riley V-Eight engine. Above is a part-section diagram.*

*The Autocar*

### New Riley V-Eight

show a very proper reluctance to make claims, but it is admitted that the V-eight produces proportionately more power than would be expected from two Nines. As the Nine is able to develop anything from 35 to 60 or more brake-horse-power, according to compression and style of special tuning, it may be guessed that the V-eight pulls something between 80 and 100 b.h.p., which is enough to give a very vivid performance indeed to a moderate-sized car. It is also said that the new engine runs with sweetness almost unexpected, and that this smoothness remains up to the maximum revolutions.

V engines of the 90 degree design are not usually easy to house under a bonnet of normal proportions, but this has been so cleverly arranged in the new car that there is no external evidence of a wide engine. Moreover, special provision for complete accessibility without need of removing panels is being made, but as this is going through the patent stage it cannot yet be illustrated.

The engine is flexibly mounted on a five-point rubber suspension to insulate it from the occupants of the car. In unit with it is the regular Riley transmission of automatic centrifugal clutch and "preselecta" self-changing four-speed gear box. The chassis for the V-eight is constructed on exactly similar lines to that of the Riley 1½-litre, with a stiff box-section under-tied frame. The wheelbase is 9ft. 4½in., the track 4ft. 3in., and tyre size is 5.25 by 18in.

Two styles of complete car will be available, the Adelphi six-light four-door saloon, and the latest six-light four-door Kestrel saloon. The price in each case is £450. The Adelphi is a new type of body introduced for 1936; it is particularly spacious, with ample room in every respect, and it has a particularly attractive appearance, whilst at the rear is a large-size luggage boot. The Kestrel is also a new design, offering more room than in previous models, but is of an even more graceful stream-line shape.

Overall sizes are: Adelphi, length 14ft. 3½in., width 5ft. 1¼in., height 5ft. 3½in.,; Kestrel, length 14ft. 7in., width 5ft. 1¼in., height 4ft. 10½in.

June 29, 1937.    The**Motor**  25

# "Hi-charge"

on the
New Rileys

# A new advance in automobile engineering

"Hi-charge"
**LOW PRICE**

9 h.p. models from £290 (Tax £6 15 0)

1½ Litre models from £315 (Tax £9 0 0)

"8-90" Saloon £475 (Tax £:3 10 0)

RILEY (COVENTRY) LIMITED COVENTRY

The principal characteristic of this new system—equalisation in length and scientific streamlining of the induction pipes—results in a substantial increase in the power of an already powerful engine.

The tremendous velocity of the petrol and air "mixture", 20,000 ft. per minute, on its way through the induction pipes to the cylinders, results in a supercharging effect without a supercharger. The consequent improvement in performance—speed, acceleration, pick-up, smoothness—is amazing.

Riley design, leading the industry from its earliest days, takes a new step forward with the new Hi-charge power system which is so valuable a feature of the new Rileys.

9 H.P. 1½-LITRE, EIGHT-NINETY

*The car that stays in front*

# CHAPTER EIGHT

# The Sporting Rileys

The association of Riley vehicles with motor sport appears to have begun (to borrow a phrase from Edward H. Reeves' '*The Riley Romance*') 'in the mists of the very dawn of the industry itself'. In the first recorded track event for which a Riley was entered, Robert Crossley won—that was in 1899. And Rileys continued to win for many years more. Indeed, in their own field they are still winning over forty years after the last real Riley was built.

Within the scope of this chapter, I propose to cover only those cars which were specifically produced as sporting cars and the data sheets at the end of the chapter will refer only to those models distinctly different in specification from the production non-sporting types. This means that there is no special data sheet for the 1909 10 h.p. Speed Model, the Two and Four Seat Sports Side Valves (the Redwingers) or the March Special Two/Four Seaters of 1933. This is because all of these cars were built on standard Riley chassis along with the other models of the range.

The reason for dealing with Sporting Rileys in a separate chapter is simple. The development of sporting models in any range of cars, no matter by whom they are made, is a process of evolution often more clearly identifiable than is true of production cars. Riley is just such a case, particularly because—more than most perhaps—the experience and knowledge gained from competition was used to improve production cars. It was a happy co-incidence (and is true today) that success in the field of motor sport brought improvements in sales figures across the range. A car which consistently succeeds is a desirable car, one which is inconsistent is not.

There is neither space nor time within the scope of this book to concentrate on the detailed competition history of Riley cars, for it would inevitably stray from the basic objective here, which is to deal with the product. Motor sport, and therefore a competition history, is as much, perhaps more, about people, for it is people who make cars come alive and be successful. That record is another task. Some of Riley's motor sporting successes will be recorded here, but no claim is made that they are the most significant and they certainly are not complete.

It is a notable fact that Riley tricycles, quadricycles, tri-cars and motor cars were consistently used in competition events in their time and among the competitors in the early days were Victor Riley, Stanley Riley and Allan Riley. All achieved success and proved, from the earliest days, the reliability of their product.

Reliability runs in the 1980's don't mean very much, because the motoring world has come to expect cars to cover mileages of 10,000 or more without maintenance and because roads have become smoother and faster. But in the first two and a half decades of this century, things were very different and it was an achievement to make a trip to Edinburgh from London without incident—or to Land's End or wherever. So, for Riley to have entered a London to Edinburgh run with eleven cars and have all eleven win First Class Awards—or to be the first manufacturer to have six of his products entered for the immortal Le Mans 24 Hours

*Harry Rignold with his 1903 2¾ h.p. Motor Bicycle—a very
successful machine in early competitions*

race and all six finish, quite apart from the distinctions won—was more than just an achievement. It was the kind of outstanding success that typified Riley reliability, quality of design
and manufacture, and character.

The first distinctly sporting Riley, unashamedly produced for that purpose, was the early
10 h.p. Speed Model. It was built on the 7 ft. 6 in. wheelbase V twin chassis, had an engine
capacity of 1390 cc. with the then usual Riley 3 speed gearbox. Bore and stroke were 96 mm.
and it seems the car was well capable of 60 m.p.h. or more—which for 1909 was pretty good
especially in a car costing only £220 (or only £188·if you wanted just the chassis for your
coachbuilder to do the rest).

The car was quite low built and featured (of course) Riley detachable wire wheels,
a rear mounted petrol tank of seven gallons capacity with air pressure feed and was a two
seater. On just such a car, Stanley Riley entered the Scottish Reliability Trials of 1909 and
won every award in his class. Mr J. Browning duplicated that success with a 12/18 h.p. at
the same event by winning all of *his* class awards too!

In that same year, Victor Riley won the Members' Event at Shelsley Walsh and the Club
Cup at the Aston Clinton Hill Climb. Riley were also second in both of these events.

After all the upheaval of the Great War, when the British Motor Industry was recovering
its feet, Riley began to think of sporting models once again and the new side valve models

*The 1909 10 h.p. Speed Model used in the Irish Trials.*

were an excellent basis. The production cars soon demonstrated to their owners that Rileys had lost none of their reliability or precision. In 1922, the first of a new generation of sporting Riley cars was born.

This new model was the Eleven Two Seat Sports which was originally priced at £520, but reduced to £495. It was joined in 1923 by the Four Seat Sports and now, in 1923, they were both given road speed guarantees. This was quite an adventurous step for the Company to take, especially when one considers that the Two Seater was guaranteed capable of 70 m.p.h. and the Four Seater 60 m.p.h. These cars were both built on the 9 ft. wheelbase chassis and were offered, with improvements, up to 1928.

The Brooklands Whitsun Meeting of 1924 resulted in resounding success for Riley, when

*1922 11 h.p. 2 Seat Sports—forerunner of the Redwingers.*

*1923 11 h.p. 2 Seat Sports—front wheel brakes came the following year.*

a standard Sports model won the Light Car Handicap, run over a distance of $5\frac{3}{4}$ miles, by $\frac{3}{4}$ of a mile! At the August Meeting a similar car won the 90 m.p.h. Long Handicap and came second in the 75 m.p.h. Short Handicap.

Also offered to special order was a Short Wheelbase Sports of 8 ft. 6 in. with a very sparse body, no windscreen and butterfly type wings. Its price was not published, clearly because the specification was almost infinitely variable and the choice of gearing and state of engine tune were matters for discussion with the customer before the question of price was settled. Two such cars are known to survive today.

When the Eleven-Forty became the Twelve in 1925, by the simple expedient of boring out the engine to 69 mm. the smaller capacity engine continued in production exclusively for the sports models so that they remained within the International Class F engine capacity limit of 1500 cc. When the Ricardo type cylinder head was fitted to the standard Twelve range, it was adapted to the sporting models too and, whilst no brake horsepower figures were ever published by the factory, it is believed that the late Two and Four Seat Sports models were producing well over 50 b.h.p.

The last development in the Redwinger family was really a bridge between the era of the Riley side-valve and the new generation of overhead-valve engined cars to be heralded by the Nine. This new sporting model was introduced at the Olympia Motor Show of 1926 for the 1927 Season. It was the 11/50/65 Supercharged Sports which was essentially a Redwinger

*Victor Gillow aboard his side-valve racer (an early fore-runner of the 11 h.p. SWB Sports?).*

fitted with an overhead valve engine and a Roots type supercharger. The car at Olympia was a four seat version, though with a longer wheelbase than the other sports models 9 ft. 6 in. This enabled the use of almost entirely standard components whilst moving the front axle six inches further forward of the radiator to make room for the supercharger which was located at the front of the engine and was crankshaft driven.

The Riley Suprohead engine was an Eleven-Forty cylinder block fitted with an overhead-valve head. The valves were vertically placed, operated by pushrods and rockers via a chain-driven camshaft. The front axle was modified from standard and the rear springs were underslung to give a lower overall height than the other two sporting models. The car had a guaranteed road speed of 80 m.p.h.—quite something for a 1500 cc. car in 1926!

With the implied power output of 65 brake horsepower and the proven side-valve reliability, this car would have been quite a sports car but it was not to be. It was suggested that the cylinder head followed too closely another, patented, design and that this was the reason for Riley hastily discontinuing the model; though it should also be borne in mind that the Nine was now a fact of life and may have been as much an influence in that decision as anything else.

In sporting terms the next decade was to be Riley's most significant, starting with the introduction of the Nine. It was the efforts of J. G. Parry-Thomas and Reid Railton, with their precursor of the Brooklands Speed Model, which persuaded Riley to embark so quickly upon the inclusion of a sports version of the Nine in their catalogue. Even then, the early cars were built by Thomson and Taylor at Brooklands. The car was originally listed just as

the Speed Model, but it soon became known as the Brooklands Speed Model, which was soon abbreviated to 'Brooklands'.

The Brooklands 9 was quickly successful and Class G records were soon being broken at surprising speeds. The prototype was driven to a new record in March 1928 and later that year, H. W. Purdy broke the 3 hr., 6 hr., 500 km. and 500 mile records at speeds between 85.2 and 87.09 m.p.h. He later added the 200 km. and 200 mile records to his count, too.

After an undistinguished Six Hours Race at Brooklands, Thomson and Taylor fielded a team of three Brooklands 9s for the 1928 R.A.C. Tourist Trophy Race at the Ards circuit in Ulster. Two other cars were entered, one by Edgar Maclure and the other by K. S. Peacock. Peacock's was the only car to finish, winning his class at a speed of 56.98 miles per hour.

And so to the next year, to try again. This time, seven Brooklands Nines were entered in the T.T. and the determination of the Riley team was to be rewarded with a first, second and third in the 1100 cc. Class—12th, 19th and 21st overall. A seven litre Mercedes won the event, but S. C. H. (Sammy) Davis led the 1100 cc. success for Riley.

Shelsley Walsh was another success story in 1929, where Riley Nines won all seven categories and took the President's Cup that year too. So by now, the Riley Nine Brooklands Speed Model was well-established as a car to be reckoned with in competition. Strange then, that only around a hundred were built and sold during its market life.

In 1930, yet another of those exciting, almost schoolboy-type, success stories took place, in which a private entrant took on the might of factory-sponsored competitors to carve another niche in motor racing history for the Riley name. This was in the Junior Car Club's Double Twelve Race at Brooklands that year, when C. R. Whitcroft entered his own two-year-old Riley Nine Brooklands for the event. He finished third overall, winning the 1100 cc. Class with ease at an average speed for the 24 hours of 69.96 m.p.h. The car was Number 83, PK2721, a Thomson and Taylor chassis—number 60/3. Second Place in Class G was taken by Mrs Scott, the first lady to finish the event, and she was sixth overall in the general classification. Quite an achievement.

The Brooklands Nine Speed Model was probably the lowest-built car Riley ever made. It had a wheelbase of 8 ft., a track of 3 ft. 11¾ in. and through its production life was fitted with a variety of two-seat bodies. The early cars had wood-framed steel-skinned bodies with two

*1925 11/40 SWB Sports*

*The Coventry Museum's 1908 12/18 h.p. Short Wheelbase Tourer, bought from the Sword Collection in 1965*

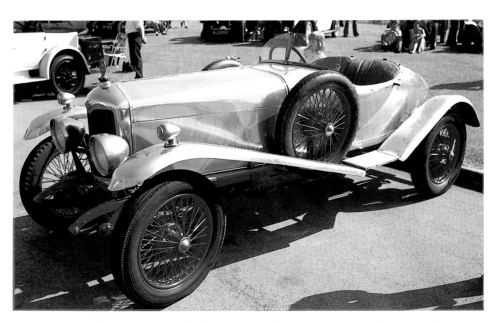

*A fine example of the Eleven-Forty Two Seat Sports (the Redwinger), this particular car had only one owner for forty years*

*A fine period picture of the 1926 11/40 Four Seat Sports*

doors, full weather equipment, a flat single panel fold-down windscreen, and long front wings which ran in a straight line from their apex over the front wheels down to the mounting brackets near the rear edge of the bonnet. The T.T. cars of 1929 had shorter-tailed doorless bodies of all-metal frame construction with alloy panelling. The cars which were so successful at Le Mans in 1933 and 1934 also had doorless lightweight bodies.

The engine of the Brooklands Nine was slightly different in appearance from the standard Nine in that it was fitted with a water pump, which was driven from an extension of the shaft driving the magneto, the water pump body being mounted vertically below the magneto. A large capacity, 16 pint, sump was fitted and it had a quick filler orifice at the front with a strongly sprung lid (impolitely known as a 'rat-trap' filler—many an innocent finger has been caught unawares in this device). Originally, the big-end journals were the same size as the production cars at $1\frac{9}{16}$ in., but then they were enlarged to $1\frac{11}{16}$ in. and finally to $1\frac{21}{32}$ in. for competition use.

Among its later competition victories a Brooklands Nine won the 1932 T.T., a race ably driven by C. R. Whitcroft: one won the 1932 J.C.C. 1,000 Miles Race at Brooklands, driven by Miss Joan Richmond & Mrs Elsie Wisdom. Its factory swan song was without doubt the 1934 Le Mans 24 Hours Race in which it secured the Rudge Whitworth Biennial Cup and played its part in securing the Team Award as well as winning the 1100 cc. class.

Following the success of the Brooklands Nine, a Brooklands Six was announced in 1932 and one such car won the 1500 cc. class in the T.T. of that year. It didn't do very well in the overall placings, but it did at least achieve something worthwhile with a class win.

The chassis of the Six was rather different from the Nine. It was of a longer wheelbase

*Dashboard of 1926 11/40 4 Seat Sports*

(9 ft.) and had a gentle sweep from the arch over the front springs down to the underslung rear, rather than the sharp gooseneck of the smaller car. The engine was a development of the now-established Six-Fourteen, but with a smaller bore (57.5 mm.) to produce 1486 cc., and enable it to comply with Class F of the International Motor Sporting Code. The centre main bearing was water-cooled, to take account of the potentially high surface speeds it was likely to be subjected to, and it had its own drain tap on the offside of the crankcase. The clutch was single dry plate with a Silent Third close ratio gearbox providing drive through the usual enclosed propeller shaft to the 4.77 : 1 rear axle.

A feature made much of in the Brooklands Six was the fuel system. At the rear of the car was the 26 gallon fuel tank which was rather saddle shaped with a central vertical slot to accommodate the spare wheel on its quite substantial brackets. The 'panniers' of the tank were each of 8 gallons capacity with the 'saddle' being 10 gallons and the feed piping was so arranged that one of the 'panniers' would be left full to act as a reserve. The driver would then operate the dash-mounted fuel tap to switch to reserve and he would know how long he had left before having to make a fuel stop—very valuable on long-distance races. The fuel was supplied by high pressure pump. The Brooklands Six was offered for sale at £595.

With an example of this car Eyston and Edgar Maclure set up a number of Class F Records at Montlhery for distances up to 2,000 km. The car they used was probably KV1862—which may have been one of only two completed, KV1861 being the 1932 T.T. car and, as

*A new model for the 1927 Season was the 11/50/65 Supercharged*
*Sports 4 Seater—photographed at Olympia in 1926.*

far as is known, the only other Brooklands Six, though a contemporary *Autocar* report of the day mentions "a batch of Brooklands sixes under construction". Perhaps a batch was only two, who knows?

However, the life of the Brooklands Six was short and by the time of the 1933 T.T., a new machine (not actually named) had been built. The new cars were the basis of the next design stage in competitive Rileys, the Grebe. They were allocated the chassis numbers R101 to R106, though it seems the chassis frames were actually stamped with the numbers 4/101 to 4/106—probably for no stranger reason than the simple fact that someone made a mistake, though whatever the cause is now lost in the depths of time.

Five of these T.T. chassis were of 8 ft. 1½ in. wheelbase and the other one was 8 ft. 6 in.— if indeed it was the sixth chassis of the type. It certainly seems to have been built at the same time, but since the wheelbase was different, the chassis could well have been intended for a new design from the outset, but simply numbered sequentially to the others for the sake of convenience. This one car was the subject of a separate brochure which announced to the world at large the Riley Grebe, and it is clear that at the time the car was intended to be offered as a real competition machine.

The five 8 ft. 1½ in. cars featured basically similar engines and gearboxes to the Brooklands Six but had rather sparse bodywork, the panelling being put over a substantial tubular

spaceframe (in later years it might have been substantial enough to form the whole chassis!) which supported the scuttle mounted tank, the rear mounted tank plus spare wheel and the front bulkhead. There were no doors, a light bonnet over the engine and a single aero screen completing the 'coachwork'. Mudwings were of the non-steering cycle type and the cars, though fitted originally with six-stud wheels, ultimately ran with Riley-built centre-lock type.

Four of the new Sixes were run in the 1933 R.A.C. Tourist Trophy race. By now they had four SU carburetters, each pair working from a single float chamber, and were fitted with large 15 in. brakes. The first Riley to finish was Dixon's Nine and another Nine, driven by Baird, was home before the first Six, driven by Whitcroft into eight place overall to win the 1500 cc. class. The other three Sixes were driven by Eyston, Edgar Maclure and Staniland. The race was won that year by the immortal Tazio Nuvolari with an MG K3 Magnette.

Despite real success eluding them, as it had in the previous year with the Brooklands Six entry at the T.T., Riley obviously thought a sporting Six had real potential so they persevered and later in 1933, the Grebe was announced. In more recent years, controversy has arisen over what was and what was not a Grebe (since the definitive type is extinct), so it is perhaps worthwhile to differentiate between them. The cars referred to here as T.T. Sixes

*Debut of the 9 h.p. Speed Model was at the 1927 Olympia Motor Show. This is the first, fabric bodied, car strikingly finished in blue and white. Victor Leverett and Bill Barrett are seen standing alongside the car.*

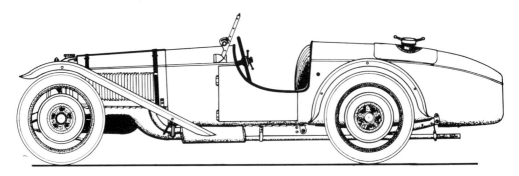

*1928 9 h.p. Speed Model*

were never referred to as Grebes in any contemporary material published either by Riley or the motoring press, though they have been so described on many occasions since. However, the Grebe by definition was the car described in a leaflet published by Riley (Coventry) Limited in 1933. Unlike the T.T. Sixes, it had a wheelbase of 8 ft. 6 in., not 8 ft. 1½ in., it had a coachbuilt body quite similar in style to the Gamecock and was fully road-equipped with lamps. The scuttle was similar to the T.T. cars, but smoother and the scuttle tank was inside the body panelling. The body featured scuttle side vents and fixed-position cycle-type mud-wings (sometimes referred to as 120° Ulster-type).

The Grebe was to be offered with three SU carburetters as standard, the 1486 cc. Six engine, an improved close ratio Silent Third gearbox, coil ignition—surprisingly, though a Scintilla Magneto was offered at £10 extra—15 in. cable-operated brakes and 5.00 in. × 19 in. tyres on Riley-built wheels. The brochure tells us that four or six carburetters were

*A Fixed-Head Coupé version of the 1928 9 h.p.*
*Brooklands Speed Model—the year is identified*
*by the five-stud wheels and 10 in. brakes.*

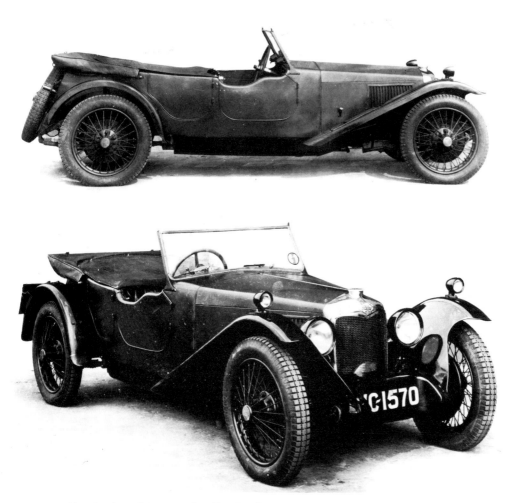

*Two fine views of the 1929 9 h.p. Four Seat Sports prototype—inspired by the Brooklands 9, but built on a long wheelbase chassis which did not have the underslung rear axle.*

available at extra cost and the price of the basic machine was £595. In fact, it was never sold to the sporting public because, despite its undoubted potential as a racing machine, Riley decided that the prettier road-going sports car design—the MPH, which was now well advanced—would have a better and wider market appeal, so the Grebe lost the day. One must reflect on that decision and, in light of the number of MPHs sold, wonder if the Company was right in view of the outstanding racing potential of the Grebe.

The Gamecock, apart from those six-cylinder models built for the 1933/34 Alpine Rallies, was never really claimed to be a sports car, though some bought it as a sporty car. It was discontinued from the range for the 1933 Season and thereby left a gap which was amplified by the decision not to put the Grebe into production.

That gap was partly filled by the March Special. The Earl of March was a partner in the firm of Kevill-Davies and March, as well as being a distinguished member of the motor-sporting fraternity. He had already been involved in the production of March Specials with

*The 1930 Brooklands 9 works demonstrator—VC6800—in
competition at a VSCC Oulton Park race meeting.*

Hillman on the Aero Minx and with AC on their 16/80 chassis before turning his attention
to Rileys. The result of his attention was a very attractive 2/4 Seater built by John Charles &
Sons of Kew and it was included in the 1932/33 Riley catalogue.

The Riley March Special was offered on the 9 h.p. Special Series chassis at £335 and on
the 6/12 Special Series chassis at £375. The September/October 1932 issue of 'The Riley
Record' mentions a 6/14 version too, though the vast majority of cars were 9 h.p. models and
it may be that only two or three 6/12s were built, because by that time the first two MPHs
were well on the way to introduction for the 1934 season. No data sheets are included in this
chapter for the March Special models, because they were built on production Special Series
chassis so the technical data is as the production cars.

It is interesting to note that the two prototype MPHs were built on to two of the T.T.
chassis, 4/101 being KV5694 and 4/105 KV6079. The latter of the two was the car which
featured in the Riley sales literature at the time. They were very pretty cars with wide flared
wings and an elegant body shape quite reminiscent of the contemporary Alfa-Romeo. Some
say the design was cribbed directly from the Alfa, but that would have been a bit too close on
the heels of Triumph's rather unfortunate experience. Triumph had introduced the eight
cylinder Dolomite Sports, a magnificent car but bearing sufficient resemblance to Alfa-
Romeo's design to enable the latter company to prevent, through legal channels, its production.
Styling similarities are a feature of the motor industry—so many cars have been branded as
copies of others.

The first two MPHs were entered for the Scottish Rally in 1934, along with four Imps,
with no mean success. A lot of heads were turned by the attractive lines of these new models.
The smaller engine in the MPH was now standard 12/6 in dimensions though not in internal

*Gordon Middleton's beautifully restored 9 h.p. Monaco at a Riley Register Coventry Rally*

*An interesting Riley-built special—a three-bearing 9 h.p. engine, No. EX/3 which was built circa 1935 using 1 11/16 in. big ends and a 3¾ in. centre main bearing. Not a very successful engine, so only a few were built. This one was rebuilt for the author by Gordon Middleton*

*Probably the last Brooklands 9 built, KV5392 competed in the 1933/34
Le Mans races, winning the Rudge Whitworth Biennial Cup.*

features, because it had duralumin connecting rods, a Scintilla magneto as standard and a
pair of H3 SU carburetters (though some cars were fitted with three SUs). The gearbox was a
choice between an Armstrong Siddeley preselector or a Silent Third close ratio manual box.
Brakes were 15 in. and the early cars were fitted with 5.00 in. × 19 in. tyres on Riley-built
wheels. An interesting feature of the MPH was that it was not catalogued with the usual
Rotax headlamps as standard—instead 5 in. diameter Salora long range lamps were specified.
They were externally adjustable for focus and apparently were extremely effective. Most
MPHs today seem to be fitted with 10 in. Rotax, suggesting that few people liked or trusted
the small Saloras.

Whilst the MPH model was classified in the 44T chassis numbering group, at least one
carried the chassis prefix 22T. This was the chassis (rumoured to have been one of two) sold
to A. C. Bertelli, once the proprietor of Aston Martin, to be fitted with special Bertelli bodywork. Its number was 22T 2255. Co-incidentally, there was already a 44T 2255—an MPH—
and it may be that this prefix was chosen by Riley, who were not quite as casual about chassis
numbering as might often be thought, because the MPH model had been officially discontinued. The Bertelli chassis could not be classified as a Sprite, however, because it was wholly
MPH in every respect. But the Sprite was already on the horizon, so the easy solution was to
take a number (or two, if two such cars were built) from the current Series, with the prefix
22T, and by pure co-incidence 2255 was the next number.

*Dashboard of another of the 1932 works team Brooklands 9s—VC8304.*

At about the same time as the MPH was announced, there came a new 9 h.p. sports model— a scaled down MPH in fact—the Imp. This was every bit as elegant as the MPH and featured a chassis of very similar design, but of 7 ft. 6 in. wheelbase. The frame had diagonal bracing, running out-from the centre of the central crossmember to the inside of the longitudinal mainframe member to increase stiffness. The bodywork was literally MPH by design, except that the spare wheel had a detachable surround instead of a cover, which was attached to the body by means of over-centre catches—whereas on the MPH, the spare wheel cover was secured by a single bolt with a hand-wheel nut.

This new sports car brought with it some changes to the appearance of the 9 h.p. engine. Firstly, it was fitted with rocker boxes which had round lids instead of square ones; secondly, it brought a return to the use of external oil feeds to the rocker shafts. The engine was the Special Series version, fitted with an inlet camshaft which corresponded in profile to the exhaust cam and produced an inlet valve timing of 25°/50°. Gearbox options were manual or preselector, the latter being an E.N.V. The original price of the car, with manual gearbox, was £298, the preselector version being £325. By 1935, the manual gearbox option had been withdrawn and the car was available with preselector, at still only £325.

That, however, is not the end of the Imp story. In fact, it isn't the beginning, because there was an earlier Imp. It was designed as a Two/Four Seater and was announced in late 1933,

*One of the 1932 Brooklands Sixes—KV1861—the T.T. car.*

one example being built and displayed at the Olympia Motor Show that year. The car was featured in the *Riley Record,* in an article entitled "Introducing a Newcomer". This article shows an artist's impression of the finished car and a photograph of the chassis and radiator, with the bonnet fitted. It is interesting to note though, that the gear change and handbrake levers are of the longer type fitted to the low-radiator 9 h.p. saloons, so this photo was obviously of a mock-up.

However, one car was built, the show car, and registered as KV5086. It bore a strong resemblance to the March Special Two/Four Seater, but being of much shorter wheelbase, looked slightly more cramped at the rear end. The original impression shows it with two spare wheels—like the March Special—but without the large petrol tank featured in the Earl of March's design. The mudwings were similar to those on other current Rileys, the bonnet was louvred on the top as well as the sides and the scuttle was faired into two deep cowls at its rear edge so that, when the windscreen was folded down, the resultant air flow was deflected from the faces of the driver and front-seat passenger.

Riley had obviously been impressed with the concept of the March Special, but with the

*The other (?) 1932 Brooklands Six—KV1862—after modification for the Class F Record run, with Capt. G.E.T. Eyston at the wheel.*

successful development of the MPH, it was decided to abandon this early design in favour of a smaller version of the six cylinder car.

In the competition world, it was decided that the Brooklands Nine had reached the peak of its development and so the Imp chassis was fitted with a doorless lightweight body, of boat-tail style, rather shorter than the Brooklands and not quite as low, since the chassis did not feature the sharp gooseneck of the earlier car. Here then, was the Ulster Imp.

Like the Brooklands before it, the Ulster Imp engine was fitted with a vertical-drive water pump. It also had a large sump of 14 pints capacity—from which a double-plunger pump still fed the engine—and a crankshaft with large, $1\frac{31}{32}$ in., crankpins. Four such cars were entered for the 1934 T.T., and, despite being overgeared, the cars all finished the race, being placed ninth, eleventh, twelfth and sixteenth overall.

Another new six-cylinder racing machine was also developed for 1934, looking very much like the Ulster Imp. This was the racing version of the MPH chassis and the forerunner of the T.T. Sprite. Two such cars finished second and third overall in the 1934 Le Mans 24 Hours, vindicating the racing six at last and justifying all the effort behind the development of these cars. It is interesting to note that it took a car with an engine of twice the power of the Riley Sixes to beat them, a 2.3 litre supercharged Alfa-Romeo. The average speed of KV9477, which came second driven by Sebilleau and de la Roche, was 70 m.p.h. exactly; and their car was followed home by the Dixon/Paul car, KV9478. Another car, registered KV9763, was also built, but not driven at Le Mans.

From the experience gained with the racing MPHs, Riley went on to produce, in 1935, the next generation of racing Rileys, the T.T. Sprites. The first four of these cars were in fact

built as MPHs in the 44T chassis number series, the other cars of that first batch being numbered in the 22T chassis series. These cars were the immortal AVC 15, AVC 16, AVC 17, AVC 18, AVC 19 and AVC 20. Some cars had six-cylinder engines and the others had the $1\frac{1}{2}$ litre four, which had been introduced in the previous year. These cars performed outstandingly well. For example, the 1935 T.T. was won by Freddie Dixon, with Cyril Paul finishing sixth and von der Becke ninth—the remaining Riley of the Team, driven by Maclure, having retired. Dixon's winning speed of 76.9 m.p.h. was the fastest ever achieved by an unsupercharged car.

Another car, with a six-cylinder 2 litre engine and streamlined radiator cowl (which was to be adopted for the production Sprite Two Seater later), was entered for the BRDC 500 Race at Brooklands, to be driven by von der Becke and Maclure. They finished second at a speed of 112.49 m.p.h., just under 9 m.p.h. slower than the 23 litre beast which beat them to the chequered flag—the Napier Railton of John Cobb and Tim Rose-Richards. So their second place was far from disgrace. Later in the same year, at Shelsley Walsh, von der Becke put up the fastest ever for a $1\frac{1}{2}$ litre car with another T.T. Sprite.

·By now Riley had introduced a new Sports Two Seater production model to succeed the MPH. It was the $1\frac{1}{2}$ Litre 4-cylinder engined Sprite. The prototype, AKV218, was actually built on to a modified MPH chassis and had a normal-type Riley radiator. The second Sprite built merits mention because only two cars were built with the earliest type of front wings, which ran in a straight line from the apex of the curve over the front wheels to the point

*1933 9 h.p. March Special*

*1933 9 h.p. March Special with hood erect.*

where they became running boards. All the later cars had a gentle double curve in the profile of the wings down to where they joined the rear wings.

These first two cars, S26S 2429 (AKV218) and S26S 2698 (BDU727), shared another common feature too, in that they were both fitted with manual gearboxes. All Sprites had long engine-mounting pedestals, capable of accepting the four or six cylinder engines, but AKV218's chassis was not fully boxed-in as were the later cars. BDU727 was eventually fitted with a radiator cowl, similar to, but not identical with, the one fitted to the production cars and it is believed that this was the car on show at Olympia in 1935. W. L. Innes, a former Riley apprentice, drove it in the 1936 Monte Carlo Rally. The radiator cowl was later removed, restoring it to pre-Motor Show appearance again.

The Sprite Two Seater was the last production sporting car to leave the Riley drawing boards, but it wasn't the last sporting Riley. More racing machines were designed and built and more racing successes amassed—both by the Factory cars, with Freddie Dixon's repeat of his 1935 T.T. win as an example, and by private entrants, such as Hector Dobbs' successes at Brooklands and Donington Park.

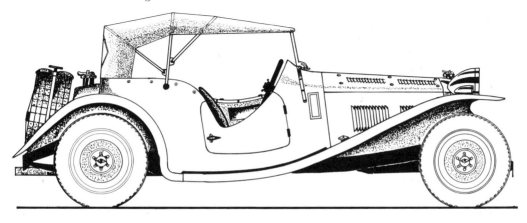

*1933 Six-Twelve March Special*

*The chassis of one of the 1933 T.T. cars, showing*
*the substantial body frame.*

In 1936, Riley produced a new 2 litre six-cylinder racing car with independent front suspension of André design and Girling manufacture. The engine of this car was basically a Six-Fifteen cylinder block bored out to 63.5 mm. and fitted with a long-throw crankshaft which gave a stroke of 104.5 mm., the capacity of the engine being 1985.66 cc. The crankshaft had disc webs and ran in a roller centre main bearing. The gearbox was a close-ratio manual type and the large 15 in. brakes were operated by Girling rods. This car was first entered for Charles Brackenbury to drive at Brooklands in the 1936 International Trophy Race. He finished sixth, being preceded by Hector Dobbs in third place and followed into eight place by von der Becke.

Riley successes continued to accumulate. In the Donington Park meeting on 9th May 1936, Hector Dobbs won the Up-to-5-Litre Handicap event with his 2 litre Riley, followed by Percy Maclure, who won the 1500 cc. Class as well as finishing second overall. Riley-based engines also powered the first four cars home in the 1939 Nuffield Trophy Race at Donington, the E.R.A.s of Bira, Mays, Whitehead and Ansell all finishing at speeds greater than 70 miles per hour.

A list of the more noteworthy competition successes is given in Appendix 8.

It seems sadly true that the tremendous catalogue of Riley successes in competition, and their contributions of innovation and development to the Automobile Industry, have never been properly recognised. For surely Riley was to Britain what Bugatti was to France and Ferrari to Italy.

For a host of the greatest names in motor sport, Riley was the oasis on the barren road to success. The car's success was their success.

*One of the 1933 Tourist Trophy Racing Sixes.*

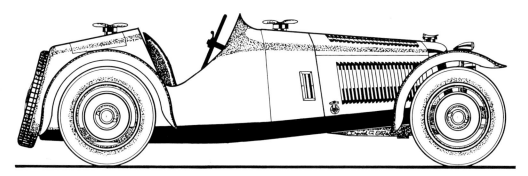

*Profile of the 1933 Grebe Sports Six*

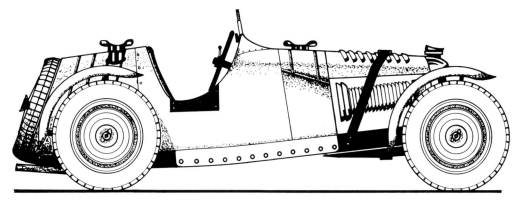

*Profile of the 1933 Racing Six T.T. Car*

SPECIFICATIONS


MODEL                 **Eleven-40 SWB Sports.**                                    *Year:* 1925

CHASSIS               Parallel channel frame, 5 cross members.
                      *Wheelbase:* 8 ft. 6 in.
                      *Track:* Front 4 ft. 4 in. Rear 4 ft. 4 in.
                      *Type of Wheels:* Wire 4 stud.
                      *Tyres:* Front 700 × 80 mm. Rear 700 × 80 mm.
                      *Braking System:* Rear wheel self compensating rod type 2 shoes footbrake, 2 handbrake.

TRANSMISSION          *Clutch Type:* Dry fabric cone.
                      *Gearbox Type:* Riley 4 speed.
                      *Gear Selecting Mechanism:* Central change.
                      *Gear Ratios:* Offered As: 1st—15.5:1, 2nd—10.8:1, 3rd—6.9:1, 4th—4.4:1, Reverse
                          15.5:1
                      *Rear Axle Type:* Semi-floating spiral bevel.
                      *Rear Axle Ratio:* 4.4:1

ENGINE                *Engine Type:* Eleven-40
                      *RAC H.P. Rating:* 10.8
                      *Cubic Capacity:* 1498 cc.
                      *Number of Cylinders:* 4
                      *Firing Order:* 1, 2, 4, 3
                      *Bore:* 65.8 mm.
                      *Stroke:* 110 mm.
                      *Cylinder Head:* Flat water-cooled detachable, with inclined spark plugs.
                      *Valve Gear:* Side valves operated from chain driven camshaft, near side, 2 per cylinder,
                          of $1\frac{1}{2}$ in diameter.
                      *Valve Timing:* Inlet opens 10° ATDC.
                      *Number of Main Bearings:* $3 \times 1\frac{5}{8}$ in.
                      *Sump Capacity:* 12 pints.
                      *Type of Oil Pump:* Gear driven, big ends splash fed.
                      *Cooling System:* Thermosyphon.
                      *Type of Ignition:* Magneto.
                      *Method of Advance/Retard:* Manual.
                      *Number, Make and Type of Carburetters:* Single Solex.
                      *Type of Inlet Manifold:* Cast bolt-on.
                      *Type of Exhaust Manifold:* Cast bolt-on.
                      *Location of Fuel Tank:* Rear mounted behind seats.
                      *Capacity of Fuel Tank:* $5\frac{1}{2}$ gallons.
                      *Method of Fuel Feed:* Air pressure-hand pump.

BODYWORK              Car offered with doorless two-seat body and butterfly-type front and rear wings.
                      Price on application from £545.


MODEL                 **11/50/65 Supercharged Sports**                            *Year:* 1927

CHASSIS               Channel section parallel frame swept up over rear axle, 5 cross members.
                      *Wheelbase:* 9 ft. 6 in.
                      *Track:* Front 4 ft. 4 in. Rear 4 ft. 4 in.
                      *Type of Wheels:* Riley wire 6 stud fixing 3.0 × 19 in.
                      *Tyres:* Front 27 × 4.40 in. Rear 27 × 4.40 in.
                      *Braking System:* Fully compensating four wheel brakes, handbrake rear. Surface area
                          203 sq. in.

TRANSMISSION          *Clutch Type:* Fabric Cone in oilbath.
                      *Gearbox Type:* Riley 4 speed.
                      *Gear Selecting Mechanism:* Central or right hand to choice.
                      *Gear Ratios:* 1st—18.2:1, 2nd—11.4:1, 3rd—7.3:1, 4th—4.7:1, Reverse—23.1:1
                      *Rear Axle Type:* Riley semi-floating spiral bevel.
                      *Rear Axle Ratio:* 4.7:1

*The ultimate development of one of the 1933 T.T. cars,
the 1934 MPH Sports Prototype*

*Rear quarter view of a production MPH*

ENGINE

*Engine Type:* 11/50/65
*RAC H.P. Rating:* 10.8
*Cubic Capacity:* 1498 cc.
*Number of Cylinders:* 4
*Firing Order:* 1, 2, 4, 3
*Bore:* 65.8 mm.
*Stroke:* 110 mm.
*Cylinder Head:* Water cooled detachable with exhaust manifold only: inclined plugs.
*Valve Gear:* Pushrod operated overhead, vertical, 2 per cylinder, $1\frac{1}{2}$ in. diameter.
*Number of Main Bearings:* $3 \times 1\frac{5}{8}$ in.
*Sump Capacity:* 12 pints.
*Type of Oil Pump:* Gear driven, splash fed big ends.
*Cooling System:* Thermosyphon and fan.
*Type of Ignition:* Magneto.
*Method of Advance/Retard:* Manual.
*Number, Make and Type of Carburetters:* Single horizontal Zenith to supercharger.
*Type of Inlet Manifold:* Cast and machined tubes.
*Type of Exhaust Manifold:* Cast bolt-on.
*Location of Fuel Tank:* Front dash mounted under bonnet.
*Capacity of Fuel Tank:* 7 gallons.
*Method of Fuel Feed:* Gravity to Carburetter thence Supercharger pressure.

MODELS AVAILABLE

11/50/65 Long wheelbase chassis only £450 (Chassis also used for Long Sports Four in 1928)
11/50/65 Long wheelbase Four Seat Sports £550
11/50/65 Two Seat Sports £550

MODEL

**9 H.P. Brooklands Speed Model**                                   *Year:* 1928–32
Because the Brooklands Nine specifications varied considerably this data sheet is based upon two known cars and the 1931 brochure.

CHASSIS

Channel section mainframe with gooseneck at front, underslung at rear.
*Wheelbase:* 8 ft. 0 in.
*Track:* Front 3 ft. $11\frac{3}{4}$ in. Rear 3 ft. $11\frac{3}{4}$ in.
*Type of Wheels:* $3.00 \times 19$ in. five stud (early) six stud (majority)
*Tyres:* Front $27 \times 4.40$ in. $(4.50 \times 19$ in) Rear $27 \times 4.40$ in. $(4.50 \times 19$ in.)
*Braking System:* Early cars—cable and rod $10\frac{1}{8}$ in. drums. Others 13 in. drums.

TRANSMISSION

*Clutch Type:* Single dry plate.
*Gearbox Type:* Silent third close ratio 4 speed.
*Gear Selecting Mechanism:* Remote central extension from gearbox with short lever in gate.
*Gear Ratios:* Plus Series 1st—11.78:1, 2nd—7.155:1, 3rd—5.96:1, 4th—4.77:1
    Reverse 18.50:1
*Gearbox Oil Capacity:* 3 pints.
*Rear Axle Oil Capacity:* $3\frac{1}{2}$ pints.
*Rear Axle Type:* Semi-floating banjo, enclosed torque tube, spiral bevel gears.
*Rear Axle Ratio:* 4.77:1

ENGINE

*Engine Type:* Riley 9
*RAC H.P. Rating:* 9.01
*Cubic Capacity:* 1087 cc.
*Number of Cylinders:* 4
*Firing Order:* 1, 2, 4, 3
*Bore:* 60.3 mm.
*Stroke:* 95.2 mm.
*Cylinder Head:* P.R. detachable, 10 stud, hemispherical combustion chambers.
*Valve Gear:* 45° overhead from high camshafts via tappets and short pushrods to lightened rockers.
*Diameter of Valve Heads:* Inlet $1\frac{3}{8}$ on. Exhaust $1\frac{3}{8}$ in.
*Tappet Clearances (Hot):* Inlet 0.002 in. Exhaust 0.003 in.
*Valve Timing:* Inlet opens 20° before T.D.C., closes 50° after BDC
    Exhaust opens 50° before BDC, closes 25° after TDC.
*Number of Main Bearings:* 2
*Diameter of Main Bearings:* $1\frac{1}{2}$ in. F & R, Later Rear $1\frac{3}{4}$ in.
*Diameter of Big End Bearings:* $1\frac{9}{16}$ in. or $1\frac{11}{16}$ in. (Competition cars fitted larger crank).

*The White Riley, restored to its former glory by Fred Rolph*

*The first four ERAs together again after over thirty-five years—at the VSCCs Oulton Park Race Meeting in June 1971. From left to right, the cars and drivers are: R3A, Hamish Moffatt; R2A, Michael Glass; R1A, Tony Merrick; R4A, John (now Sir John) Venables-Llewellyn*

*An interesting experiment in design—an MPH with
rolled-edge wings. note also the dashboard layout,
which was carried over to the 1½ Litre Sprite 2 Seater.*

*1933 9 h.p. Imp Sports 2/4 Seater—this was what the Imp was
originally intended to look like.*

*Sump Capacity:* 16 pint quick fill.
*Type of Oil Pump:* Bronze bodied eccentric drive double plunger.
*Normal Oil Pressure (Hot):* 40—60 p.s.i.
*Cooling System:* Vertical pump driven from inlet camshaft.
*Type of Ignition:* Magneto.
*Method of Advance/Retard:* Manual.
*Contact Breaker Gap:* 0.012 in.
*Plug Gap:* 0.018 in.
*Make and Type of Plug:* Champion 16.
*Number, Make and Type of Carburetters:* Standard 2 SU OM or 2 Solex 26 mm. 'Plus'—
    4 AMAL (1 per port direct feed).
*Type of Inlet Manifold:* Standard—cast alloy bolt-on: 'Plus'—Adapter plate only.
*Type of Exhaust Manifold:* Cast iron bolt-on for production models.
*Location of Fuel Tank:* Rear mounted.
*Capacity of Fuel Tank:* 10 gallons.
*Method of Fuel Feed:* Electric Pump.

MODELS AVAILABLE 1928—Speed model £395, 1929—Brooklands Speed Model £420.
1930/32—Brooklands Speed Model (Std) £420, Brooklands Speed Model (plus) £475.

MODEL **Brooklands Six** *Year:* 1932

CHASSIS Channel section mainframe, underslung at rear. 4 tubular cross members.
*Wheelbase:* 9 ft. 0 in.
*Track:* Front 3 ft. 11¾ in. Rear 3 ft. 11¾ in.
*Type of Wheels:* Centre lock wire 3.5 × 19 in.
*Tyres:* Front 5.00 × 19 in. Rear 5.00 × 19 in.
*Braking System:* Riley single continuous cable, 4 wheel, 13 in. drums.

TRANSMISSION *Clutch Type:* Single dry 10 in. plate.
*Gearbox Type:* Silent third 4 speed.
*Gear Selecting Mechanism:* Central remote lever with reverse lockout.
*Gear Ratios:* 1st—11.78:1, 2nd—7.15:1, 3rd—5.96:1, 4th—4.77:1, Reverse 18.51:1
*Gearbox Oil Capacity:* 3 pints.
*Rear Axle Oil Capacity:* 3½ pints.
*Rear Axle Type:* Semi-floating banjo type, spiral bevel gears.
*Rear Axle Ratio:* 4.77:1

ENGINE *Engine Type:* Riley 6/12
*RAC H.P. Rating:* 12.3
*Cubic Capacity:* 1486 cc.
*Number of Cylinders:* 6
*Firing Order:* 1, 5, 3, 6, 2, 4
*Bore:* 57.5 mm.
*Stroke:* 95.2 mm.
*Cylinder Head:* P.R. detachable with hemispherical combustion chambers. 14 stud
    fixing.
*Valve Gear:* 45° valves operated by high camshafts via tappets and short pushrods.
*Diameter of Valve Heads:* Inlet 1½ in. Exhaust 1⅜ in.
*Tappet Clearance (Hot):* Inlet 0.002 in. Exhaust 0.003 in.
*Valve Timing:* Inlet opens 25° before TDC, closes 50° after BDC
    Exhaust opens 60° before BDC, closes 35° after TDC.
*Number of Main Bearings:* 3
*Diameter of Main Bearings:* F—1⅝ in. C—3¾ in. R—1⅞ in.
*Diameter of Big End Bearings:* 1⅞ in.
*Sump Capacity:* 16 pints.
*Type of Oil Pump:* Eccentric drive double plunger.
*Normal Oil Pressure (Hot):* 60 p.s.i.
*Cooling System:* Pump and thermostat.
*Type of Ignition:* Scintilla Vertex magneto.
*Method of Advance/Retard:* Manual
*Contact Breaker Gap:* 0.016 in.
*Plug Gap:* 0.018 in.
*Number, Make and Type of Carburetters:* 3 SU 1⅛ in. HV2.
*Type of Inlet Manifold:* Cast alloy siamesed ports.
*Type of Exhaust Manifold:* Fabricated into two tailpieces. Two 3 branch tubular.

*The 9 h.p. sister to the MPH was the Imp, this one shown with two spare wheels.*

*Location of Fuel Tank:* Rear on top of chassis.
*Capacity of Fuel Tank:* 26½ gallons.
*Method of Fuel Feed:* High pressure pump.

MODEL AVAILABLE    Brooklands Six Speed Model £595.

| | |
|---|---|
| MODEL | **T.T. Six (4/101—4/105)**                                                                 *Year:* 1933 |
| CHASSIS | Channel section mainframe, upswept at front and underslung at rear.<br>*Wheelbase:* 8 ft. 1½ in.<br>*Track:* Front 3 ft. 11¾ in. Rear 3 ft. 11¾ in.<br>*Type of Wheels:* Riley 3.0 × 19 ft. 6 in. stud wire (later changed to centre-lock).<br>*Tyres:* Front 5.00 × 19 in. Rear 5.00 × 19 in.<br>*Braking System:* Riley continuous cable with cam-operated shoes in 15 in. drums. |
| TRANSMISSION | *Clutch Type:* Single Dry Plate.<br>*Gearbox Type:* Silent third 4 speed.<br>*Gear Selecting Mechanism:* Remote extension with central short lever in gate. Reverse lockout.<br>*Gear Ratios:* 1st—11.78: 1, 2nd—7.15: 1, 3rd—5.96: 1, 4th—4.77: 1, Reverse—18.51: 1<br>*Gearbox Oil Capacity:* 3 pints.<br>*Rear Axle Oil Capacity:* 3½ pints.<br>*Rear Axle Type:* Semi-floating banjo, enclosed torque tube, spiral bevel gears.<br>*Rear Axle Ratio:* 4.77 :1 |
| ENGINE | *Engine Type:* 1½ litre six.<br>*RAC H.P. Rating:* 12.3<br>*Cubic Capacity:* 1486 cc.<br>*Number of Cylinders:* 6<br>*Firing Order:* 1, 5, 3, 6, 2, 4<br>*Bore:* 57.5 mm.<br>*Stroke:* 95.2 mm.<br>*Cylinder Head:* P.R. detachable 14 stud with hemispherical combustion chambers.<br>*Valve Gear:* 45° overhead from high camshafts via tappets and short pushrods.<br>*Diameters of Valve Heads:* Inlet 1½ in. Exhaust 1⅜ in.<br>*Tappet Clearance (Hot):* Inlet 0.002 in. Exhaust 0.003 in.<br>*Valve Timing:* Inlet opens 25° before TDC, closes 50° after BDC.<br>Exhaust opens 60° before BDC, closes 35° after TDC.<br>*Number of Main Bearings:* 3<br>*Diameter of Main Bearings:* F—1⅝ in. C—3¾ in. R—1⅞ in.<br>*Diameter of Big End Bearings:* 1¹⁵⁄₁₆ in.<br>*Sump Capacity:* 16 pints.<br>*Type of Oil Pump:* Eccentric drive triple plunger.<br>*Normal Oil Pressure (Hot):* 40—60 p.s.i.<br>*Cooling System:* Pump & Thermostat.<br>*Type of Ignition:* Magneto.<br>*Method of Advance/Retard:* Manual.<br>*Contact Breaker Gap:* 0.012 in.<br>*Plug Gap:* 0.018 in.<br>*Number, Make and Type of Carburetters:* 4 SU HV2.<br>*Type of Inlet Manifold:* Cast alloy bolt-on.<br>*Type of Exhaust Manifold:* Fabricated six branch tubular bolt-on.<br>*Location of Fuel Tanks:* Behind seats and across scuttle.<br>*Capacity of Fuel Tanks:* 33 gallons (26+7).<br>*Method of Fuel Feed:* High pressure electric pump |
| MODELS AVAILABLE | Not developed for general sale.<br>4/101 & 4/105 Became prototype MPH cars KV 5694 and KV 6079<br>4/103 Became 'White Riley' of Raymond Mays in 1933.<br>4/102 & 4/104 Disposed of to F. W. Dixon in 1933. |

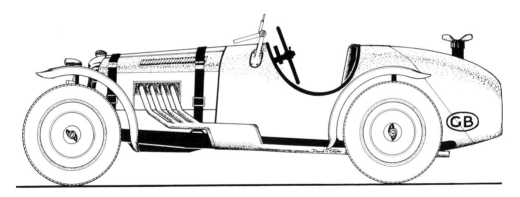

*1934 9 h.p. Ulster Imp—racing version of the Imp.*

*Ulster Imps & Racing MPHs in build at Coventry. Nine chassis are
on view here, including two Racing MPHs—KV9477, the
1934 Le Mans second-place car, can be seen clearly.*

| | | |
|---|---|---|
| MODEL | **Grebe Six** | *Year:* 1933 |

CHASSIS — Channel section mainframe, upswept at front and underslung at rear.
*Wheelbase:* 8 ft. 6 in.
*Track:* Front 3 ft. $11\frac{3}{4}$ in. Rear 3 ft. $11\frac{3}{4}$ in.
*Type of Wheels:* $3.00 \times 19$ in. centre lock wire.
*Tyres:* Front $5.00 \times 19$ in. Rear $5.00 \times 19$ in.
*Braking System:* Riley continuous cable with cam-operated shoes in 15 in. drums.

TRANSMISSION — *Clutch Type: Single dry plate.*
*Gearbox Type:* Silent 3rd, 4 speed.
*Gear Selecting Mechanism:* Central short lever in gate on remote extension.
*Gear Ratios:* 1st—11.78:1, 2nd—7.155:1, 3rd—5.96:1, 4th—4.77:1, Reverse—18.51:1
*Gearbox Oil Capacity:* 3 pints.
*Rear Axle Oil Capacity:* $3\frac{1}{2}$ pints.
*Rear Axle Type:* Semi-floating banjo with torque tube drive to bevel gears.
*Rear Axle Ratio:* 4.77:1

ENGINE — *Engine Type:* $1\frac{1}{2}$ litre six.
*RAC H.P. Rating:* 12.3
*Cubic Capacity:* 1486 cc.
*Number of Cylinders:* 6
*Firing Order:* 1, 5, 3, 6, 2, 4
*Bore:* 57.546 mm.
*Stroke:* 95.2 mm.
*Cylinder Head:* P.R. detachable 14 stud with hemispherical combustion chambers.
*Valve Gear:* 45° overhead from high camshafts via tappets and short pushrods to KE 805 rockers.
*Diameter of Valve Heads:* Inlet $1\frac{1}{2}$ in. Exhaust $1\frac{3}{8}$ in.
*Tappet Clearance (Hot):* Inlet 0.002 in. Exhaust 0.003 in.
*Valve Timing:* Inlet opens 25° before TDC, closes 50° after BDC
Exhaust opens 55° before BDC, closes 30° after TDC.
*Number of Main Bearings:* 3
*Diameter of Main Bearings:* F—$1\frac{5}{8}$ in. C—$3\frac{3}{4}$ in. R—$1\frac{7}{8}$in.
*Diameter of Big End Bearings:* $1\frac{15}{16}$ in.
*Sump Capacity:* 16 pints.
*Type of Oil Pump:* Eccentric drive triple plunger.
*Normal Oil Pressure (Hot):* 40—60 p.s.i.
*Cooling System:* Pump and thermostat.
*Type of Ignition:* Coil and distributor.
*Method of Advance/Retard:* Manual.
*Contact Breaker Gap:* 0.012—0.016 in.
*Plug Gap:* 0.018 in.
*Make and Type of Plug:* Champion 16.
*Number, Make and Type of Carburetters:* 3 SU type H2.
*Type of Inlet Manifold:* Cast alloy bolt-on with rear-fed hotspot and 2 ports per carburetter.
*Type of Exhaust Manifold:* Fabricated tubular six branch bolt-on.
*Location of Fuel Tank:* Scuttle and rear.
*Capacity of Fuel Tank:* 7+20 gallons.
*Method of Fuel Feed:* Electric pump.

MODELS AVAILABLE — 1933—Grebe 2 Seater £595 (one only built, chassis 4/106). (Scintilla vertex NV6 magneto £10 extra.
Brochure offered combinations of 4 and 6 carburetters at extra cost.

| | | |
|---|---|---|
| MODEL | **Short Six MPH (44T)** | *Year:* 1934–35 |

CHASSIS — Channel section mainframe, upswept at front and underslung at rear.

*Wheelbase:* 8 ft. $1\frac{1}{2}$ in.
*Track:* Front 3 ft. $11\frac{3}{4}$ in. Rear 3 ft. $11\frac{3}{4}$ in.
*Type of Wheels:* Dunlop centre-lock $3.00 \times 19$ in. wire.
*Tyres:* Front $5.00 \times 19$ in.* Rear $5.00 \times 19$ in.*
*Braking System:* Riley continuous cable with cam-operated shoes in 15 in. drums.

*A fine view of another Racing MPH, KV9478—the Dixon/Paul car
for the 1934 Le Mans, which finished third overall.*

*1934 Alpine Trial Gamecock Six*

**TRANSMISSION**

*Clutch Type:* Single dry plate or 2nd type centrifugal.
*Gearbox Type:* Preselector or silent 3rd 4 speed.
*Gear Selecting Mechanism:* Steering column mounted preselector quadrant or remote.
*Gear Ratios:* Manual_B 1st—11.78: 1, 2nd—7.15: 1, 3rd—5.95: 1, 4th—4.77: 1, Reverse 18.51: 1
  P.S.G_B 1st—13.35: 1, 2nd—7.5: 1  3rd—6.25: 1, 4th—5: 1, Reverse 22.99: 1
*Gearbox Oil Capacity:* Manual 3 pints, P.S.G. 4½ pints.
*Rear Axle Oil Capacity:* 3½ pints.
*Rear Axle Type:* Semi-floating banjo, enclosed torque tube drive to bevel gears.
*Rear Axle Ratio:* 4.77/5: 1

**ENGINE**

*Engine Type:* Six-twelve/Fourteen/Fifteen
*RAC H.P. Rating:* 12.01/13.1/14.3
*Cubic Capacity:* 1458 cc,/1633 cc./1726 cc.
*Number of Cylinders:* 6
*Firing Order:* 1, 5, 3, 6, 2, 4
*Bore:* 57 mm./60.3 mm./62 mm.
*Stroke:* 95.2 mm.
*Cylinder Head:* P.R. detachable 14 stud with hemispherical combustion chambers.
*Valve Gear:* 45° overhead from high camshafts operating tappets and short pushrods.
*Tappet Clearance (Hot):* Inlet 0.002 in. Exhaust 0.003 in.
*Valve Timing:* Inlet opens 25° before TDC, closes 50° after BDC.
  Exhaust opens 55° before BDC, closes 30° after TDC.
*Number of Main Bearings:* 3
*Diameter of Main Bearings:* F—1⅝ in. C—3¾ in. R—2 in.
*Diameter of Big End Bearings:* 12/14 h.p. 1¹¹⁄₁₆ in. 15 h.p. 1⅞ in.
*Sump Capacity:* 16 pints.
*Type of Oil Pump:* Eccentric drive triple plunger.
*Normal Oil Pressure (Hot):* 40—60 p.s.i.
*Cooling System:* Pump and thermosyphon.
*Type of Ignition:* Coil and distributor.
*Method of Advance/Retard:* Manual.
*Contact Breaker Gap:* 0.012 in.
*Plug Gap:* 0.018 in.
*Make and Type of Plug:* Champion 16.
*Number, Make and Type of Carburetters:* 3 SU type OM or 2 SU type H3 (Most examples had 2 SUs).
*Type of Inlet Manifold: Cast alloy bolt on with hot spot.*
*Type of Exhaust Manifold:* Cast iron bolt-on.
*Location of Fuel Tank:* Rear mounted.
*Capacity of Fuel Tank:* 15 gallons.
*Method of Fuel Feed:* Electric pump.

**MODELS AVAILABLE**

1933-4 MPH Sports 6/12 or 6/14 £550
1935  MPH Sports 6/12 or 6/15 £550
Scintilla magneto £10 extra.
*1934 Brochure shows 3.0 × 18 in. wheels, fitted with 4.75 × 18 in. tyres, though early cars fitted with 19 in. wheels & tyres.

**MODEL**   **9 H.P. Imp**                                              *Year:* 1934–35

**CHASSIS**

Channel section mainframe, upswept at front and underslung at rear.
*Wheelbase:* 7 ft. 6 in.
*Track:* Front 3 ft. 11¾ in. Rear 3 ft. 11¾ in.
*Type of Wheels:* Dunlop centre lock 2.50 × 19 in. wire.
*Tyres:* Front 4.50 × 19 in. Rear 4.50 × 19 in.
*Braking System:* Riley continuous cable with cam-operated shoes in 13 in. drums.

**TRANSMISSION**

*Clutch Type:* Single dry plate or centrifugal 2nd type.
*Gearbox Type:* All helical or ENV PSG 4 speed.
*Gear Selecting Mechanism:* Central remote lever in gate or steering column mounted preselector quadrant.
*Gear Ratios:* Manual 1st—20.37: 1, 2nd—13.13: 1, 3rd—7.67: 1, 4th—5.25: 1, Reverse —20.32: 1
  ENV 1st—20.47: 1, 2nd—12.66: 1, 3rd—7.67: 1, 4th—5.25: 1, Reverse—20.47: 1
*Gearbox Oil Capacity:* Manual 3 pints, ENV 4½ pints.

*Le Mans 1934—1500 cc. Class Winner and Second overall to a 2.9
litre Alfa Romeo was this Racing MPH KV9477, driven
by Sebilleau/de la Roche at a race average of 70 mph.*

*The first T.T. Sprite. Originally described as an MPH, AVC15
was built in 1935 and has a 44T chassis number prefix.*

*Rear Axle Oil Capacity:* 3½ pints.
*Rear Axle Type:* Semi-floating banjo, enclosed torque tube drive to bevel gears.
*Rear Axle Ratio:* 5.25:1

ENGINE

*Engine Type:* Riley Nine.
*RAC H.P. Rating:* 9.01
*Cubic Capacity:* 1087 cc.
*Number of Cylinders:* 4
*Firing Order:* 1, 2, 4, 3
*Bore:* 60.3 mm.
*Stroke:* 95.2 mm.
*Cylinder Head:* P.R. detachable 10 stud with hemispherical combustion chambers.
*Valve Gear:* 45° overhead from high camshafts with tappets and short pushrods to
  rockers.
*Diameter of Valve Heads:* Inlet 1⅜ in. Exhaust 1⅜ in.
*Tappet Clearance (Hot):* Inlet 0.002 in. Exhaust 0.003 in.
*Valve Timing:* Inlet opens 25° before TDC, closes 50° after BDC
  Exhaust opens 55° before BDC, closes 30° after TDC.
*Number of Main Bearings:* 2
*Diameter of Main Bearings:* F—1½ in. R—1½ in. (Late '35 1⅝ in.)
*Diameter of Big End Bearings:* 1¹¹⁄₁₆ in.
*Sump Capacity:* 7 pints.
*Type of Oil Pump:* Eccentric drive double plunger.
*Normal Oil Pressure (Hot):* 40—60 p.s.i.
*Cooling System:* Thermosyphon.
*Type of Ignition:* Coil and Distributor.
*Method of Advance/Retard:* Manual.
*Contact Breaker Gap:* 0.012 in—0.016 in.
*Plug Gap:* 0.018 in.
*Make and Type of Plug:* Champion 16.
*Make and Type of Carburetters:* Twin SU type OM.
*Type of Inlet Manifold:* Cast alloy bolt-on with hot spot.
*Type of Exhaust Manifold:* Cast iron bolt-on.
*Location of Fuel Tank:* Rear mounted.
*Capacity of Fuel Tank:*
*Method of Fuel Feed:* Electric Pump.

MODELS AVAILABLE 1934-5 Imp Sports 2 Seater (Manual) £298. Imp Sports 2 Seater (PSG) £325
  Scintilla Magneto £10 extra.
  Originally offered as 2/4 seater and exhibited at 1933 Motor Show, but not sold in
  that form.

MODEL

**9 H.P. Ulster Imp** *Year:* 1934-35

CHASSIS

Channel section mainframe, upswept at front and underslung at rear, with transverse
crossmembers and central diagonal bracing.
*Wheelbase:* 7 ft. 6 in.
*Track:* Front 3 ft. 11¾ in. Rear 3 ft. 11¾ in.
*Type of Wheels:* Riley centre-lock 2.50 × 19 in. wire.
*Tyres:* Front 4.50 × 19 in. Rear 4.50 × 19 in.
*Braking System:* Riley continuous cable with cam-operated shoes in 13 in. drums.

TRANSMISSION

*Clutch Type:* Single dry 10 in. plate or 2nd Type Newton centrifugal.
*Gearbox Type:* Silent 3rd manua. or ENV preselector (both 4 speed).
*Gear Selecting Mechanism:* Manual—central remote lever in gate.
  PSG—steering column-mounted quadrant.
*Gear Ratios:* 1st—11.78, 2nd—7.155, 3rd—5.96, 4th—4.77, Reverse—18.51:1
*Gearbox Oil Capacity:* Manual—3 pints. PSG—4½ pints.
*Rear Axle Oil Capacity:* 3½ pints.
*Rear Axle Type:* Semi-floating banjo type with enclosed torque-tube drive to spiral
  bevel gears.
*Final Drive Ratio:* 4.77:1, or to customer choice.

ENGINE

*Engine Type:* Riley Nine.
*RAC H.P. Rating:* 9.01
*Cubic Capacity:* 1087 cc.
*Number of Cylinders:* 4

*Another T.T. Sprite, AVC20—seen here at a VSCC Silverstone race
meeting with Colin Readey at the wheel.*

*The beautifully restored, and very fast, engine of AVC 20 with six Amal carburetters.*

*Firing Order:* 1, 2, 4, 3
*Bore:* 60.3 mm.
*Stroke:* 95.2 mm.
*Cylinder Head:* P.R. detachable 10 stud, with hemispherical combustion chambers.
*Valve Gear:* 45° overhead operated from high camshafts via tappets and short pushrods.
*Tappet Clearances Hot:* Inlet 0.002 in. Exhaust 0.003 in.
*Valve Timing:* Inlet opens 25° before TDC, closes 50° after BDC.
   Exhaust opens 55° before BDC, closes 30° after TDC.
*Number of Main Bearings:* 2
*Diameter of Main Bearings:* F—$1\frac{1}{2}$ in. R—$1\frac{5}{8}$ in.
*Diameter of Big-End Bearings:* $1\frac{31}{32}$ in.
*Sump Capacity:* 14 pints.
*Type of Oil Pump:* Eccentric drive double plunger.
*Normal Oil Pressure (Hot):* 40—60 p.s.i.
*Cooling System:* Vertical pump gear driven from inlet camshaft.
*Type of Ignition:* Scintilla magneto.
*Method of Advance/Retard:* Manual.
*Contact Breaker Gap:* 0.012 in.
*Plug Gap:* 0.018 in.
*Make and Type of Plug:* Champion 16.
*Number, Make and Type of Carburetters:* Twin SU type OM.
*Type of Inlet Manifold:* Cast alloy bolt-on.
*Type of Exhaust Manifold:* Fabricated tubular four-branch connected to single tail-
   pipe.
*Location of Fuel Tank:* Rear mounted.
*Fuel Capacity:* 10 gallons.
*Method of Fuel Feed:* Electric pump.

MODELS AVAILABLE 1934–35 Ulster Imp—£450
*Note:* A 1934 Ulster Imp leaflet was published depicting a car with a production-style body. However all the factory cars were built with Ulster-style bodies, though one car was fitted with a production-style body prior to ultimate sale.


MODEL          **Racing MPH**                                        *Year:* 1934

CHASSIS        Channel section mainframe, upswept at front and underslung at rear.
               *Wheelbase:* 8 ft. $1\frac{1}{2}$ in.
               *Track:* Front 3 ft. $11\frac{3}{4}$ in. Rear 3 ft. $11\frac{3}{4}$ in.
               *Type of Wheels:* Riley centre-lock wire 3.00 × 19 in.
               *Tyres:* Front 5.00 × 19 in. Rear 5.00 × 19 in.
               *Braking System:* Riley continuous cable with cam-operated shoes in 15 in. drums.

TRANSMISSION   *Clutch Type:* 2nd type centrifugal.
               *Gearbox Type:* ENV preselector 4 speed.
               *Gear Selecting Mechanism:* Central remote lever or steering column mounted quadrant.
               *Gear Ratios:* 1st—11.78:1, 2nd—7.155:1, 3rd—5.96:1, 4th—4.77:1, Reverse 18.51:1
               *Gearbox Oil Capacity:* $4\frac{1}{2}$ pints.
               *Rear Axle Oil Capacity:* $3\frac{1}{2}$ pints.
               *Rear Axle Type:* Semi-floating banjo with enclosed torque tube drive to spiral bevel
                  gears.
               *Rear Axle Ratio:* 4.77:1

ENGINE         *Engine Type:* Riley Six.
               *RAC H.P. Rating:* 12.3
               *Cubic Capacity:* 1486 cc.
               *Number of Cylinders:* 6
               *Firing Order:* 1, 5, 3, 6, 2, 4
               *Bore:* 57.5 mm.
               *Stroke:* 95.2 mm.
               *Cylinder Head:* P.R. detachable 14 stud with hemispherical combustion chambers.
               *Valve Gear:* 45° overhead from high camshafts via tappets and short pushrods.
               *Tappet Clearances (Hot):* Inlet 0.002 in. Exhaust 0.003 in.
               *Valve Timing:* Inlet opens 25° before TDC, closes 50° after BDC
                  Exhaust opens 60° before BDC, closes 30° after TDC
               *Number of Main Bearings:* 3
               *Diameter of Main Bearings:* F—2 in. C—$3\frac{3}{4}$ in. R—$2\frac{3}{8}$ in.

*1935 2 Litre Racing Six—note the 16 in. wheels.*

*Another view of the 2 Litre Racing Six, showing the
production Sprite type of radiator cowl.*

*Diameter of Big End Bearings:* $1\frac{15}{16}$ in.
*Sump Capacity:* 16 pints.
*Type of Oil Pump:* Triple plunger eccentric drive.
*Normal Oil Pressure (Hot):* 40—60 p.s.i.
*Cooling System:* Pump and thermostat.
*Type of Ignition:* Scintilla Magneto.
*Method of Advance/Retard:* Manual.
*Contact Breaker Gap:* 0.016 in.
*Plug Gap:* 0.018 in.
*Make and Type of Plug:* Champion 16.
*Number, Make and Type of Carburetters:* 3 SU type H2 or 4 SU H2 in 2 pairs, each with 1
    float chamber.
*Type of Inlet Manifold:* Cast Alloy bolt-on.
*Type of Exhaust Manifold:* Fabricated six-branch leading to single pipe.
*Location of Fuel Tank:* Rear
*Capacity of Fuel Tank:* 26 gallons.
*Method of Fuel Feed:* High Pressure Pump.

MODELS AVAILABLE 1934 Racing Six (Basically MPH with Ulster Imp style body).
Two examples entered in 1934 Le Mans 24 hrs. race: 2nd overall was KV9477
driven by J. Sebilleau/G. De La Roche, 3rd overall KV9478 driven by F.W. Dixon/
C. Paul, KV9763 built as spare car.


MODEL     **$1\frac{1}{2}$ & 2 Litre T.T. Sprite**            *Year:* 1935–37

CHASSIS     Channel section mainframe, upswept at front and underslung at rear, with transverse
crossmembers and partial boxing (later cars had fully-boxed frames).
*Wheelbase:* 8 ft. $1\frac{1}{2}$ in.
*Track:* Front 3 ft. $11\frac{3}{4}$ in. Rear 3 ft. $11\frac{3}{4}$ in.
*Type of Wheels:* Riley centre-lock 3.00 × 19 in. wire.
*Tyres:* Front 5.00 × 19 in. Rear 5.00 × 19 in.
*Braking System:* Girling mechanical rod with wege-operated shoes in 13 in. drums.

TRANSMISSION     *Clutch Type:* Single dry 10 in. plate or 2nd Type Newton centrifugal.
*Gearbox Type:* Manual or preselector (both 4 speed).
*Gear Selecting Mechanism:* Manual—central remote lever in gate.
        PSG—steering column-mounted quadrant.
*Gearbox Ratios:* (Example) 1st—2.47, 2nd—1.5, 3rd—1.25, 4th—1:1, Reverse—3.88:1
*Gearbox Oil Capacity:* Manual—3 pints. PSG—$4\frac{1}{2}$ pints.
*Rear Axle Oil Capacity:* $3\frac{1}{2}$ pints.
*Rear Axle Type:* Semi-floating banjo type with enclosed torque-tube drive to spiral
    bevel gears.
*Final Drive Ratio:* Various, between 3.5:1 and 6.75:1.

ENGINE     *Engine Types:* Riley $1\frac{1}{2}$ or 2 litre Six or $1\frac{1}{2}$ litre 4 cylinder.
*RAC H.P. Ratings:* 12.3, 15.1 and 11.9 respectively.
*Cubic Capacities:* 1486 cc., 1808 cc. (occasionally 1986 cc. engine, of 63.5 mm. bore
    & 106 mm. stroke, fitted) and 1496 cc.
*Number of Cylinders:* 6 or 4
*Firing Order:* 1, 5, 3, 6, 2, 4/1, 2, 4, 3
*Bore:* 6 cylinder 1486 cc. 57.5 mm, 1808 cc. 63.5 mm. 4 cylinder 69 mm.
*Stroke:* 6 cylinder models both 95.2 mm, 4 cylinder 100 mm.
*Cylinder Head:* P.R. detachable, (14 stud 6 cylinder, 12 stud 4 cylinder) with hemi-.
    spherical combustion chambers.
*Valve Gear:* 45° overhead operated from high camshafts via tappets and short pushrods,
*Tappet Clearances Hot:* 6 Cylinder Inlet 0.002 in. Exhaust 0.003 in.
    4 cylinder Inlet 0.003 in. Exhaust 0.004 in.
*Valve Timing:* 6 cylinder Inlet opens 25° before TDC, closes 50° after BDC,
    Exhaust opens 60° before BDC, closes 30° after TDC.
    4 cylinder Inlet opens 20° before TDC, closes 50° after BDC,
    Exhaust opens 55° before BDC, closes 20° after TDC.
*Number of Main Bearings:* 3
*Diameter of Main Bearings:* 6 Cylinder F—2 in. C—$3\frac{3}{4}$ in. R—$2\frac{3}{8}$ in.
    4 Cylinder F—$1\frac{3}{4}$ in. C—$2\frac{3}{4}$ in. R—$1\frac{3}{4}$ in.
*Diameter of Big End Bearings:* 6 Cylinder $1\frac{15}{16}$ in., 4 Cylinder $1\frac{7}{8}$ in.
*Sump Capacities:* 6 Cylinder—16 pints, 4 Cylinder—17 pints.

*The prototype 1½ Litre Sprite 2 Seater—AKV218—built mid-1935.*

*First production Sprite 2 Seater—BDU727—also built 1935.*

*This is how an Ulster Imp should look, except, perhaps, for the pale blue finish. This Imp once belonged to the author, who had the body built on a standard Imp chassis, but ADU301 does not belong to this car, as the original chassis is in South Africa.*

*The 1938 Lynx 1½ Litre Tourer was the ultimate version of the Lynx in production and was a first-class touring car. This is C. E. Wiles' superbly restored example*

*Type of Oil Pump:* Early 6s—triple plunger. Others—gear.
*Normal Oil Pressure (Hot):* 40—60 p.s.i.
*Cooling System:* Pump and thermostat.
*Type of Ignition:* Magneto.
*Method of Advance/Retard:* Manual.
*Contact Breaker Gap:* 0.012 in.
*Plug Gap:* 0.018 in.
*Make of Type of Plug:* Champion 16
*Number, Make and Type of Carburetters:* 6s—3 or 4 SU type HV2s.
    4s—Twin SU HV2S.
*Type of Inlet Manifold:* Cast alloy bolt-on.
*Type of Exhaust Manifold:* Fabricated tubular six or four branch.
*Location of Fuel Tank:* Rear—sometimes 7 gallon side tank extra.
*Capacity of Fuel Tank:* 25 gallons.
*Fuel Feed:* HP Pump.

MODELS AVAILABLE   1935–37 T.T. Sprite, first batch built as MPHs but later known as T.T. Sprites, not offered for general sale, though 2 litre Sprite catalogued at £550 in 1936.


MODEL              **Racing Six 2 Litre**                                                    *Year:* 1935

CHASSIS       Boxed-channel section upswept at front and underslung at rear.
*Wheelbase:* 8 ft. 1½ in.
*Track:* Front 4 ft. 0 in. Rear 4 ft. 0 in.
*Type of Wheels:* Dunlop 3.5 × 16 in. centre lock wire.
*Tyres:* Front 5.25 × 16 in. Rear 5.25 × 16 in.
*Braking System:* Girling mechanical rod with wedge operated shoes in 13 in. drums.

TRANSMISSION   *Clutch Type:* Single dry plate.
*Gearbox Type:* Manual 4 speed.
*Gear Selecting Mechanism:* Central remote lever in gate.
*Gearbox Ratios:* 1st—2.47:1, 2nd—1.5:1, 3rd—1.25:1, 4th—1:1, Reverse 3.88:1
*Gearbox Oil Capacity:* 3 pints.
*Rear Axle Oil Capacity:* 3½ pints.
*Rear Axle Type:* Semi-floating banjo with torque tube enclosed drive to spiral bevel gears.
*Rear Axle Ratio:* 4.77/5.22:1. Various, including 3.5/4.77/5.22:1

ENGINE        *Engine Type:* 2 litre six.
*RAC H.P. Rating:* 15.1
*Cubic Capacity:* 1986 cc.
*Number of Cylinders:* 6
*Firing Order:* 1, 5, 3, 6, 2, 4
*Bore:* 63.5 mm.
*Stroke:* 104.5 mm.
*Cylinder Head:* P.R. detachable 14 stud with hemispherical combustion chambers.
*Valve Gear:* 45° overhead from high camshafts via tappets and short pushrods.
*Tappet Clearance (Hot):* Inlet 0.002 in. Exhaust 0.003 in.
*Valve Timing:* Inlet opens 25° before TDC, closes 50° after BDC.
       Exhaust opens 55° before BDC, closes 30° after TDC.
*Number of Main Bearings:* 3
*Diameter of Main Bearings:* F—2 in. C—3¾ in. R—2⅞ in.
*Diameter of Big End Bearings:* 1 15/16 in.
*Sump Capacity:* 16 pints.
*Type of Oil Pump:* Gear driven.
*Normal Oil Pressure (Hot):* 40—60 p.s.i.
*Cooling System:* Pump and thermostat.
*Type of Ignition:* Scintilla magneto.
*Method of Advance/Retard:* Manual.
*Contact Breaker Bap:* 0.012 in.
*Plug Gap:* 0.018 in.
*Make and Type of Plug:* Champion 14.
*Number, Make and Type of Carburetters:* 3 SU HV2 carburetters standard with options of 4SU or 6 Amals at extra cost.
*Type of Inlet Manifold:* Cast alloy bolt-on.
*Type of Exhaust Manifold:* Six-branch to single pipe.

*1936 Sprite 2 Seater, the first works demonstrator.*

*Bob Gerard, with his wife Joan at the wheel,*
*and their new Sprite 2 Seater in 1937.*

*Location of Fuel Tank:* Rear.
*Capacity of Fuel Tank:* 15 gallons.
*Method of Fuel Feed:* High pressure pump.

MODELS AVAILABLE    One only built on MPH/TT Sprite chassis—finished 2nd in 1935 BRDC 500 Race.

MODEL                 **Sprite Two Seater**                              *Year:* 1936–38

CHASSIS               Boxed channel mainframe, upswept at front and underslung at rear, with transverse
                      crossmembers.
                      *Wheelbase:* 8 ft. 1½ in.
                      *Track:* Front 3 ft. 11¾ in. Rear 3 ft. 11¾ in.
                      *Type of Wheels:* Riley centre-lock 3.00 × 19 in. wire.
                      *Tyres:* Front 5.00 × 19 in. Rear 5.00 × 19 in.
                      *Braking System:* Girling mechanical rod with wedge-operated shoes in 13 in. drums.

TRANSMISSION          *Clutch Type:* Single dry 10 in. plate or 2nd Type Newton centrifugal.
                      *Gearbox Type:* 4 Speed Manual or Armstrong Siddeley preselector.
                      *Gear Selecting Mechanism.* Manual—central remote lever in gate.
                            PSG—steering column-mounted quadrant.
                      *Gear Ratios:* Manual 1st—20.25, 2nd—13.05, 3rd—7.63, 4th—5.22, Reverse—20.25 : 1
                            PSG 1st—17.53, 2nd—10.3, 3rd—7.4, 4th—5.22 : 1, Reverse—26 : 1
                      *Gearbox Oil Capacity:* Manual—3 pints. PSG—4½ pints.
                      *Rear Axle Oil Capacity:* 3½ pints.
                      *Rear Axle Type:* Semi-floating banjo type with enclosed torque-tube drive to spiral
                            bevel gears.
                      *Final Drive Ratio:* 5.22 : 1

ENGINE                *Engine Type:* Riley 1½ Litre.
                      *RAC H.P. Rating:* 11.9
                      *Cubic Capacity:* 1496 cc.
                      *Number of Cylinders:* 4
                      *Firing Order:* 1, 2, 4, 3
                      *Bore:* 69 mm.
                      *Stroke:* 100 mm.
                      *Cylinder Head:* P.R. detachable 12 stud with hemispherical combustion chambers.
                      *Valve Gear:* 45° overhead operated from high camshafts via tappets and short pushrods.
                      *Tappet Clearances Hot:* Inlet 0.003 in. Exhaust 0.004 in.
                      *Valve Timing:* Inlet opens 20° before TDC, closes 50° after BDC,
                            Exhaust opens 50° before BDC, closes 20° after TDC.
                      *Number of Main Bearings:* 3
                      *Diameter of Main Bearings:* F—1¾ in. C—2¾ in. R—1¾ in.
                      *Diameter of Big End Bearings:* 1⅞ in.
                      *Sump Capacities:* 17 pints.
                      *Type of Oil Pump:* Gear driven.
                      *Normal Oil Pressure (Hot):* 40—60 p.s.i.
                      *Cooling System:* Pump and thermostat.
                      *Type of Ignition:* Magneto.
                      *Method of Advance/Retard:* Manual.
                      *Contact Breaker Gap:* 0.016 in.
                      *Plug Gap:* 0.018 in.
                      *Make and Type of Plug:* Champion 16.
                      *Number, Make and Type of Carburetters:* Twin SU HV2.
                      *Type of Inlet Manifold:* Cast alloy bolt-on, without hotspot or supplementary heating.
                      *Type of Exhaust Manifold:* Cast iron bolt-on.
                      *Location of Fuel Tank:* Rear.
                      *Fuel Feed:* Electric pump.
                      *Capacity of Fuel Tank:* 15 gallons.

MODELS AVAILABLE    1936–37 Sprite 2 Seater, £425. Also 2 litre version offered at £550, but unlikely any
                            were sold.
                    1938      Sprite 2 Seater, £450.

*The 1936 2 Litre IFS Racing Six, fitted with Andre-Girling*
*independent front suspension.*

| | |
|---|---|
| MODEL | **IFS Racing Car** *Year:* 1936 |
| DESCRIPTION | Basically an offset single seat version of the T.T. Sprite with Andre-Girling coil independent from suspension, T.T. Sprite chassis, T.T. Sprite body with head fairing and cowled radiator. |

*Wheelbase:* 8 ft. 1½ in.
*Track:* Front 4 ft. 0 in. Rear 4 ft. 0 in.
*Type of Wheels:* Dunlop centre-lock 3.0 × 19 in. wire.
*Tyres:* Front 5.00 × 19 in. Rear 5.00 × 19 in.
*Braking System:* Girling mechanical rod with wedge operated shoes in 15 in. drums.

TRANSMISSION

*Clutch Type:* Single dry plate.
*Gearbox Type:* Manual 4 speed.
*Gear Selecting Mechanism:* Central remote lever in gate.
*Gearbox Ratios:* 1st—2.47:1, 2nd—1.5:1, 3rd—1.25:1, 4th—1:1, Reverse 3.88:1
*Gearbox Oil Capacity:* 3 pints.
*Rear Axle Oil Capacity:* 3½ pints.
*Rear Axle Type:* Semi-floating banjo with enclosed torque tube drive.
*Rear Axle Ratio:* 4.77—6.75:1

ENGINE

*Engine Type:* 1½ litre/2 litre six.
*RAC H.P. Rating:* 11.9/15
*Cubic Capacity:* 1496 cc./1986 cc.
*Number of Cylinders:* 4/6
*Firing Order:* 1, 2, 4, 3/1, 5, 3, 6, 2, 4
*Bore:* 69 mm./63.5 mm.
*Stroke:* 100 mm./104.5 mm.
*Cylinder Head:* P.R. detachable 12 or 14 stud.
*Valve Gear:* 45° overhead with high camshafts operating tappets and short pushrods.
*Tappet Clearances (Hot):* Inlet 0.002 in. Exhaust 0.003 in.
*Valve Timing:* 4 cylinder Inlet opens 20° before TDC, closes 50° after BDC
    6 cylinder Inlet opens 25° before TDC, closes 50° after BDC
    4 cylinder Exhaust opens 50° before BDC, closes 20° after TDC
    6 cylinder Exhaust opens 60° before BDC, closes 30° after TDC
*Number of Main Bearings:* 3
*Diameter of Main Bearings:* 4 cylinder F & R—1¾ in. C—2¾ in.
    6 cylinder F—2 in. C—3¾ in. R—2⅜ in.
*Diameter of Big End Bearings:* 1⅞ in. 1¹⁵⁄₁₆ in.
*Sump Capacity:* 17 pints/16 pints.
*Type of Oil Pump:* Gear Driven.
*Normal Oil Pressure (Hot):* 40—60 p.s.i.
*Cooling System:* Pump and thermostat.
*Type of Ignition:* Scintilla Magneto.
*Method of Advance/Retard:* Manual.
*Contact Breaker Gap:* 0.016 in.
*Plug Gap:* 0.018 in.
*Make and Type of Plug:* Champion 16 and others.
*Number, Make and Type of Carburetters:* 4 cylinder 4 Amal, 6 cylinder 6 Amal.
*Type of Inlet Manifold:* Adapter plate with carburetters feeding direct to inlet ports.
*Type of Exhaust Manifold:* Fabricated four or six branch to single pipe.
*Location of Fuel Tank:* Rear (side mounted auxiliary of 7 gallons capacity).
*Capacity of Fuel Tank:* 25 gallons.
*Method of Fuel Feed:* High pressure pump.

MODELS AVAILABLE    1936 2 litre Racing Six ⎫
                         1½ litre Four        ⎬ not available for general sale.
                                              ⎭

*The last TT Sprite, CWK171, was built in 1937 and fitted with token doors to comply with revised racing regulations.*

September 9, 1924.     257     The Motor

# A New Sports Riley.

## A Short-wheelbase Model for the Speedman.

A SIDE VIEW SHOWING THE BONNET, WHICH IS BUILT IN ONE PIECE WITH THE SCUTTLE AND THE FLARED WINGS.

A VERY attractive sporting light car model in which weight and windage have been cut down very considerably has recently been introduced by Riley (Coventry), Ltd., to sell at £545. The wheelbase has been reduced to 8 ft., while the track is 4 ft. 2 ins. and the total weight just over 10 cwt. The aluminium shell of the two-seater body scales only 22 lb., lightness having also been attained by extensive drilling of the frame, the wide central insweep which supports the four-speed box being drilled in addition to the longitudinal members. The three-piece bonnet is built in one with the scuttle and is some 5 ft. long,

THE NEAT TOP WATER JOINT.

and the sides are removable in order to provide easy access to the engine, clutch and gearbox, which closely follows

standard practice. Flared wings add to the general sporting appearance of this car, which is expected to give a good account of itself in sporting events on the road.

The engine develops well over 40 h.p.

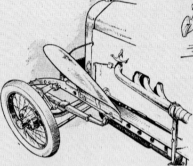

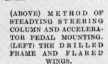

(ABOVE) METHOD OF STEADYING STEERING COLUMN AND ACCELERATOR PEDAL MOUNTING. (LEFT) THE DRILLED FRAME AND FLARED WINGS.

at between 4,000 r.p.m. and 5,000 r.p.m., and has a compression ratio of about 5½ to 1. Double springs are fitted to the side-by-side valves, the mixture being supplied by a 40 mm. Solex carburetter, and the ignition by means of an M.-L. magneto. A starter is not fitted but a

100 m.p.h. speedometer and a 6,000 r.p.m. rev. counter are provided. Two clutch stops are used, the extra one taking the form of a spring-loaded pad which presses against the disengaged member of the clutch.

The gear range varies from 4.3 down to 15 to 1, and should be suitable for every kind of condition other than at Brooklands, where a higher top would be advisable. The five-gallon petrol tank is carried at the back of the seats and supplies the carburetter by pressure from a hand pump.

The seats are very slightly staggered as the body is only 2 ft. 4 ins. wide. The rear ends of the side members of the frame have been flattened out so that

the frame members are now only 14 ins. from the ground, and the flat springs are equipped with Hartford shock absorbers. Riley wire wheels shod with 700 mm. by 80 mm. covers are fitted and are interchangeable with any of the four stud-type steel disc wheels. Both brakes are fitted to the rear wheels, a link type of adjustment without any compensating gear being provided.

AN INGENIOUS FEATURE IS THE FITTING OF AN EXTRA CLUTCH STOP.

A THREE-QUARTER REAR VIEW SHOWING THE SEMI-ELLIPTIC SPRINGING, MOUNTING OF THE HARTFORD SHOCK ABSORBERS AND THE BOAT-SHAPED TAIL.

c33

THE AUTOCAR, *August 19th, 1927.*

*331*

# A RACING RILEY NINE.

### Details of Alterations to a Standard Chassis Forming the Nucleus of a New Model.

Side and front views of the new racing Riley Nine. So low is the seating position that the driver can easily touch the ground with his hand when at the wheel. The body has been made wide purposely to accommodate two people side by side.

IT is a sad fact, but true, that the market for small sports cars of under 1,100 c.c. is almost entirely monopolised by Continental makers. Therefore any experiments made by British firms in this direction will be hailed with glee by buyers of this class of car.

As we announced at the beginning of the year, at the time of his death the late J. G. Parry Thomas was engaged in developing the 9 h.p. Riley, and his experiments, carried on by Mr. Reid Railton, who is connected with the Thomas Inventions Development Co., Ltd., at Brooklands, are now well on the way towards completion. It should clearly be understood, however, that the new racing Riley is only an attempt to evolve the nucleus of a marketable sports model from standard 9 h.p. Riley parts.

In the first place a perfectly standard Riley Nine chassis was taken, and, at the point where the frame takes a sudden outward bend, a piece 15in. long was cut out, and the two parts were then welded together with the rear ends inclined sharply inwards. The cross-members were also cut and welded, and stiffening plates placed inside the frame at the weld. The rear springs, which are underslung as standard, have been arranged inside, and parallel to, the frame, the spring pads on the rear axle being altered to suit. This, however, is only a temporary

measure. The rear axle itself, incidentally, has been left perfectly standard, except for a slightly higher gear ratio.

On the standard chassis the radiator is mounted on a broad, drilled cross-member at the front of the frame. This Mr. Railton has had cut away as much as possible, and a new and smaller radiator has been made, and dropped down very low, actually behind the cross-member. The front axle, brakes, and springs have been left quite standard, as also has the gear box.

As regards the engine, no radical changes in design have been made. Two inclined overhead valves per cylinder are operated through push rods, tappets and rockers from two camshafts carried on each side of the crank case. Special camshafts have been fitted, as well as high-compression pistons, but the connecting rods and crankshaft have not been altered. Pressure lubrication is a feature of all Riley Nine cars, but on the racer the pressure at which oil is forced to the bearings has been raised, and owing to the small size of the new radiator thermo-syphon cooling has been abandoned in favour of a very neatly fitted centrifugal pump, driven from the nose of the crankshaft.

Two large bore Solex carburetters have been arranged

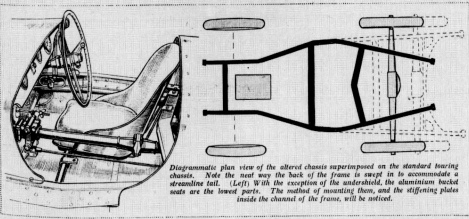

Diagrammatic plan view of the altered chassis superimposed on the standard touring chassis. Note the neat way the back of the frame is swept in to accommodate a streamline tail. (Left) With the exception of the undershield, the aluminium bucket seats are the lowest parts. The method of mounting them, and the stiffening plates inside the channel of the frame, will be noticed.

C 1

*332*

*THE AUTOCAR, August 19th, 1927.*

### A Racing Riley Nine.

at the off side of the engine, and on the near side a particularly fine example of tube bending leads the exhaust gases through four separate pipes to a Brooklands silencer, whence a tail pipe extends outside the body to the rear.

Other engine details, such as vertical drive through skew gears for the magneto, and trunnion mounting of the three-point suspended power unit, have been left alone. The alterations, however, have been to such effect that on the bench the little 1,087 c.c. engine gives off 50 b.h.p. at 5,000 r.p.m.

So far, the car has only been out on the track once or twice, but unofficial timing showed it to be capable of a speed of well over 90 m.p.h., whilst it seemed to hold the track remarkably well. Its future, therefore, seems to be very rosy.

One of the most astounding features of the neat and shapely streamlined body, which, at a glance, is somewhat reminiscent of the Bugatti, is the extreme lowness of the aluminium bucket seats, which are dropped on each side of a tunnel containing the torque tube and propeller-shaft. Apart from the undershield, which ex-

tends the whole length of the car, the seats are the lowest parts of the whole job, and are barely six inches above the ground. The rake of the steering column has also been altered, bringing the steering wheel almost vertical. At present, with right-hand gear and brake levers, it is rather difficult to get in and out of the driving seat, but we understand that a central gear-change lever is under contemplation, which should simplify this.

Modifications are also to be made in the

*How the front cross member is cut away and the new squat radiator mounted low down between the sides of the frame.*

shape of the body, giving a greater radius to the present sharpish corners, and a more rounded appearance to the tail, in which is housed a six-gallon fuel tank.

Some indication of the tiny size of this promising little racer will be given by the following figures : Wheelbase, shortened from 8ft. 11½in. to 7ft. 7½in., and greatest height of the body (at the scuttle), 36in.

*Two large-bore Solex carburetters and four separate exhaust pipes mark the chief variation from standard in the racing Riley engine. The water pump can be seen at the nose of the crankshaft.*

The **Light Car** & Cyclecar                    6                    MAY 29, 1931.

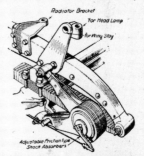

NEWS OF THE WEEK

# NEW RILEYS FOR IRISH GRAND PRIX

### First Details of Four-cylinder Four-carburetter Racers which will be Seen in Phœnix Park

SINCE the notable victory of the Riley car, piloted by Victor Gillow, in Ireland last year, the designing staff of the Riley Co. has not by any means been content to rest on its laurels. Apart from the inclusion of the " Plus " features in the new Brooklands racing

A quick-opening radiator cap. When pressed down the lever on top of the cap expands the inner face, thus ensuring a firm grip and a water-tight joint.

models, many other interesting items have been incorporated as well. The new cars are considerably lighter than their prototypes, and the layout of various parts of the chassis has received careful attention to detail, with the result that in many ways the design has been cleaned up. Additional power, too, has been obtained from the engine so that altogether these new

Riley racers should be capable of putting up thoroughly creditable performances.

We recently had an opportunity of inspecting the four special racers which are being prepared for the Dublin event next week, and it is obvious that the Riley entry will offer a serious challenge to all comers, for in appearance they are thoroughly workmanlike, and they give one the impression that they have " lasting " qualities.

### Cutting Down Weight.

In broad outline there is very little difference between last year's racing cars and the new ones, but in the latest design all unnecessary weight has been removed, at the same time maintaining adequate strength in the various components which have been machined down at non-vulnerable places. Again, the rather large and rather weighty undershield which was used on last year's cars has been replaced by an aluminium sheet tray, which is bolted directly to the underside of the frame. In other details, too, such as body supports and so forth, scientific design has enabled a lot of weight to be saved, with the result that the acceleration powers of the engine should now be more effective.

Probably the most interesting feature in regard to the power unit lies in the induction system. Four carburetters are used (one to each cylinder), the instruments being attached to a plate which covers the four inlet ports on the off side of the cylinder head. Preliminary tests have shown that this system has given an increase in power, and, coupled with the lowered weight of the complete car, has generally improved the all-round performance.

As might be expected, great care has been taken with the fuel and oiling arrangements, a large petrol tank being installed in the rear fairing of the body

The front of the Riley Brooklands model chassis has been cleaned up, and now presents a thoroughly workmanlike appearance. Note the latest type friction shock absorber with Telecontrol adjustment.

and a separate oil tank in the dash, so that the lubricant in the sump can be replenished from time to time while the car is actually under way. The usual form of pressure supply, derived from a hand pump, is employed for feeding the fuel up from the rear tank, whilst a Best and Lloyd drip-feed arrangement is installed on the dashboard so that the mechanic can operate the plunger at intervals when replenishment of the sump is deemed necessary.

(Right) A special additional oil tank is fitted to the Riley racers. It has a drip feed to the engine so that the mechanic can replenish the sump during a race. The hand pump is for supplying pressure to the rear fuel tank.

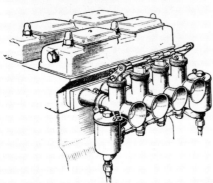

(Left) How the Amal carburetters are coupled up to the induction side of the cylinder head. Only two float chambers are employed, i.e., one at each end, but the throttle slides are worked from a common shaft. The performance of the Rileys will be watched with deep interest, for the adoption of one carburetter per cylinder is an innovation of very recent date and, for the first time, receives the prominence which we think it deserves.

MAY 20, 1932.    739    The Light Car & Cyclecar

## For This Season's Racing

# THE NEW 1½-LITRE RILEY SIX

### Efficient 1,486 c.c. Engine with Three Carburetters

FOR some time past it has been known that, following the success of the 1,100 c.c. Brooklands model Riley, the well-known Coventry concern was to produce a team of 1½-litre six-cylinder models for this season's racing. We are now able to give particulars of this interesting new chassis.

The engine to be employed is really a development of the well-known 2-litre " Alpine Six " which has been on the market for some time, whilst the chassis is built on somewhat similar lines to the latest " nine " racers, although improvements have been incorporated in the design as the dictates of experience warranted.

The frame and the mounting of the fuel tank and spare wheel are, for instance, entirely new, whilst the additional length of the 1½-litre six-cylinder power-unit over that of the 1,100 c.c. four-cylinder type has necessitated a number of alterations in lay-out.

In order to bring the capacity of the power-unit within the 1½-litre class the bore of the cylinders has been determined at 57.5 mm., with a stroke of 95.2 mm., giving a capacity of 1,486 c.c. As in the standard 2-litre product the six cylinders are cast unitwise with the crankcase, whilst inclined valves are contained in a detachable cylinder head in such a manner that the combustion chambers are truly hemispherical.

Of similar general layout to the Nine, there are two camshafts, one for the inlet valves and the other for the exhausts, each lying relatively high up in the crankcase and driven by helical gears from the forward end of the crankshaft. These operate the valves through the

medium of short push-rods and rockers, and adjustment of the valve-rocker clearance can easily be effected after removing the rocker-box lids.

Machined all over from a nickel-steel alloy forging, the crankshaft is of very stiff design and of hefty proportions. It is, of course, balanced dynamically and incorporates three main bearings, the centre one of which is of very large diameter.

The rigidity of this main rotating component in the engine, coupled with the rigid design of the crankcase, is largely responsible for the capacity of the unit to rev. at high speeds (in the neighbourhood of 5,500 r.p.m.) with extreme smoothness. We have witnessed one of the engines undergoing its bench test turning over on full throttle at the

above-mentioned speed and running so smoothly that we were surprised to learn that the compression ratio was as high as 8.2 to 1.

Three S.U. carburetters are employed, each instrument supplying two cylinders through siamesed ports. The porting arrangements in the cylinder head have, of course, received careful attention in order to make the passage of the gases as free as possible. Two main exhaust pipes convey the spent gases from the engine, each of these pipes being connected to three cylinders through short separate extension pieces.

The sump is a deeply ribbed Elektron casting which has a capacity for no less than two gallons of lubricant; baffles are incorporated in the container to prevent surging of the fluid, due to violent

TO TWO-WAY TAP    TO INSTRUMENT BOARD    TO PRESSURE PUMP

### CHASSIS DETAILS.

*(Below) A general chassis view showing how the frame slopes to the rear.*

*(Right) How the petrol tank and pipe lines are arranged.*

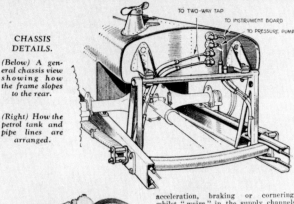

acceleration, braking or cornering, whilst " weirs " in the supply channels for the pump help to keep the circulated oil free from foreign matter which might find its way into the engine.

The clutch and gearbox are built very largely on normal Riley lines, and are mounted unitwise with the engine. When used with a standard rear-axle reduction ratio of 4.77 to 1, the indirect gears are 5.96, 7.155 and 11.78 to 1.

The layout of the chassis frame itself is of particular interest. The shape of

B23

The **Light Car** &Cyclecar                    740                    MAY 20, 1932.

## THE NEW 1½-LITRE RILEY SIX *(Contd.)*

EASY BRAKE ADJUSTMENT —— *The " as you drive " brake adjustment layout conforms closely with standard Riley practice. The deep side members and tubular cross member will be noted.*

the channels in plan view has been made to conform with the contours of a streamlined body; the top flanges are, within very narrow limits, quite flat. Furthermore, the whole of the cross-members are of tubular formation and are therefore immensely strong under all conditions of loading.

At the front there is the usual tube of relatively small diameter connecting the dumbirons; just behind the radiator there is a deeply curved tube of larger diameter which forms a support for the radiator besides acting as a very effective frame stiffener.

Amidships there are two 3-in. diameter tubes, of which the forward one is straight; the after tube—which, by the way, connects the front eyes of the rear springs—is cranked slightly in order to give clearance to the propeller shaft. Another tube connects the road spring eyes and the ends of the frame.

The general low build may be judged by the fact that the tops of the frame members in the vicinity of the seating accommodation are no more than 11 ins. above the ground; the main channels are 5½ ins. deep and both driver and passenger's seats are situated between the channels.

The wheelbase and track dimensions are 9 ft. and 3 ft. 11¾ ins. respectively. Both front and rear springs are of semi-elliptic formation, which—when the chassis is in roadworthy trim—have practically flat contours. The forward part of the frame passes over the front axle whilst the rear part is slung beneath the driving axle; sufficient clearance to allow considerable axle movement is provided.

There are many ingenious features in the layout of the chassis; the manner in which single brackets are employed at each side of the frame to carry the rear eyes of the front springs and the trunnion mountings of the engine, is a case in point. Each bracket is well stiffened by a triangulation of webs and is attached to the inner face of the frame, the lower part being formed to carry the road spring shackles whilst the top part terminates in a platform on to which is bolted a plummer block; this latter component receives the rubber insulated inner member of one of the side trunnions built into the crankcase.

The fuel tank mounting is another item in which a great deal of ingenuity is shown. The tank itself has a capacity for 26½ gallons of fuel and is made in a wide inverted U section. As an illustration shows, it is mounted at the rear part of the frame immediately behind the driver. Front and rear of the tank is a rig made up of triangular pressed-steel side plates connected by a tube; at suitable points platforms are arranged to receive the tank brackets.

### Four Gallons in Reserve.

The fuel supply system is also worthy of mention. There are two air lines and two fuel lines leading to the tank itself, one air line being taken to a gauge on the facia board, whilst the other goes to a hand-pressure pump. Each of the two fuel lines is taken from the lower extremity of the two side pieces of the tank; these pipes join up to a single line through the medium of a two-way tap, which is placed so that the driver can reach it when the car is in motion; thus, the carburetters can draw from either line, leaving four gallons (the capacity of each of the lower extremities of the tank) as a reserve. It does not matter, therefore, in which position the tap is placed when replenishing, as the system works equally well in each direction.

Braking is effected in the usual Riley style, the pedal applying by cables fully compensated internal-expanding shoes in drums of 13 ins. diameter attached to all four wheels. The lever operates the rear brakes only by means of rods. A master adjustment is provided for each system, hand screws protruding through the floorboards to enable the shoe clearances to be taken up whilst the car is in motion, if desired.

### Sells for £595.

The illustrations give an excellent impression of the general shape and disposition of the main components of the chassis. As already indicated, streamlining has been very carefully planned, and, thanks to the low overall height of the car, head resistance is extremely small. It will also be noticed that the spare wheel is mounted in the streamlined tail and a faired-off cover with a quick-release attachment is fitted at the top of the main panel in order to complete the streamlined effect. In touring trim, mudguards, a Vee screen and a hood are provided and are included in the list price of £595.

AN INTERESTING POWER-UNIT —— *An off-side view of the engine of the new Riley model showing the three S.U. carburetters and the water pump. The design is based on the well-known 2-litre Alpine Six engine but the bore and stroke are 57.5 mm. and 95.2 mm., giving a capacity of 1,486 c.c.*

B2⁴

# Introducing a Newcomer

## Details of the New 9 h.p. Riley "Imp" 2/4 Seater

*The Riley " Imp "—a newcomer to the Riley range, which is sure to make a wide appeal to the enthusiastic motorist.*

THE saloon car is definitely the most popular model on the road at the present time. There are, however, still a number of enthusiastic motorists to whom the saloon, or even the comparatively staid open tourer, is anathema. To whom the only really enjoyable kind of motoring is behind the wheel of a genuine sports car, capable of holding the road like a leech, possessing clean sporting lines, with a performance which makes it outstanding among its fellows.

In order to cater for these enthusiasts, the Riley engineers have been busy designing a car which will fulfil all the requirements outlined above. The result is the 9 h.p. Riley " Imp," which will be in production shortly.

The chassis of this model, which is shown in the picture at the bottom of the page, possesses many outstanding characteristics. The dropped frame, underslung at the rear, the deep section side members—these are actually no less than five inches deep at the centre—the short wheelbase—7 feet 6 inches—the special series engine, all these details ensure excellent performance under the severest tests which any sports car worthy of the name, has to undergo.

The bodywork, too, while by no means extreme, possesses clean, sporting lines, unspoilt, as is often the case, by mudwings which fail to harmonise with the general " flow " of the body. Nor are the mudwings of the type far too often found on so-called " sports " cars, stuck on apparently as an afterthought to satisfy the demands of the law. They are of solid, yet light construction, and definitely *do* keep the mud under control.

All weather equipment has received special consideration, and the hood, which folds neatly away when not in use, is extremely easy to erect. The side curtains too, while capable of keeping out the worst of weather, are neither heavy nor unsightly, and stow away neatly into the back of the car when not required.

The windscreen is of the single panel type, and can be folded flat along the scuttle, should occasion demand. When it is in this position, the wind is deflected from the driver's face by means of deep cowls on the trailing edge of the scuttle.

Wide doors permit easy entrance and exit, and access is gained to the rear seats by tilting those in front.

To sum up, the Riley " Imp " is a thoroughbred in every sense of the word, and, selling at the figure of £298, will undoubtedly prove extremely popular with real sports car enthusiasts.

*The chassis of the Riley " Imp." Note the short wheelbase and underslung rear axle.*

# NEW RILEY "M.P.H." SIX

### Projected to Combine Super Performance with Super Refinement in a Small Car

Near side of the engine showing the separate exhaust pipes.

## Separate Exhaust Pipes

## 70 b.h.p. for 17 Cwt.

## Body Type

*The new Riley has many interesting features and a most attractive appearance.*

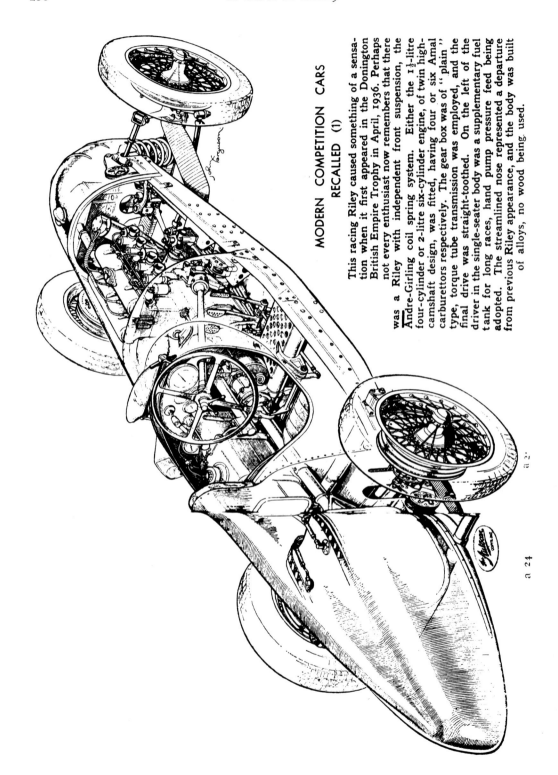

## MODERN COMPETITION CARS RECALLED (1)

This racing Riley caused something of a sensation when it first appeared in the Donington British Empire Trophy in April, 1936. Perhaps not every enthusiast now remembers that there was a Riley with independent front suspension, the Andre-Girling coil spring system. Either the 1½-litre four-cylinder or 2-litre six-cylinder engine, of twin high-camshaft design, was fitted, having four or six Amal carburettors respectively. The gear box was of " plain " type, torque tube transmission was employed, and the final drive was straight-toothed. On the left of the driver in the single-seater body was a supplementary fuel tank for long races, hand pump pressure feed being adopted. The streamlined nose represented a departure from previous Riley appearance, and the body was built of alloys, no wood being used.

a 24

# CHAPTER NINE

# 'Rileyoddities'—The Spin-offs and Riley Based Specials

The word 'Rileyoddities' might well have been conceived by the Riley company to define the odd diversions it made out of the motor industry over the years. As far as is known, the word was not coined by Riley, though it seems to serve its purpose well in the context in which it is used by this author.

Among the earliest 'spin-offs' of Riley product applications was an engine built by Percy Riley after he had successfully built his first car (completed in 1898) and which was the final inspiration to establish the Riley Engine Company in 1903.

This engine was built in Percy's spare time and was a water-cooled twin cylinder design of eight horsepower. It featured an improved mechanically operated inlet valve and a control to vary the inlet valve lift so as to control the inflow of induction gases and therefore the speed of the engine. How long this engine ultimately ran is not known, but it was still going strong in 1913 powering plant in a Coventry foundry and showing little sign of wear.

In 1904, the Riley Engine Company was approached by the South African Railways to build a number of inspection and maintenance trolleys. These rail-cars were of two types—one for those doing the work of track maintenance, without frills and equipped to tow a trailer; the other fitted with an upholstered seat to accommodate the inspectors who were overseeing the work. The first type also had a gearbox fitted with a power-take-off (a very early application of this technique) to provide rotary power for track-laying tools and their trailers were fitted with dynamos.

These early railcars were fitted with the single cylinder $4\frac{1}{2}$ h.p. engine and a two-speed constant-mesh gearbox. The inspection trolleys did not have power-take-offs. A leather-faced cone clutch was used and drive was transmitted by chain from the transverse engine and gear-box.

Shortly after these first South African rail-cars were put into service, the Indian Government bought a number of Singer cross-country vehicles and these, too, had Riley engines and gearboxes.

Then, South African Railways decided, in 1906, to buy more rail-cars. This time they were powered by the 9 h.p. V-twin engine and had the three-speed Riley gearbox as used in the cars, but again modified to provide a power-take-off on the maintenance trolleys. The engine and gearbox were again placed in the frame transversely and final drive was by chain. These were put into service in early 1907.

Singer also produced rail-cars, theirs being again for India and once more they approached Riley for engines and gearboxes. With the experience of their second batch of South African trolleys, Riley supplied 9 h.p. units and three-speed gearboxes for the Singer vehicles.

When the Riley Engine Company was moved to Aldbourne Road, Coventry in the summer

*A rare photograph of one of the Tasmanian rail-cars, believed to be a 10 h.p., in working use
as an Inspection Car and the manager's personal Transport Car.*

of 1906, the Company built its own two ton truck in the old works, using Riley mechanical components. These featured a 9 h.p. V-twin engine, a Riley 3-speed gearbox and Riley axles. The move was then made using this truck as the transport. They also built a dropside truck on the 12/18 h.p. long wheelbase chassis later, which was sold to the Coventry Radiator Company.

During 1908, a Tasmanian mining company, the Mount Lyall Mines, decided to look at, and eventually buy, the 9 h.p. Riley rail-car. The success of the South African railcars had brought the managers of the Tasmanian company to Coventry. They bought three rail-car chassis less wheels and bodies. These arrived in Tasmania late in 1908 and the company built its own bodies and fitted the wheels to make their rail-cars mobile.

Like the South African vehicles, the Tasmanian rail-cars were used by track maintenance crews. They were also employed as personnel carriers on the North Mount Lyall Railway for Mines personnel and one was used as personal transport by the Mine Manager.

Perhaps the most noteworthy task undertaken by any of these Riley rail-cars was in a terrible fire which took place in the Mount Lyall Mine on 12th October 1912. Ninety-six men were trapped in the mine and the rail cars were used to transport rescue equipment in the attempts to bring the men to the surface. On the Thursday following the fire, forty men were rescued after spending one hundred and nine hours underground. It was June 1913 before the last of the dead from that mine disaster was buried and the Riley rail-cars were used as rather unorthodox hearses to transport some of the bodies to their last resting places.

The last of these Tasmanian rail-cars survives to this day, having been retired from service

*A 1929 Australian 9 h.p. Tourer on the Colonial chassis. The tool boxes didn't
exactly aid the increased ground clearance of this model.*

in 1964—56 years after they were bought—and restored to take a place in one of Tasmania's
railway museums. A worthy end to a distinguished career.

After the Great War, during which the Riley companies had given over their entire
production capacity to the Ministry of Munitions, one of the products of the research of that
time was put to commercial success.

Little is known today of the venture, but Percy Riley was approached to design an electricity generating set, featuring the Eleven-Forty engine mounted in a channel section frame
and fitted with a starter motor but no dynamo—at least not the twelve volt variety! A lever-
operated clutch engaged and disconnected drive from the engine to the generator and the
success of these units was such that the Riley Engine Company was busy manufacturing them
until 1926.

At the same time, according to Edward H. Reeves' splendid little book *The Riley Romance*,
the Riley Engine Company was also making a marine version of the Eleven-Forty and the
later Twelve, again until 1926 when the Riley Nine took all the Company's production
capacity and time.

Now the Riley Nine was to have its turn in the realms of 'spin-offs'. J. G. Parry-Thomas
and Reid Railton busied themselves to adapt the Riley Nine for the sporting potential they

*A very elegant Continental Coupe on the 1929 9 h.p. Mk. IV chassis, believed to have been built by Tickford.*

*Dick Batho's 9 h.p. 1928/29 Amilcar-Riley at Shelsley Walsh.*

*Miss Joan Richmond's 'Jacko'—a 1931 9 h.p. chassis fitted with*
*a 2 Seater body in Australia by the Elite Motor Body Works.*

were convinced it had. Their prototype Nine Speed Model became the immortal Brooklands
Riley Nine.

Many famous names were associated with sporting Rileys and perhaps the next worthy
of mention is F. W. Dixon. Freddie Dixon had made his name racing motor-cycles in the
1920's and decided in 1932 to try his hand with cars. So he bought from Victor Gillow a
used Brooklands Nine. He set about lightening it considerably, built a new body for it,
modified the brakes and made a number of minor changes to fit the car to his needs. He then
went to work on the engine to make it go faster—and clearly succeeded, because his first race
with the car was the 1932 R.A.C. Tourist Trophy at Ards in Ulster which he led until an
infamous trip into a rhubarb patch! He probably would have won his first ever race if it had
not been that a cylinder head gasket failure caused him to have to spend more than half the
night before the race flattening the cylinder head and putting it all back together. Nonetheless
his drive in that T.T. was little short of spectacular against, amongst others, an experienced
works team. Therefore Dixon's cars are well worthy of mention here—not all as Riley-based
specials, though 'Red Mongrel' was exactly that, but as modified Rileys. That first Dixon
car is still being raced today and does the Riley marque credit.

Dixon went on to build 'Red Mongrel', a single seater based on Riley Nine components,
but rather quicker. This car was to take Class G records from 50 to 200 kilometres, the 200
being at 100.67 m.p.h. The car was first entered in the 1932 B.R.D.C. '500' but retired with a
fuel leak from its 30 gallon tank. It retired from the 1933 '500' after blowing a head gasket,
then a piston after the head gasket had been replaced without Dixon losing the lead! In
April 1934, he drove the car in the British Empire Trophy Race and was forced to retire

*Another Amilcar-Riley, the Kerr-Bate Special.*

again, this time with an oil pump failure. 'Red Mongrel' seems not to have brought Freddie Dixon a deal of good fortune, but it was an excellent development platform for his later Riley exploits.

Dixon's next cars were the T.T. chassis he bought from Riley in late 1933. He bored out the engines to 63.5 mm., giving a capacity of 1808 cc.; he fitted the now-familiar Dixon ultra-light and ultra-low bodywork; he fitted six carburetters to the engines which had throttle slide plates. The throttle slide plate was mounted into a cast alloy manifold with a direct port to each of the cylinders: it was bored in line with the manifold to ensure a constant port diameter and was mounted in roller bearings top and bottom to prevent jamming in operation. Over 30 years later, Lucas was to use a similar throttle pattern for its fuel injection system, which demonstrates Dixon's advanced thinking at the time.

These cars were a tremendous success, although on their first outing, the 1934 Mannin Moar on the Isle of Man, Dixon retired and Cyril Paul, who drove the other car, came home third. However, vindication was near at hand, for Dixon won the B.R.D.C. 500 at Brooklands in 1934 and the British Empire Trophy Race in 1935. With one of these cars he also secured a Brooklands 130 m.p.h. Badge—the only unsupercharged 2 litre car ever to lap Brooklands at that speed. The Women's Lap Record was taken in the same car by Elsie Wisdom at 126.73 m.p.h.

Talking of records leads naturally to the car which holds still, and in perpetuity, the Class G Brooklands Mountain Circuit Lap Record—the Appleton Special, built by R. J. W. Appleton in 1934 on an 1100 cc. Maserati chassis with a blown Riley Nine engine. Ulti-

*The first Dixon Riley—a Brooklands modified and re-bodied*
*by Freddie Dixon for the 1932 T.T.*

mately, he fitted a three-main-bearing 9 h.p. engine which, in supercharged form, produced 183 b.h.p. at 7400 r.p.m. The Mountain Circuit Lap Record was taken from Fairfield's E.R.A. at 76.1 m.p.h. and the car also took the British Class G Records for distances of one to ten kilometres, the one kilometre record speed being 111 m.p.h.!

Raymond Mays bought one of the 1933 T.T. chassis, 4/103 before it got as far as the T.T., and built from it another supercharged car, the White Riley. This car had a six-cylinder engine, still of 1486 cc. capacity, but with many design modifications made by Peter Berthon. It was fitted with a Roots type supercharger designed by Murray Jamieson and at 12 p.s.i., it gave 147 b.h.p. at 6500 r.p.m. and regularly ran at 8000 r.p.m. in competitive events. The White Riley's first outing was at the August Bank Holiday Meeting at Brooklands in 1933 and from it was developed the remarkably successful E.R.A.

English Racing Automobiles was formed by Mays, Berthon and Humphrey Cook. The Company built seventeen cars of Types A to D with 1100 cc., 1½ litre and 2 litre engine capacities to race in the Voiturettee Class of Grands Prix and other events such as hill-climbs. The E.R.A. success story was unmatched before the second World War. Winning was the habit and Riley took its share of the credit, by being extensively involved in the manufacture of engines and cylinder blocks.

The cylinder block was very similar to the production Riley Six except that the engine-

*Riley 9 h.p. Marine engine*

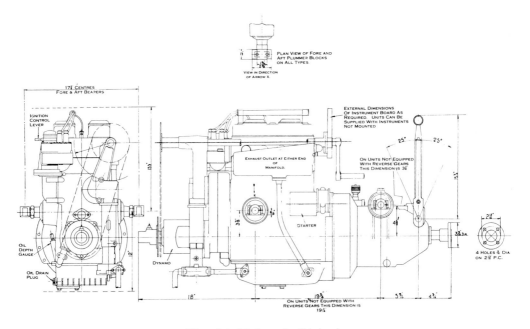

*Riley 9 h.p. Marine engine GA drawing*

mounting cross-shaft of the Riley was not used on the E.R.A. unit, so the crankcase walls were smooth, modified castings being produced to exclude the cross-shaft housing. A three-point mounting was still used, but the extensively re-designed timing case now had feet cast into it to provide the front two mounting pedestals. The engine also had more cylinder-head studs to hold down the E.R.A.-designed alloy head. The crankshafts were made by Laystall and Hyatt roller centre main bearings were used.

Eddie Maher, who was then in Riley's experimental department, recalled that Riley

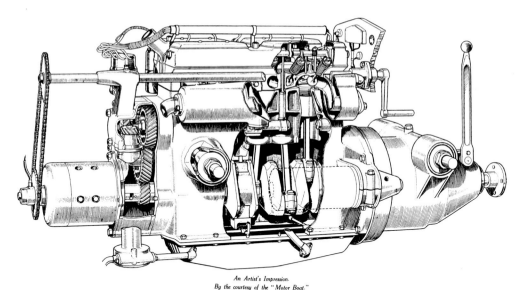

*An Artist's Impression.
By the courtesy of the " Motor Boat."*

*In view of the many outstanding features incorporated in the design of this unit, we
feel confident that no apologies are necessary from us for this method of illustrating them.*

*The "P.R." Head, inclined overhead valves, the position of the twin camshafts, the
crankshaft, rubber engine mounting, helical timing gears and many other salient features are
shown here to perfection.*

*Riley Six Marine engine*

made the finished cylinder blocks and assembled what would today be described as the
'short' engines for completion at Bourne, where cylinder heads, lubrication piping and superchargers were fitted. He remembered that numerous E.R.A. people spent a great deal of
time at the Coventry works, and that Riley people frequently went to Bourne to make their
contribution to the E.R.A. success story.

A remarkable level of co-operation existed between the two companies, particularly when
one remembers that Riley was fielding its own cars in competition, as well as supporting
several private entrants including one F. W. Dixon. Dixon, of course, gave the E.R.A.s a very
fair run for their money on many occasions with his unsupercharged Rileys.

Three other E.R.A.s were built, too, of very different chassis design and known as the E
Types. These also featured Riley-based engines, but with plain main bearings and coupled to
four-speed synchromesh gearboxes, though Riley's involvement in these cars was rather less
than was so with the earlier ones.

It is interesting to note that of the seventeen A to D Type cars built, fourteen are still in
regular use today—and two of the three E Type cars have recently re-emerged. A famous
photograph of E.R.A.s is one taken of the first four A Type cars at Brooklands in 1935. Those
same four cars came together again for the first time at a Vintage Sports Car Club meeting at
Oulton Park in 1971, R2A having been brought back to England after spending many years
in the Far East. A brief summary of the E.R.A.s follows this chapter, since no Riley history is
really complete without them in view of the close relationship between the two companies.

Riley themselves weren't above building the odd special and in 1933 and 1934 they built
three special six-cylinder cars on 44T chassis of 9 ft. 2$\frac{5}{16}$ in. wheelbase, fitting to them
Gamecock bodies. Both 1933 and 1934 cars were built to compete in the International
Alpine Rallies of those years and the 1933 cars, registered as KV5691, KV5692 and KV5693,

were fitted with engines which had roller centre main bearings. The regulations prevented the use of the roller bearing engines in 1934, so ADU27, ADU28 and ADU29 were fitted with plain bearing engines for the event.

In 1934, had it not been for an unfortunate oil leak in ADU28, the car driven by Arnold Farrar, followed by a water leak from overheating, the team would certainly have secured First Class Award—an Alpine Cup. As it was, they secured a very well-deserved Glacier Cup, the Second Class Award. There is some question about the number of bodies actually made for these cars and it has been suggested that the bodies fitted to the 1933 cars were repainted and used again in 1934. It is eminently possible that this could have been so and it certainly would have made sense, but it is not confirmed.

In 1935, the prototype MPH, 4/101 (KV5694), was loaned to E.R.A. for development work, the intention being to produce an E.R.A.-Riley sports car. The car was fitted with a supercharged engine, but the radiator had to be moved so far forward that it gave a rather ungainly appearance to the otherwise very elegant lines of the MPH. After a while, the project was abandoned, the blown engine was removed, to be fitted into Mays' Kestrel Six, and the MPH was returned to Coventry. Perhaps the realisation that the MPH was already too expensive for its market, resulting in the development of the Sprite Two Seater, was the deciding factor for the Riley company.

Hector Dobbs, a Riley dealer, built a most successful racing six-cylinder Riley on an MPH chassis, to which he fitted a very sparse offset single seat body weighing, it was said, only thirty pounds. The engine had a roller centre main bearing, six Amal carburetters and Bowden cable brakes instead of Riley type. He drove it with enormous success at Brooklands and Donington Park and the car survives to this day, though in a much less active state.

Going back to 1929, whilst the world of motor sport was notching up success after success for Rileys and Riley-engined cars of other origins, including a host of specials too numerous to

*An elegant 9 h.p. coupé by Arnold of Manchester in 1933.*

*This is one of the most famous of all Riley-based specials: one of the two racing sixes built by Freddie Dixon on the TT Six chassis he bought from Riley (Coventry) Limited in late 1933. This historic photograph shows chassis number 4/104 resting in Reg Parnell's garage just after the second World War.*

mention in these pages, the Company still displayed a strong interest in marine engines. So it produced a marine version of the Riley Nine engine, which was adopted early in that year by the Royal Motor Yacht Club as the sole power unit for their 'Puppy Dog' class of racing hydroplane.

In 1931 a Lowestoft company, J. W. Brooke and Company, produced an 18 ft. long boat known as the Brooke-Riley Special. This vessel was offered with either the Riley Nine Cruiser engine or the Six-Fourteen unit. One of the boat's most significant features was the extensive use of stainless steel for the fittings, instead of the more widely used brass.

By 1933, one of the most revered names in the marine world, Vospers, had decided to offer two versions of the Riley Nine engine for boat power. The Cruiser type had a single carburetter, electric starter motor and a forward-reverse gearbox: it was priced at £105. For £120, the Speedboat version was available with two carburetters. The power output of these two engines was 20 b.h.p. and 41 b.h.p. respectively.

Riley's own marine offerings in 1932 were the Nine Cruiser engine, the Nine Speedboat type and a single version of the Six-Fourteen. All of these engines came with a twelve volt battery; dynamo; starter motor; dash panel fitted with starter switch, ammeter, oil gauge, petrol gauge and hand crank lever; 5¼ gallon petrol tank; a water cooled exhaust manifold and an oil cooler. The prices were £110 for the 9 h.p. Cruiser version, £130 for the Speedboat Nine and £175 for the Six-Fourteen. Reverse gear cost an extra £25, a revolution counter was £5 and reduction gear for the Speedboat Nine and the Six engines cost £16. Delivery F.O.B. London, Southampton or Liverpool cost between £3 and £4!

Still in the world of marine Rileys, Mr. George White, the son of Sir Stanley White, who was then Managing Director of the Bristol Aeroplane Company, established two new world records in 1937 in the International 400 kg. Class for racing boats. The vessel he used was designed for the "Cadet" Class, but since that class was not eligible for record attempts, it was registered in the 400 kg. weight class. The boat was named "Bulldog II" (after an aeroplane built by Father's company, perhaps?), was 14 ft. long, 4 ft. 9 in. wide, and had a single seat. The 9 h.p. engine gave the boat a still-water speed of 41 m.p.h., producing an amazing 72 b.h.p. The compression ratio of this engine was 13.5 : 1, it had a 3 gallon water-cooled oil tank and ran at an optimum speed of 5,200 to 5,800 r.p.m. with a three-blade screw. Fuel consumption was about 6 g.p.h., the boat's capacity was 50 gallons and dry weight was 830 lbs.

From the very earliest days of Riley cars, it was recognised that the customer might want his own special coachwork fitted to the Riley he was about to buy. For that reason, it was always possible to buy the chassis only and fit a body to the customer's specifications. On occasions, Riley promoted specialist coachwork designs and included them in the factory catalogues, so it should be no surprise that there have been "Rileyoddities" since the days of the V-twins.

*The first E.R.A.—R1A—built in 1934 and still doing what it does best—winning.*

*A very cold picture of the last "B" type E.R.A.—R14B—the ultimate Riley-based special.*

Many Rileys were exported as chassis, acquiring coachwork on arrival in their country of destination. Australia was a particular market where this happened. Three such cars were driven overland from Australia to compete in the 1932 Monte Carlo Rally. The chassis were provided by the Riley company and the entrants, Misses Richmond and Robertson and Captain Morice, provided the Australian-built bodies. One was a rather splendid metal-bodied Two Seater whilst the other two were fabric-bodied Two/Four Seaters. These three cars were registered QA692, QA833 and QA834.

*Another view of R14B showing the offset steering wheel characteristic
of all E.R.A.s and the hill-climbing twin rear wheels.*

By the time the 1½ litre range was established, Percy Riley was thinking again about military applications and in 1936 produced a prototype for a new Army Tourer, based on the
1½ litre Lynx design, but with straight-topped doors, a top-hinged windscreen, a roll-up rear
screen in the hood, an external spare wheel carrier and oversize tyres. Naturally enough, it was
painted in olive green overall and there were no bright parts, the radiator shell and wheel
nuts even being painted. However, it was not adopted by the Army, so never went into
production.

Another military project upon which Percy Riley embarked was the design of an armoured
scout-car. This was undertaken in 1937 and was for a four-wheel-drive vehicle with a rear-
mounted engine and front-mounted gearbox, to allow a very low driving position and centre
of gravity. It was a most interesting design, which featured a central tubular backbone, to
which were attached the axles, the engine and the gearbox, and through which ran the driveline. A full-scale wooden mock-up was built, in co-operation with the Army's Motor Vehicle
Experimental Establishment, but when it was realised that the 9 h.p. engine would not be
nearly powerful enough, the design was dropped and the contract awarded to Daimler.

Perhaps the last 'spin-off', and certainly the most adventurous; was Autovia Cars Limited,

*Hector Dobb's offset racing single seater at Donington Park in 1935.*

launched by Victor Riley at the end of 1936. The chief engineer of this new company was C. M. van Eugen, who had come from Lea-Francis (perhaps that explains the shape of the Autovia radiator, quite reminiscent of the Lea-Francis style).

The Autovia was launched for the 1937 Season and the two designs of coachwork, the Saloon and Limousine, were both produced by Arthur Mulliner of Northampton. The engine was a V8, developed from the Riley 8/90 unit, but with a bore common to the $1\frac{1}{2}$ litre engine, 69 mm., and a stroke the same as the 8/90, 95.2 mm. The resultant engine capacity was 2849 cc.

The gearbox was an Armstrong Siddeley preselector, similar to that used in the 8/90, but a short open propeller-shaft took drive from the gearbox to the torque-tube, thence to the underslung worm-and-wheel rear axle. The rear suspension was underslung and behind the axle was placed the 16 gallon fuel tank. Centre-lock 19 in. wire wheels were used and the front springs, instead of being located above or below the axle, passed through it so as to provide low floor height but retain a good ground clearance. Prices for the Autovias were £685 for the chassis, £975 for the Saloon and £995 for either the Special Saloon or the Limousine.

When Riley (Coventry) Limited was put into receivership, the Bodies Branch and the Riley Engine Company (which had become known as the Engines Branch, but was still registered as a separate limited liability company) were wound up. The Autovia products and stock were taken over by the London Riley distributor, Jimmy James Limited. But the 'spin-offs' and Riley-based specials did not end there.

Over the years since the Great War of 1914–18 many coachbuilders had practised their crafts on Riley chassis. From some quite exotic two seaters on the early side-valve chassis, including one very elegant sports three seater by Hancock and Warman on the 11 h.p. Sports chassis in 1923, the 'Specials' which were built included the 1929 K.C. Special Tourer by K.C. Motor Bodies Limited; the Hoyal Coupé; the Newdigate Special Coupé by Newdigate

*The 1935 Bertelli-bodied MPH Sports*

*The Appleton Special at a VSCC Prescott Hill-Climb.*

Motor Bodies of Nuneaton; the Gloucester Special by H. J. Ripley; the Tickford Coupé on the Nine chassis; the Arnold Coupé by Arnold's of Manchester; the Two/Three Seat Coupé by Grose of Northampton on the 1½ litre chassis; the 15/6 Sedanca Coupé by Wylders of Kew and many, many more.

Racing specials were built in large numbers from Rileys. The Appleton Special has already been mentioned; in pre- and post-war times there have been the Amilcar-Riley; Cuthbert Special; the Densham Special; the Dixon Specials; the H.A.R. Special; the Kerr-Bate Special; the Treen Rileys which were basically copies of the Brooklands Nine chassis using highly tuned and modified Riley mechanical components—and last, but by no means least, there are the many post-war specials built specifically to compete in Vintage Sports Car Club and classic events. There is an argument that the building of such specials helps to keep the spirit of enthusiasm for the breed alive. It is to be hoped, though, that so many are not built as to destroy the identity of the factory-built cars, for nearly every racing special, despite the joy it gives its owner, takes an original car out of existence. There are some exceptions, of course, where a collection of parts from a number of dismantled cars are brought together and another one car returned to a life of usefulness as a result. But we should remember that, in general terms, there are already too few original, ordinary, Riley cars.

*Autovia chassis*

*1937 Autovia Saloon*

*1937 Autovia 3 litre V-8 engine*

# THE AUTOVIA—AN ENTIRELY NEW EIGHT-CYLINDER CAR

First Detailed Description of a Very Interesting New Model with a V-type Engine of 24 h.p. Rating. Saloon to Sell at £975. Road-test Impressions Show Quiet Running and Riding Comfort to be Outstanding Features

*For Further Illustrations See the Photographic Section*

## Worm-drive Advantages

## Two Body Styles

## Extensive Equipment

## Lubrication and Ignition Systems

## Novel Engine Features

(Above) Frontal appearance: the Autovia radiator is of dignified design with a character of its own. The lamps and horns show standardized.

(Left) The four-window saloon is low-built and the seats are all within the wheelbase. Note the large in-built luggage compartment.

## THE ENTIRELY NEW AUTOVIA

(Left) A D.B.S. worm drive and differential unit is built into the banjo-type rear axle casing. This provides a low propeller-shaft line and so enables a flat floor to be fitted to the body.

### Road Test Impressions

### Steady Rear-seat Ride

## A New Singer Nine Coupe

Fixed at £159 10s., this 9 h.p. two-seater coupe forms an attractive addition to the Singer range for 1937.

## THE ENTIRELY NEW AUTOVIA

Alternative to the saloon, a seven-seater limousine (also by Messrs. Arthur Mulliner) which is listed at £995 complete.

### Insulated Duplex Silencing Systems

### Special Frame Features

(Left) The facia and controls; a view which shows the large and legible dials fitted

(Right) The crankcase, inverted, and removed, showing the balanced crankshaft, with two big-ends fitted to each crankpin.

## SPECIFICATIONS

| | |
|---|---|
| MODEL | **E.R.A. Types A to D** *Year:* 1934–1937 |
| CHASSIS | Channel section mainframe arched over rear axle. |

MODEL      **E.R.A. Types A to D**          *Year:* 1934–1937

CHASSIS

Channel section mainframe arched over rear axle.
*Wheelbase:* 8 ft. 0 in.
*Track:* Front 4 ft. 4½ in. Rear 4 ft. 4½ in.
*Type of Wheels:* Dunlop centre lock wire.
*Braking System:* A & B Types—Girling mechanical rod. C & D Types—Girling hydraulic. Wedge operated shoes on all Types.
*Gearbox Type:* Armstrong Siddeley 4 speed preselector—no clutch.
*Suspension:* A & B Types—semi-elliptic all round with Hartford friction shock absorbers. C & D Types—semi-elliptic rear springs and trailing-link type independent front suspension of Porsche patent design. Three cars (R2B, R3D and R14B) fitted with de Ram hydraulic/friction shock absorbers.

ENGINE

*Type:* In-line six-cylinder based on Riley Six design.
*Bore:* 1100 cc. 57.5 mm. 1500 cc. 57.5 mm. 2 Litre 62.8 mm.
*Stroke:* 1100 cc. 69.8 mm. 1500 cc. 95.5 mm. 2 Litre 106.5 mm.
*Cubic Capacity:* 1100 1088 cc. 1500 1488 cc. 2 Litre 1980 cc.
*Ignition:* Scintilla NV6 Magneto with manual advance/retard.
*Number of Cylinders:* 6
*Firing Order:* 1, 5, 3, 6, 2, 4
*Cylinder Head:* Cast alloy with hemispherical combustion chambers.
*Valve Gear:* 45° overhead with high camshafts and 1½ in. valves.
*Sizes and Types of Main Bearings:* Front—1⅝ in. plain, Centre—3¾ in. roller, Rear—2 in plain.
*Induction System:* Jamieson/Roots or Zoller superchargers.
*Lubrication:* Dry Sump.
*Cooling System:* Inlet camshaft driven pump.
*Dry Weight:* 1100—13½ cwt, 1500—14½ cwt, 2 Litre—15½ cwt.

CARS BUILT

R1A—Works 1500 cc. car—built 1934—sold to Jean Trevoux.
R2A—Works 1100 cc. car—built 1934—sold to N. S. Embiricos.
R3A—Works 1500 cc. car—built 1934—sold to Luis Fontes.
R4A—1100 cc. car—built for Pat Fairfield—later used by F. R. Gerard.
R1B—1500 cc. car—built for Richard Seaman.
R2B—1500 cc. car—"Romulus"—built 1935 for Prince Chula of Siam as 21st birthday present to his cousin, Prince Bira.
R3B—Works 1500 cc. car—written off in 1936 at Deauville.
R4D—Works 1500 cc. car—built 1936—originally B Type, but converted to D Type at Works—retained by Raymond Mays.
R5B—1500 cc. car—"Remus"—bought by Prince Chula as 2nd car for Prince Bira in 1936.
R6B—1500 cc. car—built in 1936 for Dr. J. D. Benjafield.
R7B—1500 cc. car—built in 1936 and sold to Arthur Dobson.
R8B—1500 cc. car—built in 1936 for Earl Howe.
R9B—1500 cc. car—built for Dennis Scribbans.
R10B—1500 cc. car—built 1937 for Peter Whitehead, later converted to C Type.
R11B—1500 cc. car—built 1937 for Reggie Tongue.
R12B—Works 1500 cc. car—built 1937,—"Hanuman"—converted to C Type when purchased by Prince Chula.
R14B—1500 cc. car—built in 1937 for Johnny Wakefield.
In addition to the above-listed cars, three E Type E.R.A. chassis were built, GP1—GP3. These still used the Riley-based engine, but with a bore and stroke of 63 mm. × 80 mm., giving an engine capacity of 1487 cc. The crankshafts of these engines ran in plain main bearings and were connected to 4 speed synchromesh gearboxes.

*1937 Autovia Limousine*

*A post-war Riley-based Special, the H.A.R., with its owner Fouad Majzub.*

| | | |
|---|---|---|
| MODEL | **Autovia** | *Year:* 1937–38 |

CHASSIS

Box-section mainframe, upswept at front and underslung at rear.
*Wheelbase:* 10 ft. 9 in.
*Track:* Front 4 ft. 8½ in. Rear 4 ft. 8½ in.
*Type of Wheels:* 3.50 × 19 in. Dunlop centre-lock wire.
*Tyres:* Front 5.50 × 19 in. Rear 5.50 × 19 in.
*Braking System:* Girling mechanical rod with wedge-operated shoes in 16 in. drums.

TRANSMISSION

*Clutch Type:* Newton 3rd Type centrifugal single plate.
*Gearbox Type:* Armstrong-Siddeley 4 speed preselector.
*Gear Selecting Mechanism:* Steering-column mounted quadrant.
*Gear Ratios:* Limousine 1st—17.28, 2nd—10.05, 3rd—6.63, 4th—4.86, Reverse—21.17:1
    Saloon 1st—16.254, 2nd—9.457, 3rd—6.235, 4th—4.57, Reverse—20.42:1
*Gearbox Oil Capacity:* 9 pints.
*Rear Axle Oil Capacity:* 5 pints.
*Rear Axle Type:* Underslung worm and wheel with torque tube drive.
*Final Drive Ratio:* Limousine 4.86:1. Saloon 4.57:1.

ENGINE

*Engine Type:* Autovia V–8
*RAC H.P. Rating:* 23.8
*Cubic Capacity:* 2849 cc.
*Number of Cylinders:* 8
*Firing Order:* 1, 5, 4, 8, 6, 3, 7, 2
*Bore:* 69 mm.
*Stroke:* 95.2 mm.
*Cylinder Head:* P.R. type detachable 12 stud with hemispherical combustion chambers.
*Valve Gear:* 45° overhead valves with single central inlet and two exhaust camshafts.
*Tappet Clearances (Hot):* Inlet 0.003 in. Exhaust 0.004 in.
*Valve Timing:* Inlet opens 2° before TDC, closes 54° after BDC.
    Exhaust opens 54° before BDC, closes 20° after TDC
*Number of Main Bearings:* 3
*Type of Oil Pump:* Vertically-mounted gear driven.
*Normal Oil Pressure (Hot):* 20—40 p.s.i.
*Sump Capacity:* 15 pints.
*Cooling System:* Pump and fan with thermostat.
*Type of Ignition:* Scintilla magneto.
*Method of Advance/Retard:* Manual.
*Contact Breaker Gap:* 0.012 in.
*Plug Gap:* 0.018 in.
*Make of Type of Plug:* Champion L10S.
*Number, Make and Type of Carburetters:* Twin downdraught Zenith.
*Type of Inlet Manifold:* Cast alloy bolt-on.
*Type of Exhaust Manifold:* Cast iron bolt-on, one per cylinder bank.
*Location of Fuel Tank:* Rear mounted.
*Fuel Capacity:* 16 gallons.
*Method of Fuel Feed:* Twin electric pumps.

MODELS AVAILABLE

| | |
|---|---|
| Autovia Limousine | : £995 |
| Autovia Special Saloon | : £995 |
| Autovia Saloon | : £975 |
| Autovia Chassis only | : £685 |

sporting fraternity, remain the same in design and in price.

The six-cylinder chassis shows no change, nor does the metal-panelled saloon, known as the Deauville, but the price of the latter has been reduced from £525 to £495. There is coming along now, however, an entirely new Stelvio fabric saloon, which provides an unusually low-built body. Cunning design in the interior has contrived to give quite a normal amount of head room, despite the comparatively small overall height of the car.

This body will look extremely smart because its proportions are nicely balanced, for the rear seats are practically within the wheelbase, and the

MORE NEW CARS
(*continued*).

*Redesigned screen and visor on the Riley Nine.*

luggage box forms quite a shapely tail, rather like that of the 9 h.p. Biarritz model, but prettier. Also the luggage box is of exceptional capacity. This new Stelvio will be available at £465, and should receive a warm welcome in many quarters.

It is interesting to record that there are now some 6,000 Riley Nines on the road, and that the demand, even at this time of year, has not abated. Considerable extensions are being made to the busily humming works to meet the situation, and it is confidently anticipated they will enable the management to cope successfully with the requirements of the future, great though they are bound to be.

# ATTRACTIVE RILEY NINE SPORTS MODEL

## *Good Lines of Open Car with Cycle-type Wings and Disappearing Hood.*

THERE has recently been introduced by K.C. Bodies, 407-411, New King's Road, Fulham, S.W., a special body on a Riley Nine chassis, which has very sporting lines. The design is very similar to that of the K.C.-bodied Austin Seven, and incorporates a long bonnet extending back almost to the screen, a rounded tail in which the spare wheel and luggage can be carried, cycle-type wings, and an absence of running boards, which gives the car a very rakish appearance.

The screen is of V type and is slightly raked, while it has extensions at the side so that the occupants of

*The K.C. Riley has a very distinctive appearance.*

The body is coachbuilt, and in view of the width of the doors it should be noted that strong irons are incorporated in the body frame to strengthen the sides and prevent movement between doors and body. The price of the body is £132 10s.

Certainly the lines of this sports model are most attractive and are enhanced by the long bonnet and by the fitting of a louvred apron between the front dumb irons. Provision is also made for carrying the spare wheel on the side of the car if desired.

*The windows are contained in the doors.*

the front seats are well protected. A wide door is fitted on each side and carries a window operated by winding gear, so that when the disappearing hood is erected the car has the appearance and comfort of a coupé. The front seats are arranged to slide, and the wells for the feet of the rear pas-

sengers are extended forward beneath them, forming a convenient space for carrying tools or spare petrol tins.

Real leather upholstery is used, and the specification includes adjustable head lamps, steering adjustable for rake, and floorboards which can be quickly detached, but are rattleproof.

*The length of the bonnet is apparent even from the front.*

# WORLD'S RECORDS

*Mr. G. White's Riley-powered "Bulldog II" which has recently broken world's and national records.*

Reproduced by courtesy of "Yachting World."

# —THIS TIME ON THE WATER!

*We are indebted to Mr. George White, and to Mr. L. V. Head, of "The Yachting World," for the information upon which this article is based.*

MR. George S. M. White, son of Sir Stanley White, Managing Director of the Bristol Aeroplane Company, established two new world's records in the International 400 Kg. motor boat racing class at Poole Harbour on 6th July. Mr. White's " Bulldog II " was designed by Mr. Fred Cooper three years ago for the Royal Motor Y.C., " Cadet " class, but since this club class is not recognized for records, he registered his boat in the 400 Kg. International " Weight " class with a view to establishing long distance world's records of three, six, nine, and twelve hours.

" Bulldog " is not a stepped hydroplane, and is naturally nothing like as fast as the light supercharged racing machines in this international class, but whereas the mile record is at present 69.4 m.p.h., no attempt has been made for duration records by these out-and-out " racers." It is doubtful if any existing machine of this type could last three hours, let alone the longer periods, whereas a sturdy little boat, such as " Bulldog " is capable of standing a fair amount of rough water punishment.

This smart little Cadet, which, like several others of the type, is fitted with a Riley " Nine " engine, proved herself capable of 41 m.p.h. at full throttle in still water.

It has been raced on several occasions in the R.M.Y.C. Cadet Class with reasonable success, and results show that it is the fastest boat in its class.

The hull is a single seater, 14ft. long and 4ft. 9ins. wide. It weighs 830lbs. approximately, without fuel, oil, or water.

The engine was supplied by the Riley Company, with a brake horse power of 72 and a compression ratio of 13½ to 1. Of course, it is not fitted with a gearbox. For these long runs, the revs. are kept between 5,200 and 5,800 with a small three-bladed propeller.

The petrol consumption is about 6 gallons an hour, and there are tanks on either side of the pilot's seat, with a total capacity of 50 gallons. The hull runs quite steadily with this load. There is an extra oil tank, holding 3 gallons, which is cooled by internal water pipes. In order to run the engine at about 80 degrees and at the same time keep the oil temperature under control, there is a special bypass system, which has worked with considerable success in races. The only other point of particular interest is the method of cutting down weight by the removal of the starter and the accumulator. The starter has a small handle fitted, in a similar manner to a file handle. The method of attachment is by two butterfly nuts ; so that after starting up the engine, all that is required is the removal of the butterflies and the lifting out of the starter motor itself. The accumulator is kept in the pit.

Conditions in Poole Harbour were, however, far from perfect on the occasion of the record run, and at no time was White able to make a complete lap at full throttle. Moreover, as the mile course, up and down, is measured between the two buoys and does not make any allowance for the distance covered when actually turning, motor boat speeds in these distance records are always below that actually attained.

" Bulldog " ran extremely well up to 3 hrs. 57 mins., when she hit some floating object and damaged the propeller. Unfortunately, too, the Harbour Master stopped the trial while a new propeller was being fitted, in view of complaints having been made by residents on the score of noise.

14

The Riley Record, July, 1937

Altogether, two world's and four national records have been filed with the Marine Motoring Association, the national authority, and these will be confirmed in due course. The following are the official speeds :—

World's and National 24 nautical mile record, 25.29 knots (30.75 m.p.h.).

National 1 hr. record, 25.29 knots (29.08 m.p.h.).

National 2 hr. record, 24.67 knots (28.37 m.p.h.).

World's and National 3 hr. record, 23.39 knots.

World's records are permitted for 1 and 24 miles, and 3, 6, 9 and 12 hours, while National records embrace each individual hour, from one to twelve. A nautical mile is 1.1516 statute or land miles.

Reproduced by courtesy of " Yachting World."

" *Bulldog's* " *cockpit, very complete and business-like, is extremely like that of the famous E.R.A. racing cars.*

From *Autocar* 7 April 1933 p. 560:

# A SPECIAL RILEY NINE

BASED on a wide experience in competition work, principally on Riley cars, H. J. Ripley, of H. J. Ripley and Co., Thames Ditton, has evolved an individually prepared Riley which he is calling the Gloucester Special.

The basic Riley Nine engine and chassis are, of course, used, but a higher performance is made available for the purposes of a sports model by a number of modifications. Special care is taken with the balance of the various revolving and reciprocating parts, the flywheel is lightened, compression ratio is increased to seven to one, the ports being enlarged

and polished; the cylinder head combustion spaces are polished also, and double valve springs are used. The induction manifold is different, two self-starting type Solex carburetters being fitted, and a four-branch straight-out exhaust manifold is employed, in conjunction, if required, with the Burgess silencing system.

As to the chassis, the springs are set up, big Andre or Luvax shock absorbers are provided, a sixteen-gallon fuel tank takes the place of the ordinary tank, and fuel is fed to the carburetters under pressure, there being a hand pump in

the driving compartment to maintain pressure. Rudge-Whitworth knock-off type wheels of the special pattern for Riley cars, recently described, take the place of the standard wheels, and two spare wheels can be fitted on a special mounting. As to performance, it is stated that the specially prepared engine gives approximately 60 b.h.p. at 6,000 r.p.m., and a speed of 80 m.p.h. is claimed.

The body is a specially built close-coupled four-seater, with a windscreen that folds forward flat, there being two small extra aero-type screens. Pneumatic upholstery and cushions are provided for the separate front seats, a six-inch rev counter is fitted, as well as oil and water thermometers. The price of the car is £375, exclusive of the Rudge wheels, which cost £15. fitting being extra.

It is appropriate to mention that this firm is about to move to modern premises now nearing completion at Weston Green, on the new by-pass from Hampton Court Bridge to the Kingston by-pass and Esher. Obviously a great deal of attention has been paid to the lay-out of this new place, in order that it shall be efficient, besides being pleasing to the eye. There is a covered entrance for the vehicles which come in for re-fuelling at the electrically operated petrol pumps, and good facilities are being provided for service work.

*The Gloucester Special Riley Nine.*

C 26

CHAPTER TEN

# The Riley Colour Schemes

The identification of Riley colour schemes falls logically into three periods: the pre-Great War era when people were not yet colour conscious, the side-valve era when all kinds of colours were experimented with, and the last decade when colour choice was very definitely a selling feature.

## 1899–1914

The early quadricycles, tricycles and motor bicycles (and pedal cycles too), were all offered in the then standard finish of Black, with lining in Vermilion, though other colours were available to the customer's choice.

By Tri-car days, the market had developed and a range of four colours were now offered as standard. These were Black lined with Vermilion, Red lined with Gold and White, Red and Grey similarly lined and Napier Green lined with Black and White. Other colours were again available to customers' choice, but were "Not recommended since delivery could be delayed as a result of the choice of a special colour finish".

The early four-wheeled cars were finished in Riley Blue, Black or Green and by now a premium of £2 had been applied to the option of customer-chosen special colours. The catalogue for 1913 shows Napier Green to be the only standard colour for the 10 h.p. and 12/18 h.p. cars quoting "The bodywork is painted Napier Green, with Black mouldings and white lines. The upholstering is Green leather of good quality. Although any colour can be had, purchasers are advised to order our standard colour, as otherwise delivery may possibly be delayed". Special colours were still available, but now at prices "from £2.10.0".

The 17/30 h.p. was subject to the same colour restrictions but, like the earlier cars, and in true Riley tradition, was produced in a variety of other colours as well as Napier Green.

## 1919–1928

After the Great War, as motor cars became more reliable and so were in greater demand, all manufacturers paid more attention to the range of colours offered with their cars. Most adopted a single standard range of colours available across the range of cars. Others, like Riley, adopted, for a short while, the practice of offering a single standard colour for each model in the range. Ultimately all manufacturers were obliged to offer a range of cars and a range of colours, giving the customer the choice and the dealer a stock headache!

In 1923, Riley was offering individual models with their own colours as shown below:

| All Season Two Seater | —Normandy Blue, Black wheels, wings and valance. |
| All Season Four Seater | —Mole, Normandy Blue or Smoke Grey with Black wheels, wings and valance. |

| Sports Two Seater | —Polished aluminium body with Red wheels chassis and wings. |
| All Season Four Seater (Sporting Type) | —Normandy Blue, Black wheels, wings and valance. |
| Coupé | —Smoke Blue, Black leather head, Black wheels, wings and valance. |
| Saloon | —Painted to choice (no colours specified). |
| Four Seater Coupé | —Royal Blue, Black enamelled wings, wheels and valances. |

For 1924, the range of colours was:

| Four Seater De Luxe | —Any colour to customer's choice but wheels, wings and valances Black. |
| Four Door Four Seater | —Brown or Grey with wheels, wings and valances Black. |
| Two Door Four Seater | —Brown or Grey with wheels, wings and valances Black. |
| Two Seater | —Brown or Grey with wheels, wings and valances Black. |
| Saloon De Luxe | —To customer's choice, with wheels wings and valances Black.. |
| Saloon | —Carmine Lake or Cobalt Blue with Black wheels, wings and valances. |
| Coupé | —Cobalt Blue with Black wheels, wings and valances. |
| Four Seater Sports | —Grey or Blue with Black chassis, wings and wheels. |
| Two Seater Sports | —Polished aluminium body with Red chassis wings and wheels. |
| Two/Three Seat Clover Leaf | —Polished aluminium body with Red chassis wings and wheels. |
| Two/Three Seater | —Brown or Grey with Black chassis, wheels and valances. |
| Four Seater Coupé | —Carmine Lake or Cobalt Blue with Black wheels, wings and valances. |
| Saloon Landaulette | —Black or Cobalt Blue with Black wheels, wings and valances. |

The 1925 colour choices were:

| Five Seater De Luxe | —Any colour to choice, Black wings, wheels and valances. |
| Special Touring Car | —Blue or Grey with Black wings, wheels and valances. |
| Saloon | —Carmine Lake or Riley Blue, Black wings, wheels and valances. |
| Saloon Landaulette | —Riley Blue with Black wings, wheels and valances. |
| Saloon De Luxe | —Any colour to choice, Black wings, wheels and valances. |
| Coupé | —Riley Blue with Black wings, wheels and valances. |
| Four/Five Seat Touring Car | —Brown with Black wings, valances and wheels. |
| Two/Six Seater | —Riley Blue with Black wings, wheels and valances. |
| Two Seater Sports / Four Seater Sports | —Polished aluminium body with Red chassis, wings and wheels. |

The Riley policy of finishing specific models in their own colours continued into 1926 and for that year, the choices were:

| | |
|---|---|
| Coupé<br>Coupé with Fixed Top } | —Dark Blue, Powder Blue or Carmine Lake with Black wings and wheels. |
| Coupé de Ville | —Riley Blue, but any other colour at no extra charge. |
| De Luxe Touring | —Dark Blue with the usual Black ancillaries. |
| Foleshill Touring | —Dark Blue or Carmine Lake only. |
| Four Seat Coach | —Dark Blue or Carmine Lake. |
| Four Seat Glass<br>Enclosed | —Brown, Dark Blue, Carmine Lake, Grey or Elephant Grey. |
| Saloon<br>Saloon Landaulette } | —Dark Blue, Carmine Lake, Brown, Powder Blue. |
| Saloon De Luxe | —To customer's choice. |
| Special Touring | —Egg Shell Black, Brown, Dark Blue, Carmine Lake, Grey, Elephant Grey. |
| Sports Two Seater<br>Sports Four Seater } | —Polished aluminium body with Red chassis, wheels and wings. |
| Four/Five Seat Tourer<br>Two/Six Seater } | —Brown, Dark Blue, Carmine Lake, Grey, Elephant Grey. |
| Two/Three Seater | —Dark Blue, Carmine Lake. |

In 1926, the chassis only was all black and in all cases except the Sports models the standard colour for wheels, wings and valances was Black.

For 1927 it was 'business as before' and the colour range was:

| | |
|---|---|
| Foleshill Tourer<br>Four Door Coach } | —Dark Blue or Carmine Lake. |
| Two/Six Tourer<br>Standard Tourer<br>Two/Six Glass Enclosed } | —Brown, Carmine Lake, Dark Blue, Grey, Elephant Grey. |
| Special 2 Door Tourer | —Black, Brown, Dark Blue, Carmine Lake, Grey, Elephant Grey. |
| Glass Enclosed Tourer | —Brown, Dark Blue, Carmine Lake, Grey, Elephant Grey. |
| De Luxe Tourer | —To customer's choice. |
| Coupé<br>Four Door Saloon } | —Dark Blue, Carmine Lake, Brown, Powder Blue. |
| Sports Two Seater<br>Sports Four Seater } | —Polished aluminium body with Red chassis, wings and wheels, or any colour to choice. |
| Saloon Landaulette | —Dark Blue, Carmine Lake, Brown, Powder Blue. |
| Saloon De Luxe<br>Coupé de Ville } | —To customer's choice. |

It will be seen that an attempt was beginning to be made to standardise colour choices by 1927, and now three distinct groups of colours were available according to model. However, by 1928 the range was widened and two-tone colours were now available for the last year of the side valve's production. The choices then for 1928 were:

| | |
|---|---|
| 12 h.p. Chassis and ⎫<br>Colonial Chassis ⎭ | —All Black. |
| Lulworth Saloon ⎫<br>Lulworth Special Saloon ⎭ | —Grey, Blue, Black, Carmine, Stone. |
| Standard Touring Car | —Brown, Dark Blue, Carmine Lake. |
| Four Door Coach | —Dark Blue, Carmine Lake. |
| Two/Six Seat Glass Enclosed | —Brown, Dark Blue, Carmine Lake. |
| Two Seat Sports ⎫<br>Four Seat Sports ⎬<br>Long Sports Four ⎭ | —Polished aluminium body with Red wheels,<br>wings and chassis, but any other colour was<br>available to choice at no extra cost. |
| Wentworth Coupé | —Carmine Lake, Dark Blue, Brown, Brown roof/Neutral Grey body. |
| Special Touring Car | —Egg Shell Black, Brown, Dark Blue, Carmine Lake. |
| Chatsworth Saloon | —Dark Blue, Carmine Lake, Brown. |
| Grangeworth Saloon | —Endel Brown/Neutral Grey, Powder Blue/Ivory Buff/Ivory or Black roof<br>with Carmine Lake, Brown, Powder Blue or Dark Blue. |
| Midworth Saloon | —Blue, Red or Brown. |
| Saloon De Luxe | —Colours and upholstery to choice. |

Upholsteries during these years varied in materials used, but were always a careful blend of colour with the coachwork colours. For example, in 1923 upholstery was in leather and Black leather was matched with mole paintwork, dark Blue leather with the choices of Blue, Green leather with Grey and of course you could have any other combination to your choice by special order.

In 1924 the saloons and Coupé were upholstered in Bedford Cord, the tourers and sports cars being in leather. Again, colours were always carefully matched to coachwork and again the customer had the last word if he wanted to place a special order—and wait for delivery, though deliveries were very rarely of an extended period.

1925 again saw Bedford Cord being used to upholster the Saloons, the Saloon Landaulette and the Coupé. The tourers and sports models were again upholstered in leather, but the De Luxe and Special models were upholstered in 'antique' leather.

The colour schemes for upholstering in 1926 and 1927 were pretty straightforward. If the car was Blue then the upholstery would be Blue, if the car was Carmine Lake, then the upholstery would be Red. A Black exterior would have been fitted with Red upholstery and Elephant Grey had Green upholstery. The lighter Grey used Grey upholstery. Again, two leather finishes were offered, antique in the De Luxe, Glass Enclosed, Special and Sports models, and in the Four Door Coach and Saloon. The other cars were fitted with plain leather in the appropriate colour. Bedford Cord was not offered in the standard range of upholstery for 1926 or 1927.

The increased range of 1928 brought a wider range of colours too and whilst, again, a standard range of colours was offered, all kinds of variations were supplied if the customer wanted something different. For example, a standard range of fabrics was offered on the Lulworth Fabric Saloon, but the catalogue quickly points out that, to order, you could combine any two fabric colours to provide a colour scheme with the roof in one colour and the body in another. In this case it was usual to paint the chassis, wings and wheels in the colour

of the roof. The upholstery to the Lulworth was Grey Moquette. All the other cars were upholstered in antique leather, in colours to match the coachwork as before. The Saloon De Luxe was still available any way you wanted it, any colour and any upholstery as required.

The 9 h.p. cars were now available too and these were offered in a much more conservative selection of exterior colours and upholsteries. The Monaco, the San Remo and the Two Seater were offered with exterior fabrics in Dark Blue, Carmine or Brown. The Four Seat Tourer and the Special Tourer were offered only in Dark Blue or Carmine. The saloons were originally fitted with Moquette upholstery, but later leather was universally used, the tourers having been fitted with leather from the beginning. Only three colours of leather upholstery were offered: Blue, Red and Brown, to match the exterior colours.

There were now standard prices for non-standard finishes, when the saloons were upholstered in Moquette, a non-standard material could be fitted at £2.10.0 extra, but leather was available for £5 extra. A non-standard exterior finish on those early Nines was also £5 extra. The early Brooklands Speed Models were offered in Red or Green with leather to match.

## 1929–1938

The 1929 season brought, with the 1928 Motor Show, improvements to the Nine and a new Light Six, a 6 cylinder car which was to be known as the Stelvio. Because it was a fabric saloon along the lines of the Biarritz, but bigger, it was offered with the same colour options. These were:

| | |
|---|---|
| 9 h.p. Monaco Saloon | —Blue, Brown or Maroon with antique leather upholstery to match. |
| 9 h.p. Biarritz Saloon ⎫<br>12 h.p. Stelvio Fabric Saloon ⎭ | —Blue, Brown, Maroon or Black and Red (red wheels chassis —and upholstery). Antique upholstery to match. |
| 9 h.p. Two Seater Tourer ⎫<br>9 h.p. Open Four Seater ⎭ | —Blue or Maroon with antique leather upholstery to match. |
| 9 h.p. Special Tourer | —Blue, Brown or Maroon with antique leather to match. |
| 9 h.p. Brooklands Speed Model | —Racing Red or Racing Green with plain leather to match. |

The 6 cylinder Deauville and 5 Seat Tourer were offered with the same colours, but in slightly different variations:

| | |
|---|---|
| Deauville Six Coach-built Saloon | —Blue, Brown, Maroon or Black with matching upholstery, or either Blue, Brown or Maroon lower half with Black uppers, wings and chassis. Wheels and upholstery to match colour. |
| 14 h.p. Five Seat Special Tourer | —Blue, Brown, Maroon or Black with matching upholstery. |

With the new 'Plus' Series 9 h.p. models and the new six cylinder cars of 1930/31, the colour range was widened slightly, but a standard range of colours now firmly existed. The colours were:

Black chassis, wings and lamps with Cream wheels (and water rail where appropriate) in combination with Blue Fabric and Blue Hide, Maroon Fabric and Red Hide, Brown Fabric and Brown Hide, Green Fabric and Green Hide. If Black or Grey Fabric were chosen, the wheels and water rail were coloured to match the upholstery colour, which could be Red or Green with Black and Green or Blue with Grey.

These colours applied to the Monaco, the Fabric Tourer, the Two Seat Coupé, the Alpine Tourer and the Stelvio. The Biarritz Saloon, the Edinburgh and Alpine Saloon were cellulosed below the waistline in a matching colour for the monotones and a complementary colour for the two-tones. The single colours were Brown, Black, Green and Grey; the two-tones being Blue or Maroon below the waist with matching upholstery and Black above the waistline.

The Brooklands was offered in the standard colours of Red or Green with matching upholstery, or in any other colour to the customer's choice at no extra cost.

Again, variations from standard were available at extra cost for all of the Saloons and Tourers.

By 1932 the range of cars offered had again widened pretty considerably and the new 9 h.p. and six cylinder models combined to make a very wide range of cars, so the Company had obviously decided it was time to standardise a range of colours which would be available throughout the range of cars. The basic colours available were, between 1932 and 1934, Black, Blue, Red, Brown, Fawn, Grey, Green and Ivory and these were available to order in any two-tone combination the customer might choose, to special order. However, the standard combinations of colours were:

| Body above Waistline | Body below Waistline | Colour of Upholstery | Chassis & Wings | Colour of Wheels |
|---|---|---|---|---|
| Black | Black | Red | Black | Red |
| Black | Black | Green | Black | Green |
| Black | Black | Brown | Black | Ivory |
| Black | Blue | Blue | Black | Blue |
| Black | Red | Red | Black | Red |
| Black | Grey | Red | Black | Grey |
| Brown | Fawn | Brown | Brown | Fawn |
| Grey | Grey | Green | Grey | Green |
| * | Ivory | Red | Red | Ivory |

*Open cars only.

Certain models offered through the Riley sales organisation, like the March Special, were offered with different colour schemes, because the bodies were not made by the Riley companies and in most cases were to order anyway. The March Special did feature in the 1933 season's catalogue (published in 1932) and it was basically offered in single or two tone with any two colours available from the range of: Bright Racing Green, Italian Racing Red, French Racing Blue, Grey, Light Green, Dark Blue, Black or Cherry Red with upholsteries to tone. As before, if you did not like what you were offered, you could have what you wanted at extra cost. The prices for non-standard variations were:

| | |
|---|---|
| Chassis non-standard colour | £2.10.0 |
| Wheels non-standard colours | £2.10.0 |
| Wings (including lamps) non standard colour | £5.0.0 |
| Body above waistline non-standard colour | £5.0.0 |
| Body below waistline, or open car body, non-standard colour. | £5.0.0 |
| Upholstery non-standard colour (not quality) | £7.10.0 |

One extra colour choice was available in 1934, on cars finished in Grey. They were available with Blue upholstery.

The new range of cars offered for the 1935 season brought little variation in colours,

except that there was another upholstery colour option for the Grey cars—they were now available with Red interior and Red wheels. It appears that this was the result of popular demand; since May 1934 cars were finished in Grey with Red trim and wheels and seemingly at extra cost.

The expanded 1936 range of 1½ litre cars and the new 9 h.p. Merlin model brought a re-shuffled range of colours. The Merlin had its own special range of colours, different from the others, perhaps a clear sign of the hopes that Riley pinned on this new low priced car for their future. As had been the case since 1932, open cars took their colour schemes from 'below the waistline' of the closed cars. So, the standard range of colours for 1936 was:

| Body above Waistline | Body below Waistline | Colour of Upholstery | Chassis & Wings | Colour of Wheels |
|---|---|---|---|---|
| Black | Black | Red | Black | Red |
| Black | Black | Green | Black | Green |
| Black | Black | Brown | Black | Brown |
| Black | Blue | Blue | Black | Blue |
| Black | Red | Red | Black | Red |
| Grey | Grey | Green | Grey | Green |
| Grey | Grey | Blue | Grey | Blue |
| Battleship Grey | Battleship Grey | Red | Battleship Grey | Red |
| Battleship Grey | Battleship Grey | Blue | Battleship Grey | Blue |

The Merlin was only offered in single-tone colours, but a wider choice:

| Colour of Body, Chassis & Wings | Colour of Upholstery | Colour of Wheels |
|---|---|---|
| Brown | Brown | Ivory |
| Black | Red | Red |
| Black | Green | Green |
| Grey | Blue | Blue |
| Grey | Green | Green |
| Grey | Red | Red |
| Battleship Grey | Red | Red |
| Battleship Grey | Blue | Blue |
| Red | Red | Red |
| Blue | Blue | Blue |
| Green | Green | Green |

The variations were as before and their prices remained stable (they were to continue at the same level until 1938—option prices stable for 6 years!). The only exception was that there was an extra cost of £5 for carpeting to match a non-standard upholstery colour. Also, the price for painting the Merlin a non-standard colour was £10, because there were no two-tones so it was the sum of the prices for colours above and below the waistline on other models.

The 1937 season's cars were offered with the same colour schemes as for the previous year and the options on colours and trims revised in the same form and at the same prices. The colour schemes applying to the Merlin in 1936 now applied to the new Monaco saloon as well.

The rationalisation of the range for 1938 brought a modest revision of colours and the standard colour range for all models except the Victor Saloon was:

| Colour of Body | Colour of Upholstery | Chassis & Wings | Colour of Wheels |
|---|---|---|---|
| Black | Beige | Black | Ivory |
| Black | Red | Black | Red |
| Black | Green | Black | Green |
| Sea Green | Red | Sea Green | Red |
| Battleship Grey | Red | Battleship Grey | Red |
| Battleship Grey | Blue | Battleship Grey | Blue |
| Red | Red | Red | Red |
| Blue | Blue | Blue | Blue |
| Blue | Beige | Blue | Ivory |

The Victor Saloon was available in:

| Body, Chassis & Wings | Upholstery | Wheels |
|---|---|---|
| Black | Beige | Green |
| Black | Beige | Ivory |
| Black | Red | Red |
| Red | Red | Red |
| Red | Beige | Red |
| Sea Green | Beige | Sea Green |
| Sea Green | Red | Red |

Turning now to the subject of badge colours, the question often arises: "what colour should the badge be on my Riley?".

In the V-twin days, the horizontal badge with the Riley name in block capitals—and the oval Riley badge which was the immediate forerunner of the blue diamond-shaped badge— were finished in dark blue vitreous enamel. The side-valve cars carrying the Riley diamond had the badge finished also in dark blue vitreous enamel, though some of the later cars appear to have had light blue enamel ones. A number of early 9 h.p. cars also had light blue badges, but then, when the size of the badge was reduced the great majority were either dark blue or not coloured at all. It was during the 1938 Season that the dark blue vitreous enamel came back into use.

The end of the colourful era of Rileys came in 1938, but it can be seen that Riley was an individual in the industry, in its colour schemes as much as in its products. It was all part of 'Rileyability'.

# CHAPTER ELEVEN

# 'Rileyability'—Owners' Views and Road Tests

The word 'Rileyability' comes from a Riley advertisement of the early Twenties, when the side-valve car was approaching the peak of its success. But it serves well to describe the qualities which always set Rileys apart from the beginning.

Percy and Stanley Riley were both endowed with an obsession for quality and ease of operation in their products and this quality was always a cornerstone of the Company's advertising.

Advertising and the presentation of catalogues were always considered important features of successful sales and so Riley catalogues were meticulously prepared to lead the prospective Riley owner to his new charge. The English of the day was rather elaborate and Riley catalogues and advertisements made the most use of it.

One great feature of any campaign to sell a product is what is known as 'testimonial advertising' and Riley always made good use of that. The Company was fortunate in that the press, as well as the public, liked their cars and so they always had a very healthy fund of complimentary press statements and owners' letters from which to draw.

This chapter could well have been just an appendix with a few road tests, but if it had, much of the important material of private individuals' views would have been missed. Road tests it has, and they are set at the end of the chapter, but the owners' opinions are perhaps more important, because they were the people to whom the Riley company directed its innovative skills, design and product qualities and it was they who determined how successful the Company was in its objectives.

Some of the early Riley owners' letters make most interesting reading today, but there is a danger of reading them in the context of modern motoring, so the reader must be reminded to visualise the conditions of roads and the state of development of the industry before deciding the quality of achievement for himself.

One superb example of an owner's testimonial—and a clear demonstration of the durability and reliability of early Riley cars, in this case the V-twin—is a letter written by Mr. W. H. Smith of Kidderminster on 2nd November 1912. It reads: "I write to tell you what a splendid little car the 10 h.p. Riley is. As you known I bought one of your works demonstration cars in February 1910 and you had the tyres re-treaded before delivering it. I have driven it almost daily ever since and it has now done more than 20,000 miles. I have only had six new covers during that time and for sixteen months I have never had occasion to use the spare wheel.

In addition to the lightness on tyres I find it very economical on petrol, never doing less than 30 miles to the gallon and in a test made a few months ago, I found the actual consumption was 7 gallons for 230 miles.

By far the greatest expense I have been to with it was having a magneto fitted, of engine troubles there have been none and the car is running as well now as ever: in fact it is faster on the level and more powerful on hills than before the magneto was fitted, although it is now at least $3\frac{1}{2}$ years old."

Another, more brief, but as pertinent letter came from Mr. George N. Jessop F.A.I.:

"I have just completed 20,000 miles on my 1909 12/18 h.p. Riley Two Seated Car and I think it right to tell you that during that mileage my car ran like a clock and I had no mechanical repairs of any kind: the original spark plugs are still in use.

The whole cost of my repair bills is 12s 4d.

The Riley detachable wire wheels which you sent me last year gave me no trouble and appear today as good as when I got them."

That was the V-twin. By the time the Great War had ended and Riley had resumed motor car production, now with the side-valve four cylinder cars, the press was responding to its qualities thus:

"It is seldom one handles a car which from the first strikes one as a real thoroughbred, and this impression added to my enjoyment in driving the Riley.

There are ample evidences of real brains in its design and construction, weight has been kept down, but I have never known a car which held the road better, or was less fatiguing to drive. The steering is light and certain, and requires the absolute minimum of effort."

This quotation is from 'A Road-Farer's Log' of the *Daily Graphic* published on 10th January 1922.

Of the 11 h.p. Four Seat Coupé, J. D. of Dundalk said in January 1923: "The car is a beauty, being comfortable to drive, pulls beautifully on hills, accelerates like an eight cylinder machine, and is capable of a high average over long journeys."

The *Autocar* issue of 18th May 1923, in reviewing the Six Days Scottish Trials, said: "Walsgrave's Riley is, of course, a famous car with 48,000 miles to its credit. It seems faster than ever, and devours mountain summits as a bear eats buns at the Zoo."

The same *Autocar* article went on to say: "The knowing watchers always clear the road when the Sporting Riley takes a hill, and the speedometer must have been oscillating near the '30' mark all the way up."

So the reputation of Riley cars was sown. Owners and press alike continued to sing their praises and extol their virtues. During the middle years of the side-valve's production, a little less was made of press statements, the Company preferring now to let road test reports stand on their own as testimonials to their products, together with the log of competition successes that Riley cars had amassed.

Long-distance runs were still promotional features for any make of car and Rileys were every bit as good as, if not better than most. For example early in 1926 a Riley Twelve side-valve Overseas Tourer was driven by Mr. L. T. Galton-Fenzi over the Pioneer Trail from Nairobi to Mombasa in what was then British East Africa (Kenya). The Riley succeeded where other vehicles, even with tracks, had failed and 56 punctures were the only mishaps. No mechanical failures occurred and the road taken then is now a tarmacadam highway. The car was sent to Nairobi, after being prepared for its ordeal, by the Riley company and it is interesting to note that it is today in the hands of the East African Automobile Association in Nairobi and is on permanent display in their headquarters.

It was when the Riley Nine was introduced that the Company returned to the use of press commendations—and with very good reason. In those days the Press were generally

very complimentary to the Riley Company and its products. It was the press who dubbed the Riley Nine 'The Wonder Car'.

One of the correspondents of the *Autocar*, with the pen-name of 'Runabout', took a Riley Nine Tourer on a Continental tour of 2,500 miles, at the end of which he had this to say:

"This is a car which one can unreservedly recommend to one's friends. It averages about 36 m.p.g. of fuel and 1000 m.p.g. of oil. Capable of well over 50 m.p.h. on top, it can climb all normally steep hills on second, and should fear no freak ascent on first. The steering is perfect and the suspension really good. The engine is a glutton for work and most admirably balanced. The general impression created by our month on it is that there is no possible need to buy anything larger for work with a crew of four; it operates and handles like a large car, and the fact of its minute horse power never enters one's head."

A reprint of that article was available from Riley (Coventry) Limited upon request and doubtless served to finally convince a considerable number of prospective owners who were teetering on the brink of buying. The article was written, incidentally, in 1927, when the side-valve models were still going strong.

Another correspondent, writing of the Riley Nine shortly after its introduction, said: "It happens sometimes that an entirely new car of unusually interesting design proves in practice to be something of a disappointment, particularly in the early stages of development. But in the case of the Riley Nine, which made its first appearance at the last Olympia Show and created no little stir, the performance of the car is, on the whole, even better than the promise. The specification delineates a small car, the behaviour of the actual vehicle is comparable with that of a medium-sized automobile and, moreover, one of considerable refinement."

A beautifully presented little book appeared in 1930, written by Edward H. Reeves, who was then the Secretary of the Riley Motor Club, entitled 'The Riley Romance'. It was well written and presented a review of the Riley family business between 1890 and 1930. It was in 1890 that William Riley, we are told, bought out the cycle manufacturing business of Bonnick and Company. He was then 39. We are then told how the Riley Weaving Company was wound up in 1896 and the name of the cycle business changed to the Riley Cycle Company Limited. The book then summarises the progress of the Company into the field of mechanically-propelled vehicles and ultimately cars. We are also given a very brief glimpse into some of the events which shaped the lives of the Riley brothers. Particularly we are told of their personal successes in competition, of the sad death of their mother at the age of only 55 in 1909 and of the sacrifice of all profit in the cause of the Great War. The book was published by Riley (Coventry) Limited and was somehow the means of securing a bond between the Company and its enthusiasts. The general body of its text is an excellent insight to the Company of that time.

And so we progress. The Silent Third gearbox fitted to the Riley Nine was an immense success and of it, 'A.G.T.' of the *Sunday Dispatch* said: "I have come to the conclusion that the biggest contributor to Motor Noise is the gearbox. Of every ten cars that pass, about nine make hideous outcry when running on any but top . . . there is one solitary exception and as such it deserves honourable mention—the little Riley Nine has a gearbox so constructed that it is as silent on third as it is on top."

By the publication of the catalogue introducing the 'Plus' Series 9 h.p. models, we are presented with a mixture of views of press and public:

The *Motor* of 23 September 1930 said: "The specification of the 9 h.p. chassis is now comparable with that of much larger and more costly products."

Captain R. W. S. of London wrote in September 1930: "I bought a Riley in May, and for 6000 miles have enjoyed more care-free motoring than in my previous ten years experience on 3 wheels or 4."

The *Motor World* of 26th September 1930 commented: "We have driven few cars which revealed character so quickly, and anyone who enjoys driving will regret leaving the wheel of this very charming model."

Owners' views continued to sing the praises of Rileys long and loud, and by 1932 such quotations were being published as:

"In twenty years driving experience, I have never handled so easily controlled a car as my Riley, and the reserve power 'under the toe' is always a surprise."

Also:

"I wrote to you when my car had covered 6,000 miles and told you it had not cost me a penny piece for repairs. Today it has covered 10,900 miles and its performance has really been so excellent that, although this has been my first Riley, my next car must be a Riley too."

And:

"I have been connected with the Motor Industry for 32 years and when I retired recently, looked round for a car which would give me pleasure to drive, comfort, reliability and speed with safety . . . I have driven most makes of cars, but I don't remember any which has given me more pleasure and satisfaction than my Riley."

So it went on. By 1935 the 1½ litre cars were available and the praises continued. *The Motor*, in its issue of 15th January 1935, said: "The chief charm of the performance lies in the manner in which mile after mile can be reeled off, with the speedometer needle above the 60 m.p.h. mark, without fuss or noise. To average 40 m.p.h. over a distance of 100 miles is a simple matter without apparently forcing the pace in any way; on one journey we averaged 45 m.p.h. over a distance of 80 miles."

*The Autocar* Olympia Show Review of 12th October 1934 opens its review of Riley with: "Few cars can claim with as much justification as the Riley Nine to have given a lead in light car design."

The 1935 *Autocar* Show Review says: "The cars on this stand are worthy of the closest study, in both mechanism and coachwork, not only for their originality of conception, but also in view of the fact that their performance on the road is marked by unusual accuracy of control, and by steady safety at speed."

The same magazine in October 1936: "Famous for the way in which they hold the road, and for the charm that lies in driving behind their efficient engines the Riley reputation was built up on the 9 h.p. car, it has been more than sustained by the 1½ litre 11.9 h.p. series."

And finally, for the last Motor Show in which the products of the family business were to take part, *The Autocar* has this to say: "Honourable mention of the Riley name has been marked in so many pages of British motoring history that the activities of this old-established firm are always of immediate interest to those who take pleasure in the handling of especially roadworthy cars. Successful experience in international racing and competition has taught Rileys how to make exceptionally fine touring vehicles. . . ."

A fitting quotation upon which to end the chapter of 'Rileyability'.

*September 20, 1927.* 317 The Motor

*Read Tests Showing Principal Characteristics.*

# The 9 h.p. Riley Sports Fabric Saloon.

## A Refined Small Car with an Exceptional Road Performance.

SINCE the Riley Nine was introduced at the last Olympia Motor Show there have been one or two minor alterations made to the chassis, thereby adding to the refinement in performance. The engine is now fitted with B.H.B. pistons and a system of "rocker boxes" has been incorporated to enable valve adjustment to be more conveniently accomplished, while a "hot-spot" has been provided to the carburetter in a very ingenious manner. There has also been an alteration to the propeller shaft. It will be recalled that the transmission is enclosed. The enclosing tube is now swaged down in the centre to carry an additional bearing to the propeller shaft.

At first sight, although the car possesses extremely pleasing lines,

This view plainly illustrates the low overall height of the Riley fabric saloon.

The car is very roomy and a driver well above the average in stature can be accommodated in comfort.

one becomes a little dubious as to whether there is sufficient leg room for medium-sized passengers. In actual fact, the leg room is exceptionally good, considering the size of the vehicle, and although one can look over the top of the body with perfect ease, a six-footer can sit at the wheel with his legs straight out and with a reasonable amount of head room. The width of the body also enables two large passengers to sit in either the front or rear seats without being cramped — thanks largely to the barrel-shaped sides.

The engine is a four-cylinder monobloc, with a bore and stroke of 60 mm. and 95 mm. respectively, the crankcase being formed integral with the cylinders. The crankshaft is supported in two main bearings and is accurately balanced. Both the crankshaft bearings and the big-end bearings of the connecting rods are supplied with oil under high pressure from a plunger-type pump, the pistons and camshaft gear being

lubricated by splash. Probably the most interesting feature is the arrangement for the o.h.v. gear. Inclined overhead valves are located in a detachable cylinder head and are operated by rockers and push-rods from two camshafts that are housed in the crankcase, the push-rods lying alongside and parallel to the cylinder bores.

Mention has already been made of the new "rocker boxes." These consist of an arrangement whereby access can be obtained to the rockers for valve adjustment. Actually there are four boxes (each enclosed by a cover) which are sprung on to the rocker shafts.

A cone-type clutch and four forward-speed gearbox with right-hand control are formed unit-wise with the engine. There is an interesting feature concerning the gear control—

**TYPE:** *Sports fabric saloon, price £298.*

**ENGINE:** *Four-cylinder monobloc, inclined overhead valves operated by push-rods. Bore, 60 mm.; stroke, 95 mm.; 1,075 c.c. R.A.C. rating, 9.01 h.p.*

**GEARBOX:** *Four forward speeds, right-hand control.*

**SUSPENSION:** *Semi-elliptics front and rear. Shock absorbers all round.*

**BRAKES:** *Internal-expanding, fully compensated, operating on all four wheels by pedal.*

**MAXIMUM SPEED ON GEARS AND RATIOS:** *1st (20.3 to 1), 16 m.p.h.; 2nd (13.1 to 1), 28 m.p.h.; 3rd (7.6 to 1), 46 m.p.h.; top (5.2 to 1), 60 m.p.h.*

**TURNING CIRCLES:** *Left, 36 ft.; right, 39 ft. 10 ins.*

**PETROL CONSUMPTION:** *34 m.p.g. measured over 450 miles.*

**WHEELBASE:** *8 ft. 10½ ins.; track, 3 ft. 11 ins.; overall length, 12 ft.; overall width, 4 ft. 7 ins.; height, 5 ft. 2 ins.*

**WEIGHT:** *(As tested with two passengers) 19 cwt. 3 qrs.*

**RILEY (Coventry), Ltd., COVENTRY.**

the quadrant, complete with the lever, can be swung round to suit individual requirements of reach. Thus a tall driver with the driving seat in the rearmost position would require the lever to be inclined backwards, while a short driver with the seat well forward could very easily swing the gear quadrant forward

The neat power unit. Note the accessible position of the magneto.

until his particular requirements regarding reach are suited.

The controls are all very light, there being little difference between the amount of pressure required for the clutch, accelerator or brake pedals, while the steering, although positive, is also reasonably light. Engine starting throughout our test was practically instantaneous, a dashboard-operated strangler facilitating matters when starting up from cold. There was never any need, however, to flood the carburetter.

Gear-changing was very easy,

B31

The Motor      318      *September 20, 1927.*

## RILEY.—Contd.

upward changes requiring slight pauses to be made with the lever in neutral, if the engine was speeded up appreciably on the indirect ratios. Changing-down, however, necessitated the double-declutch method if perfectly silent changes were to be

obtained; on the other hand, the lever could be pushed straight through the gate without undue noise emanating from the gearbox, providing the road speed was not too high.

### Good Performance on Third Gear.

In passing, it might be mentioned that one of the most delightful features of this new Riley is the fine performance on third gear. When driving, it is difficult to tell whether top gear or third gear has been engaged, and there is only a very slight noise when over-running in third. This degree of silence has been obtained by making the constant-mesh pinions and the third-gear pinions with helical-gear teeth. The third gear pinions must, of course, be also in constant mesh, so that dog clutches are used for the engagement of both gears. On third speed 46 m.p.h. could be obtained without over-revving the engine in the slightest.

After 450 miles of very hard running the engine ran with its pristine silence, and the speed and power did not appear to have been affected in the slightest. On normal main-road work the car seemed to possess all the attributes of the large, powerful vehicle, with the added advantage that it was very easy to control. By virtue of its small overall dimensions one could wriggle in and out of traffic with surprising ease and perfect safety. With the throttle about one-third open the car was found to be capable of 40 m.p.h., but all the while the engine seemed to be asking for more and more speed. In a very short time the speedometer

n32

needle would creep up to 60 m.p.h., a speed which could be maintained even on slight up-hill grades. On quite severe inclines, however, the little engine would pull away merrily with the speedometer well above the 50 m.p.h. mark, the car meanwhile sitting in the road in quite a convincing manner.

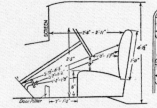

(Left) Graphs showing respectively the top gear acceleration and the retardation of the four-wheel braking system.

(Above) The chief dimensions of the four-seater saloon body.

The performance appeared to be too good to be true, so we made haste to bring out stop-watches and check the speedometer. It is sufficient to say that on several practically level stretches a mile was covered in slightly under and slightly over one minute, while at 40 m.p.h., if anything, the speedometer was inclined to read slightly slow. On one occasion under favourable circumstances with a following wind and on a slightly down-hill grade, the speedometer recorded 67 m.p.h., and on many occasions 65 m.p.h. was attained.

Although on main roads for the

majority of our run we did not find a hill sufficiently severe to necessitate a change-down into a lower ratio than top. When a detour was made, however, and hilly parts of the Cotswolds were encountered, gradients were found which required second gear but not bottom. We should say it would take a very severe single-figure freak hill to bring the Riley on to its lowest ratio, and, providing the wheels would grip, it would be almost impossible to fail.

### Stability on Corners.

The general handiness of the Riley Nine enabled good average speeds to be maintained even on roads where the contour is winding. By virtue of the low build, corners could be taken surprisingly fast without the slightest trace of a skid or any other feature which might be termed dangerous or disconcerting. The brakes, too, are a great help in maintaining a good average speed, and although the stopping distances are not exceptionally small, the brakes act with a smoothness and general sweetness that conduces to make driving a pleasure.

Summing up, we found the 9 h.p. Riley sports saloon to be a fast, well-mannered little vehicle. It is comfortable for both front and rear passengers and it is easy to drive—features which should make a distinct appeal to the lady driver.

Another view of the Riley which shows the nice lines and the large trunk provided.

April 14, 1931. 429 The **Motor**

*Road Tests Showing Principal Characteristics*

# THE RILEY SIX STELVIO SALOON

## A Car with Attractive Lines and a Good All-round Performance

A photograph which shows to advantage the attractive lines of the six-cylinder Riley Stelvio fabric four-door saloon.

THE Stelvio model Riley may be considered as the logical development of the well-established and popular Nine. Apart from the engine, which, by the way, is built on exactly the same general lines as its famous smaller brother, but has six cylinders instead of four, the chassis portrays the " Nine " in all essential respects, and as such it is obvious that the latest principles of construction are employed; moreover, the peculiar layout of the frame permits very attractive lines for the coachwork to be embodied in the design.

### Excellent Seating Accommodation

The Stelvio is not a small car, although such an impression might be created by the compact, close-coupled body, which is standardized. Actually, there is plenty of room for four passengers, in addition to the driver, to be seated in comfort, and, what is important, they are all located well within the wheelbase—an arrangement which, of course, makes for comfortable riding qualities and stability when cornering or traversing rough road surfaces. At the rear a luggage container is provided which, although of large capacity, is not at all obtrusive; a hinged back panel allows access to the interior.

In general build the Stelvio is exceptionally low, and, in consequence, one can drive almost as if it were a sports model pure and simple, taking corners at a fast pace with perfect safety.

From a driver's point of view it

The tools are stored in a container underneath the bonnet.

is very attractive, for the engine responds instantly to a touch of the starter-button, warms up quickly to its normal working temperature and is sufficiently powerful to ensure a good all-round top-gear performance. Despite the moderate capacity of the cylinders the unit produces an excellent torque figure at low and moderate rates of revolution speed, and, moreover, it is capable of high maximum revolution speeds, a noticeable feature being that the power does not fall off rapidly beyond the point where maximum power is being developed.

On the indirect gears the engine evinces marked liveliness, but combines the characteristic of refinement throughout its whole speed range; so much so, that one is always apt to under-estimate the speed at which one is travelling. First impressions gave us the idea that the speedometer was rather optimistic in its reading, but investigation against the stop-watch proved that it was recording with perfect accuracy.

It is clear, too, that the induction system has been planned after very careful investigation into the matter of distribution, because it is possible to throttle down to under 5 m.p.h. and then to accelerate quite smoothly by banging the accelerator pedal hard down—a very severe test, especially for a relatively small, high-speed power unit.

### Performance on Hills

On hills the Stelvio has a good performance. Practically all main-road gradients can be surmounted at 40 m.p.h. without rushing matters, a case in point being Meriden Hill, on the Birmingham-Coventry road. When tackling single-figure gradients the silent third speed comes in really usefully, for it is so planned that 40 m.p.h can be exceeded on this ratio of 8.39 to 1 without the engine emitting signs of distress. The maximum possible speed on third gear is in the region of 50 m.p.h., so that the engine is operating well within its powers when climbing at 40 m.p.h. Despite a fairly low top-gear ratio the power unit is quite

c1

The Motor                    430                    *April 14, 1931.*

## THE RILEY SIX STELVIO SALOON—Contd.

unobtrusive at high speeds and entirely free from vibration, while "power roar" hardly exists.

Although the steering appeared to be a trifle heavy (possibly one of the joints had run dry, so causing stiffness), there is a directness about it which gives the driver a sense of security and enables the car to be steered with great accuracy even at high speeds on rough going. The clutch pedal is light in operation

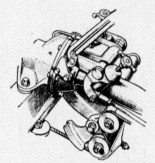

The hand and foot-operated braking system can be adjusted from the driving seat, the two screws projecting through the floorboards.

It is, of course, necessary to use the double-declutch method for a downward change when travelling fast, but no great accuracy is required. First and second gears, the pinions for which are of the ordinary plain spur type, are reasonably quiet, and the third gear, for which helical teeth are used, is to all intents and purposes silent in operation when driving, and emits only slight noise on the overrun.

Mention should be made of the braking system, for a very desirable feature has been incorporated in the layout. We refer, of course, to the manner in which both hand and foot systems can be adjusted from the driver's seat while the car is in motion. Two knobs project through the floorboards, each operating a self-locking screw, which, when turned, takes up any slackness in the operating mechanism. These adjustments were found to be particularly useful when touring in hilly districts.

Long semi-elliptic springs with fairly low frequencies ensure comfortable riding, and as most of the damping is controlled by Andre shock absorbers it is possible to alter the characteristic of the suspension to suit varied road conditions. If, for example, one intends to run about town at comparatively low speeds, a couple of turns of the shock-absorber nuts give a thoroughly delightful softness, but, on the other hand, the

Showing the ample provision for luggage, the two rear windows and the accessible petrol filler.

and the engagement of the friction surfaces is smooth, providing the driver engages the pedal slowly; the take-up of the drive occurs within comparatively narrow limits of the pedal.

Gear-changing is absurdly simple even at comparatively high speeds.

suspension is equally suitable (provided a shock-absorber adjustment is made) for fast cross-country work.

### Good Driving Vision

One small point, but a very important one, is worth recording. The windows are so arranged that the driver has very few blind spots. The windscreen pillars, for example, are narrow, and although a high waistline is provided an excellent view all round can be obtained. Thanks to large dual rear windows reversing is a simple matter, and even in a restricted space the Stelvio can be manœuvred without difficulty.

In conclusion, this Riley model successfully fills a niche in the British market. It is suitable for the enthusiast or the ordinary everyday driver.

## TABULATED DATA FOR THE DRIVER.

**CHASSIS DETAILS.**

*Riley:* Stelvio fabric saloon; six cylinders, 60.3 mm. by 95.2 mm. (1,633 c.c.). Tax £14. Inclined overhead valves; coil ignition.

*Gearbox:* Silent third and central control; ratios, 5.75, 8.39, 14.37 and 22.31 to 1. Engine speed, 1,346 r.p.m. at 20 m.p.h. on top.

**PERFORMANCE.**

*Speeds on Gears:* Top, 62 m.p.h.; third, 50 m.p.h.; second, 29 m.p.h. Minimum speed on top gear, 5 m.p.h.

*Petrol Consumption:* 19.3 m.p.g.

*Acceleration:* Standstil. to 50 m.p.h. through the gears, 32 secs.

**DIMENSIONS, Etc.**

Wheelbase, 10 ft.; track, 4 ft. 8 ins.; overall length, 13 ft.; width, 5 ft. 7 ins.

*Turning Circles:* Left and right, 40 ft.

*Weight:* (As tested with two up), 1 ton 8¼ cwt.

*Price:* £398.

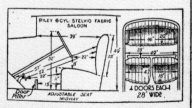

| SPEED. m.p.h. | STOP. feet. |
|---|---|
| 10 | — 7 |
| 20 | — 19 |
| 30 | — 39 |
| 40 | — 75 |
| 50 | — 140 |

BRAKES.

6-CYL RILEY STELVIO SALOON ACCELERATION CURVES ROAD—DRY TARMAC

RILEY 6CYL. STELVIO FABRIC SALOON

4 DOORS EACH 28" WIDE

Door Pillar    ADJUSTABLE SEAT MIDWAY

The Light Car 168 JUNE 29, 1934.

ROAD TESTS OF 1934 MODELS

# The
# 12 H.P. RILEY
# KESTREL

*with*

## THREE CARBURETTERS
*and*
## PRESELECTAGEAR

First Test of
a Fascinating
75 m.p.h. Model

AT once let it be said that this is an outstanding car. As no road test report of the Special Series 12 h.p. Riley has yet appeared in any motoring journal, it is probable that few people realize the excellent performance of the model.

Since "What will she do?" is commonly the first question asked about a car, let it be answered first. Against the stop-watch over a measured quarter-mile this Riley exceeded 76 m.p.h., and its average speed both ways was exactly 75 m.p.h. That is worth emphasizing—a genuine 75 m.p.h. with no advantage from wind or gradient.

As usual with Rileys, the speedometer was remarkably accurate. During the above tests, its highest reading was 77 m.p.h. According to its showing, the car just exceeded 60 m.p.h. in third gear.

Speed on the level is, of course, not the only important part of a car's performance. Equally essential are acceleration and hill-climbing. Regular readers of this series will know that anything as low as 25 secs. for the standing start ¼-mile is particularly good. The Riley clocked 24⅔ secs. Part of the credit for that must undoubtedly be given to the self-changing gearbox. The ability of the engine, however, is well shown by the way this Riley will sail at 50 m.p.h. or more in "top" up hills which bring many sports cars down to 40 m.p.h.

Speed, to be useful, must be available with safety. In this the Riley excels. Not only does it hold the road well, but its brakes are thoroughly up to their work.

B16

It has been said that streamlining brings, as a sort of by-product, better road-holding. Whether or not that is true, this Riley Kestrel is definitely above the average.

On a corner it sits square and level. To take an open bend just that little bit faster calls for no heroic work at the wheel. Most of the cars tested by us in the Midlands pass along a certain private road on which there is a shallow S-bend. Although on no previous occasion has this been taken at more than 50 m.p.h., the Riley went through it at 70 m.p.h. No doubt some other cars could have done the same, but the Riley simply pleaded for it.

Evidently this is a car for high averages. Yet it is not simply a speed machine. Pottering is just as much within its sphere, when the driver is in that mood. Despite a compression ratio which is high, the six-cylinder engine is very flexible. It will roll the car along smoothly in top gear at little more than a walking pace. By virtue of the automatic clutch, even lower speeds can be maintained without resorting to an indirect gear.

This clutch, it will be remembered, is not directly

JUNE 29, 1934.                    169                               The Light Car

(*Above*) *An off-side view of the 12 h.p. six-cylinder engine showing the three carburetters.*

(*Above*) *The engine from the exhaust side.* (*Left*) *A glimpse of the instrument board and controls.*

controlled by the driver. It depends for its drive not upon springs as usual, but upon the force exerted by weights which move outwards under centrifugal force as the clutch revolves.

Light springs oppose these weights so that when the engine is idling the clutch is not engaged. As the driver depresses the accelerator the engine speed increases and the weights exert an ever-growing force which pushes the clutch friction surfaces together. Thus engagement and disengagement of the clutch are quite automatic and depend simply on engine speed.

Owing to the very ample dimensions, this clutch will withstand a great deal of what would be abuse to any ordinary clutch. Consequently the Riley can be driven in top gear at less than a mile an hour, the clutch automatically adjusting its slip. Obviously this is an acid test.

Naturally, too, a restart can be made in "top." As an experiment, this proceeding was timed. From a standstill with top gear engaged and touching no controls but the accelerator and the steering wheel, 20 m.p.h. was reached in 11½ secs.—which is pretty good going.

In view of all that has been said, it might pardonably be imagined that this must be a vehicle in which body space has been reduced to a minimum so that every ounce shall be saved. That is not so.

The weight, as may be seen from the data panel, is substantial. The body space is ample. Its interior width is all but 4 ft. Between the armrests of the rear seat the dimension is 39½ ins. With the front seats forward, the fore-and-aft space for the rear passenger is 27 ins., and even when the bucket seats are in the rear-

## THE 12 H.P. RILEY KESTREL
### (*Continued*).

**IN BRIEF.**

ENGINE: Six cylinder, o.h. valve, 57 mm. by 95.2 mm.=1,458 c.c. Tax £12; Power output 50 b.h.p. at 4,800 r.p.m. Three Zenith carburetters.

TRANSMISSION: Automatic clutch, four-speed self-changing gearbox. Ratios 5.5, 7.84, 11.64 and 20.1 to 1. Reverse 25.2 to 1. Final drive by enclosed propeller shaft and spiral bevel.

GENERAL: Cable-operated brakes; semi-elliptic springs front and rear; 11-gallon rear tank.

DIMENSIONS: Wheelbase 9 ft. 6 ins.; track 4 ft. 0 ins.; overall length 13 ft. 9 ins.; overall width 4 ft. 9 ins.; weight 22 cwt. 3 qrs. 14 lb. Turning circle 35 ft.

PERFORMANCE: Flying ½-mile (mean speed) 75.0 m.p.h. Fastest ½-mile run, 76.26 m.p.h. Standing ¼-mile 24½ secs. Petrol consumption 21 m.p.g.

PRICE: £445.

RILEY (COVENTRY) LTD.
Coventry.

most position, there are still 7 ins. between them and the front edge of the back seats.

One point calls for criticism. For some unexplained reason large quantities of warm air invade the interior of the car. This air is apparently fume-free. At any rate, it has no smell and is objectionable solely because of its temperature, which, in summer, calls for the opening of every ventilator.

It should be emphasized that this is not due to an over-hot engine. The cooling water temperature never once rose above 80 degrees C., and was usually about 70-75 degrees C.

Apart from this one criticism, the body is a fine piece of work and is not only very well finished, but is so arranged that, despite its striking streamlined shape, comfort and convenience have not been sacrificed. One example of this is to be found in the arrangement of the doors. In the front the pronounced slope of the windscreen pillar, which is carried down in the forward line of the door, enables a distinctly greater opening to be given at running-board level, so that no contortions are called for when entering or leaving. Similarly, the door aperture is carried well over the wheel arch at the back.

These, perhaps, may seem small points, but they show the thought that has gone into the design as a whole.

Having paused to re-read what has been written, it seems quite redundant to say in summary that this Riley is a highly desirable car. Yet, apart from repeating the whole report, nothing else will describe it. Although £445 is quite a lot of money to most of us, the car is worth it.

B17

July 28th, 1934     THE PRACTICAL MOTORIST     455

# ROAD TEST of the RILEY KESTREL

"Practical Motorist" Road Tests No. 8.

AS a nation we are reputed to be conservatively-minded, and there is no reason to believe that the motorists among us are any exception to the rule. Yet it is an interesting fact that the motoring public took to its heart, at first sight,

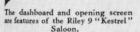

The dashboard and opening screen are features of the Riley 9 "Kestrel" Saloon.

one of the most unconventional examples of car body design yet seen ; to wit, the Riley "Kestrel," than which nothing that America or the Continent can show us is more original in line and yet which altogether escapes the charge of freakishness.

Part of the credit for this conquest of conservatism is, undoubtedly, due to the Riley concern's gradual education of the public in the matter of streamlining. Everyone remembers the impression made by the Riley "Nine" on its first appearance in 1927, and if one thinks back to that famous model it is clear that the "Kestrel," Riley's "last word" in modernity, is a logical development of that early dissenter from the dogma of a box on four wheels. The whole trend of body design since then has been the slow substitution of curve for angle and the softening of contours, until to-day there is hardly a car produced which does not conform in some degree to the new tendency. The "Kestrel," however, remains as far in advance of the generality as the 1927 "Nine" was of its contemporaries.

Besides giving such a decisive lead in body design, the first "Nine" was fitted with the first silent-third gearbox ever used as a standard feature. The makers themselves had actually built such a box as long ago as 1913, but it was not until fourteen years later that they brought it into general use.

## Four Silent Speeds

The latest Riley contribution to transmission development is a gearbox on which all four speeds are silent. This is the standard type fitted throughout the range to-day, but there is also available the "pre-selectagear" transmission —another feature which Rileys are the first to offer. The car which is the subject of this test was a "pre-selectagear" model.

The gearbox, of the now well-known pre-selective type, made

Three-quarter rear view of the Riley "Kestrel."

under Wilson patents, is used in conjunction with an automatic clutch, mechanically and centrifugally operated.

The engine specification of the "Nine" has changed very little since its introduction, which is not surprising, for it was and is an exceptionally clever design. Its four cylinders are cast en bloc and aluminium-alloy pistons of special pattern are used. The dimensions are 60.3 by 95.2 m.m., the cubic capacity being 1,089

c.c. and the Treasury rating 9.01 h.p. The "P.R." detachable head incorporates a machined hemispherical combustion chamber, straight-through inlet and exhaust ports, and valves inclined at 90 deg., and provides exceptional power, economy and sweet running. Two carburetters are fitted to the "Kestrel," which is a "Special Series" car. The "Special Series" cars have, besides, higher compression, special pistons and other detail differences which allow them to develop higher brake horse-power than the standard cars.

The carburetters are of the horizontal type, bolted direct to a specially-designed inlet manifold. A starting mixture control facilitates starting in cold weather. Lubrication is by forced feed to all bearings at high pressure, an oil gauge being mounted on the dashboard.

Cooling is by thermo-syphon, assisted by a fan, and the radiator, being flexibly mounted, is insulated from road shocks. The clutch is of the single-plate type, light and smooth in action, and a 7½-gallon petrol tank is mounted at the rear of the chassis.

The rear axle is of the banjo type, semi-floating, with spiral-bevel rear drive. The downswept frame is made unusually wide at the rear, which most effectively prevents rolling on corners, and is strongly braced by cross members. Semi-elliptic springs, fitted with spring gaiters and shock absorbers, are used all round. Both foot and hand brakes are of the internal-expanding pattern, operating in drums of large diameter, the former acting on all four wheels ; and both are adjustable from the driver's seat while the car is in motion.

## Frictionless Steering

Riley frictionless steering, of the worm-and-segment type, is employed. It is geared somewhat higher than that of the average car and is consequently exceptionally effective for the fast travel which the "Kestrel" is designed to provide. The steering

The tappet adjustment on the Riley "Kestrel" is quite accessible.

wheel and column are mounted slightly to the left of the driving seat, giving the double advantage of a little extra elbow room and a clearer forward view for the driver.

A 12-volt lighting and starting set is used, the batteries being housed at the rear of the luggage container, where they are easily accessible. The detachable wire wheels are fitted with low-pressure 4.50 by 19in. Dunlop tyres. "One-shot" chassis lubrication by pump from the steering column is provided.

The illustrations give a very clear idea of the "Kestrel's" graceful appearance, but cannot, of course, convey the essential cleverness of the body design from the points of view of comfort and stability. The downswept frame gives a low floor level, which means that entry to and exit from all seats is as easy as may be. The seats themselves, moreover, are well planned for position and pneumatically upholstered in soft leather. Foot wells make for ample leg room, while the body has an unsuspected width and height, not at all apparent from outside observation, but very accommodating to heads and elbows.

The car's exceptional stability, which remains unimpaired at all speeds and takes no account of curves and cambers, completes the tale of riding comfort.

The four wide doors open from the front and are fitted with winding windows, these and the screen and rear light being of Triplex glass. The screen is a single panel which can be opened by wind-

of performance it adds a simplicity of control which would become the staidest family saloon.

Most motorists are by now familiar with the series of operations involved in the use of a pre-selective gearbox—the flick of a little lever below the steering wheel into its appropriate notch, depression and release of the "clutch" pedal, etc. The automatic clutch of the "Kestrel" takes up

**The illustrations show the Riley automatic clutch.**

favourable circumstances the "Kestrel" is capable of as much as 70. Happy though the engine is on "flat-out" stretches, it is flexible enough to pull the car up a stiffish gradient in top gear without faltering.

Finally, in spite of its far higher than average performance, the "Kestrel" has running economy entirely in keeping with its class. We can vouch for it that its petrol consumption is well over thirty miles to the gallon, and in the course of a fairly prolonged test, including a good deal of fast travel, the oil consumption was not perceptible.

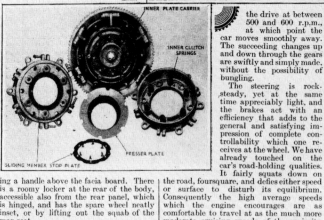

the drive at between 500 and 600 r.p.m., at which point the car moves smoothly away. The succeeding changes up and down through the gears are swiftly and simply made, without the possibility of bungling.

The steering is rock-steady, yet at the same time appreciably light, and the brakes act with an efficiency that adds to the general and satisfying impression of complete controllability which one receives at the wheel. We have already touched on the car's road-holding qualities. It fairly squats down on

ing a handle above the facia board. There is a roomy locker at the rear of the body, accessible also from the rear panel, which is hinged, and has the spare wheel neatly inset, or by lifting out the squab of the rear seat.

**On the Road**

The "Kestrel" is definitely a joy to drive. It has all the zest which its makers seem to have the secret of imparting to their products, and to its enchanting liveliness

the road, foursquare, and defies either speed or surface to disturb its equilibrium. Consequently the high average speeds which the engine encourages are as comfortable to travel at as the much more moderate cruising speeds of the majority of cars in this class.

The maximum figure obtained according to the testimony of the speedometer was 67 m.p.h., but so far from suspecting that the instrument was, as is not unusual, a little optimistic, we believe that in

### THE RILEY NINE "KESTREL" SALOON

**Specification in Brief**

**CHASSIS**

**Engine:** Four-cylinder cast en bloc, overhead valves inclined at 90 degrees, in combination with "P.R." detachable head, 60.3 x 95.2 m.m., 1,089 c.c., 9.01 h.p. Tax £9.

**Cooling:** Thermo-syphon, assisted by fan.

**Gear-Box:** Pre-selective with automatic clutch, employing mechanical and centrifugal action.

**Carburetters:** Two, horizontal type, bolted direct to specially-designed inlet manifold with hot spot.

**Suspension:** Semi-elliptic springs front and rear, enclosed in gaiters. Shock absorbers all round.

**Tyres:** Dunlop low pressure, 4.50 by 19in.

**Steering:** Worm-and-segment type. Finger-tip controls in centre of steering column for lamps, including electric dipping device.

**Brakes:** Cable operated. Foot brake on all four wheels, hand brake on rear wheels only. Both adjustable from driver's seat.

**BODY**

Streamlined, with sunshine roof, four doors hinged at rear, Triplex glass allround, single-panel opening windscreen, dual screen-wipers, speedometer, clock, luggage compartment at rear, oil and petrol gauges, electric horn, spare wheel and tyre, etc., etc.

**Wheelbase,** 8ft. 10in. **Track,** 4ft. **Ground Clearance,** 7½in.

**PRICE:** "Special Series" Model, with Pre-selectagears and two carburetters, £352. (With normal 4-speed gear-box, £325.)

**French Concession to Motorists**

CONCESSIONS granted by the French Government in respect of English cars touring France during the past month have resulted in a definite increase of cross-Channel car traffic.

Figures of the Townsend Ferry service at Dover show that during the past three weeks 707 cars were taken to France, as

against 562 in the three weeks preceding the announcement of the concessions.

**New Zealand Tariff Concessions to Britain**

GENEROUS concessions to British manufacturers are contained in the new tariff resolution approved by the New Zealand House of Representatives. Duties on numerous British goods have

been abolished, one of the most important of which is British motor-car bodies. A flat rate of 15 per cent. has been imposed on all complete United Kingdom motor vehicles.

Imports of foreign motor vehicles have recently increased, and the general tariff rate is now fixed at 73½ per cent., thus increasing the preferential margin on British motor-cars from 47 to 58 per cent.

The Light Car 343 FEBRUARY 5, 1937.

## Road Tests of 1937 Models

*With its four doors and six windows the body sacrifices nothing of ease of entrance and visibility to a fashionable appearance. The low bonnet line affords a clear view of both wings.*

*(Below) Exceptionally spacious is the luggage locker, formed in the tail, the number plate being integral with the spare-wheel cover.*

## The Kestrel-Sprite

# RILEY SALOON

## A T.T.-engined Car Combining High Performance with True Comfort

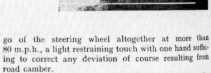

CAR buyers of a sportive turn of mind, who nevertheless crave the protection of a saloon body, have had, until a few months ago, little option but to grin and bear the heavy tax and fuel consumption inseparable from engines of 3½ or 4-litres.

With the advent of the Riley Kestrel Sprite, however, they are offered—true to the word of the man who writes those compelling advertisements—a vehicle which bears comparison with anything on the score of comfort, is taxed at only £9 per annum, and reaches 80 m.p.h. with greater willingness than many twelves do their "sixty." It will be seen, therefore, that this Riley has as good a claim to the adjective unique as any light car extant. In it, the graceful lines and supple riding of the familiar Kestrel saloon are wedded to an engine which is, as near as makes no matter, a replica of the 1936 T.T. winner; such differences as there are consist only in carburetter settings and the addition of a large air silencer, these being necessary for the sake of economy and the comfort of sensitive passengers.

The repair work to Brooklands track again made it impossible to obtain figures over the flying quarter-mile, but the best speed shown on the speedometer during our 450-mile test was exactly 85 m.p.h. Thus, even allowing for possible exaggeration on the part of that instrument, there can be no doubting the maker's claim of "over eighty." No attempt was made to produce conditions artificially favourable to the attainment of high speed; in fact, on the occasion that the above-mentioned speedometer reading was taken the Riley carried three adults and full week-end luggage.

It was found possible, perfectly easy, in fact, to leave

go of the steering wheel altogether at more than 80 m.p.h., a light restraining touch with one hand sufficing to correct any deviation of course resulting from road camber.

As for cruising speed, this, virtually, is anything the driver chooses to make it. For ourselves, we were content to keep the speedometer loitering around the 70 mark where traffic and other conditions were suitable, but our excursions further up the scale satisfied us that the stout-hearted engine would not tire if 75 m.p.h. or even more were maintained.

Of pulling power there is a great abundance, and at anything above 4,000 r.p.m. it takes a formidable main-road hill indeed to rob the Riley of its revs. in top gear. In considering acceleration it has to be remembered that with this luxurious body the weight of the car alone is over 24 cwt., so that it would be unfair to expect a pick-up comparable with that of a light two-seater. The instantaneous change obtainable with the Pre-selectagear, however, has an invaluable compensatory value in this connection, evidence of which is seen in our standing-start quarter-mile figure—23 secs.

The fame of this Pre-selectagear is already such that little need be said of it here. Suffice it to reiterate that it is entirely crash-proof, that the operating lever—placed behind and extending just beyond the rim of the steering wheel—is most conveniently situated, and

A16

that the automatic clutch incorporated simplifies traffic driving out of all knowledge.

By moving the hand throttle through a few degrees, so as to give a tick-over a few r.p.m. above the critical speed of the centrifugal clutch, the latter can, if desired, be put out of action at a second's notice. In practice we found that when taking up the drive against a considerable load, by using the gear-change pedal as though it were an ordinary clutch pedal, a sweeter get-away was effected than was possible with the automatic clutch. The slight whine which is apparently inseparable from the Pre-selectagear is not obtrusive enough to be irritating and, in any case, is absent in top gear.

No praise is too high for the springing of this car That rare thing, a back-seat ride which continues to be comfortable even up in the seventies and eighties and over surfaces by no means perfect, has positively been achieved; it was a master stroke, indeed, that effaced all trace of harshness from the suspension and yet at the same time cut out that excessively lively rise and fall motion to which sensitive passengers react so strongly.

Being high-geared, the steering does not give the utmost lightness in manœuvring at a crawl, but the extra responsiveness at higher speeds makes full recompense for a fault which would hardly be deemed such by those muscled men for whom the Kestrel Sprite came into the world.

### Powerful Braking.

Brakes by Girling. Few knowledgeable readers will ask for amplification of those three words. If the braking falls one degree short of perfection it is in a respect which has no connection with actual retardation: over choppy surfaces a rather pronounced motion—which one soon learns to ignore—is transmitted to the pedal.

Despite the low overall height of the body, and the disposition of the rear seats well within the wheelbase, the head- and leg-room provided is more than adequate, while the uninterrupted floor space in front (the brake lever lies horizontally between the seats) enables the driver or his nearest neighbour to enter and leave his seat by either door without thought of careful footwork.

Visibility is decidedly good in all directions; the rear three-quarter lights (excellent ventilators, incidentally,

| IN BRIEF |
| --- |
| **ENGINE:** Four cylinders; overhead valves; 69 mm. bore by 100 mm. stroke—1,496 c.c.; two carburetters; magneto ignition; tax, £9. |
| **TRANSMISSION:** Four-speed Pre-selectagear with right-hand control below steering wheel. Ratios: 5.22, 7.44, 11.05, and 19.07 to 1. Automatic clutch. Final drive by enclosed propeller shaft and spiral bevel. |
| **GENERAL:** Mechanically operated brakes, foot acting on all wheels, hand on rear wheels only. Semi-elliptic springs front and rear. Rear tank holds 11½ gallons. |
| **DIMENSIONS, ETC.:** Wheelbase, 9 ft. 4½ ins.; track, 4 ft. 3 ins.; overall length, 14 ft. 6½ ins.; overall width, 4 ft. 11½ ins.; width across rear seats, 42½ ins. (over arm-rests, 48 ins.); knee-room at rear, 18 ins. maximum, 14 ins. minimum; turning circle, 34 ft. left and right; weight, unladen, 24½ cwt. |
| **PERFORMANCE:** Flying quarter-mile unobtainable owing to track repairs (see text). Best standing quarter-mile, 23 secs. Petrol consumption (average conditions), 22 m.p.g. |
| **PRICE:** £398. |
| **RILEY (COVENTRY) LIMITED,** Coventry. |

being hinged) give a clear reversing view and both wings come well into range of the driver's eye.

The facia board, with its big rev. counter, matching speedometer and twin cubby holes, is well arranged and the provision of a battery master switch is one of those details which go to make the Kestrel Sprite worth its £398.

Of criticisms we have few. The windscreen wiper of the particular car tested showed a tendency to blow "over centre" in the teeth of head wind, and despite the big air silencer a good deal of power-roar, which can become tiresome on long journeys, emanates from the engine. This, however, is largely offset by the absence of wind noise. A just appreciable trace of vibration is to be felt a little below 4,000 r.p.m. Considering its racing origin, the engine calls for surprisingly little ignition-lever twiddling.

The Kestrel Sprite, in short, exerts a very strong claim on the affections of anyone who loves sustained high speeds and prides himself on the possession of a car which looks as innocent as a babe while having the heels of many out-and-out sports models.

*(Left) This off-side engine view shows the large air silencer, twin S.U. carburetters and Scintilla magneto. (Right) Spacious and comfortable rear seating.*

March 2, 1937.                            183                          The**Motor**

## "The Motor" Rationalized Road Tests

# The 9 h.p. Riley Monaco Saloon

### A Comfortable, Well-equipped and Pleasant-to-drive Car of Individual Character

Good window area is an appreciated point of this low-built model.

A RACING pedigree, 10 years of successful cultivation of the 9 h.p. type, and an awareness of those features which the critical owner values have been combined by the manufacturers to make the latest version of the Riley Monaco saloon a car of distinctive appeal.

To-day £298 may seem a lot of money, to some owners, to pay for a 9 h.p. car. That there are many who are willing to pay that amount for individuality, sturdiness and such progressive features as a self-change gearbox and a traffic clutch is proved by the popularity of the model.

Upon getting into the car, the driver (or passenger) is impressed by the practical arrangement of the seats, which gives an impression of roominess and comfort in spite of the low roof line. All the occupants can spread their legs and all-round vision is excellent. The driver can see both front wings and the flat bonnet allows a close view of the kerb in foggy weather.

#### Good Vision

The opening quarter lights and deep back light, apart from being an aid to vision when reversing, add considerably to the sense of lightness and airiness which is such a pleasant feature of the car.

The seats, with pneumatic cushions, have fairly high squabs, which, well curved, prevent rolling and the doors are wide enough to permit easy climbing in and out. This ease of access is enhanced by the unobstructed front compartment—the gear-change lever is on the steering column and the hand brake lever is between the seats—so that both the driver and front passenger can use the more convenient door.

Other features which increase the convenience of the interior are the legible instruments, the arm-rests, roll-type visor, cubby hole, door pockets, sunshine roof and a parcel's shelf behind the rear squab.

View of the facia board, spring-spoked wheel and Preselecta gear sector.

The roomy luggage boot and the neat lid-mounting of the spare wheel.

The steel bulkhead—or sub-dash—between the engine and the body.

B7

# THE RILEY MONACO SALOON . . . . . . . . Contd.

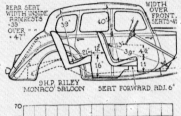

9 H.P. RILEY MONACO SALOON     SEAT FORWARD. ADJ. 6"

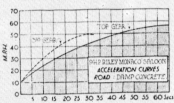

**(Left) Diagrams showing the seating dimensions and acceleration curves of the Monaco.**

The steadiness of the car is of a high order, even when very fast cornering is indulged in, and the suspension is well chosen for travelling fast 'on good roads, for it is firm. At low speeds and on pot-holed or wavy roads this firmness gives rise to a certain amount of vertical movement, but is not unpleasant except under extreme conditions.

One of the most attractive features of the car is the way in which it settles down to a tireless cruising speed of between 50 m.p.h. and 60 m.p.h. for hour after hour. So manageable is it that it does not depend upon first-class road surfaces for a high average speed to be maintained. On a Great North Road trip we found that 40 miles could be put into the hour without any sensation of hurrying unduly; and the same rate of travel was maintained on wet, rough and winding moorland roads without consciously forcing the pace.

It is the steering, roadholding and braking qualities which account for this state of affairs. The driver is possessed at all times with a feeling of real safety.

In rough, hilly country the car proves willing and untiring, even with a full load. The very simplicity of the gearchange takes much of the effort out of driving in this type of country.

At high speeds in the gears a certain amount of mechanical noise is in evidence, particularly on the overrun, and this sensation is increased by the operation of the windscreen wiper motor and the whine of the gearbox, but the car is very free from wind noise.

Weighing 22½ cwt., the car needs fairly firm handling on the indirect gears in order to regain lost speed quickly, but above 40 m.p.h., which speed is a comfortable one on third gear, it responds very well to the acceleration in top gear, and when the cruising speed has been gained the car is at its best.

Thanks to the good road-holding, which comes in part from the low centre of gravity and from the weight distribution, we found that surprisingly very good average speeds could be returned without driving consciously hard. The impeccable cornering makes the Monaco able to hold its own against many a car of twice the power. When really hard driving is indulged in the car still feels remarkably safe.

### Good Braking Qualities

The Girling type brakes perform consistently well, and heavy braking on a wet road was found to give a straight pull up. The well-placed hand brake, of the racing type, is powerful and will hold the car, fully loaded, on a 1-in-4 gradient. This makes restarting a simple matter.

A point which will be of interest to many is the fact that the car keeps clean well in dirty weather. This is due to the good mudguarding and aerodynamic shape of the car.

There is good luggage accommodation in the boot, the spare wheel is semi-recessed and Triplex glass is fitted all round. Another safety feature is the steel bulkhead behind the engine containing recesses for the tools. The provision of a battery master switch is a good point; for in the event of a short all circuits can be made dead whilst the trouble is being investigated.

Driving the car is pleasant under all conditions. The brakes, steering and generally good road manners immediately give an impression of extreme safety which remains with the driver on wet and greasy roads, in thick traffic and when travelling fast.

The steering is at its best above 30 m.p.h. High-geared, it is heavy at low speeds when cornering or manoeuvring. On the other hand, it is strongly self-centring and the wheel is comfortable to hold, both for angle and grip; and the quickness of response is appreciated when driving fast, for it inspires safe, not misleading confidence.

### Transmission Features

The Monaco saloon (as do all Riley models) incorporates the Preselecta gearchange and automatic clutch. A flick on the clutch pedal, with another ratio "preselected," gives an instantaneous change, up or down. The form of clutch allows the driver to bring the car to a standstill with the engine idling on the brakes alone, for below 600 r.p.m. the clutch drive is disengaged. Conversely a getaway from rest is made on the accelerator alone, for as the engine is speeded up the Newton clutch automatically re-engages at 600 r.p.m.

This form of transmission works very well. Very quick gearchanges save valuable time on the road, and the ease with which second can be preselected for a sharp corner when travelling in top (inter alia) places first-class driving accomplishments within the reach of the novice. The only drawback is that on a steep hill a restart can only be made by using the clutch pedal in the ordinary way: 600 r.p.m. are not enough to move away on a gradient. In other ways, the automatic clutch works well and smoothly, provided that the accelerator is smoothly pressed. The automatic operation takes a little time to get used to, for the driver may miss a "direct" touch on the clutch, but once mastered many advantages are revealed.

B8

## TABULATED DATA—RILEY MONACO SALOON

### CHASSIS DETAILS

*Engine:* Four cylinders; two - bearing crankshaft; inclined overhead valves; coil ignition : 60.3 mm. by 95.2 mm. (1,089 c.c.). Rating, 9.02 h.p.; tax, £6 15s.

*Gearbox:* Preselective type, with control beneath the steering wheel; centrifugal clutch. Ratios: 5.5, 8.32, 12.79 and 22.44 to 1.

### PERFORMANCE

*Speeds on Gears:* Top, mean speed timed after accelerating for one mile, 61 m.p.h.; best speed reached on the road, 68 m.p.h. Speed on third, 50 m.p.h. ; second, 32 m.p.h.

*Tapley Performance Figures:* Maximum pull in lb. per ton on gradient—top, 150; third, 220; second, 350. Corresponding gradients climbable at a steady speed are—1 in 15 ; 1 in 10.2 and 1 in 6.4.

*Acceleration:* Through the gears from a standstill—to 50 m.p.h., 26 secs.

Standing quarter-mile, 27½ secs. (average speed of 32.4 m.p.h.).

*Petrol Consumption:* Driven hard on long runs, 30 m.p.g.

*Braking Efficiencies:* By Tapley meter, using the pedal only—80 per cent. from 30 m.p.h. ; 80 per cent. from 40 m.p.h. Corresponding stopping distances are—37½ ft. and 67 ft.

### DIMENSIONS, ETC.

*Leading Measurements:* Wheelbase, 8 ft. 10 ins.; track, 4 ft.; overall length, 13 ft. 10½ ins.; width, 4 ft. 9½ ins.; height, 5 ft. 2 ins.; ground clearance, 6½ ins.

*Turning Circles:* Left and right, 34 ft. diameter.

*Wheels and Tyres:* Dunlop 4.50 ins. section on wire wheels with 19 ins. rims.

*Weight:* As tested, with one up, 23¾ cwt.; unladen, 22¼ cwt.

*Price:* With Preselecta gear, centrifugal clutch, etc., as tested, £298.

January 25, 1938.                              1151                              The **Motor**

## "THE MOTOR" ROAD TESTS

# The 16 h.p. Riley Adelphi Saloon

### High Performance Obtained from a Big Four-cylinder Engine Without Loss of Flexibility and Silence

THE autumn of 1937 will be remembered by motoring. enthusiasts as a time which witnessed the return of the big four-cylinder engine. There has always been a number of advantages associated with such models, but it is largely due to the improvements made in the design of flexible engine mountings that this type can once again compete with units having more cylinders.

The 16 h.p. Riley has an ancestry containing the names of many fine four-cylinder cars. The Riley Nine made history on road and track and was followed by the 1½-litre, which also gave an excellent account of itself. Going back even further there were four-cylinder Rileys of 10.8 h.p. and 12 h.p., so that we were particularly interested in this opportunity of road testing their latest, and perhaps greatest, motorcar.

#### Practical Coachwork

There has never been anything impractical or ornate about the coachwork of Riley cars so that we were not altogether surprised at the almost "family" appearance of the saloon now under review; five persons can be carried in comfort and there is head room and leg room in plenty. The body is, in fact, based on a type used with great success on the 1½-litre model and provides excellent luggage accommodation and a really exceptional degree of all-round visibility.

The steering wheel is adjustable both for rake and length, but whatever the chosen position the driver has no difficulty in obtaining ample view of both front wings together with a minimum of blind spots in any given direction.

An ingenious gearbox is fitted to the car to provide five speeds forward. It requires only three positions of the gear lever. Explained in any text book, this arrangement sounds a little formidable, so we devoted an entire morning to driving the car under a variety of conditions in order to see for ourselves what this transmission system, as applied to the Riley, is like.

We found that with intelligent use this gearbox comes very near to the

**The front seats are deep, softly sprung and have high squabs.**

ideal, and the whole matter is really bound up with the use of a lever provided for the cutting in and out of the overdrive system. Starting in heavy traffic we first pulled this lever towards us which resulted in provid-

ing the car with a perfectly normal three-speed synchromesh gearbox. The ratios of the box thus used are rather low and top gear registers 5.5 to 1. The beauty of this arrangement lies in the fact that in built-up areas one is provided with a highly accelerative and extremely flexible motorcar.

It should not, however, be imagined that the engine is called upon to stress itself in any way while proceeding thus, and it is interesting to note that a speed of 70 m.p.h. can be obtained on this ratio, although such treatment is, naturally, not advised.

No sooner does the car reach an arterial highway than the lever is pushed in and thereafter it is only necessary to lift the foot governing the accelerator at any speed in excess of 40 m.p.h. for an overdrive top of 3.9 to 1 to be engaged without a trace of shock or sound. If the speed of the car drops below 30 m.p.h. a free wheel cuts in and at the same time the lower ratio is obtained automatically.

#### Use of the Free Wheel

This cutting-in of the free wheel on the lower speeds applies only to occasions when the overdrive is desired, and in actual practice one very soon becomes accustomed to such an arrangement. There is yet another available ratio designed for "snap acceleration" and rapid hill-climbing when overdrive is engaged. Known as overdrive second, the ratio is 6.15 to 1 and is obtained by changing down in the normal way when in overdrive top.

**The 16 h.p. Riley Adelphi saloon, a six-light model capable of over 80 m.p.h.**

The**Motor**      1152      *January 25, 1938.*

# THE 16 H.P. RILEY . . . . . . . . . Contd.

We have dealt at some length with this transmission system because it is the only type available on the 16 h.p. Riley and is, naturally, one of the most discussed features of the car. On the open road one revels in the effortless speed provided by the high ratio and in towns get-away from the traffic lights was meteoric.

To meet the possible more extensive use of the brakes on account of the free wheel, Riley engineers specify 16-in. drums to the Girling layout. Besides adding materially to the appearance of the car these large brakes produce a sound feeling of security and

showed not the slightest tendency to fade or overheat when applied with considerable violence at a speed in excess of 70 m.p.h.

The car "grows" on one and it is some time before the driver realizes the performance and road-holding available. In keeping with the high maximum are the Lucas head lamps which provide an excellent beam and are augmented by a powerful fog light mounted in a central position at the base of the radiator. Incidentally, the front end of this car is a big improvement on anything attempted by the Riley concern in the past, being clean

in design, modern in appearance and yet not sacrificing the essential characteristics of a good English car in any way whatsoever.

The rear seats are provided with air cushions and a folding arm-rest. The front seats are equipped with Dunlopillo and are, therefore, commendably free from distortion, which makes for greater driving comfort and in no way impedes the hand brake, which is located between the driver and passenger.

Instruments are well laid out.

The Riley Sixteen is also available as a Kestrel model.

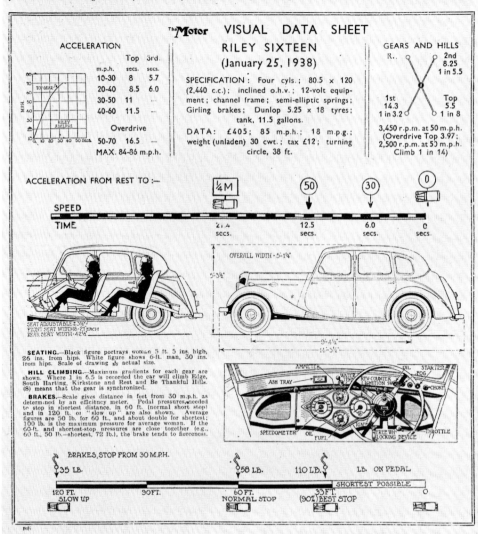

**The Motor VISUAL DATA SHEET**

**RILEY SIXTEEN**
(January 25, 1938)

**ACCELERATION**

| | Top | 3rd. |
|---|---|---|
| m.p.h. | secs. | secs. |
| 10-30 | 8 | 5.7 |
| 20-40 | 8.5 | 6.0 |
| 30-50 | 11 | — |
| 40-60 | 11.5 | — |

Overdrive

50-70   16.5

MAX. 84-86 m.p.h.

SPECIFICATION : Four cyls.; 80.5 × 120 (2,440 c.c.); inclined o.h.v.; 12-volt equipment; channel frame; semi-elliptic springs; Girling brakes; Dunlop 5.25 × 18 tyres; tank, 11.5 gallons.

DATA : £405; 85 m.p.h.; 18 m.p.g.; weight (unladen) 30 cwt.; tax £12; turning circle, 38 ft.

**GEARS AND HILLS**

R. ..    2nd 8.25   1 in 5.5

1st 14.3   1 in 3.2    Top 5.5   1 in 8

3,450 r.p.m. at 50 m.p.h. (Overdrive Top 3.97; 2,500 r.p.m. at 53 m.p.h. Climb 1 in 14)

**ACCELERATION FROM REST TO :—**

| ¼M | 50 | 30 | 0 |
|---|---|---|---|

SPEED

TIME    21.4 secs.    12.5 secs.    6.0 secs.    0 secs.

OVERALL WIDTH · 5-1¼"

SEAT ADJUSTABLE ± 5½"
FRONT SEAT WIDTH · 71 EACH
REAR SEAT WIDTH · 42½"

5-3½"

9-4½"

14-3½"

**SEATING.**—Black figure portrays woman 5 ft. 5 ins. high, 26 ins. from hips. White figure shows 6-ft. man, 30 ins. from hips. Scale of drawing 1/30 actual size.

**HILL CLIMBING.**—Maximum gradients for each gear are shown. Where 1 in 6.5 is recorded the car will climb Edge, South Harting, Kirkstone and Rest and Be Thankful Hills. (S) means that the gear is synchronized.

**BRAKES.**—Scale gives distance in feet from 30 m.p.h. as determined by an efficiency meter. Pedal pressures needed to stop in shortest distance, in 60 ft. (normal short stop) and in 120 ft. or "slow up" are also shown. Average figures are 50 lb. for 60 ft., and about double for shortest; 100 lb. is the maximum pressure for average woman. If the 60-ft. and shortest-stop pressures are close together (e.g., 60 ft., 50 lb.—shortest, 72 lb.), the brake tends to fierceness.

SPEEDOMETER   OIL   FUEL    AMMETER   WATER   REV.COUNTER   IGNITION SWITCH   OIL   STARTER   FOG   CHOKE   ASH TRAY   IGN.   FREE WH. LOCKING DEVICE   THROTTLE

**BRAKES, STOP FROM 30 M.P.H.**

35 LB.    58 LB.   110 LB.    LB. ON PEDAL

SHORTEST POSSIBLE

120 FT.    90 FT.    60 FT.   33 FT.    0
SLOW UP      NORMAL STOP   (90%) BEST STOP

The Light Car     502     MARCH 11, 1938.

## Road Tests of —— —— 1938 Models

## — THE 1½ - LITRE —

# RILEY "VICTOR"

### A Light Car of Refinement and of Excellent Performance

THE writer, who claims to have had a fair experience of Riley productions, has no hesitation in saying that the 1½-litre Victor saloon is quite one of the most pleasant motor-cars that has emanated from the Riley factory. It is roomy and substantial without being large and unduly heavy. It looks well, its lines are pleasing and its all-cream coachwork (in the case of the car tested) is striking and attractive. It is generously equipped without being overloaded with equipment, and although a modern light car priced at £325 gives the impression of being very expensive, it is not difficult to see where the money has gone in the case of the car under discussion.

From the point of view of performance, this model is also outstanding. It compares more than favourably with previous models, particularly in the way it gets off the mark; in fact, for a car of this weight and windage area, its maximum speed and a standing-start quarter-mile in 23 secs. are exceptionally good.

Flat out, the Riley Victor maintained an average of 72.6 m.p.h. under the more favourable conditions over the flying quarter-mile, whilst a mean speed of 65.8 m.p.h. was registered. Here may we explain, *mirabile dictu*, that the speedometer proved to be slow; thus at an indicated road speed of 60 m.p.h. the actual speed was just over 66 m.p.h. It tours very comfortably at "50" on the clock (just over 60 m.p.h. actual speed).

### "Such Fun to Drive. . ."

Ease of control is another characteristic of the car. The Preselecta-gear is so simple to operate; the selector pedal is light in action, the centrifugal clutch works like a charm, the brakes are powerful, whilst springing and road holding are beyond reproach. The steering, however, is heavy at low speeds. In this respect the car is like other Rileys we have tried. That it is
B12

accurate to the *n*th degree no one can deny, and at speed it is light, but for slow-motion work in traffic it is trying; it is, however, satisfyingly direct, one turn of the wheel giving full lock in either direction.

We give full marks to the hand brake. This control should receive far more attention than it does from manufacturers. It is not, as some suppose, merely a device which enables a car to conform with the law when parked. It becomes of vital importance if a car is stopped and restarted on a hill. The Riley lever lies between the seats and is controlled by a fine-toothed ratchet You lift it with one finger, and it sounds as though you are winding rather a large watch; it stops the car effectively and holds it like a vice.

### The Transmission.

The gear ratios provide for the steepest hill, thanks to a first-gear ratio of 18.79 to 1—and, *ipso facto*, at least a little care when changing to the next ratio of 10.91 if a jerk is to be avoided; but from second to third and from third to top it would indeed be hard to go wrong.

The effect of the centrifugal clutch is similar, in some respects, to that of a fluid flywheel. First gear can be engaged by moving the lever to the appropriate notch and depressing and releasing the selector pedal; then you can move off when the time comes merely by pressing the accelerator. Actually, if desired, you can, having engaged first gear, preselect second gear by means of the lever before you move, so that the first kick of the pedal after the car has rolled off from a standing start in first gear automatically engages second. You can have a free wheel if you depress the "clutch" pedal momentarily and release the accelerator.

Another big advantage of this self-engaging clutch is that when the car is motionless the epicyclic gearbox, being disconnected from the engine drive, is also motion-

MARCH 11, 1938.                    503                    *The Light Car*

# "DATAGRAPH" OF THE RILEY 1½-LITRE VICTOR SALOON

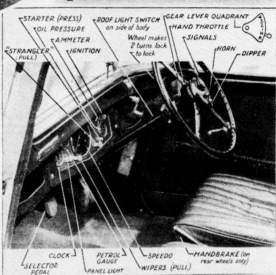

### At a Glance

#### THE SPECIFICATION.

**ENGINE:** Four-cylinder o.h.v.; 69 mm. by 100 mm. = 1,496 c.c.; tax, £9; 55 b.h.p. at 4,500 r.p.m.; compression ratio, 6.3 to 1.

**TRANSMISSION:** Centrifugal automatic clutch; four-speed epicyclic gearbox (5.22, 7.39, 10.91 and 18.79 to 1).

**GENERAL:** Girling brakes; one-shot chassis lubrication (Bijur system); 12-v. electrical equipment with automatic voltage control; AC mechanical fuel pump feeding Zenith carburetter from 10-gallon rear tank; semi-elliptic springing all round; Dunlop tyres, 5.00 by 17.

**DIMENSIONS, Etc.:** Wheelbase, 8 ft. 10 ins.; track, 4 ft. 10 ins. Overall length, 13 ft. 10½ ins.; overall width, 4 ft. 10 ins.; width across front seats, 50 ins.; back seats, 47 ins.; between rear armrests, 38 ins. Weight, as tested, tanks full, 24½ cwt.

**PERFORMANCE:** Flying ¼-mile (best run), 72.6 m.p.h.; (mean speed), 65.8 m.p.h.; ¼-mile standing start, 23 secs. Petrol consumption, 24-26 m.p.g.

**PRICE:** As tested, £325.

RILEY (COVENTRY) LTD.,
Coventry.

*Controls diagram labels:* STARTER (PRESS) — OIL PRESSURE — AMMETER — "STRANGLER" (PULL) — IGNITION — ROOF LIGHT SWITCH on side of body — Wheel makes 2 turns lock to lock — GEAR LEVER QUADRANT — HAND THROTTLE — SIGNALS — HORN — DIPPER — CLOCK — SELECTOR PEDAL — PETROL GAUGE — PANEL LIGHT — SPEEDO — WIPERS (PULL) — HANDBRAKE (on rear wheels only)

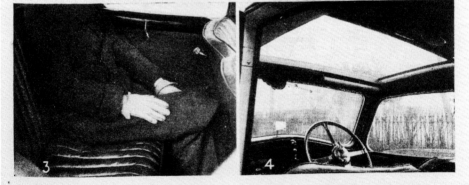

(1) Luggage: usual roomy locker at the rear. (2) Ground clearance; the photo also shows the petrol filler. (3) Rear seat accommodation. The squab affords ample support for the shoulders, the cushion is deep and there is abundant leg room and toe room. (4) Visibility: good all round. The sliding roof is easily operated and has a generous aperture. (Inset) The controls, instruments, etc. The model tested had Preselecta-gear, i.e., centrifugal clutch and epicyclic gearbox.

B13

The Light Car 504 MARCH 11, 1938.

### RILEY VICTOR SALOON *(Contd.)*

less and there is none of that rather unmelodious churning noise going on beneath the floorboards.

On the model tried, the silence, not only of the epicyclic gearbox but of engine and body, was most impressive. In such circumstances wind rush often becomes obtrusive. The car was not free from this form of noise, but, on the other hand, it was certainly not excessive, even with a fairly stiff wind blowing across the car three-quarters front.

We have become accustomed in these days to engines that start up willingly, even on the coldest morning, and if a competition were held the Riley would earn a very high position, for with a Zenith self-start carburetter at the head of affairs, as it were, the engine is off at the first touch of the button.

This brings us to a point of some importance. Starting up appears to offer complications at first because of the difficulty of threading the right arm through the steering wheel so as to press the starter button, whilst

*The engine components are more than usually accessible. This view shows the coil, junction box, battery, air cleaner and carburetter amongst other things. The oval cover on the bulk-head gives access to the tools.*

the self-start carburetter control is pulled out with the left hand. A foolish conclusion, for the controls are side by side, thus the strangler can be pulled out with the first and second fingers and the starter button pushed with the thumb of the same hand. The self-starting carburetter control is spring-loaded and can be released after two or three seconds if the revs. are "picked up" on the accelerator pedal.

Visibility is distinctly good. One sits higher than in many light cars, and well-moulded coachwork results in a minimum of blind areas. Even the near-side wing lamp can be spotted if one just lifts one's chin a little. The lights, too, are very good, although the head lamps appear at first sight to be small for the frontal appearance.

From the point of view of maintenance, the car scores heavily. It is fitted with Lucas Bi-jur automatic lubrication for one thing and, for another, the battery is easily accessible under the bonnet, a remark which also applies to other vital components which live under the bonnet. For example, on the off side of the unit the coil, the fuse and junction box, etc., the carburetter and the distributor head are all very easy to get at. On the other side of the unit there is the oil filler, incorporated in one of the rocker-box lids, the Bi-jur lubrication unit and the dip-stick. There is ample accommodation for tools, but access to the locker should be easier.

Worthy of note is the fact that the bonnet which houses all this has no louvres, and lovers of æstheticism will have to decide whether or not in their own minds they like the suggestion of severity which results. The writer preferred it—especially as there is a thermostat to look after engine temperature and a double bulkhead

*Sump oil filler orifice and Lucas Bi-jur lubrication unit are clearly revealed in this photograph: the leads to the centrally placed sparking plugs can also be seen.*

to keep fumes from entering the body. At the other end of the vehicle there is the usual Riley luggage locker, whilst inside the car and behind the rear-seat squabs there is a shelf 9 ins. wide which is invaluable for parcels, and so on.

As we suggested in our opening paragraph, the Riley 1½-litre Victor saloon with Preselecta-gear is not a cheap model; after motoring it about the country, however, for the best part of 300 miles, we feel that we cannot do more than give it a very good name and let discerning people judge for themselves.

*Frontal view. Note the absence of louvres in the bonnet and the clean lines of the wings and scuttle.*

B14

# CHAPTER TWELVE

# The Riley Legacy

Riley (Coventry) Limited came into existence by that name in March 1912. On 30th September 1938 the Company was put into voluntary liquidation and acquired by Riley (Coventry) Successors Limited. No distribution was made to creditors or shareholders and the Final Meeting Return was registered on 1st August 1939. The Board of Directors of the new company was made up of Lord Nuffield, Wilfred Hobbs and Oliver Boden, with Victor Riley appointed Managing Director.

This new company was sold, it is said, to Morris Motors Limited for the sum of £1. So began a new life for a company which one family had built up and controlled for forty years. Despite the critics and the justifiable criticisms they offered at times, the Company was kept intact as Riley Motors Limited through the stages of being 'Nuffield-ised' and 'BMC-ised' and both parents kept Riley in the upper echelons of their product ranges. There was sufficient respect left to ensure that cars carrying the Riley name were of good quality in the context of the contemporary market place, even if they did not satisfy the purist enthusiasts of the pre-1939 era.

It must always be remembered that when a company changes hands, especially after financial problems, things cannot be the same. Whatever reasons prevail, when a company has failed, people change and policies change. When the company changes hands then the whole character changes—by how much depends always on the heirs to the name and the respect they have for that name. No amount of contractual safeguards can guarantee the quality of enthusiasm, design, innovation, development and ultimately product—they have to be regenerated with leadership and team spirit. A lot of that comes from the competitive spirit of sporting involvement. Therefore, Riley could never be exactly what it was, for it was never to field a team of racing cars again, the leadership in the Company had changed and the range of cars was now to be very narrow for the rest of the marque's life.

Behind the smooth presentation of innovation and advancement which the public saw was a turbulent history of the family business. The earliest days of emergence into the motor industry were a struggle for the Riley brothers against the authority of their father and uncle, who opposed forsaking the now-familiar world of bicycles for the unfamiliar world of motor cars, and against the odds of financial survival; quite apart from the technological barriers before them. But they faced their struggles and overcame their difficulties.

Their innovative ability and foresight made a substantial contribution to their success, as the original side valve models were to testify, but those qualities were by no means the total key to that success. Determination, negotiating skills and marketing ability were all parts of the Riley story.

The path to success was relatively smooth through the era of the V-twins. The Riley brothers had designed their cars with great care, competed with them and established their reputation for themselves instead of entrusting it entirely to others. They passed through the

difficult but unifying times of the Great War to emerge into the very bouyant age of the side-valve four cylinder cars.

These side-valve cars were to be the consolidation of the Riley company's reputation and financial stability. Small wonder then that the demise of the side-valve and the emergence of the Nine were not without their problems. Some saw the end of the side-valve as a struggle for survival, one the car was inevitably to lose in the light of the new model's qualities, appeal and price.

However, the Nine survived the strain and brought with it the success which gave rise to the development of a wide range of other models—the Sixes, the $1\frac{1}{2}$ litres, the 8/90s and finally the Big Fours. The Thirties was a decade of great innovation. It is the kind of success which comes from such innovation that gives rise to a certain confident complacency. That confidence brings a sense of daring which might otherwise not exist and risks are taken such as might never be considered in a more cautious climate. Resources become overstretched and companies collapse through lack of fluidity. Today it is known as 'cash-flow', tomorrow the accountants will think of a new name, but always it is an inability to meet costs out of financial resources. Usually in the case of a successful company it is because too much investment has taken up what would otherwise be cash reserves. This is what happened to Riley (Coventry) Limited.

The Riley adventure came after the six-cylinder cars, which had originally, sensibly, been developed from the Nine and used many parts in common with its smaller relative—a sensible strategy because it allowed extension of the range without major extra production costs. However, when the $1\frac{1}{2}$ litre car came on to the scene, it moved away from the policy of having interchange of parts. That was not a harmful decision in itself, but the modifications to the Sixes were the first signs that production costs must rise, because there was very little interchangeability of parts now between any of the engine models. The 8/90 was to add to those costs, as was the Big Four.

Neither the 8/90 nor the Big Four could really have recovered the tooling costs from sales and the only saving, once they had been launched, which could be quickly effective was the use of common chassis and bodywork. As far as possible this was done but the range of cars displayed at the 1937 Motor Show gave not the slightest hint of the depth of the Company's problems. Only the Victor saloon suggested any effort to build down to a price and whilst it was a fine car for the price, it seems to have been too late.

The other part of the Riley adventure which did little to help the stability or survival of the Company was the creation of Autovia Cars. Autovias were very fine cars, built to a high engineering standard, as one would expect, but again they were launched at the wrong time, and probably at the wrong market. It was a market well-provided for by Humber and Daimler with cars which were simpler and longer established. The big saloon/limousine market was in any case rather precarious, Rolls Royce and Bentley being at the top and Austin, Morris and Vauxhall at the bottom in price terms. Autovia was entering a difficult market at a difficult time with a new V8 engined car and unfortunately it went down with the collapse of Riley.

The Riley legacy began in 1898 with the first car built by Percy Riley. That car has deliberately not featured as a model in Chapter 2 because it was never offered for sale as a product of the Company, although without it the Riley marque would never have become the force to be reckoned with that it was. That car was sold in Belfast and, despite Victor Riley's efforts to trace it, with a reward of £50 being offered for some years, it was never

recovered. The Company did recognise the value of history and bought a number of its early cars to form a small collection for use in appropriate events, however.

The Riley Motor Club was formed in 1925 and became the largest one-make car club in the world before the end of a decade. This club was the cornerstone of the Riley heritage after the demise of Riley (Coventry) Limited and it inherited a momentous legacy. Riley enthusiasm was certainly not exclusive to the motor sporting fraternity and after some years the Riley Register came into existence to promote the continued existence of Riley cars of all types built before 1939. Originally the Register was seen as a club to promote the Riley Nine's interests—then it was realised that there was rather more to Riley than the 9 h.p. models!

The tremendous enthusiasm for Rileys and dedication to their survival has retained its strength over the years and, whilst there are less Rileys left in the world today, those which remain are probably better kept than ever they were in their own time. Riley clubs exist worldwide, most catering for Rileys of all years and models between 1899 and 1969, the year in which the Riley badge was last offered on the front of a car. Even though it bore no resemblance to its forebears, the passing of the last Riley badged car was with the regret of many thousands of car buyers. It was decided by the board of British Leyland in 1969 that cars bearing the Riley name would only ever sell at the rate of perhaps 8,000—10,000 per year maximum and so the name was withdrawn—after its third reorganisation. Regrettably, because the Riley name still represented a better-than-average car, the would-be Riley buyer was now encouraged to buy imported cars as a result of this decision and so the once-great British industry suffered yet another indignity.

However, even in the blackest days of Riley history, those following the collapse of the original company, Rileys were being driven in quite remarkable style round circuits and up hills faster than their adversaries. Riley engines were powering other cars to continuing success in races and hill-climbs too. What great satisfaction the Riley brothers would surely have enjoyed from seeing cars and engines they built winning races so many years after they were built—in most cases forty years and in some even fifty.

In their day, Rileys established a proud record of competition successes and speed records at Brooklands, at Donington Park, at Montlhery, at Le Mans and many other locations. To quote one set of interesting statistics from all of these, in the six years of racing pre-war at Donington Park, Riley and Riley-based engines brought 142 places between First and Third in 135 eligible events. Riley cars won 43 races, took 33 second places and 16 third places. E.R.A.s, with Riley-based engines, won all six Nuffield Trophy Races between 1934 and 1939, one of the two J.C.C. 200s run there, two British Empire Trophy Races and the 1938 Coronation Handicap. The 1939 British Empire Trophy Race was the last to be run on the old Donington Park circuit and was won by Tony Rolt in the E.R.A. R5B.

Nearly forty years on, the revived British Empire Trophy Race in 1977, organised by Tom Wheatcroft, owner of the Donington Collection and reviver of the Donington Park circuit, was won by Neil Corner in a car which owed its origins entirely to Riley (via the White Riley and the E.R.A.s), the B.R.M. P25. An E.R.A. was to win its event, the Pre-War All Comers Scratch Race, at the first V.S.C.C. meeting run post-war at Donington—exactly forty years after the last race meeting held there before the second World War, which was also organised by the Vintage Sports Car Club.

A wide range of cars, both contemporary and of later years, owe their origins to Riley. Imitation, it is said, is the highest form of flattery. If that is so then many manufacturers have

paid homage to Riley, either by direct copy or by basing their designs on emulations. The styling of the 1937/8 B.M.W. 328 bore a striking similarity to the Riley Sprite, as did the Squire Two Seater (which bore more than a styling resemblance to the Riley).

When Hugh Rose, the designer of the 1½ litre, left Riley in 1934, he went to Lea Francis who introduced 12 h.p. and 14 h.p. engines in 1937/8 almost identical to the Riley design. So it might be said that the post-war Connaught whose engine was a development from the Lea Francis owed the origins of its engine to Riley. Even the Morgan sports car of the 1970s and 1980s had more than a passing similarity to the coachwork of the Riley Sprite. And of course, the concept of the B.R.M., British Racing Motors, owed its origins entirely to the White Riley. Appropriate perhaps then that the 1962 World Grand Prix Championship for Constructors was won by B.R.M.; the Driver's Championship being won by a man who was probably Britain's greatest racing champion—not just for the races he won, but for the sportmanship he displayed in winning or losing, the late Graham Hill.

Today, the world's Riley clubs hold all kinds of events from reliability runs and social drives to highly competitive sporting events which test the mettle of car and driver. All of those clubs have one common aim, the perpetuation of the breed. For breed it is. At the heart of all of those events and at the heart of Riley enthusiasm itself is the Riley Register's annual Coventry Rally. Here, each summer, usually the first weekend of July, Riley enthusiasts gather from all over the world on their own special pilgrimage—perhaps in a subconscious effort of rejuvenation for them and their beloved Rileys. Spare parts are bought and exchanged and cars are physically rejuvenated as a result. For that special weekend each year, Coventry becomes Mecca and the pilgrims gather for their Haj, the great annual pilgrimage.

Throughout the rest of the summer there are all kinds of events held specifically for Rileys and others in which Rileys compete with other makes. Vintage and Historic race meetings are numerous at many of England's premier circuits, Silverstone, Oulton Park and Donington Park, and cars are driven to win. Rileys, Riley based specials of pre- and post-war origins and Riley engined cars are all winning races.

A great feature of these gatherings is always speculation: 'What would have happened if Riley had developed the Sixes further?' 'How much better would a 2¼ litre six-cylinder version of the 1½ litre have sold than the 8/90? 'Would they then have bothered with the Big 4?' 'Could Riley have survived into the present age if they had been a little less adventurous and managed to stay in business until the War?' These and many other questions are part of the mystique of Riley, part of our enthusiasm.

We must hope that these pilgrimages continue, for as long as they do, Rileys will retain their 'raison d'être'. This then is the legacy of Riley (Coventry) Limited. What treasures that family left us.

# Riley Model Identification to 1938

The very earliest of Riley 'chassis numbers' are the frame numbers on bicycles, motor bicycles, motor tricycles and motor quadricycles. As far as can be established, these started in 1896 with a series of three-digit numbers on the bottom bracket. Later it appears they were stamped, as four-digit numbers, on the saddle clamp bracket. No numerical or alphabetical prefixes seem to have been used so it was not possible to identify a model by its frame number.

The fore-cars and tri-cars continued this system of simple numbering and the V-twin cars also used straightforward sequential numbers. The side-valve cars of the Twenties were numbered originally with four digit numbers and, again, no identifying prefix. However, a number of cars showed the first two digits of a six-digit number as 69 and all such cars were those fitted with the larger, 1645 cc., engine the bore of which was 69 mm. After 1922, most side valve models had engine numbers which carried a letter suffix and it was that letter which identified the model—at least the model from which the engine came! It was still not too accurate a system though, because 'T' denoted all tourer bodies, 'S' denoted Standard and DeLuxe Saloons as well as the Four Door Coach, 'C' denoted all the Coupés (except the Wentworth which had 'W' as its suffix) and the Clover Leaf. Mostly, it was the initial letter of the model of coachwork which was added to the engine numbers to identify the model.

As ever with Rileys, there are exceptions and some side-valves had odd numbers, like an X suffix used on odd engines built out of the normal sequence. The 11/50/65 supercharged engine (as far as is known, only one was built) was numbered thus, being 101X.

With the introduction of the 9 h.p. model, there was still no means of identifying an individual model from its chassis number, cars carrying a six-digit number commencing 60 from 1926. The numbering sequence ran thus:

| DATE FROM | CHASSIS NUMBERS | COMMENT |
|---|---|---|
| July 1926 | 600001—601000 | Mk I chassis, r.h. gearchange, cone clutch. |
| | 601001—602964 | Mk II chassis (Mk I body). |
| | 602965—604293 | Mk III chassis (Mk I body). |
| | 604294—6011012 | ⌠ Mk IV chassis— <br> ⟨ Mk II bodies on all models except Monaco. <br> ⌊ Monaco Mk II body from C/n 606770. |
| 1927/1928 | 60/1—  60/? | First 9 h.p. Speed Models (Brooklands) built by Thompson & Taylor Limited. |
| 1938/1932 | 8001—  8093* | Brooklands 9 h.p. Speed Models. *There are suggestions that the last Brooklands 9 chassis number was 8098, but evidence available so far reveals numbers to 8093 only. |
| Oct. 1930 | 6011013—6014999 | Plus Series. Internal rocker oil feed from 6012013. Long-shank pinion from 6013196. |
| Oct. 1931 | 6015000—6018999 | Plus Ultra Series. |
| Oct. 1932 | 6019000—6019799 | Silent Third gearbox & magneto ignition. |
| | 6019800—6022600 | All-helical gearbox & coil ignition. |

| Oct. 1933 | 6022601—6023600 | 1934 9 h.p. models with all-helical gearbox. |
| | 6023601—6025048 | 1934 9 h.p. models with ENV psg and 1st-type centrifugal clutch. Imps from 6025044 had external rocker oil feed. |
| | 6025049—6025600 | 1934 9 h.p. models with ENV psg and 2nd-type clutch. |
| | 6025601—6027000 | 1934 9 h.p. models with all-helical gearbox. |
| Oct. 1934 | 6027001—6027030 | 1935 9 h.p. models with ENV psg and external rocker oil feed. |
| | 6027031—6027900 | Armstrong-Siddeley preselector gearbox & Luvax shock absorbers. Imps continued with ENV gearboxes and Hartford shock absorbers. |
| Aug. 1935 | S66K/M101—2200 | S—Special Series, M—Merlin, K—Kestrel. |
| Oct. 1936 | 67M/S67C/S67Z | M—Merlin, C—Touring Saloon, Z—Monaco, |
| | 2201        3399 | Prefix S—Special Series, Suffix X—Overdrive transmission. |
| Oct. 1937 | From 68V   3400 | 9 h.p. Victor. |

Example of late-type chassis number, giving specification of car: S67ZX is Special Series 1937 Monaco with overdrive transmission. The Kestrel, Monaco and Touring Saloons were only offered with Special Series engines in 66 and 67 Series 9 h.p. models.

The chassis numbers on the 9 h.p. models built before August 1935 (up to chassis number 6027900) were stamped on to the front left hand dumb-iron as well as being on the brass chassis plate which was fixed to the car bulkhead. This applies also to 6 cylinder models before chassis number 44T 2499. All later models had the chassis number stamped on to the left hand engine mounting bracket.

In the early series of six-cylinder cars, it was now possible to identify certain models of cars from their chassis numbers. For example, 14S represented the Stelvio Saloon, 14L represented the Light Six Saloon (named 'Alpine' from October 1930) and 14 without a suffix showed the chassis was either a Deauville or a Tourer. It was possible to identify the later Stelvios, the Family Saloon (later named 'Winchester') and the Edinburgh models all by their chassis number prefixes, but those models built on the 44T series of chassis numbers were not identifiable. In fact the 44T series did not even use a common chassis frame, there being three different wheelbases under that prefix, making identification by chassis number impossible. However, with the 1936 model year came the new numbering system used by Riley, so it was now possible to identify all models by their chassis numbers.

The first two chassis number sequences for the Six-cylinder cars overlapped until 1934, because Edinburghs, Stelvios and Winchesters were still being produced alongside their 44T counterparts. The actual numbers for that early series were all taken from the same block, with the exception of the Edinburgh and Winchester models, running from 200 to 1120, but produced in small batches, hence the late Stelvios appearing to be out of sequence. The 88E series was produced as the Edinburgh and the Family Saloon (later Winchester), with chassis numbers up to 263 allocated to Edinburghs. The first Winchester was number 264, but thereafter numbers were allocated out of the 200–1120 block (for example 88E 1017 was a Winchester 15/6, factory registered as ADU802 in 1934). So the six-cylinder number sequences ran thus:

| DATE FROM | CHASSIS NUMBERS | COMMENT |
|---|---|---|
| Oct. 1928 | 14/14S 200–699 (From blocks of numbers 200–1120) 14L up to 1117 | No letter prefix used for the 5 Seat Tourer or Deauville Saloon. S=Stelvio, produced up to 1935; L=Light Six (Alpine Saloon from Oct 1930). Internal rocker oil feed on 14/14S (LWB) models from chassis number 369 and on 14L (SWB) model from number 567. |
| Oct. 1932 | 88E up to 263 | Edinburgh Saloon/Limousine. |

| Oct. 1932 | 88E 264 upwards | Family Saloon, later named Winchester (after c/n 264, Winchester numbers were taken in sequence with other models from the 200–1120 block). |
| | 14S 700–799 | Stelvio Six-Fourteen Saloon. |
| | 14L Series | Very small number of Alpines built. |
| | 44T 101–1300 | Ascot, Kestrel, Lincock, Lynx, MPH, March Special 6/12, Mentone 6/12. All-helical gearbox from December 1932. |
| Oct. 1933 | 14S 800–929 | Stelvio Six-Fourteen Saloon. |
| | 44T 1301–2243 | All short wheelbase models as 44T 101–1300 with addition of Alpine 6/14. |
| Sep. 1934 | 15S 930 upwards | Stelvio Six-Fifteen Saloon. |
| Oct. 1934 | 44T 2244–2499 | Six-Fifteen Falcon, Kestrel, Lynx, MPH. |
| Apr 1935 | 14L 1120 allocated | Last of 200–1120 block, Alpine Saloon 14/6, factory registered as AVC 9. |
| July 1935 | 46A/F/K/L 2500–3000 | 6/12 or 6/15 Adelphi, Falcon, Kestrel or Lynx 1936 series. |
| Oct. 1936 | 47A/K 3001–3299 | 6/15 Adelphi or Kestrel 1937 series. |
| Oct. 1937 | 48A/K 3300 upwards | 6/15 Adelphi or Kestrel 1938 series. |

The $1\frac{1}{2}$ litre 12 h.p. four-cylinder models are the easiest of all to identify from their chassis numbers, except for the first year of their production, when all the models—Falcon, Kestrel and Lynx—had the same chassis number prefix, 22T. But after the change in the chassis numbering system of July 1935, for the 1936 series of cars, all models in all ranges were identifiable from the chassis number. In the case of the $1\frac{1}{2}$ litre, it was possible to tell whether a Standard Series, Special Series or Sprite Series engine was fitted. The Sprite Two Seaters of course were only fitted with Sprite Series engines and so the letter prefix used to identify them was simply 'S' followed by the year code 26, 27 or 28 a suffix 'S' and the actual number of the chassis.

From July 1935 each model was identified by a two digit year code followed by a letter code for the model and then the number of the frame. For example:

|  | 26 | — | K | — | 2200 |
|---|---|---|---|---|---|
|  | Year of build 1936 | | Kestrel | | Chassis Number |
| or: | S—26 | — | K | — | 2200 |
|  | Special Series—1936 build— | | Kestrel | — | Chassis Number |
| or: | SS—26— | | K | — | 2200 |
|  | Sprite Series—1936— | | Kestrel | — | Chassis Number |

and the Sprite Two Seater: S 26S | | — | 2698
Sprite 1936 | | — | Chassis Number

The individual model letters were:

A=Adelphi C=Touring Saloon (Continental) F=Falcon & 1938 Touring Saloon K=Kestrel M=Merlin L=Lynx V=Victor.

In 1937 and 1938, models were offered with dual overdrive transmission and so a suffix letter 'X' was used to denote that a particular car was fitted with overdrive and its chassis number would appear thus:

| SS | 28 | KX | | 7200 |
|---|---|---|---|---|
| Sprite Series—1938— | | Kestrel overdrive— | | Chassis Number |

The $1\frac{1}{2}$ litre chassis number sequences ran:

| Date from | Commencing Chassis Number | Comment |
|---|---|---|
| Oct. 1934 | 22T 101– | 1935 Series Kestrel, Lynx, Falcon. |
| July 1935 | 26A/K/L/M/F & S26S 2201 | 1936 Series models. |
| Oct. 1936 | S27S & 27A/C/F/K/L 5001 | 1937 Series models. |
| Oct. 1937 | S28S & 28A/F/K/L/V 7201 | 1938 Series models. |

The chassis number on the 1½ litre models can be found stamped on the near (left) side engine mounting bracket, as well as on the chassis plate mounted on the bulkhead.

On the early 1½ litres, the battery master switch was mounted on the offside of the scuttle panel, but from chassis number 22T108 it was located on the rear shelf behind the rear seats. Engines up to 22T333 had chain driven camshafts, gear drive being used from 22T334.

The Eight-Ninety 'Silver Streak' and Big Four 'Blue Streak' ranges had easily identified models and their numbers ran as follows:

| Date from | Commencing Chassis Number | | Comment |
|---|---|---|---|
| Oct. 1935 | 86A/K | 101 | Offered as 9 ft. 4½ in. W.B., then on 9 ft. 8½ in. W.B. Changeover |
| Oct. 1936 | 87A/K | 201 | number probably 86A 109 to 87A 201. |
| Oct. 1937 | 87A | 212 | 9 ft. 8½ in. W.B., Adelphi only, PSG. |
| Oct. 1937 | 38A/B/K/L | 1001 | All models fitted dual overdrive gearbox & model letters followed by 'X'. |

In the case of the Big Four 16 h.p. models, A denoted Adelphi, B was either version of Touring Saloon, K was Kestrel and L the only Big Four Lynx built.

From the introduction of the new numbering system in July 1935, when a set of numbers was embarked upon in each range, the numbers ran in straight sequence, regardless of model, so that chassis number 2201 might have been a Kestrel (26K2201) and 2202 might have been a Lynx (26L2202). From this we can see, by comparison with the early Nine and Six chassis numbers, that production fell after the introduction of the 1½ litre range. This seems to be the result of introducing other ranges as well as widening the choice of models, so that at one time the prospective Riley owner had the choice of 9 h.p., 1½ litre, 8/90, Six-Fifteen or Big Four with as many as five types of coachwork on any one chassis.

A final point about chassis numbers in the period of the 11.9 h.p. side-valve and the early 9 h.p. models is that the first two digits of both are identifying features. The 11.9s went to a six digit number starting '69' and the 9 h.p. also used a six digit number, later extending to a seven digit number starting '60'. The only logical reason for the Nines suddenly switching to a seven digit number at chassis number 6010000 is that the number really was 60–10,000: number 10,000 in the series. It is logical because the bore of the side valve engine was 69 mm., and the bore of the 9 was 60.3 mm., suggesting '60' as the identifying feature.

And so, at chassis number ?29? 8001, Rileys become something different—for ever.

# GLOSSARY OF TERMS USED IN APPENDICES TWO AND THREE

Most models listed in these two Appendices are listed by their full name but, for the sake of space in column widths, it has been necessary to abbreviate some and, whilst most are obvious to the seasoned Riley owner and enthusiast, some readers will need advice on the terminology used.

| *Term.* | *Explanation.* |
|---|---|
| $1\frac{1}{2}$ | $1\frac{1}{2}$ Litre (12/4) Model. |
| 2D | 2 Door Model. |
| 2S | 2 Seater Model. |
| 4/5 | 4/5 Seater (as 4/5 Seat Tourer). |
| 9 | 9 H.P. Model. |
| 8–90 | 18 H.P. V8 Models (Silver Streak). |
| 10.8 | 10.8 H.P. Side-valve Model (11/40). |
| 11.9 | 11.9 H.P. Side-valve Model (Twelve). |
| 12/6 | 12 H.P. Six Cylinder Model. |
| 14/6 | 14 H.P. Six Cylinder Model. |
| 15/6 | 15 H.P. Six Cylinder Model. |
| 16/4 | 16 H.P. Big Four Model (Blue Streak). |
| CC TRG SAL | Close Coupled Touring Saloon. |
| COL OR COLNL | Colonial Model (Export). |
| CONCRS OR CNCRS | Concours Model (as Lynx-Concours). |
| CONTNTL | Continental (as in Continental Coupé). |
| DHC | Drop Head Coupé. |
| EXP | Experimental. |
| FHC | Fixed Head Coupé. |
| LIM | Limousine (as Autovia Limousine). |
| M/CYCLE | Motor Cycle. |
| SAL | Saloon (as Alpine Saloon). |
| SPL | Special (as March Special). |
| SPR (as a suffix to a name) | Sprite Series (e.g. Lynx-Sprite). |
| TR | Tourer (as Alpine Tourer). |
| TRG SAL | Touring Saloon. |

It will be noticed that no model years have been included in either Appendix, because the dating information appears in Appendix 1. Therefore, by referring a chassis number to Appendix 1, the reader will easily be able to identify the model year of a car listed.

Looking through these appendices, the question must inevitably arise: "How many Rileys were built in those first forty years?" The precise answer is not available, of course, but the chassis numbers we do know tell us quite a lot and when we add these to the loose statistics published in the very early days of the motor industry, we can at least produce a reasonably well educated guess.

For example, the early press talks of Riley car production being at the rate of seven cars a week in 1907, in addition to the production of tricars and pedal bicycles. This and other evidence leads us, with the aid of known chassis numbers, to estimate the pre-1914 production of motor bicycles, tricars and four wheeled cars to have been around 4000, averaging five vehicles per week, which is well in line with production statistics of the day. On the basis of the same kind of information, bicycle output between 1896 and 1911 was probably around 3000, knowing that production had reduced to just a trickle by 1911, when bicycle manufacture ceased, and that it had been low for two years before that.

The side-valve era yields very little more really concrete information, since chassis number issues are again not available, but we do know a little more than of the pre-war situation. We know, for example, that the first 11 h.p. (better known now as 10.8) chassis numbers started at 101 and that the sequence started again at 69101 for the 12 h.p. (11.9) in the 1925 model year. We know the Sports models continued in the 11/40 series of numbers and we know, from late examples of cars on record, that 11 h.p. production ran to around 5000 cars and that 12 h.p. production seems to have been not more than 4000.

With the introduction of the Nine, statistics become much easier to produce because most numbers are on record, though there a few oddities even here. From the published chassis numbers we know that some 27900 Nines were built between 1926 and 1935, excluding the Brooklands cars which had a different chassis number sequence. From the information known of the Brooklands Nine, it can be concluded that Thomson and Taylor probably built 20 cars and Riley built the remaining 93, making 113 in all. The last chassis number recorded in these appendices for the second series of Nines, which began with the Merlin and ended with the Victor, is 3468 and we know that production was at a very low ebb in 1938, so it is reasonable to suggest that it is unlikely more than 150 9 h.p. Victors were built, making the total second generation of Nines produced around 3450 (remembering that the series began with chassis number 101).

Six-cylinder cars account for about 1000 cars in the first (14S/14L/15S/88E) series, 2400 in the second (44T) series and 850 in the third (46/47/48) series, making a total of 4550.

Around 7800 1½ Litres were built in the 22T/26/27/28 Series and it seems 313 Big Fours left the factory. The last 86 Series 8-90 (an Adelphi) was number 109, with the series beginning at 101, and the last 87 Series 8-90 recorded here was 228, the number sequence beginning again in 1937 at 201. That makes a total of 37 V8 Rileys, to which may fairly be added the Autovias, since they were really Riley-built. The last Autovia known is chassis number S63141, a saloon, giving us 78 Riley and Autovia V8s.

So our final estimate can now be put together. To the 4000 motor vehicles and 3000 pedal cycles of the pre-1914 period, we can add 9000 side-valve cars, 31463 first and second-generation Nines (including the Brooklands models), 4550 Sixes, 7800 1½ Litres, 313 Big Fours, 78 V8s and 20 odd numbers used for experimental and non-production chassis (such as the Brooklands Sixes, the 1933 TT Sixes and other odd racing and experimental cars) and we have a grand total of just over 60,200 units in forty years. Some 4,500-odd are recorded here, representing about 7½% of the total or just under 8% of the number of motorised vehicles built by Riley (Coventry) Limited.

# Known Rileys in Registration Number Sequence

This Appendix aims to provide the reader with a list of all the known Riley registration numbers which can be identified to cars. It will be seen that the list aims to give three pieces of information for each car listed—the registration number, the model of car and the chassis number. Where one of two pieces of information is missing—for example, if the registration number and chassis number are known, or if the registration number and model are known, the car has been included in the list. It should be noted that the list was sorted in strict alpha-numeric sequence, which means that three-letter registration numbers appear before two-letter ones. Cars located overseas are identified with the international identification letters shown against the registration number. Appendices 2 and 3 are intended to cross-refer as far as possible. However, a number of registration and chassis numbers are not known for particular cars, so those without registration numbers are not included in this list and those without chassis numbers are excluded from Appendix 3, making this list somewhat longer, as would be expected.

To find a particular car, simply seek out the registration number and you can identify the model, its chassis number and, with the aid of Appendix 1, the year of build.

An asterisk against the registration number denotes a Riley factory-registered car. The mark # against the registration number of a Brooklands 9 car indicates that it was reported as registered by Thomson and Taylor Limited.

In lists such as these, errors are inevitable, so whilst it is appropriate to say that every effort has been made to eliminate them, the author hopes the reader will forgive those which may be found.

| REG NUMBER | MODEL | CHASSIS NO | |
|---|---|---|---|
| AAA427 | KESTREL 1½ | 22T | ---- |
| AAC346 | FALCON 1½ | 22T | ---- |
| AAD566 | IMP 9 | 60 | 25410 |
| AAD659 | FALCON 1½ | 22T | ---- |
| AAD848 | FALCON 1½ | 22T | ---- |
| AAE 32 | FALCON 9 | 60 | 22345 |
| AAF497 | KESTREL 12/6 | 44T | ---- |
| AAF697 | KESTREL 12/6 | 44T | 2004 |
| AAH674 | FALCON 1½ | 26F | ---- |
| AAH716 | KESTREL 1½ | 22T | ---- |
| AAJ 7 | KESTREL SPR 1½ | SS27K | ---- |
| AAJ624 | TRG SAL 9 | S68C | ---- |
| AAL804 | KESTREL 9 | 60 | 22440 |
| AAM488 | ADELPHI 1½ | 26A | ---- |
| AAO336 | KESTREL 9 | 60 | ---- |
| AAP276 | MONACO 9 | S67Z | ---- |
| AAP336 | KESTREL 9 | 60 | ---- |
| AAP682 | MONACO 9 | S67Z | ---- |
| AAP994 | FALCON 1½ | 27F | ---- |
| AAT165 | MONACO 9 | 60 | ---- |
| AAT166 | MONACO 9 | 60 | ---- |
| AAT939 | KESTREL 9 | 60 | 25606 |
| AAY 36 | MONACO 9 | S67Z | ---- |
| AAY338 | ADELPHI 1½ | 27A | 5237 |
| ABA525 | SPRITE 1½ | S28S | 7829 |
| ABC 3 | MERLIN 1½ | 26M | ---- |
| ABH431 | TOURER 9 | 60 | 21707 |
| ABJ336 | LYNX 9 | 60 | ---- |
| ABJ475 | LYNX 9 | 60 | ---- |
| ABK 23 | KESTREL 15/6 | 46K | ---- |
| ABK595 | MONACO 9 | S67Z | ---- |
| ABL 6 | ADELPHI 1½ | 26A | ---- |
| ABL147 | KESTREL 1½ | S27K | 5403 |
| ABL250 | KESTREL 1½ | 26K | ---- |
| ABL400 | KESTREL 1½ | 27K | ---- |
| ABM132 | ADELPHI 1½ | 26A | 3846 |
| ABR 23 | KESTREL 15/6 | 46K | ---- |
| ABT161 | FALCON 1½ | 27F | ---- |
| ABU616 | KESTREL 1½ | 28K | ---- |
| ABU775 | KESTREL 1½ | 28K | 7532 |
| ABY915 | KESTREL 1½ | 22T | 593 |
| AB1390 | 10 HP 2 SEATER | ---- / | 2018 |
| ACA167 | ADELPHI 1½ | 27A | ---- |
| ACA367 | MONACO 9 | S67Z | 2893 |
| ACA447 | CC TRG SAL 1½ | 27C | ---- |
| ACA677 | LINCOCK 14/6 | 44T | ---- |
| ACA736 | FALCON 1½ | 27F | ---- |
| ACA944 | MONACO 9 | S67Z | ---- |
| ACD 11 | KESTREL 12/6 | 44T | ---- |
| ACD590 | KESTREL SPR 1½ | SS26K | ---- |
| ACD897 | KESTREL 9 | 60 | ---- |
| ACE 40 | MONACO 9 | 60 | 24452 |
| ACE100 | MENTONE 12/6 | 44T | 1996 |
| ACE108 | KESTREL 12/6 | 44T | ---- |
| ACE370 | MONACO 9 | 60 | 23404 |
| ACE677 | LINCOCK 14/6 | 44T | 1690 |
| ACG684 | FALCON 1½ | 27F | ---- |
| ACJ 70 | ADELPHI 1½ | 27A | ---- |

| REG NUMBER | MODEL | CHASSIS NO. | |
|---|---|---|---|
| ACR205 | KESTREL 1½ | 27K | ---- |
| ACR308 | LYNX SPR 1½ | SS27L | ---- |
| ACR634 | LYNX 1½ | 27L | ---- |
| ACR864 | FALCON 1½ | 27F | ---- |
| ACR909 | MONACO 9 | S67Z | 2627 |
| ACV852 | FALCON 1½ | 26F | ---- |
| ADA456 | KESTREL SPR 1½ | SS27K | 5341 |
| ADA885 | KESTREL 1½ | 26K | ---- |
| ADF715 | FALCON 1½ | 22T | 1942 |
| ADG 3 | LYNX 1½ | 27L | ---- |
| ADG217 | FALCON 1½ | 26F | ---- |
| ADG406 | MERLIN 9 | S66M | 1315 |
| ADG549 | MERLIN 1½ | 27M | ---- |
| ADG888 | MPH 12/6 | 44T | 2249 |
| ADL190 | KESTREL 1½ | 26K | 3421 |
| ADM477 | MERLIN 9 | 67M | ---- |
| ADP191 | LYNX SPR 1½ | SS28L | ---- |
| ADR 48 | FALCON 1½ | 27F | ---- |
| ADR891 | KESTREL 1½ | 26K | ---- |
| ADU 22* | MENTONE 12/6 | 44T | 2207 |
| ADU 23* | MONACO 9 | 60 | 26012 |
| ADU 24* | MENTONE 12/6 | 44T | 2122 |
| ADU 25* | MENTONE 12/6 | 44T | 2164 |
| ADU 26* | MONACO 9 | 60 | 26040 |
| ADU 27* | GAMECOCK 14/6 | 44T | 1733 |
| ADU 28* | GAMECOCK 14/6 | 44T | 1734 |
| ADU 29*-DK | GAMECOCK 14/6 | 44T | 1735 |
| ADU 30* | LYNX 14/6 | 44T | ---- |
| ADU 31* | KESTREL 9 | 60 | 26005 |
| ADU 32* | KESTREL 9 | 60 | 24976 |
| ADU 33* | MONACO 9 | 60 | 24941 |
| ADU154* | MONACO 9 | 60 | 24956 |
| ADU155* | MONACO 9 | 60 | 24890 |
| ADU156* | MENTONE 12/6 | 44T | 1433 |
| ADU157* | KESTREL 9 | 60 | 24680 |
| ADU158* | MONACO 9 | 60 | 24481 |
| ADU159* | MENTONE 12/6 | 44T | 2219 |
| ADU160* | MONACO 9 | 60 | 24487 |
| ADU161* | MENTONE 12/6 | 44T | 2172 |
| ADU162* | ULSTER IMP 9 | 60 | 24992 |
| ADU163* | KESTREL 9 | 60 | 24985 |
| ADU164* | KESTREL 9 | 60 | 24851 |
| ADU165* | MONACO 9 | 60 | 24886 |
| ADU293* | KESTREL 9 | 60 | 24908 |
| ADU294* | STELVIO 15/6 | 15S | 940 |
| ADU295* | MONACO 9 | 60 | 24281 |
| ADU296* | MONACO 9 | 60 | 24904 |
| ADU297* | MONACO 9 | 60 | 24604 |
| ADU298* | MENTONE 12/6 | 44T | 2155 |
| ADU299* | KESTREL 9 | 60 | 24822 |
| ADU300* | ULSTER IMP 9 | 60 | 25034 |
| ADU301* | ULSTER IMP 9 | 60 | 25035 |
| ADU302* | ULSTER IMP 9 | 60 | 25038 |
| ADU303* | ULSTER IMP 9 | 60 | 25036 |
| ADU304* | MONACO 9 | 60 | 24528 |
| ADU529* | MPH 12/6 | 44T | 2248 |
| ADU530* | KESTREL 9 | 60 | 25000 |
| ADU531* | FALCON 1½ | 22T | 102 |

| REG NUMBER | MODEL | CHASSIS NO | |
|---|---|---|---|
| ADU532* | KESTREL 1½ | 22T | 103 |
| ADU533* | FALCON 1½ | 22T | 104 |
| ADU534* | MONACO 9 | 60 | 24619 |
| ADU535* | KESTREL 9 | 60 | 25019 |
| ADU536* | KESTREL 9 | 60 | 25011 |
| ADU537* | KESTREL 9 | 60 | 24999 |
| ADU538* | KESTREL 9 | 60 | 25013 |
| ADU539* | MONACO 9 | 60 | 24732 |
| ADU540* | STELVIO 15/6 | 15S | 946 |
| ADU709* | FALCON 1½ | 26F | 3376 |
| ADU801* | IMP 9 | 60 | 25044 |
| ADU802* | WINCHESTER 15/6 | 88E | 1017 |
| ADU803* | KESTREL 9 | 60 | 25166 |
| ADU804* | FALCON 15/6 | 44T | 2250 |
| ADU805* | KESTREL 9 | 60 | 25165 |
| ADU806* | STELVIO 15/6 | 15S | 939 |
| ADU807* | MONACO 9 | 60 | 24888 |
| ADU808* | MONACO 9 | 60 | 25239 |
| ADU809* | MONACO 9 | 60 | 24887 |
| ADU810* | FALCON 1½ | 22T | 122 |
| ADU811* | FALCON 1½ | 22T | 125 |
| ADU812* | FALCON 1½ | 22T | 121 |
| ADV159 | MENTONE 12/6 | 44T | ---- |
| ADV709 | FALCON 1½ | 26F | ---- |
| ADV758 | FALCON 1½ | 27F | ---- |
| ADV904 | MERLIN 9 | 66M | ---- |
| ADW507 | MONACO 9 | S67Z | ---- |
| ADW872 | CC TRG SAL 1½ | 27C | 6342 |
| AED 25 | MERLIN 1½ | 26M | 4271 |
| AED573 | KESTREL 1½ | 27K | ---- |
| AED971 | ADELPHI 1½ | 27A | ---- |
| AEE186 | MONACO 9 | 60 | ---- |
| AEH746 | MONACO 9 | 60 | ---- |
| AEL826 | ASCOT 9 | 60 | 25936 |
| AER 22 | KESTREL SPR 1½ | SS27K | ---- |
| AEV324 | MONACO 9 | 60 | ---- |
| AEV388 | MONACO 9 | 60 | 20653 |
| AEW962 | VICTOR 1½ | 28V | ---- |
| AFC176 | LYNX 9 | 60 | 25912 |
| AFG172 | FALCON 1½ | 22T | ---- |
| AFM254 | FALCON 1½ | 26F | ---- |
| AFR384 | KESTREL 16/4 | 38KX | 1243 |
| AFV388 | MONACO 9 | 60 | ---- |
| AF7747-NZ | FALCON 1½ | 26F | 4654 |
| AGA288 | FALCON 1½ | 26F | ---- |
| AGB407 | FALCON 1½ | 26F | ---- |
| AGB594 | ADELPHI 15/6 | 46A | ---- |
| AGD 11 | KESTREL 14/6 | 44T | ---- |
| AGD590 | KESTREL SPR 1½ | SS27K | 5994 |
| AGF581 | KESTREL 12/6 | 44T | 439 |
| AGF801 | MONACO 9 | 60 | 21218 |
| AGG214 | MERLIN 9 | 67M | ---- |
| AGJ 45 | LYNX 9 | 60 | 20169 |
| AGJ 88 | KESTREL 14/6 | 44T | ---- |
| AGJ518 | MONACO 9 | 60 | ---- |
| AGJ528 | MONACO 9 | 60 | 20843 |
| AGK809 | ADELPHI 15/6 | 47K | ---- |
| AGK944 | KESTREL 12/6 | 44T | 602 |

| REG NUMBER | MODEL | CHASSIS NO. | |
|---|---|---|---|
| AGK947 | MENTONE 12/6 | 44T | ---- |
| AGN256 | LYNX 9 | 60 | ---- |
| AGN257 | MONACO 9 | 60 | ---- |
| AGN603 | MENTONE 12/6 | 44T | ---- |
| AGN740 | ALPINE SPL 12/6 | 44T | ---- |
| AGO328 | LYNX 9 | 60 | ---- |
| AGO405 | FALCON 9 | 60 | ---- |
| AGP253 | TRINITY 9 | 60 | 21749 |
| AGU426 | MONACO 9 | 60 | ---- |
| AGU653 | MENTONE 12/6 | 44T | 634 |
| AGW268 | LYNX 9 | 60 | 21726 |
| AGW270 | KESTREL 6 | 44T | ---- |
| AGX947 | MONACO 9 | 60 | 21776 |
| AGY515 | MARCH SPL 9 | 60 | 19006 |
| AG7384 | MONACO 9 | 60 | 16779 |
| AG8512 | - - 9 | 60 | 20297 |
| AHK400 | MONACO 9 | 60 | 21732 |
| AHK714 | MONACO 9 | 60 | ---- |
| AHK883 | FALCON 9 | 60 | ---- |
| AHM103 | KESTREL 1½ | 28K | ---- |
| AHP201* | MONACO 9 | 60 | 26115 |
| AHP202* | KESTREL 9 | 60 | 25313 |
| AHP203* | MPH 12/6 | 44T | 2257 |
| AHP204* | MONACO 9 | 60 | 25308 |
| AHP205* | KESTREL 1½ | 22T | 138 |
| AHP206* | KESTREL 9 | 60 | 25326 |
| AHP207* | FALCON 1½ | 22T | 156 |
| AHP208* | KESTREL 9 | 60 | 26087 |
| AHP209* | FALCON 1½ | 22T | 171 |
| AHP210* | FALCON 1½ | 22T | 665 |
| AHP211* | FALCON 1½ | 22T | 211 |
| AHP212* | FALCON 1½ | 22T | 239 |
| AHP541* | FALCON 15/6 | 44T | 2244 |
| AHP542* | IMP 9 | 60 | 25444 |
| AHP543* | KESTREL 9 | 60 | 27203 |
| AHP544* | KESTREL 1½ | 22T | 419 |
| AHP545* | IMP 9 | 60 | 26133 |
| AHP546* | FALCON 1½ | 22T | 507 |
| AHP547* | MONACO COLNL 9 | 60 | 26132 |
| AHP548* | FALCON 1½ | 22T | 340 |
| AHP549* | FALCON 1½ | 22T | 530 |
| AHP550* | FALCON 1½ | 22T | 615 |
| AHP551* | KESTREL 1½ | 22T | 349 |
| AHP552* | FALCON 1½ | 22T | 563 |
| AHP883* | FALCON 1½ | 22T | --- |
| AHP925* | FALCON 1½ | 22T | 1918 |
| AHP981* | FALCON 1½ | 22T | 564 |
| AHP982* | FALCON 1½ | 22T | 567 |
| AHP983* | FALCON 1½ | 22T | 699 |
| AHP984* | KESTREL 15/6 | 44T | 2245 |
| AHP985* | FALCON 1½ | 22T | 642 |
| AHP986* | KESTREL 1½ | 22T | 787 |
| AHP987* | FALCON 1½ | 22T | 788 |
| AHP988* | FALCON 1½ | 22T | 793 |
| AHP989* | KESTREL 1½ | 22T | 591 |
| AHP990* | FALCON 1½ | 22T | 754 |
| AHP991* | KESTREL 9 | 60 | 27126 |
| AHP992* | KESTREL 9 | 60 | 27119 |

| REG NUMBER | MODEL | CHASSIS NO | |
|---|---|---|---|
| AHS 29 | ADELPHI 1½ | 27A | 6953 |
| AHT941 | ALPINE SAL 14/6 | 44T | ---- |
| AHU 58 | KESTREL 9 | 60 | 23471 |
| AHU 96 | KESTREL 9 | 60 | ---- |
| AHU233 | MONACO 9 | 60 | 23584 |
| AHV183 | KESTREL 9 | 60 | ---- |
| AHW484 | KESTREL 9 | 60 | ---- |
| AHW623 | LYNX 9 | 60 | ---- |
| AHX 73 | MONACO 9 | 60 | 19846 |
| AHX490 | KESTREL 9 | 60 | 20324 |
| AHY368 | KESTREL 9 | 60 | 2511R |
| AJA331 | MONACO 9 | 60 | ---- |
| AJB324 | ADELPHI 1½ | 27A | ---- |
| AJG528 | MONACO 9 | 60 | 20843 |
| AJH331 | MONACO 9 | S67Z | ---- |
| AJH378 | KESTREL 1½ | 22T | ---- |
| AJH531 | IMP 9 | 60 | ---- |
| AJK351 | MONACO 9 | 60 | ---- |
| AJO497 | KESTREL 1½ | 22T | 957 |
| AJU121 | MONACO 9 | S67Z | ---- |
| AJX309 | VICTOR 1½ | 28V | ---- |
| AJY283 | TRG SAL 1½ | 28F | ---- |
| AKA582 | KESTREL 9 | 60 | ---- |
| AKA704 | KESTREL 9 | 60 | ---- |
| AKB211 | FALCON 15/6 | 46F | 2505 |
| AKB212 | MONACO 9 | 60 | 27624 |
| AKC257 | FALCON 1½ | 22T | ---- |
| AKD106 | MONACO 9 | 60 | ---- |
| AKD401 | KESTREL 1½ | 22T | ---- |
| AKD410 | KESTREL 1½ | 22T | ---- |
| AKF 3 | FALCON 1½ | 22T | 1833 |
| AKF975 | LYNX 1½ | 22T | ---- |
| AKH228 | FALCON 1½ | 22T | 152 |
| AKH275 | MONACO 9 | 60 | ---- |
| AKH696 | MONACO 9 | 60 | ---- |
| AKJ710 | LYNX 9 | 60 | 20168 |
| AKK637 | LYNX 9 | 60 | 21070 |
| AKK971-I | MONACO 9 | 60 | ---- |
| AKO902 | KESTREL 12/6 | 44T | ---- |
| AKP878 | LINCOCK 9 | 60 | ---- |
| AKR827 | LYNX 9 | 60 | ---- |
| AKT566 | MONACO 9 | 60 | 25622 |
| AKT618 | MENTONE 12/6 | 44T | ---- |
| AKU633 | KESTREL 1½ | 22T | 1011 |
| AKV207 | KESTREL 1½ | 22T | ---- |
| AKV210* | FALCON 1½ | 26F | 2264 |
| AKV213* | FALCON 1½ | 26F | 2384 |
| AKV214* | FALCON 1½ | 26F | 2394 |
| AKV215* | FALCON 1½ | 26F | 2413 |
| AKV216* | IMP 9 | 60 | 27685 |
| AKV217* | MERLIN 1½ | 26M | 2476 |
| AKV218* | SPRITE 1½ | S26S | 2429 |
| AKV241* | FALCON 1½ | 26F | 2386 |
| AKV242* | LYNX 1½ | 26L | 2420 |
| AKV243* | FALCON 1½ | 26F | 2523 |
| AKV244* | FALCON 1½ | 26F | 2427 |
| AKV245* | MERLIN 9 | 66M | 101 |
| AKV246* | FALCON 1½ | 26F | 2499 |

| REG NUMBER | MODEL | CHASSIS NO. | |
|---|---|---|---|
| AKV247* | FALCON 1½ | 26F | 2524 |
| AKV248* | FALCON 1½ | 26F | 2564 |
| AKV249* | FALCON 1½ | 26F | 2538 |
| AKV250* | FALCON 1½ | S26F | 2484 |
| AKV251* | FALCON 15/6 | 46F | 2528 |
| AKV252* | MERLIN 9 | 66M | 140 |
| AKV278 | FALCON 1½ | 22T | ---- |
| AKV655 | MERLIN 1½ | 26M | 2905 |
| AKV757* | FALCON 1½ | 26F | 2664 |
| AKV758* | FALCON 1½ | 26F | 2646 |
| AKV759* | LYNX 1½ | 26L | 2684 |
| AKV760* | KESTREL COL 9 | S66K | 194 |
| AKV761* | FALCON 1½ | 26F | 2880 |
| AKV762* | FALCON 1½ | S26F | 2763 |
| AKV892* | KESTREL 1½ | 26K | 3504 |
| AKW 38 | KESTREL 1½ | 26K | ---- |
| AKW620 | KESTREL 1½ | 26K | ---- |
| AKX203 | KESTREL 1½ | 26K | ---- |
| AKY 8 | ADELPHI 1½ | S26A | 4299 |
| AKY203 | KESTREL 9 | S66K | ---- |
| AKY317 | FALCON 1½ | 26F | ---- |
| AKY345 | KESTREL 9 | S66K | 1773 |
| AKY830 | MERLIN 9 | 66M | 1517 |
| ALA870 | MONACO 9 | 60 | 21996 |
| ALB 42 | LYNX 9 | 60 | ---- |
| ALB147 | KESTREL 1½ | 27K | ---- |
| ALB196 | FALCON 9 | 60 | ---- |
| ALB608 | MONACO 9 | 60 | 19127 |
| ALC245 | LYNX 9 | 60 | ---- |
| ALE 99 | MONACO 9 | 60 | 20571 |
| ALE429 | LYNX 9 | 60 | ---- |
| ALE873 | TOURER 9 | 60 | ---- |
| ALF758 | LINCOCK 9 | 60 | 21700 |
| ALJ186 | KESTREL 9 | 60 | 25174 |
| ALJ325 | KESTREL 9 | 60 | 25355 |
| ALJ454 | IMP 9 | 60 | 25492 |
| ALJ914 | FALCON 1½ | 22T | ---- |
| ALM909 | LINCOCK 9 | 60 | 21245 |
| ALO100 | KESTREL 9 | 60 | ---- |
| ALO450 | KESTREL 12/6 | 44T | ---- |
| ALO562 | MONACO 9 | 60 | ---- |
| ALO569 | TRINITY 9 | 60 | 21575 |
| ALO604 | MONACO 9 | 60 | ---- |
| ALT325 | KESTREL 9 | 60 | ---- |
| ALU 5 | LINCOCK 9 | 60 | 22203 |
| ALU876 | ASCOT 9 | 60 | 21363 |
| ALV700 | KESTREL 1½ | 22T | ---- |
| ALV999 | FALCON 1½ | 26F | ---- |
| ALX170 | ASCOT 9 | 60 | 21351 |
| ALX466 | ASCOT 9 | 60 | ---- |
| ALY944 | MONACO 9 | 60 | ---- |
| AMA 70 | MONACO 9 | 60 | 21128 |
| AMA202 | MONACO 9 | 60 | 21535 |
| AMB 86 | LYNX 9 | 60 | ---- |
| AMC314 | MONACO 9 | 60 | ---- |
| AMD239 | MONACO 9 | 60 | ---- |
| AMD327 | KESTREL 12/6 | 44T | ---- |
| AME790 | MONACO 9 | 60 | 21541 |

| REG NUMBER | MODEL | CHASSIS NO. | |
|---|---|---|---|
| AMF818 | MONACO 9 | 60 | 22193 |
| AMH122 | MONACO 9 | 60 | 23831 |
| AMH202 | MONACO 9 | 60 | ---- |
| AMH874 | MONACO 9 | 60 | 22117 |
| AMJ245 | ADELPHI 1½ | 27A | ---- |
| AMJ454 | LYNX CONCRS 1½ | S27L | 6027 |
| AML713 | LYNX 9 | 60 | 22357 |
| AMM526 | KESTREL 9 | 60 | ---- |
| AMN874 | MONACO 9 | 60 | ---- |
| AMO547 | MONACO 9 | S67Z | ---- |
| AMR433 | KESTREL 1½ | 26K | ---- |
| AMV 11 | KESTREL 6 | 44T | ---- |
| AMV 41 | LINCOCK 12/6 | 44T | 1519 |
| AMV909 | LYNX 12/6 | 44T | 1022 |
| AMW774 | ADELPHI 1½ | 27A | 6406 |
| AMX 71 | MONACO 9 | 60 | 23076 |
| AMY818 | LINCOCK 9 | 60 | ---- |
| AM5344-NZ | KESTREL 15/6 | 47K | 3017 |
| ANB251 | MONACO 9 | 60 | 21282 |
| ANB320 | MONACO 9 | 60 | 22772 |
| ANB444 | KESTREL 6 | 44T | ---- |
| ANB956 | MONACO 9 | 60 | ---- |
| ANC462 | LYNX 12/6 | 44T | 1509 |
| ANC817 | MONACO 9 | 60 | 23727 |
| ANC992 | MONACO 9 | 60 | ---- |
| AND530 | KESTREL 9 | 60 | 23287 |
| AND916 | LYNX 9 | 60 | ---- |
| ANE519 | MONACO 9 | 60 | 24419 |
| ANF846 | KESTREL 12/6 | 44T | ---- |
| ANG177 | LYNX 6 | 44T | ---- |
| ANG466 | LYNX 1½ | 26L | ---- |
| ANM 22 | LYNX 1½ | 26L | ---- |
| ANM439 | ADELPHI 1½ | 26A | ---- |
| ANO290 | MONACO 9 | 60 | 21826 |
| ANO976 | LYNX 9 | 60 | ---- |
| ANP999 | KESTREL 9 | S66K | 1694 |
| ANR702 | ADELPHI 16/4 | 38AX | ---- |
| ANU202 | MONACO 9 | 60 | ---- |
| ANW837 | KESTREL 9 | 60 | 24911 |
| ANX 83 | MERLIN 1½ | 26M | 2934 |
| ANX305 | SPRITE 1½ | S26S | 3377 |
| ANX513 | ADELPHI 1½ | 26A | ---- |
| AOB281 | KESTREL 9 | 60 | ---- |
| AOC886 | KESTREL 9 | 60 | ---- |
| AOE500 | LYNX 9 | 60 | 25817 |
| AOE770 | KESTREL 14/6 | 44T | 2125 |
| AOG888 | MPH 14/6 | 44T | ---- |
| AOH231 | MONACO 9 | 60 | ---- |
| AOJ139 | KESTREL 1½ | 26K | ---- |
| AOJ431 | IMP 9 | 60 | ---- |
| AOJ849 | KESTREL 9 | 60 | ---- |
| AOJ888 | MPH 14/6 | 44T | ---- |
| AOK500 | MONACO 9 | 60 | 25496 |
| AOL763 | MPH 15/6 | 44T | 2256 |
| AOL793 | KESTREL 1½ | 22T | ---- |
| AOM450 | KESTREL 15/6 | 44T | 2320 |
| AON139 | KESTREL 1½ | 22T | ---- |
| AON434 | IMP 9 | 60 | 27305 |

| REG NUMBER | MODEL | CHASSIS NO | |
|---|---|---|---|
| AON837 | FALCON 1½ | 22T | ---- |
| AON948 | KESTREL 1½ | 22T | ---- |
| AOP900 | FALCON 1½ | 22T | ---- |
| AOP910 | FALCON 1½ | 22T | ---- |
| AOP912 | FALCON 1½ | 22T | 1368 |
| AOR 8 | FALCON 1½ | 22T | 1144 |
| AOT855 | MPH(BERTELLI)15 | 22T | 2255 |
| AOT889 | LYNX SPR 1½ | SS26L | ---- |
| AOT899 | LYNX 1½ | 22T | ---- |
| AOU934 | LYNX 1½ | 22T | ---- |
| AOV934 | LYNX 1½ | 22T | 1573 |
| AOV935 | LYNX 1½ | 22T | ---- |
| AOV973 | KESTREL 9 | 60 | ---- |
| AOY935 | LYNX 1½ | 22T | ---- |
| AO6609-NZ | CC TRG SAL 1½ | 27C | ---- |
| APA273 | MONACO 9 | 60 | 19845 |
| APA520 | TRINITY 9 | 60 | ---- |
| APA839 | SPRITE 1½ | S28S | 7917 |
| APA871 | MARCH SPL 9 | 60 | ---- |
| APB231 | LYNX 9 | 60 | 20254 |
| APB442 | MONACO 9 | 60 | 20402 |
| APB451 | MONACO 9 | 60 | ---- |
| APC 81 | LYNX 9 | 60 | ---- |
| APC246 | MARCH SPL 9 | 60 | ---- |
| APC436 | ASCOT 9 | 60 | 20880 |
| APC629 | MONACO 9 | 60 | 20841 |
| APD210 | BROOKLANDS 9 | 80 | -- |
| APF531 | LYNX 9 | 60 | 21300 |
| APG299 | ASCOT 9 | 60 | ---- |
| APG382 | LYNX 9 | 60 | 21762 |
| APG728 | LYNX 9 | 60 | 20892 |
| APH366 | LYNX 9 | 60 | ---- |
| APH982 | FALCON 1½ | 27F | ---- |
| APJ396 | MONACO 9 | 60 | ---- |
| APJ564 | KESTREL 9 | 60 | 22484 |
| APK263 | KESTREL 9 | 60 | 22503 |
| APK586 | LYNX 9 | 60 | 22362 |
| APK853 | KESTREL 9 | 60 | ---- |
| APM200 | KESTREL 9 | 60 | ---- |
| APM253 | ADELPHI 1½ | 27A | ---- |
| APM351 | SPRITE 1½ | S27S | 7069 |
| APM397 | TRG SAL 9 | 67C | ---- |
| APM485 | FALCON 1½ | 27F | 7074 |
| APN438 | ADELPHI 16/4 | 38AX | ---- |
| APN522 | LYNX 9 | 60 | 19394 |
| APN580 | ADELPHI 16/4 | 38AX | 1222 |
| APO681 | KESTREL 1½ | 22T | 1116 |
| APP 22 | LINCOCK 9 | 60 | 25696 |
| APP166 | KESTREL 12/6 | 44T | 1617 |
| APT466 | KESTREL 1½ | 27K | ---- |
| APT590 | IMP 9 | 60 | ---- |
| APU 54 | MONACO 9 | 60 | 21035 |
| APU200 | KESTREL 9 | 60 | ---- |
| APU821 | MENTONE 12/6 | 44T | ---- |
| APW808 | ADELPHI 1½ | 26A | 4078 |
| APX114 | FALCON 1½ | 22T | ---- |
| APX910 | KESTREL 1½ | 22T | 1316 |
| APY 76 | KESTREL 16/4 | 38KX | 1028 |

| REG NUMBER | MODEL | CHASSIS NO. |
|---|---|---|
| AR 3 | 9 HP CAR | ---- / 1058 |
| ARA996 | KESTREL 9 | 60 ---- |
| ARB399 | MONACO 9 | 60 ---- |
| ARE1932-NZ | MONACO 9 | 60 ---- |
| ARE230 | MONACO 9 | 60 ---- |
| ARE999 | KESTREL 9 | 60 25067 |
| ARF275 | ALPINE 14/6 | 44T ---- |
| ARF941 | LYNX 9 | 60 ---- |
| ARF951 | MONACO 9 | 60 21562 |
| ARF960 | MONACO 9 | 60 21711 |
| ARH248 | FALCON 1½ | 22T ---- |
| ARH258 | FALCON 1½ | 22T ---- |
| ARK741 | LYNX 1½ | 22T 2015 |
| ARL609 | KESTREL 1½ | 22T ---- |
| ARL859 | LYNX 1½ | 22T 1443 |
| ARM267 | KESTREL 9 | 60 27166 |
| ARM513 | KESTREL 1½ | 22T ---- |
| AR0225 | KESTREL 1½ | 22T 1959 |
| AR0247 | KESTREL 1½ | 22T 2003 |
| ARU824 | KESTREL 1½ | 22T 821 |
| ARV488 | ADELPHI 15/6 | 47A ---- |
| ARW271* | KESTREL 1½ | 22T 987 |
| ARW272* | KESTREL 1½ | 22T 937 |
| ARW273* | KESTREL 9 | 60 27132 |
| ARW274* | FALCON 1½ | 22T 958 |
| ARW275* | FALCON 1½ | 22T 881 |
| ARW276* | FALCON 1½ | 22T 971 |
| ARW277* | FALCON 1½ | 22T 1016 |
| ARW278* | KESTREL 9 | 60 27188 |
| ARW279* | FALCON 1½ | 22T 1032 |
| ARW280* | KESTREL 1½ | 22T 1035 |
| ARW281* | FALCON 1½ | 22T 1047 |
| ARW282* | KESTREL 1½ | 22T 1051 |
| ARW421* | MONACO 9 | 60 27223 |
| ARW422* | LYNX 9 | 60 27213 |
| ARW423* | FALCON 15/6 | 44T 2340 |
| ARW424* | KESTREL 1½ | 22T 1067 |
| ARW425* | KESTREL 1½ | 22T 1153 |
| ARW427* | FALCON 1½ | 22T 1092 |
| ARW428* | KESTREL 1½ | 22T 1052 |
| ARW429* | FALCON 1½ | 22T 1094 |
| ARW430* | FALCON 1½ | 22T 1174 |
| ARW431* | KESTREL 9 | 60 27197 |
| ARW432* | MONACO 9 | 60 27293 |
| ARW481* | KESTREL 1½ | 22T 1215 |
| ARW482* | FALCON 1½ | 22T 1169 |
| ARW483* | FALCON 1½ | 22T 1102 |
| ARW484* | FALCON 1½ | 22T 1180 |
| ARW485* | MPH 15 (COE354) | 44T 2246 |
| ARW486* | KESTREL 1½ | 22T 1347 |
| ARW487* | KESTREL 1½ | 22T 1216 |
| ARW488* | KESTREL 1½ | 22T 1298 |
| ARW489* | KESTREL 1½ | 22T 1404 |
| ARW490* | MONACO 9 | 60 27361 |
| ARW491* | IMP 9 | 60 27421 |
| ARW492* | FALCON 15/6 | 44T 2335 |
| ARY148 | KESTREL 9 | S66K ---- |
| ARY389 | LYNX 1½ | 28L 7484 |

| REG NUMBER | MODEL | CHASSIS NO. |
|---|---|---|
| AR1932-NZ | MONACO 9 | 60 ---- |
| AR1934-NZ | MONACO 9 | 60 ---- |
| AR1936-NZ | KESTREL 9 | S66K ---- |
| AR5685-NZ | ADELPHI 1½ | 27A ---- |
| AR6558-NZ | ADELPHI 1½ | 27A 5685 |
| AS 505-NZ | MENTONE 12/6 | 44T 1466 |
| ASC 55 | FALCON 1½ | 26F ---- |
| ASC544 | ADELPHI 1½ | 27A 5838 |
| ASC962 | FALCON 1½ | 27F 5853 |
| ASF522 | SPRITE 1½ | S27S 6299 |
| ASF772 | FALCON 1½ | 27F ---- |
| ASG279 | AUTOVIA SAL | S 63--- |
| ASP578 | KESTREL 15/6 | 47K ---- |
| ASP984 | ADELPHI 1½ | 26A 4364 |
| ASR292 | ADELPHI 15/6 | 47A ---- |
| ASR325 | ADELPHI 1½ | 27A ---- |
| ASR885 | FALCON 1½ | 27F ---- |
| AS2855-NZ | KESTREL 15/6 | 44T ---- |
| ATA779 | KESTREL 9 | 60 25003 |
| ATA948 | KESTREL 9 | 60 ---- |
| ATC158 | ADELPHI 1½ | 26A ---- |
| ATD346 | FALCON 1½ | 26F ---- |
| ATE157 | KESTREL 1½ | 26K 3655 |
| ATE220 | MERLIN 9 | 66M ---- |
| ATM 21 | ADELPHI 1½ | 26A 4916 |
| ATM277 | MERLIN 9 | 66M ---- |
| ATM504 | MONACO 9 | S67Z ---- |
| ATM709 | ADELPHI 1½ | 27A 5619 |
| ATM900 | KESTREL SPR 1½ | SS27K 5607 |
| AT0176 | MONACO 9 | 60 22839 |
| AT0393 | MONACO 9 | 60 26015 |
| ATP765 | ADELPHI 8-90 | 87A ---- |
| ATR341 | KESTREL 15/6 | 47K 3139 |
| ATR717 | KESTREL 1½ | 27K ---- |
| ATR718 | KESTREL 1½ | 27K ---- |
| ATT360 | FALCON 1½ | 22T ---- |
| ATT392 | IMP 9 | 60 25511 |
| ATT485 | KESTREL 1½ | 22T 815 |
| ATT956 | LYNX 9 | 60 27327 |
| ATV 60 | FALCON 1½ | 22T 115 |
| ATX891 | MERLIN 9 | 66M ---- |
| AUA324 | MONACO 9 | 60 ---- |
| AUA327 | MONACO 9 | 60 ---- |
| AUB920 | ULSTER IMP 9 | 60 ---- |
| AUC332 | KESTREL 6 | 44T ---- |
| AUE170 | MERLIN 1½ | 26M 4164 |
| AUF187 | MONACO 9 | 60 ---- |
| AUG 16 | FALCON 1½ | 22T 232 |
| AUG865 | IMP 9 | 60 ---- |
| AUG977 | MONACO 9 | 60 27218 |
| AUK210 | KESTREL 9 | 60 ---- |
| AUK328 | ADELPHI 1½ | 27A ---- |
| AUL 81 | MENTONE 12/6 | 44T 1378 |
| AUL718 | KESTREL 9 | 60 ---- |
| AUL763-IRL | MPH 14/6 | 44T ---- |
| AUM170 | MONACO 9 | S67Z ---- |
| AUM220 | MONACO 9 | S67Z ---- |
| AUM370 | KESTREL 1½ | 22T ---- |

| REG NUMBER | MODEL | CHASSIS NO |
|---|---|---|
| AUM772 | KESTREL 1½ | 26K ---- |
| AUN139 | KESTREL 1½ | 27K ---- |
| AUN169 | GAMECOCK 9 | 60 11594 |
| AUN170 | MONACO 9 | S67Z 2307 |
| AUN173 | MONACO 9 | S67Z 3055 |
| AUN220 | SPRITE 1½ | S26S ---- |
| AUN306 | KESTREL 1½ | 27K ---- |
| AUN352 | MONACO 9 | S67Z 3143 |
| AUN917 | CC TRG SAL 16/4 | 38BX 1217 |
| AUP912 | FALCON 1½ | 27F ---- |
| AUU298 | MONACO 9 | 60 23779 |
| AUU336 | MONACO 9 | 60 23810 |
| AUV395 | LYNX 9 | 60 ---- |
| AUV408 | KESTREL 9 | 60 ---- |
| AUW 44 | MENTONE 12/6 | 44T ---- |
| AUW 50 | MONACO 9 | 60 ---- |
| AUW267 | MONACO 9 | 60 ---- |
| AUW495 | TRINITY 9 | 60 ---- |
| AUW637 | MONACO 9 | 60 ---- |
| AU5536 | 3½ HP M/CYCLE | 2035 / 434 |
| AU6692-NZ | KESTREL 15/6 | 47K ---- |
| AVB430 | FALCON 1½ | 26F ---- |
| AVB756 | KESTREL 9 | 60 ---- |
| AVC 9* | ALPINE 14/6 | 14L 1120 |
| AVC 10* | FALCON 1½ | 22T 1770 |
| AVC 11* | LYNX 1½ | 22T 1917 |
| AVC 12* | FALCON 1½ | 22T 1805 |
| AVC 13* | FALCON 1½ | 22T 1886 |
| AVC 14* | FALCON 1½ | 22T 1737 |
| AVC 15* | TT SPRITE(MPH) | 44T 2407 |
| AVC 16* | TT SPRITE(MPH) | 44T 2418 |
| AVC 17* | TT SPRITE(MPH) | 44T 2419 |
| AVC 18* | TT SPRITE(MPH) | 44T 2420 |
| AVC 19* | TT SPRITE | 22T 1750 |
| AVC 20* | TT SPRITE | 22T 1916 |
| AVC189* | FALCON 1½ | 22T 1760 |
| AVC190* | KESTREL 15/6 | 44T 2388 |
| AVC191* | FALCON 1½ | 22T 1807 |
| AVC192* | KESTREL 1½ | 22T 1909 |
| AVC193* | LYNX COLNL 15/6 | 44T 2423 |
| AVC194* | FALCON 15/6 | 44T 2393 |
| AVC195* | MONACO COLNL 9 | 60 27634 |
| AVC196* | FALCON 1½ | 22T 1845 |
| AVC197* | LYNX 1½ | 22T 1976 |
| AVC198* | FALCON COLNL 1½ | 22T 2009 |
| AVC199* | FALCON 1½ | 22T 1965 |
| AVC200* | FALCON COL 15/6 | 44T 2430 |
| AVC333 | GAMECOCK CPE 9 | 60 ---- |
| AVC401* | KESTREL 1½ | 22T 1950 |
| AVC402* | FALCON 1½ | 22T 1848 |
| AVC403* | FALCON 1½ | 22T 1875 |
| AVC404* | KESTREL 1½ | 22T 2059 |
| AVC405* | KESTREL COL 1½ | 22T 1941 |
| AVC406* | FALCON 1½ | 22T 1987 |
| AVC407* | KESTREL 15/6 | 44T 2411 |
| AVC408* | BIARRITZ 9 | 60 15042 |
| AVC409* | FALCON COL 1½ | 22T 1942 |
| AVC410* | FALCON 15/6 | 44T 2413 |

| REG NUMBER | MODEL | CHASSIS NO |
|---|---|---|
| AVC411* | FALCON 15/6 | 44T 2435 |
| AVC412* | FALCON 1½ | 22T 2200 |
| AVC611* | FALCON 1½ | 22T 2007 |
| AVC612* | FALCON 1½ | 22T 2052 |
| AVC613* | FALCON 1½ | 22T 2067 |
| AVC614* | KESTREL 15/6 | 44T 2373 |
| AVC615* | FALCON 15/6 | 44T 2323 |
| AVC616* | FALCON COL 15/6 | 44T 2443 |
| AVC617* | MONACO 9 | 60 27585 |
| AVC618* | FALCON 15/6 | 44T 2448 |
| AVC619* | LYNX 1½ | 22T 2096 |
| AVC620* | MONACO 9 | 60 27652 |
| AVC621* | FALCON 1½ | 26F 2201 |
| AVC622* | FALCON 1½ | 26F 2251 |
| AVC973* | FALCON 1½ | 22T 1344 |
| AVC974* | FALCON 1½ | 22T 2139 |
| AVC975* | FALCON 1½ | 26F 2211 |
| AVC976* | FALCON 15/6 | 46F 2501 |
| AVC977* | FALCON 1½ | 26F 2235 |
| AVC978* | FALCON 1½ | 26F 2244 |
| AVC979* | FALCON 1½ | 26F 2288 |
| AVC980* | FALCON 1½ | S26F 2310 |
| AVC981* | FALCON 1½ | 26F 2296 |
| AVC982* | FALCON 1½ | 26F 2232 |
| AVC983* | FALCON 1½ | 26F 2305 |
| AVC984* | FALCON 1½ | 26F 2256 |
| AVE 6 | KESTREL 1½ | 22T 1302 |
| AVE196 | KESTREL 9 | 60 ---- |
| AVE500-USA | KESTREL 1½ | 22T 1951 |
| AVE888 | KESTREL 1½ | 22T ---- |
| AVG672 | KESTREL 1½ | 27K ---- |
| AVH 6 | MONACO 9 | S67Z ---- |
| AVK283 | KESTREL 15/6 | 44T ---- |
| AVK295 | KESTREL 9 | 60 ---- |
| AVK528 | KESTREL 9 | 60 24549 |
| AVK980 | MONACO 9 | 60 ---- |
| AVL207 | KESTREL 9 | 60 ---- |
| AVL718 | KESTREL 9 | 60 22512 |
| AVM772 | KESTREL 1½ | 22T 1570 |
| AVN 61 | VICTOR 1½ | 28VX 7778 |
| AVN206 | VICTOR 9 | 68V ---- |
| AVR 35 | KESTREL 12/6 | 44T 2204 |
| AVR520 | KESTREL 9 | 60 24859 |
| AVT997 | KESTREL 9 | 60 25175 |
| AVU808 | IMP 9 | 60 25144 |
| AV5437 | GAMECOCK 9 | 60 18151 |
| AV7144 | MONACO 9 | 60 24921 |
| AV7829 | MERLIN 9 | 66M ---- |
| AV8471 | ADELPHI 1½ | 26A 4827 |
| AV8942 | MERLIN 1½ | 27M ---- |
| AWA195 | KESTREL 9 | 60 ---- |
| AWA203 | LYNX 9 | 60 ---- |
| AWA204 | KESTREL 9 | 60 24826 |
| AWA287 | KESTREL 9 | 60 . 24219 |
| AWD436 | KESTREL 1½ | 27K ---- |
| AWD503 | LYNX 1½ | 26L ---- |
| AWD745 | LYNX SPR 1½ | SS27L ---- |
| AWD906 | MONACO 9 | S67Z ---- |

| REG NUMBER | MODEL | CHASSIS NO. | |
|---|---|---|---|
| AWE519 | MONACO 9 | 60 | ---- |
| AWE533 | FALCON 1½ | 22T | ---- |
| AWE969 | KESTREL 6 | 44T | ---- |
| AWF975 | KESTREL 16/4 | 38KX | 1121 |
| AWK193* | KESTREL 9 | 60 | 27395 |
| AWK194* | KESTREL 1½ | 22T | 1458 |
| AWK195* | MPH 12/6 | 44T | 2251 |
| AWK196* | FALCON 1½ | 22T | 1387 |
| AWK197* | MONACO 9 | 60 | 27424 |
| AWK198* | KESTREL 1½ | 22T | 1477 |
| AWK199* | FALCON 1½ | 22T | 1439 |
| AWK200* | FALCON 1½ | 22T | 1444 |
| AWK201* | D/H COUPE 9 | 60 S | 22531 |
| AWK202* | KESTREL 1½ | 22T | 1526 |
| AWK203* | KESTREL COL 15 | 44T | 2350 |
| AWK204* | FALCON 15/6 | 44T | 2368 |
| AWK381* | KESTREL COL 1½ | 22T | 1430 |
| AWK382* | FALCON COL 1½ | 22T | 1349 |
| AWK383* | FALCON 15/6 | 44T | 2371 |
| AWK384* | FALCON 1½ | 22T | 1521 |
| AWK385* | MONACO 9 | 60 | 27364 |
| AWK386* | FALCON 15/6 | 44T | 2386 |
| AWK387* | FALCON 1½ | 22T | 1403 |
| AWK388* | FALCON 1½ | 22T | 1426 |
| AWK389* | KESTREL COL 1½ | 22T | 1423 |
| AWK390* | KESTREL 1½ | 22T | 1528 |
| AWK391* | FALCON 1½ | 22T | 1529 |
| AWK392* | KESTREL 15/6 | 44T | 2403 |
| AWK601* | KESTREL COL 1½ | 22T | 1559 |
| AWK602* | KESTREL 1½ | 22T | 1620 |
| AWK603* | LYNX 1½ | 22T | 1586 |
| AWK604* | FALCON 1½ | 22T | 1544 |
| AWK605* | FALCON 1½ | 22T | 1637 |
| AWK606* | FALCON 1½ | 22T | 1655 |
| AWK607* | KESTREL COL 1½ | 22T | 1625 |
| AWK608* | KESTREL 15/6 | 44T | 2390 |
| AWK609* | FALCON 1½ | 22T | 1702 |
| AWK610* | MONACO 9 | 60 | 27543 |
| AWK611* | LYNX COL 1½ | 22T | 1574 |
| AWK612* | FALCON 1½ | 22T | 1476 |
| AWK701* | KESTREL COL 9 | 60 | 27586 |
| AWK702* | KESTREL 1½ | 22T | 1766 |
| AWK703* | FALCON 1½ | 22T | 1709 |
| AWK704* | FALCON 15/6 | 44T | 2392 |
| AWK705* | FALCON 15/6 | 44T | 2406 |
| AWK706* | MONACO 9 | 60 | 27544 |
| AWK708* | FALCON 1½ | 22T | 1467 |
| AWK709* | FALCON 1½ | 22T | 1675 |
| AWK710* | KESTREL 1½ | 22T | 1764 |
| AWK711* | KESTREL 1½ | 22T | 1724 |
| AWK712* | KESTREL 1½ | 22T | 1665 |
| AWK713* | MONACO 9 | 60 | 20428 |
| AWN185 | ADELPHI 1½ | 26A | ---- |
| AWN230 | KESTREL 1½ | 27K | ---- |
| AWR603 | FALCON 1½ | 22T | 1114 |
| AWR702 | ADELPHI 16/4 | 38AX | 1089 |
| AWS 66 | KESTREL SPR 1½ | SS27K | 6714 |
| AWS 87 | FALCON 1½ | 27F | 6134 |

| REG NUMBER | MODEL | CHASSIS NO | |
|---|---|---|---|
| AWT594 | FALCON 1½ | 26F | ---- |
| AWU432 | KESTREL 1½ | 22T | 2127 |
| AWU580 | FALCON 1½ | 26F | 2372 |
| AWW675 | FALCON 1½ | 27F | ---- |
| AWX160 | LYNX 1½ | 26L | ---- |
| AWX421 | MERLIN 9 | 66M | ---- |
| AXA202 | KESTREL 9 | 60 | ---- |
| AXA916 | MONACO 9 | 60 | 23941 |
| AXB339 | KESTREL 1½ | 26K | ---- |
| AXF147 | LYNX 9 | 60 | 22047 |
| AXF986 | LYNX 9 | 60 | 23075 |
| AXG859 | MONACO 9 | 60 | ---- |
| AXH 32 | KESTREL 9 | 60 | ---- |
| AXJ289 | KESTREL 1½ | 22T | ---- |
| AXJ383 | MONACO 9 | 60 | ---- |
| AXJ681 | LYNX 9 | 60 | 25499 |
| AXJ993 | IMP 9 | 60 | 25340 |
| AXK393 | KESTREL 12/6 | 44T | ---- |
| AXL111 | MONACO 9 | 60 | ---- |
| AXL514 | MONACO 9 | 60 | ---- |
| AXL646 | LYNX 9 | 60 | ---- |
| AXL649 | KESTREL 15/6 | 44T | ---- |
| AXM 53 | LYNX 12/6 | 44T | 1031 |
| AXM275 | LYNX 1½ | 22T | ---- |
| AXM555 | LYNX 9 | 60 | 22438 |
| AXN319 | LYNX 12/6 | 44T | 1123 |
| AXN841 | MONACO 9 | 60 | 23331 |
| AXO923 | - - 9 | 60 | 23579 |
| AXP 96 | KESTREL 9 | 60 | ---- |
| AXP 99 | KESTREL 9 | 60 | 23429 |
| AXP307 | LYNX 12/6 | 44T | 1877 |
| AXP495 | KESTREL 9 | 60 | ---- |
| AXP499 | MONACO 9 | 60 | 24114 |
| AXP923 | KESTREL 9 | 60 | 23295 |
| AXR 46 | MONACO 9 | 60 | ---- |
| AXT 16 | LYNX 12/6 | 44T | ---- |
| AXU178 | MONACO 9 | 60 | 24257 |
| AXU987 | LYNX 9 | 60 | 25712 |
| AXV178 | MONACO 9 | 60 | ---- |
| AXW 17 | KESTREL 9 | 60 | ---- |
| AXW496 | KESTREL 9 | 60 | 24341 |
| AXX 98-MW | LYNX 9 | 60 | ---- |
| AXX126 | KESTREL 9 | 60 | ---- |
| AXY293 | KESTREL 9 | 60 | 24322 |
| AXY299 | MENTONE 12/6 | 44T | 1998 |
| AYA 90 | MONACO 9 | 60 | ---- |
| AYB564 | FALCON 1½ | 22T | ---- |
| AYB756 | KESTREL 9 | 60 | ---- |
| AYB888 | KESTREL 9 | 60 | 27244 |
| AYC 1 | KESTREL 1½ | 22T | 1924 |
| AYD686 | FALCON 15/6 | 44T | ---- |
| AYE100 | KESTREL 9 | 60 | ---- |
| AYE622 | LYNX 12/6 | 44T | 1165 |
| AYE634 | MONACO 9 | 60 | 14552 |
| AYE640 | MENTONE 12/6 | 44T | 2058 |
| AYK597 | IMP 9 | 60 | ---- |
| AYK599 | KESTREL 9 | 60 | ---- |
| AYL 66 | KESTREL 12/6 | 44T | ---- |

| REG NUMBER | MODEL | CHASSIS NO. | |
|---|---|---|---|
| AYM275 | LYNX 14/6 | 44T | 1603 |
| AYN 23 | LYNX 9 | 60 | 25066 |
| AYN562 | MONACO 9 | 60 | ---- |
| AYP524 | MONACO 9 | 60 | 22833 |
| AYP831 | MONACO 9 | 60 | ---- |
| AYP833 | MONACO 9 | 60 | 23589 |
| AYP838 | KESTREL 9 | 60 | ---- |
| AYP840 | KESTREL 14/6 | 44T | 1686 |
| AYR598 | KESTREL 9 | 60 | 25662 |
| AYR644 | MONACO 9 | 60 | ---- |
| AYR645 | KESTREL 12/6 | 44T | 1683 |
| AYS149 | MONACO 9 | S67Z | ---- |
| AYT475 | LYNX 9 | 60 | ---- |
| AYW505 | LYNX 9 | 60 | 25637 |
| AYW562 | LYNX 9 | 60 | ---- |
| AYX557 | LYNX 9 | 60 | ---- |
| AYY868 | LYNX 9 | 60 | ---- |
| AZ1189-IRL | BROOKLANDS 9 | 80 | 21 |
| AZ1275-NZ | KESTREL 12/6 | 44T | ---- |
| AZ3641-IRL | BROOKLANDS 9 | 80 | 57 |
| AZ7879-IRL | TOURER 9 | 60 | ---- |
| AZ9153-IRL | GAMECOCK 9 | 60 | 16161 |
| AZ9504-IRL | GAMECOCK 9 | 60 | ---- |
| BAA371 | KESTREL 1½ | 26K | ---- |
| BAA597 | MERLIN 9 | 66M | ---- |
| BAB433 | FALCON 1½ | 27F | ---- |
| BAB798 | MERLIN 9 | 67M | ---- |
| BAC360 | ADELPHI 1½ | 26A | ---- |
| BDK691 | ADELPHI 1½ | 27A | 5617 |
| BDU 3* | ADELPHI 1½ | 26A | 2775 |
| BDU 4* | KESTREL 9 | S66K | 150 |
| BDU 5* | FALCON 1½ | 26F | 2750 |
| BDU 6* | ADELPHI 15/6 | 46A | 2533 |
| BDU 7* | FALCON 15/6 | 46F | 2530 |
| BDU 8* | ADELPHI 8-90 | 86A | 101 |
| BDU 61* | FALCON 1½ | 26F | 2734 |
| BDU 62* | FALCON 1½ | 26F | 2713 |
| BDU 63* | MERLIN 1½ | 26M | 2866 |
| BDU 64* | KESTREL 1½ | S26K | 2733 |
| BDU 65* | LYNX 1½ | S26L | 2998 |
| BDU 66* | FALCON 1½ | 26F | 2892 |
| BDU 67* | MERLIN 9 | 66M | 379 |
| BDU 68* | FALCON 1½ | 26F | 2845 |
| BDU 69* | KESTREL SPR 1½ | SS26K | 2964 |
| BDU 70* | FALCON COL 1½ | 26F | 2946 |
| BDU 71* | MERLIN 1½ | S26M | 2950 |
| BDU 72* | FALCON 1½ | 26F | 3014 |
| BDU341* | ADELPHI 1½ | 26A | 3204 |
| BDU342* | FALCON 1½ | S26F | 2762 |
| BDU343* | FALCON 1½ | 26F | 2776 |
| BDU344* | FALCON 1½ | 26F | 2833 |
| BDU345* | FALCON 1½ | 26F | 3010 |
| BDU346* | MERLIN 1½ | 26M | 2989 |
| BDU347* | ADELPHI 1½ | 26A | 2980 |
| BDU348* | FALCON 1½ | 26F | 2786 |
| BDU349* | FALCON 1½ | 26F | 2957 |
| BDU350* | FALCON 1½ | 26F | 2809 |
| BDU351* | ADELPHI 1½ | 26A | 3073 |

| REG NUMBER | MODEL | CHASSIS NO | |
|---|---|---|---|
| BDU352* | MERLIN 9 | 66M | 562 |
| BDU412* | MERLIN 9 | 66M | 1850 |
| BDU511* | KESTREL SPR 1½ | SS26K | 3075 |
| BDU512* | MERLIN 1½ | 26M | 3127 |
| BDU513* | MERLIN 9 | S66M | 610 |
| BDU514* | MERLIN 9 | S66M | 695 |
| BDU515* | FALCON 1½ | 26F | 2789 |
| BDU516* | FALCON 1½ | 26F | 3040 |
| BDU517* | MERLIN 9 | 66M | 657 |
| BDU518* | FALCON 1½ | 26F | 2972 |
| BDU519* | FALCON 1½ | S26F | 3120 |
| BDU520* | MERLIN 1½ | 26M | 3060 |
| BDU521* | MERLIN 1½ | 26M | 3061 |
| BDU592 | MERLIN 9 | 66M | ---- |
| BDU700* | FALCON 1½ | S26F | 3333 |
| BDU721* | ADELPHI 1½ | 26A | 3307 |
| BDU722* | ADELPHI 1½ | S26A | 3256 |
| BDU723* | MERLIN 9 | S66M | 740 |
| BDU724* | MERLIN 1½ | 26M | 3230 |
| BDU725* | ADELPHI 1½ | 26A | 3252 |
| BDU726* | KESTREL 1½ | S26K | 3380 |
| BDU727* | SPRITE 1½ | S26S | 2698 |
| BDU728* | KESTREL 1½ | 26K | 3395 |
| BDU729* | ADELPHI 1½ | 26A | 3433 |
| BDU730* | KESTREL 1½ | S26K | 3381 |
| BDU731* | LYNX SPR 1½ | SS26L | 3904 |
| BDU820 | KESTREL 1½ | 26K | ---- |
| BDU939 | MERLIN 9 | 66M | ---- |
| BAE677 | LYNX 9 | 60 | 26135 |
| BAF903 | KESTREL 1½ | 22T | ---- |
| BAH900 | SPRITE 1½ | S27S | 5675 |
| BAH997 | LYNX 1½ | 26L | ---- |
| BAL383 | FALCON 1½ | 22T | 812 |
| BAL662 | MONACO 9 | 60 | 23204 |
| BAO359 | MERLIN 1½ | 26M | ---- |
| BAO928 | MERLIN 9 | 66M | 1065 |
| BAP175 | VICTOR 1½ | 28V | ---- |
| BAT473 | FALCON 1½ | 26F | ---- |
| BAU519 | IMP 9 | 60 | 27493 |
| BAX514 | KESTREL 1½ | 27K | ---- |
| BAX951 | MONACO 9 | S67Z | 2702 |
| BBH405 | KESTREL 9 | 60 | 25267 |
| BBH461 | MONACO 9 | 60 | ---- |
| BBH517 | MONACO 9 | 60 | 26131 |
| BBH670 | LYNX 1½ | 22T | 112 |
| BBJ869 | KESTREL 1½ | 26K | ---- |
| BBJ925 | MERLIN 9 | 66M | 213 |
| BBJ930 | KESTREL 1½ | 26K | ---- |
| BBK764 | VICTOR 9 | 68V | ---- |
| BBL312 | ADELPHI 1½ | 28A | ---- |
| BBM363 | LYNX COLNL 1½ | 27L | 6420 |
| BBM628 | MERLIN 9 | S67M | 3027 |
| BBO114 | VICTOR 1½ | 28V | ---- |
| BBP 20 | KESTREL 1½ | 22T | 2040 |
| BBP459 | FALCON 1½ | 26F | 2575 |
| BBP974 | LYNX 9 | 60 | ---- |
| BBV885 | KESTREL 9 | S66K | 1442 |
| BBY152 | ADELPHI 1½ | 26A | ---- |

| REG NUMBER | MODEL | CHASSIS NO. | |
|---|---|---|---|
| BBY181 | MERLIN 9 | 66M | ---- |
| BBY182 | ADELPHI 1½ | 26A | ---- |
| BBY351 | MERLIN 9 | 66M | ---- |
| BBY885 | KESTREL 1½ | 28KX | 7584 |
| BB2838 | TOURER 9 | 60 | ---- |
| BCA229 | MONACO 9 | S67Z | ---- |
| BCE293 | KESTREL 9 | 60 | ---- |
| BCE345 | KESTREL 9 | 60 | ---- |
| BCE551 | KESTREL 1½ | 26K | 3289 |
| BCE660 | KESTREL 1½ | 26K | 3384 |
| BCE770 | KESTREL 1½ | 26K | ---- |
| BCG540 | ADELPHI 15/6 | 46A | ---- |
| BCG550 | KESTREL SPR 1½ | SS26K | 4685 |
| BCR153 | TRG SAL 1½ | 28F | 7419 |
| BCR252 | KESTREL 1½ | 28K | ---- |
| BCR490 | KESTREL 16/4 | 38KX | 1076 |
| BCR668 | KESTREL 16/4 | 38KX | ---- |
| BCR723 | ADELPHI 16/4 | 38AX | ---- |
| BCR810 | SPRITE 1½ | S28S | 7693 |
| BCR811 | KESTREL 1½ | 28K | ---- |
| BCR812 | TRG SAL 1½ | 28FX | 7445 |
| BCY968 | VICTOR 1½ | 28VX | 7577 |
| BDA 33 | KESTREL 1½ | 27K | ---- |
| BDF877 | FALCON 1½ | 26F | ---- |
| BDG598 | CC TRG SAL 1½ | 27C | ---- |
| BDK502 | KESTREL SPR 1½ | SS27K | 5413 |
| BDK547 | KESTREL SPR 1½ | SS27K | ---- |
| BDK690 | ADELPHI 1½ | 27A | ---- |
| BHP 98* | ADELPHI 1½ | 26A | 3682 |
| BHP349* | LYNX 1½ | S26L | 3628 |
| BHP350* | KESTREL 1½ | 26K | 3612 |
| BHP351* | AUTOVIA LIM | L | 63101 |
| BHP352* | ADELPHI 1½ | 26A | 3563 |
| BHP353* | FALCON 1½ | 26F | 3044 |
| BHP354* | KESTREL 1½ | S26K | 3594 |
| BHP355* | ADELPHI 1½ | 26A | 3521 |
| BHP356* | MERLIN 9 | 66M | 781 |
| BHP357* | MERLIN COL 9 | 66M | 1124 |
| BHP358* | KESTREL 1½ | 26K | 3720 |
| BHP359* | MERLIN COL 1½ | 26M | 3634 |
| BHP360* | ADELPHI 1½ | 26A | 3751 |
| BHP403 | MERLIN 9 | 26M | ---- |
| BHP461* | ADELPHI 1½ | 26A | 3703 |
| BHP462* | MERLIN 1½ | S26M | 3686 |
| BHP463* | MERLIN 9 | 66M | 1230 |
| BHP464* | ADELPHI 1½ | 26A | 3700 |
| BHP465* | ADELPHI 15/6 | 46A | 2625 |
| BHP466* | KESTREL 1½ | 26K | 3856 |
| BHP467* | FALCON 1½ | S26F | 3953 |
| BHP468* | MERLIN 1½ | 26M | 3193 |
| BHP469* | ADELPHI 1½ | 26A | 3896 |
| BHP470* | MERLIN 9 | 66M | 1257 |
| BHP471* | MERLIN 1½ | S26M | 3841 |
| BHP534* | KESTREL 1½ | S26K | 4437 |
| BHP681* | KESTREL 1½ | S26K | 3906 |
| BHP682* | ADELPHI 15/6 | 46A | 2644 |
| BHP683* | MERLIN 9 | 66M | 1263 |
| BHP684* | ADELPHI 1½ | 26A | 3711 |

| REG NUMBER | MODEL | CHASSIS NO. | |
|---|---|---|---|
| BHP685* | KESTREL 1½ | S26K | 3915 |
| BHP686* | KESTREL 15/6 | S46K | 2659 |
| BHP687* | MERLIN 1½ | 26M | 3861 |
| BHP688* | ADELPHI 1½ | 26A | 3887 |
| BHP690* | ADELPHI 1½ | 26A | 3965 |
| BHP691* | KESTREL 1½ | 26K | 4026 |
| BHP692* | KESTREL 1½ | 26K | 4004 |
| BHP881* | ADELPHI COL 1½ | 26A | 3997 |
| BHP882* | KESTREL 1½ | 26K | 3725 |
| BHP883* | KESTREL SPR 1½ | SS26K | 4081 |
| BHP884* | KESTREL 1½ | S26K | 4087 |
| BHP885* | ADELPHI 1½ | 26A | 3519 |
| BHP886* | ADELPHI 1½ | 26A | 3490 |
| BHP887* | MERLIN 9 | S66M | 1300 |
| BHP888* | ADELPHI 1½ | S26A | 3556 |
| BHP889* | LYNX 1½ | S26L | 4086 |
| BHP890* | ADELPHI 1½ | 27A | 5231 |
| BHP891* | ADELPHI 1½ | 26A | 4145 |
| BHP892* | LYNX 1½ | S26L | 4065 |
| BHP893* | KESTREL 9 | S66K | 1832 |
| BHP963 | MERLIN 9 | 66M | 1399 |
| BHR180 | VICTOR 1½ | 28V | ---- |
| BHT189 | KESTREL 1½ | 22T | ---- |
| BHT508 | KESTREL 1½ | 22T | 1328 |
| BHU767 | FALCON 1½ | 22T | ---- |
| BHU771 | KESTREL 1½ | 22T | 1957 |
| BHU942 | LYNX 1½ | 22T | 1930 |
| BHX315 | FALCON 1½ | 22T | ---- |
| BDV959 | ADELPHI 1½ | 26A | 3942 |
| BEE324 | MONACO 9 | 60 | ---- |
| BEL131 | KESTREL 1½ | 22T | ---- |
| BEL425 | FALCON 1½ | 22T | ---- |
| BEL878 | FALCON 1½ | 22T | ---- |
| BER 12 | MERLIN 1½ | 26M | ---- |
| BER283 | KESTREL 9 | S66K | ---- |
| BER696 | KESTREL 9 | S66K | 1874 |
| BER919 | MERLIN 9 | 66M | ---- |
| BE6098-NZ | KESTREL 1½ | 26K | ---- |
| BFC272 | FALCON 1½ | 22T | ---- |
| BFG 1 | SPRITE 1½ | S26S | 3754 |
| BFG206 | MERLIN 1½ | 26M | 4669 |
| BFJ208 | FALCON 1½ | 22T | ---- |
| BFJ516 | KESTREL 1½ | 26K | ---- |
| BFM257 | KESTREL SPR 1½ | SS27K | 5473 |
| BFM447 | FALCON 1½ | 27F | 5628 |
| BG 916 | ALPINE 14/6 | 14L | 782 |
| BGC509 | KESTREL 9 | 60 | ---- |
| BGE156 | KESTREL 16/4 | 38KX | ---- |
| BGF570 | KESTREL 12/6 | 44T | ---- |
| BGK272 | MENTONE 12/6 | 44T | 2138 |
| BG0503 | MONACO 9 | 60 | 23396 |
| BGP104 | KESTREL 9 | 60 | 24987 |
| BGT263 | KESTREL 9 | 60 | ---- |
| BGT949 | MONACO 9 | 60 | 24108 |
| BGU475 | KESTREL 9 | 60 | 25221 |
| BGW119 | IMP 9 | 60 | 25441 |
| BGY 73 | KESTREL 9 | 60 | ---- |
| BG2257 | KESTREL 1½ | 22T | ---- |

| REG NUMBER | MODEL | CHASSIS NO | |
|---|---|---|---|
| BG2296 | KESTREL 9 | 60 | ---- |
| BG4945 | LYNX 9 | 60 | ---- |
| BHK444 | KESTREL 9 | 60 | 24742 |
| BHK674 | KESTREL 9 | 60 | ---- |
| BHN440 | FALCON 1½ | 26F | ---- |
| BHP 11* | ADELPHI 1½ | 26A | 3402 |
| BHP 12* | KESTREL 1½ | 26K | 3759 |
| BHP 13* | MERLIN COL 1½ | 26M | 3426 |
| BHP 14* | MERLIN 1½ | 26M | 3128 |
| BHP 15* | MERLIN 9 | 66M | 923 |
| BHP 16* | FALCON 1½ | 26F | 3450 |
| BHP 17* | KESTREL 1½ | S26K | 3540 |
| BHP 18* | MERLIN COL 1½ | 26M | 3496 |
| BHP 19* | KESTREL 9 | S66K | 879 |
| BHP 20* | ADELPHI 15/6 | 46A | 2580 |
| BHP 45* | MERLIN 9 | S66M | 952 |
| BHP 46* | ADELPHI 1½ | 26A | 3551 |
| BHP 53* | ADELPHI 1½ | 26A | 3491 |
| BHP 54* | ADELPHI 1½ | 26A | 3483 |
| BHP 56* | MERLIN 9 | S66M | 993 |
| BHP 57* | MERLIN 1½ | 26M | 3447 |
| BHP 91* | KESTREL 9 | S66K | 905 |
| BHP 92* | KESTREL 1½ | S26K | 3606 |
| BHP 93* | FALCON 1½ | 26F | 3345 |
| BHP 94* | KESTREL 15/6 | 46K | 2593 |
| BHP 95* | FALCON 1½ | S26F | 3386 |
| BHP 96* | ADELPHI 1½ | 26A | 3524 |
| BHP 97* | KESTREL 1½ | S26K | 3369 |
| BKV714* | ADELPHI 1½ | S27A | 5758 |
| BKV715* | CC TRG SAL 1½ | 27C | 5710 |
| BKV716* | CC TRG SAL 1½ | 27C | 5665 |
| BKV717* | ADELPHI 15/6 | 47A | 3051 |
| BKV718* | KESTREL SPR 1½ | SS27K | 5810 |
| BKV719* | ADELPHI 1½ | 27A | 5684 |
| BKV720* | ADELPHI 1½ | S27A | 5868 |
| BKV915* | KESTREL 1½ | 27K | 5846 |
| BKV935* | KESTREL 1½ | 27K | 5846 |
| BKV936* | ADELPHI 1½ | 27A | 5849 |
| BKV937* | KESTREL 15/6 | 47K | 3095 |
| BKV938* | KESTREL SPR 1½ | SS27K | 5827 |
| BKV939* | EXP IFS SAL 1½ | | ---- |
| BKV939* | ADELPHI 1½ | 27A | 7128 |
| BKV940* | CC TRG SAL 1½ | 27C | 5889 |
| BKW475 | KESTREL SPR 1½ | SS27K | 5055 |
| BKW769 | SPRITE 1½ | S27S | 6843 |
| BKX244 | KESTREL 9 | 60 | ---- |
| BKX269 | KESTREL 1½ | 26K | ---- |
| BK6844 | 2DR TOURER 10.8 | | 850 |
| BLA540 | MENTONE 12/6 | 44T | 2130 |
| BLA902 | KESTREL 9 | 60 | 25211 |
| BLA907 | FALCON 1½ | 22T | 109 |
| BLC150 | - - 6 | 44T | 446 |
| BLD737 | STELVIO 15/6 | 15S | 950 |
| BLE 5 | KESTREL 9 | 60 | ---- |
| BLE730 | LYNX 1½ | 22T | 1852 |
| BLE863 | FALCON 1½ | 22T | ---- |
| BLF 74 | KESTREL 9 | 60 | 25099 |
| BLF776 | MONACO 9 | 60 | 25347 |

| REG NUMBER | MODEL | CHASSIS NO | |
|---|---|---|---|
| BLJ385 | MERLIN 9 | 66M | ---- |
| BLJ948 | ADELPHI 1½ | 26A | 3002 |
| BLK780 | KESTREL 1½ | 22T | 388 |
| BLL625 | FALCON 1½ | 22T | ---- |
| BLM667 | LYNX 9 | 60 | ---- |
| BLN 39 | MPH 12/6 | 44T | 2258 |
| BLN289 | LINCOCK 9 | 60 | ---- |
| BL0737 | STELVIO 15/6 | 15S | ---- |
| BLP164 | KESTREL 9 | 60 | ---- |
| BLP170 | FALCON 1½ | 22T | ---- |
| BLT141 | LYNX 9 | 60 | ---- |
| BLT581 | MERLIN 9 | 66M | ---- |
| BLT582 | KESTREL 9 | 60 | ---- |
| BLT834 | FALCON 1½ | 22T | ---- |
| BLU220 | FALCON 1½ | 22T | ---- |
| BLU255 | LYNX 1½ | 22T | 600 |
| BLU257 | KESTREL 9 | 60 | 25345 |
| BLU678 | KESTREL 9 | 60 | 27005 |
| BLU876 | KESTREL 1½ | 22T | ---- |
| BLV173 | MERLIN 9 | 66M | ---- |
| BLX371 | KESTREL 9 | 60 | 27056 |
| BLX372 | KESTREL 9 | 60 | 25362 |
| BMB118 | FALCON 1½ | 22T | 496 |
| BMB240 | FALCON 1½ | 22T | 643 |
| BMC111 | KESTREL 9 | 60 | ---- |
| BME424 | LINCOCK 9 | 60 | ---- |
| BME672 | KESTREL 9 | 60 | ---- |
| BME729 | LYNX 9 | 60 | 25743 |
| BHX464 | KESTREL 1½ | 22T | 466 |
| BHX676 | FALCON 1½ | 22T | 572 |
| BHY327 | IMP 9 | 60 | 25512 |
| BHY408 | FALCON 1½ | 22T | ---- |
| BHY770 | FALCON 1½ | 22T | ---- |
| BI3798-NZ | KESTREL SPR 1½ | SS27K | ---- |
| BJ 733-NZ | MONACO 9 | 60 | 24164 |
| BJJ214 | MENTONE 12/6 | 44T | 2123 |
| BJO 22 | LYNX 1½ | 22T | ---- |
| BJ0665 | FALCON 1½ | 22T | ---- |
| BJ0669 | FALCON 1½ | 22T | ---- |
| BJW699 | KESTREL 1½ | 26K | ---- |
| BJW738 | KESTREL 16/4 | 38KX | ---- |
| BKB858 | MERLIN 1½ | 26M | ---- |
| BKD547 | KESTREL SPR 1½ | SS26K | ---- |
| BKD619 | ADELPHI 1½ | 27A | ---- |
| BKE213 | LYNX 9 | 60 | 25879 |
| BKE654 | MONACO 9 | 60 | ---- |
| BKE840 | LINCOCK 9 | 60 | ---- |
| BKH 73 | FALCON 1½ | 26F | 2568 |
| BKH966 | MERLIN 9 | 66M | ---- |
| BKL273 | KESTREL 9 | 60 | ---- |
| BKL753 | KESTREL 9 | 60 | ---- |
| BKL981 | MONACO 9 | 60 | 24994 |
| BK0423 | MONACO 9 | 60 | 27248 |
| BKP648 | FALCON 1½ | 22T | 1374 |
| BKV 82* | MONACO 9 | S67Z | 2421 |
| BKV 83* | ADELPHI 1½ | S27A | 5393 |
| BKV 84* | ADELPHI 8-90 | 87A | 201 |
| BKV 85* | LYNX 1½ | 27L | 5434 |

| REG NUMBER | MODEL | CHASSIS NO | |
|---|---|---|---|
| BKV 86* | ADELPHI 15/6 | 47A | 3033 |
| BKV 87* | FALCON 1½ | S27F | 5375 |
| BKV 88* | SPRITE 1½ | S27S | 5379 |
| BKV 89* | MONACO 9 | S67Z | 2482 |
| BKV 90* | KESTREL SPR 1½ | SS27K | 5404 |
| BKV 91* | MONACO 9 | S67Z | 2498 |
| BKV 92* | CC TRG SAL 1½ | 27C | 5387 |
| BKV 93* | KESTREL 1½ | 27K | 5360 |
| BKV178 | KESTREL 1½ | 27K | ---- |
| BKV304* | MONACO 9 | S67Z | 2475 |
| BKV305* | ADELPHI 1½ | 27A | 5539 |
| BKV306* | KESTREL SPR 1½ | SS27K | 5560 |
| BKV307* | FALCON 1½ | S27F | 5541 |
| BKV308* | FALCON 1½ | 27F | 5546 |
| BKV309* | ADELPHI 1½ | S27A | 5449 |
| BKV310* | FALCON 1½ | 27F | 5558 |
| BKV311* | FALCON 1½ | 27F | 5581 |
| BKV312* | KESTREL SPR 1½ | SS27K | 5452 |
| BKV313* | ADELPHI 1½ | 27A | 5609 |
| BKV314* | KESTREL SPR 1½ | SS27K | 5630 |
| BKV315* | FALCON COL 1½ | 27F | 5739 |
| BKV363* | KESTREL SPR 1½ | SS27K | 5655 |
| BKV666 | ADELPHI 1½ | 26A | ---- |
| BKV699 | CC TRG SAL 1½ | 27C | ---- |
| BKV710* | MONACO 9 | S67Z | 2619 |
| BKV711* | FALCON 1½ | 27F | 5719 |
| BKV712*IRL | KESTREL SPR 1½ | SS27K | 5744 |
| BKV713* | MONACO 9 | S67Z | 2719 |
| BMH920 | MENTONE 12/6 | 44T | ---- |
| BMH942 | KESTREL 9 | 60 | 24970 |
| BMK491 | KESTREL 9 | 60 | ---- |
| BMK597 | KESTREL 9 | 60 | ---- |
| BMN876 | KESTREL SPR 1½ | SS28K | ---- |
| BMP267 | KESTREL 1½ | 22T | ---- |
| BMP475 | LYNX 1½ | 26L | 4134 |
| BMT878 | MONACO 9 | 60 | ---- |
| BMT879 | MONACO 9 | 60 | ---- |
| BMT881 | FALCON 1½ | 22T | ---- |
| BMV 10 | KESTREL 12/6 | 44T | ---- |
| BMV845 | KESTREL 9 | 60 | 25451 |
| BMY173 | MONACO 9 | 60 | ---- |
| BMY315 | FALCON 1½ | 26F | ---- |
| BMY498 | KESTREL 1½ | 22T | 514 |
| BN 975-NZ | FALCON 1½ | 22T | ---- |
| BNA204 | KESTREL 9 | 60 | 25316 |
| BNB331 | KESTREL 9 | 60 | 27191 |
| BNB713 | FALCON 1½ | 22T | ---- |
| BND 74 | KESTREL 9 | 60 | 27111 |
| BND334 | KESTREL 1½ | 22T | ---- |
| BNE573 | KESTREL 9 | 60 | ---- |
| BNE717 | KESTREL 9 | 60 | ---- |
| BNE975 | FALCON 1½ | 22T | ---- |
| BNG842 | KESTREL 1½ | 27K | ---- |
| BNM876 | KESTREL 1½ | 28K | ---- |
| BNN203 | FALCON 1½ | 22T | ---- |
| BNO189 | KESTREL 9 | 60 | 24282 |
| BNW 22 | KESTREL 1½ | 22T | ---- |
| BNW 51-USA | IMP 9 | 60 | 27430 |

| REG NUMBER | MODEL | CHASSIS NO. | |
|---|---|---|---|
| BNW265 | FALCON 1½ | 22T | 1651 |
| BNW333 | KESTREL 1½ | -- | ---- |
| BNX635 | KESTREL 1½ | 27K | 6850 |
| BNY914 | MERLIN 9 | 66M | ---- |
| BOA300 | KESTREL 1½ | -- | ---- |
| BOC423 | FALCON 1½ | 26F | 2215 |
| BOC751 | FALCON 1½ | 26F | ---- |
| BOD434 | ADELPHI 1½ | 26A | 4847 |
| BOE822 | FALCON 1½ | 26F | 2441 |
| BOE987 | FALCON 1½ | 26F | ---- |
| BOJ652 | MERLIN 9 | 66M | ---- |
| BOK103 | FALCON 1½ | 26F | ---- |
| BOK856 | ADELPHI 1½ | 26A | 3138 |
| BOL 5 | KESTREL 1½ | 26K | ---- |
| BOM956 | SPRITE 1½ | S27S | ---- |
| BON221 | KESTREL | 26K | ---- |
| BOP567 | ADELPHI 1½ | 26A | ---- |
| BOR131 | FALCON 1½ | 26F | 4765 |
| BOR401 | D/H COUPE 1½ | 26L | ---- |
| BOR707 | FALCON 1½ | 27F | 5326 |
| BOT109 | FALCON 1½ | 27F | ---- |
| BOT348 | MONACO 9 | S67Z | 2537 |
| BOV465 | MERLIN 1½ | 26M | ---- |
| BOW 19 | VICTOR 1½ | 28VX | 7615 |
| BOW423 | ADELPHI 16/4 | 38AX | 1313 |
| BOY711 | ADELPHI 1½ | 26A | ---- |
| BP 19 | 9 HP TRI-CAR | ---- / | 914 |
| BPB974 | LYNX 9 | 60 | ---- |
| BPC478 | KESTREL 12/6 | 44T | 1917 |
| BPC641 | LINCOCK 9 | 60 | 21347 |
| BPC709 | MERLIN 1½ | 26M | 2828 |
| BPC740 | STELVIO 14/6 | 14S | 901 |
| BPC886 | LYNX 9 | 60 | 23457 |
| BPC902 | LYNX 12/6 | 44T | ---- |
| BPE848 | KESTREL 9 | 60 | 24773 |
| BPE903 | KESTREL 9 | 60 | 24688 |
| BPF519 | KESTREL 9 | 60 | 25814 |
| BPF920 | KESTREL 9 | 60 | 24783 |
| BPG146 | LYNX 9 | 60 | 24806 |
| BPG267 | - - 9 | 60 | 25714 |
| BPG740 | STELVIO 14/6 | 14S | ---- |
| BPH422 | KESTREL 9 | 60 | ---- |
| BPH437 | LYNX 9 | 60 | ---- |
| BPH842 | MONACO 9 | 60 | ---- |
| BPH849 | LINCOCK 9 | 60 | ---- |
| BPH901 | FALCON 9 | 60 | ---- |
| BPH905 | KESTREL 9 | 60 | 24140 |
| BPJ158 | LYNX 14/6 | 44T | ---- |
| BPJ574 | LYNX 9 | 60 | ---- |
| BPJ575 | FALCON 9 | 60 | 24957 |
| BPJ616 | KESTREL 9 | 60 | ---- |
| BPK547 | MENTONE 12/6 | 44T | ---- |
| BPL146 | FALCON 1½ | 22T | 135 |
| BPL784 | FALCON 1½ | 22T | ---- |
| BPO132 | MERLIN 9 | 66M | ---- |
| BPO629 | MERLIN 1½ | 26M | 2668 |
| BPO697 | KESTREL 1½ | 26K | ---- |
| BPO723 | MERLIN 9 | 66M | ---- |

| REG NUMBER | MODEL | CHASSIS NO | |
|---|---|---|---|
| BPR662R | ADELPHI 1½ | 26A | ---- |
| BPW548 | FALCON 1½ | 26F | ---- |
| BPX674 | MONACO 9 | 60 | 6728 |
| BPX916 | LYNX 1½ | 26L | ---- |
| BRB406 | FALCON 1½ | 26F | ---- |
| BRD492 | ADELPHI 15/6 | 46A | ---- |
| BRF723 | MENTONE 12/6 | 44T | ---- |
| BRH551 | MERLIN 9 | 66M | ---- |
| BRK744 | KESTREL 9 | S66K | 1696 |
| BRK872 | MERLIN 9 | 66M | 1916 |
| BRO397 | KESTREL 1½ | 26K | ---- |
| BRO649 | LYNX 1½ | 26L | 4672 |
| BRT348 | LYNX 1½ | 26L | ---- |
| BRT467 | MERLIN 9 | 66M | ---- |
| BRU342 | MERLIN 1½ | 26M | 3284 |
| BRU349 | FALCON 1½ | 26F | 2655 |
| BRU350 | MERLIN 9 | 66M | ---- |
| BRV312 | KESTREL SPR 1½ | SS27K | 5452 |
| BRW 3 | KESTREL | 26K | ---- |
| BRW194 | MERLIN 9 | 66M | ---- |
| BRW301* | ADELPHI 15/6 | 46A | 2650 |
| BRW302* | MERLIN 1½ | 26M | 4122 |
| BRW303* | SPRITE 1½ | S26S | 3878 |
| BRW304* | ADELPHI 1½ | 26A | 3771 |
| BRW305* | FALCON 1½ | 26F | 2895 |
| BRW306* | MERLIN 9 | 66M | 984 |
| BRW307* | ADELPHI 1½ | 26A | 3950 |
| BRW308* | KESTREL 9 | S66K | 1459 |
| BRW309* | ADELPHI 1½ | 26A | 3845 |
| BRW310* | MERLIN 9 | S66M | 1566 |
| BRW311* | ADELPHI COL 1½ | 26A | 4177 |
| BRW312* | ADELPHI 1½ | 26A | 3993 |
| BRW398* | ADELPHI 1½ | 26A | 4172 |
| BRW399* | FALCON 1½ | 26F | 4157 |
| BRW511* | KESTREL SPR 1½ | SS26K | 4217 |
| BRW512* | KESTREL 1½ | S26K | 3886 |
| BRW513* | ADELPHI 1½ | 26A | 4251 |
| BRW514* | ADELPHI 1½ | 26A | 3626 |
| BRW515* | FALCON 1½ | 26F | 2737 |
| BRW516* | ADELPHI 1½ | 26A | 4258 |
| BRW517* | ADELPHI COL 1½ | 26A | 4077 |
| BRW518* | KESTREL 1½ | S26K | 4235 |
| BRW519* | KESTREL SPR 1½ | SS26K | 4240 |
| BRW520* | FALCON 1½ | 26F | 4510 |
| BRW534* | AUTOVIA SAL | S | 63102 |
| BRW700* | ADELPHI 1½ | S26A | 4303 |
| BRW842* | FALCON 1½ | 26F | 4133 |
| BRW843* | ADELPHI 1½ | 26A | 4374 |
| BRW844* | ADELPHI 1½ | 26A | 4520 |
| BRW845* | ADELPHI 1½ | 26A | 4400 |
| BRW846* | ADELPHI 1½ | 26A | 4430 |
| BRW847* | ADELPHI 1½ | 26A | 4350 |
| BRW848* | LYNX SPR 1½ | SS26L | 4241 |
| BRW849* | KESTREL SPR 1½ | SS26K | 4457 |
| BRW850* | MERLIN 1½ | 26M | 4293 |
| BRW851* | KESTREL 1½ | S26K | 4584 |
| BRY752 | ADELPHI 1½ | 28A | 7362 |
| BR9284 | MONACO 9 | 60 | ---- |

| REG NUMBER | MODEL | CHASSIS NO. | |
|---|---|---|---|
| BSC165 | ADELPHI 8-90 | 87A | ---- |
| BSC190 | KESTREL 1½ | 27K | ---- |
| BSC249 | ADELPHI 1½ | 28A | ---- |
| BSC692 | KESTREL 1½ | 28K | 7351 |
| BSC761 | ADELPHI 16/4 | 38AX | 1093 |
| BSM 29 | KESTREL 9 | 60 | ---- |
| BSM940 | MERLIN 9 | 66M | ---- |
| BSP 1 | KESTREL SPR 1½ | SS27K | 6073 |
| BSP 7 | TRG SAL 1½ | 28F | ---- |
| BSP294 | MONACO 9 | S67Z | ---- |
| BSP296 | FALCON 1½ | 27F | ---- |
| BSP867 | ADELPHI 1½ | 27A | ---- |
| BTA910 | FALCON 1½ | 22T | 408 |
| BTB963 | SPRITE 1½ | S26S | 4883 |
| BTC924 | MONACO 9 | S67Z | ---- |
| BTF996 | KESTREL SPR 1½ | SS27K | ---- |
| BTG577 | KESTREL SPR 1½ | SS27K | ---- |
| BTG706 | MONACO 9 | S67Z | 3172 |
| BTJ915 | MERLIN 9 | S67M | ---- |
| BTM878 | MONACO 9 | 60 | ---- |
| BTN351 | KESTREL 1½ | 22T | ---- |
| BTN808 | FALCON 1½ | 22T | ---- |
| BTR408 | LYNX 16/4 | 38LX | 1181 |
| BTR533 | TRG SAL 1½ | 28F | ---- |
| BTR730 | KESTREL 16/4 | 38KX | ---- |
| BTT354 | FALCON 1½ | 27F | ---- |
| BTT915 | MERLIN 9 | 67M | ---- |
| BTT988 | KESTREL 15/6 | 47K | ---- |
| BTU128 | MERLIN 9 | 66M | ---- |
| BTV258 | FALCON 1½ | 22T | ---- |
| BTV466 | IMP 9 | 60 | ---- |
| BTV693 | KESTREL 1½ | S26K | 3661 |
| BTW128 | MERLIN 9 | 66M | ---- |
| BTW768 | FALCON 1½ | 26F | ---- |
| BU 490 | FALCON 1½ | 26F | ---- |
| BUC911 | KESTREL 1½ | 22T | 1453 |
| BUC915 | LYNX 9 | 60 | ---- |
| BUF 15 | KESTREL 1½ | 22T | ---- |
| BUL270 | FALCON 1½ | 22T | ---- |
| BUL411 | KESTREL 1½ | 22T | 978 |
| BU0945 | MERLIN 9 | S66M | 301 |
| BUR164 | MERLIN 9 | S66M | 1811 |
| BUR872 | ADELPHI 1½ | 26A | 4871 |
| BUW 77 | LYNX 1½ | 22T | 1415 |
| BUW152 | FALCON 1½ | 22T | ---- |
| BUW256 | KESTREL 1½ | 22T | ---- |
| BUY250 | LYNX SPR 1½ | SS27L | ---- |
| BU7485 | MARCH SPL 9 | 60 | ---- |
| BU8300 | KESTREL 16/4 | 38KX | ---- |
| BVB161 | KESTREL 1½ | 27K | 5069 |
| BVB162 | ADELPHI 1½ | 27A | 5028 |
| BVB410 | ADELPHI 1½ | 27A | 5463 |
| BVC 49* | ADELPHI 1½ | 26A | 4741 |
| BVC 50* | ADELPHI 1½ | 26A | 4835 |
| BVC 51* | MERLIN 9 | 66M | 1868 |
| BVC 52* | ADELPHI 1½ | S26A | 4758 |
| BVC 53* | ADELPHI 1½ | 26A | 4844 |
| BVC 54* | KESTREL 1½ | 26K | 4614 |

| REG NUMBER | MODEL | CHASSIS NO | |
|---|---|---|---|
| BVC 55* | LYNX 1½ | S26L | 4870 |
| BVC 56* | ADELPHI 1½ | 26A | 4843 |
| BVC 57* | ADELPHI 1½ | 26A | 4795 |
| BVC 58* | ADELPHI 1½ | 26A | 4755 |
| BVC 59* | MERLIN 1½ | 26M | 4680 |
| BVC 60* | ADELPHI 1½ | S26A | 4661 |
| BVC 71 | MERLIN 1½ | 26M | ---- |
| BVC 79 | MERLIN 9 | 66M | ---- |
| BVC201* | MERLIN 1½ | 26M | 4872 |
| BVC202* | ADELPHI 1½ | S26A | 4378 |
| BVC203* | ADELPHI 1½ | 26A | 4888 |
| BVC204* | 2D EXP SALOON 9 | 66X | 1519 |
| BVC205* | ADELPHI 1½ | 26A | 4896 |
| BVC206* | KESTREL 15/6 | 46K | 2771 |
| BVC207* | MERLIN 9 | S66M | 1984 |
| BVC208* | MERLIN 9 | S66M | 1982 |
| BVC209* | ADELPHI 8-90 | 86A | 109 |
| BVC210* | MONACO 9 | S67Z | 2201 |
| BVC211* | ADELPHI 1½ | 27A | 5002 |
| BVC521* | MERLIN 9 | 66M | 2075 |
| BVC522* | ADELPHI 1½ | 27A | 5067 |
| BVC523* | KESTREL SPR 1½ | SS27K | 5103 |
| BVC524* | ADELPHI 1½ | 27A | 5001 |
| BVC525* | ADELPHI 1½ | 27A | 5021 |
| BVC526* | MERLIN 9 | 66M | 1897 |
| BVC527* | MERLIN 9 | 66M | 2098 |
| BVC528* | FALCON 1½ | 27F | 5137 |
| BVC529* | FALCON 1½ | 27F | 5111 |
| BVC530* | ADELPHI 1½ | 27A | 5094 |
| BVC531* | ADELPHI 1½ | 27A | 5073 |
| BVC532* | ARMY TOURER 1½ | 26AT | 4076 |
| BVC534* | ADELPHI 1½ | 27A | 5300 |
| BVC542 | ADELPHI 1½ | 27A | ---- |
| BVC821* | FALCON 1½ | 27F | 5109 |
| BVC822* | MONACO 9 | S67Z | 2295 |
| BVC823* | ADELPHI COL 1½ | 27A | 5139 |
| BVC824* | ADELPHI 1½ | 27A | 5079 |
| BVC825* | MERLIN 9 | 66M | 2041 |
| BVC826* | MONACO 9 | S67Z | 2289 |
| BVC827* | ADELPHI 1½ | 27A | 5216 |
| BVC828* | FALCON 1½ | 27F | 5190 |
| BVC829* | FALCON 1½ | 27F | 5175 |
| BVC830* | KESTREL 1½ | 27K | 5278 |
| BVC831* | ADELPHI 1½ | 27A | 5330 |
| BVC832* | KESTREL SPR 1½ | SS27K | 5310 |
| BVC944* | KESTREL 1½ | 26K | 4085 |
| BVE171 | MONACO 9 | S67Z | ---- |
| BVE510 | CC TRG SAL 1½ | 27C | 5667 |
| BVE604 | MONACO 9 | S67Z | 2613 |
| BVE792 | KESTREL SPR 1½ | SS27K | 5776 |
| BVE863 | TRG SAL 1½ | 28F | ---- |
| BVK850 | KESTREL 1½ | 26K | ---- |
| BVM735 | KESTREL 9 | 60 | ---- |
| BVO160 | FALCON 1½ | 26F | 2839 |
| BVR 15 | IMP 9 | 60 | ---- |
| BVT 14 | MONACO 9 | 60 | ---- |
| BVW523 | KESTREL 9 | 60 | ---- |
| BVW735 | KESTREL 9 | 60 | 27175 |
| REG NUMBER | MODEL | CHASSIS NO. | |
| BVX761 | KESTREL 9 | 60 | ---- |
| BVX868 | KESTREL 9 | 60 | 25219 |
| BV2067 | MARCH SPL 9 | 60 | ---- |
| BV4293 | FALCON 1½ | 27F | ---- |
| BV5152 | MERLIN 9 | 66M | 288 |
| BV6322 | MONACO 9 | S67Z | 2515 |
| BV7415 | LYNX SPR 1½ | SS28L | ---- |
| BV8300 | KESTREL 16/4 | 38KX | ---- |
| BV8448 | KESTREL 1½ | 28K | ---- |
| BW 36 | 4½ HP FORECAR | ---- / | 416 |
| BWE999 | KESTREL 1½ | 26K | 3670 |
| BWJ699 | KESTREL 1½ | 26K | ---- |
| BWK 68 | ADELPHI 15/6 | 46A | 2741 |
| BWK101* | MERLIN COL 1½ | 26M | 4231 |
| BWK102* | FALCON COL 1½ | 26F | 4500 |
| BWK103* | ADELPHI 1½ | 26A | 4511 |
| BWK104* | ADELPHI 1½ | 26A | 3578 |
| BWK105* | FALCON 1½ | 26F | 4541 |
| BWK106* | KESTREL 1½ | S26K | 4513 |
| BWK107* | ADELPHI COL 1½ | 26A | 4543 |
| BWK108* | FALCON COL 1½ | 26F | 4538 |
| BWK109* | MERLIN COL 1½ | 26M | 4491 |
| BWK110* | ADELPHI 1½ | 26A | 3933 |
| BWK111* | ADELPHI 1½ | 26A | 4366 |
| BWK112* | ADELPHI 15/6 | 46A | 2711 |
| BWK323* | ADELPHI 15/6 | 46A | 2715 |
| BWK324* | TT SPRITE | S26S | 4634 |
| BWK325* | ADELPHI 1½ | 26A | 4382 |
| BWK326* | ADELPHI 1½ | 26A | 4601 |
| BWK327* | ADELPHI 1½ | 26A | 4589 |
| BWK328* | MERLIN 1½ | 26M | 4668 |
| BWK329* | ADELPHI 1½ | 26A | 4575 |
| BWK330* | ADELPHI 1½ | 26A | 4425 |
| BWK331* | KESTREL SPR 1½ | SS26K | 4470 |
| BWK334* | ADELPHI 1½ | 26A | 4626 |
| BWK335* | ADELPHI 1½ | 26A | 4600 |
| BWK571* | MERLIN 9 | S66M | 1151 |
| BWK572* | ADELPHI COL 1½ | 26A | 4675 |
| BWK573* | ADELPHI COL 1½ | 26A | 4691 |
| BWK574* | KESTREL SPR 1½ | SS26K | 4606 |
| BWK575* | LYNX SPR 1½ | SS26L | 4670 |
| BWK576* | ADELPHI 1½ | 26A | 4545 |
| BWK577* | KESTREL 9 | S66K | 1836 |
| BWK578* | ADELPHI 1½ | 26A | 4386 |
| BWK579* | KESTREL 1½ | S26K | 4488 |
| BWK580* | MERLIN COL 1½ | 26M | 4695 |
| BWK581* | ADELPHI 1½ | 26A | 4390 |
| BWK582* | ADELPHI 1½ | S26A | 4735 |
| BWK741* | ADELPHI 1½ | 26A | 4381 |
| BWK742* | LYNX 1½ | 26L | 4792 |
| BWK743* | MERLIN 9 | S66M | 1381 |
| BWK744* | ADELPHI 1½ | 26A | 4717 |
| BWK745* | ADELPHI 1½ | S26A | 4749 |
| BWK746* | ADELPHI 1½ | 26A | 4793 |
| BWK747* | ADELPHI 1½ | 26A | 4772 |
| BWK748* | ADELPHI 1½ | 26A | 4774 |
| BWK749* | ADELPHI 1½ | 26A | 4751 |
| BWK750* | ADELPHI 1½ | 26A | 4747 |
| REG NUMBER | MODEL | CHASSIS NO | |
| BWK751* | LYNX CNCRS 1½ | S26L | 4819 |
| BWK752* | KESTREL 1½ | 26K | 4791 |
| BWM276 | FALCON 1½ | 26F | 4072 |
| BWM365 | ADELPHI 1½ | 26A | ---- |
| BWN141 | CC TRG SAL 16/4 | 38BX | 1188 |
| BWT105 | LYNX SPR 1½ | SS26L | ---- |
| BWU 85 | KESTREL 1½ | 27K | 5411 |
| BWX171 | FALCON 1½ | 27F | ---- |
| BWY572 | FALCON 1½ | 27F | 7102 |
| BWY574 | FALCON 1½ | 27F | ---- |
| BXA740 | KESTREL 1½ | 22T | 1359 |
| BXB250 | FALCON 1½ | 22T | ---- |
| BXC117 | FALCON 15/6 | 44T | 2332 |
| BXC494 | KESTREL 1½ | 22T | 1337 |
| BXC874 | FALCON 1½ | 22T | ---- |
| BXC879 | FALCON 1½ | 22T | ---- |
| BXD864 | LYNX 1½ | 22T | ---- |
| BXD868 | KESTREL 1½ | 22T | ---- |
| BXE213 | LYNX 9 | 60 | ---- |
| BXF621 | FALCON 1½ | 22T | ---- |
| BXH 6 | FALCON 1½ | 22T | ---- |
| BXH 70 | KESTREL 15/6 | 44T | ---- |
| BXJ482 | MERLIN 9 | 66M | ---- |
| BXL451 | KESTREL 15/6 | 44T | ---- |
| BXL550 | IMP 9 | 60 | ---- |
| BXL876 | KESTREL 15/6 | 44T | 2363 |
| BXM777 | KESTREL 1½ | 22T | ---- |
| BXM820 | IMP 9 | 60 | 27462 |
| BXN 4 | KESTREL 1½ | 22T | ---- |
| BXN572 | KESTREL 15/6 | 44T | ---- |
| BXT 91 | FALCON 1½ | 22T | ---- |
| BXT 93 | KESTREL 1½ | 22T | ---- |
| BXT 96 | FALCON 1½ | 22T | ---- |
| BXT 97 | KESTREL 9 | S66K | ---- |
| BXT538 | FALCON 1½ | 22T | 1956 |
| BXU294 | LYNX 9 | 60 | 27501 |
| BXU295 | KESTREL 1½ | 22T | 1834 |
| BXU296 | KESTREL 1½ | 22T | ---- |
| BXU598 | KESTREL 9 | 60 | ---- |
| BXU988 | LYNX SPR 1½ | SS27L | ---- |
| BXV294 | LYNX 9 | 60 | ---- |
| BXV623 | FALCON 1½ | 22T | 1968 |
| BXV671 | IMP 9 | 60 | ---- |
| BXV988 | LYNX 1½ | 22T | ---- |
| BXW166 | KESTREL 1½ | 27K | ---- |
| BXX226 | FALCON 1½ | 22T | ---- |
| BXX456 | KESTREL 1½ | 22T | ---- |
| BXY988 | LYNX 1½ | 22T | 929 |
| BYA233 | LYNX SPR 1½ | SS26L | ---- |
| BYA572 | FALCON 1½ | 22T | ---- |
| BYA943 | ADELPHI 15/6 | 46A | 2579 |
| BYB 30 | ADELPHI 1½ | 26A | 3579 |
| BYB162 | ADELPHI 1½ | 27A | ---- |
| BYC407 | MERLIN 9 | 66M | ---- |
| BYD587 | LYNX 1½ | 27L | 5311 |
| BYD983 | ADELPHI 1½ | 27A | 5431 |
| BYF867 | KESTREL 1½ | 22T | 2047 |
| BYG893 | KESTREL 1½ | 27K | ---- |
| REG NUMBER | MODEL | CHASSIS NO. | |
| BYK947 | IMP 9 | 60 | 27447 |
| BYN 12 | KESTREL 1½ | 22T | 1905 |
| BY0887 | MERLIN 9 | 66M | ---- |
| BYP491 | KESTREL 9 | 60 | ---- |
| BYU211 | LYNX 1½ | 22T | ---- |
| BYU220 | FALCON 1½ | 26F | 2361 |
| BYU655 | KESTREL 1½ | 22T | ---- |
| BYX 82 | LYNX 1½ | 26L | ---- |
| BYY502 | LYNX 1½ | S26L | 2527 |
| BYY575 | IMP 9 | 60 | 27439 |
| BYY909 | IMP 9 | 60 | ---- |
| BY1963 | 10 HP 2 SEATER | ---- / | 2859 |
| BZ4015-IRL | MERLIN 9 | 66M | ---- |
| BZ4581-IRL | ADELPHI 1½ | 27A | ---- |
| BZ6133-IRL | ADELPHI 16/4 | 38AX | 1309 |
| C 1337-NZ | ADELPHI 1½ | 28A | ---- |
| C 2570-S | SPRITE 1½ | S27S | 6320 |
| CAA263 | ADELPHI 1½ | 27A | ---- |
| CAC 82 | VICTOR | | ---- |
| CAC531 | LYNX 1½ | 28LX | 7866 |
| CAE242 | ADELPHI 1½ | 26A | ---- |
| CAE266 | FALCON 1½ | 26F | ---- |
| CAE620 | MERLIN 1½ | 26M | ---- |
| CAF 58 | MERLIN 1½ | 26M | ---- |
| CAF 80 | RILEY/ERA | -- | ---- |
| CAF226 | FALCON 1½ | 26F | 4268 |
| CAF593 | LYNX SPR 1½ | SS26L | 4671 |
| CAK 1 | KESTREL 16/4 | 38KX | 1067 |
| CAL302 | KESTREL SPR 1½ | SS26K | ---- |
| CAR613 | MONACO 9 | S67Z | ---- |
| CA5907-TAS | FALCON 1½ | 27F | 5594 |
| CA9407-ZA | ADELPHI 1½ | 28A | ---- |
| CBB880 | MERLIN 9 | 66M | ---- |
| CBJ570 | MONACO 9 | S67Z | 2683 |
| CBM858 | ADELPHI 16/4 | 38AX | ---- |
| CBY279 | KESTREL 1½ | 27K | 5856 |
| CBY897 | LYNX SPR 1½ | SS26L | ---- |
| CBY898 | MONACO 9 | S67Z | 2239 |
| CCD542 | MERLIN 9 | 66M | 777 |
| CCE110 | FALCON 1½ | 27F | ---- |
| CCE914 | ADELPHI 1½ | 27A | ---- |
| CCF501 | KESTREL 1½ | 26K | ---- |
| CCG294 | SPRITE 1½ | S27S | 7070 |
| CCV724 | KESTREL 1½ | 27K | ---- |
| CDC152 | BROOKLANDS 9/ DIXON SPECIAL | 80 | -- |
| CDE416 | ADELPHI 8-90 | 87A | ---- |
| CDK 92 | MONACO 9 | S67Z | ---- |
| CDK223 | LYNX 1½ | 27L | 6548 |
| CDK907 | TRG SAL 1½ | 28F | ---- |
| CDU 54* | FALCON 1½ | S27F | 5476 |
| CDU 55* | CC TRG SAL 1½ | 27C | 5753 |
| CDU 56* | FALCON 1½ | 27F | 5482 |
| CDU 57* | ADELPHI 1½ | 27A | 5747 |
| CDU 58* | ADELPHI 1½ | 27A | 5750 |
| CDU 59* | KESTREL SPR 1½ | SS27K | 5778 |
| CDU 60* | FALCON 1½ | 27F | 5515 |
| CDU 61* | ADELPHI 15/6 | 47A | 3108 |

| REG NUMBER | MODEL | CHASSIS NO | |
|---|---|---|---|
| CDU 62* | CC TRG SAL 1½ | 27C | 5852 |
| CDU 63* | SPRITE 1½ | S27S | 6031 |
| CDU 64* | MONACO 9 | S67Z | 2643 |
| CDU 65* | MONACO 9 | S67Z | 2759 |
| CDU469* | ADELPHI 1½ | 27A | 5967 |
| CDU470* | KESTREL SPR 1½ | SS27K | 5741 |
| CDU471* | KESTREL SPR 1½ | SS27K | 5506 |
| CDU472* | ADELPHI 1½ | 27A | 5169 |
| CDU473* | ADELPHI 1½ | 27A | 5876 |
| CDU474* | ADELPHI 15/6 | 47A | 3105 |
| CDU475* | KESTREL SPR 1½ | SS27K | 5453 |
| CDU613* | ADELPHI 1½ | 27A | 6064 |
| CDU614* | ADELPHI 1½ | 27A | 5977 |
| CDU615* | FALCON 1½ | 27F | 6067 |
| CDU616* | CC TRG SAL 1½ | 27C | 5610 |
| CDU617* | MONACO 9 | S67Z | 2804 |
| CDU618* | LYNX SPR 1½ | SS27L | 6166 |
| CDU619* | KESTREL 1½ | 27K | 6102 |
| CDU620* | KESTREL 1½ | S27K | 6129 |
| CDU621* | ADELPHI 1½ | 27A | 6143 |
| CDU622* | ADELPHI 1½ | 27A | 7046 |
| CDU623* | KESTREL SPR 1½ | SS27K | 6162 |
| CDU624* | MONACO 9 | S67Z | 2486 |
| CDU681 | LYNX SPR 1½ | SS27L | ---- |
| CDU921* | KESTREL SPR 1½ | SS27K | 6146 |
| CDU922* | ADELPHI COL 15 | 47A | 3127 |
| CDU923* | ADELPHI 15/6 | 47A | 3066 |
| CDU924* | MONACO 9 | S67Z | 2427 |
| CDU925* | LYNX SPR 1½ | SS27L | 6200 |
| CDU926* | ADELPHI 1½ | 27A | 6241 |
| CDU927* | FALCON 1½ | 27F | 6260 |
| CDU928* | CC TRG SAL 1½ | 27C | 6272 |
| CDU929* | MONACO 9 | S67Z | 2783 |
| CDU930* | FALCON 1½ | 27F | 6302 |
| CDU931* | ADELPHI 1½ | 27A | 5068 |
| CDU932* | KESTREL SPR 1½ | SS27K | 6319 |
| CDV591 | VICTOR 1½ | 28V | ---- |
| CEF827 | KESTREL 1½ | 28K | ---- |
| CEH397 | LYNX 1½ | 22T | ---- |
| CEH435 | FALCON 1½ | 26F | 2581 |
| CEH914 | ADELPHI 1½ | 26A | ---- |
| CEL482 | KESTREL 1½ | 26K | ---- |
| CEL900 | ADELPHI 1½ | 26A | 4204 |
| CER666 | MONACO 9 | S67Z | ---- |
| CER804 | VICTOR 1½ | 28VX | 7592 |
| CER827 | KESTREL 1½ | 28K | 7309 |
| CFG663 | MONACO 9 | S67Z | ---- |
| CFG687 | VICTOR 1½ | 28V | ---- |
| CFJ209 | ADELPHI 1½ | 27A | 5164 |
| CFJ663 | MONACO 9 | S67Z | ---- |
| CFY 8 | KESTREL SPR 1½ | SS27K | 5070 |
| CFY258 | KESTREL SPR 1½ | SS26K | ---- |
| CFY347 | KESTREL 1½ | 27K | ---- |
| CFY610 | CC TRG SAL 1½ | 27C | ---- |
| CF3737-NZ | KESTREL 1½ | 26K | ---- |
| CG 555 | GAMECOCK 9 | 60 | 16326 |
| CG 751 | GAMECOCK 9 | 60 | ---- |
| CGC 55 | LYNX 1½ | 26L | ---- |

| REG NUMBER | MODEL | CHASSIS NO. | |
|---|---|---|---|
| CGF 52 | FALCON 1½ | 26F | 2443 |
| CGH397 | LYNX 1½ | 22T | 2111 |
| CGH969 | FALCON 1½ | 26F | ---- |
| CGK208 | FALCON 1½ | 26F | ---- |
| CGK293 | MERLIN 9 | 66M | 157 |
| CGN961 | FALCON 1½ | 26F | 2602 |
| CGN964 | MERLIN 1½ | 26M | ---- |
| CGP793 | FALCON 1½ | 26F | ---- |
| CGV611 | KESTREL 9 | 66K | ---- |
| CGV615 | KESTREL 1½ | 26K | ---- |
| CGX 51 | KESTREL 9 | S66K | ---- |
| CGX 54 | KESTREL 9 | 60 | ---- |
| CGY658 | MERLIN 9 | 66M | ---- |
| CG1045 | GAMECOCK 9 | 60 | ---- |
| CG1629 | ALPINE TR 14/6 | 14L | ---- |
| CG1898 | ASCOT 9 | 60 | ---- |
| CG3028 | MONACO 9 | 60 | 19951 |
| CG3691 | MONACO 9 | 60 | 20587 |
| CG4433 | MONACO 9 | 60 | ---- |
| CG6192 | MONACO 9 | 60 | ---- |
| CG7307 | LINCOCK 9 | 60 | ---- |
| CG8460 | KESTREL 9 | 60 | ---- |
| CG8880 | FALCON 1½ | 22T | 240 |
| CG9071 | KESTREL 9 | 60 | ---- |
| CG9320 | KESTREL 9 | 60 | ---- |
| CHB477 | MERLIN 1½ | 26M | ---- |
| CHP101* | KESTREL SPR 1½ | SS27K | 6126 |
| CHP102* | MONACO 9 | S67Z | 2866 |
| CHP103* | KESTREL SPR 1½ | SS27K | 6363 |
| CHP104* | MONACO 9 | S67Z | 2458 |
| CHP105* | FALCON COL 1½ | 27F | 6357 |
| CHP106* | ADELPHI 1½ | 27A | 6413 |
| CHP107* | MONACO 9 | S67Z | 2636 |
| CHP108* | ADELPHI 1½ | 27A | 6452 |
| CHP109*USA | SPRITE 1½ | S27S | 6445 |
| CHP110* | FALCON 1½ | 27F | 6368 |
| CHP111* | KESTREL SPR 1½ | SS27K | 6458 |
| CHP112* | ADELPHI COL 1½ | 27A | 6483 |
| CHP781* | ADELPHI COL 1½ | 27A | 6572 |
| CHP782* | ADELPHI COL 1½ | 27A | 6481 |
| CHP785* | FALCON COL 1½ | 27F | 6502 |
| CHP786* | KESTREL COL 1½ | 27K | 6207 |
| CHP787* | LYNX COL 1½ | 27L | 6537 |
| CHP788* | FALCON COL 1½ | 27F | 6630 |
| CHP789* | AUTOVIA SAL | S | 63110 |
| CHP790* | MERLIN 9 | S67M | 2928 |
| CHP791* | KESTREL SPR 1½ | SS27K | 6609 |
| CHP792* | KESTREL SPR 1½ | SS27K | 6835 |
| CHT500 | KESTREL 1½ | 26K | ---- |
| CHT754 | FALCON 1½ | 26F | 4106 |
| CHU169 | ADELPHI 1½ | 26A | ---- |
| ChW 41 | ADELPHI 1½ | 26A | ---- |
| CHY467 | FALCON 1½ | 27F | ---- |
| CHY468 | ADELPHI 1½ | 27A | ---- |
| CHY676 | MONACO 9 | S67Z | ---- |
| CI 336-NZ | LYNX SPR 1½ | SS28L | ---- |
| CJH164 | FALCON 1½ | 27F | ---- |
| CJH350 | MERLIN 9 | 66M | ---- |

| REG NUMBER | MODEL | CHASSIS NO | |
|---|---|---|---|
| CJJ105 | MERLIN 1½ | 26M | 2928 |
| CJJ242 | FALCON 1½ | 22T | ---- |
| CJ8600 | TOURER 9 | 60 | ---- |
| CK 965 | MONACO 9 | 60 | ---- |
| CKB384 | MERLIN 1½ | 26M | 4276 |
| CKC 67 | MONACO 9 | S67Z | ---- |
| CKC210 | KESTREL SPR 1½ | SS27K | 5471 |
| CKD968 | KESTREL 1½ | 27K | ---- |
| CKE550 | FALCON 1½ | 22T | ---- |
| CKE675 | FALCON 1½ | 26F | ---- |
| CKE685 | KESTREL 9 | 60 | ---- |
| CKF455 | MONACO 9 | S67Z | ---- |
| CKF735 | ADELPHI 1½ | 27A | 6429 |
| CKF810 | ADELPHI 1½ | 27A | ---- |
| CKG 84 | KESTREL 1½ | 22T | ---- |
| CKJ127 | FALCON 1½ | 22T | ---- |
| CKJ760 | MERLIN 9 | 66M | 409 |
| CKK796 | FALCON 1½ | 26F | ---- |
| CKM582 | KESTREL 1½ | 26K | ---- |
| CKM635 | ADELPHI 1½ | 26A | ---- |
| CKM818 | FALCON 1½ | 22T | ---- |
| CKM927 | MERLIN 9 | 66M | 1168 |
| CKN324 | KESTREL 1½ | S26K | 3357 |
| CKN465 | FALCON 1½ | 26F | ---- |
| CK0838 | LYNX CONCRS 1½ | S26L | 4131 |
| CK0960 | MERLIN 9 | 66M | ---- |
| CKR 21 | KESTREL 9 | S66K | ---- |
| CKR 96 | ADELPHI 1½ | 26A | ---- |
| CKR328 | LYNX 1½ | 26L | 2591 |
| CKT225 | ADELPHI 1½ | 26A | ---- |
| CKT777 | KESTREL 1½ | 26K | ---- |
| CKT898 | ADELPHI 1½ | 26A | ---- |
| CKV100* | ADELPHI 1½ | 28A | 7404 |
| CKV280* | ADELPHI 1½ | 28A | 7376 |
| CKV313* | KESTREL 16/4 | 38KX | 1016 |
| CKV314* | ADELPHI 8-90 | 87A | 220 |
| CKV315* | ADELPHI 1½ | 28A | 7399 |
| CKV316* | ADELPHI 16/4 | 38AX | 1014 |
| CKV317* | ADELPHI 16/4 | 38AX | 1026 |
| CKV318* | VICTOR 1½ | 28VX | 7381 |
| CKV319* | ADELPHI 1½ | 28A | 7479 |
| CKV320* | LYNX 1½ | 28L | 7478 |
| CKV321* | KESTREL 16/4 | 38KX | 1056 |
| CKV322*IRL | KESTREL 1½ | 28K | 7393 |
| CKV410 | ADELPHI 1½ | 27A | ---- |
| CKV573* | ADELPHI 16/4 | 38AX | 1061 |
| CKV574* | KESTREL 1½ | 28K | 7458 |
| CKV575* | ADELPHI 8-90 | 87A | 223 |
| CKV576* | VICTOR 1½ | 28VX | 7540 |
| CKV577* | ADELPHI 16/4 | 38AX | 1087 |
| CKV578* | KESTREL 1½ | 28K | 7605 |
| CKV579* | VICTOR 1½ | 28VX | 7598 |
| CKV580* | ADELPHI 16/4 | 38AX | 1071 |
| CKV581* | KESTREL 16/4 | 38KX | 1124 |
| CKV582* | KESTREL 16/4 | 38KX | 1153 |
| CKV583* | VICTOR 1½ | 28VX | 7629 |
| CKV584* | KESTREL 1½ | 28K | 7348 |
| CKX228 | FALCON 1½ | 26F | ---- |

| REG NUMBER | MODEL | CHASSIS NO. | |
|---|---|---|---|
| CKX371 | MERLIN 9 | 66M | ---- |
| CKX740 | KESTREL 9 | S66K | 1589 |
| CLA528 | LYNX 1½ | 26L | 3359 |
| CLA716 | LYNX 1½ | 22T | 2109 |
| CLA797 | LYNX 1½ | 22T | ---- |
| CLB503 | KESTREL 9 | S66K | ---- |
| CLB504 | KESTREL 9 | S66K | 189 |
| CLB749 | KESTREL 1½ | 26K | ---- |
| CLC489 | FALCON 15/6 | 46F | ---- |
| CLC961 | MERLIN 9 | 66M | ---- |
| CLC966 | KESTREL 15/6 | 46K | ---- |
| CLD 72 | KESTREL 1½ | 26K | ---- |
| CLE409 | FALCON 1½ | 22T | ---- |
| CLE905 | LYNX 1½ | 26L | ---- |
| CLF456 | ADELPHI 1½ | 26A | 3200 |
| CLG367 | FALCON 1½ | 22T | 1859 |
| CLJ178 | MERLIN 1½ | 26M | ---- |
| CLJ498 | MONACO 9 | S67Z | ---- |
| CLJ780 | KESTREL 15/6 | 47K | 3144 |
| CLJ836 | ADELPHI 1½ | 26A | ---- |
| CLJ877 | ADELPHI 1½ | 27A | ---- |
| CLJ931 | MONACO 9 | S67Z | 2467 |
| CLK455 | KESTREL 9 | S66K | ---- |
| CLK526 | MERLIN 9 | 66M | ---- |
| CLL909 | KESTREL 1½ | 22T | ---- |
| CLM324 | MERLIN 1½ | 26M | ---- |
| CLM520 | ADELPHI 1½ | 26A | 3680 |
| CLN658 | ADELPHI 15/6 | 46K | ---- |
| CL0677 | KESTREL 9 | S66K | ---- |
| CL0716 | MERLIN 9 | 66M | ---- |
| CL0868 | MERLIN 9 | 66M | 577 |
| CLR372 | MERLIN 9 | 66M | ---- |
| CLR853 | ADELPHI 1½ | 26A | 3791 |
| CLT174 | MERLIN 1½ | 26M | 2992 |
| CLU 99 | KESTREL SPR 1½ | SS26K | ---- |
| CLU569 | KESTREL 1½ | 27K | ---- |
| CLU671 | KESTREL 1½ | 26K | 3668 |
| CLU674 | MERLIN 9 | 66M | ---- |
| CLU679 | MERLIN 1½ | 26M | ---- |
| CLU681 | LYNX 1½ | 26L | ---- |
| CLU684 | KESTREL 15/6 | 46K | ---- |
| CLV931 | MONACO 9 | S67Z | ---- |
| CLW497 | ADELPHI 1½ | 26A | 3688 |
| CLW680 | ADELPHI 15/6 | 46A | ---- |
| CLX 25 | KESTREL 1½ | S26K | 4155 |
| CLY595 | KESTREL 9 | S66K | ---- |
| CLY667 | MERLIN 9 | 66M | ---- |
| CMA378 | LYNX 1½ | 22T | ---- |
| CMB205 | FALCON 1½ | 22T | ---- |
| CMC627 | KESTREL 15/6 | 44T | ---- |
| CMD861 | KESTREL 1½ | 22T | ---- |
| CME419 | KESTREL 1½ | 22T | 1078 |
| CMF 47 | KESTREL 1½ | 22T | 1997 |
| CMF209 | KESTREL 1½ | 22T | ---- |
| CMG 4 | FALCON 1½ | 26F | 2594 |
| CMG384 | LYNX 1½ | 22T | 1442 |
| CMP947 | KESTREL 9 | 60 | ---- |
| CMV 91 | IMP 9 | 60 | ---- |

| REG NUMBER | MODEL | CHASSIS NO | |
|---|---|---|---|
| CMV518 | KESTREL 1½ | 26K | ---- |
| CMV519 | FALCON 1½ | 26F | 2955 |
| CMY470 | ADELPHI 1½ | 26A | ---- |
| CMY755 | MERLIN 9 | 66M | ---- |
| CMY977 | MERLIN 9 | 66M | ---- |
| CM9338 | TOURER 9 | 60 | 8511 |
| CNA285 | KESTREL 1½ | 26K | ---- |
| CNC206 | MERLIN 9 | 66M | ---- |
| CNC645 | KESTREL 9 | S66K | ---- |
| CNE853 | KESTREL 1½ | 26K | ---- |
| CNF640 | SPRITE 1½ | S26S | 4394 |
| CNP 56 | VICTOR 9 | 68V | ---- |
| CNU 58 | FALCON 1½ | 26F | 2739 |
| CNW125 | LYNX 1½ | 22T | ---- |
| CNY342 | ADELPHI 1½ | 27A | 5161 |
| CN4727 | MONACO 9 | 60 | ---- |
| CN5309 | BROOKLANDS 9 | 80 | -- |
| CN5393 | MONACO 9 | 60 | ---- |
| CN6761 | KESTREL 1½ | 22T | 2123 |
| CN7737 | MONACO 9 | S67Z | ---- |
| COB848-USA | LYNX 1½ | 26L | 4659 |
| COE354-USA | MPH 14(ARW485*) | 44T | 2246 |
| COE766 | LYNX 1½ | 26L | 4848 |
| COL793 | MONACO 9 | S67Z | ---- |
| COM313 | KESTREL 1½ | 27K | ---- |
| CON 59 | LYNX 1½ | 27L | 5887 |
| COP649 | MERLIN 9 | 67M | ---- |
| COU619 | KESTREL 1½ | 27K | ---- |
| COU658 | KESTREL SPR 1½ | SS27K | ---- |
| COV 33 | KESTREL SPR 1½ | SS27K | 6082 |
| COV591 | VICTOR 1½ | 28V | ---- |
| COV658 | KESTREL SPR 1½ | SS27K | ---- |
| COX 51 | KESTREL 9 | 66K | 204 |
| COY481 | LYNX SPR 1½ | SS27L | 5470 |
| COY552 | KESTREL 1½ | S27K | 6417 |
| COY553 | LYNX 1½ | 28L | ---- |
| COY901 | KESTREL 1½ | 27K | 5629 |
| CP 778-NZ | KESTREL 1½ | 22T | 2037 |
| CPA346 | MONACO 9 | 60 | ---- |
| CPB461 | KESTREL 1½ | 22T | 468 |
| CPB660 | ADELPHI 15/6 | 46A | 2635 |
| CPC500 | KESTREL 1½ | 22T | ---- |
| CPC649 | KESTREL 9 | 60 | ---- |
| CPC897 | KESTREL 9 | 60 | 27007 |
| CPC900 | KESTREL 1½ | 22T | 655 |
| CPC954 | FALCON 1½ | 22T | 927 |
| CPD531 | KESTREL 9 | 60 | 27142 |
| CPD722 | FALCON 1½ | 22T | ---- |
| CPD723 | FALCON 1½ | 22T | ---- |
| CPD813 | MONACO 9 | 60 | 27231 |
| CPE424 | KESTREL 1½ | 22T | ---- |
| CPE426 | FALCON 1½ | 22T | 1122 |
| CPE695 | FALCON 15/6 | 44T | ---- |
| CPE721 | FALCON 1½ | 22T | ---- |
| CPF640 | FALCON 1½ | 22T | 1332 |
| CPG 1 | FALCON 1½ | 22T | ---- |
| CPG 9 | FALCON 1½ | 22T | 1499 |
| CPG177 | KESTREL 15/6 | 44T | ---- |
| CPG587 | KESTREL 1½ | 22T | 1309 |
| CPG951 | LYNX 1½ | 22T | 1736 |
| CPH250 | MONACO 9 | 60 | 27641 |
| CPH256 | KESTREL 1½ | 26K | ---- |
| CPH852 | KESTREL 1½ | 22T | 2019 |
| CPH922 | FALCON 1½ | 22T | ---- |
| CPJ322 | KESTREL 15/6 | 44T | 2402 |
| CPJ401 | FALCON 1½ | 22T | 2042 |
| CPJ800 | LYNX 9 | 60 | ---- |
| CPK 6 | KESTREL 1½ | 22T | ---- |
| CPO 63 | FALCON 1½ | 26F | ---- |
| CPO302 | SPRITE 1½ | S27S | 5732 |
| CPP528 | MERLIN 9 | 66M | ---- |
| CPP602 | MERLIN 9 | 66M | ---- |
| CPP707 | LYNX 1½ | S26L | 4897 |
| CPP755 | KESTREL SPR 1½ | SS26K | ---- |
| CPU 1 | KESTREL 1½ | 22T | ---- |
| CP7161 | TOURER 9 | 60 | ---- |
| CP7811 | TOURER 9 | 60 | 6276 |
| CP8620 | BIARRITZ 9 | 60 | ---- |
| CR 187 | MONACO 9 | 60 | ---- |
| CRA 66 | FALCON 15/6 | 46F | ---- |
| CRA 67 | FALCON 1½ | 26F | ---- |
| CRA228 | FALCON 1½ | 22T | ---- |
| CRB880 | MERLIN 9 | 66M | ---- |
| CRC971 | KESTREL 1½ | 27K | ---- |
| CRD270 | KESTREL 1½ | 27K | ---- |
| CRF902 | LYNX 9 | 60 | 25970 |
| CRH205 | KESTREL 1½ | 26K | ---- |
| CRH477 | MERLIN 9 | 66M | ---- |
| CRH852 | KESTREL 1½ | 26K | ---- |
| CRK125 | MONACO 9 | SS67Z | ---- |
| CRL309 | KESTREL 15/6 | 47K | ---- |
| CRL313 | MONACO 9 | S67Z | ---- |
| CRL971 | KESTREL 15/6 | 47K | ---- |
| CRO270 | KESTREL SPR 1½ | SS27K | 6202 |
| CRR800 | MERLIN 9 | 66M | ---- |
| CRR806 | KESTREL 1½ | 27K | ---- |
| CRR865 | MERLIN 9 | 66M | 2005 |
| CRR898 | KESTREL SPR 1½ | SS27K | 5727 |
| CRT 30 | MONACO 9 | S67Z | 2550 |
| CRW373* | KESTREL 15/6 | 47K | 3178 |
| CRW374* | ADELPHI COL 1½ | 27A | 6697 |
| CRW375* | FALCON 1½ | 27F | 6629 |
| CRW376* | ADELPHI 1½ | 27A | 6749 |
| CRW377* | FALCON 1½ | S27F | 6719 |
| CRW378* | FALCON 1½ | 27F | 6742 |
| CRW379* | FALCON 1½ | 27F | 6736 |
| CRW380* | ADELPHI 1½ | 27A | 6778 |
| CRW381* | FALCON COL 1½ | 27F | 6678 |
| CRW382* | FALCON 1½ | 27F | 6634 |
| CRW384* | AUTOVIA LIM | L | 63111 |
| CRW447 | MERLIN 9 | 67M | 3013 |
| CRW902* | MONACO 9 | S67Z | 2988 |
| CRW903* | MONACO 9 | S67Z | 2952 |
| CRW904* | MONACO 9 | S67Z | 3008 |
| CRW905* | EXP SAL 16/4 | 16. | 082RP |
| CRW906* | LYNX SPR 1½ | SS27L | 6830 |
| CRW907* | MONACO 9 | S67Z | 3009 |
| CRW908* | FALCON 1½ | 27F | 7018 |
| CRW909* | AUTOVIA SAL | S | 63109 |
| CRW910* | SPRITE 1½ | S27S | 6653 |
| CRW911* | TRG SAL 9 | S67C | 3038 |
| CRW912* | MONACO 9 | S67Z | 2925 |
| CRW913* | MONACO 9 | S67Z | 3031 |
| CSP531 | VICTOR 1½ | 28VX | 7477 |
| CS1212 | FALCON | 22T | ---- |
| CS3038 | KESTREL 1½ | 26K | 3667 |
| CS3732 | MERLIN 9 | 66M | 1677 |
| CS5069 | ADELPHI 1½ | 28A | ---- |
| CS6244 | FALCON 1½ | 27F | ---- |
| CTD144 | FALCON 1½ | 27F | ---- |
| CTD925 | ADELPHI 1½ | 28A | 7430 |
| CTG487 | MONACO 9 | S67Z | ---- |
| CTO639 | KESTREL 1½ | 26K | ---- |
| CTU304 | MERLIN 9 | 66M | ---- |
| CTX 69 | ADELPHI 16/4 | 38AX | ---- |
| CTX397 | VICTOR 1½ | 28V | ---- |
| CT1909-AUS | KESTREL 1½ | 27K | ---- |
| CUB477 | MERLIN 9 | 66M | ---- |
| CUB987 | ADELPHI 1½ | 27A | ---- |
| CUC 19 | KESTREL 1½ | 26K | ---- |
| CUC139 | KESTREL 1½ | S26K | 3731 |
| CUD 54 | KESTREL 1½ | 28K | ---- |
| CUL176 | KESTREL 1½ | S26K | 3970 |
| CUL793 | MONACO 9 | S67Z | 2641 |
| CUN272-AUS | IMP 9 | 60 | ---- |
| CUR571 | KESTREL 1½ | 26K | ---- |
| CUR679 | KESTREL 1½ | 27K | ---- |
| CUU154 | KESTREL 1½ | 26K | ---- |
| CUU285 | IMP 9 | 60 | ---- |
| CUV137 | KESTREL 1½ | S26K | 4211 |
| CUV139 | KESTREL 1½ | 26K | ---- |
| CUV142 | ADELPHI 1½ | 26A | 4126 |
| CUV143 | KESTREL 1½ | 26K | ---- |
| CUV144 | ADELPHI 1½ | 26A | ---- |
| CUV146 | ADELPHI 1½ | 26A | ---- |
| CUV147 | KESTREL 1½ | 26K | 4333 |
| CUV148 | MERLIN 9 | 66M | ---- |
| CUV235 | MERLIN 9 | 66M | 729 |
| CUY482 | MONACO 9 | S67Z | ---- |
| CVB341 | TRG SAL 9 | S67CX | 3164 |
| CVB989 | KESTREL 1½ | 28K | ---- |
| CVC128* | ADELPHI 1½ | 27A | 6438 |
| CVC129* | ADELPHI 1½ | 27AX | 7200 |
| CVC130* | ADELPHI COL 1½ | 27A | 7042 |
| CVC131* | ADELPHI 1½ | 27A | 7123 |
| CVC132* | TRG SAL 1½ | 28F | 7237 |
| CVC473* | ADELPHI 1½ | 28A | 7211 |
| CVC474* | ADELPHI 8-90 | 87A | 212 |
| CVC475* | TRG SAL 1½ | 28FX | 7201 |
| CVC476* | ADELPHI 1½ | 28AX | 7229 |
| CVC477* | FALCON 1½ | 27F | 6766 |
| CVC478* | ADELPHI 1½ | 28AX | 7231 |
| CVC479* | TRG SAL 1½ | 28FX | 7212 |
| CVC480* | ADELPHI 1½ | 28AX | 7216 |
| CVC481* | KESTREL 1½ | 28KX | 7326 |
| CVC482* | LYNX 1½ | 28L | 7255 |
| CVC483* | ADELPHI 1½ | 28A | 7371 |
| CVC534* | AUTOVIA SAL | S | 63124 |
| CVC884* | VICTOR 1½ | 28VX | 7374 |
| CVC885* | ADELPHI 15/6 | 48A | 3301 |
| CVC886* | ADELPHI 16/4 | 38AX | 1001 |
| CVC887* | VICTOR 9 | S68V | 3400 |
| CVC888* | VICTOR 1½ | 28VX | 7369 |
| CVC889* | ADELPHI 16/4 | 38AX | 1007 |
| CVC890* | KESTREL 16/4 | 38KX | 1005 |
| CVC891* | KESTREL 1½ | 28KX | 7271 |
| CVC892* | ADELPHI 16/4 | 38AX | 1010 |
| CVC893* | ADELPHI 1½ | 28A | 7258 |
| CVC894* | ADELPHI 1½ | 28A | 7397 |
| CVC895* | KESTREL 1½ | 28KX | 7392 |
| CVE 7 | KESTREL 16/4 | 38AX | 1226 |
| CVK425 | MERLIN 1½ | S26M | 3802 |
| CVK770 | MERLIN 1½ | 26M | 4035 |
| CVK947 | MERLIN 1½ | 26M | 4107 |
| CVM208 | SPRITE 1½ | S26S | 4920 |
| CVO 2 | MONACO 9 | S67Z | ---- |
| CVO628 | MONACO 9 | SS67Z | ---- |
| CVU158 | ADELPHI 15/6 | 46A | ---- |
| CVU296 | KESTREL 1½ | 27K | ---- |
| CVU346 | ADELPHI 1½ | 27A | ---- |
| CVU783 | SPRITE 1½ | S27S | 5443 |
| CVW781 | LYNX 1½ | 27L | ---- |
| CV2914 | MONACO 9 | 60 | ---- |
| CV3788 | MONACO 9 | 60 | 11679 |
| CV6231 | GAMECOCK 9 | 60 | ---- |
| CV7363 | MONACO 9 | 60 | ---- |
| CV7667 | MONACO 9 | 60 | ---- |
| CWE289 | KESTREL 1½ | S27K | 5076 |
| CWJ844 | ADELPHI 1½ | 26A | ---- |
| CWK161* | KESTREL SPR 1½ | SS27K | 6828 |
| CWK162* | LYNX SPR 1½ | SS27L | 6903 |
| CWK163* | MONACO 9 | S67Z | 2036 |
| CWK164* | FALCON COL 1½ | 27F | 6885 |
| CWK165* | ADELPHI COL 1½ | 27A | 6792 |
| CWK166* | CC TRG SAL 1½ | S27C | 6801 |
| CWK167* | ADELPHI 1½ | S27A | 6198 |
| CWK168* | ADELPHI 1½ | 27A | 5953 |
| CWK169* | ADELPHI COL 1½ | 27A | 6930 |
| CWK170* | ADELPHI 8-90 | 87A | 202 |
| CWK171* | TT SPRITE | S27S | 6950 |
| CWK172* | ADELPHI 1½ | 27A | 6878 |
| CWK442* | ADELPHI 1½ | 27A | 6879 |
| CWK443* | ADELPHI 1½ | 27A | 6898 |
| CWK445* | ADELPHI 1½ | 27A | 6876 |
| CWK446* | CC TRG SAL 1½ | 27C | 6960 |
| CWK447* | MONACO 9 | S67ZX | 2680 |
| CWK448* | MONACO 9 | S67Z | 3163 |
| CWK449* | FALCON 1½ | 27F | 6887 |
| CWK451* | ADELPHI 1½ | 27A | 6947 |
| CWK452* | ADELPHI 1½ | 27A | 6985 |
| CWK453* | KESTREL 1½ | 27K | 6956 |
| CWK454* | MONACO 9 | S67Z | 3127 |

| REG NUMBER | MODEL | CHASSIS NO | |
|---|---|---|---|
| CWK455* | MONACO 9 | S67Z | 3145 |
| CWK816* | LYNX SPR 1½ | SS27L | 6978 |
| CWK817* | ADELPHI 1½ | 27A | 6834 |
| CWK818* | ADELPHI 1½ | 27A | 7015 |
| CWK819* | ADELPHI 1½ | 27A | 6958 |
| CWK820* | TRG SAL 9 | S67CX | 3199 |
| CWK821* | ADELPHI 1½ | 27A | 7038 |
| CWK822* | TRG SAL 9 | S67C | 3228 |
| CWK823* | ADELPHI 1½ | 27A | 6997 |
| CWK824* | FALCON 1½ | 27F | 7055 |
| CWK825* | ADELPHI 8-90 | 87A | 205 |
| CWK826* | MONACO 9 | S67Z | 3185 |
| CWK827* | KESTREL 1½ | 27K | 7064 |
| CWL115 | MERLIN 9 | 66M | ---- |
| CWM115 | KESTREL SPR 1½ | SS27K | ---- |
| CWM356 | ADELPHI 1½ | 27A | ---- |
| CWM557 | KESTREL 1½ | 27K | ---- |
| CWM739 | MONACO 9 | S67Z | ---- |
| CWN213 | IMP 9 | 60 | ---- |
| CWT753 | VICTOR 1½ | 28VX | 7617 |
| CWT907 | VICTOR 1½ | 28VX | 7841 |
| CW6221 | MONACO 9 | 60 | ---- |
| CW8475 | TOURER 9 | 60 | ---- |
| CXB507 | MERLIN 9 | 66M | ---- |
| CXC278 | KESTREL 9 | S66K | ---- |
| CXC761 | MERLIN 9 | 66M | ---- |
| CXC794 | MERLIN 9 | 66M | ---- |
| CXF226 | ADELPHI 1½ | 26A | 4419 |
| CXH 65 | ADELPHI 1½ | 26A | ---- |
| CXJ945 | KESTREL 1½ | 27K | ---- |
| CXL182 | MERLIN 9 | 66M | ---- |
| CXL713 | MERLIN 9 | 66M | ---- |
| CXL715 | KESTREL 1½ | 26K | ---- |
| CXR110 | KESTREL 9 | S66K | ---- |
| CXU569 | IMP 9 | 60 | ---- |
| CXU853 | MERLIN 1½ | 26M | 4557 |
| CXV 17 | FALCON 15/6 | 46F | 2738 |
| CXV426 | MERLIN 9 | 66M | ---- |
| CXV569 | IMP 9 | 60 | ---- |
| CXW448 | ADELPHI 1½ | 26A | 3620 |
| CXW834 | MERLIN 1½ | S26M | 4441 |
| CXW912 | MERLIN 9 | 66M | 1400 |
| CXW932 | ADELPHI 1½ | 26A | 4629 |
| CXY 58 | KESTREL 15/6 | 46K | ---- |
| CXY 59 | MERLIN 9 | 66M | ---- |
| CXY 60 | KESTREL SPR 1½ | SS26K | 4606 |
| CXY 67 | KESTREL SPR 1½ | SS26K | ---- |
| CXY382 | LYNX 1½ | 26L | 2519 |
| CXY386 | SPRITE 1½ | S26S | 4631 |
| CXY388 | VICTOR 9 | 68V | ---- |
| CYA605 | ADELPHI 15/6 | 47A | 3101 |
| CYD404 | MONACO 9 | S67Z | ---- |
| CYE688 | KESTREL 1½ | 26K | 4433 |
| CYH 67 | ADELPHI 1½ | 26A | ---- |
| CYH121 | KESTREL 15/6 | 46K | ---- |
| CYH604 | LYNX SPR 1½ | SS26L | 2486 |
| CYK302 | MERLIN 9 | 66M | ---- |
| CYL 55 | KESTREL 9 | S66K | 1758 |

| REG NUMBER | MODEL | CHASSIS NO. | |
|---|---|---|---|
| CYL715 | KESTREL 1½ | 26K | ---- |
| CY0761 | MERLIN 9 | 66M | ---- |
| CYP967 | KESTREL 1½ | 27K | 5166 |
| CYR247 | KESTREL 15/6 | 46K | ---- |
| CYR533-NL | FALCON 1½ | 26F | ---- |
| CYT474 | ADELPHI 1½ | 26A | ---- |
| CYT475 | KESTREL 15/6 | 46K | ---- |
| CYT477 | KESTREL SPR 1½ | SS26K | ---- |
| CYT488 | STELVIO 15/6 | 15S | ---- |
| CYV644 | ADELPHI 1½ | 26A | 3346 |
| CYX382 | LYNX 1½ | S26L | 2519 |
| CY7680 | SPRITE 1½ | S26S | ---- |
| CZ3026-IRL | MONACO 9 | 60 | 21817 |
| CZ4421-IRL | LYNX 9 | 60 | 24290 |
| CZ6620-IRL | FALCON 1½ | 22T | ---- |
| CZ7740-IRL | KESTREL 1½ | 22T | 1037 |
| CZ9134-IRL | KESTREL 9 | 60 | ---- |
| D 1894 | TRI-CAR | 862 / | 122 |
| DAA742 | LYNX 1½ | 22T | 1574 |
| DAD460 | VICTOR | -- | ---- |
| DAE738 | MERLIN 1½ | 26M | 4901 |
| DAE866 | FALCON 1½ | S27F | 6717 |
| DAL713 | TRG SAL 9 | S67CX | ---- |
| DAR 67 | ADELPHI 1½ | 27A | ---- |
| DAR873 | TRG SAL 1½ | 28F | ---- |
| DAU572 | LYNX SPR 1½ | SS27L | ---- |
| DAU573 | FALCON 1½ | 27F | 6308 |
| DBB537 | KESTREL 9 | S66K | 1700 |
| DBP408 | KESTREL 1½ | 26K | ---- |
| DBY859 | KESTREL 1½ | 28K | ---- |
| DCT712 | LYNX SPR 1½ | SS28L | ---- |
| DCY968 | VICTOR | -- | ---- |
| DDG908 | LYNX 9 | 60 | ---- |
| DDK296 | ADELPHI 1½ | 28A | ---- |
| DDU386* | VICTOR 9 | S68V | 3423 |
| DDU387* | VICTOR 1½ | 28VX | 7699 |
| DDU388* | CC TRG SAL 16/4 | 38BX | 1182 |
| DDU389* | ADELPHI 1½ | 28A | 7737 |
| DDU390* | KESTREL 16/4 | 38KX | 1221 |
| DDU391* | VICTOR 1½ | 28V | 7606 |
| DDU392* | ADELPHI 1½ | 28A | 7771 |
| DDU393* | KESTREL 16/4 | 38KX | 1214 |
| DDU394* | ADELPHI 16/4 | 38AX | 1238 |
| DDU395* | LYNX 1½ | 28L | 7840 |
| DDU396* | LYNX 1½ | 28L | 7818 |
| DDU397* | ADELPHI 16/4 | 38AX | 1211 |
| DDV987 | CC TRG SAL 16/4 | 38BX | 1232 |
| DEL130 | MONACO 9 | S67Z | ---- |
| DER560-AUS | FALCON 1½ | 27F | 6652 |
| DEV101 | MERLIN 9 | 66M | ---- |
| DE4127 | KESTREL 1½ | 22T | ---- |
| DE9660 | KESTREL 9 | 60 | ---- |
| DE9745 | LYNX 9 | 60 | ---- |
| DFC789 | SPRITE 1½ | S26S | 4884 |
| DFD 44 | TRG SAL 1½ | 28F | ---- |
| DFJ762 | ADELPHI 16/4 | 38AX | ---- |
| DFM254 | BROOKLANDS 9 | 80 | -- |
| DFY383 | ADELPHI 15/6 | 47A | ---- |

| REG NUMBER | MODEL | CHASSIS NO | |
|---|---|---|---|
| DFY611 | TRG SAL 1½ | 28F | 7869 |
| DF1936-NZ | KESTREL 1½ | 26K | 4022 |
| DF8549 | 2 SEATER 9 | 60 | 6590 |
| DGF972 | KESTREL SPR 1½ | SS27K | 5227 |
| DGF986 | MONACO 9 | S67Z | 2420 |
| DGF987 | MONACO 9 | S67Z | 3442 |
| DGJ759 | KESTREL 1½ | 27K | ---- |
| DGN 8 | FALCON 1½ | S27F | 5343 |
| DGO 7 | KESTREL SPR 1½ | SS26K | ---- |
| DG0748 | KESTREL SPR 1½ | SS27K | 5501 |
| DGP408 | KESTREL 1½ | 26K | ---- |
| DGT711 | ADELPHI 1½ | 27A | ---- |
| DGT712 | LYNX SPR 1½ | SS27L | 5542 |
| DGT713 | FALCON 1½ | 27F | ---- |
| DGT718 | CC TRG SAL 1½ | 27C | 5799 |
| DGT720 | MONACO 9 | S67Z | ---- |
| DGT727 | CC TRG SAL 1½ | 27C | ---- |
| DGT729 | KESTREL 1½ | S27K | 5837 |
| DGU748 | KESTREL SPR 1½ | SS26K | ---- |
| DGW542 | ADELPHI 15/6 | 47A | 3055 |
| DG4925 | GAMECOCK 9 | 60 | ---- |
| DG5080 | GAMECOCK 9 | 60 | ---- |
| DG6796 | KESTREL 12/6 | 44T | 783 |
| DG7407 | LYNX 9 | 60 | 22415 |
| DG9635 | MONACO 9 | 60 | ---- |
| DH0776 | ADELPHI 16/4 | 38AX | ---- |
| DHP722* | VICTOR 1½ | 28VX | 7817 |
| DHP723* | VICTOR 1½ | 28V | 7716 |
| DHP724* | ADELPHI 15/6 | 48A | 3321 |
| DHP725* | KESTREL 16/4 | 38KX | 1270 |
| DHP726* | ADELPHI 16/4 | 38AX | 1262 |
| DHP727* | KESTREL 16/4 | 38KX | 1266 |
| DHP728* | VICTOR EXP 1½ | 28VX | EXP- |
| DHP730* | ADELPHI 16/4 | 38AX | 1276 |
| DHP731* | ADELPHI 1½ | 28AX | 7436 |
| DHP732* | KESTREL 16/4 | 38KX | 1289 |
| DHP733* | TRG SAL 1½ | 28F | 7872 |
| DHU799 | MONACO 9 | S67Z | ---- |
| DHW 61 | MONACO 9 | S67Z | 2916 |
| DHW216 | ADELPHI 1½ | 27A | ---- |
| DH8908 | KESTREL 9 | 60 | ---- |
| DH9991 | ASCOT 9 | 60 | ---- |
| DI2796-IRL | MERLIN 9 | 66M | 1080 |
| DJH393 | FALCON 1½ | 26F | ---- |
| DJJ 29 | KESTREL 1½ | S27K | 6661 |
| DJJ678 | SPRITE 1½ | S27S | 5548 |
| DJO 76 | MONACO 9 | S67Z | ---- |
| DKD 33 | CC TRG SAL 1½ | 27C | ---- |
| DKE480 | LINCOCK 9 | 60 | ---- |
| DKF506 | KESTREL 16/4 | 38KX | 1196 |
| DKF778 | KESTREL 16/4 | 38KX | 1078 |
| DKH275 | MONACO 9 | S67Z | ---- |
| DKJ385-B | LYNX SPR 1½ | SS26L | ---- |
| DKJ961 | KESTREL SPR 1½ | SS26K | ---- |
| DKJ970 | MERLIN 9 | 66M | ---- |
| DKM818 | KESTREL SPR 1½ | SS27K | 6131 |
| DKN510 | FALCON 1½ | 27F | 5716 |
| DKN977 | KESTREL 1½ | 27K | ---- |

| REG NUMBER | MODEL | CHASSIS NO | |
|---|---|---|---|
| DK0714 | ADELPHI 1½ | 27A | 6387 |
| DKR746 | FALCON 1½ | 27F | ---- |
| DKV431* | ADELPHI 1½ | 28A | 7918 |
| DKW977 | KESTREL 1½ | 27K | 5571 |
| DK6603 | MONACO 9 | 60 | ---- |
| DK6780 | TOURER 9 | 60 | 10603 |
| DK8078 | GAMECOCK 9 | 60 | 18048 |
| DK9922 | FALCON 1½ | 22T | ---- |
| DLA402 | KESTREL 1½ | 27K | 5677 |
| DLA906-USA | KESTREL 1½ | 27K | ---- |
| DLC222 | LYNX 1½ | 26L | ---- |
| DLC474 | MONACO 9 | S67Z | ---- |
| DLC950 | FALCON 1½ | 27F | 5545 |
| DLE366 | CC TRG SAL 1½ | 27C | ---- |
| DLF361 | MONACO 9 | S67Z | ---- |
| DLF366 | CC TRG SAL 1½ | 27C | ---- |
| DLF370 | KESTREL SPR 1½ | SS27K | 5968 |
| DLF377 | MERLIN 9 | 66M | 2036 |
| DLF378 | CC TRG SAL 1½ | 27C | 6080 |
| DLJ293 | TRG SAL 9 | S67CX | ---- |
| DLJ786 | CC TRG SAL 16/4 | 38BX | 1022 |
| DLJ875 | ADELPHI 1½ | 27A | ---- |
| DLL222 | LYNX 1½ | 26L | ---- |
| DLM358 | FALCON 1½ | -- | ---- |
| DLM467 | LYNX 1½ | 27L | ---- |
| DLN 2 | KESTREL 1½ | S27K | 5927 |
| DLO 87 | ADELPHI 1½ | 27A | ---- |
| DL0753 | KESTREL SPR 1½ | SS27K | ---- |
| DLP468 | KESTREL SPR 1½ | SS27K | 6071 |
| DLP495 | ADELPHI 15/6 | 47A | 3123 |
| DLP890 | KESTREL SPR 1½ | SS27K | 6193 |
| DLR372 | KESTREL 1½ | 26K | ---- |
| DLT295 | ADELPHI 1½ | 27A | ---- |
| DLT298 | MERLIN 1½ | 27M | ---- |
| DLT310 | FALCON 1½ | 27F | ---- |
| DLT693 | MONACO 9 | S67Z | ---- |
| DLW353 | KESTREL 1½ | 27K | 6300 |
| DL7676 | MONACO 9 | 60 | 11346 |
| DMA 13 | ADELPHI 1½ | 27A | 5258 |
| DMA123 | KESTREL 1½ | 27K | 5650 |
| DMA791 | KESTREL 15/6 | 47K | ---- |
| DMB300 | MERLIN 9 | 67M | ---- |
| DMD354 | KESTREL 1½ | 26K | ---- |
| DME 62 | MERLIN 9 | 66M | ---- |
| DME 65 | KESTREL 1½ | 26K | 3501 |
| DME 74 | KESTREL 1½ | 26K | ---- |
| DME158 | MERLIN 9 | 66M | ---- |
| DMG301 | FALCON 1½ | 26F | ---- |
| DMG818 | ADELPHI 1½ | 26A | ---- |
| DMH292 | KESTREL 1½ | 26K | ---- |
| DMK 51 | MERLIN 9 | 66M | 1250 |
| DMK612 | KESTREL 9 | S66K | ---- |
| DMP475 | LYNX 1½ | 26L | ---- |
| DMP520 | IMP 9 | 60 | 27673 |
| DMP767 | MERLIN 9 | 66M | 1568 |
| DMY655 | LYNX SPR 1½ | SS26L | 4781 |
| DMY657 | MERLIN 9 | 66M | ---- |
| DM8414 | KESTREL 6 | 44T | ---- |

| REG NUMBER | MODEL | CHASSIS NO | |
|---|---|---|---|
| DM8564 | KESTREL 1½ | 22T | ---- |
| DM8898 | KESTREL 9 | 60 | 25073 |
| DM8908 | KESTREL 9 | 60 | 25113 |
| DM9115 | KESTREL 9 | 60 | ---- |
| DM9841 | ADELPHI 1½ | 26A | 3613 |
| DNC157 | KESTREL 9 | 66K | ---- |
| DND162 | SPRITE 1½ | S27S | 6667 |
| DND309 | KESTREL 1½ | 27K | ---- |
| DNF795 | MONACO 9 | S67Z | ---- |
| DNU339 | ADELPHI 1½ | 27A | 5670 |
| DNY540 | VICTOR 1½ | 28VX | 7849 |
| DOB443 | MERLIN 9 | 66M | ---- |
| DOB896 | LYNX 1½ | 27L | ---- |
| DOC600 | KESTREL 1½ | 27K | ---- |
| DOH 58 | FALCON 1½ | 27F | ---- |
| DOI294-AUS | SPECIAL 1½ | 22T | 949 |
| DOJ321 | KESTREL SPR 1½ | SS28K | 7281 |
| DON735 | ADELPHI 16/4 | 38AX | ---- |
| DON753 | VICTOR 1½ | 28V | ---- |
| DON755 | ADELPHI 16/4 | 38AX | ---- |
| DON906 | KESTREL 16/4 | 38KX | 1155 |
| DOP165 | KESTREL 16/4 | 38KX | ---- |
| DOP678 | KESTREL 1½ | 28K | ---- |
| DPB783-USA | LYNX 1½ | 22T | ---- |
| DPB788 | LYNX 1½ | 22T | 2074 |
| DPC208 | MERLIN 1½ | 26M | 3063 |
| DPC709 | MERLIN 9 | 66M | ---- |
| DPC793 | FALCON 1½ | 26F | ---- |
| DPD503 | LYNX 1½ | 22T | 2098 |
| DPE 31 | KESTREL SPR 1½ | SS27K | ---- |
| DPE 83 | MERLIN 9 | 66M | ---- |
| DPE248 | MERLIN 1½ | 26M | ---- |
| DPE271 | KESTREL 1½ | 26K | ---- |
| DPE569 | KESTREL 1½ | 22T | ---- |
| DPE588 | MERLIN 9 | 67M | ---- |
| DPE589 | KESTREL 9 | S66K | 717 |
| DPE754 | MERLIN 1½ | 26M | 3125 |
| DPF524 | MERLIN 9 | 66M | ---- |
| DPF829 | KESTREL 1½ | S26K | 3546 |
| DPG292 | MERLIN 9 | 66M | ---- |
| DPG553 | KESTREL 1½ | 22T | ---- |
| DPG573 | KESTREL 1½ | 26K | ---- |
| DPG928 | LYNX 1½ | 22T | 1975 |
| DPH175 | KESTREL 1½ | 26K | ---- |
| DPH433-DK | ADELPHI 15/6 | 46A | 2692 |
| DPJ 41 | KESTREL 9 | S66K | ---- |
| DPJ362 | FALCON 1½ | 26F | ---- |
| DPJ454-ZA | LYNX 1½ | 26L | ---- |
| DPJ991 | KESTREL 15/6 | 46K | 2660 |
| DPK 41 | KESTREL 9 | S66K | 1430 |
| DPK165 | KESTREL 1½ | S26K | 4289 |
| DPK449 | ADELPHI 1½ | 26A | ---- |
| DPK949 | ADELPHI 15/6 | 46A | ---- |
| DPK956 | KESTREL 15/6 | 46K | 2674 |
| DPL378 | ADELPHI 1½ | 26A | 4554 |
| DPL409 | ADELPHI 1½ | 26A | ---- |
| DPL765 | LYNX 15/6 | 46L | 2723 |
| DPO577 | KESTREL 1½ | 28K | ---- |

| REG NUMBER | MODEL | CHASSIS NO. | |
|---|---|---|---|
| DP0919 | VICTOR | -- | ---- |
| DPP467 | FALCON 1½ | 27F | 6838 |
| DPU437 | MERLIN 9 | 66M | ---- |
| DPU991 | MERLIN 9 | 66M | 1797 |
| DPX 11 | VICTOR 1½ | 28V | ---- |
| DPX 84 | ADELPHI 16/4 | 38AX | ---- |
| DPX479 | ADELPHI 1½ | 28A | ---- |
| DR 378 | MONACO 9 | 60 | 25171 |
| DRA968 | MONACO 9 | SS67Z | ---- |
| DRE149 | FALCON 1½ | 26F | ---- |
| DRE263 | FALCON 1½ | 26F | ---- |
| DRL246 | ADELPHI 1½ | 28AX | 7593 |
| DRO684 | VICTOR 1½ | 28VX | 7792 |
| DRU575 | VICTOR 1½ | 28VX | 7755 |
| DRW147* | LYNX 1½ | 28L | 7875 |
| DRW148* | ADELPHI 1½ | 28A | 7874 |
| DRW149* | VICTOR 1½ | 28VX | 7884 |
| DRW150* | VICTOR 1½ | 28V | 7902 |
| DRW151* | KESTREL 16/4 | 38KX | 1039 |
| DRW152* | MONACO 1½ | 28V | 7796 |
| DRW154* | ADELPHI 16/4 | 38AX | 1311 |
| DRW155* | CC TRG SAL 16/4 | 38BX | 1300 |
| DRW156* | ADELPHI 16/4 | 38AX | 1310 |
| DR7872 | BIARRITZ 9 | 60 | 11717 |
| DS1769 | LINCOCK 9 | 60 | 18176 |
| DS2097 | MONACO 9 | S67Z | ---- |
| DTA772 | KESTREL 1½ | 27K | ---- |
| DTN152 | ADELPHI 1½ | 26A | ---- |
| DT0283 | MONACO 9 | S67Z | 2841 |
| DT0500 | KESTREL SPR 1½ | SS27K | ---- |
| DT0543 | KESTREL 1½ | 27K | ---- |
| DTT354 | ADELPHI 1½ | 27A | ---- |
| DTT657 | TICKFORD 1½ | SS27K | 6663 |
| DTU439 | ADELPHI | 27A | ---- |
| DTU450 | MONACO 9 | S67Z | ---- |
| DTV992 | CC TRG SAL 1½ | 27C | ---- |
| DT3113 | MONACO 9 | 60 | 13646 |
| DT3343 | GAMECOCK 9 | 60 | ---- |
| DT3533 | GAMECOCK 9 | 60 | 16138 |
| DT6255 | MONACO 9 | 60 | 27608 |
| DU 458* | 4½ HP FORECAR | ---- / | 394 |
| DUB351 | MERLIN 9 | 66M | ---- |
| DUE331 | ADELPHI 1½ | 26A | ---- |
| DUG497 | SPRITE 1½ | S27S | 6030 |
| DUL669 | ADELPHI 1½ | 27A | 6447 |
| DU0947 | ADELPHI 1½ | 26A | ---- |
| DUR482 | LYNX 1½ | 28L | 7838 |
| DUT519 | MONACO 9 | S67Z | 2424 |
| DUU830 | MERLIN 9 | 67M | ---- |
| DUU837 | CC TRG SAL 1½ | 27C | 6468 |
| DUV119 | FALCON 1½ | 27F | 6115 |
| DV0404 | VICTOR 1½ | 28VX | 7834 |
| DVR310 | MONACO 9 | S67Z | 2257 |
| DVT 43 | MERLIN 9 | 66M | 2013 |
| DVW374 | KESTREL 1½ | 27K | 5018 |
| DVW957 | KESTREL 1½ | 26K | ---- |
| DV3084 | TOURER 9 | 60 | 7900 |
| DV3176 | VERNON DERBY/RILEY | | ---- |

| REG NUMBER | MODEL | CHASSIS NO | |
|---|---|---|---|
| DV7600 | GAMECOCK 9 | 60 | ---- |
| DV9008 | MONACO 9 | 60 | ---- |
| DWB486 | FALCON 1½ | 27F | 6486 |
| DWJ465 | FALCON 1½ | 27F | ---- |
| DWJ475 | FALCON 1½ | 27F | ---- |
| DWL484 | MERLIN 9 | 66M | ---- |
| DWL835 | MONACO 9 | S67Z | 2570 |
| DW4653-NZ | KESTREL 12/6 | 44T | ---- |
| DW4865 | MONACO 9 | S67Z | ---- |
| DW7035 | MONACO 9 | 60 | ---- |
| DW9286 | KESTREL 9 | 60 | ---- |
| DW9528 | MONACO 9 | 60 | ---- |
| DXA923 | LYNX SPR 1½ | SS27L | ---- |
| DXB916 | FALCON 1½ | S27F | 6680 |
| DXD256 | KESTREL 1½ | 27K | ---- |
| DXD704 | KESTREL 15/6 | 47K | ---- |
| DXE 31 | KESTREL 15/6 | 46K | ---- |
| DXE 41 | KESTREL 15/6 | 46K | 3147 |
| DXE644 | LYNX 1½ | 27L | ---- |
| DXJ477 | ADELPHI 16/4 | 38AX | 1012 |
| DXJ732 | KESTREL 16/4 | 38KX | ---- |
| DXK 66 | LYNX 1½ | 27L | ---- |
| DXL509 | KESTREL 1½ | 27K | ---- |
| DXM 49 | ADELPHI 15/6 | 47A | ---- |
| DXM181 | TRG SAL 1½ | 28F | ---- |
| DXM660 | KESTREL 1½ | 27K | ---- |
| DXP298 | AUTOVIA SAL | S | 63121 |
| DXT363 | CC TRG SAL 1½ | 27C | ---- |
| DXT798 | ADELPHI 1½ | 27A | ---- |
| DXV326 | MONACO 9 | S67Z | 2739 |
| DXV590 | KESTREL SPR 1½ | SS27K | 6054 |
| DXW285 | LYNX SPR 1½ | SS27L | ---- |
| DXW409 | LYNX 1½ | 27L | 6780 |
| DXX732 | KESTREL 1½ | 26K | 6851 |
| DX9170 | MONACO 9 | 60 | ---- |
| DX9609 | MONACO 9 | 60 | ---- |
| DYA 2 | ADELPHI 1½ | 27A | 6355 |
| DYB 85 | VICTOR 9 | S68V | 3436 |
| DYH149 | CC TRG SAL 1½ | 27C | ---- |
| DYH151 | KESTREL SPR 1½ | SS27K | ---- |
| DYH160 | MERLIN 9 | 67M | ---- |
| DYH436 | FALCON 1½ | 27F | ---- |
| DYH443 | SPRITE 1½ | S27S | ---- |
| DYH816 | KESTREL 1½ | 27K | ---- |
| DYM429 | LYNX 1½ | 27L | 6877 |
| DYR539 | KESTREL SPR 1½ | SS27K | 6974 |
| DYU171 | KESTREL SPR 1½ | SS27K | 6971 |
| DYV 90 | KESTREL 1½ | 27K | 6952 |
| DYV241 | SPRITE 1½ | S27S | 6797 |
| DYW153 | TRG SAL 9 | 67C | ---- |
| DYW897 | KESTREL 1½ | 27K | 7035 |
| DYW898 | LYNX SPR 1½ | SS27L | 6739 |
| DYW899 | ADELPHI 1½ | 26A | ---- |
| DYW900 | TRG SAL 9 | 67C | ---- |
| DYW909 | TRG SAL 9 | 67C | ---- |
| DY5457 | LINCOCK 9 | 60 | ---- |
| DY5668 | BIARRITZ 9 | 60 | ---- |
| DY7467 | LYNX 9 | 60 | ---- |

| REG NUMBER | MODEL | CHASSIS NO. | |
|---|---|---|---|
| DY7777 | LYNX 9 | 60 | ---- |
| DZ1065-IRL | LYNX 9 | 60 | 23455 |
| DZ3737-IRL | ADELPHI 1½ | 27A | 5926 |
| DZ4742-IRL | LYNX 1½ | 27L | ---- |
| DZ4747-IRL | LYNX 1½ | 28L | 7439 |
| DZ4999-IRL | ADELPHI 16/4 | 38AX | 1127 |
| DZ9792-IRL | LYNX 1½ | 28L | ---- |
| EAF180 | FALCON 1½ | 27F | ---- |
| EAF545 | ADELPHI 16/4 | 38AX | ---- |
| EAF668 | VICTOR 1½ | 28V | ---- |
| EAL437 | MONACO 9 | 60 | ---- |
| EB9736 | MONACO 9 | 60 | 17882 |
| ECD712 | TRG SAL 1½ | 28F | ---- |
| ECV228 | KESTREL 16/4 | 38KX | 1302 |
| EC2636 | MONACO 9 | 60 | ---- |
| ED 609 | MONACO 9 | 60 | ---- |
| EDY633-S | ADELPHI 1½ | 27A | 5127 |
| ED7481 | MONACO 9 | 60 | ---- |
| ED8306-NZ | KESTREL 12/6 | 44T | 1714 |
| ED9689 | MERLIN 9 | 66M | ---- |
| EEL 24 | VICTOR | 28V | ---- |
| EEV 17 | ADELPHI 1½ | 27A | ---- |
| EEV502 | ADELPHI 1½ | 27A | 5274 |
| EF3776 | 2 SEATER 9 | 60 | 950 |
| EF5320 | LYNX 9 | 60 | 23412 |
| EF5795 | FALCON 1½ | 26F | ---- |
| EF6365 | MONACO 9 | S67Z | ---- |
| EF6830 | CC TRG SAL 16/4 | 38BX | 1301 |
| EG 206 | GAMECOCK 9 | 60 | ---- |
| EG 774 | FALCON 9 | 60 | 22126 |
| EGF768 | FALCON 1½ | 27F | 7091 |
| EGH144 | MONACO 9 | S67Z | ---- |
| EGH194 | MONACO 9 | S67Z | ---- |
| EGH198 | SPRITE 1½ | S27S | ---- |
| EGJ400 | ADELPHI 15/6 | 47A | ---- |
| EGJ825 | MONACO 9 | S67Z | ---- |
| EGM198 | SPRITE 1½ | S27S | 7126 |
| EGN542 | KESTREL 1½ | 28K | ---- |
| EG0202 | FALCON 1½ | 27F | ---- |
| EG0203 | CC TRG SAL 1½ | 27C | 5908 |
| EG0204 | MONACO 9 | S67Z | ---- |
| EG0207 | CC TRG SAL 1½ | 27C | ---- |
| EG0214 | MONACO 9 | S67Z | ---- |
| EG0216 | LYNX 1½ | 27L | ---- |
| EG0217 | MONACO 9 | S67Z | ---- |
| EG0220 | KESTREL 1½ | 27K | ---- |
| EGP388 | TRG SAL 9 | S67CX | 3325 |
| EGP464 | FALCON 1½ | 27F | 7125 |
| EGW674 | MONACO 9 | S67Z | ---- |
| EGY631 | FALCON 1½ | 27F | 7111 |
| EGY635 | MONACO 9 | S67Z | 3251 |
| EGY636 | ADELPHI 1½ | 27A | ---- |
| EGY637 | TRG SALOON 9 | S67C | 3271 |
| EG1395 | KESTREL 9 | 60 | 24817 |
| EG1617 | MONACO 9 | 60 | ---- |
| EG2510 | FALCON 1½ | 26F | ---- |
| EG2652 | ADELPHI 15/6 | 46A | 2598 |
| EG2745 | KESTREL 1½ | 26K | ---- |

| REG NUMBER | MODEL | CHASSIS NO | |
|---|---|---|---|
| EG2840 | MERLIN 9 | 66M | ---- |
| EG3324 | KESTREL SPR 1½ | SS26K | ---- |
| EG3348 | MERLIN 9 | 66M | 2612 |
| EG3660 | ADELPHI 1½ | 27A | ---- |
| EG3676 | SPRITE 1½ | S26S | ---- |
| EG3700 | MONACO 9 | S67Z | ---- |
| EG7636 | ADELPHI 1½ | 27A | ---- |
| EHK300 | KESTREL 15/6 | 47K | 3090 |
| EHN814 | KESTREL 1½ | 28K | ---- |
| EHT455 | KESTREL 1½ | 27K | ---- |
| EHU992 | KESTREL 1½ | 28K | ---- |
| EHY702 | KESTREL 1½ | 28K | ---- |
| EJJ573 | MONACO 9 | S67Z | ---- |
| EJ0429 | MONACO 9 | S67Z | ---- |
| EJ3214 | MONACO 9 | 60 | ---- |
| EJ3653 | MONACO 9 | 60 | 21479 |
| EJ3824 | MONACO 9 | 60 | ---- |
| EKA 70 | KESTREL 16/4 | 38KX | ---- |
| EKA439 | KESTREL 1½ | 28K | 7359 |
| EKA544 | VICTOR | -- | ---- |
| EKE560 | MONACO 9 | S67Z | ---- |
| EKF986 | FALCON 1½ | 27F | ---- |
| EKM281 | ADELPHI 1½ | 27A | 5125 |
| EKM596 | CC TRG SAL 1½ | 27C | ---- |
| EK0910 | VICTOR 9 | 68V | ---- |
| EKT335 | MALTBY TR 16/4 | 38BX | 1224 |
| EK9816 | MONACO 9 | 60 | 24483 |
| EK9974 | MONACO 9 | 60 | 20349 |
| ELB193 | ADELPHI 1½ | 28A | ---- |
| ELB663 | TRG SAL 1½ | 28F | ---- |
| ELC893 | KESTREL 1½ | 28K | 7268 |
| ELD468 | ADELPHI 1½ | 28A | ---- |
| ELD482 | ADELPHI 1½ | 28A | ---- |
| ELD486 | ADELPHI 1½ | 28A | ---- |
| ELE651 | LYNX 1½ | 28L | 7368 |
| ELM144 | LYNX 1½ | 28L | 7566 |
| ELM294 | KESTREL 1½ | 28K | 7538 |
| ELM417 | KESTREL 16/4 | 38KX | ---- |
| ELP 65 | ADELPHI 1½ | 28A | 7385 |
| ELP 79 | ADELPHI 16/4 | 38AX | 1099 |
| ELR721 | KESTREL 16/4 | 38KX | 1229 |
| ELR854 | KESTREL 16/4 | 38KX | ---- |
| ELT883 | ADELPHI 1½ | 28A | 7750 |
| ELU491 | VICTOR | -- | ---- |
| ELY169 | TRG SAL 9 | 67C | ---- |
| EMA890 | ADELPHI 16/4 | 38AX | ---- |
| EMB136 | SPRITE 1½ | S28S | 7723 |
| EMC726 | LYNX 1½ | 27L | ---- |
| EMD100 | MERLIN 1½ | 26M | ---- |
| EMD715 | MERLIN 9 | S66M | 2027 |
| EMD722 | ADELPHI 1½ | 27A | 5134 |
| EMD834 | KESTREL 1½ | 27K | ---- |
| EMF483 | MERLIN 9 | 66M | ---- |
| EMH 4 | FALCON 1½ | 26F | ---- |
| EMH590 | FALCON 1½ | 27F | 5242 |
| EML678 | ADELPHI 1½ | 27A | 5620 |
| EML863 | KESTREL 15/6 | 47K | ---- |
| EMP133 | LYNX 1½ | 26L | ---- |

| REG NUMBER | MODEL | CHASSIS NO. | |
|---|---|---|---|
| EMT124 | ADELPHI 1½ | 26A | ---- |
| EMT131 | ADELPHI 1½ | 27A | ---- |
| EMT132 | KESTREL 1½ | 27K | 5569 |
| EMT133 | LYNX 1½ | 27L | ---- |
| EMT135 | KESTREL 1½ | 26K | ---- |
| EMW 61 | CC TRG SAL 1½ | 27C | 5896 |
| EMX 90 | KESTREL 1½ | 26K | ---- |
| EMX 94 | MONACO 9 | S67Z | ---- |
| EMX 97 | KESTREL 1½ | 27K | ---- |
| EMX102 | CC TRG SAL 1½ | 27C | ---- |
| EMX105 | KESTREL 1½ | 27K | ---- |
| EMX364 | FALCON 1½ | 27F | ---- |
| EMX796 | CC TRG SAL 1½ | 27C | 5829 |
| EMX845 | KESTREL SPR 1½ | SS27K | ---- |
| EM3441 | KESTREL 16/4 | 38KX | 1279 |
| EM5495 | MONACO 9 | 60 | ---- |
| ENA 59 | KESTREL 1½ | 28K | 7587 |
| ENA152 | ADELPHI 16/4 | 38AX | 1041 |
| ENE358 | VICTOR 9 | S68V | 3446 |
| ENE589 | VICTOR 9 | S68V | 3466 |
| EN0151 | FALCON 1½ | 27F | 6186 |
| EN0291 | ADELPHI 1½ | 27A | ---- |
| EN0586 | MONACO 9 | S67Z | ---- |
| EN0835 | ADELPHI 1½ | 27A | ---- |
| EN0841 | KESTREL 1½ | 27K | 6150 |
| ENU864 | MONACO 9 | S67Z | 2244 |
| EOB622 | ADELPHI 16/4 | 38AX | 1110 |
| EOH357 | ADELPHI 16/4 | 38AX | 1308 |
| E04810 | MONACO 9 | 60 | 5426 |
| EPA723 | FALCON 15/6 | 46F | 2535 |
| EPB323 | FALCON 1½ | 26F | ---- |
| EPB768 | KESTREL SPR 1½ | SS26K | 4897 |
| EPC107 | LYNX 1½ | 26L | ---- |
| EPC320 | MERLIN 9 | 66M | ---- |
| EPC740 | FALCON 1½ | 27F | ---- |
| EPC962 | KESTREL 1½ | 27K | ---- |
| EPD158 | MERLIN 9 | 66M | ---- |
| EPG328 | ADELPHI 1½ | 26A | ---- |
| EPH250 | ADELPHI 1½ | 26A | ---- |
| EPH357 | ADELPHI 1½ | 27A | 5551 |
| EPH508 | ADELPHI 1½ | 27A | ---- |
| EPH583 | MONACO 9 | S67Z | ---- |
| EPJ434 | FALCON 1½ | 27F | ---- |
| EPK 44 | KESTREL 1½ | S27K | 5036 |
| EPK436 | LYNX 1½ | 27L | ---- |
| EPL100 | ADELPHI 1½ | 27A | ---- |
| EPL221 | LYNX 1½ | 27L | ---- |
| EPL453 | FALCON 1½ | 27F | ---- |
| EPL612 | ADELPHI 1½ | 27A | 6289 |
| EPL771 | KESTREL 1½ | 27K | 6362 |
| EPL845 | MONACO 9 | S67Z | ---- |
| EP4302 | TOURER 9 | 60 | 5072 |
| ER2750 | KESTREL 16/4 | 38KX | 1258 |
| ESP464 | FALCON 1½ | 27F | ---- |
| ES7436 | 4/5 TOURER 11.9 | 69 | ---- |
| ETA357 | SPRITE 1½ | S27S | 6344 |
| ETN460 | MERLIN 9 | 67M | ---- |
| ETT 3 | FALCON 1½ | 27F | ---- |

| REG NUMBER | MODEL | CHASSIS NO | |
|---|---|---|---|
| ETT470 | LYNX SPR 1½ | SS27L | ---- |
| ETT733 | TRG SAL 1½ | 28F | 7493 |
| ETW493 | ADELPHI 1½ | 27A | ---- |
| ETW660 | ADELPHI 1½ | 27A | ---- |
| ET1936-NZ | KESTREL 1½ | 26K | ---- |
| ET9579 | ADELPHI 1½ | 26A | ---- |
| EUB278 | MERLIN 9 | 66M | 1889 |
| EUG494 | MONACO 9 | S67Z | 3071 |
| EUW 88 | KESTREL 15/6 | 48K | ---- |
| EUW 92 | KESTREL 1½ | 28K | ---- |
| EUW 98 | KESTREL 16/4 | 38KX | ---- |
| EU5963 | LYNX 1½ | 26L | 4070 |
| EU7642 | MERLIN 9 | 66M | ---- |
| EVK509 | KESTREL 1½ | 28K | 7303 |
| EVW381 | FALCON 1½ | 27F | ---- |
| EVW583 | ADELPHI 1½ | 27A | 6675 |
| EVW723 | MERLIN 9 | S67M | ---- |
| EV4014 | GAMECOCK 9 | 60 | ---- |
| EV4374 | MONACO 9 | 60 | ---- |
| EV6218 | GAMECOCK 9 | 60 | ---- |
| EV6682 | MONACO 9 | 60 | ---- |
| EV7642 | MERLIN 9 | 66M | ---- |
| EV9574 | MONACO 9 | S67Z | ---- |
| EWJ118 | KESTREL 1½ | 27K | 5089 |
| EWL134 | LYNX 1½ | S27L | 6587 |
| EWL325 | LYNX SPR 1½ | SS27L | ---- |
| EW9277 | ADELPHI 1½ | 26A | 4901 |
| EXA587 | AUTOVIA SAL | S | 63--- |
| EXK157 | VICTOR 1½ | 28V | ---- |
| EX0561 | KESTREL 1½ | 26K | ---- |
| EXR340 | KESTREL 1½ | 28KX | 7325 |
| EXR342 | ADELPHI 16/4 | 38AX | ---- |
| EXX627 | KESTREL 16/4 | 38KX | 1277 |
| EXX741 | TRG SAL 1½ | 28FX | 7812 |
| EX3202 | LYNX 14/6 | 44T | 487 |
| EYE942 | TRG SAL 1½ | 28F | ---- |
| EYM 75 | ADELPHI 16/4 | 38AX | 1009 |
| EYO 11 | VICTOR 9 | 68V | ---- |
| EY0117 | TRG SAL | 28F | ---- |
| EY0126 | ADELPHI 16/4 | 38AX | 1060 |
| EYU482 | AUTOVIA SAL | S | 63--- |
| EYX464 | AUTOVIA SAL | S | 63--- |
| EY5518 | KESTREL 9 | S66K | ---- |
| EY6333 | KESTREL 16/4 | 38KX | 1253 |
| EZ 210-IRL | KESTREL 9 | 60 | ---- |
| EZ 497-IRL | MERLIN 9 | 66M | ---- |
| EZ 789-IRL | MERLIN 1½ | 26M | 3191 |
| EZ 860-IRL | ADELPHI 1½ | 26A | 3094 |
| EZ1082-IRL | MERLIN 9 | 66M | 711 |
| EZ2743-IRL | FALCON 1½ | 26F | 4239 |
| EZ2867-IRL | KESTREL 1½ | 26K | 4463 |
| EZ4581-IRL | ADELPHI 1½ | 27A | 5353 |
| EZ4796-IRL | ADELPHI 1½ | 26A | ---- |
| EZ5982-IRL | ADELPHI 1½ | 27A | 5038 |
| EZ6210-IRL | LYNX 1½ | 27L | 5636 |
| EZ6496-IRL | KESTREL 1½ | 27K | ---- |
| EZ7951-IRL | MONACO 9 | S67Z | ---- |
| EZ8402-IRL | 9 HP TRI-CAR | ---- / | 578 |

| REG NUMBER | MODEL | CHASSIS NO | |
|---|---|---|---|
| EZ8765-IRL | KESTREL 1½ | 28K | 7266 |
| FAE279 | ADELPHI 16/4 | 38AX | 1296 |
| FA5568 | ALPINE SAL 14/6 | 44T | ---- |
| FA5958 | FALCON 1½ | 22T | ---- |
| FB8604 | MONACO 9 | 60 | 10530 |
| FB9620 | MONACO 9 | 60 | ---- |
| FD 999 | KESTREL 1½ | 22T | ---- |
| FD8322 | KESTREL 9 | 60 | 23217 |
| FD8999 | KESTREL 9 | 60 | 27151 |
| FD9143 | FALCON 1½ | 22T | 498 |
| FEV102 | ADELPHI 1½ | 26A | ---- |
| FEV666 | ADELPHI 1½ | 27A | ---- |
| FE9612 | MONACO 9 | SS67Z | ---- |
| FFC534 | MONACO 9 | S67Z | ---- |
| FF3398 | MONACO 9 | 60 | ---- |
| FF3637 | TOURER 9 | 60 | ---- |
| FGU260 | ADELPHI 1½ | 28A | ---- |
| FG9562 | MONACO 9 | 60 | ---- |
| FG9860 | MONACO 9 | 60 | ---- |
| FH5984 | MONACO 9 | 60 | ---- |
| FH8118 | MONACO 9 | 60 | 20866 |
| FH8367 | MONACO 9 | 60 | 22310 |
| FJN220 | SPRITE 1½ | S28S | ---- |
| FJ1938-NZ | LYNX SPR 1½ | SS28L | 7533 |
| FJ3108 | KESTREL 9 | 60 | ---- |
| FJ9322 | KESTREL 9 | 60 | 22981 |
| FJ9407 | MONACO 9 | 60 | 23898 |
| FJ9429 | MONACO 9 | 60 | 23940 |
| FJ9519 | KESTREL 9 | 60 | 22800 |
| FJ9607 | KESTREL 9 | 60 | ---- |
| FJ9715 | LYNX 9 | 60 | ---- |
| FKE597 | ADELPHI 16/4 | 38AX | 1304 |
| FK5428 | MONACO 9 | 60 | 19626 |
| FK5534 | MARCH SPL 9 | 60 | 20948 |
| FK6552 | FALCON 1½ | 22T | 274 |
| FLD468 | ADELPHI 1½ | 28A | ---- |
| FLG979 | ADELPHI 1½ | 28A | ---- |
| FL6839 | WENTWORTH 11.9 | 69 | 2248 |
| FL6863 | WENTWORTH 11.9 | 69 | ---- |
| FL7669 | BIARRITZ 9 | 60 | 4331 |
| FL7878 | MONACO 9 | 60 | ---- |
| FMC224 | LYNX 1½ | 26L | ---- |
| FMC613 | MERLIN 9 | 66M | ---- |
| FMC726 | LYNX 1½ | 27L | 6028 |
| FMD607 | KESTREL SPR 1½ | SS27K | 5676 |
| FMD613 | FALCON 1½ | 27F | ---- |
| FMF 26 | ADELPHI 1½ | S27A | 5958 |
| FMK340 | MONACO 9 | S67Z | ---- |
| FML285 | KESTREL SPR 1½ | SS27K | 6661 |
| FML549 | KESTREL 1½ | 27K | ---- |
| FML934 | KESTREL SPR 1½ | SS27K | ---- |
| FMP631 | KESTREL SPR 1½ | SS27K | 6606 |
| FMP873 | KESTREL 1½ | 27K | ---- |
| FMT428 | FALCON 1½ | 27F | ---- |
| FMT950 | FALCON 1½ | 27F | ---- |
| FMV933 | KESTREL SPR 1½ | SS27K | 6806 |
| FM8881 | LYNX 9 | 60 | ---- |
| FM8934 | MPH | 44T | ---- |

| REG NUMBER | MODEL | CHASSIS NO | |
|---|---|---|---|
| FM9304 | KESTREL 9 | 60 | ---- |
| FM9324 | KESTREL 1½ | 22T | ---- |
| FPA121 | ADELPHI 1½ | 27A | ---- |
| FPB 2 | LYNX 1½ | 27L | 6457 |
| FPB620 | ADELPHI 1½ | 27A | 5170 |
| FPC933 | FALCON 1½ | 27F | ---- |
| FPC944 | KESTREL 1½ | 27K | ---- |
| FPC962 | KESTREL 1½ | 27K | 6499 |
| FPD155 | MERLIN 9 | 67M | ---- |
| FPE676 | TRG SAL 1½ | 28F | ---- |
| FPE766 | CC TRG SAL 1½ | 27C | 5668 |
| FPF200 | WYLDER COUPE 15 | 47K | 3179 |
| FPF704 | TRG SAL 9 | 67C | ---- |
| FPG100 | CC TRG SPR SAL | SS27C | 7005 |
| FPG106 | TRG SAL 1½ | 28F | ---- |
| FPG215 | ADELPHI 1½ | 27A | ---- |
| FPG454 | ADELPHI 1½ | 27A | ---- |
| FPG643 | ADELPHI 1½ | 27A | ---- |
| FPH299 | LYNX SPR 1½ | SS27L | 7024 |
| FPH376 | CC TRG SAL 1½ | 27C | ---- |
| FPJ681 | MONACO 9 | S67ZX | 2324 |
| FPJ717 | TRG SAL 9 | 67C | ---- |
| FPK199 | MONACO 9 | S67Z | 3057 |
| FPU 22 | TRG SAL 9 | S67CX | 3183 |
| FPU948 | ADELPHI 16/4 | 38AX | ---- |
| FP2717 | KESTREL 9 | 60 | ---- |
| FP2959 | FALCON 1½ | 26F | ---- |
| FP2985 | KESTREL 1½ | 26K | ---- |
| FRA 61 | TRG SALOON 1½ | 28FX | 7343 |
| FRF429 | KESTREL 16/4 | 38KX | ---- |
| FRL512 | TRG SAL 1½ | 28F | ---- |
| FS 484 | MONACO 9 | 60 | ---- |
| FS1927 | KESTREL 9 | 60 | ---- |
| FS4953 | FALCON 9 | 60 | ---- |
| FS8712 | KESTREL 9 | 60 | 23364 |
| FS9150 | LYNX 9 | 60 | 23546 |
| FS9570 | MONACO 9 | 60 | ---- |
| FTF134 | MONACO 9 | 60 | ---- |
| FTJ470 | LYNX 1½ | 28L | ---- |
| FTJ851 | SPRITE 1½ | S26S | ---- |
| FTN200 | SPRITE 1½ | S28S | 7850 |
| FTN562 | ADELPHI 16/4 | 38AX | 1170 |
| FTW476 | ADELPHI 1½ | 28A | ---- |
| FTW476 | ADELPHI 1½ | 28A | ---- |
| FT2835 | MONACO 9 | 60 | 19812 |
| FT3884 | MERLIN 9 | 66M | ---- |
| FT3936 | MERLIN 9 | 66M | 2034 |
| FT3953 | MONACO 9 | S67Z | ---- |
| FUA 3 | KESTREL SPR 1½ | SS28K | 7295 |
| FUA232 | KESTREL 16/4 | 38KX | ---- |
| FUG521 | ADELPHI 16/4 | 38AX | ---- |
| FU3482 | MONACO 9 | 60 | ---- |
| FVK810 | VICTOR 1½ | 28V | ---- |
| FVT597 | ADELPHI 16/4 | 38AX | 1199 |
| FV3369 | MONACO 9 | 60 | ---- |
| FV3482 | MONACO 9 | 60 | ---- |
| FV3690 | MONACO 9 | 60 | ---- |
| FV3763 | KESTREL 9 | 60 | ---- |

| REG NUMBER | MODEL | CHASSIS NO. | |
|---|---|---|---|
| FV3973 | KESTREL 9 | 60 | 22508 |
| FV4300 | MONACO 9 | 60 | 23059 |
| FV4533 | MENTONE 12/6 | 44T | 1383 |
| FV4772 | KESTREL 12/6 | 44T | ---- |
| FV4825 | KESTREL 9 | 60 | ---- |
| FV5622 | KESTREL 9 | 60 | ---- |
| FV5816 | KESTREL 1½ | 26K | ---- |
| FV6054 | KESTREL 9 | 60 | ---- |
| FV6354 | FALCON 1½ | 26F | 2283 |
| FV6649 | MERLIN 9 | 66M | 124 |
| FV6757 | ADELPHI 1½ | 26A | ---- |
| FV6968 | KESTREL 1½ | 26K | 3422 |
| FV7636 | MERLIN 9 | 66M | 1650 |
| FV7642 | MERLIN 9 | 66M | ---- |
| FV7818 | MERLIN 9 | 66M | ---- |
| FV8091 | MONACO 9 | S67Z | ---- |
| FV8417 | FALCON 1½ | 27F | 5809 |
| FV8423 | MONACO 9 | S67Z | 2746 |
| FV8517 | KESTREL SPR 1½ | SS27K | ---- |
| FV8556 | CC TRG SPR SAL | SS27C | 6165 |
| FV8564 | KESTREL 1½ | 27K | ---- |
| FV8642 | CC TRG SAL 1½ | 27C | ---- |
| FV9612 | MONACO 9 | S67Z | ---- |
| FV9831 | MONACO 9 | S67ZX | 3205 |
| FWL765 | CC TRG SAL 1½ | 38BX | 1240 |
| FW1936-NZ | KESTREL 15/6 | 46K | 2618 |
| FW3369 | MONACO 9 | 60 | 20426 |
| FW6933 | FALCON 1½ | 26F | ---- |
| FW8079 | KESTREL SPR 1½ | SS26K | ---- |
| FX6552 | VICTOR 1½ | 28VX | 7679 |
| FYX413 | AUTOVIA SAL | S | 63141 |
| FY8825 | COACH 11.9 | 69 | ---- |
| FZ 4-IRL | KESTREL 16/4 | 38KX | 1167 |
| FZ 665-IRL | VICTOR 1½ | 28VX | 7679 |
| FZ1637-IRL | VICTOR 1½ | 28V | ---- |
| FZ2040-IRL | ADELPHI 16/4 | 38AX | ---- |
| FZ2867-IRL | KESTREL 1½ | 26K | ---- |
| GB0671 | FALCON 1½ | 22T | 1623 |
| GC1770 | TOURER 9 | 60 | ---- |
| GC2675 | IMP 9 | 60 | ---- |
| GE2123 | MONACO 9 | 60 | ---- |
| GE6583 | TOURER 9 | 60 | ---- |
| GF 738 | - - 9 | 60 | 7392 |
| GF3055 | MONACO 9 | 60 | ---- |
| GF6427 | MONACO 9 | 60 | ---- |
| GG0398 | KESTREL 9 | 60 | ---- |
| GGP670 | BROOKLANDS 9 | 80 | -- |
| GG3558 | MONACO 9 | 60 | 12280 |
| GG5796 | MONACO 9 | 60 | 15799 |
| GG5904 | TOURER 9 | 60 | ---- |
| GG6139 | ASCOT 9 | 60 | ---- |
| GG6973 | GAMECOCK 9 | 60 | ---- |
| GG7108 | ASCOT 9 | 60 | ---- |
| GG7524 | ASCOT 9 | 60 | ---- |
| GG8048 | ALPINE TR 14/6 | 14L | 1116 |
| GG8249 | TOURER 9 | 60 | 17571 |
| GG8810 | LYNX 9 | 60 | 19108 |
| GG9395 | MONACO 9 | 60 | 19225 |

| REG NUMBER | MODEL | CHASSIS NO. | |
|---|---|---|---|
| GG9759 | MONACO 9 | 60 | ---- |
| GH5336 | TOURER 9 | 60 | ---- |
| GH5497 | MONACO 9 | 60 | ---- |
| GH5696 | MONACO 9 | 60 | 10891 |
| GJ 18 | BROOKLANDS 9 | 80 | -- |
| GJ1209 | TOURER 9 | 60 | ---- |
| GJ3824 | MONACO 9 | 60 | 24072 |
| GJ4325 | TOURER 9 | 60 | 7372 |
| GJ5809 | TOURER 9 | 60 | ---- |
| GJ8601 | BROOKLANDS 9 | 80 | -- |
| GK 354 | TOURER 9 | 60 | ---- |
| GK3249 | BROOKLANDS 9 | 80 | 44 |
| GK4244 | BROOKLANDS 9 | 80 | 74 |
| GK4407-S | BROOKLANDS 9 | 80 | 76 |
| GK8825 | MONACO 9 | 60 | 11263 |
| GK9814 | MONACO 9 | 60 | ---- |
| GL 211 | MONACO 9 | 60 | ---- |
| GL 562 | MONACO 9 | 60 | ---- |
| GLI584-IRL | TOURER 9 | 60 | ---- |
| GL1180 | MONACO 9 | 60 | 24186 |
| GL3547 | MERLIN 9 | 66M | ---- |
| GMD465 | KESTREL 1½ | 27K | ---- |
| GMH275-USA | KESTREL 15/6 | 47K | 3217 |
| GMH853 | KESTREL 1½ | 27K | ---- |
| GMH860 | KESTREL 1½ | 27K | ---- |
| GMH865 | KESTREL 1½ | 27K | 6752 |
| GML672 | FALCON 1½ | 27F | ---- |
| GML881 | MONACO 9 | S67Z | ---- |
| GMV543 | KESTREL 16/4 | 38KX | 1160 |
| GMX683 | ADELPHI 16/4 | 38AX | ---- |
| GMX700 | ADELPHI 1½ | 27A | 6174 |
| GMY958 | IMP 9 | 60 | ---- |
| GN 7 | MONACO 9 | 60 | ---- |
| GNJ 57 | FALCON 1½ | 22T | ---- |
| GN0332 | KESTREL 1½ | 28K | ---- |
| GNW 99 | ADELPHI 1½ | 28A | ---- |
| GNW265 | SPRITE 1½ | S28S | 7914 |
| GN1297 | MONACO 9 | 60 | 11079 |
| GN3198 | MONACO 9 | 60 | 11834 |
| GN3425 | MONACO 9 | 60 | ---- |
| GN4267 | MONACO 9 | 60 | ---- |
| GN6048 | MONACO 9 | 60 | ---- |
| GN6188 | MONACO 9 | 60 | ---- |
| GN7037 | BIARRITZ 9 | 60 | ---- |
| GN8171 | ALPINE SAL 14/6 | 14L | ---- |
| GO 276 | MONACO 9 | 60 | 12966 |
| GOG830 | - - 9 | 60 | 13552 |
| GO1413 | MONACO 9 | 60 | 11987 |
| GO1413 | MONACO 9 | 60 | ---- |
| GO1927 | STELVIO 14/6 | 14S | 285 |
| GO2399 | MONACO 9 | 60 | 13140 |
| GO6646 | MONACO 9 | 60 | ---- |
| GO7267 | MONACO 9 | 60 | 13675 |
| GO8531 | MONACO 9 | 60 | 13505 |
| GO8596 | DEAUVILLE 14/6 | 14 | ---- |
| GP 17 | BROOKLANDS 9 | 80 | ---- |
| GP 171 | 2 SEATER 9 | 60 | ---- |
| GPA229 | VICTOR 9 | 68V | ---- |

| REG NUMBER | MODEL | CHASSIS NO. | |
|---|---|---|---|
| GPA522 | KESTREL 1½ | 28K | 7434 |
| GPB 3 | KESTREL 16/4 | 38KX | ---- |
| GPB 66 | KESTREL 1½ | 28K | ---- |
| GPC932 | KESTREL 16/4 | 38KX | 1180 |
| GPD800 | LYNX 1½ | 28L | 7764 |
| GPD999 | ADELPHI 16/4 | 38AX | ---- |
| GPG 55 | MONACO 9 | S67Z | ---- |
| GPG587 | KESTREL 1½ | 22T | ---- |
| GPH235 | VICTOR 1½ | 28V | ---- |
| GPH520 | CC TRG SAL 16/4 | 38BX | ---- |
| GPJ401 | FALCON 1½ | 22T | ---- |
| GPJ440 | VICTOR | -- | ---- |
| GPJ697 | MERLIN 9 | 66M | ---- |
| GP4682 | MONACO 9 | 60 | 14129 |
| GP5351 | MONACO 9 | 60 | ---- |
| GP7748 | MONACO 9 | 60 | 14161 |
| GP8998 | TOURER 9 | 60 | ---- |
| GR 187 | MONACO 9 | 60 | 22001 |
| GRB880 | MERLIN 9 | 66M | ---- |
| GR1401 | FALCON 1½ | 22T | ---- |
| GR2490 | KESTREL 1½ | 26K | ---- |
| GR2574 | MERLIN 9 | 66M | ---- |
| GR3572 | CC TRG SAL 1½ | 27C | 5843 |
| GR4358 | ADELPHI 1½ | 27A | ---- |
| GR5407 | VICTOR | -- | ---- |
| GS1750 | BIARRITZ 9 | 60 | ---- |
| GS3273 | MONACO 9 | 60 | 17949 |
| GS4180 | LYNX 9 | 60 | 22970 |
| GS4779 | ADELPHI 8-90 | 87A | 219 |
| GS5738 | LYNX 1½ | 27L | ---- |
| GS6245 | ADELPHI 1½ | 26A | ---- |
| GS7683 | LYNX 1½ | 28L | 7481 |
| GS8774 | ADELPHI 8-90 | 87A | ---- |
| GT1137 | MONACO 9 | 60 | ---- |
| GT1171 | MONACO 9 | 60 | ---- |
| GT1831 | TOURER 9 | 60 | ---- |
| GT2484 | MONACO 9 | 60 | ---- |
| GT3513 | HOYAL 9 | 60 | 14361 |
| GT3523 | MONACO 9 | 60 | ---- |
| GT5989 | ALPINE SAL 14/6 | 14L | 736 |
| GT5990 | MONACO 9 | 60 | ---- |
| GT7855 | MONACO 9 | 60 | 15538 |
| GT7939 | TOURER 9 | 60 | ---- |
| GU 584 | TOURER 9 | 60 | ---- |
| GUP389-AUS | IMP 9 | 60 | ---- |
| GU1188 | BROOKLANDS 9 | 80 | -- |
| GU4267 | MONACO 9 | 60 | ---- |
| GV4500 | KESTREL 15/6 | 46K | 2757 |
| GW 428 | MONACO 9 | 60 | 15612 |
| GW2899 | GAMECOCK 9 | 60 | ---- |
| GW2974 | MONACO 9 | 60 | ---- |
| GW3220 | GAMECOCK 9 | 60 | 15536 |
| GW3224 | MONACO 9 | 60 | 16071 |
| GW3805 | GAMECOCK 9 | 60 | 15746 |
| GW3989 | MONACO 9 | 60 | ---- |
| GW4157 | MONACO 9 | 60 | ---- |
| GW4379 | KESTREL 9 | S66K | ---- |
| GW6221 | MONACO 9 | 60 | 17163 |

| REG NUMBER | MODEL | CHASSIS NO | |
|---|---|---|---|
| GW6226 | GAMECOCK 9 | 60 | ---- |
| GW6450 | GAMECOCK 9 | 60 | ---- |
| GW6880 | GAMECOCK 9 | 60 | ---- |
| GW7008 | MONACO 9 | 60 | 16282 |
| GW8085 | MONACO 9 | 60 | 15962 |
| GW8097 | TOURER 9 | 60 | 16891 |
| GW8475 | TOURER 9 | 60 | 14499 |
| GW9630 | GAMECOCK 9 | 60 | 16675 |
| GW9646 | TOURER 9 | 60 | 16522 |
| GX 17 | GAMECOCK 9 | 60 | 16735 |
| GX 165 | MONACO 9 | 60 | ---- |
| GXR764-AUS | MONACO 9 | 60 | ---- |
| GX1285 | GAMECOCK 9 | 60 | 15924 |
| GX1741 | MONACO 9 | 60 | ---- |
| GX2320 | 2 SEATER 9 | 60 | ---- |
| GX2846 | GAMECOCK 9 | 60 | 16325 |
| GX2962 | MONACO 9 | 60 | ---- |
| GX3160 | GAMECOCK 9 | 60 | ---- |
| GX3497 | MONACO 9 | 60 | 15986 |
| GX3977 | MONACO 9 | 60 | ---- |
| GX3997 | MONACO 9 | 60 | 16534 |
| GX6173 | ALPINE SAL 14/6 | 14L | ---- |
| GX7200 | GAMECOCK 9 | 60 | ---- |
| GX7815 | MONACO 9 | 60 | ---- |
| GX8229 | GAMECOCK 9 | 60 | ---- |
| GX9572 | GAMECOCK 9 | 60 | 17131 |
| GX9834 | MONACO 9 | 60 | ---- |
| GX9910 | MONACO 9 | 60 | ---- |
| GX9919 | TOURER 9 | 60 | 18257 |
| GY 10 | TOURER 9 | 60 | ---- |
| GY 60 | GAMECOCK 9 | 60 | ---- |
| GY 61 | GAMECOCK 9 | 60 | ---- |
| GY 61 | LYNX 9 (PROTO) | 60 | ---- |
| GY 62 | GAMECOCK 9 | 60 | ---- |
| GY 68 | MARCH SPL 9 | 60 | ---- |
| GY 257 | GAMECOCK 9 | 60 | 17583 |
| GYM958 | IMP 9 | 60 | ---- |
| GY1204 | MONACO 9 | 60 | 17749 |
| GY1325 | ALPINE SAL 14/6 | 14L | ---- |
| GY1729 | GAMECOCK 9 | 60 | ---- |
| GY4076 | MONACO 9 | 60 | ---- |
| GY7346 | MONACO 9 | 60 | ---- |
| GY7966 | MONACO 9 | 60 | ---- |
| GY8333 | GAMECOCK 9 | 60 | ---- |
| GY8605 | TOURER 9 | 60 | 17960 |
| GZ5021-J | BROOKLANDS 9 | 80 | 20 |
| H 3714 | 3 HP FORECAR | ---- / | 11? |
| HE7341 | LYNX 1½ | 26F | ---- |
| HE8023 | MONACO 9 | S67Z | ---- |
| HE8345 | MONACO 9 | S67Z | ---- |
| HF4420 | MONACO 9 | 60 | 25225 |
| HF4544 | KESTREL 9 | 60 | ---- |
| HF5526 | MERLIN 9 | 66M | ---- |
| HF6950 | TRG SAL 1½ | 28F | ---- |
| HF8097 | GAMECOCK 9 | 60 | ---- |
| HG 202 | MONACO 9 | 60 | ---- |
| HG3408 | KESTREL 1½ | 22T | ---- |
| HG3959 | KESTREL 1½ | 22T | ---- |

| REG NUMBER | MODEL | CHASSIS NO. | |
|---|---|---|---|
| HG4918-S | LYNX 1½ | 27L | ---- |
| HG5227 | KESTREL 1½ | 27K | ---- |
| HG9295 | KESTREL 1½ | 27K | ---- |
| HH7280 | LYNX 9 | 60 | ---- |
| HJ7494 | FALCON 1½ | -- | ---- |
| HJ8211 | TOURER 9 | 60 | ---- |
| HJ8976 | MONACO 9 | 60 | ---- |
| HJ9525 | MONACO 9 | 60 | ---- |
| HJ9902 | TOURER 9 | 60 | 9905 |
| HKX626 | TOURER 9 | 60 | ---- |
| HL8531 | TRG SAL 1½ | 28F | ---- |
| HMK492 | MONACO 9 | SS67Z | ---- |
| HMX 69 | VICTOR 9 | 68V | ---- |
| HMX326 | ADELPHI 15/6 | 48A | 3305 |
| HPA839 | SPRITE 1½ | S28S | 7917 |
| HP5772 | SALOON 10.8 | S | ---- |
| HP6433* | A-W COUPE 10.8 | C | 1404 |
| HP9675 | TOURER 10.8 | T | ---- |
| HP9679* | COUPE 10.8 | C | 2339 |
| HP9683 | SALOON 10.8 | S | ---- |
| HRL256-AUS | TOURER 9 | 60 | ---- |
| HS7091 | LINCOCK 9 | 60 | ---- |
| HS7336 | LYNX 9 | 60 | ---- |
| HS7723 | LYNX 12/6 | 44T | ---- |
| HS9727 | KESTREL SPR 1½ | SS27K | ---- |
| HV2680 | KESTREL 12/6 | 44T | 412 |
| HV9127 | MERLIN 9 | 67M | ---- |
| HW6427 | TOURER 9 | 60 | ---- |
| HW8306 | MONACO 9 | 60 | ---- |
| HW8837 | MONACO 9 | 60 | ---- |
| HX 544 | MONACO 9 | 60 | ---- |
| HX2748 | STELVIO 14/6 | 14S | ---- |
| HX3975 | MONACO 9 | 60 | ---- |
| HX5747 | MONACO 9 | 60 | ---- |
| HX5874 | GAMECOCK 9 | 60 | ---- |
| HX6175 | WD TOURER 9 | 60 | 12996 |
| HX6472 | TOURER 9 | 60 | ---- |
| HX6507 | WD TOURER 9 | 60 | 14408 |
| HY 49 | MONACO 9 | 60 | ---- |
| HYV 6-AUS | KESTREL 15/6 | 44T | 2412 |
| HY3603 | GAMECOCK 9 | 60 | 16152 |
| HY6571 | MONACO 9 | 60 | 17596 |
| HY7966 | LYNX 9 | 60 | ---- |
| IB6066-IRL | KESTREL 9 | 60 | ---- |
| II 940-IRL | FALCON 1½ | 26F | ---- |
| IIL659-USA | KESTREL 1½ | 26K | ---- |
| ILL461-AUS | LYNX SPR 1½ | SS27L | ---- |
| IWX000-AUS | LYNX SPR 1½ | SS26L | 4670 |
| IW4989 | KESTREL 9 | 60 | ---- |
| IW5136-IRL | FALCON 1½ | 22T | ---- |
| IW5925-IRL | MERLIN 9 | 66M | ---- |
| IYF865-AUS | FALCON 1½ | 26F | 4012 |
| JAW610-AUS | KESTREL 16/4 | 38KX | 1253 |
| JA2125 | MONACO 9 | 60 | 15190 |
| JA7892 | ADELPHI 15/6 | 47A | 3028 |
| JA9800 | VICTOR 9 | S68V | 3403 |
| JB 34 | MONACO 9 | 60 | ---- |
| JB 147 | MONACO 9 | 60 | 16837 |

| REG NUMBER | MODEL | CHASSIS NO | |
|---|---|---|---|
| JB 444 | MONACO 9 | 60 | 17657 |
| JB1229 | MONACO 9 | 60 | ---- |
| JB1346 | MARCH SPL 9 | 60 | 19322 |
| JB3672 | KESTREL 9 | 60 | 24217 |
| JB4301 | KESTREL 9 | 60 | ---- |
| JB4361 | KESTREL 12/6 | 44T | ---- |
| JB5593 | FALCON 1½ | 22T | 671 |
| JB5655 | LYNX 9 | 60 | 27074 |
| JB5877 | KESTREL 1½ | 22T | 1172 |
| JB7402 | FALCON 1½ | 22T | ---- |
| JB7830 | KESTREL 9 | S66K | 713 |
| JB7836 | MERLIN 9 | S66M | 570 |
| JB8059 | ADELPHI 1½ | 26A | ---- |
| JB8128 | MERLIN 1½ | 26M | ---- |
| JB8284 | SPRITE 1½ | S26S | 2766 |
| JB8308 | ADELPHI 1½ | 26A | ---- |
| JB8666 | KESTREL 15/6 | S46K | 2673 |
| JB8852 | SPRITE 1½ | S27S | 4088 |
| JB8890 | FALCON 1½ | 26F | ---- |
| JB9291 | ADELPHI 1½ | 26A | 4599 |
| JCC091-S | BROOKLANDS 9 | 80 | -- |
| JC4086 | FALCON 1½ | 26F | ---- |
| JC5016 | KESTREL 16/4 | 38KX | 1213 |
| JC5167 | ADELPHI 1½ | 28A | 7654 |
| JD 544 | 2 SEATER 9 | 60 | 10398 |
| JD 988 | TOURER 9 | 60 | ---- |
| JD2483-USA | GAMECOCK 9 | 60 | ---- |
| JD3939 | KESTREL 12/6 | 44T | ---- |
| JD5390 | KESTREL 9 | 60 | ---- |
| JD5492 | KESTREL 9 | 60 | 25469 |
| JD5508 | KESTREL 9 | 60 | ---- |
| JD6501 | KESTREL 1½ | 26K | 4159 |
| JD7593 | LYNX | -- | ---- |
| JD9169-DK | KESTREL SPR 1½ | SS27K | ---- |
| JE6451 | KESTREL 9 | 60 | ---- |
| JFM868 | KESTREL 12/6 | 44T | 639 |
| JF1076 | MONACO 9 | 60 | ---- |
| JF3589 | GAMECOCK 9 | 60 | 18163 |
| JF6451 | KESTREL 9 | 60 | 24653 |
| JF7222 | KESTREL 9 | 60 | ---- |
| JF7438 | KESTREL 9 | 60 | ---- |
| JF7457 | FALCON 1½ | 22T | 411 |
| JF7602 | FALCON 1½ | 22T | ---- |
| JF7888 | FALCON 1½ | 22T | 1145 |
| JF8228 | KESTREL 9 | 60 | ---- |
| JF8474 | KESTREL 1½ | 22T | ---- |
| JF9625 | KESTREL 9 | 60 | 27357 |
| JF9804 | MERLIN 9 | 66M | ---- |
| JG4867 | MONACO 9 | 60 | 23084 |
| JG5472 | KESTREL 9 | 60 | ---- |
| JG8265 | MONACO 9 | S67Z | ---- |
| JG9527 | MONACO 9 | S67Z | ---- |
| JG9823 | ADELPHI 1½ | 27A | ---- |
| JH 378 | KESTREL 1½ | 22T | ---- |
| JH 622 | MONACO 9 | 60 | 15087 |
| JH 954 | MONACO 9 | 60 | ---- |
| JHZ932-S | MERLIN 9 | S66M | 586 |
| JH3589 | LYNX 9 | 60 | 19293 |

| REG NUMBER | MODEL | CHASSIS NO. | |
|---|---|---|---|
| JH3905 | LYNX 9 | 60 | 20557 |
| JH4058 | MONACO 9 | 60 | ---- |
| JH4456 | ASCOT 9 | 60 | 21271 |
| JH4614 | KESTREL 12/6 | 44T | ---- |
| JH4924 | MONACO 9 | 60 | ---- |
| JH6516 | KESTREL 9 | 60 | 22878 |
| JH7043 | LYNX 9 | 60 | ---- |
| JH7179 | KESTREL 9 | 60 | 23899 |
| JH8152 | ALPINE SAL 14/6 | 44T | ---- |
| JH9506 | MPH 14/6 | 44T | 1739 |
| JH9977 | FALCON 1½ | 22T | ---- |
| JIS292-IRL | MONACO 9 | 60 | ---- |
| JI5292-IRL | MONACO 9 | 60 | 15787 |
| JI7305-IRL | SPRITE 1½ | 26S | ---- |
| JJ 813 | MONACO 9 | 60 | 19923 |
| JJ 919 | MARCH SPL 9 | 60 | 19567 |
| JJG244 | MARCH SPL 9 | 60 | ---- |
| JJ1320 | MARCH SPL 9 | 60 | 19478 |
| JJ1493 | MONACO 9 | 60 | ---- |
| JJ1865 | LYNX 9 | 60 | 20167 |
| JJ2100 | MONACO 9 | 60 | 20484 |
| JJ2398 | KESTREL 12/6 | 44T | 280 |
| JJ3350 | - - 9 | 60 | 19206 |
| JJ3563-IRL | LYNX 9 | 60 | 20862 |
| JJ3569 | KESTREL 9 | 60 | ---- |
| JJ4166 | ASCOT 9 | 60 | 20221 |
| JJ4244 | MARCH SPL 9 | 60 | 19307 |
| JJ4826 | MONACO 9 | 60 | ---- |
| JJ6591 | MONACO 9 | 60 | ---- |
| JJ7541 | LYNX 9 | 60 | ---- |
| JJ8150 | LINCOCK 9 | 60 | 21046 |
| JJ8869 | LINCOCK 9 | 60 | ---- |
| JJ9255 | LYNX 9 | 60 | ---- |
| JJ9272 | MONACO 9 | 60 | 20422 |
| JJ9303 | MENTONE 12/6 | 44T | ---- |
| JJ9317 | MARCH SPL 9 | 60 | ---- |
| JKP209 | KESTREL 15/6 | 46K | ---- |
| JKU186-AUS | FALCON 1½ | 26F | ---- |
| JK4308 | IMP 9 | 60 | ---- |
| JK4454 | IMP 9 | 60 | 27369 |
| JK4949 | IMP 9 | 60 | 27677 |
| JK5185 | FALCON 1½ | 22T | ---- |
| JK5644 | KESTREL 1½ | 26K | 4462 |
| JK6285 | MERLIN 9 | 66M | 1990 |
| JK7353 | ADELPHI 16/4 | 38AX | 1021 |
| JM 327 | LYNX 15/6 | 47L | ---- |
| JM 641 | MONACO 9 | 60 | 20918 |
| JM3248 | ADELPHI 1½ | 27A | ---- |
| JM3576 | ADELPHI 8-90 | 87A | 224 |
| JM4370 | IMP 9 | 60 | 27310 |
| JN 316 | BIARRITZ 9 | 60 | 10463 |
| JN 719 | KESTREL 15/6 | 46K | 2772 |
| JN1178 | BIARRITZ 9 | 60 | ---- |
| JN1741 | LYNX 9 | 60 | 16268 |
| JN2271 | MONACO 9 | 60 | 18004 |
| JN2468 | LINCOCK 9 | 60 | ---- |
| JN2807 | MONACO 9 | 60 | ---- |
| JN2896 | MONACO 9 | 60 | ---- |

| REG NUMBER | MODEL | CHASSIS NO | |
|---|---|---|---|
| JN3040 | LYNX 9 | 60 | ---- |
| JN4438 | MONACO 9 | 60 | 25731 |
| JN4684 | MONACO 9 | 60 | ---- |
| JN5195 | FALCON 1½ | 26F | ---- |
| JN5703 | FALCON 1½ | 26F | ---- |
| JN6181 | FALCON 1½ | 26F | 2501 |
| JN6312 | LYNX 1½ | 22T | 1852 |
| JN6622 | KESTREL 9 | S66K | ---- |
| JN7134 | LYNX 1½ | 26F | 4005 |
| JN7919 | KESTREL 15/6 | 46K | ---- |
| JN8268 | MERLIN 9 | 66M | 2094 |
| JN8845 | FALCON 1½ | 27F | ---- |
| JN9103 | FALCON 1½ | 27F | ---- |
| JO 117 | LYNX 12/6 | 44T | ---- |
| JO1605 | MONACO 9 | 60 | 12504 |
| JO2483 | GAMECOCK 9 | 60 | ---- |
| JO4750-USA | TOURER 9 | 60 | ---- |
| JO5202 | MONACO 9 | 60 | ---- |
| JO5826 | KESTREL 9 | 60 | ---- |
| JO6116 | MONACO 9 | 60 | ---- |
| JO6371 | LINCOCK 14/6 | 44T | 833 |
| JO7117 | LYNX 12/6 | 44T | 686 |
| JO8314 | MONACO 9 | 60 | 19807 |
| JO8558 | KESTREL 9 | 60 | 23864 |
| JO8561 | MONACO 9 | 60 | 23825 |
| JO8629 | MONACO 9 | 60 | 23955 |
| JO9401 | KESTREL 12/6 | 44T | ---- |
| JO9688 | RANALAGH D/H 9 | 60 | 24415 |
| JO9700 | KESTREL 9 | 60 | 23573 |
| JP 271 | FALCON 1½ | 22T | 1447 |
| JPD124 | HUDLASS SPL SV | - | ---- |
| JPG818 | ADELPHI 1½ | 26A | ---- |
| JP8866 | KESTREL 15/6 | 46K | ---- |
| JR1746 | KESTREL 9 | 60 | ---- |
| JR3581 | FALCON 1½ | 22T | ---- |
| JR6000 | GAMECOCK 9 | 60 | ---- |
| JR6057 | FALCON 1½ | 27F | ---- |
| JR6095 | CC TRG SAL 1½ | 27C | ---- |
| JT 203 | MONACO 9 | 60 | ---- |
| JT 707 | KESTREL 1½ | 22T | ---- |
| JTR512 | LYNX 1½ | 28L | ---- |
| JTU512 | IMP 9 | 60 | ---- |
| JTY257-S | LYNX 1½ | 27L | 5766 |
| JT1105 | MONACO 9 | 60 | 19557 |
| JT1144 | KESTREL 9 | 60 | ---- |
| JT4291 | LYNX 1½ | 26L | ---- |
| JT4515 | MERLIN 9 | 66M | 755 |
| JT5187 | KESTREL 9 | S66K | 1890 |
| JT6340 | MONACO 9 | S67Z | ---- |
| JT6537 | ADELPHI 1½ | 27A | 5253 |
| JU 51 | GAMECOCK 9 | 60 | 17688 |
| JU 840 | GAMECOCK 9 | 60 | 17912 |
| JU2273 | MONACO 9 | 60 | 21289 |
| JU2607 | KESTREL 12/6 | 44T | 2023 |
| JU2641 | MONACO 9 | 60 | 22050 |
| JU3587 | KESTREL 9 | 60 | ---- |
| JU3993 | MONACO 9 | 60 | ---- |
| JU5206 | KESTREL SPR 1½ | SS27K | ---- |

| REG NUMBER | MODEL | CHASSIS NO. | |
|---|---|---|---|
| JU5453 | KESTREL 1½ | 22T | 681 |
| JU5695 | KESTREL 9 | 60 | 27131 |
| JU5826 | KESTREL 1½ | 22T | 1150 |
| JU6301 | TRG SAL 9 | 27C | ---- |
| JU6365 | KESTREL 9 | 60 | ---- |
| JU6414 | KESTREL 9 | 60 | ---- |
| JU8343 | MERLIN 9 | 66M | ---- |
| JU8877 | ADELPHI 1½ | 26A | 4369 |
| JU8887-USA | ADELPHI 1½ | 26A | 4642 |
| JU9153 | KESTREL 1½ | 26K | 4435 |
| JV1105 | GAMECOCK 9 | 60 | 16308 |
| JV1171 | MONACO 9 | 60 | 16688 |
| JV1753 | KESTREL 12/6 | 44T | ---- |
| JV2665 | KESTREL 9 | 60 | 25697 |
| JV2667 | KESTREL 12/6 | 44T | 2023 |
| JV2888 | KESTREL 9 | 60 | ---- |
| JV3301 | FALCON 1½ | 22T | 598 |
| JV3397 | FALCON 1½ | 22T | 1209 |
| JV3506 | IMP 9 | 60 | ---- |
| JV3511 | KESTREL 1½ | 22T | 1457 |
| JV3824 | KESTREL 1½ | 22T | ---- |
| JV3885 | FALCON 1½ | 26F | 2367 |
| JV3905 | FALCON 1½ | 26F | ---- |
| JV4147 | ADELPHI 1½ | 26A | ---- |
| JV4409 | KESTREL 1½ | 26K | 3908 |
| JV4549 | MERLIN 9 | 66M | ---- |
| JV4773 | KESTREL 1½ | 26K | 4432 |
| JV5206 | KESTREL SPR 1½ | SS27K | 5455 |
| JV5453 | KESTREL 1½ | 22T | ---- |
| JV5507 | ADELPHI 15/6 | 47A | ---- |
| JV5665 | FALCON 1½ | 27F | 6176 |
| JV5826 | KESTREL 1½ | 22T | ---- |
| JV5885 | ADELPHI 15/6 | 47A | ---- |
| JV6220 | ADELPHI 8-90 | 87A | ---- |
| JV6301 | CC TRG SAL 1½ | 27C | ---- |
| JV6400 | KESTREL 16/4 | 38KX | 1058 |
| JW3030 | MONACO 9 | 60 | ---- |
| JW3040 | LYNX 9 | 60 | ---- |
| JW3314 | LYNX 9 | 60 | ---- |
| JW6471 | FALCON 15/6 | 44T | 2305 |
| JW9103 | FALCON 1½ | 27F | 7010 |
| JW9447 | KESTREL 1½ | 26K | ---- |
| JX3656 | KESTREL 1½ | S26K | 3674 |
| JX5971 | KESTREL 16/4 | 38KX | ---- |
| JY2630 | MONACO 9 | 60 | ---- |
| JY3421 | MONACO 9 | 60 | 24468 |
| JY3660 | LYNX 12/6 | 44T | 2062 |
| JY4542 | KESTREL 9 | 60 | ---- |
| JY6791 | FALCON 1½ | 26F | 2795 |
| JY7950 | SPRITE 1½ | S26S | 4242 |
| JY8249 | MERLIN 9 | 66M | 1351 |
| JY9284 | KESTREL SPR 1½ | SS27K | 5475 |
| K 2022 | MONACO 9 | 60 | ---- |
| KB5901 | LYNX 9 | 60 | ---- |
| KC2675 | MONACO 9 | 60 | 21605 |
| KD2817 | MONACO 9 | 60 | 1797 |
| KD3887 | 2 SEATER 9 | 60 | 2944 |
| KD5340 | BROOKLANDS 9 | 80 | 43 |

| REG NUMBER | MODEL | CHASSIS NO. | |
|---|---|---|---|
| KD5603 | TOURER 9 | 60 | 1732 |
| KD9605 | TOURER 9 | 60 | ---- |
| KF3398 | MONACO 9 | 60 | 11146 |
| KF9265 | GAMECOCK 9 | 60 | 11208 |
| KG 526 | ADELPHI 16/4 | 38AX | 1222 |
| KG1175 | MONACO 9 | 60 | ---- |
| KG1387 | MONACO 9 | 60 | 18036 |
| KG2339 | KESTREL 12/6 | 44T | 601 |
| KG2675 | MONACO 9 | 60 | ---- |
| KG3332 | MONACO 9 | 60 | ---- |
| KG3353 | MONACO 9 | 60 | ---- |
| KG3739 | LYNX 9 | 60 | 23437 |
| KG3928 | LYNX 9 | 60 | 25360 |
| KG4151 | KESTREL 12/6 | 44T | 2078 |
| KG4377 | FALCON 9 | 60 | ---- |
| KG5102 | MONACO 9 | 60 | ---- |
| KG6077 | KESTREL 9 | 60 | ---- |
| KG6493 | KESTREL 1½ | 22T | 2002 |
| KG6711 | FALCON 1½ | 26F | ---- |
| KG7783 | KESTREL 9 | 60 | ---- |
| KG8148 | KESTREL 1½ | 26K | ---- |
| KG8303 | KESTREL 1½ | 26K | 4396 |
| KG8510 | KESTREL 1½ | 26K | ---- |
| KG8616 | ADELPHI 1½ | 26A | 4716 |
| KG9045 | MONACO 9 | S67Z | ---- |
| KH9918 | BIARRITZ 9 | 60 | 7383 |
| KJ1245 | BIARRITZ 9 | 60 | ---- |
| KJ2481 | MONACO 9 | 60 | ---- |
| KJ3453 | HOYAL COUPE 9 | 60 | 12975 |
| KJ44220-DK | FALCON 1½ | 22T | 1742 |
| KJ6272 | MONACO 9 | 60 | ---- |
| KJ7777 | MONACO 9 | S67Z | ---- |
| KJ8665 | GAMECOCK 9 | 60 | ---- |
| KLF647 | LYNX 9 | 60 | ---- |
| KN 312 | MONACO 9 | 60 | ---- |
| KO7735 | TOURER 9 | 60 | 116 |
| KO9870 | MONACO 9 | 60 | 1288 |
| KR8625 | BROOKLANDS 9 | 80 | -- |
| KR9162 | ALPINE SAL 14/6 | 14L | 243 |
| KS5901 | LYNX 9 | 60 | 21889 |
| KS7279 | KESTREL 1½ | 27K | ---- |
| KV 113 | MONACO 9 | 60 | ---- |
| KV 235* | MONACO 9 | 60 | ---- |
| KV 246 | ASCOT 9 | 60 | 15979 |
| KV 536 | MONACO 9 | 60 | ---- |
| KV 693 | MONACO 9 | 60 | ---- |
| KVN164-AUS | KESTREL 1½ | 22T | ---- |
| KVT208-AUS | IMP 9 | 60 | 25503 |
| KV1151 | GAMECOCK 9 | 60 | ---- |
| KV1199 | MONACO 9 | 60 | ---- |
| KV1861* | BROOKLANDS 6 | 12R | 102 |
| KV1862* | BROOKLANDS 6 | 12R | 101 |
| KV1869 | MONACO 9 | 60 | ---- |
| KV2197 | MONACO 9 | 60 | 1845 |
| KV2329 | MONACO 9 | 60 | 17834 |
| KV2481* | KESTREL 6 2D | 44T | 101 |
| KV2702 | MONACO 9 | 60 | ---- |
| KV2709 | WD TOURER 9 | 60 | ---- |

| REG NUMBER | MODEL | CHASSIS NO. | |
|---|---|---|---|
| KV2712 | TRINITY 9 | 60 | ---- |
| KV2925 | STELVIO 14/6 | 14S | ---- |
| KV2943 | LINCOCK 6 | 44T | ---- |
| KV2945* | MENTONE 12/6 | 44T | ---- |
| KV3056 | KESTREL 14/6 | 44T | 364 |
| KV3087 | MONACO 9 | 60 | ---- |
| KV3092* | WD TOURER 9 | 60 | ---- |
| KV3239 | MONACO 9 | 60 | ---- |
| KV3310 | ALPINE SAL 14/6 | 14L | 1024 |
| KV3498* | MARCH SPL 9 | 60 | 19430 |
| KV3621 | MONACO 9 | 60 | 20151 |
| KV3933 | MONACO 9 | 60 | ---- |
| KV4063 | FALCON 9 | 60 | ---- |
| KV4250 | MENTONE 12/6 | 44T | ---- |
| KV4302 | MONACO 9 | 60 | ---- |
| KV4490 | MONACO 9 | 60 | ---- |
| KV4738 | LYNX 9 | 60 | ---- |
| KV5082* | KESTREL 12/6 | 44T | ---- |
| KV5086* | IMP 9 2/4 STR | 60 | ---- |
| KV5089 | MONACO 9 | 60 | ---- |
| KV5204* | LYNX 12/6 | 44T | 687 |
| KV5209 | MONACO 9 | 60 | 21796 |
| KV5212 | LYNX 9 | 60 | 21699 |
| KV5392* | BROOKLANDS 9 | 80 | 93 |
| KV5485 | LINCOCK 9 | 60 | 21988 |
| KV5490 | KESTREL 12/6 | 44T | 948 |
| KV5691* | GAMECOCK 14/6 | 44T | ---- |
| KV5692* | GAMECOCK 14/6 | 44T | ---- |
| KV5693* | GAMECOCK 14/6 | 44T | ---- |
| KV5694* | TT SIX/MPH 14 | 4/ | 101 |
| KV5695* | TT6/DIXON CAR | 4/ | 102 |
| KV5696* | TT6/WHITE RILEY | 4/ | 103 |
| KV5804 | MONACO 9 | 60 | ---- |
| KV5810 | GAMECOCK 14/6 | 44T | ---- |
| KV5835 | KESTREL 9 | 60 | ---- |
| KV5902 | LYNX 12/6 | 44T | ---- |
| KV5929 | WHITE RILEY | 4/ | 103 |
| KV6072* | LYNX 14/6 | 44T | 1007 |
| KV6077* | TT6/GREBE 12 | 4/ | 106 |
| KV6078* | TT6/DIXON CAR | 4/ | 104 |
| KV6079* | TT6/MPH 12 | 4/ | 105 |
| KV6080* | MONACO 9 | 60 | ---- |
| KV6183 | MONACO 9 | 60 | 22267 |
| KV6483 | MONACO 9 | 60 | ---- |
| KV6485 | KESTREL 9 | 60 | ---- |
| KV6492 | MONACO 9 | 60 | ---- |
| KV6541 | MENTONE 12/6 | 44T | ---- |
| KV6544* | KESTREL 12/6 | 44T | ---- |
| KV6684 | LYNX 12/6 | 44T | ---- |
| KV6685 | MONACO 9 | 60 | 22815 |
| KV7123 | MENTONE 12/6 | 44T | ---- |
| KV7125 | KESTREL 9 | 60 | ---- |
| KV7423 | MONACO 9 | 60 | ---- |
| KV7431 | KESTREL 9 | 60 | ---- |
| KV7596 | MENTONE 12/6 | 44T | ---- |
| KV7677 | KESTREL 9 | 60 | 24212 |
| KV7763 | MONACO 9 | 60 | 24063 |
| KV7765 | MONACO 9 | 60 | ---- |

| REG NUMBER | MODEL | CHASSIS NO | |
|---|---|---|---|
| KV7766 | MONACO 9 | 60 | ---- |
| KV7771 | MONACO 9 | 60 | 23361 |
| KV7837 | MONACO 9 | 60 | 23467 |
| KV8025* | IMP 9 | 60 | ---- |
| KV8031 | KESTREL 9 | 60 | ---- |
| KV8157 | MONACO 9 | 60 | ---- |
| KV8445 | KESTREL 9 | 60 | ---- |
| KV8446 | KESTREL 12/6 | 44T | 1929 |
| KV8517 | MONACO 9 | 60 | ---- |
| KV8726 | KESTREL 9 | 60 | 24622 |
| KV8932* | IMP 9 | 60 | 24757 |
| KV8933* | IMP 9 | 60 | ---- |
| KV9029 | LYNX 9 | 60 | ---- |
| KV9206 | LYNX 9 | 60 | ---- |
| KV9475* | ULSTER IMP 9 | 60 | ---- |
| KV9476* | ULSTER IMP 9 | 60 | ---- |
| KV9477* | MPH (RACING) | 44T | 2127 |
| KV9478* | MPH (RACING) | 44T | 2128 |
| KV9480 | KESTREL 9 | 60 | ---- |
| KV9548 | BROOKLANDS 9 | 80 | -- |
| KV9555 | KESTREL 9 | 60 | 24692 |
| KV9763* | MPH (RACING) | 44T | 2142 |
| KV9764 | MONACO 9 | 60 | ---- |
| KV9765 | LYNX 9 | 60 | ---- |
| KV9982 | ALPINE SAL 14/6 | 44T | ---- |
| KX1272 | MONACO 9 | 60 | 2599 |
| KX3599 | TOURER 9 | 60 | 6948 |
| KX6073 | MONACO 9 | 60 | ---- |
| KX7486 | MONACO 9 | 60 | 15329 |
| KX8685 | GAMECOCK 9 | 60 | 17687 |
| KX8735 | GAMECOCK 9 | 60 | 17226 |
| KX9892 | LYNX 9 | 60 | 21010 |
| KY 220 | BROOKLANDS 9 | 80 | 77 |
| KY 743 | MONACO 9 | 60 | ---- |
| KY2296 | GAMECOCK 9 | 60 | ---- |
| KY2684 | GAMECOCK 9 | 60 | ---- |
| KY7727 | KESTREL 9 | 60 | ---- |
| KY8909 | MPH 14/6 | 44T | 2252 |
| L 902-AUS | ALPINE SAL 14/6 | 14L | ---- |
| L 1930-L | MONACO 9 | 60 | ---- |
| LBF591-AUS | TOURER 9 | 60 | ---- |
| LB4612 | 5 HP TRI-CAR | ---- | / 1324 |
| LDD393-AUS | KESTREL | 28K | 7465 |
| LFJ663 | MONACO 9 | S67Z | ---- |
| LG0457 | BROOKLANDS 9 | 80 | -- |
| LG2533 | GILLOW SPL 9 | 60 | ---- |
| LG2825 | MONACO 9 | 60 | 7203 |
| LG9575 | GAMECOCK 9 | 60 | ---- |
| LG9667 | MONACO 9 | 60 | ---- |
| LG9897 | MENTONE 12/6 | 44T | ---- |
| LHX182 | KESTREL 9 | S66K | ---- |
| LJ4909 | MONACO 9 | 60 | 15360 |
| LJ5003 | 2 SEATER 9 | 60 | 11200 |
| LJ5087 | GAMECOCK 9 | 60 | ---- |
| LJ6719 | MONACO 9 | 60 | 19928 |
| LJ7010 | MONACO 9 | 60 | 20257 |
| LJ7019 | MONACO 9 | 60 | ---- |
| LJ7170 | MONACO 9 | 60 | ---- |

| REG NUMBER | MODEL | CHASSIS NO. | |
|---|---|---|---|
| LJ8002 | MONACO 9 | 60 | 21979 |
| LJ8874 | MONACO 9 | 60 | ---- |
| LJ8876 | MONACO 9 | 60 | ---- |
| LJ9084 | LYNX 9 | 60 | 23065 |
| LJ9817 | LYNX 12/6 | 44T | ---- |
| LMC109 | MONACO 9 | 60 | 8710 |
| LN2637-USA | 6 HP TRI-CAR | ---- | / 564 |
| LRL467 | KESTREL 9 | 60 | ---- |
| LS2869 | TOURER 9 | 60 | 16935 |
| LV 804 | MONACO 9 | 60 | ---- |
| LV5512 | MONACO 9 | 60 | ---- |
| LV7667 | MONACO 9 | 60 | 24469 |
| LV7860 | KESTREL 9 | 60 | 23498 |
| LV8374 | KESTREL 12/6 | 44T | 2031 |
| LV8683 | KESTREL 9 | 60 | ---- |
| LWU425-AUS | TOURER 9 | 60 | 19360 |
| LXH 83 | LYNX 9 | 60 | 22219 |
| LYT489 | LYNX 1½ | 26L | 4910 |
| MCR794 | FALCON 1½ | 27F | 6544 |
| MER198 | KESTREL 1½ | 22T | ---- |
| MF4444 | MONACO 9 | 60 | 27651 |
| MF7108 | MONACO 9 | S67Z | ---- |
| MG 437 | 2 SEATER 9 | 60 | 9450 |
| MG1820 | GAMECOCK 9 | 60 | ---- |
| MG2056 | MONACO 9 | 60 | ---- |
| MG3434 | KESTREL 1½ | 22T | 1677 |
| MG3443 | LYNX 9 | 60 | ---- |
| MG3637 | FALCON 1½ | 22T | 755 |
| MG3871 | KESTREL 1½ | 22T | ---- |
| MG3959 | KESTREL 1½ | 22T | 1677 |
| MJ2999 | MONACO 9 | 60 | 22686 |
| MJ3148 | MONACO 9 | 60 | 23851 |
| MJ3487 | KESTREL 12/6 | 44T | ---- |
| MJ3789 | KESTREL 9 | 60 | ---- |
| MJ4147 | MONACO 9 | 60 | ---- |
| MJ4606 | KESTREL 9 | 60 | 25927 |
| MJ5536 | KESTREL 9 | 60 | 25364 |
| MJ5872 | KESTREL 9 | 60 | 25432 |
| MJ6475 | FALCON 1½ | 22T | ---- |
| MJ7340 | FALCON 1½ | 22T | ---- |
| MJ8778 | MERLIN 9 | 66M | ---- |
| MJ8919 | MERLIN 1½ | 26M | ---- |
| MJ8984 | FALCON 1½ | 22T | ---- |
| MJ9035 | KESTREL 9 | S66K | ---- |
| MJ9040 | FALCON 1½ | 26F | 2732 |
| MJ9694 | KESTREL 1½ | 26K | ---- |
| MMF271 | BROOKLANDS 9 | 80 | 24 |
| MON837 | FALCON 1½ | 22T | ---- |
| MS1932-NZ | MARCH SPL 9 | 60 | 19061 |
| MS7336 | LYNX 9 | 60 | 22432 |
| MT3205 | MONACO 9 | 60 | 24724 |
| MV1172 | GAMECOCK 9 | 60 | ---- |
| MV1844 | GAMECOCK 9 | 60 | 16101 |
| MV2291 | MONACO 9 | 60 | ---- |
| MV5431 | WD TOURER 9 | 60 | 14562 |
| MV6906 | MONACO 9 | 60 | ---- |
| MW3040 | LYNX 9 | 60 | 21501 |
| MW6404 | TOURER 9 | 60 | 8442 |

| REG NUMBER | MODEL | CHASSIS NO | |
|---|---|---|---|
| MY 440 | TOURER 9 | 60 | 5954 |
| MY 804 | TOURER 9 | 60 | 6063 |
| MY 805 | TOURER 9 | 60 | ---- |
| MY1326 | 2 SEATER 9 | 60 | ---- |
| MY2203 | TOURER 9 | 60 | 8015 |
| MY2447 | BIARRITZ 9 | 60 | 8096 |
| MY2858 | BIARRITZ 9 | 60 | ---- |
| MY5100 | MONACO 9 | 60 | ---- |
| MY8910 | MONACO 9 | 60 | 19289 |
| N 2-NZ | FALCON 15/6 | 44T | ---- |
| NCV906 | GAMECOCK 9 | 60 | 16730 |
| ND1217-NL | LYNX SPR 1½ | SS27L | ---- |
| NE9104-CH | KESTREL 1½ | S26K | 3787 |
| NF2507 | SPL TOURER 11.9 | 69 | 1326 |
| NG 75 | TOURER 9 | 60 | ---- |
| NG 314 | BIARRITZ 9 | 60 | ---- |
| NG2018 | MONACO 9 | 60 | ---- |
| NG2393 | MONACO 9 | 60 | ---- |
| NG2893 | LYNX 9 | 60 | 17309 |
| NG6646 | TRG SAL 9 | 67C | ---- |
| NG8290 | MONACO 9 | 60 | ---- |
| NH5575 | TOURER 10.8 | | 1105 |
| NH9595 | TOURER 9 | 60 | 41 |
| NH9599 | MONACO 9 | 60 | 6951 |
| NJ 495 | MONACO 9 | 60 | 19925 |
| NJ 656 | MONACO 9 | 60 | ---- |
| NJ 801 | KESTREL 14/6 | 44T | ---- |
| NJ 935 | MONACO 9 | 60 | ---- |
| NJ1809 | WINCHESTER 14/6 | 88E | ---- |
| NJ1819 | WINCHESTER 14/6 | 88E | 78 |
| NJ2014 | LYNX 9 | 60 | 22439 |
| NJ2565 | MONACO 9 | 60 | ---- |
| NJ2790 | LYNX 9 | 60 | ---- |
| NJ2807 | MONACO 9 | 60 | 23962 |
| NJ2831 | MENTONE 12/6 | 44T | ---- |
| NJ2873 | ASCOT 9 | 60 | ---- |
| NJ3045 | MONACO 9 | 60 | ---- |
| NJ3120 | ASCOT9 | 60 | 23038 |
| NJ3253 | KESTREL 9 | 60 | ---- |
| NJ3875 | MONACO 9 | 60 | ---- |
| NJ4483 | KESTREL 9 | 60 | 25083 |
| NJ5896 | KESTREL 1½ | 22T | ---- |
| NJ5955 | KESTREL 1½ | 22T | ---- |
| NJ6087 | KESTREL 1½ | 22T | 1686 |
| NJ6176 | LYNX 1½ | 22T | 1919 |
| NJ6180 | MPH 14/6 | 44T | 2247 |
| NJ6895 | FALCON 1½ | 22T | ---- |
| NJ7494 | FALCON 1½ | 26F | 2970 |
| NJ7705 | MERLIN 9 | 66M | ---- |
| NJ7907 | FALCON 1½ | 26F | 3149 |
| NJ7938 | KESTREL 9 | 60 | ---- |
| NJ8108 | KESTREL 1½ | 26K | ---- |
| NJ8109 | KESTREL 1½ | S26K | 3739 |
| NJ8837 | ADELPHI 1½ | 26A | ---- |
| NJ8903 | KESTREL 1½ | 26K | ---- |
| NJ9388 | MERLIN 1½ | 26M | 4790 |
| NJ9562 | FALCON 1½ | 26F | 4317 |
| NJ9632 | MERLIN 9 | 66M | ---- |

| REG NUMBER | MODEL | CHASSIS NO. | |
|---|---|---|---|
| NKD494 | IMP 9 | 60 | 25217 |
| NS 105 | 12/18 HP SWB CAR | ---- | / 1478 |
| NSW017-AUS | BROOKLANDS 9 | 80 | -- |
| NSW018-AUS | LINCOCK 9 | 60 | 24693 |
| NV1054 | GAMECOCK 9 | 60 | ---- |
| NV1172 | GAMECOCK 9 | 60 | ---- |
| NV4282 | KESTREL 9 | 60 | ---- |
| NV4639 | MONACO 9 | 60 | 25297 |
| NV4645 | KESTREL 9 | 60 | 25418 |
| NV5432 | FALCON 9 | 22T | 1824 |
| NV7456 | MERLIN 1½ | 26M | ---- |
| NV9627 | MONACO 9 | S67Z | 2342 |
| NXA202 | KESTREL 9 | 60 | ---- |
| NX3316 | 2ST SPORTS 10.8 | | ---- |
| OA18A -USA | BROOKLANDS 9 | 80 | -- |
| OC 99 | LYNX 9 | 60 | ---- |
| OC 354 | LYNX 12/6 | 44T | 863 |
| OC 604 | KESTREL 12 | 44T | 802 |
| OC1845 | MONACO 9 | 60 | ---- |
| OC2690 | KESTREL 9 | 60 | ---- |
| OC3798 | KESTREL 9 | 60 | ---- |
| OC5673 | MENTONE 12/6 | 44T | ---- |
| OC5720 | - - 9 | 60 | 23960 |
| OC7985-NL | KESTREL 9 | 60 | 24200 |
| OC8831 | LYNX 9 | 60 | 25625 |
| OC8835 | KESTREL 9 | 60 | ---- |
| OC8836 | MONACO 9 | 60 | 24363 |
| OD1357 | MONACO 9 | 60 | 16123 |
| OD1827 | GAMECOCK 9 | 60 | ---- |
| OD1865 | TOURER 9 | 60 | ---- |
| OD3101 | MONACO 9 | 60 | ---- |
| OD4310 | MONACO 9 | 60 | ---- |
| OD4481 | MARCH SPL 9 | 60 | 19578 |
| OD4814 | LINCOCK 9 | 60 | 20592 |
| OD4817 | LINCOCK 9 | 60 | ---- |
| OD5014 | MONACO 9 | 60 | ---- |
| OD5019 | MONACO 9 | 60 | ---- |
| OD5084 | MONACO 9 | 60 | ---- |
| OD5760 | LYNX 9 | 60 | ---- |
| OD6862 | KESTREL 9 | 60 | ---- |
| OD7723 | MONACO 9 | 60 | 23930 |
| OD8379 | LYNX 12/6 | 44T | 1912 |
| OD9245 | KESTREL 9 | 60 | 24698 |
| OF 282 | 2 SEATER 9 | 60 | 5464 |
| OF2289 | MONACO 9 | 60 | ---- |
| OF3245 | MONACO 9 | 60 | 6100 |
| OF4506 | MONACO 9 | 60 | 7088 |
| OF5722 | BIARRITZ 9 | 60 | ---- |
| OF6320 | MONACO 9 | 60 | ---- |
| OF7267 | 2 SEATER 9 | 60 | ---- |
| OG1585 | BIARRITZ 9 | 60 | ---- |
| OG3184 | TOURER 9 | 60 | 10539 |
| OG6128 | MONACO 9 | 60 | ---- |
| OG6497 | TOURER 9 | 60 | 11167 |
| OG6787 | MONACO 9 | 60 | ---- |
| OG8254 | MONACO 9 | 60 | 11548 |
| OJ 418 | GAMECOCK 9 | 60 | ---- |
| OJ 891 | GAMECOCK 9 | 60 | 17867 |

| REG NUMBER | MODEL | CHASSIS NO | |
|---|---|---|---|
| OJ1445 | GAMECOCK 9 | 60 | ---- |
| OJ5898 | MONACO 9 | 60 | ---- |
| OJ6078 | TRINITY 9 | 60 | ---- |
| OJ6481 | KESTREL 12/6 | 44T | ---- |
| OJ7482 | MONACO 9 | 60 | 19312 |
| OJ8040 | LYNX 9 | 60 | ---- |
| OJ8442 | MONACO 9 | 60 | 24524 |
| OJ9058 | LYNX 12/6 | 44T | 724 |
| OK7892 | MONACO 9 | 60 | ---- |
| OMH 9 | MERLIN 1½ | 26M | ---- |
| OND309 | KESTREL 1½ | 27K | 6676 |
| OO 003-AUS | KESTREL SPR 1½ | SS27K | ---- |
| OPG928 | LYNX SPR 1½ | SS26L | ---- |
| OPJ991 | KESTREL 15/6 | 46K | 2660 |
| OPP959 | KESTREL 15/6 | 4?K | ---- |
| ORE600 | SPRITE 1½ | S2?S | ---- |
| OS3975 | MONACO 9 | 60 | ---- |
| OU2170 | MONACO 9 | 60 | ---- |
| OU2313 | TOURER 9 | 60 | ---- |
| OU3643 | MONACO 9 | 60 | ---- |
| OU8546 | MONACO 9 | 60 | ---- |
| OVK947 | MERLIN 1½ | 26M | ---- |
| OV1227 | TOURER 9 | 60 | ---- |
| OV2806 | DEAUVILLE 14/6 | 14 | 397 |
| OV2933 | TRINITY 9 | 60 | ---- |
| OV5286 | GAMECOCK 9 | 60 | 15312 |
| OV5829 | GAMECOCK 9 | 60 | ---- |
| OV6763 | GAMECOCK 9 | 60 | ---- |
| OV7306 | 2 SEATER 9 | 60 | ---- |
| OV7600 | GAMECOCK 9 | 60 | ---- |
| OV8357 | ALPINE SAL 14/6 | 14L | 908 |
| OW1763 | GAMECOCK 9 | 60 | ---- |
| OW1891 | MONACO 9 | 60 | ---- |
| OW3162 | MONACO 9 | 60 | 21447 |
| OW4319 | MONACO 9 | 60 | ---- |
| OW4427 | MONACO 9 | 60 | 6771 |
| OW4557 | MONACO 9 | 60 | ---- |
| OW4767 | LYNX 9 | 60 | ---- |
| OW4771 | LYNX 9 | 60 | 25858 |
| OW5343 | KESTREL 9 | 60 | ---- |
| OW5506 | IMP 9 | 60 | ---- |
| OW6276 | IMP 9 | 60 | ---- |
| OW6390 | KESTREL 1½ | 22T | ---- |
| OW6590 | KESTREL 9 | 60 | ---- |
| OW7166 | LYNX 1½ | 22T | 2004 |
| OW7859 | IMP 9 | 60 | 27359 |
| OW7925 | MPH 14/6 | 44T | 2255 |
| OW8196 | KESTREL 1½ | 26K | ---- |
| OW8796 | KESTREL 1½ | 22T | ---- |
| OW9001 | KESTREL SPR 1½ | SS26K | ---- |
| OW9193 | KESTREL 1½ | 26K | 4460 |
| OW9280 | LYNX 1½ | 26L | 4459 |
| OXW767 | ADELPHI 1½ | 27A | ---- |
| OX7786 | TOURER 9 | 60 | ---- |
| OX7999 | COUPE 9 | 60 | 513 |
| OY 83 | BIARRITZ 9 | 60 | ---- |
| OY 412 | LINCOCK 9 | 60 | ---- |
| OYY555 | KESTREL 9 | 60 | ---- |

| REG NUMBER | MODEL | CHASSIS NO. | |
|---|---|---|---|
| OY1355 | MONACO 9 | 60 | ---- |
| OY2596 | GAMECOCK 9 | 60 | 16811 |
| OY2717 | MONACO 9 | 60 | ---- |
| OY4112 | MONACO 9 | 60 | 19571 |
| OY4441 | MONACO 9 | 60 | 20251 |
| OY4911 | LYNX 9 | 60 | 20943 |
| OY5457 | LINCOCK 9 | 60 | ---- |
| OY5541 | LYNX 9 | 60 | 21395 |
| OY5652 | MENTONE 12/6 | 44T | ---- |
| OY5656 | MONACO 9 | 60 | ---- |
| OY5847 | LINCOCK 9 | 60 | 21164 |
| OY6999 | MONACO 9 | 60 | ---- |
| OY7467 | LYNX 9 | 60 | 23144 |
| OY7554 | KESTREL 6 | 44T | ---- |
| OY7555 | KESTREL 9 | 60 | ---- |
| OY7992 | LINCOCK 9 | 60 | 22436 |
| OY8471 | MONACO 9 | 60 | 25640 |
| OY8474 | MONACO 9 | 60 | 23660 |
| OY9710 | KESTREL 9 | 60 | ---- |
| OZ2796-IRL | MERLIN 9 | 66M | ---- |
| O39583-S | MONACO 9 | 60 | 20197 |
| PF8905 | SPL TOURER 11.9 | 69 | 1482 |
| PG 472 | BROOKLANDS 9 | 80 | 55 |
| PG1154 | TOURER 9 | 60 | 5800 |
| PG3601 | TOURER 9 | 60 | ---- |
| PG3609 | TOURER 9 | 60 | 7014 |
| PG3811 | BROOKLANDS 9 | 80 | -- |
| PG6378 | BROOKLANDS 9 | 80 | -- |
| PG7160 | STELVIO 14/6 | 14S | 803 |
| PG7598 | TOURER 9 | 60 | 2966 |
| PG8541 | BROOKLANDS 9 | 80 | 46 |
| PG8793 | MONACO 9 | 60 | ---- |
| PH7527 | TOURER 9 | 60 | 824 |
| PH7546 | TOURER 9 | 60 | 703 |
| PH8195 | TOURER 9 | 60 | 918 |
| PJ1114 | GAMECOCK 9 | 60 | ---- |
| PJ1978 | MONACO 9 | 60 | ---- |
| PJ2192 | TOURER 9 | 60 | 13974 |
| PJ2915 | TOURER 9 | 60 | ---- |
| PJ3336 | MONACO 9 | 60 | ---- |
| PJ3847 | GAMECOCK 9 | 60 | ---- |
| PJ4042 | ALPINE TR 14/6 | 14L | ---- |
| PJ4280 | TOURER 9 | 60 | 16863 |
| PJ5073 | GAMECOCK 9 | 60 | 16497 |
| PJ5410 | MONACO 9 | 60 | 17508 |
| PJ5592 | MONACO 9 | 60 | ---- |
| PJ5610 | MONACO 9 | 60 | ---- |
| PJ5671 | GAMECOCK 9 | 60 | 17579 |
| PJ6968 | GAMECOCK 9 | 60 | ---- |
| PJ7662 | MONACO 9 | 60 | ---- |
| PK2499# | BROOKLANDS 9 | 80 | 71 |
| PK2705# | BROOKLANDS 9 | 60/ | 16 |
| PK2706# | BROOKLANDS 9 | 60/ | 17 |
| PK2707# | BROOKLANDS 9 | 60/ | 18 |
| PK2708# | BROOKLANDS 9 | 60/ | 19 |
| PK2721# | BROOKLANDS 9 | 60/ | 3 |
| PK3891 | MONACO 9 | 60 | ---- |
| PK4395 | TOURER 9 | 60 | ---- |

| REG NUMBER | MODEL | CHASSIS NO | |
|---|---|---|---|
| PK4420 | TOURER 9 | 60 | 3074 |
| PK7028 | TOURER 9 | 60 | ---- |
| PK8170 | TOURER 9 | 60 | ---- |
| PL1120 | TOURER 9 | 60 | ---- |
| PL2924 | TOURER 9 | 60 | 10554 |
| PL3697 | MONACO 9 | 60 | ---- |
| PL5491 | BIARRITZ 9 | 60 | 12507 |
| PL6447 | MONACO 9 | 60 | 11992 |
| PL6648 | TOURER 9 | 60 | ---- |
| PL7385 | MONACO 9 | 60 | ---- |
| PL8617 | DEAUVILLE 14/6 | 14 | 238 |
| PL9352 | MONACO 9 | 60 | ---- |
| PM2965 | COUPE 10.8 | C | 1242 |
| PN3026 | 2 SEATER 9 | 60 | 4098 |
| PN4231 | TOURER 9 | 60 | ---- |
| PN4632 | TOURER 9 | 60 | 6848 |
| PN8003 | MONACO 9 | 60 | ---- |
| PO2113 | 2 SEATER 9 | 60 | 9407 |
| PO5441 | STELVIO 14/6 | 14S | 518 |
| PO6844 | LYNX 9 | 60 | 20255 |
| PO6860 | MONACO 9 | 60 | 17349 |
| PO8915 | MONACO 9 | 60 | 23203 |
| PP0697 | KESTREL 1½ | 26K | ---- |
| PR7845 | WENTWORTH 11.9 | 69 | 846 |
| PT3641 | MONACO 9 | 60 | ---- |
| PV4088 | MONACO 9 | S67Z | ---- |
| QA 692-AUS | SPL TOURER | 60 | ---- |
| QA 833-AUS | SPL TOURER | 60 | ---- |
| QA 834-AUS | SPL TOURER | 60 | ---- |
| RB5343 | MONACO 9 | 60 | 15402 |
| RB6330 | MONACO 9 | 60 | 17460 |
| RB9097 | LYNX 1½ | 22T | 993 |
| RC 566 | MONACO 9 | 60 | ---- |
| RC1040 | FALCON 9 | 60 | ---- |
| RC4497 | ADELPHI 15/6 | 46A | ---- |
| RDV566 | KESTREL SPR 1½ | SS27K | 5883 |
| RD6370 | FALCON 1½ | 22T | ---- |
| RD6987 | MONACO 9 | 60 | 27391 |
| RD7007 | KESTREL 1½ | 22T | ---- |
| RF3361 | CHATSWORTH 11.9 | 69 | ---- |
| RGO 99-AUS | TOURER 9 | 60 | ---- |
| RG1700 | MONACO 9 | 60 | 11387 |
| RG1917 | BIARRITZ 9 | 60 | ---- |
| RG3131 | MONACO 9 | 60 | ---- |
| RG4060 | MONACO 9 | 60 | ---- |
| RG5549 | FALCON 1½ | 26F | 3572 |
| RG6366 | ADELPHI 1½ | 26A | ---- |
| RH3557 | BIARRITZ 9 | 60 | ---- |
| RH6857 | MONACO 9 | 60 | 21126 |
| RH7497 | STELVIO 14/6 | 14S | 745 |
| RH7775 | MONACO 9 | 60 | ---- |
| RH7819 | LINCOCK 9 | 60 | ---- |
| RH8647 | MONACO 9 | 60 | 24017 |
| RH8780 | KESTREL 12/6 | 44T | 1586 |
| RH9059 | MONACO 9 | 60 | ---- |
| RH9424 | KESTREL 9 | 60 | 23438 |
| RLY 9 | IMP 9 | 60 | ---- |
| RM5479 | 2 SEATER 9 | 60 | ---- |

| REG NUMBER | MODEL | CHASSIS NO. | |
|---|---|---|---|
| RM6436 | TOURER 9 | 60 | ---- |
| RM8270 | GAMECOCK 9 | 60 | 15156 |
| RM8545 | ALPINE SAL 14/6 | 14L | ---- |
| RM9263 | MONACO 9 | 60 | ---- |
| RM9901 | MONACO 9 | 60 | 23768 |
| RN1159 | MONACO 9 | 60 | ---- |
| RN5290 | KESTREL 1½ | 27K | 5350 |
| RP 925 | CHATSWORTH 11.9 | 69 | 3479 |
| RP6334 | TOURER 9 | 60 | 2048 |
| RT8798 | MONACO 9 | 60 | ---- |
| RT9473 | MARCH SPL 9 | 60 | ---- |
| RU7993 | - - 9 | 60 | 1937? |
| RU8199 | BROOKLANDS 9 | -- | -- |
| RU8857 | TOURER 9 | 60 | 5213 |
| RV 845 | MONACO 9 | 60 | 14073 |
| RVK234 | FALCON 1½ | 27F | ---- |
| RV1250 | TOURER 9 | 60 | 15034 |
| RV3333 | LYNX 9 | 60 | ---- |
| RV3469 | MONACO 9 | 60 | ---- |
| RV4166 | MONACO 9 | 60 | 22295 |
| RV4745 | LYNX 12/6 | 44T | 2028 |
| RV4747 | MONACO 9 | 60 | ---- |
| RV5827 | KESTREL 9 | 60 | ---- |
| RV6062 | KESTREL 1½ | 22T | 877 |
| RV6170 | FALCON 1½ | 22T | ---- |
| RV6230 | MONACO 9 | 60 | ---- |
| RV6524 | LYNX 9 | 60 | ---- |
| RV6525 | KESTREL 1½ | 22T | 1688 |
| RV6860 | KESTREL 1½ | 22T | ---- |
| RV7381 | FALCON 1½ | 26F | ---- |
| RV8152 | KESTREL 1½ | 26K | ---- |
| RV8487 | KESTREL 15/6 | 46K | 2680 |
| RV9552 | LYNX SPR 1½ | SS27L | 5207 |
| RW 104* | SWB SPORTS 10.8 | | 2116A |
| RW2686* | TOURER 11.9 | 69 | ---- |
| RW9891* | SPL TOURER 11.9 | 69 | ---- |
| RX1656 | TOURER 9 | 60 | 698 |
| RX2347 | BROOKLANDS 9 | 80 | 09 |
| RX3565 | MONACO 9 | 60 | 3553 |
| RX9753 | GAMECOCK 9 | 60 | 16243 |
| RX9772 | ASCOT 9 | 60 | 16405 |
| RYB814-AUS | KESTREL 1½ | 26K | ---- |
| SAA 27 | IMP 9 | 60 | 25492 |
| SB4492 | LYNX 14/6 | 44T | 1737 |
| SCV552 | KESTREL 12/6 | 44T | 770 |
| SC3475 | MONACO 9 | 60 | ---- |
| SC5006 | TOURER 9 | 60 | 3273 |
| SE2386 | 4D COACH 11.9 | 69 | 285 |
| SHM517 | IMP 9 | 60 | ---- |
| SH5654 | KESTREL 1½ | 27K | ---- |
| SJN283R | MPH 14/6 | 44T | ---- |
| SK2056 | FALCON 1½ | 22T | ---- |
| SK2766 | KESTREL 15/6 | 46K | ---- |
| SL2026 | FALCON 1½ | 27F | ---- |
| SL2221 | KESTREL SPR 1½ | SS27K | 6151 |
| SMH106 | FALCON 9 | 60 | ---- |
| SM5654 | KESTREL 1½ | 27K | 6237 |
| SN6019 | LYNX 12/6 | 44T | ---- |

| REG NUMBER | MODEL | CHASSIS NO | |
|---|---|---|---|
| SN6094 | LYNX 9 | 60 | 22447 |
| SN6129 | MONACO 9 | 60 | ---- |
| SN6380 | LYNX 12/6 | 44T | ---- |
| SN7145 | MERLIN 9 | 66M | 1094 |
| SN7326 | KESTREL 1½ | 26K | ---- |
| SN8499 | ADELPHI 1½ | 28A | ---- |
| SO4872 | MENTONE 12/6 | 44T | ---- |
| SR9434 | KESTREL 1½ | 22T | 1723 |
| ST6365 | MONACO 9 | 60 | 11481 |
| SU0543-AUS | TOURER 9 | 60 | 6648 |
| SVE604 | MONACO 9 | S67Z | ---- |
| SX4220 | SPRITE 1½ | S26S | 3753 |
| SX4300 | LYNX 1½ | 26L | ---- |
| SY1729 | GAMECOCK 9 | 60 | 18058 |
| T 59 | LYNX 1½ | 22T | 1919 |
| T 194 | TOURER 12/18 | -- | ---- |
| T 1915 | 12/18 HP CAR | ---- / | 1374 |
| TA7711 | TOURER 9 | 60 | ---- |
| TC1183 | 4ST COUPE 10.8 | C | 826 |
| TC8804 | KESTREL 9 | 60 | ---- |
| TF3030 | 2 SEATER 9 | 60 | ---- |
| TF6732 | MONACO 9 | 60 | 13828 |
| TF6898 | MONACO 9 | 60 | 16022 |
| TF7539 | GAMECOCK 9 | 60 | ---- |
| TF8731 | GAMECOCK 9 | 60 | ---- |
| TF9131 | MONACO 9 | 60 | ---- |
| TF9427 | MONACO 9 | 60 | ---- |
| TF9740 | TOURER 9 | 60 | 19463 |
| TGB569 | ADELPHI 1½ | 28AX | 7256 |
| TGB569 | ADELPHI 16/4 | 38AX | ---- |
| TG5687 | FALCON 9 | 60 | 21640 |
| TG6322 | KESTREL 9 | 60 | ---- |
| TG9349 | KESTREL 9 | 60 | ---- |
| TH7970 | LYNX SPR 1½ | SS27L | 5885 |
| TH8306 | MONACO 9 | SS67Z | ---- |
| TJ 419 | MONACO 9 | 60 | 20396 |
| TJ1298 | FALCON 9 | 60 | 21502 |
| TJ1332 | LYNX 9 | 60 | 21394 |
| TJ1365 | MONACO 9 | 60 | ---- |
| TJ1567 | MONACO 9 | 60 | 20569 |
| TJ2113 | MONACO 9 | 60 | ---- |
| TJ2612 | LYNX 9 | 60 | 22351 |
| TJ2614 | LYNX 9 | 60 | ---- |
| TJ4757 | KESTREL 9 | 60 | 23441 |
| TJ5258 | LYNX 9 | 60 | ---- |
| TJ8552 | KESTREL 6 | 44T | ---- |
| TJ8720 | MONACO 9 | 60 | ---- |
| TK9227 | MENTONE 12/6 | 44T | 578 |
| TL1679 | ASCOT 9 | 60 | ---- |
| TL2807 | LINCOCK 9 | 60 | ---- |
| TL4000 | FALCON 1½ | 22T | ---- |
| TM 235 | GAMECOCK 9 | 60 | ---- |
| TP8072 | TOURER 9 | 60 | ---- |
| TP8433 | TOURER 9 | 60 | ---- |
| TR7711-S | TOURER 9 | 60 | 7532 |
| TS9053 | BIARRITZ 9 | 60 | 12159 |
| TS9280 | BIARRITZ 9 | 60 | 13637 |
| TT3563 | LYNX 9 | 60 | ---- |

| REG NUMBER | MODEL | CHASSIS NO. | |
|---|---|---|---|
| TU6615 | MONACO 9 | 60 | ---- |
| TU7055 | LYNX 9 | 60 | ---- |
| TU9039 | BIARRITZ 9 | 60 | 1804 |
| TV 690 | TOURER 9 | 60 | ---- |
| TV3497 | KESTREL 1½ | 22T | 1356 |
| TV4052 | MONACO 9 | 60 | ---- |
| TV5055 | MONACO 9 | 60 | ---- |
| TV6615 | MONACO 9 | 60 | ---- |
| TV6617 | MONACO 9 | 60 | ---- |
| TV7055 | LYNX 9 | 60 | ---- |
| TV7057 | LINCOCK 9 | 60 | 20170 |
| TV7287 | MONACO 9 | 60 | 19114 |
| TV8011 | MARCH SPL 12/6 | 44T | 618 |
| TV8048 | LYNX 9 | 60 | ---- |
| TV9390 | MONACO 9 | 60 | ---- |
| TW8640 | FALCON 1½ | 26F | ---- |
| TX4056 | MERLIN 9 | 66M | ---- |
| TY 225 | 2D TOURER 10.8 | | 3868 |
| TYS59G | MONACO 9 | 60 | ---- |
| TY7075 | 2 SEATER 9 | 60 | ---- |
| TY7271 | MONACO 9 | 60 | ---- |
| TY8015 | MONACO 9 | 60 | ---- |
| TY8249 | MERLIN 9 | 66M | ---- |
| TY9253 | ASCOT 9 | 60 | 16245 |
| TY9968 | MONACO 9 | 60 | 19220 |
| UB3468 | MONACO 9 | 60 | ---- |
| UB6552 | ALPINE SAL 14/6 | 14L | 400 |
| UB9316 | MONACO 9 | 60 | 5249 |
| UB9711 | ALPINE SAL 14/6 | 14L | 895 |
| UD4481 | MARCH SPL 9 | 60 | ---- |
| UD4817 | LINCOCK 9 | 60 | ---- |
| UD7635 | KESTREL 1½ | 26K | 4479 |
| UD8092 | MONACO 9 | S67Z | 2566 |
| UE9825 | TOURER 9 | 60 | ---- |
| UF4285 | MONACO 9 | 60 | ---- |
| UF4506 | MONACO 9 | 60 | ---- |
| UF8047 | MONACO 9 | 60 | ---- |
| UF9709 | LYNX 14/6 | 44T | ---- |
| UG 511 | TOURER 9 | 60 | 16808 |
| UG 990 | MONACO 9 | 60 | ---- |
| UG3427 | KESTREL 12/6 | 44T | 317 |
| UG3855 | MONACO 9 | 60 | ---- |
| UG4139 | MONACO 9 | 60 | 21336 |
| UG6031 | MONACO 9 | 60 | 21825 |
| UG8286 | KESTREL 9 | 60 | ---- |
| UG8347 | KESTREL 9 | 60 | ---- |
| UG9093 | MONACO 9 | 60 | 23230 |
| UIZ973-IRL | MERLIN 9 | 66M | 1228 |
| UJ1393 | KESTREL 12/6 | 44T | 441 |
| UJ1526 | MENTONE 12/6 | 44T | ---- |
| UJ2482 | MONACO 9 | 60 | ---- |
| UJ3701 | MONACO 9 | 60 | ---- |
| UJ4028 | KESTREL 9 | 60 | 25301 |
| UJ4895 | LYNX 1½ | 22T | ---- |
| UJ5307 | KESTREL 9 | 60 | ---- |
| UJ6154 | FALCON 1½ | 22T | ---- |
| UJ6793 | KESTREL 9 | S66K | ---- |
| UJ7052 | MERLIN 9 | 66M | ---- |

| REG NUMBER | MODEL | CHASSIS NO | |
|---|---|---|---|
| UK6991 | TOURER 9 | 60 | ---- |
| UL5266 | MONACO 9 | 60 | 3927 |
| UL7459 | MONACO 9 | 60 | 4033 |
| UM4913 | BROOKLANDS 9 | 80 | -- |
| UM5742 | MONACO 9 | 60 | ---- |
| UN5665 | FALCON 1½ | 27F | ---- |
| UN6313 | MONACO 9 | 60 | ---- |
| UN6679 | TRINITY 9 | 60 | 21526 |
| UN6829 | KESTREL 12/6 | 44T | ---- |
| UN6878 | KESTREL 9 | S66K | ---- |
| UN7024 | MONACO 9 | 60 | ---- |
| UN7402 | MONACO 9 | 60 | ---- |
| UN8186 | KESTREL 1½ | 22T | ---- |
| UN9099 | MERLIN 9 | 66M | ---- |
| UN9412 | MERLIN 9 | 66M | ---- |
| UN9501 | KESTREL 1½ | 26K | ---- |
| UN9585 | FALCON 1½ | 26F | ---- |
| UN9621 | MERLIN 9 | 66M | ---- |
| UN9676 | FALCON 1½ | 26F | 3152 |
| UP3919 | MONACO 9 | 60 | 15457 |
| UP6127 | MONACO 9 | 60 | ---- |
| UP8625 | MONACO 9 | 60 | ---- |
| UR 609 | TRG SAL 1½ | 28F | ---- |
| UR2699 | TOURER 9 | 60 | 4313 |
| UR4211 | BIARRITZ 9 | 60 | 6283 |
| UR6236 | MONACO 9 | 60 | ---- |
| US1426 | LYNX 9 | 60 | ---- |
| US1451 | LYNX 12/6 | 44T | ---- |
| US1514 | LYNX 9 | 60 | 21295 |
| US2661 | MONACO 9 | 60 | ---- |
| US3568 | KESTREL 9 | 60 | 22760 |
| US4630 | LYNX 9 | 60 | 24163 |
| US4847 | KESTREL 9 | 60 | ---- |
| US5148 | LYNX 9 | 60 | ---- |
| US6187 | LYNX 14/6 | 44T | 1646 |
| US6808 | LYNX 9 | 60 | ---- |
| US8803 | IMP 9 | 60 | ---- |
| UT2535 | MONACO 9 | 60 | 901 |
| UT8254 | BROOKLANDS 9 | 80 | 79 |
| UU1662 | BIARRITZ 9 | 60 | 4876 |
| UU2994 | MONACO 9 | 60 | 5354 |
| UU6913 | MONACO 9 | 60 | 5647 |
| UU8996 | 2 SEATER 9 | 60 | 2867 |
| UV1180 | TOURER 9 | 60 | 5832 |
| UV4155 | MONACO 9 | 60 | ---- |
| UV5840 | MONACO 9 | 60 | ---- |
| UV6685 | 2 SEATER 9 | 60 | 6672 |
| UV6763 | GAMECOCK 9 | 60 | ---- |
| UW 629 | MONACO 9 | 60 | 6983 |
| UW 649-CH | TOURER 9 | 60 | 7012 |
| UW2303 | TOURER 9 | 60 | ---- |
| UW4427 | MONACO 9 | 60 | ---- |
| UW5374 | TOURER 9 | 60 | 7043 |
| UX3940 | MONACO 9 | 60 | ---- |
| UX4218-NL | BROOKLANDS 9 | 80 | 23 |
| UY4322 | BROOKLANDS 9 | 80 | 32 |
| UY5457 | LINCOCK 9 | 60 | ---- |
| UY6362 | MONACO 9 | 60 | 6533 |

| REG NUMBER | MODEL | CHASSIS NO. | |
|---|---|---|---|
| UY6685 | 2 SEATER 9 | 60 | ---- |
| UY7800 | TOURER 9 | 60 | ---- |
| UY9178 | MONACO 9 | 60 | 11696 |
| VB5039 | SAN REMO 9 | 60 | ---- |
| VB6041 | MONACO 9 | 60 | ---- |
| VB6148 | MONACO 9 | 60 | 5884 |
| VB9975 | MONACO 9 | 60 | 11859 |
| VC 483* | BROOKLANDS 9 | 80 | 47 |
| VC 484* | BROOKLANDS 9 | 80 | 48 |
| VC 485* | BROOKLANDS 9 | 80 | 49 |
| VC 833* | BROOKLANDS 9 | 80 | 50 |
| VC 834* | BROOKLANDS 9 | 80 | 52 |
| VC 835* | BROOKLANDS 9 | 80 | 51 |
| VC1570* | 4S SPTS 9 PROTO | 60 | ---- |
| VC2189 | MONACO 9 | 60 | ---- |
| VC3993 | TOURER 9 | 60 | ---- |
| VC4415 | TOURER 9 | 60 | 9718 |
| VC6782 | MONACO 9 | 60 | 11508 |
| VC6787 | BROOKLANDS 9 | 80 | -- |
| VC6788 | BROOKLANDS 9 | 80 | -- |
| VC6800 | BROOKLANDS 9 | 80 | 81 |
| VC7066 | STELVIO 14/6 | 14S | ---- |
| VC7072 | BIARRITZ 9 | 60 | ---- |
| VC7552 | TOURER 9 | 60 | ---- |
| VC7856 | WD TOURER 9 | 60 | ---- |
| VC8302* | BROOKLANDS 9 | 80 | 87 |
| VC8303* | BROOKLANDS 9 | 80 | 88 |
| VC8304*USA | BROOKLANDS 9 | 80 | 89 |
| VC8305* | BROOKLANDS 9 | 80 | 90 |
| VC8306* | BROOKLANDS 9 | 80 | 91 |
| VC8309 | MONACO 9 | 60 | ---- |
| VC8602 | BIARRITZ 9 | 60 | 13091 |
| VC8804 | GAMECOCK 9 | 60 | ---- |
| VC9116 | GAMECOCK 9 | 60 | 16324 |
| VC9199* | ALPINE SAL 14/6 | 14L | ---- |
| VC9204* | BROOKLANDS 9 | 80 | 92 |
| VC9484 | MONACO 9 | 60 | 15028 |
| VC9722* | ALPINE TR 14/6 | 14L | ---- |
| VC9725 | GAMECOCK 9 | 60 | ---- |
| VC9859* | CONTNTL COUPE 9 | 60 | 14534 |
| VC9898 | GAMECOCK 9 | 60 | ---- |
| VC9899 | WD TOURER 9 | 60 | ---- |
| VD 515 | BIARRITZ 9 | 60 | ---- |
| VD2243 | MONACO 9 | 60 | 20012 |
| VD3083 | KESTREL 9 | 60 | 22706 |
| VD3110 | KESTREL 9 | 60 | 23011 |
| VD5224 | FALCON 1½ | 22T | ---- |
| VD5254 | FALCON 1½ | 22T | ---- |
| VD6228 | MERLIN 9 | 66M | 1647 |
| VD7498 | MERLIN 9 | 67M | 2828 |
| VD8092 | MONACO 9 | S67Z | ---- |
| VD8395 | MONACO 9 | S67Z | ---- |
| VD9059 | KESTREL 1½ | 28K | ---- |
| VD9170 | MONACO 9 | 60 | 23114 |
| VE 609 | MONACO 9 | 60 | ---- |
| VE1701 | BEAVIS SPL 9 | 60 | 6294 |
| VE4847 | BROOKLANDS 9 | 80 | -- |
| VE4849 | BIARRITZ 9 | 60 | 12490 |

| REG NUMBER | MODEL | CHASSIS NO | |
|---|---|---|---|
| VE7627 | HOYAL COUPE 9 | 60 | 17546 |
| VE8778 | LINCOCK 9 | 60 | ---- |
| VE8947 | LYNX 9 | 60 | 21900 |
| VE9043 | LYNX 9 | 60 | 22124 |
| VE9077 | FALCON 9 | 60 | ---- |
| VE9171 | MONACO 9 | 60 | 21821 |
| VE9559 | KESTREL 9 | 60 | ---- |
| VE9825 | TOURER 9 | 60 | ---- |
| VF4937 | TOURER 9 | 60 | 3563 |
| VF6134 | BROOKLANDS 9 | 80 | -- |
| VG2367 | COUPE 9 | 60 | 7819 |
| VG4530 | MONACO 9 | 60 | ---- |
| VG5654 | MONACO 9 | 60 | ---- |
| VG6527 | KESTREL 9 | 60 | ---- |
| VG6556 | LYNX 9 | 60 | 25853 |
| VG6583 | KESTREL 9 | 60 | ---- |
| VG7007 | FALCON 1½ | 22T | 200 |
| VG7251 | MONACO 9 | 60 | ---- |
| VG8101 | MERLIN 9 | 66M | ---- |
| VG8286 | KESTREL 9 | 60 | ---- |
| VH6012 | MONACO 9 | 60 | ---- |
| VH7450 | FALCON 1½ | 22T | ---- |
| VH7457 | KESTREL 15/6 | 44T | 2303 |
| VH7503 | IMP 9 | 60 | 27414 |
| VH7568 | FALCON 15/6 | 44T | ---- |
| VH7963 | FALCON 15/6 | 44T | ---- |
| VH8857 | KESTREL 1½ | 26K | 3796 |
| VH9623 | KESTREL SPR 1½ | SS27K | 5527 |
| VJ1813 | TOURER 9 | 60 | ---- |
| VJ3389 | TOURER 9 | 60 | ---- |
| VJ4915 | MONACO 9 | 60 | 19101 |
| VJ5460 | MARCH SPL 9 | 60 | ---- |
| VJ5515 | MARCH SPL 9 | 60 | 19308 |
| VJ5519 | MARCH SPL 9 | 60 | ---- |
| VJ6243 | LYNX 9 | 60 | ---- |
| VJ6411 | KESTREL 9 | 60 | 25850 |
| VJ6717 | LYNX 9 | 60 | ---- |
| VJ7151 | KESTREL 1½ | 22T | ---- |
| VJ9040 | LYNX 1½ | 26L | ---- |
| VK2768 | MONACO 9 | 60 | ---- |
| VK3712 | MONACO 9 | 60 | ---- |
| VK3968 | BIARRITZ 9 | 60 | 12384 |
| VK6861 | MONACO 9 | 60 | 16630 |
| VK7300 | MONACO 9 | 60 | 18098 |
| VK7883 | MONACO 9 | 60 | 19013 |
| VK9627 | MONACO 9 | 60 | ---- |
| VL4555 | MARCH SPL 9 | 60 | 19581 |
| VL4986 | MONACO 9 | 60 | ---- |
| VL7836 | MERLIN 9 | 66M | ---- |
| VMC003-AUS | BROOKLANDS 9 | 80 | -- |
| VM1558 | TOURER 9 | 60 | ---- |
| VM3049 | TOURER 9 | 60 | 1541 |
| VM4913 | BROOKLANDS 9 | 80 | 26 |
| VM5742 | MONACO 9 | 60 | 3038 |
| VM7451 | MONACO 9 | 60 | 3667 |
| VM9134 | TOURER 9 | 60 | 2088 |
| VN3061 | MONACO 9 | 60 | ---- |
| VN4893 | MONACO 9 | 60 | 22113 |
| VN5665 | FALCON 1½ | 27F | ---- |
| VN9041 | KESTREL 1½ | 22T | ---- |
| VN9108 | ADELPHI 1½ | 26A | ---- |
| VN9185 | MERLIN 9 | 66M | ---- |
| VOL500 | TOURER 9 | 60 | ---- |
| VO1588 | 2 SEATER 9 | 60 | 4857 |
| VO6888 | HOYAL COUPE 9 | 60 | 14533 |
| VO7685 | TOURER 9 | 60 | 16982 |
| VO8445 | MONACO 9 | 60 | ---- |
| VO8888 | ALPINE TR 14/6 | 14L | 1066 |
| VP2373 | 2 SEATER 9 | 60 | 2222 |
| VP8554 | TOURER 9 | 60 | 4784 |
| VR4077 | TOURER 9 | 60 | 14095 |
| VR7401 | TOURER 9 | 60 | 9722 |
| VS 970 | ALPINE SAL 14/6 | 14L | ---- |
| VS2274 | MONACO 9 | 60 | ---- |
| VS2386 | LYNX 9 | 60 | 22125 |
| VS2457 | KESTREL 12/6 | 44T | ---- |
| VT2188 | 2 SEATER 9 | 60 | ---- |
| VT3382 | TOURER 9 | 60 | ---- |
| VT4915 | MONACO 9 | 60 | ---- |
| VU 309 | TOURER 9 | 60 | 10422 |
| VU 362 | TOURER 9 | 60 | 10874 |
| VU5132 | TOURER 9 | 60 | 14027 |
| VU5916 | MONACO 9 | 60 | 14026 |
| VU7634 | GAMECOCK 9 | 60 | 15673 |
| VU8336 | GAMECOCK 9 | 60 | ---- |
| VU8732 | ALPINE SAL 14/6 | 14L | 843 |
| VU8733 | GAMECOCK 9 | 60 | 16172 |
| VU9364 | GAMECOCK 9 | 60 | ---- |
| VV1477 | GAMECOCK 9 | 60 | ---- |
| VV1727 | MARCH SPL 9 | 60 | ---- |
| VV1882 | FALCON 9 | 60 | 21370 |
| VV2520 | KESTREL 12/6 | 44T | ---- |
| VV5720 | KESTREL 1½ | 27K | ---- |
| VV5722 | FALCON 1½ | 22T | 735 |
| VV5750 | KESTREL 1½ | 22T | ---- |
| VV6509 | MONACO 9 | S67Z | ---- |
| VV7021 | ADELPHI 16/4 | 38AX | ---- |
| VW 629 | TOURER 9 | 60 | 6938 |
| VW5132 | MONACO 9 | 60 | 14072 |
| VX3538 | CHASSIS 9 | 60 | 8038 |
| VX4869 | MONACO 9 | 60 | 7359 |
| VX6594 | MONACO 9 | 60 | 10725 |
| VX9166 | BIARRITZ 9 | 60 | ---- |
| VY1039 | TOURER 9 | 60 | ---- |
| VY3983 | MONACO 9 | 60 | ---- |
| VY4240 | KESTREL 12/6 | 44T | 434 |
| VY4254 | MONACO 9 | 60 | ---- |
| VY4274 | MONACO 9 | 60 | 21496 |
| VY5630 | KESTREL 1½ | 26K | ---- |
| VY6804 | MENTONE 12/6 | 44T | 1881 |
| VY7838 | MERLIN 9 | 66M | ---- |
| VY8728 | MERLIN 9 | 66M | 2042 |
| VY9706 | ADELPHI 1½ | 27A | ---- |
| W 258 | DEAUVILLE 14/6 | 14 | ---- |
| W 6509 | MONACO 9 | S67Z | ---- |
| WAR976 | MONACO 9 | S67Z | ---- |
| WD2245 | TOURER 9 | 60 | ---- |
| WD3467 | GAMECOCK 9 | 60 | ---- |
| WD3502 | GAMECOCK 9 | 60 | 16564 |
| WD3648 | BROOKLANDS 9 | 80 | -- |
| WD4135 | GAMECOCK 9 | 60 | ---- |
| WD4483 | MONACO 9 | 60 | ---- |
| WD4943 | LYNX 9 | 60 | ---- |
| WD6949 | KESTREL 14/6 | 44T | 1961 |
| WD8853 | IMP 9 | 60 | ---- |
| WE5733 | MONACO 9 | 60 | 6259 |
| WF3735 | MONACO 9 | 60 | 11208 |
| WF5354 | LINCOCK 9 | 60 | ---- |
| WF6491 | LINCOCK 9 | 60 | ---- |
| WF6686 | KESTREL 9 | 60 | ---- |
| WF7464 | KESTREL 1½ | 27K | ---- |
| WF7732 | KESTREL 9 | 60 | ---- |
| WF8585 | ADELPHI 1½ | 26A | ---- |
| WF8713 | KESTREL 9 | S66K | 1438 |
| WF8743 | MERLIN 9 | 66M | ---- |
| WF9392 | MONACO 9 | S67Z | ---- |
| WF9594 | ADELPHI 15/6 | 4?A | ---- |
| WF9790 | FALCON 1½ | 27F | 6084 |
| WG2488 | LYNX 9 | 60 | 23512 |
| WG3688 | IMP 9 | 60 | ---- |
| WG4379 | KESTREL 9 | S66K | 184 |
| WG5843 | MONACO 9 | S67Z | ---- |
| WG5937 | MERLIN 9 | 66M | 2090 |
| WG6006 | MERLIN 9 | 67M | ---- |
| WG6646 | TRG SALOON 9 | S67CX | 3148 |
| WH5650 | KESTREL 9 | 60 | ---- |
| WH7196 | MERLIN 9 | 66M | ---- |
| WH7738 | MONACO 9 | 60 | ---- |
| WH8170 | ADELPHI 1½ | 26A | ---- |
| WJ 935 | MONACO 9 | 60 | 13037 |
| WJ 971 | MONACO 9 | 60 | 12854 |
| WJ 975 | MONACO 9 | 60 | ---- |
| WJ6717 | LYNX 9 | 60 | ---- |
| WJ6895 | FALCON 1½ | 26F | 2546 |
| WK3181 | TOURER 9 | 60 | 41 |
| WK4321 | TOURER 9 | 60 | ---- |
| WK4894 | TOURER 9 | 60 | ---- |
| WK6547 | TOURER 9 | 60 | 1633 |
| WK6652 | BROOKLANDS 9 | 80 | 19 |
| WK7162* | BROOKLANDS 9 | 60/ | 4 |
| WK9030 | BROOKLANDS 9 | 80 | -- |
| WL4707 | TOURER 9 | 60 | ---- |
| WL9117 | TOURER 9 | 60 | 8912 |
| WL9707 | MONACO 9 | 60 | 10140 |
| WMN946 | MERLIN 1½ | 26M | 4497 |
| WM7248 | GAMECOCK 9 | 60 | 15810 |
| WM7738 | MONACO 9 | 60 | 17518 |
| WM8584 | MONACO 9 | 60 | 20715 |
| WM9033 | MONACO 9 | 60 | ---- |
| WN5519 | ALPINE SAL 14/6 | 44T | ---- |
| WN7872 | KESTREL 9 | 60 | 27375 |
| WN8075 | FALCON 1½ | -- | ---- |
| WN8201 | FALCON 1½ | 22T | 1639 |
| WN9586 | MERLIN 1½ | 26M | ---- |
| WO4564 | MONACO 9 | 60 | 10622 |
| WP 444 | KESTREL 9 | 60 | 13977 |
| WP1400 | MONACO 9 | 60 | ---- |
| WP1500 | GAMECOCK 9 | 60 | 16242 |
| WP1589 | GAMECOCK 9 | 60 | 16391 |
| WP2372 | TOURER 9 | 60 | ---- |
| WP2996 | MONACO 9 | 60 | 19253 |
| WP4012 | MONACO 9 | 60 | ---- |
| WP4110 | LYNX 12/6 | 44T | 716 |
| WP4573 | KESTREL 12/6 | 44T | 1138 |
| WP5274 | MONACO 9 | 60 | ---- |
| WP6200 | KESTREL 9 | 60 | 25869 |
| WP6226 | KESTREL 14/6 | 44T | 1666 |
| WP7742 | KESTREL 9 | 60 | ---- |
| WP9114 | KESTREL 1½ | 22T | ---- |
| WP9199 | KESTREL 1½ | 22T | ---- |
| WP9727 | FALCON 1½ | 22T | ---- |
| WRU 43 | TOURER 9 | 60 | 11416 |
| WS 914 | LYNX 9 | 60 | 25758 |
| WS2869 | FALCON 1½ | 22T | ---- |
| WS3008 | MONACO 9 | 60 | ---- |
| WS4558 | KESTREL 9 | 60 | ---- |
| WS4933 | KESTREL 1½ | 22T | ---- |
| WS6214 | KESTREL 9 | S66K | 479 |
| WS6253 | FALCON 1½ | 22T | ---- |
| WS6660 | KESTREL 9 | 60 | ---- |
| WS6767 | KESTREL 15/6 | 46K | ---- |
| WS7076 | ADELPHI 1½ | 26A | 4127 |
| WS8094 | ADELPHI 1½ | 26A | ---- |
| WS9002 | ADELPHI 1½ | 26A | ---- |
| WS9169 | ADELPHI 1½ | 26A | ---- |
| WUS845 | MENTONE 12/6 | 44T | ---- |
| WV4852 | LYNX 9 | 60 | ---- |
| WV5805 | MONACO 9 | 60 | ---- |
| WV5844 | KESTREL 9 | 60 | 24716 |
| WV6621 | FALCON 15/6 | 44T | 2424 |
| WV9545 | MERLIN 9 | 66M | ---- |
| WW6292 | MONACO 9 | 60 | ---- |
| WW9162 | BIARRITZ 9 | 60 | 4265 |
| WX2754 | TOURER 9 | 60 | 8240 |
| WY7800 | TOURER 9 | 60 | 9588 |
| XG1626 | MONACO 9 | 60 | ---- |
| XG3423-NL | KESTREL 9 | 60 | 25136 |
| XG3663 | FALCON 1½ | 26F | 2858 |
| XI2007-IRL | STD TOURER 10.8 | | 1124 |
| XJ 78 | MONACO 9 | 60 | ---- |
| XJ 897 | MONACO 9 | 60 | 17276 |
| XJ1868 | MONACO 9 | 60 | 15610 |
| XJ2576 | GAMECOCK 9 | 60 | ---- |
| XJ2953 | TOURER 9 | 60 | ---- |
| XJ3751 | WD TOURER 9 | 60 | ---- |
| XJ3885 | MONACO 9 | 60 | 19835 |
| XJ4284 | ARNOLD COUPE 9 | 60 | 19107 |
| XJ4905 | MONACO 9 | 60 | ---- |
| XJ5808 | LYNX 9 | 60 | 20840 |
| XJ8151 | LYNX 9 | 60 | 21746 |
| XJ9500 | LYNX 9 | 60 | ---- |
| XPW335-AUS | KESTREL 1½ | 22T | ---- |

| REG NUMBER | MODEL | CHASSIS NO | |
|---|---|---|---|
| XP5306 | COUPE 10.8 | C | 1243 |
| XU 4 | KESTREL 6 | 44T | ---- |
| XV1334 | MONACO 9 | 60 | ---- |
| XV1407 | TOURER 9 | 60 | 2630 |
| XV3488 | TOURER 9 | 60 | 2449 |
| XV7681 | 2 SEATER 9 | 60 | ---- |
| XW7559 | 4ST SPORTS 10.8 | | ---- |
| XW8032 | 4/5 TOURER 11.9 | 69 | ---- |
| XY8388 | TOURER 9 | 60 | ---- |
| Y 9747 | GAMECOCK 9 | 60 | ---- |
| YC4373 | MONACO 9 | 60 | 2546 |
| YC6787 | 2 SEATER 9 | 60 | 14450 |
| YC7391ZA | SAN REMO 9 | 60 | 6616 |
| YC7870 | 2 SEATER 9 | 60 | 7673 |
| YD1392 | MONACO 9 | 60 | ---- |
| YD3964 | MONACO 9 | 60 | 15992 |
| YD4761 | GAMECOCK 9 | 60 | 17556 |
| YD5609 | MONACO 9 | 60 | 19267 |
| YD8274 | MONACO 9 | 60 | 22749 |
| YD9076 | KESTREL 14/6 | 44T | 1943 |
| YD9901 | MONACO 9 | 60 | ---- |
| YE9707 | LYNX 12/6 | 44T | 1657 |
| YF5943 | TOURER 10.8 | T | ---- |
| YF6321 | AMIL/RILEY 9 | | ---- |
| YG 797 | GAMECOCK 9 | 60 | 16297 |
| YG1146 | ASCOT 9 | 60 | 17946 |
| YG1463 | TOURER 9 | 60 | ---- |
| YG2496 | MONACO 9 | 60 | ---- |
| YG3383 | LYNX 9 | 60 | ---- |
| YG3919 | KESTREL 6 | 44T | ---- |
| YG5522 | MONACO 9 | 60 | 22798 |

| REG NUMBER | MODEL | CHASSIS NO. | |
|---|---|---|---|
| YH 455 | SPL TOURER 11.9 | 69 | 1581 |
| YJ1321 | MONACO 9 | 60 | ---- |
| YJ2969 | FALCON 1½ | 26F | ---- |
| YJ3098 | ADELPHI 1½ | 26A | ---- |
| YJ5130 | ADELPHI 1½ | 27A | 7041 |
| YO9253 | TOURER 11.9 | 69 | ---- |
| YS 216 | FALCON 1½ | 22T | ---- |
| YS 344 | MONACO 9 | 60 | ---- |
| YS1412 | KESTREL 1½ | 22T | 1519 |
| YS1534 | KESTREL 9 | 60 | ---- |
| YS2692 | MONACO 9 | 60 | 27512 |
| YS3157 | KESTREL 1½ | 22T | ---- |
| YS4764 | ADELPHI 1½ | 26A | ---- |
| YS5021 | MERLIN 9 | 66M | 670 |
| YS6164 | KESTREL 1½ | 26K | 3596 |
| YS6394 | MERLIN 9 | 66M | 1156 |
| YS7561 | KESTREL 1½ | 26K | ---- |
| YS7816 | KESTREL 9 | S66K | 1419 |
| YU4031 | 9 HP CAR | ---- / | 1112 |
| YW6311 | TOURER 9 | 60 | 1455 |
| YW8926 | TOURER 9 | 60 | ---- |
| YW9445 | TOURER 9 | 60 | ---- |
| YX8068 | 2 SEATER 9 | 60 | 2741 |
| YY 747 | GAMECOCK 9 | 60 | 16790 |
| YY1485 | GAMECOCK 9 | 60 | ---- |
| YY3962 | GAMECOCK 9 | 60 | 16529 |
| YY3968 | MONACO 9 | 60 | 19211 |
| YY5037 | MONACO 9 | 60 | ---- |
| YY7237 | TOURER 9 | 60 | ---- |
| YY7668 | MARCH SPL 9 | 60 | 19111 |
| YY8923 | MONACO 9 | 60 | 19608 |

| REG NUMBER | MODEL | CHASSIS NO. | |
|---|---|---|---|
| Z 2776-CL | LYNX 1½ | 27L | ---- |
| Z 5397-IRL | MONACO 9 | 60 | 23125 |
| Z 6603-IRL | FALCON 1½ | 26F | 3322 |
| Z 6880-IRL | ADELPHI 1½ | 26A | 4624 |
| ZA 916-IRL | MONACO 9 | 60 | ---- |
| ZA1007-IRL | MONACO 9 | 60 | ---- |
| ZA1158-IRL | KESTREL 9 | 60 | ---- |
| ZA2960-IRL | KESTREL 9 | 60 | 25002 |
| ZC1979-IRL | FALCON 1½ | 26F | ---- |
| ZI8896-IRL | MONACO 9 | 60 | ---- |
| Z65508-NZ | MONACO 9 | 60 | ---- |
| 0 11-AUS | ULSTER IMP 9 | 60 | ---- |
| 0 12-AUS | ADELPHI 15/6 | 47A | ---- |
| 0 16-AUS | TOURER 9 | 60 | ---- |
| 0 18-AUS | LINCOCK 9 | 60 | ---- |
| 0 23-AUS | FALCON 1½ | 27F | ---- |
| 0241EJ-NL | MONACO 9 | 60 | 9127 |
| 1 YPD | KESTREL 16/4 | 38KX | ---- |
| 100634-AUS | KESTREL 1½ | 27K | 6487 |
| 112923-NZ | ADELPHI 1½ | 28A | ---- |
| 11969 -M | TOURER 9 | 60 | 5800 |
| 11-940-AUS | FALCON 1½ | 27F | ---- |
| 134787-AUS | TOURER 9 | 60 | 22524 |
| 141158-AUS | TOURER 9 | 60 | ---- |
| 145529-AUS | KESTREL 1½ | 26K | 3956 |
| 169784-NZ | KESTREL 1½ | 27K | ---- |
| 174165-AUS | LYNX 9 | 60 | 21660 |
| 215820-AUS | FALCON 1½ | 22T | ---- |
| 216913-NZ | KESTREL 1½ | 27K | 5834 |
| 225488-AUS | 4ST SPORTS 10.8 | - | ---- |
| 262793-ZA | MONACO 9 | 60 | ---- |

| REG NUMBER | MODEL | CHASSIS NO | |
|---|---|---|---|
| 269MHX | MERLIN 1½ | 27M | ---- |
| 303333-NZ | TOURER 9 | 60 | ---- |
| 316493-NZ | KESTREL 16/4 | 38KX | ---- |
| 34 IMP | IMP 9 | 60 | 25340 |
| 373221-AUS | MONACO 9 | 60 | ---- |
| 400MPA | IMP 9 | 60 | ---- |
| 429980 | FALCON 9 | 60 | ---- |
| 447827-NZ | MONACO 9 | 60 | ---- |
| 471 U3-B | KESTREL 1½ | 28K | 7458 |
| 49UA41-NL | FALCON 1½ | 22T | ---- |
| 496383 | LYNX 9 | 60 | ---- |
| 5 DOR | 2¼ HP TRICYCLE | ---- / | ---- |
| 512JTU-S | IMP 9 | 60 | 27682 |
| 541437-NZ | KESTREL 1½ | 22T | 845 |
| 64 LMB | MONACO 9 | 60 | 10109 |
| 683756-NZ | MONACO 9 | 60 | 19213 |
| 712EVE | VICTOR 1½ | 28VX | 7615 |
| 781YYC | KESTREL 1½ | 22T | ---- |
| 79-431 | MONACO 9 | 60 | ---- |
| 80 138-AUS | KESTREL 9 | 60 | 22467 |
| 800257-NZ | TOURER 10.8 | C | 938 |
| 8344WI | SPRITE 1½ | | ---- |
| 8537BR-NL | ADELPHI 1½ | 26A | ---- |
| 8877 U | KESTREL SPR 1½ | SS28K | 7295 |
| 89 704-NZ | KESTREL 1½ | 27K | ---- |
| 949CMD | LINCOCK 12/6 | 44T | ---- |
| 966DMG | MERLIN 9 | 66M | 2078 |
| 996NOD | LINCOCK 9 | 60 | ---- |
| ---006-AUS | KESTREL 1½ | 27K | 7078 |
| ---019-AUS | MERLIN 1½ | 26M | 4295 |

# Known Rileys in Chassis Number Sequence

Like its predecessor, Appendix 3 seeks to list known Rileys. Also as in the case of Appendix 2, this does not pretend to be a total list of all surviving Rileys. Indeed it cannot be that because there are less cars in this list than in Appendix 2, simply because less chassis numbers are known than registration numbers. However, it is the result of research into a number of sources, including information provided by members of the Riley Register, people's research into individual models, a search for Factory-registered cars and the information provided by a number of casual observers of this work, who happened to know of particular Rileys they or their relatives and friends had owned. For ease of reference, the list is presented in model groups by age priority. So, logically, the pre-1914 vehicles are listed first, followed by the Side-valve models, then the Nines, the Sixes, the $1\frac{1}{2}$ Litre 12/4s, the 8–90s, the Big Fours and finally the Autovias. If a reader finds that his car is not listed, it will either be because it was not known or because insufficient information was known about it. Cars which today are home-built specials are listed, if possible, as the types they were when built. Pre-war specials are listed as such.

It will be seen that the list shows a prefix and the basic number. To locate a particular car simply look for the complete number, but remember that the list is in chassis series sequence, so a 1936 $1\frac{1}{2}$ Litre Lynx-Sprite built immediately after a Kestrel will follow it in the list; thus 26K 3000 would be followed by SS26L 3001. Again, Model Years can be identified by reference to Appendix 1. It may be noticed that occasional chassis numbers can reflect two registration numbers: this is either because a vehicle will have been re-registered at some time and the later number included as well as the original, or because there are two claimants to a given chassis number and evidence is not available to disprove one or the other.

**PRE - 1914 MODELS (SINGLE CYLINDER AND V - TWIN ENGINED VEHICLES.**

| CH/ENG. NO. | REG NUMBER | MODEL |
|---|---|---|
| ---- | ---   5 DDR | 2¾ HP TRICYCLE |
| ---- | 112 H 3714 | 3 HP FORECAR |
| 862 | 122 D 1894 | TRI-CAR |
| ---- | 394 DU 458* | 4½ HP FORECAR |
| ---- | 416 BW 36 | 4½ HP FORECAR |
| 2035 | 434 AU5536 | 3½ HP M/CYCLE |
| ---- | 564 LN2637-USA | 6 HP TRI-CAR |
| ---- | 578 E28402-IRL | 9 HP TRI-CAR |
| ---- | 914 BP 19 | 9 HP TRI-CAR |
| ---- | 1058 AR  3 | 9 HP CAR |
| ---- | 1112 YU4031 | 9 HP CAR |
| ---- | 1324 LB4612 | 9 HP TRI-CAR |
| ---- | 1374 T 1915 | 12/18 HP SWB CAR |
| ---- | 1478 NS 105 | 12/18 HP SWB CAR |
| ---- | 2018 AB1390 | 10 HP 2 SEATER |
| ---- | 2859 BY1963 | 10 HP 2 SEATER |

**10.8HP (ELEVEN-40) AND 11.9 (TWELVE) SIDE - VALVE MODELS.**

| | CHASSIS NO. | REG NUMBER | MODEL |
|---|---|---|---|
| C | 826 | TC1183 | 4ST COUPE 10.8 |
| | 850 | BK6844 | 2DR TOURER 10.8 |
| | 938 | BOO257-NZ | WENTWORTH 10.8 |
| | 1105 | NH5575 | TOURER 10.8 |
| C | 1124 | X12007-IRL | STD TOURER 10.8 |
| | 1242 | PM2965 | COUPE 10.8 |
| C | 1243 | XP5306 | COUPE 10.8 |
| C | 1404 | HP6433* | A-W COUPE 10.8 |
| C | 2116A | RW 104* | SWB SPORTS 10.8 |
| C | 2339 | HP9679* | COUPE 10.8 |
| | 3868 | TY 225 | 2D TOURER 10.8 |
| | 4696 | NR -S | 2S REDWING 10.8 |
| S | 101X | NR | 11/50/65 SPTS 4 |
| | 285 | SE2386 | 4D COACH 11.9 |
| 69 | 846 | PR7845 | WENTWORTH 11.9 |
| | 966 | NR-AUS | TOURER 11.9 |
| 69 | 1326 | NF2507 | SPL TOURER 11.9 |
| 69 | 1482 | NF8905 | SPL TOURER 11.9 |
| 69 | 1581 | YH 455 | SPL TOURER 11.9 |
| 69 | 2248 | FL6839 | WENTWORTH 11.9 |
| 69 | 3479 | RP 925 | CHATSWORTH 11.9 |

**9HP MODELS - ALL YEARS.**

| | CHASSIS NO. | REG NUMBER | MODEL |
|---|---|---|---|
| 60 | 41 | NH9595 | TOURER 9 |
| 60 | 41 | WK3181 | TOURER 9 |
| 60 | 116 | KO7735 | TOURER 9 |
| 60 | 259 | WE5733 | MONACO 9 |
| 60 | 513 | OX7999 | TOURER 9 |
| 60 | 698 | RX1656 | COUPE 9 |
| 60 | 703 | PH7546 | TOURER 9 |
| 60 | 824 | PH7527 | TOURER 9 |

| | CHASSIS NO. | REG NUMBER | MODEL |
|---|---|---|---|
| 60 | 901 | UT2535 | MONACO 9 |
| 60 | 918 | PH8195 | 2 SEATER 9 |
| 60 | 950 | EF3776 | 2 SEATER 9 |
| 60 | 1288 | KO9870 | MONACO 9 |
| 60 | 1455 | YW6311 | TOURER 9 |
| 60 | 1541 | VM3049 | TOURER 9 |
| 60 | 1633 | WK6547 | TOURER 9 |
| 60 | 1732 | KD5603 | TOURER 9 |
| 60 | 1797 | KD2817 | MONACO 9 |
| 60 | 1804 | TU9039 | BIARRITZ 9 |
| 60 | 1845 | KV2197 | TOURER 9 |
| 60 | 2048 | RP6334 | MONACO 9 |
| 60 | 2088 | VM9134 | TOURER 9 |
| 60 | 2222 | VP2373 | 2 SEATER 9 |
| 60 | 2449 | XV3488 | TOURER 9 |
| 60 | 2546 | YC4373 | MONACO 9 |
| 60 | 2599 | KX1272 | TOURER 9 |
| 60 | 2630 | XV1407 | 2 SEATER 9 |
| 60 | 2741 | YX8068 | 2 SEATER 9 |
| 60 | 2867 | UU8996 | 2 SEATER 9 |
| 60 | 2944 | KD3887 | TOURER 9 |
| 60 | 2966 | PG7598 | MONACO 9 |
| 60 | 3038 | VM5742 | TOURER 9 |
| 60 | 3074 | PK4420 | MONACO 9 |
| 60 | 3273 | SC5006 | MONACO 9 |
| 60 | 3553 | RX3565 | TOURER 9 |
| 60 | 3563 | VF4937 | TOURER 9 |
| 60 | 3667 | YM7451 | MONACO 9 |
| 60 | 3927 | UL5266 | MONACO 9 |
| 60 | 4033 | UL7459 | MONACO 9 |
| 60 | 4098 | PN3026 | 2 SEATER 9 |
| 60 | 4265 | WW9162 | BIARRITZ 9 |
| 60 | 4313 | UR2699 | TOURER 9 |
| 60 | 4331 | FL7669 | BIARRITZ 9 |
| 60 | 4784 | VP8554 | TOURER 9 |
| 60 | 4857 | VO1588 | 2 SEATER 9 |
| 60 | 4876 | UU1662 | BIARRITZ 9 |
| 60 | 5072 | EP4302 | TOURER 9 |
| 60 | 5213 | RU8857 | MONACO 9 |
| 60 | 5249 | UB9316 | MONACO 9 |
| 60 | 5354 | UU2994 | MONACO 9 |
| 60 | 5426 | EO4810 | MONACO 9 |
| 60 | 5464 | QF 282 | 2 SEATER 9 |
| 60 | 5647 | UU6913 | MONACO 9 |
| 60 | 5800 | PG1154 | TOURER 9 |
| 60 | 5800 | 11969 -M | |
| 60 | 5832 | UV1180 | TOURER 9 |
| 60 | 5884 | VB6148 | TOURER 9 |
| 60 | 5954 | MY 440 | MONACO 9 |
| 60 | 6063 | MY 804 | TOURER 9 |
| 60 | 6100 | OF3245 | MONACO 9 |
| 60 | 6259 | WE5733 | MONACO 9 |
| 60 | 6276 | CP7811 | TOURER 9 |
| 60 | 6283 | UR4211 | BIARRITZ 9 |
| 60 | 6294 | VE1701 | BEAVIS SPL 9 |
| 60 | 6533 | LJ5003 | MONACO 9 |
| 60 | 6590 | DF8549 | MONACO 9 |
| 60 | 6616 | YC7391 | SAN REMO 9 |

| | CHASSIS NO. | REG.NUMBER | MODEL |
|---|---|---|---|
| 60 | 6648 | SU0543-AUS | TOURER 9 |
| 60 | 6672 | UV6685 | 2 SEATER 9 |
| 60 | 6728 | BPX674 | MONACO 9 |
| 60 | 6771 | OW4427 | TOURER 9 |
| 60 | 6848 | PN4632 | TOURER 9 |
| 60 | 6938 | VW 629 | TOURER 9 |
| 60 | 6948 | KX3599 | TOURER 9 |
| 60 | 6951 | NH9599 | MONACO 9 |
| 60 | 6983 | UW 629 | MONACO 9 |
| 60 | 7012 | UW 649 | TOURER 9 |
| 60 | 7014 | PG3609 | TOURER 9 |
| 60 | 7043 | UW5374 | TOURER 9 |
| 60 | 7088 | OF4506 | MONACO 9 |
| 60 | 7203 | LG2825 | MONACO 9 |
| 60 | 7359 | VX4869 | TOURER 9 |
| 60 | 7372 | GJ4325 | MONACO 9 |
| 60 | 7383 | KH9918 | BIARRITZ 9 |
| 60 | 7392 | GF 738 | - - 9 |
| 60 | 7532 | TR7711 | TOURER 9 |
| 60 | 7673 | YC7870 | 2 SEATER 9 |
| 60 | 7819 | VG2367 | COUPE 9 |
| 60 | 7900 | DV3084 | TOURER 9 |
| 60 | 8015 | MY2203 | TOURER 9 |
| 60 | 8038 | VX3538 | CHASSIS 9 |
| 60 | 8096 | MY2447 | BIARRITZ 9 |
| 60 | 8240 | WX2754 | TOURER 9 |
| 60 | 8442 | MW6404 | TOURER 9 |
| 60 | 8511 | CM9338 | TOURER 9 |
| 60 | 8710 | LMC109 | MONACO 9 |
| 60 | 8805 | NR | GARDEN SPL 9 |
| 60 | 8912 | WL9117 | TOURER 9 |
| 60 | 9127 | O241EJ-NL | 2 SEATER 9 |
| 60 | 9407 | PO2113 | 2 SEATER 9 |
| 60 | 9450 | MG 437 | MONACO 9 |
| 60 | 9588 | WY7800 | TOURER 9 |
| 60 | 9718 | VC4415 | MONACO 9 |
| 60 | 9722 | VR7401 | TOURER 9 |
| 60 | 9905 | HJ9902 | MONACO 9 |
| 60 | 10109 | 64 LMB | WD TOURER 9 |
| 60 | 10140 | WL9707 | WD TOURER 9 |
| 60 | 10398 | JD 544 | 2 SEATER 9 |
| 60 | 10422 | VU 309 | TOURER 9 |
| 60 | 10463 | JN 316 | WD TOURER 9 |
| 60 | 10530 | FB8604 | BIARRITZ 9 |
| 60 | 10539 | OG3184 | TOURER 9 |
| 60 | 10554 | PL2924 | TOURER 9 |
| 60 | 10603 | DK6780 | MONACO 9 |
| 60 | 10622 | WO4564 | MONACO 9 |
| 60 | 10725 | VX6594 | MONACO 9 |
| 60 | 10798 | NR -ZA | MONACO 9 |
| 60 | 10874 | VU 362 | MONACO 9 |
| 60 | 10891 | GH5696 | MONACO 9 |
| 60 | 11070 | NR | TOURER 9 |
| 60 | 11079 | GN1297 | MONACO 9 |
| 60 | 11146 | KF3398 | MONACO 9 |
| 60 | 11167 | OG6497 | MONACO 9 |
| 60 | 11200 | LJ5003 | MONACO 9 |
| 60 | 11208 | KF9265 | MONACO 9 |

| | CHASSIS NO. | REG.NUMBER | MODEL |
|---|---|---|---|
| 60 | 11208 | WF3735 | MONACO 9 |
| 60 | 11263 | GK8825 | MONACO 9 |
| 60 | 11346 | DL7676 | MONACO 9 |
| 60 | 11387 | RG1700 | MONACO 9 |
| 60 | 11416 | WRU 43 | MONACO 9 |
| 60 | 11481 | ST6365 | TOURER 9 |
| 60 | 11508 | VC6782 | TOURER 9 |
| 60 | 11548 | OG8254 | MONACO 9 |
| 60 | 11594 | AUN169 | GAMECOCK 9 |
| 60 | 11679 | CV3788 | MONACO 9 |
| 60 | 11696 | UY9178 | MONACO 9 |
| 60 | 11717 | DR7872 | BIARRITZ 9 |
| 60 | 11834 | GN3198 | MONACO 9 |
| 60 | 11859 | VB9975 | MONACO 9 |
| 60 | 11987 | GO1413 | MONACO 9 |
| 60 | 11992 | PL6447 | MONACO 9 |
| 60 | 12159 | TS9053 | BIARRITZ 9 |
| 60 | 12280 | GG3558 | BIARRITZ 9 |
| 60 | 12384 | VK3968 | BIARRITZ 9 |
| 60 | 12490 | VE4849 | BIARRITZ 9 |
| 60 | 12504 | JO1605 | MONACO 9 |
| 60 | 12507 | PL5491 | MONACO 9 |
| 60 | 12854 | WJ 971 | MONACO 9 |
| 60 | 12966 | GO 276 | MONACO 9 |
| 60 | 12975 | KJ3453 | HOYAL COUPE 9 |
| 60 | 12996 | HX6175 | WD TOURER 9 |
| 60 | 13037 | WJ 935 | MONACO 9 |
| 60 | 13091 | VC8602 | BIARRITZ 9 |
| 60 | 13140 | GO2399 | BIARRITZ 9 |
| 60 | 13505 | GO8531 | MONACO 9 |
| 60 | 13552 | GOG830 | MONACO 9 |
| 60 | 13637 | TS9280 | BIARRITZ 9 |
| 60 | 13646 | DT3113 | MONACO 9 |
| 60 | 13675 | GO7267 | MONACO 9 |
| 60 | 13828 | TF6732 | MONACO 9 |
| 60 | 13974 | PJ2192 | KESTREL 9 |
| 60 | 13977 | WP 444 | MONACO 9 |
| 60 | 14026 | VU5916 | MONACO 9 |
| 60 | 14072 | VU5132 | MONACO 9 |
| 60 | 14073 | RV 845 | TOURER 9 |
| 60 | 14095 | VR4077 | MONACO 9 |
| 60 | 14129 | GP4682 | MONACO 9 |
| 60 | 14161 | GP7748 | MONACO 9 |
| 60 | 14170 | OV2933 | COUPE 9 |
| 60 | 14361 | GT3513 | ASCOT 9 |
| 60 | 14408 | HX6507 | 2 SEATER 9 |
| 60 | 14450 | YC6787 | 2 SEATER 9 |
| 60 | 14499 | GW8475 | TOURER 9 |
| 60 | 14533 | VO6888 | HOYAL COUPE 9 |
| 60 | 14534 | VC9859* | CONTNTL COUPE 9 |
| 60 | 14552 | AYE634 | WD TOURER 9 |
| 60 | 14562 | MY5431 | WD TOURER 9 |
| 60 | 15028 | VC9484 | TOURER 9 |
| 60 | 15034 | RV1250 | TOURER 9 |
| 60 | 15042 | AVC408* | BIARRITZ 9 |
| 60 | 15087 | JH 622 | MONACO 9 |
| 60 | 15156 | RM8270 | GAMECOCK 9 |

| CHASSIS NO. | REG.NUMBER | MODEL |
|---|---|---|
| 60 15190 | JA2125 | MONACO 9 |
| 60 15312 | OV5286 | GAMECOCK 9 |
| 60 15329 | KX7486 | MONACO 9 |
| 60 15360 | LJ4909 | MONACO 9 |
| 60 15402 | RB5343 | MONACO 9 |
| 60 15457 | UP3919 | MONACO 9 |
| 60 15536 | GW3220 | GAMECOCK 9 |
| 60 15538 | GT7855 | MONACO 9 |
| 60 15610 | XJ1868 | MONACO 9 |
| 60 15612 | GW 428 | MONACO 9 |
| 60 15673 | VU7634 | GAMECOCK 9 |
| 60 15746 | GW3805 | GAMECOCK 9 |
| 60 15787 | J15292-IRL | HOYAL COUPE 9 |
| 60 15799 | GG5796 | TOURER 9 |
| 60 15810 | WM7248 | GAMECOCK 9 |
| 60 15924 | GX1285 | GAMECOCK 9 |
| 60 15962 | GW8085 | MONACO 9 |
| 60 15979 | KV 246 | ASCOT 9 |
| 60 15986 | GX3497 | MONACO 9 |
| 60 15992 | YD3964 | MONACO 9 |
| 60 16022 | TF6898 | MONACO 9 |
| 60 16071 | GX3224 | MONACO 9 |
| 60 16101 | MV1844 | GAMECOCK 9 |
| 60 16123 | OD1357 | MONACO 9 |
| 60 16138 | DT3533 | GAMECOCK 9 |
| 60 16152 | HY3603 | GAMECOCK 9 |
| 60 16161 | AZ9153-IRL | GAMECOCK 9 |
| 60 16172 | VU8733 | GAMECOCK 9 |
| 60 16242 | WP1500 | MONACO 9 |
| 60 16243 | RX9753 | GAMECOCK 9 |
| 60 16245 | TY9253 | ASCOT 9 |
| 60 16268 | JN1741 | MONACO 9 |
| 60 16282 | GW7008 | GAMECOCK 9 |
| 60 16297 | JV 797 | GAMECOCK 9 |
| 60 16308 | JV1105 | GAMECOCK 9 |
| 60 16324 | VC9116 | GAMECOCK 9 |
| 60 16325 | GX2846 | GAMECOCK 9 |
| 60 16326 | CG 555 | GAMECOCK 9 |
| 60 16391 | WP1589 | GAMECOCK 9 |
| 60 16405 | RX9772 | GAMECOCK 9 |
| 60 16497 | PJ5073 | ASCOT 9 |
| 60 16522 | GW9646 | GAMECOCK 9 |
| 60 16529 | YY3962 | GAMECOCK 9 |
| 60 16534 | GX3997 | MONACO 9 |
| 60 16564 | WD3502 | GAMECOCK 9 |
| 60 16630 | VK6861 | MONACO 9 |
| 60 16675 | GW9630 | GAMECOCK 9 |
| 60 16688 | JV1171 | MONACO 9 |
| 60 16730 | NCV906 | GAMECOCK 9 |
| 60 16735 | GX 17 | GAMECOCK 9 |
| 60 16779 | AG7384 | GAMECOCK 9 |
| 60 16790 | YW 747 | GAMECOCK 9 |
| 60 16808 | UG 511 | TOURER 9 |
| 60 16811 | OY2596 | MONACO 9 |
| 60 16837 | JB 147 | MONACO 9 |
| 60 16863 | PJ4280 | TOURER 9 |
| 60 16891 | GW8097 | TOURER 9 |
| 60 16935 | LS2869 | TOURER 9 |
| 60 16982 | V07685 | TOURER 9 |
| 60 17131 | GX9572 | GAMECOCK 9 |
| 60 17163 | GW6221 | MONACO 9 |
| 60 17226 | KX8735 | GAMECOCK 9 |
| 60 17276 | XJ 897 | MONACO 9 |
| 60 17302 | NR | MONACO 9 |
| 60 17309 | NG2893 | LYNX 9 |
| 60 17349 | P06860 | GAMECOCK 9 |
| 60 17460 | R86330 | MONACO 9 |
| 60 17508 | PJ5410 | MONACO 9 |
| 60 17518 | WM7738 | MONACO 9 |
| 60 17546 | VE7627 | HOYAL COUPE 9 |
| 60 17556 | YD4761 | GAMECOCK 9 |
| 60 17571 | GG8249 | TOURER 9 |
| 60 17579 | PJ5671 | GAMECOCK 9 |
| 60 17583 | GY 257 | GAMECOCK 9 |
| 60 17596 | HY6571 | MONACO 9 |
| 60 17657 | JB 444 | MONACO 9 |
| 60 17687 | KX8685 | GAMECOCK 9 |
| 60 17688 | JU 51 | MONACO 9 |
| 60 17749 | GY1204 | MONACO 9 |
| 60 17834 | KV2329 | MONACO 9 |
| 60 17867 | OJ 891 | GAMECOCK 9 |
| 60 17882 | EB9736 | MONACO 9 |
| 60 17912 | JU 840 | GAMECOCK 9 |
| 60 17946 | YG1146 | ASCOT 9 |
| 60 17949 | GS3273 | MONACO 9 |
| 60 17960 | GY8605 | GAMECOCK 9 |
| 60 18004 | JN2271 | MONACO 9 |
| 60 18036 | KG1387 | GAMECOCK 9 |
| 60 18048 | DK8078 | MONACO 9 |
| 60 18058 | SY1729 | GAMECOCK 9 |
| 60 18098 | VK7300 | GAMECOCK 9 |
| 60 18151 | AV5437 | MONACO 9 |
| 60 18163 | JF3589 | GAMECOCK 9 |
| 60 18176 | DS1769 | LINCOCK 9 |
| 60 18257 | GX9919 | TOURER 9 |
| 60 19006 | AGY515 | MARCH SPL 9 |
| 60 19013 | VK7883 | MONACO 9 |
| 60 19061 | MS1932 | MARCH SPL 9 |
| 60 19101 | VJ4915 | MONACO 9 |
| 60 19107 | XJ4284 | ARNOLD COUPE 9 |
| 60 19108 | GG8810 | LYNX 9 |
| 60 19111 | YY7668 | MARCH SPL 9 |
| 60 19114 | YY7287 | MONACO 9 |
| 60 19127 | ALB608 | MONACO 9 |
| 60 19206 | JJ3350 | - - 9 |
| 60 19211 | YY3968 | MONACO 9 |
| 60 19213 | 683756-NZ | MONACO 9 |
| 60 19220 | TY9968 | MONACO 9 |
| 60 19225 | GG9395 | GAMECOCK 9 |
| 60 19253 | WP2996 | MONACO 9 |
| 60 19267 | YD5609 | MONACO 9 |
| 60 19289 | WY8910 | MONACO 9 |
| 60 19293 | JH3589 | LYNX 9 |
| 60 19307 | JJ4244 | MARCH SPL 9 |
| 60 19308 | VJ5515 | MARCH SPL 9 |
| 60 19362 | NR-AUS | TOURER 9 |
| 60 19377 | RJ7993 | - - 9 |
| 60 19394 | APN522 | LYNX 9 |
| 60 19430 | KY3498* | MARCH SPL 9 |
| 60 19463 | TF 9740 | TOURER 9 |
| 60 19478 | OJ1320 | MARCH SPL 9 |
| 60 19557 | JT1105 | MONACO 9 |
| 60 19567 | JJ 919 | MARCH SPL 9 |
| 60 19571 | OY4112 | MARCH SPL 9 |
| 60 19578 | OD4481 | MARCH SPL 9 |
| 60 19581 | VL4555 | MONACO 9 |
| 60 19608 | YY8923 | MONACO 9 |
| 60 19626 | FK5428 | MONACO 9 |
| 60 19807 | J08314 | MONACO 9 |
| 60 19812 | FT2835 | MONACO 9 |
| 60 19835 | X33885 | MONACO 9 |
| 60 19845 | APA273 | MONACO 9 |
| 60 19846 | AHX 73 | MONACO 9 |
| 60 19923 | JJ 813 | MONACO 9 |
| 60 19925 | NJ 495 | MONACO 9 |
| 60 19928 | LJ6719 | MONACO 9 |
| 60 19961 | CG3028 | MONACO 9 |
| 60 20012 | VD2243 | MONACO 9 |
| 60 20064 | NR-SA | LYNX 9 |
| 60 20151 | KV3621 | LYNX 9 |
| 60 20167 | JJ1865 | MONACO 9 |
| 60 20168 | AKJ710 | LYNX 9 |
| 60 20169 | AGJ 45 | LYNX 9 |
| 60 20170 | TV7057 | LINCOCK 9 |
| 60 20197 | 039583-S | MONACO 9 |
| 60 20221 | JJ4166 | ASCOT 9 |
| 60 20251 | OY4441 | LYNX 9 |
| 60 20254 | APB231 | MONACO 9 |
| 60 20255 | P06844 | LYNX 9 |
| 60 20257 | LJ7010 | MONACO 9 |
| 60 20297 | AG8512 | MONACO 9 |
| 60 20324 | AHX490 | - - 9 |
| 60 20349 | EK9974 | KESTREL 9 |
| 60 20392 | AGN256 | MONACO 9 |
| 60 20396 | TJ 419 | LYNX 9 |
| 60 20402 | APB442 | MONACO 9 |
| 60 20422 | JJ9272 | MONACO 9 |
| 60 20426 | FW3369 | MONACO 9 |
| 60 20428 | AWK713* | LYNX 9 |
| 60 20484 | JJ2100 | MONACO 9 |
| 60 20557 | JH3905 | MONACO 9 |
| 60 20569 | TJ1567 | LYNX 9 |
| 60 20571 | ALE 99 | MONACO 9 |
| 60 20587 | CG3691 | MONACO 9 |
| 60 20592 | OD4814 | LINCOCK 9 |
| 60 20653 | AEY388 | MONACO 9 |
| 60 20715 | WM8584 | MONACO 9 |
| 60 20840 | X35808 | MONACO 9 |
| 60 20841 | APC629 | MONACO 9 |
| 60 20843 | AGJ528 | MONACO 9 |
| 60 20843 | AJ6528 | LYNX 9 |
| 60 20862 | JJ3563 | MONACO 9 |
| 60 20866 | FH8118 | MONACO 9 |
| 60 20880 | APC436 | ASCOT 9 |
| 60 20892 | APG728 | LYNX 9 |
| 60 20918 | JM 641 | MONACO 9 |
| 60 20943 | 0Y4911 | LYNX 9 |
| 60 20948 | FK5534 | MARCH SPL 9 |
| 60 21010 | KX9892 | LYNX 9 |
| 60 21035 | APU 54 | MONACO 9 |
| 60 21046 | J.J8150 | LINCOCK 9 |
| 60 21070 | AKK637 | LYNX 9 |
| 60 21126 | RH6857 | MONACO 9 |
| 60 21128 | AMA 70 | LYNX 9 |
| 60 21164 | 0Y5847 | LINCOCK 9 |
| 60 21218 | AGF801 | LINCOCK 9 |
| 60 21245 | ALM909 | MONACO 9 |
| 60 21271 | JH4456 | ASCOT 9 |
| 60 21273 | AGN257 | MONACO 9 |
| 60 21282 | ANB251 | MONACO 9 |
| 60 21289 | JU2273 | LYNX 9 |
| 60 21295 | US1514 | MONACO 9 |
| 60 21300 | APF531 | MONACO 9 |
| 60 21336 | UG4139 | MONACO 9 |
| 60 21347 | BPC641 | LINCOCK 9 |
| 60 21351 | ALX170 | MONACO 9 |
| 60 21363 | ALU876 | MONACO 9 |
| 60 21365 | NR-SA | MONACO 9 |
| 60 21370 | VV1882 | FALCON 9 |
| 60 21394 | TJ1332 | LYNX 9 |
| 60 21395 | 0Y5541 | LYNX 9 |
| 60 21447 | 0W3162 | MONACO 9 |
| 60 21479 | EJ3653 | MONACO 9 |
| 60 21496 | VY4274 | MONACO 9 |
| 60 21501 | MW3040 | LYNX 9 |
| 60 21502 | TJ1298 | FALCON 9 |
| 60 21526 | UN66779 | TRINITY 9 |
| 60 21535 | AMA202 | MONACO 9 |
| 60 21541 | AME790 | MONACO 9 |
| 60 21562 | ARF951 | MONACO 9 |
| 60 21575 | AL0569 | TRINITY 9 |
| 60 21699 | KV5212 | LYNX 9 |
| 60 21700 | ALF758 | LINCOCK 9 |
| 60 21707 | ABH431 | TOURER 9 |
| 60 21711 | ARF960 | MONACO 9 |
| 60 21726 | AGW268 | MONACO 9 |
| 60 21732 | AHK400 | MONACO 9 |
| 60 21746 | XJ8151 | LYNX 9 |
| 60 21749 | AGP253 | TRINITY 9 |
| 60 21762 | APG382 | LYNX 9 |
| 60 21776 | AGX947 | MONACO 9 |
| 60 21796 | KV5209 | MONACO 9 |
| 60 21817 | CZ3026 | MONACO 9 |
| 60 21821 | VE 9171 | MONACO 9 |
| 60 21825 | UG6031 | MONACO 9 |
| 60 21826 | ANO290 | MONACO 9 |
| 60 21889 | KS5901 | LYNX 9 |
| 60 21900 | VE8947 | MONACO 9 |
| 60 21979 | LJ8002 | MONACO 9 |
| 60 21988 | KV5485 | LYNX 9 |
| 60 21996 | ALA870 | MONACO 9 |
| 60 22001 | GR 187 | MONACO 9 |

| CHASSIS NO. | REG.NUMBER | MODEL |
|---|---|---|
| 60 22047 | AXF147 | LYNX 9 |
| 60 22050 | JU2641 | MONACO 9 |
| 60 22113 | VN4893 | MONACO 9 |
| 60 22117 | AMH874 | MONACO 9 |
| 60 22124 | VE9043 | LYNX 9 |
| 60 22125 | VS2386 | LYNX 9 |
| 60 22126 | EG 774 | FALCON 9 |
| 60 22156 | NR | LYNX 9 |
| 60 22193 | AMF818 | MONACO 9 |
| 60 22203 | ALU 5 | LINCOCK 9 |
| 60 22219 | LXH 83 | LYNX 9 |
| 60 22267 | KV6183 | KESTREL 9 |
| 60 22295 | RV4166 | MONACO 9 |
| 60 22310 | FHB367 | MONACO 9 |
| 60 22345 | AAE 32 | FALCON 9 |
| 60 22351 | TJ2612 | LYNX 9 |
| 60 22357 | AML713 | LYNX 9 |
| 60 22362 | APK586 | LYNX 9 |
| 60 22406 | NR-SA | LYNX 9 |
| 60 22415 | DG7407 | LYNX 9 |
| 60 22432 | MS7336 | LYNX 9 |
| 60 22436 | 0Y7992 | LINCOCK 9 |
| 60 22438 | AXM555 | LYNX 9 |
| 60 22439 | NJ2014 | LYNX 9 |
| 60 22440 | AAL804 | KESTREL 9 |
| 60 22443 | NR | LYNX 9 |
| 60 22447 | SN6094 | LYNX 9 |
| 60 22467 | 80 138-AUS | KESTREL 9 |
| 60 22484 | APJ564 | KESTREL 9 |
| 60 22503 | APK263 | KESTREL 9 |
| 60 22508 | FV3973 | KESTREL 9 |
| 60 22512 | AVL718 | KESTREL 9 |
| 60 22524 | 134787-AUS | TOURER 9 |
| 60 22686 | MJ2999 | KESTREL 9 |
| 60 22706 | VD3083 | KESTREL 9 |
| 60 22749 | Y08274 | MONACO 9 |
| 60 22760 | US3568 | KESTREL 9 |
| 60 22772 | ANB320 | MONACO 9 |
| 60 22798 | YG5522 | MONACO 9 |
| 60 22800 | FJ9519 | KESTREL 9 |
| 60 22815 | KV6685 | MONACO 9 |
| 60 22833 | AYP524 | MONACO 9 |
| 60 22839 | AT0176 | MONACO 9 |
| 60 22878 | JH6516 | KESTREL 9 |
| 60 22970 | GS4180 | LYNX 9 |
| 60 22981 | FJ9322 | KESTREL 9 |
| 60 23011 | VD3110 | KESTREL 9 |
| 60 23038 | NJ3120 | ASCOT 9 |
| 60 23059 | FV4300 | MONACO 9 |
| 60 23065 | LJ9084 | LYNX 9 |
| 60 23075 | AXF986 | LYNX 9 |
| 60 23076 | AWX 71 | MONACO 9 |
| 60 23084 | JG4867 | MONACO 9 |
| 60 23114 | VD9170 | MONACO 9 |
| 60 23125 | Z 5397-IRL | LYNX 9 |
| 60 23144 | 0Y7467 | LYNX 9 |
| 60 23203 | P08915 | MONACO 9 |
| 60 23204 | BAL662 | MONACO 9 |
| 60 23217 | FD8322 | KESTREL 9 |
| 60 23230 | UG9093 | MONACO 9 |
| 60 23287 | AND530 | KESTREL 9 |
| 60 23295 | AXP923 | KESTREL 9 |
| 60 23331 | AXN841 | MONACO 9 |
| 60 23361 | KY7771 | MONACO 9 |
| 60 23364 | FS8712 | KESTREL 9 |
| 60 23396 | BG0503 | MONACO 9 |
| 60 23404 | ACE370 | MONACO 9 |
| 60 23412 | EF5320 | LYNX 9 |
| 60 23429 | AXP 99 | KESTREL 9 |
| 60 23432 | NR | LYNX 9 |
| 60 23437 | KG3739 | LYNX 9 |
| 60 23438 | RH9424 | KESTREL 9 |
| 60 23441 | TJ4757 | KESTREL 9 |
| 60 23455 | DZ1065-IRL | LYNX 9 |
| 60 23467 | KY7837 | LYNX 9 |
| 60 23546 | FS9150 | MONACO 9 |
| 60 23573 | J09700 | KESTREL 9 |
| 60 23579 | AX0923 | LYNX 9 |
| 60 23584 | AHU233 | - - 9 |
| 60 23589 | AYP833 | MONACO 9 |
| 60 23660 | 0Y8474 | MONACO 9 |
| 60 23727 | ANC817 | MONACO 9 |
| 60 23768 | RM9901 | MONACO 9 |
| 60 23779 | AUU298 | MONACO 9 |
| 60 23810 | AUU336 | MONACO 9 |
| 60 23825 | J08561 | MONACO 9 |
| 60 23831 | AMH122 | MONACO 9 |
| 60 23851 | MJ3148 | MONACO 9 |
| 60 23864 | J08558 | KESTREL 9 |
| 60 23898 | FJ9407 | KESTREL 9 |
| 60 23899 | JH7179 | KESTREL 9 |
| 60 23930 | 007723 | MONACO 9 |
| 60 23940 | FJ9429 | MONACO 9 |
| 60 23941 | AXA916 | MONACO 9 |
| 60 23955 | J08629 | MONACO 9 |
| 60 23960 | 0C5720 | MONACO 9 |
| 60 23962 | NJ2807 | - - 9 |
| 60 24017 | RH8647 | MONACO 9 |
| 60 24063 | KY7763 | MONACO 9 |
| 60 24072 | GJ3824 | MONACO 9 |
| 60 24108 | BGT949 | MONACO 9 |
| 60 24114 | AXP499 | MONACO 9 |
| 60 24140 | BPH905 | KESTREL 9 |
| 60 24163 | US4630 | LYNX 9 |
| 60 24164 | BJ 733 | MONACO 9 |
| 60 24186 | GL1180 | MONACO 9 |
| 60 24200 | 0C7985 | KESTREL 9 |
| 60 24212 | KY7677 | KESTREL 9 |
| 60 24217 | JB3672 | KESTREL 9 |
| 60 24219 | AWA287 | KESTREL 9 |
| 60 24257 | AXU178 | MONACO 9 |
| 60 24281 | ADU295* | KESTREL 9 |
| 60 24282 | BN0189 | KESTREL 9 |
| 60 24290 | C24421 | LYNX 9 |
| 60 24322 | AXY293 | KESTREL 9 |
| 60 24341 | AXW496 | KESTREL 9 |
| 60 24363 | 0C8836 | MONACO 9 |
| 60 24415 | J09688 | R AN ALAGH D/H 9 |
| 60 24419 | ANE519 | MONACO 9 |
| 60 24452 | ACE 40 | MONACO 9 |
| 60 24468 | JY3421 | MONACO 9 |
| 60 24469 | LV7667 | MONACO 9 |
| 60 24481 | ADU158* | MONACO 9 |
| 60 24483 | EK9816 | MONACO 9 |
| 60 24487 | ADU160* | MONACO 9 |
| 60 24524 | 0J8442 | MONACO 9 |
| 60 24528 | 0J3304* | MONACO 9 |
| 60 24549 | AVK528 | KESTREL 9 |
| 60 24604 | ADU297* | MONACO 9 |
| 60 24619 | ADU534* | KESTREL 9 |
| 60 24622 | KY8726 | KESTREL 9 |
| 60 24653 | JF6451 | KESTREL 9 |
| 60 24680 | ADU157* | KESTREL 9 |
| 60 24688 | BPE903 | KESTREL 9 |
| 60 24692 | KV9555 | KESTREL 9 |
| 60 24693 | NSW018-AUS | LINCOCK 9 |
| 60 24698 | 0D9245 | KESTREL 9 |
| 60 24716 | WV5844 | KESTREL 9 |
| 60 24724 | MT3205 | MONACO 9 |
| 60 24732 | ADU539* | MONACO 9 |
| 60 24742 | BHK444 | KESTREL 9 |
| 60 24757 | KV8932* | KESTREL 9 |
| 60 24773 | BPE848 | KESTREL 9 |
| 60 24783 | BPF920 | KESTREL 9 |
| 60 24806 | BPG146 | LYNX 9 |
| 60 24817 | EGI395 | KESTREL 9 |
| 60 24822 | ADU299* | KESTREL 9 |
| 60 24826 | AWA204 | KESTREL 9 |
| 60 24851 | ADU164* | MONACO 9 |
| 60 24859 | AVR520 | MONACO 9 |
| 60 24886 | ADU165* | MONACO 9 |
| 60 24887 | ADU809* | MONACO 9 |
| 60 24888 | ADU807* | MONACO 9 |
| 60 24890 | ADU155* | MONACO 9 |
| 60 24904 | ADU296* | MONACO 9 |
| 60 24908 | ADU293* | KESTREL 9 |
| 60 24911 | ANW837 | KESTREL 9 |
| 60 24921 | AVT144 | MONACO 9 |
| 60 24941 | ADU 33* | MONACO 9 |
| 60 24956 | ADU154* | MONACO 9 |
| 60 24957 | BPJ575 | FALCON 9 |
| 60 24970 | BMH942 | KESTREL 9 |
| 60 24976 | ADU 32* | KESTREL 9 |
| 60 24985 | ADU163* | KESTREL 9 |
| 60 24987 | BGP104 | KESTREL 9 |
| 60 24992 | ADU162* | ULSTER IMP 9 |
| 60 24994 | BKL981 | MONACO 9 |
| 60 24999 | ADU537* | KESTREL 9 |
| 60 25000 | ADU530* | KESTREL 9 |
| 60 25002 | ZA2960-IRL | MONACO 9 |
| 60 25003 | AT A779 | KESTREL 9 |
| 60 25011 | ADU536* | KESTREL 9 |
| 60 25035 | ADU301* | ULSTER IMP 9 |
| 60 25036 | ADU303* | ULSTER IMP 9 |
| 60 25038 | ADU302* | ULSTER IMP 9 |
| 60 25044 | ADU801* | IMP 9 |
| 60 25066 | AYN 23 | LYNX 9 |
| 60 25067 | ARE999 | KESTREL 9 |
| 60 25073 | DM8898 | KESTREL 9 |
| 60 25083 | NJ4483 | KESTREL 9 |
| 60 25099 | BLF 74 | KESTREL 9 |
| 60 25113 | DM8908 | KESTREL 9 |
| 60 25114 | AHY368 | KESTREL 9 |
| 60 25136 | XG3423-NL | KESTREL 9 |
| 60 25144 | AVU808 | IMP 9 |
| 60 25165 | ADU805* | KESTREL 9 |
| 60 25166 | ADU803* | KESTREL 9 |
| 60 25171 | DR 378 | MONACO 9 |
| 60 25175 | AVT997 | KESTREL 9 |
| 60 25211 | BLA902 | KESTREL 9 |
| 60 25217 | NK0494 | IMP 9 |
| 60 25219 | BVX868 | KESTREL 9 |
| 60 25221 | BGU475 | KESTREL 9 |
| 60 25225 | HF4420 | MONACO 9 |
| 60 25239 | ADU808* | MONACO 9 |
| 60 25267 | BBH405 | KESTREL 9 |
| 60 25297 | NV4639 | MONACO 9 |
| 60 25301 | UJ4028 | KESTREL 9 |
| 60 25308 | AHP204* | MONACO 9 |
| 60 25313 | AHP202* | KESTREL 9 |
| 60 25316 | BN A204 | KESTREL 9 |
| 60 25326 | AHP206* | KESTREL 9 |
| 60 25340 | 34 IMP | IMP 9 |
| 60 25340 | AXJ993 | IMP 9 |
| 60 25345 | BLU257 | KESTREL 9 |
| 60 25347 | BLF776 | MONACO 9 |
| 60 25355 | ALJ325 | KESTREL 9 |
| 60 25360 | KG3928 | LYNX 9 |
| 60 25362 | BLX372 | KESTREL 9 |
| 60 25364 | MJ5536 | KESTREL 9 |
| 60 25410 | AAD566 | IMP 9 |
| 60 25418 | NV4645 | KESTREL 9 |
| 60 25432 | MJ5872 | KESTREL 9 |
| 60 25441 | BGW119 | IMP 9 |
| 60 25444 | AHP542* | IMP 9 |
| 60 25451 | BMW845 | KESTREL 9 |
| 60 25469 | JD5492 | KESTREL 9 |
| 60 25492 | SAA 27 | IMP 9 |
| 60 25492 | ALJ454 | IMP 9 |
| 60 25496 | A0K500 | MONACO 9 |
| 60 25499 | AXJ681 | LYNX 9 |
| 60 25503 | KVT208-AUS | IMP 9 |
| 60 25511 | ATT392 | IMP 9 |
| 60 25512 | BHY327 | IMP 9 |
| 60 25606 | AAT939 | KESTREL 9 |
| 60 25622 | AKT566 | MONACO 9 |
| 60 25625 | 0C8831 | LYNX 9 |
| 60 25637 | AYW505 | LYNX 9 |
| 60 25640 | 0Y8471 | MONACO 9 |
| 60 25662 | AYR598 | KESTREL 9 |
| 60 25696 | APP 22 | LINCOCK 9 |

| CHASSIS NO. | REG.NUMBER | MODEL |
|---|---|---|
| 60 | 25697 JV2665 | KESTREL 9 |
| 60 | 25712 AXU987 | LYNX 9 |
| 60 | 25714 BPG267 | - - 9 |
| 60 | 25727 NR | MONACO 9 |
| 60 | 25731 JN4438 | MONACO 9 |
| 60 | 25743 BME729 | LYNX 9 |
| 60 | 25758 WS 914 | LYNX 9 |
| 60 | 25814 BPF519 | KESTREL 9 |
| 60 | 25817 AOE500 | LYNX 9 |
| 60 | 25850 VJ6411 | KESTREL 9 |
| 60 | 25853 VG6556 | LYNX 9 |
| 60 | 25858 OW4771 | LYNX 9 |
| 60 | 25869 WP6200 | KESTREL 9 |
| 60 | 25879 BKE213 | LYNX 9 |
| 60 | 25912 AFC176 | LYNX 9 |
| 60 | 25927 NR | KESTREL 9 |
| 60 | 25936 AEL826 | ASCOT 9 |
| 60 | 25970 CRF902 | LYNX 9 |
| 60 | 26005 ADU 31* | KESTREL 9 |
| 60 | 26012 ADU 23* | MONACO 9 |
| 60 | 26015 ATO393 | MONACO 9 |
| 60 | 26040 ADU 26* | KESTREL 9 |
| 60 | 26087 AHP208 | MONACO 9 |
| 60 | 26115 AHP201* | MONACO 9 |
| 60 | 26131 BBH517 | MONACO 9 |
| 60 | 26132 AHP547* | MONACO COLNL 9 |
| 60 | 26133 AHP545* | IMP 9 |
| 60 | 26135 BAE677 | LYNX 9 |
| 60 | 27005 BLU678 | KESTREL 9 |
| 60 | 27007 CPC897 | KESTREL 9 |
| 60 | 27056 BLX371 | KESTREL 9 |
| 60 | 27074 JB5655 | LYNX 9 |
| 60 | 27111 BND 74 | KESTREL 9 |
| 60 | 27119 AHP 992* | KESTREL 9 |
| 60 | 27126 AHP991 | KESTREL 9 |
| 60 | 27131 JU5695 | KESTREL 9 |
| 60 | 27132 ARW273* | KESTREL 9 |
| 60 | 27142 CPD531 | KESTREL 9 |
| 60 | 27188 ARW278* | KESTREL 9 |
| 60 | 27191 BNB331 | KESTREL 9 |
| 60 | 27197 ARW431* | KESTREL 9 |
| 60 | 27203 AHP543* | KESTREL 9 |
| 60 | 27213 ARW422* | LYNX 9 |
| 60 | 27218 AUG397 | MONACO 9 |
| 60 | 27223 ARW421* | MONACO 9 |
| 60 | 27231 CPD813 | KESTREL 9 |
| 60 | 27244 AYB888 | KESTREL 9 |
| 60 | 27248 BKO423 | MONACO 9 |
| 60 | 27293 ARW432* | MONACO 9 |
| 60 | 27305 AON434 | MONACO 9 |
| 60 | 27310 JMJ4370 | IMP 9 |
| 60 | 27327 ATT956 | IMP 9 |
| 60 | 27357 JF9625 | KESTREL 9 |
| 60 | 27359 OW7859 | IMP 9 |
| 60 | 27361 ARW490* | MONACO 9 |
| 60 | 27364 AWK385* | MONACO 9 |
| 60 | 27369 JK4454 | IMP 9 |
| 60 | 27375 WN7872 | KESTREL 9 |

| CHASSIS NO. | REG.NUMBER | MODEL |
|---|---|---|
| 60 | 27391 RD6987 | MONACO 9 |
| 60 | 27395 AWK193* | KESTREL 9 |
| 60 | 27414 VH7503 | IMP 9 |
| 60 | 27421 ARW491* | IMP 9 |
| 60 | 27424 AWK197* | MONACO 9 |
| 60 | 27430 BNW 51 | IMP 9 |
| 60 | 27433 NR | IMP 9 |
| 60 | 27439 BYY575 | IMP 9 |
| 60 | 27447 BYK947 | IMP 9 |
| 60 | 27462 BXM820 | IMP 9 |
| 60 | 27493 BAU519 | IMP 9 |
| 60 | 27501 BXU294 | LYNX 9 |
| 60 | 27512 YS2692 | MONACO 9 |
| 60 | 27543 AWK610* | MONACO 9 |
| 60 | 27544 AWK706* | MONACO 9 |
| 60 | 27585 AVC617* | KESTREL COL 9 |
| 60 | 27586 AWK701* | LYNX 9 |
| 60 | 27608 DT6255 | KESTREL 9 |
| 60 | 27624 AKB212 | MONACO 9 |
| 60 | 27634 AVC195* | MONACO COLNL 9 |
| 60 | 27641 CPH250 | MONACO 9 |
| 60 | 27651 WF4444 | MONACO 9 |
| 60 | 27652 AVC620* | KESTREL 9 |
| 60 | 27673 DMP520 | MONACO 9 |
| 60 | 27677 JK4949 | IMP 9 |
| 60 | 27682 512JTU-S | IMP 9 |
| 60 | 27685 AKV216* | D/H COUPE 9 |
| 60 S | 22531 AWK171* | BROOKLANDS 9 |
| 60/ | 1 NR | BROOKLANDS 9 |
| 60/ | 2 NR | BROOKLANDS 9 |
| 60/ | 3 PK2721# | BROOKLANDS 9 |
| 60/ | 4 WK7162* | BROOKLANDS 9 |
| 60/ | 5 NR | BROOKLANDS 9 |
| 60/ | 6 NR | BROOKLANDS 9 |
| 60/ | 7 NR | BROOKLANDS 9 |
| 60/ | 8 NR | BROOKLANDS 9 |
| 60/ | 9 NR | BROOKLANDS 9 |
| 60/ | 10 NR | BROOKLANDS 9 |
| 60/ | 11 NR | BROOKLANDS 9 |
| 60/ | 12 NR | BROOKLANDS 9 |
| 60/ | 13 NR | BROOKLANDS 9 |
| 60/ | 14 NR | BROOKLANDS 9 |
| 60/ | 15 NR | BROOKLANDS 9 |
| 60/ | 16 NR | BROOKLANDS 9 |
| 60/ | 17 NR | BROOKLANDS 9 |
| 60/ | 18 PK2707# | BROOKLANDS 9 |
| 80 | 01 NR | BROOKLANDS 9 |
| 80 | 02 NR | BROOKLANDS 9 |
| 80 | 03 NR | BROOKLANDS 9 |
| 80 | 04 NR | BROOKLANDS 9 |
| 80 | 05 NR | BROOKLANDS 9 |
| 80 | 06 NR | BROOKLANDS 9 |
| 80 | 07 NR | BROOKLANDS 9 |
| 80 | 08 NR | BROOKLANDS 9 |
| 80 | 09 RX2347 | BROOKLANDS 9 |
| 80 | 10 NR | BROOKLANDS 9 |
| 80 | 11 NR | BROOKLANDS 9 |
| 80 | 12 NR | BROOKLANDS 9 |

| CHASSIS NO. | REG. NUMBER | MODEL |
|---|---|---|
| 80 | 13 NR | BROOKLANDS 9 |
| 80 | 14 NR | BROOKLANDS 9 |
| 80 | 15 NR | BROOKLANDS 9 |
| 80 | 16 NR | BROOKLANDS 9 |
| 80 | 17 NR | BROOKLANDS 9 |
| 80 | 18 NR | BROOKLANDS 9 |
| 80 | 19 HK6652 | BROOKLANDS 9 |
| 80 | 20 GZ5021-IRL | BROOKLANDS 9 |
| 80 | 21 AZ1189-IRL | BROOKLANDS 9 |
| 80 | 22 CO1134-IRL | BROOKLANDS 9 |
| 80 | 23 UX4218-NL | BROOKLANDS 9 |
| 80 | 24 MWF271 | BROOKLANDS 9 |
| 80 | 25 NR | BROOKLANDS 9 |
| 80 | 26 VM4913 | BROOKLANDS 9 |
| 80 | 27 NR | BROOKLANDS 9 |
| 80 | 28 NR | BROOKLANDS 9 |
| 80 | 29 NR | BROOKLANDS 9 |
| 80 | 30 NR | BROOKLANDS 9 |
| 80 | 31 NR | BROOKLANDS 9 |
| 80 | 32 UY4322 | BROOKLANDS 9 |
| 80 | 33 NR | BROOKLANDS 9 |
| 80 | 34 NR | BROOKLANDS 9 |
| 80 | 35 NR | BROOKLANDS 9 |
| 80 | 36 NR | BROOKLANDS 9 |
| 80 | 37 NR | BROOKLANDS 9 |
| 80 | 38 NR | BROOKLANDS 9 |
| 80 | 39 NR | BROOKLANDS 9 |
| 80 | 40 NR | BROOKLANDS 9 |
| 80 | 41 NR | BROOKLANDS 9 |
| 80 | 42 NR | BROOKLANDS 9 |
| 80 | 43 KD5340 | BROOKLANDS 9 |
| 80 | 44 GK3249 | BROOKLANDS 9 |
| 80 | 45 NR | BROOKLANDS 9 |
| 80 | 46 PG8541 | BROOKLANDS 9 |
| 80 | 47 VC 483* | BROOKLANDS 9 |
| 80 | 48 VC 484* | BROOKLANDS 9 |
| 80 | 49 VC 485* | BROOKLANDS 9 |
| 80 | 50 VC 833* | BROOKLANDS 9 |
| 80 | 51 VC 835* | BROOKLANDS 9 |
| 80 | 52 VC 834* | BROOKLANDS 9 |
| 80 | 53 NR | BROOKLANDS 9 |
| 80 | 54 NR | BROOKLANDS 9 |
| 80 | 55 PG 472 | BROOKLANDS 9 |
| 80 | 56 NR | BROOKLANDS 9 |
| 80 | 57 AZ3641-IRL | BROOKLANDS 9 |
| 80 | 58 NR | BROOKLANDS 9 |
| 80 | 59 NR | BROOKLANDS 9 |
| 80 | 60 NR | BROOKLANDS 9 |
| 80 | 61 NR-AUS | BROOKLANDS 9 |
| 80 | 62 NR | BROOKLANDS 9 |
| 80 | 63 NR-ZA | BROOKLANDS 9 |
| 80 | 64 NR | BROOKLANDS 9 |
| 80 | 65 NR | BROOKLANDS 9 |
| 80 | 66 NR | BROOKLANDS 9 |
| 80 | 67 NR | BROOKLANDS 9 |
| 80 | 68 NR | BROOKLANDS 9 |
| 80 | 69 NR | BROOKLANDS 9 |
| 80 | 70 NR | BROOKLANDS 9 |

| CHASSIS NO. | REG.NUMBER | MODEL |
|---|---|---|
| 80 | 71 PK2499# | BROOKLANDS 9 |
| 80 | 72 NR | BROOKLANDS 9 |
| 80 | 73 NR | BROOKLANDS 9 |
| 80 | 74 GK4244 | BROOKLANDS 9 |
| 80 | 75 NR -NZ | BROOKLANDS 9 |
| 80 | 76 GK4407-S | BROOKLANDS 9 |
| 80 | 77 KY 220 | BROOKLANDS 9 |
| 80 | 78 NR | BROOKLANDS 9 |
| 80 | 79 UT8254 | BROOKLANDS 9 |
| 80 | 80 NR | BROOKLANDS 9 |
| 80 | 81 VC6800* | BROOKLANDS 9 |
| 80 | 82 NR | BROOKLANDS 9 |
| 80 | 83 NR | BROOKLANDS 9 |
| 80 | 84 NR | BROOKLANDS 9 |
| 80 | 85 NR-AUS | BROOKLANDS 9 |
| 80 | 86 NR | BROOKLANDS 9 |
| 80 | 87 VC8302* | BROOKLANDS 9 |
| 80 | 88 VC8303* | BROOKLANDS 9 |
| 80 | 89 VC8304* | BROOKLANDS 9 |
| 80 | 90 VC8305* | BROOKLANDS 9 |
| 80 | 91 VC8306* | BROOKLANDS 9 |
| 80 | 92 VC9204* | BROOKLANDS 9 |
| 80 | 93 KV5392* | BROOKLANDS 9 |

NEW SERIES 9HP MODELS COMMENCING MODEL
YEAR 1936 (CHASSIS PREFIXES 66/67/768.

| CHASSIS NO. | REG.NUMBER | MODEL |
|---|---|---|
| 66M | 101 AKV245* | MERLIN 9 |
| 66M | 124 FV6649 | MERLIN 9 |
| 66M | 140 AKV252* | MERLIN 9 |
| 66M | 142 NR | MERLIN 9 |
| S66K | 150 BDU 4* | KESTREL 9 |
| 66M | 157 CGK293 | MERLIN 9 |
| S66K | 184 WG4379 | KESTREL 9 |
| S66K | 189 CLB504 | KESTREL 9 |
| S66K | 192 NR-USA | KESTREL 9 |
| S66K | 194 AKV760* | KESTREL COL 9 |
| 66K | 204 COX 51 | KESTREL 9 |
| 66M | 213 BBJ925 | MERLIN 9 |
| 66M | 288 BV5152 | MERLIN 9 |
| 66M | 301 BU0945 | MERLIN 9 |
| 66M | 379 BDU 67* | MERLIN 9 |
| 66M | 409 CKJ760 | MERLIN 9 |
| S66K | 479 WS6214 | KESTREL 9 |
| 66M | 562 BDU352* | MERLIN 9 |
| S66M | 570 JB7836 | MERLIN 9 |
| 66M | 577 CLO868 | MERLIN 9 |
| 66M | 580 NR | MERLIN 9 |
| S66M | 586 JHZ932-S | KESTREL 9 |
| S66K | 610 BDU513* | MERLIN 9 |
| 66M | 657 BDU517* | MERLIN 9 |
| 66M | 670 YS5021 | MERLIN 9 |
| S66M | 695 BDU514* | MERLIN 9 |
| 66M | 711 EZ1082-IRL | MERLIN 9 |
| S66K | 713 JB7830 | KESTREL 9 |
| S66K | 717 DPE589 | KESTREL 9 |

| CHASSIS NO. | | REG.NUMBER | MODEL |
|---|---|---|---|
| 66M | 729 | CUV235 | MERLIN 9 |
| S66M | 740 | BDU723* | MERLIN 9 |
| 66M | 755 | JT4515 | MERLIN 9 |
| 66M | 777 | CCD542 | MERLIN 9 |
| 66M | 781 | BHP356* | MERLIN 9 |
| S66K | 879 | BHP 19* | KESTREL 9 |
| S66K | 905 | BHP 91* | KESTREL 9 |
| 66M | 923 | BHP 15* | MERLIN 9 |
| S66M | 952 | BHP 45* | MERLIN 9 |
| 66M | 984 | BRW306* | MERLIN 9 |
| S66M | 993 | BHP 56* | MERLIN 9 |
| 66M | 998 | NR | MERLIN 9 |
| 66M | 1065 | BAO928 | MERLIN 9 |
| 66M | 1080 | D12796-IRL | MERLIN 9 |
| 66M | 1094 | SN7145 | MERLIN COL 9 |
| 66M | 1124 | BHP357* | MERLIN 9 |
| S66M | 1151 | BWK571* | MERLIN 9 |
| 66M | 1156 | YS6394 | MERLIN 9 |
| 66M | 1168 | CKM927 | MERLIN 9 |
| 66M | 1228 | UIZ973-IRL | MERLIN 9 |
| 66M | 1230 | BHP463* | MERLIN 9 |
| 66M | 1250 | DMK 51 | MERLIN 9 |
| 66M | 1257 | BHP470* | MERLIN 9 |
| 66M | 1263 | BHP683* | MERLIN 9 |
| 66M | 1300 | BHP887* | MERLIN 9 |
| S66M | 1315 | ADG406 | MERLIN 9 |
| 66M | 1351 | JY8249 | MERLIN 9 |
| S66M | 1381 | BWK743* | MERLIN 9 |
| 66M | 1399 | BHP963 | MERLIN 9 |
| 66M | 1400 | CXW912 | MERLIN 9 |
| S66K | 1419 | YS7816 | KESTREL 9 |
| S66K | 1430 | DPK 41 | KESTREL 9 |
| S66K | 1438 | WF8173 | KESTREL 9 |
| S66K | 1442 | BBV885 | KESTREL 9 |
| S66K | 1459 | BRW308* | KESTREL 9 |
| 66M | 1517 | AKY830 | MERLIN 9 |
| 66X | 1519 | BVC204* | 2D EXP SALOON 9 |
| S66M | 1566 | BRW310* | MERLIN 9 |
| 66M | 1568 | DMP767 | MERLIN 9 |
| S66K | 1589 | CKX740 | KESTREL 9 |
| 66M | 1647 | VD6228 | MERLIN 9 |
| 66M | 1650 | FV7636 | MERLIN 9 |
| 66M | 1677 | CS3732 | MERLIN 9 |
| S66K | 1694 | ANP999 | KESTREL 9 |
| S66K | 1696 | BRK744 | KESTREL 9 |
| 66M | 1700 | DBB537 | MERLIN 9 |
| S66K | 1758 | CYL 55 | KESTREL 9 |
| S66K | 1773 | AKY345 | KESTREL 9 |
| 66M | 1811 | BUR164 | MERLIN 9 |
| S66K | 1832 | BHP893* | KESTREL 9 |
| S66K | 1836 | BWK577* | KESTREL 9 |
| S66K | 1850 | BDU412* | KESTREL 9 |
| 66M | 1868 | BVC 51* | MERLIN 9 |
| 66M | 1874 | BER696 | MERLIN 9 |
| 66M | 1889 | EUB278 | MERLIN 9 |
| S66M | 1890 | JT5187 | KESTREL 9 |
| 66M | 1897 | BVC526* | MERLIN 9 |
| 66M | 1916 | BRK872 | MERLIN 9 |

| CHASSIS NO. | | REG.NUMBER | MODEL |
|---|---|---|---|
| 66M | 1980 | AKV208* | MERLIN 9 |
| S66M | 1982 | BVC208* | MERLIN 9 |
| S66M | 1984 | BVC207* | MERLIN 9 |
| 66M | 2005 | CRR865 | MERLIN 9 |
| S66M | 2027 | EMD715 | MERLIN 9 |
| 66M | 2036 | CWK163* | MERLIN 9 |
| 66M | 2041 | BYC825* | MERLIN 9 |
| 66M | 2075 | BYC521* | MERLIN 9 |
| 66M | 2098 | BYC527* | MERLIN 9 |
| 66M | 2200 | NR | MERLIN 9 |
| S67Z | 2201 | BYC210* | MONACO 9 |
| S67Z | 2229 | NR | MONACO 9 |
| S67Z | 2239 | CBY898 | MONACO 9 |
| S67Z | 2244 | ENU864 | MONACO 9 |
| S67Z | 2257 | DVR310 | MONACO 9 |
| S67Z | 2286 | ACA367 | MONACO 9 |
| S67Z | 2289 | BVC826* | MONACO 9 |
| S67Z | 2295 | BYC822* | MONACO 9 |
| S67Z | 2307 | AUN170 | MONACO 9 |
| S67ZX | 2324 | FPJ681 | MONACO 9 |
| S67Z | 2342 | NV9627 | MONACO 9 |
| S67Z | 2420 | DGF986 | MONACO 9 |
| S67Z | 2421 | BKV 82* | MONACO 9 |
| S67Z | 2424 | DUT519 | MONACO 9 |
| S67Z | 2427 | CDU924* | MONACO 9 |
| S67Z | 2458 | CHP104* | MONACO 9 |
| S67Z | 2467 | CL3931 | MONACO 9 |
| S67Z | 2475 | BKV304* | MONACO 9 |
| S67Z | 2482 | BKV 89* | MONACO 9 |
| S67Z | 2486 | CDU624* | MONACO 9 |
| S67ZX | 2498 | BKV 91* | MONACO 9 |
| S67Z | 2515 | BV6322 | MONACO 9 |
| S67Z | 2537 | BOT348 | MONACO 9 |
| S67Z | 2550 | CRT 30 | MONACO 9 |
| S67Z | 2566 | UD8092 | MONACO 9 |
| S67Z | 2570 | DWL835 | MONACO 9 |
| S67Z | 2613 | BVE604 | MONACO 9 |
| S67Z | 2619 | BKV710* | MONACO 9 |
| S67Z | 2627 | ACR909 | MONACO 9 |
| 66M | 2636 | CHP107* | MERLIN 9 |
| 66M | 2641 | CUL793 | MERLIN 9 |
| S67Z | 2643 | CDU 64* | MONACO 9 |
| S67ZX | 2680 | CWK447* | MONACO 9 |
| S67Z | 2683 | CBJ570 | MONACO 9 |
| S67Z | 2702 | BAX951 | MONACO 9 |
| S67Z | 2719 | BKV713* | MONACO 9 |
| S67Z | 2739 | DXV326 | MONACO 9 |
| S67Z | 2746 | FV8423 | MONACO 9 |
| S67Z | 2759 | CDU 65* | MONACO 9 |
| S67Z | 2783 | CDU929* | MONACO 9 |
| S67Z | 2804 | CDU617* | MONACO 9 |
| S67Z | 2841 | DT0283 | MONACO 9 |
| S67Z | 2866 | CHP102* | MONACO 9 |
| S67Z | 2893 | ACA367 | MONACO 9 |
| S67Z | 2916 | DHW 61 | MONACO 9 |
| S67Z | 2925 | CRW912* | MONACO 9 |
| S67M | 2928 | CHP790* | MERLIN 9 |
| 66M | 2952 | CRW903* | MONACO 9 |

| CHASSIS NO. | | REG.NUMBER | MODEL |
|---|---|---|---|
| S67Z | 2988 | CRW902* | MONACO 9 |
| S67Z | 3008 | CRW904* | MONACO 9 |
| S67Z | 3009 | CRW907* | MONACO 9 |
| 67M | 3013 | CRW447 | MERLIN 9 |
| S67M | 3027 | BBM628 | MERLIN 9 |
| S67Z | 3031 | CRW913* | MONACO 9 |
| S67C | 3038 | CRW911* | MONACO 9 |
| S67Z | 3055 | AUN173 | MONACO 9 |
| S67Z | 3057 | FPK199 | MONACO 9 |
| S67Z | 3071 | EUG494 | MONACO 9 |
| S67Z | 3127 | CWK454* | MONACO 9 |
| S67Z | 3143 | AUN352 | MONACO 9 |
| S67Z | 3145 | CWK455* | MONACO 9 |
| S67CX | 3148 | WG6646 | MONACO 9 |
| S67Z | 3162 | CVC122* | MONACO 9 |
| S67Z | 3163 | CWK448* | MONACO 9 |
| S67CX | 3164 | CVB341 | TRG SAL 1½ |
| S67Z | 3172 | BTG706 | MONACO 9 |
| S67Z | 3183 | FPU 22 | TRG SAL 9 |
| S67Z | 3185 | CWK826* | MONACO 9 |
| S67CX | 3199 | CWK820* | TRG SAL 9 |
| S67ZX | 3205 | FV9831 | MONACO 9 |
| S67C | 3228 | CWK822* | TRG SAL 9 |
| S67CX | 3251 | EGY635 | TRG SAL 9 |
| S67C | 3271 | EGY637 | TRG SAL 9 |
| S67Z | 3283 | NR | MONACO 9 |
| S67CX | 3325 | EGP388 | TRG SALOON 9 |
| S68V | 3400 | CVC887* | VICTOR 9 |
| S68V | 3403 | JA9800 | VICTOR 9 |
| S68V | 3415 | NR | VICTOR 9 |
| S68V | 3423 | DDU386* | VICTOR 9 |
| S68V | 3436 | DYB 85 | VICTOR 9 |
| S68V | 3442 | DGF987 | MONACO 9 |
| S68V | 3446 | ENE358 | VICTOR 9 |
| S68V | 3466 | ENE589 | VICTOR 9 |

SIX CYLINDER MODELS - ALL VERSIONS.

| CHASSIS NO. | | REG.NUMBER | MODEL |
|---|---|---|---|
| 14 | 238 | PL8617 | DEAUVILLE 14/6 |
| 14L | 243 | KR9162 | ALPINE SAL 14/6 |
| 14L | 250 | NR-NZ | ALPINE 14/6 |
| 14S | 285 | GO1927 | STELVIO 14/6 |
| 14S | 290 | NR | STELVIO 14/6 |
| 14 | 397 | OV2806 | DEAUVILLE 14/6 |
| 14L | 400 | UB6552 | ALPINE SAL 14/6 |
| 14S | 518 | P05441 | STELVIO 14/6 |
| 14L | 736 | GT5989 | ALPINE SAL 14/6 |
| 14L | 745 | RH7497 | ALPINE SAL 14/6 |
| 14L | 766 | NR-NZ | ALPINE 14/6 |
| 14L | 782 | BG 916 | ALPINE 14/6 |
| 14L | 802 | NR-NZ | ALPINE 14/6 |
| 14S | 803 | PG7160 | STELVIO 14/6 |
| 14L | 843 | VU8732 | ALPINE SAL 14/6 |
| 14L | 895 | UB9711 | ALPINE SAL 14/6 |
| 14L | 901 | BPC740 | ALPINE 14/6 |
| 14L | 908 | OV8357 | ALPINE SAL 14/6 |
| 14L | 939 | ADU806* | ALPINE SAL 14/6 |
| 15S | 940 | ADU294* | STELVIO 15/6 |
| 15S | 946 | ADU540* | STELVIO 15/6 |

| CHASSIS NO. | | REG.NUMBER | MODEL |
|---|---|---|---|
| 15S | 950 | BLD737 | STELVIO 15/6 |
| 14L | 1024 | KV3310 | ALPINE SAL 14/6 |
| 14L | 1066 | V08888 | ALPINE TR 14/6 |
| 14L | 1116 | GG8048 | ALPINE TR 14/6 |
| 14L | 1120 | AVC 9* | ALPINE 14/6 |
| 14L | ---- | VC9199* | ALPINE SAL 14/6 |
| 14L | ---- | VC9722* | ALPINE TR 14/6 |
| 14S | ---- | P05441 | STELVIO 14/6 |
| 88E | 78 | NJ1819 | EDINBURGH 14/6 |
| 88E | 1017 | ADU802* | WINCHESTER 15/6 |
| 4/ | 101 | KV5694* | TT SIX/MPH 14 |
| 4/ | 102 | KV5695* | TT6/DIXON CAR |
| 4/ | 103 | KV5696* | TT6/WHITE RILEY |
| 4/ | 103 | KV5929 | WHITE RILEY |
| 4/ | 104 | KV6078* | TT6/DIXON CAR |
| 4/ | 105 | KV6079* | TT6/MPH 12 |
| 4/ | 106 | KV6077* | TT6/GREBE 12 |
| 4/ | 101 | KV2481* | KESTREL 12/6 2D |
| 44T | 159 | NR-NZ | KESTREL 12/6 |
| 44T | 234 | NJ 801 | KESTREL 14/6 |
| 44T | 280 | JJ2398 | KESTREL 12/6 |
| 44T | 300 | NR-NZ | MENTONE 12/6 |
| 44T | 317 | UG3427 | KESTREL 12/6 |
| 44T | 364 | KV3056 | KESTREL 14/6 |
| 44T | 412 | HV2680 | KESTREL 12/6 |
| 44T | 434 | VY4240 | KESTREL 12/6 |
| 44T | 438 | NR-NZ | ALPINE 14/6 |
| 44T | 439 | ACF581 | KESTREL 14/6 |
| 44T | 441 | UJ1393 | KESTREL 14/6 |
| 44T | 446 | BLC150 | KESTREL 12/6 |
| 44T | 487 | EX3202 | LYNX 14/6 |
| 44T | 544 | NR-NZ | KESTREL 12/6 |
| 44T | 578 | TK9227 | MENTONE 12/6 |
| 44T | 580 | OW2960 | MENTONE 12/6 |
| 44T | 601 | KG2339 | KESTREL 12/6 |
| 44T | 602 | AGK944 | KESTREL 12/6 |
| 44T | 606 | JH4614 | KESTREL 12/6 |
| 44T | 618 | TV8011 | MARCH SPL 12/6 |
| 44T | 628 | WN5519 | ALPINE SAL 14/6 |
| 44T | 634 | AGU653 | MENTONE 12/6 |
| 44T | 639 | JFM868 | KESTREL 12/6 |
| 44T | 646 | NR-NZ | MENTONE 12/6 |
| 44T | 686 | J07117 | LYNX 12/6 |
| 44T | 687 | KV5204* | LYNX 12/6 |
| 44T | 716 | WP4110 | LYNX 12/6 |
| 44T | 724 | OJ9058 | LYNX 12/6 |
| 44T | 754 | NR-NZ | LYNX 12/6 |
| 44T | 770 | SCV552 | KESTREL 12/6 |
| 44T | 783 | DG6796 | KESTREL 12/6 |
| 44T | 802 | OC 604 | KESTREL 12/6 |
| 44T | 833 | J06371 | LINCOCK 14/6 |
| 44T | 863 | OC 354 | LYNX 12/6 |
| 44T | 939 | NR-NZ | KESTREL 14/6 |
| 44T | 948 | KV5490 | KESTREL 12/6 |
| 44T | 1007 | KV6072* | LYNX 14/6 |
| 44T | 1022 | AMW909 | LYNX 12/6 |
| 44T | 1031 | AXM 53 | LYNX 12/6 |
| 44T | 1123 | AXN319 | LYNX 12/6 |

| CHASSIS NO. | | REG.NUMBER | MODEL |
|---|---|---|---|
| 44T | 1138 | WP4573 | KESTREL 12/6 |
| 44T | 1151 | NR-NZ | KESTREL 12/6 |
| 44T | 1164 | NR-NZ | KESTREL 12/6 |
| 44T | 1165 | AYE622 | LYNX 12/6 |
| 44T | 1318 | NR-NZ | NZ SPECIAL 12/6 |
| 44T | 1378 | AUL 81 | MENTONE 12/6 |
| 44T | 1383 | FV4533 | MENTONE 12/6 |
| 44T | 1433 | ADU156* | MENTONE 12/6 |
| 44T | 1466 | AS 505-NZ | MENTONE 12/6 |
| 44T | 1498 | NR-NZ | MENTONE 12/6 |
| 44T | 1509 | ANC462 | LYNX 12/6 |
| 44T | 1519 | AMV 41 | LINCOCK 12/6 |
| 44T | 1531 | NR-NZ | MENTONE 12/6 |
| 44T | 1536 | NR | LYNX 12/6 |
| 44T | 1586 | RH8780 | KESTREL 12/6 |
| 44T | 1594 | NR-NZ | MENTONE 12/6 |
| 44T | 1603 | AYM275 | LYNX 14/6 |
| 44T | 1617 | APP166 | KESTREL 12/6 |
| 44T | 1646 | US6187 | LYNX 14/6 |
| 44T | 1657 | YE9707 | LYNX 12/6 |
| 44T | 1666 | WP6226 | KESTREL 14/6 |
| 44T | 1683 | AYR645 | KESTREL 12/6 |
| 44T | 1686 | AYP840 | KESTREL 14/6 |
| 44T | 1690 | ACE677 | LINCOCK 12/6 |
| 44T | 1714 | ED8306-NZ | KESTREL 12/6 |
| 44T | 1733 | ADU 27* | GAMECOCK 14/6 |
| 44T | 1734 | ADU 28* | GAMECOCK 14/6 |
| 44T | 1735 | ADU 29* | GAMECOCK 14/6 |
| 44T | 1736 | ADU 30* | LYNX 14/6 |
| 44T | 1737 | SB4492 | LYNX 14/6 |
| 44T | 1739 | JH9506 | MPH 14/6 |
| 44T | 1877 | AXP307 | LYNX 12/6 |
| 44T | 1881 | VY6804 | MENTONE 12/6 |
| 44T | 1908 | NR-NZ | KESTREL 12/6 |
| 44T | 1912 | OD8379 | LYNX 12/6 |
| 44T | 1917 | BPC478 | KESTREL 12/6 |
| 44T | 1929 | KV8446 | KESTREL 12/6 |
| 44T | 1943 | YD9076 | KESTREL 14/6 |
| 44T | 1961 | WD6949 | KESTREL 14/6 |
| 44T | 1985 | BPD773 | LINCOCK 12/6 |
| 44T | 1996 | ACE100 | MENTONE 12/6 |
| 44T | 1998 | AXY299 | MENTONE 12/6 |
| 44T | 2004 | AAF497 | KESTREL 12/6 |
| 44T | 2023 | JV2667 | KESTREL 12/6 |
| 44T | 2028 | RV4745 | LYNX 12/6 |
| 44T | 2031 | LV8374 | KESTREL 12/6 |
| 44T | 2058 | AYE640 | MENTONE 12/6 |
| 44T | 2062 | JY3660 | LYNX 15/6 |
| 44T | 2078 | KG4151 | KESTREL 12/6 |
| 44T | 2097 | NR | LYNX 12/6 |
| 44T | 2109 | NR-NZ | KESTREL 14/6 |
| 44T | 2122 | ADU 24* | MENTONE 12/6 |
| 44T | 2123 | BJJ214 | MENTONE 12/6 |
| 44T | 2125 | AOE770 | KESTREL 14/6 |
| 44T | 2127 | KV9477* | MPH (RACING) |
| 44T | 2128 | KV9478* | MPH (RACING) |
| 44T | 2130 | BLA540 | MENTONE 12/6 |
| 44T | 2138 | BGK272 | MENTONE 12/6 |

| CHASSIS NO. | | REG.NUMBER | MODEL |
|---|---|---|---|
| 44T | 2142 | KV9763* | MPH (RACING) |
| 44T | 2155 | ADU298* | MENTONE 12/6 |
| 44T | 2164 | ADU 25* | MENTONE 12/6 |
| 44T | 2172 | ADU161* | MENTONE 12/6 |
| 44T | 2204 | AVR 35 | KESTREL 12/6 |
| 44T | 2207 | ADU 22* | MENTONE 12/6 |
| 44T | 2219 | ADU159* | MENTONE 12/6 |
| 44T | 2227 | NR-NZ | MENTONE 12/6 |
| 44T | 2244 | AHP541* | FALCON 15/6 |
| 44T | 2245 | AHP984* | KESTREL 15/6 |
| 44T | 2246 | ARW485* | MPH 15 (COE354) |
| 44T | 2246 | COE354-USA | MPH 15(ARW485*) |
| 44T | 2247 | NJ6180 | MPH 14/6 |
| 44T | 2248 | ADU529* | MPH 12/6 |
| 44T | 2249 | ADG888 | MPH 12/6 |
| 44T | 2250 | ADU804* | FALCON 15/6 |
| 44T | 2251 | AWK195* | MPH 12/6 |
| 44T | 2252 | KY8909 | MPH 14/6 |
| 44T | 2255 | OW7925 | MPH 14/6 |
| 22T | 2255 | AOT855 | MPH 15 BERTELLI |
| 44T | 2256 | AOL763 | MPH 15/6 |
| 44T | 2257 | AHP203* | MPH 12/6 |
| 44T | 2258 | BLN 39 | MPH 12/6 |
| 44T | 2303 | VH7457 | KESTREL 15/6 |
| 44T | 2305 | JW6471 | FALCON 15/6 |
| 44T | 2320 | AOM450 | KESTREL 15/6 |
| 44T | 2323 | AVC615* | FALCON 15/6 |
| 44T | 2332 | BXC117 | FALCON 15/6 |
| 44T | 2335 | ARW492* | FALCON 15/6 |
| 44T | 2340 | ARW423* | FALCON 15/6 |
| 44T | 2347 | NJ6180 | MPH 14/6 |
| 44T | 2350 | AWK203* | KESTREL COL 15 |
| 44T | 2363 | BXL876 | KESTREL 15/6 |
| 44T | 2368 | AWK204* | FALCON 15/6 |
| 44T | 2371 | AWK383* | FALCON 15/6 |
| 44T | 2373 | AVC614* | KESTREL 15/6 |
| 44T | 2386 | AWK386* | FALCON 15/6 |
| 44T | 2388 | AVC190* | KESTREL 15/6 |
| 44T | 2390 | AWK608* | KESTREL 15/6 |
| 44T | 2392 | AWK704* | FALCON 15/6 |
| 44T | 2393 | AVC194* | FALCON 15/6 |
| 44T | 2402 | CPJ322 | KESTREL 15/6 |
| 44T | 2403 | AWK392* | KESTREL 15/6 |
| 44T | 2403 | NR-NZ | KESTREL 15/6 |
| 44T | 2406 | AWK705* | FALCON 15/6 |
| 44T | 2407 | AVC 15* | TT SPRITE(MPH) |
| 44T | 2411 | AVC407* | KESTREL 15/6 |
| 44T | 2412 | HYV 6-AUS | KESTREL 15/6 |
| 44T | 2413 | AVC410* | FALCON 15/6 |
| 44T | 2417 | NR | KESTREL 15/6 |
| 44T | 2418 | AVC 16* | TT SPRITE(MPH) |
| 44T | 2419 | AVC 17* | TT SPRITE(MPH) |
| 44T | 2420 | AVC 18* | TT SPRITE(MPH) |
| 44T | 2421 | NR-NZ | KESTREL 15/6 |
| 44T | 2423 | AVC193* | LYNX COLNL 15/6 |
| 44T | 2424 | WV6621 | FALCON 15/6 |
| 44T | 2430 | AVC200* | FALCON COL 15/6 |
| 44T | 2435 | AVC411* | FALCON 15/6 |

| CHASSIS NO. | | REG.NUMBER | MODEL |
|---|---|---|---|
| 44T | 2443 | AVC616* | FALCON COL 15/6 |
| 44T | 2448 | AVC618* | FALCON 15/6 |
| 46F | 2501 | AVC976* | FALCON 15/6 |
| 46F | 2505 | AKB211 | FALCON 15/6 |
| 46F | 2528 | AKV251* | FALCON 15/6 |
| 46F | 2530 | BDU 7* | FALCON 15/6 |
| 46A | 2533 | BDU 6* | ADELPHI 15/6 |
| 46F | 2535 | EPA723 | FALCON 15/6 |
| 46F | 2540 | NR-NZ | FALCON 15/6 |
| 44T | 2552 | NR | LYNX 15/6 |
| 46A | 2579 | BYA943 | ADELPHI 15/6 |
| 46A | 2580 | BHP 20* | ADELPHI 15/6 |
| 46K | 2593 | BHP 94* | KESTREL 15/6 |
| 46A | 2598 | EG2652 | ADELPHI 15/6 |
| 46F | 2613 | NR-NZ | FALCON 15/6 |
| 46K | 2618 | FW1936-NZ | KESTREL 15/6 |
| 46A | 2625 | BHP465* | ADELPHI 15/6 |
| 46A | 2635 | CPB660 | ADELPHI 15/6 |
| 46A | 2644 | BHP682* | ADELPHI 15/6 |
| 46A | 2650 | BRW301* | ADELPHI 15/6 |
| 46K | 2660 | DPJ991 | KESTREL 15/6 |
| 46K | 2660 | OPJ991 | KESTREL 15/6 |
| 46K | 2674 | DPK956 | KESTREL 15/6 |
| 46K | 2680 | RV8487 | KESTREL 15/6 |
| 46A | 2692 | DPH433-DK | ADELPHI 15/6 |
| 46A | 2711 | BWK112* | ADELPHI 15/6 |
| 46A | 2715 | BWK323* | ADELPHI 15/6 |
| 46L | 2723 | DPL765 | LYNX 15/6 |
| 46F | 2738 | CXV 17 | FALCON 15/6 |
| 46A | 2741 | BWK 68 | ADELPHI 15/6 |
| 46K | 2757 | GV4500 | KESTREL 15/6 |
| 46K | 2771 | BVC206* | KESTREL 15/6 |
| 46K | 2772 | JN 719 | KESTREL 15/6 |
| 46K | 3012 | NR-NZ | KESTREL 15/6 |
| 47A | 3015 | NR-NZ | ADELPHI 15/6 |
| 47K | 3017 | AM5344 | KESTREL 15/6 |
| 47K | 3017 | NR-NZ | KESTREL 15/6 |
| 47A | 3028 | JA7892 | ADELPHI 15/6 |
| 47A | 3033 | BKV 86* | ADELPHI 15/6 |
| 47A | 3051 | BKV717* | ADELPHI 15/6 |
| 47A | 3055 | DGW542 | ADELPHI 15/6 |
| 47A | 3066 | CDU923* | ADELPHI 15/6 |
| 47A | 3073 | NR | ADELPHI 15/6 |
| 47K | 3095 | BKV937* | KESTREL 15/6 |
| 47A | 3101 | CYA605 | ADELPHI 15/6 |
| 47K | 3102 | NR-NZ | KESTREL 15/6 |
| 47A | 3105 | CDU474* | ADELPHI 15/6 |
| 47A | 3108 | CDU 61* | ADELPHI 15/6 |
| 47A | 3123 | DLP495 | ADELPHI 15/6 |
| 47A | 3127 | CDU922* | ADELPHI COL 15 |
| 47K | 3139 | ATR341 | KESTREL 15/6 |
| 47K | 3144 | CLJ780 | KESTREL 15/6 |
| 47K | 3147 | DXE 41 | KESTREL 15/6 |
| 47K | 3178 | CRW373* | KESTREL 15/6 |
| 47K | 3179 | FPF200 | KESTREL 15/6 |
| 47A | 3182 | NR-NZ | ADELPHI 15/6 |
| 47K | 3186 | NR | KESTREL 15/6 |
| 47K | 3217 | GMH275 | KESTREL 15/6 |

| CHASSIS NO. | | REG.NUMBER | MODEL |
|---|---|---|---|
| 48A | 3301 | CVC885* | ADELPHI 15/6 |
| 48A | 3305 | HMX326 | ADELPHI 15/6 |
| 48A | 3321 | DHP724* | ADELPHI 15/6 |
| 46A | ---- | RC4497 | ADELPHI 15/6 |
| 47K | ---- | BTT988 | KESTREL 15/6 |
| 48K | ---- | EUW 88 | KESTREL 15/6 |

1½ LITRE (12HP, 4 CYLINDER) MODELS.

| CHASSIS NO. | | REG.NUMBER | MODEL |
|---|---|---|---|
| 22T | 102 | ADU531* | FALCON 1½ |
| 22T | 103 | ADU532* | KESTREL 1½ |
| 22T | 104 | ADU533* | FALCON 1½ |
| 22T | 109 | BLA907 | FALCON 1½ |
| 22T | 112 | BBH670 | LYNX 1½ |
| 22T | 115 | ATV 60 | FALCON 1½ |
| 22T | 121 | ADU812* | FALCON 1½ |
| 22T | 122 | ADU810* | FALCON 1½ |
| 22T | 125 | ADU811* | FALCON 1½ |
| 22T | 135 | BPL146 | FALCON 1½ |
| 22T | 138 | AHP205* | KESTREL 1½ |
| 22T | 152 | AKH228 | FALCON 1½ |
| 22T | 156 | AHP207* | FALCON 1½ |
| 22T | 171 | AHP209* | FALCON 1½ |
| 22T | 196 | NR | FALCON 1½ |
| 22T | 200 | VG7007 | FALCON 1½ |
| 22T | 211 | AHP211* | FALCON 1½ |
| 22T | 222 | NR | FALCON 1½ |
| 22T | 232 | NR | FALCON 1½ |
| 22T | 239 | AHP212* | FALCON 1½ |
| 22T | 240 | CG8880 | FALCON 1½ |
| 22T | 246 | NR | FALCON 1½ |
| 22T | 258 | NR | FALCON 1½ |
| 22T | 262 | NR | FALCON 1½ |
| 22T | 270 | BHX315 | FALCON 1½ |
| 22T | 274 | FK6552 | FALCON 1½ |
| 22T | 340 | AHP548* | FALCON 1½ |
| 22T | 349 | AHP551* | KESTREL 1½ |
| 22T | 388 | BLK780 | KESTREL 1½ |
| 22T | 408 | BTA910 | FALCON 1½ |
| 22T | 411 | JF7457 | FALCON 1½ |
| 22T | 419 | AHP544* | KESTREL 1½ |
| 22T | 466 | BHX464 | KESTREL 1½ |
| 22T | 496 | BMB118 | FALCON 1½ |
| 22T | 498 | FD9143 | FALCON 1½ |
| 22T | 507 | AHP546* | FALCON 1½ |
| 22T | 514 | BMY498 | KESTREL 1½ |
| 22T | 530 | AHP549* | FALCON 1½ |
| 22T | 544 | NR | FALCON 1½ |
| 22T | 563 | AHP552* | FALCON 1½ |
| 22T | 564 | AHP981* | FALCON 1½ |
| 22T | 567 | AHP982* | FALCON 1½ |
| 22T | 572 | BHX676 | FALCON 1½ |
| 22T | 591 | AHP989* | KESTREL 1½ |
| 22T | 593 | ABY915 | KESTREL 1½ |
| 22T | 598 | JV3301 | FALCON 1½ |
| 22T | 600 | BLU255 | LYNX 1½ |
| 22T | 615 | AHP550* | FALCON 1½ |

| CHASSIS NO. | REG.NUMBER | MODEL |
|---|---|---|
| 22T 616 | NR | FALCON 1½ |
| 22T 642 | AHP985* | FALCON 1½ |
| 22T 643 | BMB240 | FALCON 1½ |
| 22T 655 | CPC900 | KESTREL 1½ |
| 22T 665 | AHP210* | FALCON 1½ |
| 22T 671 | JB5593 | FALCON 1½ |
| 22T 681 | JU5453 | KESTREL 1½ |
| 22T 699 | AHP983* | FALCON 1½ |
| 22T 729 | NR | FALCON 1½ |
| 22T 735 | VV5722 | FALCON 1½ |
| 22T 754 | AHP990* | FALCON 1½ |
| 22T 755 | MG3637 | FALCON 1½ |
| 22T 757 | NR | FALCON 1½ |
| 22T 778 | NR | KESTREL 1½ |
| 22T 787 | AHP986* | FALCON 1½ |
| 22T 788 | AHP987* | FALCON 1½ |
| 22T 793 | AHP988* | FALCON 1½ |
| 22T 812 | BAL383 | FALCON 1½ |
| 22T 815 | ATT485 | KESTREL 1½ |
| 22T 821 | ARU824 | KESTREL 1½ |
| 22T 845 | 541437-NZ | KESTREL 1½ |
| 22T 877 | RV6062 | KESTREL 1½ |
| 22T 881 | ARW275* | FALCON 1½ |
| 22T 927 | CPC954 | LYNX 1½ |
| 22T 929 | BXY998 | FALCON 1½ |
| 22T 937 | ARW272* | SPECIAL 1½ |
| 22T 949 | D01294-AUS | SPECIAL 1½ |
| 22T 957 | AJ0497 | FALCON 1½ |
| 22T 958 | ARW274* | KESTREL 1½ |
| 22T 971 | ARW276* | KESTREL 1½ |
| 22T 978 | BUL411 | FALCON 1½ |
| 22T 987 | ARW271* | LYNX 1½ |
| 22T 993 | RB9097 | KESTREL 1½ |
| 22T 1011 | AKU633 | FALCON 1½ |
| 22T 1016 | ARW277* | KESTREL 1½ |
| 22T 1032 | ARW279* | FALCON 1½ |
| 22T 1035 | ARW280* | KESTREL 1½ |
| 22T 1037 | C27740-IRL | KESTREL 1½ |
| 22T 1047 | ARW281* | FALCON 1½ |
| 22T 1051 | ARW282* | KESTREL 1½ |
| 22T 1052 | ARW428* | FALCON 1½ |
| 22T 1078 | CME419 | KESTREL 1½ |
| 22T 1092 | ARW427* | FALCON 1½ |
| 22T 1094 | ARW429* | KESTREL 1½ |
| 22T 1102 | ARW483* | FALCON 1½ |
| 22T 1114 | AMR603 | KESTREL 1½ |
| 22T 1116 | AP0681 | KESTREL 1½ |
| 22T 1117 | JB5877 | KESTREL 1½ |
| 22T 1122 | CPE426 | FALCON 1½ |
| 22T 1144 | AOR 8 | FALCON 1½ |
| 22T 1145 | JF7888 | NR |
| 22T 1150 | JU5826 | KESTREL 1½ |
| 22T 1153 | ARW425* | FALCON 1½ |
| 22T 1169 | ARW482* | KESTREL 1½ |
| 22T 1174 | ARW430* | FALCON 1½ |
| 22T 1180 | ARW484* | FALCON 1½ |
| 22T 1209 | JV3397 | FALCON 1½ |
| 22T 1215 | ARW481* | KESTREL 1½ |
| 22T 1216 | ARW487* | KESTREL 1½ |
| 22T 1260 | NR | FALCON 1½ |
| 22T 1298 | ARW488* | KESTREL 1½ |
| 22T 1302 | AVE 6 | KESTREL 1½ |
| 22T 1309 | CPG587 | FALCON 1½ |
| 22T 1316 | APX910 | KESTREL 1½ |
| 22T 1328 | BHT508 | KESTREL 1½ |
| 22T 1332 | CPF640 | FALCON 1½ |
| 22T 1337 | BXC494 | KESTREL 1½ |
| 22T 1344 | AVC973* | FALCON 1½ |
| 22T 1347 | ARW486* | KESTREL 1½ |
| 22T 1349 | AWK382* | FALCON COL 1½ |
| 22T 1356 | TY3497 | KESTREL 1½ |
| 22T 1359 | BXA740 | FALCON 1½ |
| 22T 1368 | AOP912 | FALCON 1½ |
| 22T 1374 | BKP648 | FALCON 1½ |
| 22T 1387 | AWK196* | KESTREL 1½ |
| 22T 1391 | NR | LYNX 1½ |
| 22T 1403 | AWK387* | FALCON COL 1½ |
| 22T 1404 | ARW489* | KESTREL 1½ |
| 22T 1415 | BUW 77 | KESTREL COL 1½ |
| 22T 1423 | AWK389* | FALCON 1½ |
| 22T 1426 | AWK388* | FALCON 1½ |
| 22T 1430 | AWK381* | KESTREL 1½ |
| 22T 1439 | AWK199* | LYNX 1½ |
| 22T 1442 | CMG384 | LYNX 1½ |
| 22T 1443 | ARL859 | FALCON 1½ |
| 22T 1444 | AWK200* | KESTREL 1½ |
| 22T 1447 | JP 271 | KESTREL 1½ |
| 22T 1453 | BUC911 | FALCON 1½ |
| 22T 1457 | JV3511 | KESTREL 1½ |
| 22T 1458 | AWK194* | FALCON 1½ |
| 22T 1467 | AWK708* | KESTREL 1½ |
| 22T 1476 | AWK612* | FALCON 1½ |
| 22T 1477 | AWK198* | KESTREL 1½ |
| 22T 1499 | CPG 9 | FALCON 1½ |
| 22T 1519 | YS1412 | KESTREL 1½ |
| 22T 1521 | AWK384* | FALCON 1½ |
| 22T 1526 | AWK202* | KESTREL 1½ |
| 22T 1528 | AWK390* | KESTREL 1½ |
| 22T 1529 | AWK391* | FALCON 1½ |
| 22T 1533 | APX114 | KESTREL 1½ |
| 22T 1544 | AWK604* | FALCON 1½ |
| 22T 1559 | AWK601* | KESTREL COL 1½ |
| 22T 1570 | AVM772 | FALCON 1½ |
| 22T 1573 | AOU934 | KESTREL 1½ |
| 22T 1574 | DAA742 | LYNX 1½ |
| 22T 1574 | AWK611* | LYNX COL 1½ |
| 22T 1586 | AWK603* | DOBBS SPL |
| 22T 1612 | NR | LYNX 1½ |
| 22T 1620 | AWK602* | LYNX 1½ |
| 22T 1623 | GB0671 | FALCON 1½ |
| 22T 1625 | AWK607* | KESTREL COL 1½ |
| 22T 1637 | AWK605* | FALCON 1½ |
| 22T 1639 | WN8201 | FALCON 1½ |
| 22T 1651 | BNW265 | FALCON 1½ |
| 22T 1655 | ARW606* | FALCON 1½ |
| 22T 1665 | AWK712* | KESTREL 1½ |
| 22T 1675 | AWK709* | FALCON 1½ |
| 22T 1677 | MG3434 | KESTREL 1½ |
| 22T 1680 | NR | FALCON 1½ |
| 22T 1686 | NJ6087 | KESTREL 1½ |
| 22T 1688 | RV6525 | KESTREL 1½ |
| 22T 1702 | AWK609* | FALCON 1½ |
| 22T 1709 | AWK703* | KESTREL 1½ |
| 22T 1723 | SR9434 | FALCON 1½ |
| 22T 1724 | AWK711* | KESTREL 1½ |
| 22T 1736 | CPG951 | LYNX 1½ |
| 22T 1737 | AVC 14* | FALCON 1½ |
| 22T 1742 | KJ44220-DK | FALCON 1½ |
| 22T 1750 | AVC 19* | TT SPRITE |
| 22T 1760 | AVC189* | FALCON 1½ |
| 22T 1764 | AWK710* | KESTREL 1½ |
| 22T 1766 | AWK702* | FALCON 1½ |
| 22T 1770 | AVC 10* | FALCON 1½ |
| 22T 1805 | AVC 12* | FALCON 1½ |
| 22T 1807 | AVC191* | FALCON 1½ |
| 22T 1824 | NV5432 | FALCON 9 |
| 22T 1831 | AVC207* | KESTREL 1½ |
| 22T 1833 | AKF 3 | FALCON 1½ |
| 22T 1834 | BXU295 | KESTREL 1½ |
| 22T 1845 | AVC196* | FALCON 1½ |
| 22T 1848 | AVC402* | FALCON 1½ |
| 22T 1852 | JN6312 | FALCON 1½ |
| 22T 1859 | CLG367 | FALCON 1½ |
| 22T 1875 | AVC403* | FALCON 1½ |
| 22T 1886 | AVC 13* | LYNX 1½ |
| 22T 1905 | BYN 12 | FALCON 1½ |
| 22T 1909 | AVC192* | KESTREL 1½ |
| 22T 1916 | AVC 20* | TT SPRITE |
| 22T 1917 | AVC 11* | FALCON 1½ |
| 22T 1918 | AHP925* | LYNX 1½ |
| 22T 1919 | NJ6176 | LYNX 1½ |
| 22T 1919 | T 59 | LYNX 1½ |
| 22T 1922 | NR | KESTREL 1½ |
| 22T 1924 | AYC 1 | FALCON 1½ |
| 22T 1929 | NR | LYNX 1½ |
| 22T 1930 | BHU942 | KESTREL COL 1½ |
| 22T 1941 | AVC405* | FALCON 1½ |
| 22T 1942 | ADF715 | KESTREL COL 1½ |
| 22T 1950 | AVC409* | KESTREL 1½ |
| 22T 1951 | AVC401* | FALCON 1½ |
| 22T 1951 | AVE500-USA | KESTREL 1½ |
| 22T 1956 | BXT538 | FALCON 1½ |
| 22T 1957 | BHU771 | KESTREL 1½ |
| 22T 1959 | AR0225 | KESTREL 1½ |
| 22T 1965 | AVC199* | FALCON 1½ |
| 22T 1968 | BXV623 | LYNX 1½ |
| 22T 1975 | DPG928 | LYNX 1½ |
| 22T 1976 | AVC197* | FALCON 1½ |
| 22T 1987 | AVC406* | KESTREL 1½ |
| 1997 | CMF 47 | FALCON 1½ |
| 22T 2002 | KG6493 | KESTREL 1½ |
| 22T 2003 | AR0247 | KESTREL 1½ |
| 22T 2004 | 0W7166 | LYNX 1½ |
| 22T 2007 | AVC611* | FALCON 1½ |
| 22T 2009 | AVC198* | FALCON COLNL 1½ |
| 22T 2015 | ARK741 | LYNX 1½ |
| 22T 2019 | CPH852 | KESTREL 1½ |
| 22T 2037 | CP 778-NZ | KESTREL 1½ |
| 22T 2040 | BBP 20 | KESTREL 1½ |
| 22T 2042 | CPJ401 | FALCON 1½ |
| 22T 2047 | BYF 867 | KESTREL 1½ |
| 22T 2052 | AVC612* | FALCON 1½ |
| 22T 2059 | AVC404* | KESTREL 1½ |
| 22T 2067 | AVC613* | FALCON 1½ |
| 22T 2074 | DPB788 | FALCON 1½ |
| 22T 2096 | AVC619* | LYNX 1½ |
| 22T 2098 | DPD503 | LYNX 1½ |
| 22T 2109 | CLA716 | LYNX 1½ |
| 22T 2111 | CGH397 | KESTREL 1½ |
| 22T 2123 | CN6761 | KESTREL 1½ |
| 22T 2127 | AWU432 | FALCON 1½ |
| 26F 2139 | AVC974* | FALCON 1½ |
| 26F 2200 | AVC412* | FALCON 1½ |
| 26F 2201 | AVC621* | FALCON 1½ |
| 26F 2211 | AVC975* | FALCON 1½ |
| 26F 2215 | B0G423 | FALCON 1½ |
| 26F 2232 | AVC982* | FALCON 1½ |
| 26F 2235 | AVC977* | FALCON 1½ |
| 26F 2244 | AVC978* | FALCON 1½ |
| 26F 2251 | AVC622* | FALCON 1½ |
| 26F 2256 | AVC984* | FALCON 1½ |
| 26F 2263 | AKV209* | FALCON 1½ |
| 26F 2264 | AKV210* | FALCON 1½ |
| 26F 2283 | FV6354 | FALCON 1½ |
| 26F 2288 | AVC979* | FALCON 1½ |
| 26F 2296 | AVC981* | FALCON 1½ |
| 26F 2305 | AVC983* | FALCON 1½ |
| S26F 2310 | AVC980* | FALCON 1½ |
| 26F 2361 | BYU220 | KESTREL 1½ |
| 26F 2367 | JV3885 | FALCON 1½ |
| 26F 2372 | AWU580 | FALCON 1½ |
| 26F 2384 | AKV213* | FALCON 1½ |
| 26F 2386 | AKV241* | FALCON 1½ |
| 26F 2394 | AKV214* | FALCON 1½ |
| 26F 2413 | AKV215* | FALCON 1½ |
| 26L 2420 | AKV242* | LYNX 1½ |
| 26F 2427 | AKV244* | FALCON 1½ |
| 26S 2429 | AKV218* | FALCON 1½ |
| 26F 2441 | B0E822 | SPRITE |
| 26M 2443 | CGF 52 | FALCON 1½ |
| 26M 2476 | AKV217* | MERLIN 1½ |
| S26F 2484 | AKV250* | FALCON 1½ |
| 26L 2486 | CYH604 | LYNX 1½ |
| 26F 2499 | AKV246* | LYNX 1½ |
| 26F 2501 | JN6181 | FALCON 1½ |
| S26L 2519 | CYX382 | LYNX 1½ |
| 26F 2523 | AKV243* | FALCON 1½ |
| 26F 2524 | AKV247* | KESTREL 1½ |
| S26L 2527 | BYY502 | LYNX 1½ |
| 26F 2538 | AKV249* | FALCON 1½ |

| CHASSIS NO. | REG.NUMBER | MODEL |
|---|---|---|
| 26F 2546 | WJ6895 | FALCON 1½ |
| 26L 2563 | NR | LYNX 1½ |
| 26F 2564 | AKY248* | FALCON 1½ |
| 26F 2568 | BKH 73 | FALCON 1½ |
| 26F 2575 | BBP459 | FALCON 1½ |
| 26F 2581 | CEH435 | FALCON 1½ |
| 26L 2591 | CKR328 | LYNX 1½ |
| 26F 2594 | CMG 4 | FALCON 1½ |
| 26F 2602 | CGN961 | FALCON 1½ |
| 26F 2605 | NR | FALCON 1½ |
| 26F 2646 | AKY758* | FALCON 1½ |
| 26F 2655 | BRU349 | FALCON 1½ |
| 26F 2664 | AKY757* | FALCON 1½ |
| 26M 2668 | BPO629 | MERLIN 1½ |
| S26L 2668 | AKY759* | LYNX SPR 1½ |
| S26S 2698 | BDU727* | SPRITE 1½ |
| 26F 2713 | BDU 62* | FALCON 1½ |
| S26K 2732 | MJ9040 | KESTREL 1½ |
| 26F 2733 | BDU 64* | FALCON 1½ |
| 26F 2734 | BDU 61* | FALCON 1½ |
| 26F 2737 | BRW515* | FALCON 1½ |
| 26F 2739 | CNU 58 | FALCON 1½ |
| 26F 2750 | BDU 5* | FALCON 1½ |
| S26F 2762 | BDU342* | FALCON 1½ |
| 26F 2763 | AKY762* | FALCON 1½ |
| S26S 2766 | J88284 | SPRITE 1½ |
| 26A 2775 | BDU 3* | ADELPHI 1½ |
| 26F 2776 | BDU343* | FALCON 1½ |
| 26A 2778 | CRW380 | ADELPHI 1½ |
| 26F 2786 | BDU348* | FALCON 1½ |
| 26F 2789 | BDU515* | FALCON 1½ |
| 26F 2795 | JY6791 | FALCON 1½ |
| 26F 2809 | BDU350* | FALCON 1½ |
| 26M 2828 | BPC709 | MERLIN 1½ |
| 26F 2833 | BDU344* | FALCON 1½ |
| 26F 2839 | BVO160 | FALCON 1½ |
| 26F 2845 | BDU 68* | FALCON 1½ |
| 26F 2858 | X63663 | FALCON 1½ |
| 26M 2880 | BDU 63* | MERLIN 1½ |
| 26F 2880 | AKY761* | FALCON 1½ |
| 26F 2892 | BDU 66* | FALCON 1½ |
| 26F 2895 | BRW305* | FALCON 1½ |
| 26M 2905 | AKV655 | MERLIN 1½ |
| 26M 2916 | NR | MERLIN 1½ |
| 26M 2917 | NR | MERLIN 1½ |
| 26M 2928 | CJJ105 | MERLIN 1½ |
| 26M 2934 | ANX 83 | MERLIN 9 |
| 26F 2946 | BDU 70* | FALCON COL 1½ |
| 26M 2950 | BDU 71* | MERLIN 1½ |
| 26M 2955 | CMV519 | MERLIN 1½ |
| 26F 2957 | BDU349* | FALCON 1½ |
| 26F 2962 | NR | FALCON 1½ |
| S26K 2964 | BDU 69* | KESTREL SPR 1½ |
| 26F 2970 | NJ7494 | FALCON 1½ |
| 26F 2972 | BDU518* | FALCON 1½ |
| 26A 2980 | BDU347* | ADELPHI 1½ |
| 26M 2989 | BDU346* | MERLIN 1½ |
| 26M 2992 | CLT174 | MERLIN 1½ |
| S26L 2998 | BDU 65* | LYNX 1½ |
| 26A 3002 | BLJ948 | ADELPHI 1½ |
| 26F 3010 | BDU345* | FALCON 1½ |
| 26F 3014 | BDU 72* | FALCON 1½ |
| 26F 3020 | NR | FALCON 1½ |
| 26F 3040 | BDU516* | FALCON 1½ |
| 26F 3044 | BHP353* | FALCON 1½ |
| 26M 3060 | BDU520* | FALCON 1½ |
| 26M 3061 | BDU521* | MERLIN 1½ |
| 26M 3063 | DPC208 | MERLIN 1½ |
| 26A 3073 | BDU351* | ADELPHI 1½ |
| S26K 3075 | BDU511* | KESTREL SPR 1½ |
| 26F 3094 | EZ 860-IRL | FALCON 1½ |
| 26F 3120 | BDU519* | FALCON 1½ |
| 26M 3125 | DPE754 | MERLIN 1½ |
| 26M 3127 | BDU512* | MERLIN 1½ |
| 26M 3128 | BHP 14* | MERLIN 1½ |
| 26A 3138 | BOK856 | ADELPHI 1½ |
| 26F 3149 | NJ7907 | FALCON 1½ |
| 26A 3152 | UN9676 | ADELPHI 1½ |
| 26A 3183 | NR | ADELPHI 1½ |
| 26A 3191 | NR | MERLIN 1½ |
| 26M 3193 | BHP468* | MERLIN 1½ |
| 26A 3200 | CLF456 | ADELPHI 1½ |
| 26A 3204 | BDU341* | ADELPHI 1½ |
| 26M 3221 | NR | MERLIN 1½ |
| 26M 3230 | BDU724* | MERLIN 1½ |
| 26A 3252 | BDU725* | ADELPHI 1½ |
| S26A 3256 | BDU722* | ADELPHI 1½ |
| 26M 3284 | BRU342 | MERLIN 1½ |
| 26F 3289 | BCE551 | KESTREL 1½ |
| 26A 3307 | BDU721* | FALCON 1½ |
| 26F 3322 | Z 6603-IRL | FALCON 1½ |
| S26F 3333 | BDU700* | MERLIN 1½ |
| 26F 3345 | BHP 93* | FALCON 1½ |
| 26A 3346 | CYV644 | ADELPHI 1½ |
| 26K 3357 | CKN324 | KESTREL 1½ |
| 26L 3359 | CLA528 | LYNX 1½ |
| S26K 3369 | BHP 97 | KESTREL 1½ |
| 26F 3376 | ADV709 | FALCON 1½ |
| S26S 3377 | ANX305 | SPRITE 1½ |
| S26K 3380 | BDU726* | KESTREL 1½ |
| S26K 3381 | BDU730* | KESTREL 1½ |
| 26K 3384 | BCE660 | KESTREL 1½ |
| S26F 3386 | BHP 95* | FALCON 1½ |
| 26F 3390 | NR | FALCON 1½ |
| 26K 3395 | BDU728* | KESTREL 1½ |
| 26A 3402 | BHP 11* | ADELPHI 1½ |
| 26K 3421 | ADL190 | MERLIN 1½ |
| 26K 3422 | FV6968 | KESTREL 1½ |
| 26A 3426 | BHP 13* | MERLIN COL 1½ |
| 26A 3433 | BDU729* | MERLIN 1½ |
| 26M 3447 | BHP 57* | FALCON 1½ |
| 26A 3450 | BHP 16* | FALCON 1½ |
| 26A 3483 | BHP 54* | ADELPHI 1½ |
| 26M 3490 | BHP886* | ADELPHI 1½ |
| 26A 3491 | BHP 53* | ADELPHI 1½ |
| 26M 3496 | BHP 18* | MERLIN COL 1½ |
| 26K 3501 | DME 65 | KESTREL 1½ |
| 26K 3504 | AKY892* | KESTREL 1½ |
| 26A 3519 | BHP885* | ADELPHI 1½ |
| 26A 3521 | BHP355* | ADELPHI 1½ |
| 26A 3524 | BHP 96* | ADELPHI 1½ |
| S26K 3540 | BHP 17* | KESTREL 1½ |
| 26A 3546 | DPF829 | KESTREL 1½ |
| 26A 3551 | BHP 46* | ADELPHI 1½ |
| S26A 3556 | BHP888* | ADELPHI 1½ |
| 26A 3563 | BHP352* | ADELPHI 1½ |
| 26F 3572 | RG5549 | FALCON 1½ |
| 26K 3573 | NR | KESTREL 1½ |
| 26M 3576 | NR | MERLIN 1½ |
| 26A 3577 | NR | ADELPHI 1½ |
| 26A 3578 | BWK104* | ADELPHI 1½ |
| 26A 3579 | BYB 30 | ADELPHI 1½ |
| S26K 3594 | BHP354* | KESTREL 1½ |
| 26K 3596 | YS6164 | KESTREL 1½ |
| 26K 3598 | NR | KESTREL 1½ |
| 26K 3606 | BHP 92* | KESTREL 1½ |
| 26K 3612 | BHP350* | KESTREL 1½ |
| 26A 3613 | DM9841 | ADELPHI 1½ |
| 26A 3620 | CXW448 | ADELPHI 1½ |
| 26A 3626 | BRW514* | ADELPHI 1½ |
| 26L 3628 | BHP349* | ADELPHI 1½ |
| 26M 3634 | BHP359* | LYNX 1½ |
| 26K 3655 | ATE157 | MERLIN COL 1½ |
| 26K 3661 | BTY693 | KESTREL 1½ |
| 26M 3663 | NR | KESTREL 1½ |
| 26K 3667 | CS3038 | MERLIN 1½ |
| 26K 3668 | CLU671 | KESTREL 1½ |
| S26K 3669 | BHP 97* | KESTREL 1½ |
| 26K 3670 | BWE999 | KESTREL 1½ |
| 26K 3674 | JX3656 | KESTREL 1½ |
| 26A 3680 | CLM520 | ADELPHI 1½ |
| 26M 3682 | BHP 98* | MERLIN 1½ |
| 26A 3686 | BHP462* | KESTREL 1½ |
| 26A 3688 | CLW497 | ADELPHI 1½ |
| 26A 3700 | BHP464* | ADELPHI 1½ |
| 26A 3703 | BHP461* | ADELPHI 1½ |
| 26A 3711 | BHP684* | ADELPHI 1½ |
| 26K 3720 | BHP358* | KESTREL 1½ |
| 26K 3725 | BHP882* | KESTREL 1½ |
| 26K 3731 | CUC139 | ADELPHI 1½ |
| S26K 3739 | NJ8108 | KESTREL 1½ |
| 26A 3751 | BHP360* | ADELPHI 1½ |
| S26S 3753 | SX4220 | SPRITE 1½ |
| 26S 3754 | BFG 1 | SPRITE 1½ |
| 26K 3755 | BHP 12* | KESTREL 1½ |
| 26A 3771 | BRW304* | KESTREL 1½ |
| S26K 3783 | NR | KESTREL 1½ |
| 26K 3787 | NE9104-CH | KESTREL 1½ |
| 26A 3791 | CLR853 | ADELPHI 1½ |
| S26K 3796 | VH8857 | MERLIN 1½ |
| 26M 3802 | CVK425 | MERLIN 1½ |
| 26M 3841 | BHP471* | ADELPHI 1½ |
| 26A 3845 | BRW309* | ADELPHI 1½ |
| 26M 3846 | ABM132 | ADELPHI 1½ |
| 26K 3856 | BHP466* | KESTREL 1½ |
| 26M 3861 | BHP687* | MERLIN 1½ |
| S26S 3878 | BRW303* | SPRITE 1½ |
| S26K 3886 | BRW512* | KESTREL 1½ |
| 26A 3887 | BHP688* | ADELPHI 1½ |
| 26A 3896 | BHP469* | ADELPHI 1½ |
| S26K 3904 | BDU731* | LYNX SPR 1½ |
| S26K 3906 | BHP681* | KESTREL 1½ |
| 26K 3908 | JV4409 | KESTREL 1½ |
| S26K 3915 | BHP685* | KESTREL 1½ |
| 26A 3933 | BWK110* | ADELPHI 1½ |
| 26A 3942 | BDV959 | ADELPHI 1½ |
| 26A 3950 | BRW307* | ADELPHI 1½ |
| S26F 3953 | BHP467* | FALCON 1½ |
| 26A 3956 | 145529-AUS | KESTREL 1½ |
| 26A 3965 | BHP690* | ADELPHI 1½ |
| 26M 3968 | NR | MERLIN 1½ |
| 26K 3970 | CUL176 | KESTREL 1½ |
| 26K 3977 | NR | KESTREL 1½ |
| 26A 3993 | BRW312* | KESTREL 1½ |
| 26A 3997 | BHP881* | ADELPHI 1½ |
| 26K 4004 | BHP692* | ADELPHI COL 1½ |
| 26K 4005 | JN7134 | KESTREL 1½ |
| 26F 4012 | 1YF865-AUS | LYNX 1½ |
| 26K 4022 | DF1936-NZ | FALCON 1½ |
| 26K 4026 | BHP691* | KESTREL 1½ |
| 26M 4035 | CYK770 | MERLIN 1½ |
| S26L 4065 | BHP892* | LYNX 1½ |
| 26L 4070 | EU5963 | LYNX 1½ |
| 26F 4072 | BWM276 | FALCON 1½ |
| 26AT 4076 | BVC532* | KESTREL 1½ |
| 26A 4077 | BHP517* | ARMY TOURER 1½ |
| 26A 4078 | APW808 | ADELPHI COL 1½ |
| S26K 4081 | BHP883* | KESTREL 1½ |
| 26A 4085 | BVC944* | KESTREL 1½ |
| 26L 4086 | BHP889* | KESTREL SPR 1½ |
| S26K 4087 | BHP884* | LYNX 1½ |
| S26S 4088 | JB8852 | KESTREL 1½ |
| S27S 4106 | CHT754 | SPRITE 1½ |
| 26F 4107 | CVK947 | FALCON 1½ |
| 26M 4119 | NR | MERLIN 1½ |
| 26M 4122 | BRW302* | MERLIN 1½ |
| 26A 4126 | CUV142 | ADELPHI 1½ |
| 26A 4127 | W57076 | ADELPHI 1½ |
| S26L 4131 | CK0838 | LYNX CONCRS 1½ |
| 26M 4132 | NR | MERLIN 1½ |
| 26M 4133 | BRW842* | FALCON 1½ |
| 26L 4134 | BMP475 | LYNX 1½ |
| 26A 4145 | BHP891* | ADELPHI 1½ |
| S26K 4155 | CLX 25 | KESTREL 1½ |
| 26A 4157 | BRW399* | KESTREL 1½ |
| S26F 4158 | NR | FALCON 1½ |
| 26K 4159 | JD6501 | KESTREL 1½ |
| 26A 4164 | AUE170 | ADELPHI 1½ |
| 26A 4172 | BRW398* | ADELPHI COL 1½ |
| 26A 4177 | BHP311* | FALCON 1½ |
| 26A 4204 | CEL900 | ADELPHI COL 1½ |
| S26K 4211 | CUV137 | KESTREL 1½ |

| CHASSIS NO. | REG.NUMBER | MODEL |
|---|---|---|
| SS26K | 4217 | KESTREL SPR 1½ |
| 26M | 4231 | MERLIN COL 1½ |
| 26M | 4232 | NR MERLIN 1½ |
| 26M | 4234 | DMG818 MERLIN 1½ |
| S26K | 4235 | BRW518* KESTREL 1½ |
| 26F | 4239 | E22743-IRL FALCON 1½ |
| SS26K | 4240 | BRW519* KESTREL SPR 1½ |
| SS26L | 4241 | BRW848* LYNX SPR 1½ |
| S26S | 4242 | JY7950 SPRITE 1½ |
| 26A | 4251 | BRW513* ADELPHI 1½ |
| 26A | 4258 | BRW516* ADELPHI 1½ |
| 26F | 4268 | CAF226 FALCON 1½ |
| 26F | 4271 | AED 25 MERLIN 1½ |
| 26M | 4276 | CKB384 MERLIN 1½ |
| S26K | 4289 | DPK165 KESTREL 1½ |
| 26M | 4293 | BRW850* MERLIN 1½ |
| 26M | 4295 | ---019-AUS MERLIN 1½ |
| S26A | 4299 | AKY 8 ADELPHI 1½ |
| 26A | 4303 | BRW700* ADELPHI 1½ |
| 26A | 4317 | NJ9562 FALCON 1½ |
| 26K | 4333 | CUV147 KESTREL 1½ |
| 26A | 4350 | BRW847* ADELPHI 1½ |
| 26A | 4364 | ASP984 ADELPHI 1½ |
| 26A | 4366 | BWK111* ADELPHI 1½ |
| 26A | 4369 | JU8877 ADELPHI 1½ |
| 26M | 4371 | NR MERLIN 1½ |
| 26A | 4374 | BRW843* ADELPHI 1½ |
| 26A | 4375 | NR ADELPHI 1½ |
| S26A | 4378 | BVC202* ADELPHI 1½ |
| 26A | 4381 | BWK741* ADELPHI 1½ |
| 26A | 4382 | BWK325* ADELPHI 1½ |
| 26A | 4386 | BWK578* ADELPHI 1½ |
| 26A | 4387 | NR ADELPHI 1½ |
| 26A | 4390 | BWK581* MERLIN 1½ |
| S26S | 4394 | CNF640 SPRITE 1½ |
| 26K | 4396 | KGB303 KESTREL 1½ |
| 26A | 4400 | BRW845* ADELPHI 1½ |
| 26A | 4419 | CXF226 KESTREL 1½ |
| 26A | 4425 | BWK330* ADELPHI 1½ |
| 26A | 4430 | BRW846* ADELPHI 1½ |
| 26K | 4432 | JV4773 KESTREL 1½ |
| 26K | 4433 | CYE688 KESTREL 1½ |
| 26K | 4435 | JU9153 KESTREL 1½ |
| 26A | 4437 | BHP534* KESTREL 1½ |
| 26A | 4441 | CXW834 KESTREL 1½ |
| SS26K | 4457 | BRW849* KESTREL SPR 1½ |
| 26L | 4459 | 0W9280 LYNX 1½ |
| 26K | 4460 | 0W9193 KESTREL 1½ |
| 26K | 4462 | JK5644 KESTREL 1½ |
| 26K | 4463 | E22867-IRL KESTREL 1½ |
| 26K | 4469 | NR KESTREL 1½ |
| SS26K | 4470 | BWK331* KESTREL SPR 1½ |
| 26K | 4479 | UD7635 KESTREL 1½ |
| S26K | 4488 | BWK579* KESTREL 1½ |
| 26M | 4491 | BWK109* MERLIN COL 1½ |
| 26M | 4497 | WMM946 MERLIN 1½ |
| 26F | 4500 | BWK102* FALCON COL 1½ |
| 26A | 4502 | NR ADELPHI 1½ |

| CHASSIS NO. | REG.NUMBER | MODEL |
|---|---|---|
| 26F | 4510 | BRW520* FALCON 1½ |
| | 4511 | BKW103* ADELPHI 1½ |
| 26K | 4513 | BKW106* KESTREL 1½ |
| 26A | 4520 | BRW844* KESTREL 1½ |
| 26F | 4538 | BKW108* FALCON COL 1½ |
| 26F | 4541 | BKW105* FALCON COL 1½ |
| 26A | 4543 | BKW107* ADELPHI COL 1½ |
| 26A | 4545 | BKW576* ADELPHI 1½ |
| 26A | 4554 | DPL378 MERLIN 1½ |
| 26A | 4557 | CXU853 ADELPHI 1½ |
| 26A | 4575 | BRW851* ADELPHI 1½ |
| S26K | 4584 | BRW851* KESTREL 1½ |
| 26A | 4589 | BKW327* ADELPHI 1½ |
| 26A | 4599 | JB9291 MERLIN 1½ |
| 26A | 4600 | BKW335* ADELPHI 1½ |
| 26A | 4601 | BKW326* KESTREL 1½ |
| S26K | 4606 | BKW574* KESTREL SPR 1½ |
| S26K | 4606 | CXY 60 KESTREL SPR 1½ |
| 26K | 4614 | BVC 54* KESTREL 1½ |
| 26A | 4624 | Z 6880-IRL ADELPHI 1½ |
| 26A | 4626 | BKW334* ADELPHI 1½ |
| 26A | 4629 | CXW932 ADELPHI 1½ |
| S26S | 4631 | CXY386 SPRITE 1½ |
| S26S | 4634 | BKW324* TT SPRITE |
| 26A | 4642 | JU8887 ADELPHI 1½ |
| 26F | 4654 | AF7747-NZ FALCON 1½ |
| 26L | 4659 | COB848 LYNX 1½ |
| S26A | 4661 | BVC 60* ADELPHI 1½ |
| 26M | 4668 | BKW328* MERLIN 1½ |
| 26M | 4669 | BFG206 MERLIN 1½ |
| 26A | 4670 | 1WX000-AUS ADELPHI 1½ |
| SS26L | 4670 | BKW575* LYNX SPR 1½ |
| SS26L | 4671 | CAF593 LYNX SPR 1½ |
| 26L | 4672 | BRO649 LYNX 1½ |
| 26A | 4675 | BKW748* ADELPHI COL 1½ |
| 26M | 4680 | BVC 59* MERLIN 1½ |
| S26K | 4685 | BCG550 KESTREL SPR 1½ |
| 26M | 4691 | BKW573* ADELPHI COL 1½ |
| 26A | 4695 | BKW560* MERLIN COL 1½ |
| 26A | 4716 | KGB616 ADELPHI 1½ |
| 26A | 4717 | BKW744* ADELPHI 1½ |
| 26L | 4725 | NR LYNX 1½ |
| S26A | 4735 | BKW582* KESTREL 1½ |
| 26A | 4741 | BVC 49* KESTREL 1½ |
| 26A | 4747 | BKW750* KESTREL 1½ |
| S26A | 4749 | BKW745* KESTREL 1½ |
| 26A | 4751 | BKW749* KESTREL 1½ |
| 26A | 4755 | BVC 58* KESTREL 1½ |
| S26A | 4758 | BVC 52* KESTREL 1½ |
| 26F | 4765 | B0R131 FALCON 1½ |
| 26A | 4772 | BKW747* ADELPHI 1½ |
| 26A | 4774 | BKW748* KESTREL 1½ |
| S26L | 4781 | DMY655 LYNX SPR 1½ |
| 26M | 4790 | NJ9388 MERLIN 1½ |
| 26K | 4791 | BKW752* KESTREL 1½ |
| 26L | 4792 | BKW742* KESTREL 1½ |
| 26A | 4793 | BKW746* ADELPHI 1½ |
| 26A | 4795 | BVC 57* ADELPHI 1½ |

| CHASSIS NO. | REG.NUMBER | MODEL |
|---|---|---|
| S26S | 4818 | NR SPRITE 1½ |
| S26L | 4819 | BWK751* LYNX CNCRS 1½ |
| 26A | 4827 | AV8471 ADELPHI 1½ |
| 26A | 4835 | BVC 50* ADELPHI 1½ |
| 26A | 4843 | BVC 56* ADELPHI 1½ |
| 26A | 4844 | BVC 53* ADELPHI 1½ |
| 26A | 4847 | B0D434 ADELPHI 1½ |
| 26L | 4848 | C0E766 LYNX 1½ |
| 26A | 4870 | BVC 55* LYNX 1½ |
| S26L | 4871 | BUR872 ADELPHI 1½ |
| 26M | 4872 | BVC201* MERLIN 1½ |
| S26S | 4883 | BTB963 SPRITE 1½ |
| S26S | 4884 | DFC789 SPRITE 1½ |
| 26A | 4896 | BVC203* ADELPHI 1½ |
| 26A | 4896 | BVC205* ADELPHI 1½ |
| SS26K | 4897 | EPB768 KESTREL SPR 1½ |
| 26L | 4901 | EW9277 LYNX 1½ |
| 26A | 4910 | LYT489 ADELPHI 1½ |
| 26A | 4916 | ATM 21 ADELPHI 1½ |
| 26S | 4920 | CVM208 SPRITE 1½ |
| 26A | 4987 | CPP707 LYNX 1½ |
| 26L | 5001 | BVC524* ADELPHI 1½ |
| 27A | 5002 | BVC211* ADELPHI 1½ |
| 27L | 5006 | NR LYNX 1½ |
| 27K | 5008 | NR KESTREL 1½ |
| SS27K | 5012 | NR KESTREL SPR 1½ |
| 27K | 5018 | DYW374 KESTREL 1½ |
| 27A | 5021 | BVC525* ADELPHI 1½ |
| 27A | 5028 | BVB162 ADELPHI 1½ |
| 27K | 5036 | EPK 44 KESTREL 1½ |
| 27A | 5038 | EZ5982-IRL ADELPHI 1½ |
| SS27K | 5055 | BKW475 KESTREL SPR 1½ |
| 27A | 5067 | BVC522* ADELPHI 1½ |
| 27K | 5068 | CDU931* ADELPHI 1½ |
| 27K | 5069 | BVB161 ADELPHI 1½ |
| SS27K | 5070 | CFY 8 KESTREL SPR 1½ |
| 27A | 5073 | BVC531* ADELPHI 1½ |
| S27K | 5076 | CWE289 KESTREL 1½ |
| 27K | 5079 | BVC824* ADELPHI 1½ |
| 27K | 5089 | EWJ118 ADELPHI 1½ |
| 27A | 5094 | BVC530* ADELPHI 1½ |
| SS27K | 5103 | BVC523* KESTREL SPR 1½ |
| 27F | 5109 | BVC821* FALCON 1½ |
| 27A | 5111 | BVC529* FALCON 1½ |
| 27A | 5125 | EKM281 ADELPHI 1½ |
| 27A | 5127 | EDY633-S ADELPHI 1½ |
| 27A | 5134 | EM0722 ADELPHI 1½ |
| 27F | 5137 | BVC528* FALCON 1½ |
| 27A | 5139 | BVC823* ADELPHI COL 1½ |
| 27A | 5161 | CNY342 ADELPHI 1½ |
| SS27L | 5164 | CF3209 ADELPHI 1½ |
| 27K | 5166 | CYP967 KESTREL 1½ |
| 27K | 5169 | CDU472* ADELPHI 1½ |
| 27L | 5170 | FPB620 FALCON 1½ |
| 27F | 5175 | BVC829* ADELPHI 1½ |
| 27F | 5190 | BVC828* FALCON 1½ |
| 27K | 5206 | NR KESTREL 1½ |
| SS27L | 5207 | RV9552 LYNX SPR 1½ |

| CHASSIS NO. | REG.NUMBER | MODEL |
|---|---|---|
| 27A | 5216 | BVC827* ADELPHI 1½ |
| SS27K | 5227 | DGF972 KESTREL SPR 1½ |
| 27A | 5231 | BHP890* ADELPHI 1½ |
| 27A | 5237 | AAY338 ADELPHI 1½ |
| 27F | 5242 | EMH590 FALCON 1½ |
| 27A | 5253 | JT6537 ADELPHI 1½ |
| 27A | 5258 | DMA 13 ADELPHI 1½ |
| 27A | 5274 | EEV502 ADELPHI 1½ |
| 27K | 5278 | BVC830* KESTREL 1½ |
| SS27K | 5300 | BVC534* ADELPHI 1½ |
| SS27K | 5310 | BVC832* KESTREL SPR 1½ |
| 27L | 5311 | BYD587 FALCON 1½ |
| 27F | 5326 | B0R707 FALCON 1½ |
| 27A | 5330 | BVC831* KESTREL SPR 1½ |
| SS27F | 5341 | AD A456 ADELPHI 1½ |
| S27F | 5343 | DGN 8 FALCON 1½ |
| SS27K | 5350 | RN5290 KESTREL 1½ |
| S27K | 5352 | NR KESTREL 1½ |
| 27A | 5353 | EZ4581-IRL ADELPHI 1½ |
| 27K | 5360 | BKV 93* KESTREL 1½ |
| S27F | 5375 | BKV 87* FALCON 1½ |
| S27S | 5379 | BKV 88* SPRITE 1½ |
| 27C | 5387 | BKV 92* CC TRG SAL 1½ |
| S27A | 5393 | BKV 83* ADELPHI 1½ |
| 27A | 5403 | ABL147 KESTREL 1½ |
| SS27K | 5404 | BKV 90* KESTREL SPR 1½ |
| 27K | 5411 | BWJ 85 KESTREL 1½ |
| SS27K | 5413 | BDK502 KESTREL 1½ |
| 27A | 5431 | BYD983 ADELPHI 1½ |
| 27K | 5453 | NR ADELPHI 1½ |
| S27F | 5434 | BKV 85* FALCON 1½ |
| 27L | 5443 | CVU783 LYNX SPR 1½ |
| S27A | 5449 | BKV309* ADELPHI 1½ |
| SS27K | 5452 | BKV312* KESTREL 1½ |
| SS27K | 5453 | CDU475* KESTREL SPR 1½ |
| SS27K | 5455 | JV5206 KESTREL 1½ |
| SS27K | 5457 | NR KESTREL SPR 1½ |
| 27A | 5463 | B0Y410 FALCON 1½ |
| S27K | 5470 | C0Y481 LYNX SPR 1½ |
| S27K | 5471 | CKC210 KESTREL 1½ |
| S27K | 5473 | BFM257 ADELPHI 1½ |
| SS27K | 5475 | JY9284 KESTREL SPR 1½ |
| 27F | 5476 | CDU 54* FALCON 1½ |
| 27F | 5482 | CDU 56* FALCON 1½ |
| SS27K | 5501 | DG0748 KESTREL 1½ |
| SS27K | 5506 | CDU471* KESTREL 1½ |
| 27F | 5515 | CDU 60* FALCON 1½ |
| SS27K | 5527 | VH9623 ADELPHI 1½ |
| 27A | 5539 | BKV305* ADELPHI 1½ |
| S27F | 5541 | BKV307* FALCON 1½ |
| SS27L | 5542 | DGT712 LYNX SPR 1½ |
| 27F | 5545 | DLC950 FALCON 1½ |
| 27F | 5546 | BKV308* KESTREL 1½ |
| 27S | 5548 | DJ3678 SPRITE 1½ |
| 27F | 5551 | EPH357 ADELPHI 1½ |
| 27A | 5558 | BKV310* FALCON 1½ |
| 27F | 5569 | EMT132 FALCON 1½ |
| SS27K | 5560 | BKV306* KESTREL SPR 1½ |

| CHASSIS NO. | REG.NUMBER | MODEL |
|---|---|---|
| 27K 5571 | DKW977 | KESTREL 1½ |
| 27K 5579 | DJJ 29 | KESTREL 1½ |
| 27F 5581 | BKV311* | FALCON 1½ |
| 27A 5587 | NR | ADELPHI 1½ |
| 27F 5594 | CAS907-TAS | FALCON 1½ |
| SS27K 5607 | ATM900 | KESTREL SPR 1½ |
| 27A 5609 | BKV313* | KESTREL 1½ |
| 27C 5610 | CDU616* | CC TRG SAL 1½ |
| 27A 5617 | BDK691 | ADELPHI 1½ |
| 27A 5619 | ATM709 | ADELPHI 1½ |
| 27F 5620 | EML678 | ADELPHI 1½ |
| SS27K 5628 | BFM447 | KESTREL SPR 1½ |
| 27K 5629 | COY901 | KESTREL 1½ |
| SS27K 5630 | BKV314* | KESTREL SPR 1½ |
| 27L 5636 | E26210-IRL | LYNX 1½ |
| 27K 5650 | DMA123 | FALCON 1½ |
| SS27K 5655 | BKV363* | KESTREL SPR 1½ |
| 27C 5665 | BKV716* | CC TRG SAL 1½ |
| 27C 5667 | BVE510 | CC TRG SAL 1½ |
| 27C 5668 | FPE766 | CC TRG SAL 1½ |
| 27A 5669 | AD6609 | ADELPHI 1½ |
| 27A 5670 | DNU339 | ADELPHI 1½ |
| S27S 5675 | BAH900 | SPRITE 1½ |
| 27F 5676 | FMO607 | KESTREL 1½ |
| 27K 5677 | DLA402 | KESTREL 1½ |
| 27A 5684 | BKV719* | ADELPHI 1½ |
| 27A 5685 | AR6558-NZ | ADELPHI 1½ |
| 27C 5710 | BKV715* | CC TRG SAL 1½ |
| 27F 5716 | DKN510 | FALCON 1½ |
| 27K 5727 | CRR898 | KESTREL 1½ |
| SS27K 5732 | CPD302 | KESTREL SPR 1½ |
| S27S 5739 | BKV315* | SPRITE 1½ |
| 27F 5741 | CDU470* | FALCON COL 1½ |
| SS27K 5744 | BKV712* | KESTREL SPR 1½ |
| SS27K 5747 | CDU 57* | KESTREL SPR 1½ |
| 27A 5750 | CDU 58* | ADELPHI 1½ |
| 27C 5753 | CDU 55* | CC TRG SAL 1½ |
| 27A 5758 | BKV714* | ADELPHI 1½ |
| 27L 5766 | JTY257-S | LYNX 1½ |
| SS27K 5776 | BVE792 | KESTREL SPR 1½ |
| 27C 5778 | CDU 59* | CC TRG SAL 1½ |
| SS27K 5799 | DGT718 | KESTREL SPR 1½ |
| 27F 5809 | FVB417 | FALCON 1½ |
| SS27K 5810 | BKV718* | KESTREL SPR 1½ |
| SS27K 5827 | BKV938* | KESTREL SPR 1½ |
| 27C 5829 | EMX796 | CC TRG SAL 1½ |
| 27K 5834 | 216913-NZ | KESTREL 1½ |
| S27K 5837 | DGT729 | KESTREL 1½ |
| 27A 5838 | ASC544 | ADELPHI 1½ |
| 27C 5843 | GR3572 | CC TRG SAL 1½ |
| 27K 5846 | BKV935* | KESTREL COL 1½ |
| 27A 5849 | BKV933* | KESTREL 1½ |
| 27C 5852 | CDU 62* | ADELPHI 1½ |
| 27C 5853 | ASC962 | CC TRG SAL 1½ |
| 27K 5856 | CBY279 | KESTREL 1½ |
| 27K 5868 | CDU720* | ADELPHI 1½ |
| 27A 5876 | CDU473* | ADELPHI 1½ |
| 27A 5881 | NR | ADELPHI 1½ |
| SS27K 5883 | RDV566 | KESTREL SPR 1½ |
| 27L 5887 | CON 59 | LYNX 1½ |
| 27C 5889 | BKV940* | CC TRG SAL 1½ |
| 27C 5896 | EMW 61 | CC TRG SAL 1½ |
| 27C 5908 | EG0203 | ADELPHI 1½ |
| 27A 5926 | D23737-IRL | ADELPHI 1½ |
| S27K 5927 | DLN  2 | ADELPHI 1½ |
| 27A 5953 | CWK168* | ADELPHI 1½ |
| S27A 5958 | FMF 26 | ADELPHI 1½ |
| 27A 5967 | CDU469* | KESTREL SPR 1½ |
| SS27K 5968 | DLF370 | ADELPHI 1½ |
| 27A 5977 | CDU614* | ADELPHI 1½ |
| SS27K 5994 | AGD590 | KESTREL SPR 1½ |
| 27F 6003 | NR | FALCON 1½ |
| 27C 6014 | NR | CC TRG SAL 1½ |
| S27L 6027 | AM1454 | LYNX CONCRS 1½ |
| 27L 6028 | FMC726 | LYNX 1½ |
| 27L 6030 | DUG497 | SPRITE 1½ |
| S27S 6031 | CDU 63* | SPRITE 1½ |
| 27F 6041 | NR | FALCON 1½ |
| SS27K 6054 | DXV590 | KESTREL SPR 1½ |
| 27A 6064 | CDU613* | ADELPHI 1½ |
| 27F 6067 | CDU615* | KESTREL 1½ |
| SS27K 6071 | DLP468 | KESTREL SPR 1½ |
| 27K 6073 | BSP  1 | KESTREL SPR 1½ |
| SS27K 6080 | DLF378 | KESTREL SPR 1½ |
| 27C 6082 | COV 33 | CC TRG SAL 1½ |
| 27K 6084 | WF 9790 | FALCON 1½ |
| 27F 6102 | CDU619* | FALCON 1½ |
| 27F 6115 | DUV119 | FALCON 1½ |
| SS27K 6126 | CHP101* | KESTREL SPR 1½ |
| 27C 6129 | CDU620* | KESTREL 1½ |
| SS27K 6131 | DKM818 | KESTREL 1½ |
| 27A 6134 | AWS 87 | ADELPHI 1½ |
| SS27K 6143 | CDU621* | KESTREL SPR 1½ |
| 27K 6146 | CDU921* | ADELPHI 1½ |
| 27C 6149 | NR-AUS | CC TRG SAL 1½ |
| 27K 6150 | EN0841 | ADELPHI 1½ |
| 27A 6151 | SL2221 | KESTREL SPR 1½ |
| S27K 6157 | NR-AUS | KESTREL SPR 1½ |
| SS27K 6162 | CDU623* | KESTREL 1½ |
| SS27C 6165 | FVB556 | CC TRG SPR SAL |
| 27F 6166 | CDU618* | LYNX SPR 1½ |
| 27A 6174 | GMX700 | ADELPHI 1½ |
| 27F 6176 | JV5665 | FALCON 1½ |
| 27K 6186 | EN0151 | FALCON 1½ |
| 27K 6193 | DLP890 | KESTREL SPR 1½ |
| SS27A 6198 | CWK167* | ADELPHI 1½ |
| SS27K 6200 | CDU925* | KESTREL SPR 1½ |
| SS27K 6202 | CRO270 | KESTREL SPR 1½ |
| 27A 6207 | CHP786* | KESTREL COL 1½ |
| 27K 6237 | SM5654 | KESTREL 1½ |
| 27A 6241 | CDU926* | ADELPHI 1½ |
| 27A 6253 | NR | ADELPHI 1½ |
| 27A 6260 | CDU927* | FALCON 1½ |
| 27C 6272 | CDU928* | CC TRG SAL 1½ |
| 27A 6289 | EPL612 | ADELPHI 1½ |
| S27S 6299 | ASF522 | SPRITE 1½ |
| 27K 6300 | DLW353 | KESTREL 1½ |
| 27F 6302 | CDU930* | FALCON 1½ |
| 27F 6307 | NR | FALCON 1½ |
| 27K 6308 | DAU573 | FALCON 1½ |
| 27A 6315 | FPA121 | ADELPHI 1½ |
| 27A 6319 | CDU932* | KESTREL SPR 1½ |
| S27S 6320 | C 2570-S | SPRITE 1½ |
| 27C 6342 | ADW872 | CC TRG SAL 1½ |
| S27S 6344 | ET A357 | SPRITE 1½ |
| 27A 6355 | DYA  2 | ADELPHI 1½ |
| 27F 6357 | CHP105* | FALCON COL 1½ |
| 27K 6362 | EPL175* | ADELPHI 1½ |
| SS27K 6363 | CHP103* | KESTREL SPR 1½ |
| 27A 6368 | CHP110* | FALCON 1½ |
| 27A 6371 | NR | ADELPHI 1½ |
| 27A 6387 | DK0714 | ADELPHI 1½ |
| 27A 6406 | AMW774 | ADELPHI 1½ |
| 27A 6413 | CHP106* | ADELPHI 1½ |
| S27K 6417 | COY552 | ADELPHI 1½ |
| 27L 6420 | BBM363 | LYNX COLNL 1½ |
| 27A 6429 | CKF735 | ADELPHI 1½ |
| 27A 6438 | CVC128* | ADELPHI 1½ |
| S27S 6445 | CHP109* | SPRITE 1½ |
| 27A 6447 | DUL669 | ADELPHI 1½ |
| 27C 6452 | CHP108* | ADELPHI 1½ |
| 27C 6456 | NR | CC TRG SAL 1½ |
| 27L 6457 | FPB  2 | LYNX 1½ |
| SS27K 6458 | CHP111* | KESTREL SPR 1½ |
| 27C 6468 | DUU837 | KESTREL SPR 1½ |
| 27A 6481 | CHP782* | ADELPHI COL 1½ |
| 27A 6483 | CHP112* | ADELPHI COL 1½ |
| 27K 6487 | 100634-AUS | ADELPHI 1½ |
| 27F 6499 | FPC962 | KESTREL SPR 1½ |
| 27F 6502 | CHP785* | KESTREL SPR 1½ |
| 27L 6537 | CHP787* | LYNX COL 1½ |
| 27A 6544 | MCR794 | FALCON 1½ |
| 27L 6548 | CDK223 | LYNX 1½ |
| 27A 6572 | CHP781* | KESTREL SPR 1½ |
| S27K 6587 | EWL134 | LYNX 1½ |
| S27L 6606 | FMP631 | KESTREL SPR 1½ |
| SS27K 6609 | CHP791* | KESTREL SPR 1½ |
| 27F 6629 | CRW375* | FALCON 1½ |
| 27F 6630 | CHP788* | FALCON COL 1½ |
| 27A 6634 | CRW382* | FALCON 1½ |
| 27F 6652 | DER560 | FALCON 1½ |
| S27S 6653 | CRW910* | SPRITE 1½ |
| SS27K 6661 | FML285 | KESTREL SPR 1½ |
| SS27K 6663 | CRW911* | KESTREL SPR 1½ |
| S27S 6667 | DTT657 | TICKFORD 1½ |
| 27A 6675 | DND162 | SPRITE 1½ |
| 27A 6676 | EVW583 | KESTREL 1½ |
| 27K 6676 | OND309 | KESTREL COL 1½ |
| 27F 6678 | CRW381* | FALCON COL 1½ |
| 27A 6680 | DXB916 | FALCON 1½ |
| 27A 6697 | CRW374* | ADELPHI COL 1½ |
| SS27K 6714 | AWS 66 | KESTREL SPR 1½ |
| S27F 6717 | DAE866 | FALCON 1½ |
| S27F 6719 | CRW377* | FALCON 1½ |
| 27F 6736 | CRW379* | FALCON 1½ |
| SS27L 6739 | DYW898 | LYNX SPR 1½ |
| 27F 6742 | CRW378* | ADELPHI 1½ |
| 27A 6749 | CRW376* | KESTREL 1½ |
| 27K 6752 | GMH865 | FALCON 1½ |
| 27F 6766 | CVC477* | FALCON 1½ |
| 27A 6778 | CRW380* | ADELPHI 1½ |
| 27L 6780 | DXW409 | LYNX 1½ |
| 27A 6792 | CWK165* | ADELPHI COL 1½ |
| S27S 6797 | DTY241 | SPRITE 1½ |
| 27K 6801 | CWK166* | CC TRG SAL 1½ |
| SS27K 6806 | FMW933 | KESTREL SPR 1½ |
| SS27K 6828 | CWK161* | KESTREL SPR 1½ |
| SS27L 6830 | CRW906* | LYNX SPR 1½ |
| 27L 6832 | DXX 66 | LYNX CONCRS 1½ |
| 27A 6834 | CWK817* | ADELPHI 1½ |
| SS27K 6835 | CHP792* | KESTREL 1½ |
| 27F 6838 | DPP467 | ADELPHI 1½ |
| S27S 6843 | BKW769 | SPRITE 1½ |
| 27K 6850 | BNX635 | KESTREL 1½ |
| 26K 6851 | DXX732 | ADELPHI 1½ |
| 27A 6876 | CWK445* | ADELPHI 1½ |
| 27L 6877 | DYM429 | LYNX 1½ |
| 27A 6878 | CWK172* | ADELPHI 1½ |
| 27A 6879 | CWK442* | ADELPHI 1½ |
| 27F 6885 | CWK164* | FALCON COL 1½ |
| 27F 6887 | CWK449* | FALCON 1½ |
| SS27L 6898 | CWK443* | LYNX SPR 1½ |
| 27A 6903 | CWK162* | ADELPHI 1½ |
| SS27K 6930 | CWK169* | ADELPHI COL 1½ |
| 27L 6947 | CWK451* | FALCON COL 1½ |
| 27L 6949 | CVC121* | ADELPHI 1½ |
| S27S 6950 | CWK171* | LYNX 1½ |
| 27A 6952 | DYV 90 | TT SPRITE |
| 27A 6953 | AHS 29 | ADELPHI 1½ |
| 27K 6956 | CWK453* | ADELPHI 1½ |
| 27K 6958 | CWK819* | ADELPHI 1½ |
| 27C 6960 | CWK446* | CC TRG SAL 1½ |
| SS27K 6971 | DYU171 | KESTREL SPR 1½ |
| SS27K 6974 | DYR539 | KESTREL SPR 1½ |
| SS27K 6978 | CWK816* | ADELPHI 1½ |
| 27A 6985 | CWK452* | KESTREL SPR 1½ |
| 27A 6997 | CWK823* | ADELPHI 1½ |
| SS27C 7005 | FPG100 | CC TRG SPR SAL |
| 27F 7010 | JW9103 | FALCON 1½ |
| 27F 7015 | CWK818* | ADELPHI 1½ |
| 27F 7018 | CRW908* | FALCON 1½ |
| SS27L 7021 | NR | ADELPHI 1½ |
| 27K 7024 | FPH299 | LYNX SPR 1½ |
| 27K 7035 | DYW897 | KESTREL 1½ |
| 27A 7038 | CWK821* | KESTREL SPR 1½ |
| SS27K 7039 | GMH860 | KESTREL 1½ |
| 27A 7041 | YJ5130 | ADELPHI 1½ |
| 27A 7042 | CVC130* | KESTREL COL 1½ |
| 27A 7046 | CDU622* | ADELPHI COL 1½ |
| 27F 7055 | CWK825* | FALCON 1½ |
| 27K 7064 | CWK827* | KESTREL 1½ |

| CHASSIS NO. | | REG.NUMBER | MODEL |
|---|---|---|---|
| S27S | 7069 | APM351 | SPRITE 1½ |
| S27S | 7070 | CCG294 | SPRITE 1½ |
| 27F | 7074 | APM485 | FALCON 1½ |
| 27K | 7078 | ---006-AUS | KESTREL 1½ |
| SS27K | 7080 | CVC127* | KESTREL SPR 1½ |
| 27F | 7091 | EGF768 | FALCON 1½ |
| 27F | 7097 | CVC126* | FALCON COL 1½ |
| 27F | 7100 | NR | FALCON 1½ |
| 27F | 7102 | BWY572 | FALCON 1½ |
| SS27K | 7106 | CVC124* | KESTREL SPR 1½ |
| 27F | 7111 | EGY631 | FALCON 1½ |
| 27F | 7114 | CVC125* | FALCON COL 1½ |
| 27A | 7123 | CVC131* | ADELPHI 1½ |
| 27F | 7125 | EGP464 | FALCON 1½ |
| S27S | 7126 | EGM198 | SPRITE 1½ |
| 27A | 7128 | BKV939* | ADELPHI 1½ |
| 27AX | 7200 | CVC129* | ADELPHI 1½ |
| 28FX | 7201 | CVC475* | TRG SAL 1½ |
| 28A | 7211 | CVC473* | ADELPHI 1½ |
| 28FX | 7212 | CVC479* | TRG SAL 1½ |
| 28AX | 7216 | CVC480* | ADELPHI 1½ |
| 28AX | 7229 | CVC476* | ADELPHI 1½ |
| 28AX | 7231 | CVC478* | ADELPHI 1½ |
| 28F | 7237 | CVC132* | TRG SAL 1½ |
| 28L | 7255 | CVC482* | LYNX 1½ |
| 28AX | 7256 | TGB569 | ADELPHI 1½ |
| 28A | 7258 | CVC893* | ADELPHI 1½ |
| 28K | 7266 | EZ8765-IRL | KESTREL 1½ |
| 28K | 7268 | ELC893 | KESTREL 1½ |
| 28KX | 7271 | CVC891* | KESTREL 1½ |
| SS28K | 7281 | DOJ321 | KESTREL SPR 1½ |
| SS28K | 7295 | FUA 3 | KESTREL SPR 1½ |
| SS28K | 7295 | 8877 U | KESTREL SPR 1½ |
| 28K | 7303 | EVK509 | KESTREL 1½ |
| 28K | 7309 | CER809 | KESTREL 1½ |
| 28KX | 7325 | EXR340 | KESTREL 1½ |
| 28KX | 7326 | CVC481* | KESTREL 1½ |
| 28FX | 7343 | FRA 61 | TRG SALOON 1½ |
| 28K | 7348 | CKV584* | KESTREL 1½ |
| 28K | 7351 | BSC692 | KESTREL 1½ |
| 28K | 7359 | EKA439 | KESTREL 1½ |
| 28A | 7362 | BRY752 | ADELPHI 1½ |
| 28L | 7368 | ELE651 | LYNX 1½ |
| 28VX | 7369 | CVC888* | VICTOR 1½ |
| 28A | 7371 | CVC483* | ADELPHI 1½ |
| 28VX | 7374 | CVC884* | VICTOR 1½ |
| 28A | 7376 | CKV280* | ADELPHI 1½ |
| 28VX | 7381 | CKV318* | VICTOR 1½ |
| 28A | 7385 | ELP 65 | ADELPHI 1½ |
| 28KX | 7392 | CVC895* | KESTREL 1½ |
| 28K | 7393 | CKV322* | KESTREL 1½ |
| 28A | 7394 | CKV410 | ADELPHI 1½ |
| 28A | 7397 | CVC894* | ADELPHI 1½ |
| 28A | 7399 | CKV315* | ADELPHI 1½ |
| 28A | 7404 | CKV100* | ADELPHI 1½ |
| 28F | 7419 | BCR153 | TRG SAL 1½ |
| 28A | 7430 | CTD925 | ADELPHI 1½ |
| 28K | 7434 | GPA522 | KESTREL 1½ |

| CHASSIS NO. | | REG.NUMBER | MODEL |
|---|---|---|---|
| 28AX | 7436 | DHP731* | ADELPHI 1½ |
| 28K | 7438 | NR | KESTREL 1½ |
| 28L | 7439 | DZ4742-IRL | LYNX 1½ |
| 28FX | 7445 | BCR812 | TRG SAL 1½ |
| 28K | 7458 | 471 U3-B | KESTREL 1½ |
| 28K | 7458 | CKV574* | KESTREL 1½ |
| 28K | 7465 | LDD393-AUS | KESTREL |
| 28VX | 7477 | CSP531 | VICTOR 1½ |
| 28L | 7478 | CKV320* | LYNX 1½ |
| 28A | 7479 | CKV319* | ADELPHI 1½ |
| 28L | 7481 | GS7683 | LYNX 1½ |
| 28L | 7484 | ARY389 | LYNX 1½ |
| 28F | 7493 | ETT733 | TRG SAL 1½ |
| 28K | 7532 | ABU775 | KESTREL 1½ |
| SS28L | 7533 | FJ1938-NZ | LYNX SPR 1½ |
| 28K | 7538 | ELM294 | KESTREL 1½ |
| 28VX | 7540 | CKV576* | VICTOR 1½ |
| 28L | 7566 | ELM144 | LYNX 1½ |
| 28VX | 7577 | BCY968 | VICTOR 1½ |
| 28KX | 7584 | BBY885 | KESTREL 1½ |
| 28K | 7587 | ENA 59 | KESTREL 1½ |
| 28VX | 7592 | CER804 | VICTOR 1½ |
| 28AX | 7593 | DRL246 | ADELPHI 1½ |
| 28VX | 7598 | CKV579* | VICTOR 1½ |
| 28K | 7605 | CKV578* | KESTREL 1½ |
| 28V | 7606 | DDU391* | VICTOR 1½ |
| 28VX | 7610 | NR | VICTOR 1½ |
| 28VX | 7615 | 712EVE | VICTOR 1½ |
| 28VX | 7615 | BOW 19 | VICTOR 1½ |
| 28VX | 7617 | CWT753 | VICTOR 1½ |
| 28VX | 7629 | CKV583* | VICTOR 1½ |
| 28A | 7654 | JC5167 | ADELPHI 1½ |
| 28VX | 7679 | FZ 665-IRL | VICTOR 1½ |
| S28S | 7693 | BCR810 | SPRITE 1½ |
| 28VX | 7699 | DDU387* | VICTOR 1½ |
| 28V | 7716 | DHP723* | VICTOR 1½ |
| S28S | 7721 | ORE600 | SPRITE 1½ |
| 28K | 7722 | NR | KESTREL 1½ |
| S28S | 7723 | EMB136 | SPRITE 1½ |
| 28A | 7737 | DDU389* | ADELPHI 1½ |
| 28A | 7750 | ELT883 | ADELPHI 1½ |
| 28VX | 7755 | DRU575 | VICTOR 1½ |
| 28L | 7764 | GPD800 | LYNX 1½ |
| 28A | 7771 | DDU392* | ADELPHI 1½ |
| 28VX | 7778 | AVN 61 | VICTOR 1½ |
| 28VX | 7792 | DRO684 | VICTOR 1½ |
| 28V | 7796 | DRW152* | VICTOR 1½ |
| 28A | 7799 | NR | ADELPHI 1½ |
| 28FX | 7810 | NR | TRG SAL 1½ |
| 28FX | 7812 | EXX741 | TRG SAL 1½ |
| 28VX | 7816 | DHP729* | VICTOR 1½ |
| 28VX | 7816 | NR | VICTOR 1½ |
| 28VX | 7817 | DHP722* | VICTOR 1½ |
| 28L | 7818 | DDU396* | LYNX 1½ |
| S28S | 7829 | ABA525 | SPRITE 1½ |
| 28L | 7832 | DUR482 | LYNX 1½ |
| 28VX | 7834 | DVO404 | VICTOR 1½ |
| 28L | 7838 | DUR482 | LYNX 1½ |

| CHASSIS NO. | | REG.NUMBER | MODEL |
|---|---|---|---|
| 28L | 7840 | DDU395* | LYNX 1½ |
| 28VX | 7841 | CWT907 | VICTOR 1½ |
| 28VX | 7849 | DNY540 | VICTOR 1½ |
| S28S | 7850 | FTN200 | SPRITE 1½ |
| 28VX | 7852 | NR | VICTOR 1½ |
| 28LX | 7866 | CAC531 | LYNX 1½ |
| 28F | 7869 | DFY611 | TRG SAL 1½ |
| 28F | 7872 | DHP733* | TRG SAL 1½ |
| 28A | 7874 | DRW148* | ADELPHI 1½ |
| 28L | 7875 | DRW147* | LYNX 1½ |
| 28A | 7883 | NR | ADELPHI 1½ |
| 28VX | 7884 | DRW149* | VICTOR 1½ |
| S28S | 7892 | ABA525 | SPRITE 1½ |
| 28F | 7900 | NR | TRG SAL 1½ |
| 28V | 7902 | DRW150* | VICTOR 1½ |
| S28S | 7914 | GNW265 | SPRITE 1½ |
| S28S | 7917 | HPA839 | SPRITE 1½ |
| 28A | 7918 | DKV431* | ADELPHI 1½ |
| 28VX | -EXP | DHP728* | VICTOR EXP 1½ |

8-90 (18HP V8) 'SILVER STREAK' MODELS.

| CHASSIS NO. | | REG.NUMBER | MODEL |
|---|---|---|---|
| 86A | 101 | BDU 8* | ADELPHI 8-90 |
| 86A | 109 | BVC209* | ADELPHI 8-90 |
| 87A | 201 | BKV 84* | ADELPHI 8-90 |
| 87A | 202 | CWK170* | ADELPHI 8-90 |
| 87A | 205 | CWK825* | ADELPHI 8-90 |
| 87A | 208 | CVC123* | ADELPHI 8-90 |
| 87A | 211 | NR -AUS | ADELPHI 8-90 |
| 87A | 212 | CVC474* | ADELPHI 8-90 |
| 87A | 219 | GS4779 | ADELPHI 8-90 |
| 87A | 220 | CKV314* | ADELPHI 8-90 |
| 87A | 223 | CKV575* | ADELPHI 8-90 |
| 87A | 224 | JM3576 | ADELPHI 8-90 |
| 87A | 228 | NR | ADELPHI 8-90 |

2½ LITRE (16HP BIG FOUR) 'BLUE STREAK' MODELS.

| CHASSIS NO. | | REG.NUMBER | MODEL |
|---|---|---|---|
| 16. | 082RP | CRW905* | EXP SAL 16/4 |
| 38AX | 1001 | CVC886* | ADELPHI 16/4 |
| 38AX | 1002 | NR | ADELPHI 16/4 |
| 38KX | 1003 | NR | KESTREL 16/4 |
| 38KX | 1005 | CVC890* | KESTREL 16/4 |
| 38AX | 1007 | CVC889* | ADELPHI 16/4 |
| 38AX | 1009 | EYM 75 | ADELPHI 16/4 |
| 38AX | 1010 | CVC892* | ADELPHI 16/4 |
| 38AX | 1012 | DXJ477 | ADELPHI 16/4 |
| 38AX | 1014 | CKV316* | ADELPHI 16/4 |
| 38KX | 1016 | CKV313* | KESTREL 16/4 |
| 38KX | 1016 | 1 YDP | KESTREL 16/4 |
| 38AX | 1021 | JK7353 | ADELPHI 16/4 |
| 38BX | 1022 | DLJ786 | CC TRG SAL 16/4 |
| 38AX | 1026 | CKV317* | ADELPHI 16/4 |
| 38KX | 1028 | APY 76 | KESTREL 16/4 |

| CHASSIS NO. | | REG.NUMBER | MODEL |
|---|---|---|---|
| 38KX | 1039 | DRW151* | KESTREL 16/4 |
| 38AX | 1041 | ENA152 | ADELPHI 16/4 |
| 38KX | 1044 | NR | KESTREL 16/4 |
| 38KX | 1056 | CKV321* | KESTREL 16/4 |
| 38KX | 1058 | JV6400 | KESTREL 16/4 |
| 38AX | 1060 | EY0126 | ADELPHI 16/4 |
| 38AX | 1061 | CKV573* | ADELPHI 16/4 |
| 38KX | 1066 | ELM417 | KESTREL 16/4 |
| 38KX | 1067 | CAK 1 | KESTREL 16/4 |
| 38AX | 1071 | CKV580* | ADELPHI 16/4 |
| 38KX | 1076 | BCR490 | KESTREL 16/4 |
| 38KX | 1078 | DKF778 | KESTREL 16/4 |
| 38KX | 1078 | RLY 16 | KESTREL 16/4 |
| 38BX | 1082 | NR | CC TRG SAL 16/4 |
| 38AX | 1087 | CKV577* | ADELPHI 16/4 |
| 38AX | 1089 | AWR702 | ADELPHI 16/4 |
| 38KX | 1090 | NR | KESTREL 16/4 |
| 38AX | 1093 | BSC761 | ADELPHI 16/4 |
| 38AX | 1099 | ELP 79 | ADELPHI 16/4 |
| 38AX | 1110 | EOB622 | ADELPHI 16/4 |
| 38KX | 1121 | AWF975 | KESTREL 16/4 |
| 38KX | 1124 | CKV581* | KESTREL 16/4 |
| 38AX | 1127 | DZ4999-IRL | ADELPHI 16/4 |
| 38AX | 1152 | NR | ADELPHI 16/4 |
| 38KX | 1153 | CKV582* | KESTREL 16/4 |
| 38KX | 1155 | DON906 | KESTREL 16/4 |
| 38AX | 1159 | NR | ADELPHI 16/4 |
| 38KX | 1160 | GMV543 | KESTREL 16/4 |
| 38AX | 1162 | NR | ADELPHI 16/4 |
| 38KX | 1167 | FZ 4-IRL | KESTREL 16/4 |
| 38AX | 1170 | FTN562 | ADELPHI 16/4 |
| 38KX | 1180 | GPC932 | KESTREL 16/4 |
| 38LX | 1181 | BTR408 | LYNX 16/4 |
| 38BX | 1182 | DDU388* | CC TRG SAL 16/4 |
| 38BX | 1188 | BWN141 | CC TRG SAL 16/4 |
| 38AX | 1189 | NR | ADELPHI 16/4 |
| 38KX | 1196 | DKF506 | KESTREL 16/4 |
| 38AX | 1199 | FVT597 | ADELPHI 16/4 |
| 38KX | 1208 | APN580 | KESTREL 16/4 |
| 38AX | 1211 | DDU397* | ADELPHI 16/4 |
| 38KX | 1213 | JC5016 | KESTREL 16/4 |
| 38KX | 1214 | DDU393* | KESTREL 16/4 |
| 38BX | 1217 | AUN917 | CC TRG SAL 16/4 |
| 38KX | 1221 | DDU390* | KESTREL 16/4 |
| 38AX | 1222 | APN580 | ADELPHI 16/4 |
| 38BX | 1224 | ENA152 | MALTBY TR 16/4 |
| 38KX | 1226 | CVE 7 | KESTREL 16/4 |
| 38KX | 1229 | ELR721 | KESTREL 16/4 |
| 38BX | 1232 | DDV987 | CC TRG SAL 16/4 |
| 38AX | 1238 | DDU394* | ADELPHI 16/4 |
| 38BX | 1240 | FWL765 | CC TRG SAL 16/4 |
| 38KX | 1243 | AFR384 | KESTREL 16/4 |
| 38KX | 1253 | EY6333 | KESTREL 16/4 |
| 38KX | 1255 | NR | KESTREL 16/4 |
| 38KX | 1258 | JAW610-AUS | KESTREL 16/4 |
| 38AX | 1262 | DHP726* | ADELPHI 16/4 |
| 38KX | 1266 | DHP727* | KESTREL 16/4 |
| 38BX | 1267 | NR | CC TRG SAL 16/4 |

| CHASSIS NO. | REG.NUMBER | MODEL |
|---|---|---|
| 38KX | 1270 DHP725* | KESTREL 16/4 |
| 38AX | 1273 NR- ZA | ADELPHI 16/4 |
| 38AX | 1276 DHP730* | ADELPHI 16/4 |
| 38KX | 1277 EXX627 | KESTREL 16/4 |
| 38KX | 1279 EM3441 | KESTREL 16/4 |
| 38BX | 1288 GPH520 | CC TRG SAL 16/4 |
| 38KX | 1289 DHP732* | KESTREL 16/4 |
| 38AX | 1296 FAE279 | ADELPHI 16/4 |
| 38BX | 1300 DRW155* | CC TRG SAL 16/4 |
| 38BX | 1301 EF6830 | CC TRG SAL 16/4 |
| 38KX | 1302 ECV228 | KESTREL 16/4 |
| 38AX | 1304 FKE597 | ADELPHI 16/4 |
| 38AX | 1308 EOH357 | ADELPHI 16/4 |
| 38AX | 1309 BZ6133-IRL | ADELPHI 16/4 |
| 38AX | 1310 DRW156* | ADELPHI 16/4 |
| 38AX | 1311 DRW154* | ADELPHI 16/4 |

| CHASSIS NO. | REG.NUMBER | MODEL |
|---|---|---|
| 38AX | 1313 BOW423 | ADELPHI 16/4 |
| 38AX | ---- JK7353 | ADELPHI 16/4 |

AUTOVIA 24HP V8 SALOONS AND LIMOUSINES

| | CHASSIS NO. | REG.NUMBER | MODEL |
|---|---|---|---|
| L | 63101 | BHP351* | AUTOVIA LIM |
| S | 63102 | BRW534* | AUTOVIA SAL |
| S | 63109 | CRW909* | AUTOVIA SAL |
| S | 63110 | CHP789* | AUTOVIA SAL |
| L | 63111 | CRW384* | AUTOVIA LIM |
| S | 63121 | DXP298 | AUTOVIA SAL |
| S | 63124 | CVC534* | AUTOVIA SAL |
| S | 63141 | FYX413 | AUTOVIA SAL |

# Riley Patents

Listed here are all of the known patents taken out by the Riley companies or members of the Riley family. It will be seen that some are dated after 1938, because the date of patent may have been some time after the date of the design to which a patent relates. The years shown for all patents are the years in which the patent numbers were issued. However, in the case of those patents issued before 1919, the patent year is significant because the number sequence started again annually. After that date a straight-through numbering system was adopted. Since the date of the patent was the date of issue, it was always possible that the year in which the patent was finally granted could be some considerable time later than the date of application. Because Riley took out so many patents, it is not possible to reproduce them all in facsimile within this book, but some of the more interesting ones are reproduced.

This list attempts to represent all of the Riley patents related to road vehicles, though the description given here may differ from the official title. That is because a number of the original titles under which patents have been granted are either rather vague, brief or even slightly misleading.

The list is laid out in such a way that a person wishing to obtain copies of patents can extract all of the information needed in an application for them from the first three columns:

| Year. | Pat. No. | Applicant. | Subject of Patent. |
| --- | --- | --- | --- |
| 1901 | 19422 | V & P Riley & Riley Cycle Co. Ltd. | Clutch freewheel. |
| 1902 | 21689 | V & P Riley. | Back-pedalling brake. |
| 1902 | 23684 | V & P Riley. | Bicycle free-wheel clutch. |
| 1903 | 7246 | P & V Riley. | Hand brake mechanism. |
| 1903 | 14391 | P Riley. | Engine valve gear. |
| 1903 | 14392 | V Riley. | Gear hardening. |
| 1904 | 20344 | P Riley. | Steering gear. |
| 1904 | 20597 | P Riley. | Expanding ring clutch. |
| 1904 | 20860 | P Riley. | Gearbox (Tricar). |
| 1905 | 24211 | P Riley. | Shaft-driven differential. |
| 1906 | 13762 | P Riley. | Built-up shafts (including ball-race crank). |
| 1907 | 21457 | P Riley. | Carburetter. |
| 1908 | 13857 | P Riley. | Detachable wheels. |
| 1908 | 23390 | P Riley. | Sleeve-valve engine. |
| 1909 | 2297 | V Riley. | Self-locking hub cap. |
| 1910 | 19797 | V Riley. | Hub nut & spanner. |
| 1911 | 4942 | P Riley. | Engine sleeve valves. |

| Year. | Pat. No. | Applicant. | Subject of Patent. |
|---|---|---|---|
| 1912 | 18604 | V & S Riley. | Detachable hub & spanner. |
| 1912 | 21942 | V & S Riley. | Detachable wheels. |
| 1912 | 25001 | S Riley & Rapide Detachable Wheel Syndicate. | Detachable wheels. |
| 1914 | 18204 | P Riley. | Internal combust. engine. |
| 1915 | 11933 | P Riley. | Disc valve gear. |
| 1919 | 138500 | Riley (Coventry) Ltd & H Rush. | Swivel pin lubrication. |
| 1919 | 139351 | Riley (Coventry) Ltd & H Rush. | Piston design. |
| 1919 | 143005 | Riley (Coventry) Ltd & H Rush. | Cam brakes. |
| 1919 | 143360 | Riley (Coventry) Ltd & H Rush. | Disc wheels. |
| 1919 | 148000 | Riley (Coventry) Ltd & H Rush. | Air-cooled brakes. |
| 1919 | 150795 | Riley (Coventry) Ltd & H Rush. | Laminated disc wheels. |
| 1921 | 183539 | Riley (Coventry) Ltd & H Rush. | Coupé glazing. |
| 1923 | 216356 | A Riley. | Dashboard lockers. |
| 1923 | 223676 | A Riley. | Vehicle luggage carrier. |
| 1923 | 223989 | A & S Riley. | Sidescreen tensioner. |
| 1923 | 229012 | A & S Riley. | Vehicle interior heater. |
| 1924 | 236380 | A & S Riley. | Hinged sidescreens. |
| 1924 | 240923 | A & S Riley. | Foldaway sidescreens. |
| 1924 | 242412 | A Riley. | Draught excluders. |
| 1924 | 243490 | A & S Riley. | Windscreen/door pillar. |
| 1924 | 243541 | A & S Riley. | Vehicle windscreens. |
| 1924 | 245909 | A Riley. | Draught Excluders. |
| 1924 | 246287 | P Riley. | Engine slide-valves. |
| 1925 | 244283 | A & S Riley. | Windscreen/door pillar. |
| 1925 | 250372 | A & S Riley. | Draught excluders. |
| 1925 | 250387 | A Riley & J Wiggins. | Windscreen fastenings. |
| 1925 | 257413 | P Riley. | Silent Third gearbox. |
| 1926 | 270519 | P Riley. | Engine mountings. |
| 1926 | 282188 | Riley (Coventry) Ltd & H Rush. | Engine mountings. |
| 1926 | 282192 | Riley (Coventry) Ltd & H Rush. | Windscreen fastenings. |
| 1927 | 290822 | P Riley. | Carburetter heating. |
| 1927 | 303257 | A Riley & R Hallwood. | Vehicle bonnets. |
| 1928 | 305804 | A Riley. | Pedal draught excluders. |
| 1928 | 306730 | A Riley. | Vehicle bonnets. |
| 1928 | 313340 | A Riley & R Hallwood. | Body mountings. |
| 1928 | 317251 | A Riley. | Underbonnet tool holder. |
| 1928 | 318755 | A Riley. | Floor sound proofing. |
| 1928 | 320503 | Riley (Coventry) Ltd & S Riley. | Front brake cable guide. |
| 1928 | 320759 | A Riley. | Mudguards. |
| 1928 | 321508 | Riley (Coventry) Ltd & S Riley. | Brake compensator. |
| 1928 | 322030 | Riley (Coventry) Ltd & S Riley. | Adjustable hand brake. |
| 1928 | 322267 | Riley (Coventry) Ltd & S Riley. | Brake compensator. |
| 1928 | 325059 | Riley (Coventry) Ltd & S Riley. | Brake actuating mechanism. |

| *Year.* | *Pat. No.* | *Applicant.* | *Subject of Patent.* |
|---|---|---|---|
| 1929 | 323380 | A Riley & R Hallwood. | Window winding mechanism. |
| 1929 | 323938 | A Riley. | Vehicle mudguards. |
| 1929 | 330396 | A Riley & R Hallwood. | Swivelling seats. |
| 1929 | 339087 | P Riley. | Variable speed gearing. |
| 1930 | 354424 | A Riley. | Vehicle bonnet design. |
| 1930 | 354867 | A Riley. | Vehicle bonnet design. |
| 1930 | 356939 | A Riley. | Door with hinged mudguard. |
| 1931 | 371981 | A Riley. | Vehicle bonnet design. |
| 1931 | 375041 | A Riley. | Pedal draught excluders. |
| 1931 | 375591 | A Riley. | Draught excluders. |
| 1931 | 376535 | P Riley. | Silent helical gearbox. |
| 1932 | 382362 | A Riley & H Rush. | Door check mechanism. |
| 1932 | 384631 | A Riley & H Rush. | Door retaining mechanism. |
| 1932 | 391387 | P Riley. | Engine/gearbox mountings. |
| 1933 | 391588 | P Riley. | Water-cooled bearings. |
| 1933 | 392330 | P Riley. | Silent helical gearbox. |
| 1933 | 394093 | P Riley. | Synchronised gearbox. |
| 1933 | 394652 | Riley (Coventry) Limited. | Gearbox gate lock. |
| 1933 | 405429 | P Riley. | Fluid clutches. |
| 1933 | 422217 | Houdaille Hydraulic Suspension Co/ AW King/Midland Motor Body Co & R Hallwood. | Windscreen wipers. |
| 1934 | 412742 | A Riley & H Rush. | Draught excluders. |
| 1934 | 414816 | A Riley & H Rush. | Door lock mechanism. |
| 1934 | 420433 | P Riley. | Independent suspension. |
| 1935 | 423454 | P Riley. | Change-speed mechanism. |
| 1935 | 423455 | P Riley. | Change-speed mechanism. |
| 1935 | 433896 | A Riley. | Ventilator mechanism. |
| 1935 | 435331 | A Riley. | Boot locking mechanism. |
| 1935 | 435497 | P Riley. | Change-speed mechanism. |
| 1936 | 441925 | P Riley. | Hydraulic gear-change. |
| 1936 | 449077 | P Riley. | Hydraulic clutch. |
| 1936 | 449637 | Riley (Coventry) Ltd & H Rush. | Handbrake mechanism. |
| 1937 | 450394 | H Rush & Riley (Coventry) Ltd. | Handbrake lever. |
| 1937 | 457633 | Riley (Coventry) Limited. | Door interior panelling. |
| 1937 | 459084 | Riley (Coventry) Ltd & S Riley. | Propeller shaft design. |
| 1937 | 459905 | S Riley & Riley (Coventry) Ltd. | V8 bonnet design. |
| 1937 | 464712 | P Riley. | Engine valve mechanism. |
| 1937 | 465006 | P Riley. | Hydraulic tappets. |
| 1937 | 467640 | A Riley & R Hallwood. | Window/screen mechanism. |
| 1937 | 468647 | Riley (Coventry) Ltd & AWK von der Becke. | Crossflow cylinder/head cooling. |
| 1937 | 471823 | Riley (Coventry) Ltd & S Riley. | Ind. front suspension. |
| 1937 | 471824 | Riley (Coventry) Ltd & S Riley. | Front & rear suspension. |

| Year. | Pat. No. | Applicant. | Subject of Patent. |
|-------|----------|------------|--------------------|
| 1937 | 472781 | Midland Motor Body Co/R Hallwood. | Sliding seat mechanism. |
| 1937 | 472872 | Midland Motor Body Co/R Hallwood. | Slidable seats. |
| 1937 | 476786 | Riley (Coventry) Ltd & S Riley. | Ind. front suspension. |
| 1938 | 488172 | P Riley. | Ind. suspension system. |
| 1938 | 496831 | P Riley. | 4WD Military vehicle. |
| 1939 | 499048 | P Riley. | Limited slip differential. |

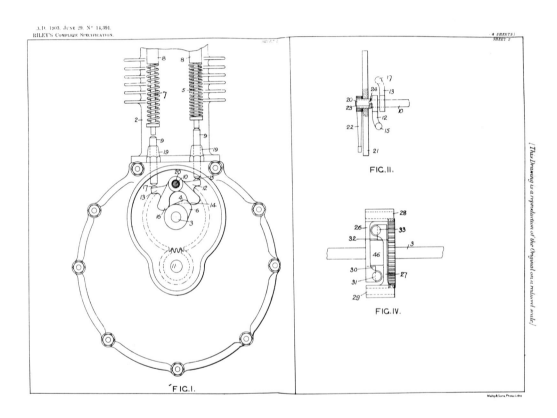

A.D. 1903. JUNE 29. N° 14,391.
RILEY'S COMPLETE SPECIFICATION.

FIG. I.

FIG. II.

FIG. IV.

(*This Drawing is a reproduction of the Original on a reduced scale.*)

Malby & Sons. Photo-Litho.

# N° 14,391

# A.D. 1903

*Date of Application, 29th June, 1903—Accepted, 20th Aug., 1903*

## COMPLETE SPECIFICATION.

### Improvements in or relating to Internal Combustion Motors.

I, PERCY RILEY, of Hollybank, Radford Road, Coventry, Warwickshire, Engineer, do hereby declare the nature of this invention and in what manner the same is to be performed to be particularly described and ascertained in and by the following statement:—

5   My invention relates to internal combustion motors such as used on motor cycles and other automobiles; and has for its objects to provide simple means for operating both the inlet and the exhaust valves mechanically, and for holding open one or other of such valves when required. And in order that the manner in which I attain my objects may be properly understood I will describe

10 the same with the aid of the accompanying drawings, wherein.

Figure I is a side elevation of part of an internal combustion motor fitted with valve operating mechanism constructed according to my invention, the cover plate being omitted to disclose the mechanism.

Figures III and V are similar views showing modifications.

15   Figures II and IV are detail views in plan.

Figure VI is a front elevation of the valve operating and holding mechanisms shown in Figure V.

The same numerals refer to the same parts throughout the drawings.

I operate both the inlet valve and the exhaust valve from one shaft and

20 according to the method of carrying out my invention shown in Figs. I and II, as applied to a four phase internal combustion motor 2 provided with the usual half speed shaft 3, I mount upon the said shaft two cam projections, one (4) of comparatively wide angle for actuating the exhaust valve 5, and the other (6) of comparatively narrow angle for actuating the inlet valve 7. The valves may have

25 their stems arranged parallel to one another and be provided with the usual return springs. The valve stems work in guides 8, and plungers 9 carried in other guides 19 operate upon the feet of the said stems. On a pivot 10, the axis of which is parallel to and may be in line with the axes of both the crank shaft 11 and the half speed shaft 3, I mount two rocking arms 12, 13, each of

30 which is provided with two striking faces, *viz* 14 and 15 on the arm 12, and 16 and 17 on the arm 13. The striking faces 14, 16 are adapted to be operated upon by the cam projections 4 and 6 respectively, and the faces 15 and 17 are adapted to operate upon the feet of the plungers 9 of the exhaust valve 5 and the inlet valve 7 respectively.

35   The striking surfaces of the respective faces are preferably suitably curved, and the arms 12, 13 are set at suitable angles.

In action, as the half speed shaft 3 rotates the cam projection 6 operates upon the arm 13 which transmits the motion to the plunger of the inlet valve 7. and the combustible mixture is admitted to the cylinder. As the cam projection 6

40 leaves the said arm 13 the inlet valve is closed by its spring and the mixture is compressed by the return stroke of the piston, both the inlet and the exhaust valves for the time being remaining closed. The charge is next fired, and, preferably before the driving stroke of the piston is completed, the cam projection 4 commences to act upon the arm 12 which transmits the motion to the

45 plunger of the exhaust valve 5 and the said exhaust valve is held open during

[*Price 8d.*]

**2**                       N° 14,391.—A.D. 1903.

*Riley's Improvements in or relating to Internal Combustion Motors.*

the remainder of that stroke and until the end of the next return stroke, when the cam projection 4 leaves the said arm 12, and the series of operations is repeated.

Upon the stud or the like 10 upon which the arms are pivotted I mount a sleeve 20 (Fig. II) which preferably passes through the cover 21, if any, en- 5 closing the valve actuating mechanism. Upon the outer end of the said sleeve I secure a lever 22 by which the same may be rotated through a suitable angle, and upon the inner end of the said sleeve I provide a projection 23 adapted to engage a corresponding projection 24 upon preferably the arm 12 of the exhaust valve operating mechanism. Normally the sleeve 20 and lever 22 stand in 10 such a position that the projection 23 on the sleeve clears the projection 24 on the arm; but when it is desired to hold open the valve 5 the sleeve 20 is rotated by the lever 22 until the projection 23 obstructs the projection 24 and so holds up the arm 12 and with it the exhaust valve 5.

According to the method of carrying out my invention shown in Figs. III 15 and IV, I operate both the valves from the one half speed shaft 3, as before, but provide it with a single cam projection 46 of comparatively narrow angle. The arms 26, 27 operating the plungers 9 of the respective valves 5, 7 are pivotted upon separate studs 28, 29 with the ends carrying the striking faces 30, 32 overlapping. The single cam 46 operates upon both the arms 26, 27 and 20 is made wide enough for that purpose; and in order to obtain the proper periods of holding open the inlet and exhaust valves respectively I make the striking faces 30, 32 which come in contact with the cam projection 46 of different lengths or angles, the face 32 on the inlet valve arm 27 being comparatively short or narrow, and the face 30 on the exhaust valve arm 26 being comparatively 25 long or wide. The striking faces 31 and 33 operating upon the plungers 9 of the exhaust and inlet valves respectively are preferably set over into the axial lines of those valves as shown in Fig. IV. When the cam projection 46 operates upon the arm 27 and inlet valve 7 is held open for a comparatively short period, while when the said cam projection operates upon the arm 26 30 the exhaust valve 5 is held open for a comparatively long period.

In this case one of the valves, may be held open by a lever 35 pivotted to the plunger guide 19 and provided with projections 36 on its upper surface adapted to engage a collar 37 or other stop upon the plunger 9 when the said lever is raised, but the said collar or the like normally clears the said projections. 35

The method of carrying out my invention shown in Figs. V and VI is more particularly applicable to motors in which the valves are arranged in a plane parallel to, instead of at right angles to, the crank shaft. I employ a single half-speed shaft 3 and a single cam 46 to operate both the valves 5 and 7, but the two arms 40 and 41, which are pivotted on the stud 42, are in one piece. 40 The arms 40 and 41 are provided with striking faces 43 and 44 of dimensions adapted to the respective periods of the exhaust and inlet valves respectively which they are adapted to operate. The arms 40 and 41 are connected, as by the link 45, to a lever 47 pivotted at 48 and provided with striking faces 49 and 50 adapted to act upon the plungers 9 of the exhaust valve 5 45 and inlet valve 7 respectively. When the cam projection 46 operates on the striking face 44 the arm 41 is raised and the arm 40 is depressed. Consequently the adjacent end of the lever 47 is depressed and the other end, i.e the end carrying the striking face 50, is raised and the inlet valve is held open for a suitable period, while the striking face 49 50 falls away from the plunger of the exhaust valve 5. The charge is next compressed and exploded. Then the cam projection begins to operate on the striking face 43, when the arm 40 is raised and the arm 41 is depressed. The raising of the arm 40 causes the raising of the striking face 49 and hence opens the exhaust valve 5, while the striking face 50 falls away from the plunger of 55 the inlet valve 7. The same means may be employed for holding open the exhaust valve as shown in Fig. III.

## Nº 14,391.—A.D. 1903.                                                3

*Riley's Improvements in or relating to Internal Combustion Motors.*

'1 he valve operating mechanism shown in Ł gs. V and V1 may be adapted to a motor in which the valves are arranged in a plane at right angles to the crank shaft, by setting the axes of the half speed shaft 3 and stud 42 in the central transverse plane of the motor, and providing the arms 40 and 41 with
5 striking faces 49 and 50 (indicated by dotted lines in Fig. V) adapted to operate directly upon the plungers of the respective valves.

I do not confine myself strictly to the above description but hold myself at liberty to make such modifications and applications of my invention as fairly fall within the scope thereof; the method of varying the periods during which
10 valves operated from a single cam projection may be operated being, in particular, capable of being carried out in other ways and applied to other similar purposes.

Having now particularly described and ascertained the nature of my said invention and in what manner the same is to be performed, I declare that what
15 I claim is :—

1. In the inlet and exhaust valve operating mechanism of internal combustion motors, a single cam projection, and striking faces adapted to be operated upon by such single cam projection and of dimensions proportioned to the periods of the valves to which they respectively relate, substantially as set forth.
20 2. In internal combustion motors, operating both the inlet and exhaust valves from one shaft with two cam projections, substantially as herein described with reference to Figs. I and II of the accompanying drawings.
3. In internal combustion motors, operating both the inlet and the exhaust valves from one shaft with one cam projection, substantially as herein described
25 with reference to Figs. III and IV of the accompanying drawings.
4. In internal combustion motors, operating both the inlet and the exhaust valves from one shaft with one cam projection, substantially as herein described with reference to Figs. V and VI of the accompanying drawings.
5. In internal combustion motors, operating both the inlet and the exhaust
30 valves from one shaft with one cam projection substantially as herein described with reference to the modification indicated in Fig. V of the accompanying drawings.
6. In internal combustion motors, means for holding open the exhaust valve or the inlet valve substantially as herein described with reference to Fig. I of
35 the accompanying drawings.
7. In internal combustion motors, means for holding open the exhaust valve or the inlet valve substantially as herein described with reference to Figs. III, V and V1 of the accompanying drawings.

Dated this 27th day of June 1903.

40                     DOUGLAS LEECHMAN, A.I.M.E.
              Fellow of the Chartered Institute of Patent Agents.
                       18 Hertford Street, Coventry,
              9, Exchange Chambers, New Street, Birmingham, and
                         32 York Street, Dublin,
45                     Patent Agent for the Applicant.

Redhill Printed for His Majesty's Stationery Office, by Love & Malcomson, Ltd.—1903.

**20,860. Variable-speed &c. gearing.** RILEY, P., Hollybank, Radford Road, Coventry Sept. 28.

Relates to step-by-step change-speed and reversing clutch toothed gearing in which the driving and driven shafts are co-axial and clutched together to give one speed, each of the other speeds being obtained through a separate counter-shaft. Figs. 1, 2, and 3 show a form of gearing giving three forward speeds and one reverse. The ends of the driving and driven shafts A, D may extend into and support one another, and the driving-shaft A carries two toothed wheels B, C, the wheel C being formed with clutch jaws $C^1$ adapted to be engaged by jaws $E^1$ formed on a broad toothed wheel E which rotates with, but slides longitudinally on, the driven shaft D. A reduced speed is obtained through toothed wheels G, $H^1$, mounted freely on the countershaft F, which gear con-

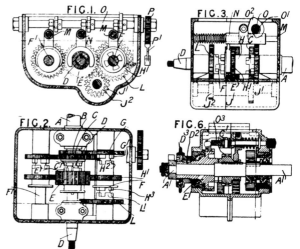

tinually with the wheels B, E, the sleeve on which the wheel $H^1$ is mounted being moved longitudinally so that clutch jaws $H^2$ formed on it engage jaws $G^1$ formed on the wheel G. Another speed is obtained similarly through wheels mounted on the countershaft $F^1$. The reverse speed is obtained by means of two toothed wheels $J^1$, $J^2$ fixed to a freely-rotating sleeve J, the wheel $J^1$ being continually in gear with the wheel C on the driving-shaft, and the wheel $J^2$ with the wheel L which is freely mounted on the countershaft F ; the gear is brought into action by moving the sleeve carrying the wheel $H^1$ so that the clutch jaws $H^3$, $L^1$ engage. The sliding of the various parts is preferably brought about as follows :—Each sliding part is connected by a fork to a sleeve N mounted on a fixed spindle M and acted on by a spring which tends to force the sliding part into engagement. Arranged transversely to these rods M is a shaft O carrying cams with recesses $O^1$ which allow the springs to press the sliding parts into

engagement when the cam shaft is in the proper position. For reversal, the sliding sleeve H is pressed into position by a cam-swell $O^2$. The cam shaft is provided with a pinion P engaging a sector $P^1$ which is suitably operated from the speed lever. In a modified construction, shown in Fig. 6, suitable for a tricar, the driving-shaft $A^1$ passes through the gear box, and carries the hollow driven shaft $D^2$, which is provided with a chain sprocket $D^3$ and toothed wheel $E^1$. The direct drive is obtained by moving the pinion $C^1$ keyed on the driving-shaft, until clutch jaws formed on it engage with similar jaws on the wheel $E^1$. The reduced speeds and reversal are obtained through counter-shafts as in the first construction. The method of operation by sliding the several parts is similar, but the rotating cam shaft is replaced by a longitudinally-sliding rod $O^3$, having recesses for the forward speeds, and operating a rocking lever for the reversal.

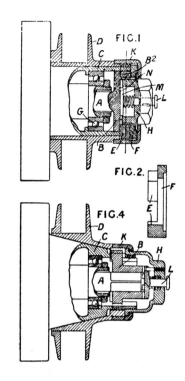

**13,857. Vehicle wheels.** RILEY, P., Holly Bank, Radford Road, Coventry. June 30.

*Hubs.*—In detachable wheels having fixed and removable hub parts, the drive is transmitted direct from the live axle to the removable hub. The axle A, Fig. 1, has made integral with it or fixed to it a dog B, flanged over as at B² on to which screws the fixed hub C enclosing the bearings G. The detachable hub D, fixed hub C, and dog B² are notched radially and engage a floating disk F with projections E, Fig. 2. The nut H screws into the dog B and is locked by the non-return spring plunger L carrying a disk M with projections N engaging recesses in the dog, and is adapted to positively remove the wheel through the cap K. As shown in Fig. 4, the dog B fits on the squared axle end and enters slots in the fixed and detachable hubs, the nut H being locked by the spring plunger L carrying a plate on which are formed teeth engaging corresponding teeth on the dog.

**23,390. Internal-combustion engines.** RILEY, P., Hollybank, Radford Road, Coventry. Nov. 2.

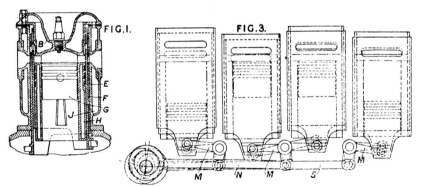

Engines having one or more distributing slide valves, concentric with and surrounding the working piston, are provided with a stationary sleeve arranged between the valves and the working piston. Fig. 1 shows a four-stroke-cycle engine having a pair of slide valves E, F and a stationary cooling-chamber H. The valves are actuated by rocking arms M through eccentric rods N, S, which may also be driven by cams or cranks. The water spaces H, J may each communicate with the cooling-space B ; or if preferred, the water space in the chamber H may be dispensed with, and the outer space J may be air-cooled. In a multi-cylinder engine the water jackets J may be cast in a single piece. The engine is suitable for use with motor road vehicles.

**18,204. Internal-combustion engines.** RILEY, P., Castle Works, Coventry. Aug. 1. [*Cognate Application*, 3209/15.] [*Classes* 7 (ii), 7 (v), *and* 7 (vi).]

*Two - stroke - cycle engines ; four - stroke - cycle engines ; driving - gear ; starting ; valves.* — Relates to internal-combustion engines of the kind in which a number of cylinders are arranged around and parallel to the crank-shaft, and comprises improvements chiefly in the valve mechanism and in the means for converting reciprocating piston movement into rotary movement of the crank-shaft. Fig. 1 shows a two-stroke-cycle engine having four working and four pumping cylinders 1, 2 respectively. The connecting-rods 4 are each ball-jointed to a piston at one end and to the cross-head 7 at the other end. The cross-head is carried at one end on a crank-pin 16 inclined to the crank-disk 15, and its other end is mounted on gimbals in the following manner. Brackets 9 on the cylinder carry pivoted to them a ring 10, which carries pivoted to it, at right-angles to the

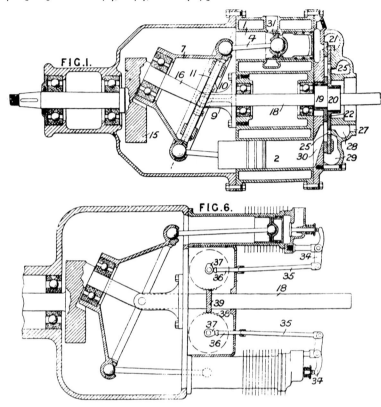

FIG.1.

FIG.6.

bracket pivots, a rod 11, which enters bearings in the cross-head. The end of the crank-pin is attached to or formed in one with a spindle 18 co-axial with the crank-shaft. The rod 11 is bifurcated in the middle to enable it to pass this spindle. Eccentrics 19, 20 on the spindle 18 operate two valve slides 21, 22. Mixture is admitted at 27 to an annular space 28 in the cover-plate, in which is also an annular receiver 29. On the suction stroke of the pump, mixture passes from the space 28 through a port 25 in the valve 22 and through the valve 21 and passage 30 to the pump cylinder. On completion of the stroke, the valve 22 closes to the passage 28 and opens to the receiver 29, into which mixture is forced on the next stroke. On the outer stroke of the power piston, immedi-

ately after the exhaust 31 is uncovered, the valve 21 admits mixture from the receiver 29, first for scavenging, and subsequently for charging. At starting, one port 30 must necessarily be open, and this admits mixture which presses out the piston, rotating the crank-shaft and uncovering the next passage. Mixture is thus pumped into the receiver, and from there enters the power cylinders and is fired. Two cross-heads and crank-pins, arranged tandem on the same shaft with two sets of cylinders working on each cross-head, are also described. Fig. 6 shows a four-cycle engine. Each cylinder has similar inlet and exhaust valves worked by levers 34 rocked by rods 35 from tappets 36 actuated by cams 37 rotated by two-to-one skew gears 38, 39 from the spindle 18.

**150,795. Vehicle wheels.** RILEY, LTD. and RUSH, H., City Works, Coventry. June 4, 1919, No. 14212. [*Class* 144 (i).]

Dished wheels comprise two or more disks 1, 2 spaced apart at the hub by a ring 4 and braced intermediate the hub and rim by a series of washers 5 and rivets 6 or by a ring. In one construction, the disks are dished in the same direction to different angles, and in an alternative construction one of the disks may be flat. Fig. 3 shows a further modification in which only one disk 1 extends the full depth of the wheel, a second disk 7 of less diameter being riveted to the disk 1 at its periphery, and a third disk 9 of still smaller diameter being riveted at its periphery to the disk 7. The disks are mutually spaced at the hub by rings 4 and the disks 1 and 7 are braced at an intermediate part by a ring or washers 5 and the rivets 10 that secure the smallest disk.

**257,413. Riley, P.** Sept. 16, 1925.

*Variable-speed gearing* comprises a gear or gears 11, 12 slidably splined upon a double-ended dog clutch sleeve 9, which is in turn splined on a driven shaft 3. A gear-box containing the usual driving and lay shafts 2, 6 is thus shortened. The shaft 6 is constantly driven from the shaft 2 through a pair 4, 5. The sleeve 9 when moved to the left engages clutch 20, 20¹ for direct driving. When moved to the right it engages clutch 21, 21¹ for fourth speed through train 4, 5, 7, 8. Second and third speeds are effected by sliding the coupled gears 11, 12 to left and right into mesh with fixed gears 13, 14.

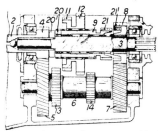

The constant mesh gears have preferably helical teeth to lessen noise. The shaft 3 may be the driver.

**391,588. Cooling bearings.** RILEY, P., Castle Works, Aldbourne Road, Coventry. March 23, 1932, No. 8630. [Class 12 (i).]

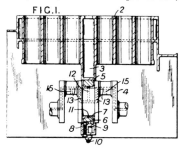

In a water-cooled internal-combustion engine in which the crank shaft 4 is supported by a hollow web 3 extending from the cylinder water-jacket 2, the interior of which is in communication with the web 3, the cooling water is applied all round the bearing. As shown in the Figure, an intermediate crank shaft bearing comprising a split ring 6 having a white metal liner 7 has a snug fit in the circular wall 5 of the web 3. An oil feed tube 10 passes through the wall 5 and the ring 6 and communicates with a peripheral groove 11 extending a substantial way round the interior of the bearing. Oil passes into the radial duct 12 and thence into ducts 13, 15 to lubricate the crank-pin bearings. The hole in the web 3 is preferably large enough to allow the crank webs to be passed through it. The ring 6 is located angularly by a peg 8 entering a notch 9.

---

**468,647. Cylinders.** RILEY (COVENTRY), Ltd., and BECKE, A. W. K. VON DER. Feb. 7, 1936, No. 3768. [Class 7 (ii)]

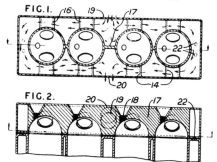

A partition 17 extends along the water space of a cylinder head, in which the exhaust and inlet passages 16, 14 are on opposite sides, and cooling water enters at 19 on the exhaust side, and flows round the ends of the partition before it leaves at 20. The only communication with the water in the cylinder barrel jackets is by ports 22. The combustion chambers are hemispherical and have sparking-plug sockets 18.

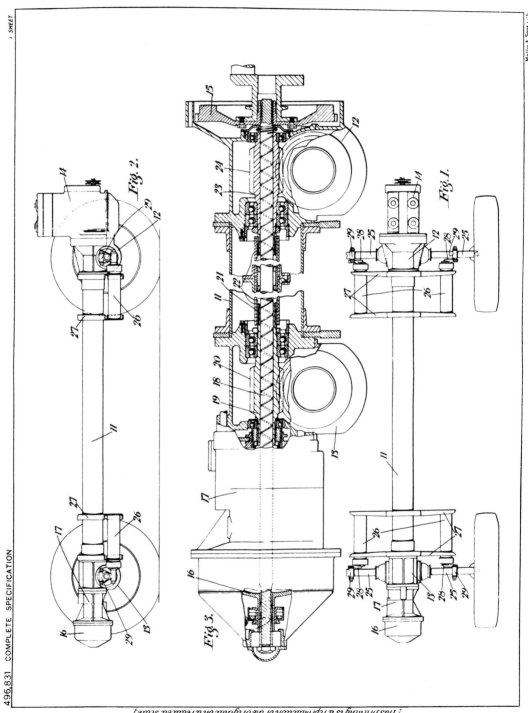

# PATENT SPECIFICATION

Application Date: Sept. 15, 1937.   No. 25038/37.

Complete Specification Left: Sept. 9, 1938.

Complete Specification Accepted: Dec. 7, 1938.

## 496,831

## PROVISIONAL SPECIFICATION

### Military and like Motor Vehicles

I, PERCY RILEY, a British Subject, of the Riley Engine Company Limited, Castle Works, Aldbourne Road, Coventry, Warwickshire, do hereby declare the
5 nature of this invention to be as follows:—

This invention relates to military and like motor-vehicles, particularly for carrying machine-guns, searchlights,
10 sound-receiving apparatus, wireless apparatus or the like, such as have road wheels at opposite ends of the chassis which are both driven and steerable and, in addition, independently connected
15 with the chassis-frame for supporting the latter.

My main object is to provide an improved vehicle of this kind which whilst having desirable characteristics
20 from the point of view of speed and control at speed, and whilst being capable of negotiating very rough surfaces, will afford material accessibility both for the engine and for the change-speed mech-
25 anism.

According to the invention, there is disposed at one end of the chassis an engine connected to drive a change-speed mechanism, at the other end of the
30 chassis, which is in turn connected to drive two spaced, coaxial worms from which drives are taken, respectively, to two differential mechanisms driving to road wheels, at opposite ends of the
35 chassis, which are independently connected thereto for supporting purposes and are steerable.

In a simple construction according to the invention, the chassis-frame mainly
40 comprises a tubular backbone member secured at its ends to the casings of two differential mechanisms. Secured to one of these, on the side remote from the backbone member, is an engine, which is
45 conveniently a four-cylinder unit arranged with its flywheel inwardly (i.e., adjacent the associated differential mechanism), the crankshaft axis being just above the differential mechanism and
50 coaxial with the backbone member. The main clutch may be incorporated in the engine unit in a known manner, but it is preferably arranged at the remote end of

the chassis adjacent or incorporated in a change-speed mechanism, the latter being 55 mounted on that side of the other differential mechanism remote from the backbone member. The crankshaft drives to the gear-box, by way of the main clutch, by means of a shaft coaxial with the 60 backbone member. Driven from the gear-box is a tubular shaft carrying a worm by which the drive is transmitted to the adjacent differential mechanism. This tubular shaft is also connected, as 65 by splines, to a tubular sleeve, coaxial with and extending along the main driving shaft, to drive a tubular shaft carrying a worm by which the differential mechanism adjacent the engine can be 70 driven. The tubular sleeve and the tubular worm shafts, which may be formed integrally, may be journalled in the backbone member. Similarly the driving shaft may be journalled in the 75 tubular sleeve. From the differential mechanisms drives are taken to the four road wheels through swinging half-axles. All the four wheels can be steered.

A preferred method of connecting each 80 of the road wheels with the chassis-frame for supporting the latter includes the use of a longitudinally-disposed cylinder substantially midway between the associated road wheel and the backbone member and 85 extending from the associated swinging half-axle towards the centre of the chassis, and the two cylinders at each end of the chassis are connected with the backbone member by transverse channels 90 or other members. These latter may also be interconnected by longitudinal channel or other members parallel to the backbone member. Extending into each of the cylinders is a spindle formed with 95 a crank arm at the end adjacent the associated swinging half-axle, which is connected by means of a bracket thereto. Preferably the connection is to the underside of the swinging half-axle. Disposed 100 within the cylinder is a screw-and-nut means operating in both directions against substantial compression springs. The suspension may, for example, be as disclosed in my prior patent specification 105 No. 420,433.

2         496,831

In this way it is possible to build a vehicle of the kind in question which is very satisfactory and with which the engine and change-speed mechanism are
5   very accessible, as either can be removed for replacement without the rest of the chassis being disturbed. These two components can also be arranged so that they do not project forwardly or rearwardly
10 beyond planes inclined at 45 degrees to the vertical passing through the points of

contact of the associated road wheels. Thus, these components are out-of-the-way when the vehicle is negotiating ditches and the like the inclinations of **15** which do not exceed 45 degrees.

Dated this 14th day of September, 1937.
WALFORD & HARDMAN BROWN,
Chartered Patent Agents,
Roslyn Chambers, Warwick Road,
Coventry, Warwickshire.

**488,172.** **Vehicle spring-suspensions.** RILEY, P. Jan. 27, 1938, No. 2588. [Class 108 (ii)]

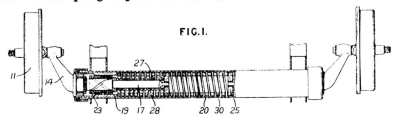

FIG.1.

In a spring-suspension for a motor vehicle of the kind such as is described in Specification 420,433, in which each wheel 11 is carried by a substantially horizontal crank 14 having a screw-threaded or equivalent connection with a non-rotatable member 23 that is slidable axially against resilient means 27, the crank 14 is also connected with a torsion spring 28 surrounding the spring 27, so that both springs 27, 28 act together to resist movement of the road wheel. In the construction shown in Fig. 1, the cranks 14 with their shafts 17 are supported at the opposite ends of a transverse casing 20, and the inner ends of the shafts 17 are engaged with a rotatable element 25, which serves both as an abutment for the inner spring 27 and also as the means for stressing the torsion spring 28, the other end of which is held by a stationary sleeve 19. Preferably an additional torsion spring 30 is coupled to the two abutments 25 so as to function as an anti-roll device. In a modification, Fig. 4, the horizontal cranks 35 are associated with a pair of swinging semi-

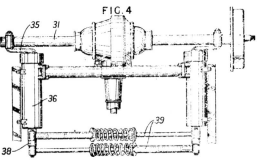

FIG.4

axles 31 and are journalled in casings 36 for rotation about longitudinal axes. Rotation of the shafts of the cranks 35 is resisted by the spring combination as in the construction of Fig. 1, while the ends of the shafts remote from the cranks are provided with cross-arms 38, the diametrically opposed ends of which are cross-connected by resilient telescopic links 39 forming a stabilizing device.

# The Factory Listed Riley Models, 1896–1938

| Model | Years | Model | Years |
|---|---|---|---|
| Riley Bicycle | 1896–1911 | 11 h.p. All Season Tourer | 1921–23 |
| Royal Riley Tricycle 2¼ h.p. | 1899–1900 | 11/40 h.p. Saloon | 1921–25 |
| Royal Riley Quadricycle 2¼ h.p. | 1899–1901 | 11/40 h.p. Sports 2 Seater | 1922–28 |
| Royal Riley Quadricycle 2¾ h.p. | 1901–02 | 11/40 h.p. Touring (4dr, 4 seat) | 1922–24 |
| 1½ h.p. Motor Bicycle | 1902–03 | 11/40 h.p. All Season 2 Seater | 1923–25 |
| 2¼ h.p. Motor Bicycle | 1903–04 | 11/40 h.p. All Season 4st 2dr | 1923–25 |
| 3 h.p. Motor Bicycle | 1903–04 | 11/40 h.p. 4 Seat Coupé | 1923–25 |
| 3½ h.p. Motor Bicycle | 1903–04 | 11/40 h.p. 4 Seat De Luxe | 1924–25 |
| 3 h.p. Forecar | 1903–04 | 11/40 h.p. Saloon De Luxe | 1924–25 |
| 4½ h.p. Forecar | 1903–04 | 11/40 h.p. Four Seat Sports | 1924–28 |
| 4 h.p. Tricar (Air cooled) | 1905–07 | 11/40 h.p. 2/3 Seat Cloverleaf | 1924–25 |
| 4½ h.p. Tricar (water cooled) | 1905–07 | 11/40 h.p. 2/3 Seater | 1924–25 |
| 6 h.p. Tricar (water cooled) | 1905–07 | 11/40 h.p. Saloon Landaulette | 1924–25 |
| 9 h.p. Tricar (water cooled) | 1905–07 | 11/40 h.p. SWB Sports | 1925 |
| 5 h.p. Tricar | 1907 | 11/40 h.p. Special Tourer (2dr 4st) | 1925–27 |
| 9 h.p. V-twin Car | 1905–10 | 11.9 h.p. 5st De Luxe Tourer | 1925–27 |
| 12/18 h.p. SWB 2 Seater | 1907–10 | 11.9 h.p. Saloon | 1925–27 |
| 12/18 h.p. SWB 5 Seater | 1907–09 | 11.9 h.p. Saloon De Luxe | 1925–28 |
| 12/18 h.p. LWB 5 Seater | 1907–14 | 11.9 h.p. Coupé | 1925–27 |
| 12/18 h.p. LWB Landaulette | 1909–14 | 11.9 h.p. 4/5 Seat Tourer | 1925–28 |
| 10 h.p. 2 Seat Car (V-twin) | 1909–10 | 11.9 h.p. 2/6 Seater | 1925–27 |
| 10 h.p. Speed Model | 1909–10 | 11.9 h.p. Saloon Landaulette | 1925–27 |
| 10 h.p. 2 Seat Torpedo | 1911–14 | 11.9 h.p. Coupé Fixed Top | 1926–27 |
| 12/18 h.p. 2 Seat Torpedo | 1911–14 | 11.9 h.p. Coupé de Ville | 1926 |
| 12/18 h.p. LWB 2 Seater | 1911–14 | 11.9 h.p. Foleshill Tourer | 1926–27 |
| 12/18 h.p. Medico Coupé | 1913–14 | 11.9 h.p. Four Door Coach | 1926–28 |
| 12/18 h.p. 4 Seat Torpedo | 1913–14 | 11.9 h.p. Glass Enclosed Tourer | 1926–27 |
| 17/30 h.p. 2 Seat Car | 1913–14 | 11.9 h.p. 4 Door Special Tourer | 1926 |
| 17/30 h.p. 3 Seat Car | 1913–14 | 11.9 h.p. 2/6 Seat Glass Enclosed | 1926–28 |
| 17/30 h.p. 5 Seat Tourer | 1913–22 | 11.9 h.p. 2/3 Seater | 1926–27 |
| 10 h.p. 4 cylinder 2 Seater | 1914 | 11/50/65 S/charged Sports | |
| 11 h.p. 4 Seater | 1919–21 | 2 seater | 1927 |
| 11 h.p. Family Tourer | 1919–22 | 11/50/65 S/charged Sports | |
| 11 h.p. 2 Seater | 1919–23 | 4 seater | 1927 |
| 11/40 h.p. Coupé | 1919–25 | 11/40 h.p. Long Sports Four | 1928 |

| | | |
|---|---|---|
| 11.9 h.p. Lulworth Saloon | 1928 | |
| 11.9 h.p. Lulworth Special Saloon | 1928 | |
| 11.9 h.p. Midworth Saloon | 1928 | |
| 11.9 h.p. Wentworth Coupé | 1928 | |
| 11.9 h.p. Chatsworth Saloon | 1928 | |
| 11.9 h.p. Grangeworth Saloon | 1928 | |
| 9 h.p. Monaco Saloon | 1926–29 | |
| 9 h.p. 4 Seat Tourer | 1926–27 | |
| 9 h.p. 2 Seater | 1928–30 | |
| 9 h.p. 4 Seater | 1928–30 | |
| 9 h.p. San Remo Saloon | 1928 | |
| 9 h.p. Sports Four | 1928 | |
| 9 h.p. Brooklands Speed Model | 1928–32 | |
| 6/14 5 Seat Tourer | 1928–29 | |
| 6/14 Stelvio I Saloon | 1928–30 | |
| 9 h.p. Biarritz Silent Saloon | 1929–30 | |
| 6/14 Deauville Saloon | 1929–30 | |
| 9 h.p. Special 4st Tourer | 1929–30 | |
| 6/14 Light Six Saloon | 1929–30 | |
| 9 h.p. 'Plus Series' Monaco Saloon | 1930–31 | |

9 h.p. 'Plus' Biarritz ½ Panel
Saloon                                1930–31
9 h.p. 'Plus' 4 Seat Tourer          1930–31
9 h.p. 'Plus' Army Tourer            1930–31
9 h.p. 'Plus' 2 Seat Coupé           1930–31
6/14 Alpine Fabric Saloon            1931–32
6/14 Alpine ½ Panelled Saloon        1931–32
6/14 Alpine Tourer                   1931–32
9 h.p. 'Plus Ultra' Monaco
(Fabric)                             1931–32
9 h.p. 'Plus Ultra' ½ Panel
Monaco                               1931–32
9 h.p. 'Plus Ultra' Army Tourer      1931–32
9 h.p. 'Plus Ultra' 2st D/H Coupé    1931–32
6/14 Stelvio II Saloon               1931–34
6/12 Brooklands Speed Model          1932
6/14 Winchester Limousine            1933
6/14 Winchester Saloon               1933–34
6/14 Edinburgh Saloon                1933–34
6/14 Edinburgh Limousine             1933–34
9 h.p. Monaco Coachbuilt
Saloon                               1933–35
6/12 Grebe 2 Seater                  1933
6/12 TT Racing Car                   1933
9 h.p. Falcon Saloon (1st type)      1933
9 h.p. Lincock F/H Coupé             1933–34

| | | |
|---|---|---|
| 6/12 Lincock F/H Coupé | 1933–34 | |
| 6/14 Lincock F/H Coupé | 1933–34 | |
| 6/12 Mentone Saloon | 1933–34 | |
| 9 h.p. Gamecock 2 Seater | 1933 | |
| 9 h.p. Lynx 2 Door Tourer | 1933 | |
| 6/12 Lynx 2 Door Tourer | 1933 | |
| 6/14 Lynx 2 Door Tourer | 1933 | |
| 6/12 March Special 2/4 Seater | 1933 | |
| 9 h.p. March Special 2/4 Seater | 1933 | |
| 9 h.p. Trinity 2/4 Seat Coupé | 1933 | |
| 9 h.p. Kestrel Saloon (1st type) | 1933–35 | |
| 6/12 Kestrel Saloon (1st type) | 1933–34 | |
| 6/14 Kestrel Saloon (1st type) | 1933–34 | |
| 9 h.p. Ascot D/H Coupé | 1933–34 | |
| 6/12 Ascot D/H Coupé | 1933–34 | |
| 6/14 Ascot D/H Coupé | 1933–34 | |
| 6/14 Alpine Saloon | 1933–34 | |
| 9 h.p. Falcon Spl. Series Saloon | 1934 | |
| 9 h.p. Imp 2 Seat Sports | 1934–35 | |
| 9 h.p. Ulster Imp | 1934–35 | |
| 9 h.p. Lynx 4 Door Tourer | 1934–35 | |
| 6/12 Lynx 4 Door Tourer | 1934 | |
| 6/14 Lynx 4 Door Tourer | 1934 | |
| 6/12 MPH 2 Seat Sports | 1934–35 | |
| 6/14 MPH 2 Seat Sports | 1934–35 | |
| 6/12 Racing MPH | 1934 | |
| 6/14 Gamecock 2 Seater | 1934 | |
| 6/15 MPH 2 Seat Sports | 1935 | |
| 6/15 Stelvio Saloon | 1935 | |
| 12/4 Kestrel Saloon (22T) | 1935 | |
| 12/4 TT Sprite 2 Seater | 1935–37 | |
| 12/4 Falcon Saloon | 1935–37 | |
| 6/12 Kestrel Saloon (44T) | 1935 | |
| 6/15 Kestrel Saloon (44T) | 1935 | |
| 6/12 Falcon Saloon | 1935–36 | |
| 6/15 Falcon Saloon | 1935–36 | |
| 12/4 Lynx Tourer | 1935–38 | |
| 6/15 Lynx Tourer | 1936 | |
| 9 h.p. Kestrel Saloon (2nd type) | 1936 | |
| 12/4 Merlin Saloon | 1936 | |
| 9 h.p. Merlin Saloon | 1936–37 | |
| 12/4 Adelphi Saloon | 1936–38 | |
| 15/6 Adelphi Saloon | 1936–38 | |
| 8/90 Adelphi Saloon | 1936–38 | |
| 12/4 6 Light Kestrel Saloon | 1936–38 | |
| 15/6 6 Light Kestrel Saloon | 1936–38 | |

| | | | |
|---|---|---|---|
| 8/90 6 Light Kestrel Saloon | 1936–37 | 9 h.p. Monaco Saloon | 1937 |
| 12/4 Sprite 2 Seater | 1936–38 | 9 h.p. Touring Saloon | 1937 |
| 2 Litre Sprite Six | 1936 | 12/4 Touring Saloon | 1938 |
| I.F.S. Racing $1\frac{1}{2}$/2 litre | 1936 | 9 h.p. Victor Saloon | 1938 |
| 12/4 Kestrel-Sprite Saloon | 1936–38 | 12/4 Victor Saloon | 1938 |
| 12/4 Lynx-Sprite Tourer | 1936–38 | 16 h.p. Adelphi Saloon | 1938 |
| 12/4 Adelphi Sprite Saloon | 1937 | 16 h.p. Close Coupled Touring | |
| 12/4 Close-Coupled Touring | | Saloon | 1938 |
| Saloon | 1937 | 16 h.p. Kestrel Saloon | 1938 |
| 12/4 Touring Sprite Saloon | 1937 | 16 h.p. Lynx Tourer | 1938 |
| 12/4 Falcon-Sprite Saloon | 1937 | 16 h.p. Touring Saloon | 1938 |

The years shown against each model are the years in which that model was offered.

No distinction has been drawn between Standard Series and Special Series Models, except where only a Special Series model was available, though Special Series versions of the 9 h.p., six-cylinder and 12/4 cars were available. The Sprite Series $1\frac{1}{2}$ litre models are listed as separate models because they were sufficiently different from Standard Series cars to merit separate mention and they were catalogued separately.

A total of 176 models are listed here. These do not include development models which were never catalogued, nor the early railcars.

# The Riley Family, their Companies and Trade Names

The founder of this particular Riley dynasty was William Riley's father, the William Riley of William Riley and Son. William Riley junior took over the management of the family weaving business, under his father's guidance, in 1870, at the remarkably tender age of 19. So, by the time he bought out the interests of Bonnick and Company Limited he had twenty years management experience behind him and he was still only 39.

Bonnick continued to produce bicycles under that name for another six years, when the weaving company was wound up and all of the Riley interests put into the cycle company which was re-formed as the Riley Cycle Company in 1896. The company continued under that name until 1912 when it was reconstructed as Riley (Coventry) Limited. It was re-constituted under Lord Nuffield as Riley (Coventry) Successors Limited in September 1938.

The Riley Engine Company was formed in 1903 under Percy Riley's management. It was the supplier of engines to other companies as well as the Riley Cycle Company. It was absorbed into Riley (Coventry) Limited in 1931.

The Nero Engine Company was formed under Victor Riley's guidance in 1912 and was the manufacturer of the engines for the 17/30 h.p. and the 10 h.p. four cylinder car of Stanley Riley's design. Riley (Coventry) Limited took over the assets of this company in 1919.

The Riley Motor Manufacturing Company was established by the Riley brothers in 1913 when their father had decided that Riley (Coventry) Limited should concentrate its whole attention on the manufacture of wheels. When the reorganisation of the companies took place in 1919, the name of this company was changed to Midland Motor Bodies Limited under Allan Riley. It was eventually absorbed, as the Bodies Division, into Riley (Coventry) Limited in 1931.

Autovia Cars Limited was established in 1936 to build the luxury Autovia range. Victor Riley was Chairman and the Company produced only the Saloon and Limousine models until it was sold to Jimmy James Limited in 1938.

After Riley had passed into Nuffield hands, with Victor Riley continuing in office as Chairman and Managing Director, it became known as Riley (Coventry) Successors Limited but in 1940 began to be known once more as Riley (Coventry) Limited. This continued until the 1948 move to Abingdon when the Company was re-named Riley Motors Limited. The Company finally became known as the Riley Motors Division of the British Motor Corporation until finally dissolved in 1969.

*The Riley Family Companies*

William Riley and Son:                                        to 1896

| Bonnick & Company Limited: | 1890 to 1896 |
| Riley Cycle Company Limited: | 1896 to 1912 |
| Riley Engine Company Limited: | 1903 to 1931 |
| Nero Engine Company Limited: | 1912 to 1919 |
| Riley Motor Manufacturing Company Limited: | 1913 to 1919 |
| Riley (Coventry) Limited: | 1912 to 1938 |
| Midland Motor Bodies Limited: | 1919 to 1931 |
| Coventry Disc Wheels Limited: | 1920 |
| Autovia Cars Limited: | 1936 to 1938 |

*The Riley Family*

| William Riley | 1851—1944 |
| Victor Riley | 1876—1958 |
| Allan Riley | 1881—1963 |
| Percy Riley | 1883—1941 |
| Stanley Riley | 1885—1952 |
| Cecil Riley | 1895—1961 |

*The Riley Trade Marks*

1: Riley bicycles and cars between 1906 and 1912.

2: Riley motor bicycles and forecars/tricars.

4: Riley 12/18 1908.

3: Riley 9 V-Twin badge.

5: Riley car badge 1913 onwards. (Periodically used on earlier models).

6: Riley cars: 1919 without motto, 1920–24 with motto 'As old as the Industry', 1925–38 with full motto. (Badge continued in use without motto after Nuffield takeover to demise of Riley name in 1969).

*William Riley Jr*

*Victor Riley & Lord Nuffield*

*Percy Riley*

*Allan Riley*

*Stanley Riley*

*Cecil Riley*

# Riley Clubs Worldwide

The intention of this appendix is to give the prospective Riley owner—or the owner who is not at present a club member—some idea of the clubs which exist to cater for his favourite breed of car. Of course it holds good too for the Riley owner who is a club member in one country but moves to another.

Club officials' names and addresses change—sometimes frequently, sometimes not so frequently—but this presents a problem in a book of this kind, because it can so easily become out of date if such details are included. It was decided to make the prospective club member aware of the clubs available to him in the presumption that he could quickly find out who would be the right official to contact once he knew the name of the club. Indeed, such is the interest in older cars today that many specialist periodicals regularly give information about club activities, and people to contact, on a news basis.

The one-make clubs which cater for the Riley enthusiast are:

### The Riley Motor Club Limited

The oldest Riley club, formed in 1925 at the Peebles Hydro in Scotland. Once the largest one-make car club in the world, it has centres in most areas of the United Kingdom and caters for Rileys of all ages, 1898–1969. It had an overseas Centre in Victoria, Australia, until that Centre became part of R.M.C. Australia. *The Riley Record*, first published 1927 is produced bi-monthly.

### The Riley Register

Based in Great Britain, this club was formed in 1954 to bring together owners and enthusiasts of those Rileys built by the family Riley Company between 1898 and 1938. It holds area meetings in most parts of Britain, generally monthly. A Bulletin of very high quality is published quarterly.

### The Riley Motor Club of Australia

Formed out of the Victoria Centre of the Riley Motor Club, it is now a very strong club in its own right. Victoria Centre publishes a monthly magazine, *The Blue Diamond*, duplicated but always of excellent editorial quality. It caters for all Riley models up to 1969 and has very active centres in Victoria, New South Wales, South Australia and Western Australia.

### The Riley Car Club of New Zealand

A small club catering for the interests of owners and enthusiasts of Rileys of all periods. Very active centres in North and South Islands. A duplicated quarterly magazine of high editorial quality is produced.

*The Riley Motor Club of Ireland*
This is a small group of Riley enthusiasts catering for all ages of cars.

*The Riley Motor Club of Sweden*
Again, this is a small club with a very keen membership catering for all Riley types.

*The Riley Motor Club of Holland*
Another very strong, but small, group of enthusiasts, welcoming owners of all ages of cars.

*The Riley Car Club U.S.A. Inc.*
Though larger than the mainland European clubs, this is still a small club in terms of the U.S., having under 1000 members, seemingly concentrated mostly in California. A regular duplicated magazine with news and technical information is published.

*The Riley R.M. Club*
Not strictly at home in this appendix, since this club caters only for post-World War 2 cars—1946 to 1955, up to the Pathfinder. Formed in 1969, it is a large and growing club with centres in the U.K. as well having overseas membership. High quality magazine with eight issues per year.

In addition to the one-make Riley clubs, there are others which cater for vintage, historic or classic cars in general for which most Riley models are eligible. For example in Great Britain all pre-1940 Riley models are catered for by the Vintage Sports Car Club and their owners are eligible to compete in appropriate events with their cars under Vintage (pre-1931) or Post Vintage Thoroughbred (post-1930) classifications. Still in Britain, the Historic Sports Car Club includes R.M. Series cars in its eligibility for events.

Elsewhere in the world, there are clubs of a similar general nature which also provide for various Rileys, the Vintage Sports Car Club of America to quote but one.

There are also clubs which cater for some of those spin-offs and Riley-based specials. Considering the very few cars made, the E.R.A. Club is particularly strong, catering as it does for E.R.A. owners and enthusiasts (it is really a revival of the E.R.A. Club which existed before the second World War). At the other, and pretty extreme, end of the scale, the Rochdale Register caters for the Rochdale Olympic owners—whose cars used Riley (B.M.C. variety) mechanical components.

There is still not, at the time of writing, any club catering exclusively for those cars built under the B.M.C. banner after the R.M. Series, though they are, of course, catered for by the Riley Motor Club.

APPENDIX EIGHT

# Some Noteworthy Riley Competition Successes

Records of Riley's earliest successes with motor bicycles and tricycles are scant, but it is known that Robert Crossley entered a Riley tricycle for a track event in 1899 and won it. In the very early 1900s H. Rignold competed in several events with a Riley motor bicycle, as did Allan Riley and others. Rignold won the 1903 Preston Speed Trial with an M.M.C. engined Riley motor bicycle. In the Southport Speed Trial of the same year, Rileys won First, Second and Third in their classes and set up a new standing-start mile time of 1 minute 24.2 seconds in July 1903.

And so, competition successes began to amass:

*1905*

A.C.C. Tricar Trials, Dashwood—Riley 9—F.T.D.—1:40.4
A.C.C. 6-Day Reliability Trial—Riley 9 Tricar—1st Class & Silver Medal.

*1906*

Skegness Speed Trials—Riley 9 V-twin car—1st in class.
Kettleby Hill Climb—Riley 9 V-twin car—1st in class; F.T.D.

*1907*

S.M.C. Reliability Trial—Riley 9 Tricar—1st.
Herts M.C. Consumption Trial—Riley 9 Tricar—57.14 m.p.g.
Shelsley Walsh Hill Climb—Riley 9 V-twin—2nd overall on handicap.
Notts M.C. Speed Trial—Riley 9 V-twin—1st Flying kilometre.
London-Edinburgh Reliability Trial—Riley 9 V-twin—1st Class Award.

*1908*

Ballinaslaughter Hill Climb—Riley 12–18—1st Class C.
Welbeck Speed Trials—Riley 12–18—1st, Flying Kilometre.
Coventry-Holyhead Trial—Riley 9, 12–18—1st Class Awards.
Essex M.C. Open Hill Climb—Riley 9—1st, Light Car Class.
Kettleby Hill Climb—Riley 9—F.T.D.; 1st in Class A.
Aston Clinton Hill Climb—Riley 12–18—1st Class C.

*1909*

Kettleby Hill Climb—Riley 10—1st Class A; F.T.D.
Irish Trials—Riley 12–18—1st Class C.
Aston Clinton Hill Climb—Riley 12–18—1st Class C; Club Cup.
Scottish Reliability Trials—Riley 10, 12–18—1st Class A & C.
Shelsley Walsh Hill Climb—Riley 12–18—1st & 2nd, Members event.

*1910–1913*

Fintry Hill Climb—Riley 10—1st.
Derby County Hill Climb—Riley 12–18—1st in Class.
Sudbourne Park Speed Trials—Riley 10—Class Win.
Coventry M.C. Hill Climb—Riley 10—Class Win.
Rivington Pike Hill Climb—Riley 12–18—Class Win.
M.C.C. Flexibility Tests—Riley 10, 12–18 —1st Class Awards.
Herts A.C. Hill Climb—Riley 10—Class Win.
Essex Motor Club 24 hours Reliability Trial—Riley 10—1st Class Award.
Southern M.C. Reliability Trial—Riley 12–18—1st Class Award.
Ipswich & East Suffolk A.C. Hill Climb—Riley 12–18—Class Win.
Crystal Palace Hill Climb—Riley 12–18—Class Win.
Frome Hill Climb—Riley 10, 12–18—Class Win.
M.C.C. Reliability Non-Stop Trials—Riley 12–18—1st Class Award.
Notts A.C. Reliability Trial—Riley 10, 12–18—1st Class Awards.
Birdlip Hill Climb—Riley 12–18—1st, Class C.
Essex M.C. 200 Mile Reliability Trial—Riley 12–18—1st Class Award.
Cardiff Hill Climb—Riley 12–18—1st Class C.
Sudbourne Park Speed Trials—Riley 12–18—Class Award.
Southern M.C. Hill Climb—Riley 10—Class Win.

*1923*

London-Lands End Trial—Riley 11/40—Class Win, Gold Medal.
J.C.C. General Efficiency Trial—Riley 11/40—1st overall.
R.A.C. Consumption Trial—Riley 11/40—Class Win, Special Award.
Scottish Reliability Trial—Riley 11/40—Class Wins.

*1924*

J.C.C. General Efficiency Trial—Riley 11/40—1st Class Award.
Liverpool 24 hour Trial—Riley 11/40—1st Class Award.
London to Lands End Trial—Riley 11/40—7 1st Class; 2 2nd Class, 1 3rd Class Awards.
Travers Trophy, Newcastle—Riley 11/40—2 1st Class Awards.
London to Holyhead Trial—Riley 11/40—2 1st Class Awards.
Coventry to Torquay & Return Trial—Riley 11/40—1st Class Award.
London to Edinburgh Trial—Riley 11/40—11 1st Class Awards.
Lands End to John O'Groats—Riley 11/40—41 1st Class Awards.

Scottish 6 Days Trial—Riley 11/40—2 1st Class Awards.
Southport Speed Trials—Riley 11/40—1st Class, 1 2nd Class Award.
Norfolk Hill Climb—Riley 11/40—F.T.D.
Saffron Walden Hill Climb—Riley 11/40—6 1st Class Awards.
Essex & Southend Hill Climb—Riley 11/40—13 1st Class, 7 2nd Class Awards.
Southampton to Exeter Trial—Riley 11/40—1st Class Award, 2 3rd Class Awards.
London to Barnstaple Trial—Riley 11/40—1st Class Award.
Brooklands Whitsun Light Car Handicap—Riley 11/40—1st.
Brooklands August 90 m.p.h. Long Handicap—Riley 11/40—1st.
Brooklands August 75 m.p.h. Short Handicap—Riley 11/40—2nd.

*1925*

R.A.C. Economy Trial—Riley 11/40—Class Win.
M.C.C. 100 Mile High Speed Reliability Trial—Riley 11/40, 12 h.p.—5 1st Class Awards.
London-Exeter-London Trial—Riley 11/40—3 1st, 17 2nd Class Awards.
London to Edinburgh Trial—Riley 11/40, 12 h.p.—6 1st Class Awards (Formation of Riley
    Motor Club).

*1926*

Nairobi-Mombasa, Kenya—Riley 12—first ever successful car journey.

*1927*

Brooklands Short Handicap—Riley 9—1st.
M.C.C. High Speed Trial, Brooklands—Riley 9—1st Class, Gold Medal.
Australian 700 Mile Alpine Tour—Riley 9—2 1sts.
Class G Records 5 km, 5 miles, 10 km, 10 miles, Brooklands—Riley 9 (97.38–97.89 m.p.h.)

*1928*

Brooklands Six Hours—Riley 9—1st (Class 3).
Ulster Tourist Trophy—Riley 9—1100 cc. Class—1st & Fastest Lap.
Brooklands—Class G Records 3 hrs, 4 hrs, 500 km, 500 miles—Riley 9—(85–87.12 m.p.h.).
J.C.C. High Speed Reliability Trial—Riley 9—7 Gold Medals.

*1929*

Australian Trans Continental Record (Fremantle-Sydney)—Riley 9—2850 miles in 5 days
    8 hours.
Shelsley Walsh Hill Climb—Riley 9—1st and 2nd in Class.
Brooklands Double 12 Race—Riley 9—2nd in Class, 6th overall.
Brooklands 47th 76 m.p.h. Handicap—Riley 9—1st at 86.30 m.p.h.
Irish International Grand Prix—Riley 9—1st in Class, 4th, 6th, 8th, 10th and 11th overall.
Ulster T.T.—Riley 9—1st in Class, 1st non-supercharged car to finish.
Canberra R.A.C. Reliability Trial—Riley 9—1st in Class.

Shelsley Walsh Open Hill Climb—Riley 9—5 Cups, 4 seconds, 4 thirds, 1st–8th overall on
    formula.
R.A.C. Mudgee (Australia) Trial—Riley 9—1st in Class, with full points.
B.R.D.C. 500, Brooklands—Riley 9—1st in Class, 8th overall.
Class G Record, Montlhery—Riley 9—1000 miles at 65.83 m.p.h. (Monaco).

## 1930

Monte Carlo Rally—Riley 9—Class G, 2nd, 3rd, 4th and 5th.
Brooklands Double Twelve Race—Riley 9—3rd & 6th overall, 1st & 2nd in Class.
Class G Records, Montlhery—Riley 9—1000, 2000, 4000 miles; 2000, 3000, 4000, 5000 km;
    24 & 48 hours. Speeds between 64.36 and 67.79 m.p.h.
Slovensky M.C. International Trial—Riley 9—Overall winner, only certificate award.
Shelsley Walsh Hill Climb—Riley 9—Class Win.
New York to Los Angeles Record—Riley 9—4,200 miles at 41 m.p.h. average.
Irish International Grand Prix—Riley 9—Won 1st day's race beating 19 supercharged cars.
Ulster T.T. Race—Riley 9—1st in Class, Class G lap record.

## 1931

Monte Carlo Rally Mont des Mules Hill Climb—Riley 9—Class win, 3rd F.T.D.
Monte Carlo Rally Coupé de Riviera—Riley 9—1st & 4th in Class, Class F.T.D.
Brooklands March Mountain Speed Handicap—Riley 9—1st.
Brooklands March Lincoln Short Handicap—Riley 9—1st.
Brooklands Somerset Junior Short Handicap—Riley 9—1st.
Irish International Grand Prix—Riley 9—1st, 2nd, 3rd in Class G.
Class G Records at Montlhery—Riley 9—50, 100, 200 km; 50, 100 miles; 1 hour Speeds
    between 108.29 & 108.9 m.p.h.
German 10,000 km. Trial—Riley 9—2 First Class Awards, Hungarian Cup.
R.A.C. Tourist Trophy Race—Riley 9—5th, 11th, 13th overall, 1st Class G, Class G Record.
German Grand Prix—Riley 9—Class Win, driven to and from event.
Class G Records—Riley 9—200, 500 miles; 500, 1000 km.; 3 & 6 hours. Speeds between
    98.14 & 104.08 m.p.h.
B.R.D.C. 500 Race, Brooklands—Riley 9—Class Win, 4th overall.

## 1932

Monte Carlo Rally—Riley 6/14, 9—Overall 3rd, 4th, 10th, 11th, 15th, 16th, 17th, 18th,
    19th: 2nd, 3rd Coupé des Dames, Aftenposten Cup, 2nd Concours de Confort, Mont des
    Mules Hill Climb 1st 1100 cc., 3rd F.T.D., Barclays Bank Cup, Prix du Docteur Monde.
Durban to Johannesburg Record—Riley 9—Light Car Record, Unlimited Record 55.26
    m.p.h.
Capetown to Johannesburg Record—Riley 9—Unlimited Record.
R.A.C. 1000 Mile Rally—Riley 9, 14/6—Class II 1st, 2nd, 4th, 5th, 7th. Over 1100 cc. 3rd.
    *Light Car & Cycle Car* Trophy, Leamington Cup, Eastbourne Cup, Ladies Prize, R.A.C.
    Trophy, *Daily Despatch* Trophy.

J.C.C. 1000 Miles Race—Riley 9—Overall 1st, 5th: 1st & 2nd 1100 cc. Class: S.M.M.T. Gold Challenge Trophy, Austin £100 Award, Wakefield Cup, Mobiloid Prize, Rootes Cup.

Class F 200 km. & 200 mile Records—Riley 6 Twelve—111.12 & 111.65 m.p.h.

Brooklands Guy's Gala Day—Riley 9—1st, Duke of York's Race.

Alpine Rally—Riley 9—Coupé des Alpes 1100 cc. Class, 4 Coupés des Glaciers.

Ulster Tourist Trophy—Riley 9, Six Twelve—Overall 1st, 2nd, 8th: Class G 1st, 2nd: Class F 1st: Lap Record, Race Record, Tourist Trophy, Lady Houston Prize, Wakefield Trophy, 2 *Autocar* Plaques.

B.R.D.C. 500 Mile Race, Brooklands—Riley 9—Overall 2nd, 4th, 5th: Class G 1st, 2nd, 3rd: R.A.C. Trophy, Barnato Trophy, Mobiloil Trophy, 3 B.R.D.C. Plaques.

## 1933

R.A.C. Rally—Riley 9, Six Twelve—Class III 1st, 4th, 5th, 6th, 7th, 8th, 9th; Class II 1st: Team Prize, Ladies Prize, 3 Concours D'Elegance 1st Class Awards.

Le Mans—Riley 9—4th overall, 1st on Handicap, 1st 1100/1500 cc. Classes, 1100 cc. Record.

R.S.A.C. 1000 Mile Rally—Riley Six Twelve—Small Car Class 1st, 2nd, 3rd, 6th: Ladies Prize: 2nd Concours.

Mannin Beg Race—Riley 9—1st overall, lap record.

International Alpine Trial—Riley 6/12, 9—Group 4 1st, 2nd, 3rd, Alpine Cup, Glacier Cup: Group 5 Glacier Cup 2nd.

Australian 200 mile Grand Prix—Riley 9—Overall 1st, lap record.

Johannesburg-Durban-Johannesburg Record—Riley Six—18 hours 12 minutes.

Ulster Tourist Trophy—Riley 9, 6/12—Overall 6th, 8th. Class F 1st.

Shelsley Walsh Hill Climb—Riley 9, 6/12—1500 cc. F.T.D., 1100 cc. F.T.D., U/S Sports Cars F.T.D.

Class G Records Brooklands—Riley 9—50 km. to 200 km.—109.18 m.p.h. to 110.67 m.p.h.

Brooklands Autumn Senior Mountain Handicap—Riley 9—1st.

Brooklands Autumn Ladies Mountain Handicap—Riley 9—1st.

Brooklands Oxford & Cambridge Mountain Handicap—Riley 6/12—1st: 1500 cc. Record.

## 1934

Monte Carlo Rally—Riley 9—2nd Small Car Class.

Class F Records Montlhery—Riley 6/12—1000 miles, 12 hrs, 2000 km.—102.35 m.p.h., 101.1 m.p.h., 101.04 m.p.h.

Australian Grand Prix—Riley 9—1st and 3rd overall.

B.A.R.C. Easter Meeting, Brooklands—Riley 9, 6/12—5 wins, 1 3rd, 1 5th.

Mannin Moar Race—Riley 2 litre—3rd.

Mannin Beg Race—Riley 2 litre—6th.

R.S.A.C. Scottish Rally—Riley 9, 6/12—14 Premier Awards, 10 Silver Awards, 1 Bronze Award.

Shelsley Walsh Hill Climb—Riley 6/12—2nd F.T.D.

Le Mans 24 hours—Riley 9, 6/12—Overall 2nd, 3rd, 5th, 6th, 12th, 13th: Rudge Whitworth Cup, 1500 cc./1100 cc. Class Wins, Ladies Prize, Team Prize.

International Alpine Rally—Riley 9, 6/14 –3 Vergold Plaques, 1 Glacier Plaque.
Ulster Tourist Trophy—Riley 9—9th, 11th, 12th & 16th overall.
B.R.D.C. 500 Brooklands—Riley 9, 2 litre—Overall 1st, 2nd: Team Prize: B.A.R.C. Cup,
    Wakefield Cup, Dunlop Trophy, Gibson Trophy, Maxwell Colegrave Trophy.


*1935*

New Zealand M.R.D.A. One Day Trial—Riley 9—1st, 2nd & 3rd.
Gloucester Park Speedway Inaugural Meeting N.Z.—Riley 9—1st overall.
Brooklands New Haw Mountain Handicap—Riley Six—1st.
1st Donington Park Race Meeting—Riley Six—2 wins, 1 second.
May Donington Park Race Meeting—Riley Six—3 firsts, 1 second.
Brooklands Whitsun Long Handicap—Riley 9—1st.
Mannin Beg Race—Riley Six—2nd (E.R.A. 1st).
Brooklands International Trophy Race—Riley Six, 9—2nd, 4th, 9th.
Le Mans 24 Hours—Riley 1½ Litre—4th, 7th (3rd & 4th Rudge Whitworth Cup).
British Empire Trophy Race—Riley Six—1st, 2nd, 3rd, 8th: Team Prize.
4th Mountain Handicap, Brooklands—Riley 9—1st (Appleton Special 2nd).
Ulster Tourist Trophy Race—Riley 1½ Litre—1st, 6th, 9th.
B.R.D.C. 500, Brooklands—Riley 2 Litre, 9—2nd overall & Team Prize.
Shelsley Walsh Hill Climb—Riley 1½ Litre, Six—Fastest 1500 Sports Car, M.A.C. Ladies
    Cup, Fastest unblown Racing Car.
M.C.C. High Speed Trials Brooklands—Riley 1½ Litre, 9—3 1st Class Awards, 1 Third.


*1936*

Brooklands British Mountain Handicap—Riley Six—Win 2nd Heath, 3rd Final.
International Trophy Race, Brooklands—Riley Six—3rd, 6th, 8th.
French Grand Prix Montlhery—Riley 1½ Litre—2 Litre Class—1st, 2nd, 3rd, 4th.
Ulster Tourist Trophy Race—Riley 1½ Litre—1st, 6th, 10th, 11th, 12th.
B.R.D.C. 500 Brooklands—Riley Six, 1½ Litre—1st, Team Prize.


*1937*

South African Grand Prix—Riley 9, 1½ Litre—2nd, 3rd, 7th.
Monte Carlo Rally—Riley 1½ Litre—Concours de Confort under 1500 cc., 1st.
British Empire Trophy Race, Donington Park—Riley 9—2nd (E.R.A.s 1st, 3rd & 4th).
Nuffield Trophy Race, Donington Park—Riley 1½ Litre—4th.
Twelve Hour Sports Car Race, Donington Park—Riley 1½ Litre—2nd & 3rd overall, 1st
    & 2nd Class B.
R.A.C. Tourist Trophy Race, Donington Park—Riley 1½ Litre—1500 cc. 1st & 2nd: 7th,
    9th overall.
B.R.D.C. 500 Brooklands—Riley 2 Litre, 1½ Litre—2nd, 3rd, 5th: Team Prize.
Sporting Commission Cup Race, Montlhery—Riley 1½ Litre—1st and 2nd.

*1938*

South African Grand Prix—Riley Six, 9—1st and 3rd.
International Trophy Race, Brooklands—Riley Six—1st.
British Empire Trophy Race, Donington Park—Riley Six, $1\frac{1}{2}$ Litre—Class B 1st; Team Prize.
R.A.C. Tourist Trophy, Donington Park—Riley $1\frac{1}{2}$ Litre, 9—1500 cc. Class 1st, 2nd, 3rd:
1100 cc. Class 3rd. Team Prize.


This list of competition achievements does not claim to represent all of Riley's successes, nor does it claim to be all Factory sponsored. It is far from complete and many of the awards and places won were secured without the financial or technical support of Riley (Coventry) Limited. Riley owners entered for the sport and took their chances. A tremendous catalogue of success exists far beyond this list and the sense of sportsmanship and cameraderie which prevailed then—and indeed does today—cannot possibly be done justice on these pages. Rileys continue to win and will surely do so for a long time yet.

VOLUME II

# 'THE PHOENIX RISES'
## 1939–1969

# Foreword

There has to be a first time for forewords and, in this case, it will probably be the last one also! Having helped David Styles with one or two questions he had raised, I was then asked to look through the draft of his proposed book and add any useful comments. This I did, finding and correcting the small number of mistakes, and I felt my job finished until he had the book in production. Not so; as he then asked if I would write for him a foreword.

You will probably know that, for some years David has been the Registrar and Historian for the Riley Register. My copies of their Bulletin suggest that he took over from Dr. Tony Birmingham at the end of March 1970.

I was very glad to hear of another book on Rileys and I do not feel that it replaces the Tony Birmingham book, but is supplementary to it. This latest book also covers post-1938 Rileys, which I think will give it a wider appeal. David has spent a lot of time in research and I feel Riley owners' thanks will go out to him.

So, in future I shall have two Riley Gospels to consult when in doubt. I am not yet making any real advance offers to the writer of a third Riley history, if it should occur!

ARNOLD C. FARRAR,
Director and Secretary, the Riley Motor Club,
Vice-President, the Riley Register.                                        *Oxford*, 1982.

# Introduction

I cannot, and therefore would not attempt to, hide the fact that the prime objective of this volume was always to present the product history of the family Riley Companies. I originally had no intention of giving space to consider the post-World War 2 cars, because I, like many others, had always nursed the thought that real Riley cars stopped being made when Riley (Coventry) Limited was sold to Lord Nuffield. To many, cars built thereafter were somehow 'cars with Riley badges'. But then one has to think logically—how many times are we reminded today that things cannot remain as they were? So why should Rileys be exempt? After all, there was not a sudden exodus of personnel from the Company when it changed hands and so there must have been continuity of ideas and designs.

Then I realised that I had covered 176 models in the first Book—it surely could not take too long to review the history of another 17 types built over the next thirty years. What is more, whether the 'purists' like it or not, post-war Rileys are now classics in their own right and many are very desirable cars. With this in mind, I set about accumulating the material needed to cover their history—it was rather more readily available than had been the pre-war material, though it still took some digging.

So, without apology, here it is—Volume II. I have deliberately prepared it in this fashion to draw the distinction between the pre-1939 and post-1938 cars. It does seem entirely logical to cover the seventy years of Riley product history within one book and my justification, if I need any, for covering seventy and not just forty years is that it makes a *complete* history. It is as appropriate that the enthusiast for the pre-1939 cars should be reminded or made aware of Riley's continuity of existence as it is for the post-1938 car enthusiast to be reminded or made aware of their heritage.

Quite apart from all this ideology, I am reminded that the oldest Riley club —and once the largest one-make car club in the world—still caters for *all* cars made under the various Riley badges. That club is the Riley Motor Club. I am further reminded of some rather pleasurable motoring I have enjoyed from just two post-war Rileys with twenty years between their ages. The first was a 1948 2½ Litre Saloon and the other was a 1968 1300 Saloon—it was quite remarkable how many characteristics they had in common. It may just be that such commonality of characteristics exists between the owners of the cars which span those seventy years. One thing is certain—just as the pre-1939 cars have, so the post-1938 cars will *all* ultimately become cherished motor cars. It *is* a cherished breed.

D.G.S.

# CHAPTER ONE

# The Nuffield Rileys—
# the 1939 and RM Series Cars

After the Nuffield takeover of Riley (Coventry) Limited and the establishment of Riley (Coventry) Successors Limited, the new Company, now owned by Morris Motors made a rather inconspicuous revival of the name 'Riley' with the new models they introduced. It is perhaps not fair to lay all the blame at the door of the Nuffield Organisation, because much of the groundwork for those new models was done by the old Company. However, the coachwork had a distinct Morris influence.

Nonetheless, Riley continued and six new models were produced. They were the Twelve Saloon at £310, the Twelve Sprite Saloon at £335, the Twelve Drophead at £335, the Drophead Sprite Tourer at £360, the Sixteen Saloon at £385 and the Sixteen Drophead at £410. As can be seen, prices took a fairly drastic fall and of course this was related to a similar reduction in production costs.

By July 1939, in response to market demand, the 16 h.p. Kestrel was re-introduced, but now, like its Nuffield Riley counterparts, it had a four speed synchromesh gearbox instead of the dual overdrive of the earlier Big Fours. This revived Kestrel was also priced at £410, in line with the Drophead.

Also in July, the Company took a very bold step in its sales campaign by introducing a guaranteed fuel consumption for the 12 h.p. model. With each car purchased came a certificate, signed by the Managing Director—Victor Riley—and by the head tester. They guaranteed that the Riley Twelve would give at least 30 miles per gallon at an average speed of 30 m.p.h. Who said that the last quarter of the 20th Century was the period of fuel conservation?

The 12 h.p. model was different in many ways from its predecessors. Firstly the preselector gearbox was gone, replaced with a four-speed unit with synchromesh on second, third and top. There was now a short open propeller shaft to the torque tube and a central straight gear lever on the floor. Wheels were now bolt-on pressed steel of 16 in. diameter equipped with 5.75 × 16 in. tyres. Steering was no longer of the worm and segment type, Bishop cam and roller type having been adopted instead.

The six-light bodywork was rather more bulbous than had been usual for Riley and one could have been forgiven for mistaking the profile for a Wolseley or a Morris—or even an MG Saloon. However one saw it, the car was produced and at least retained something of the Riley character inside the car. Leather was still used to upholster the seats and the doors were still capped with walnut trim. The dash was still wood faced and the instruments were now three dials, giving speedometer, oil pressure gauge, ammeter and petrol gauge. Lights and ignition switch were on the dash capping, as were the individual windscreen wiper controls. The handbrake was now a rather frail-looking umbrella-handle type pulling on a ratchet from under the parcel shelf and the headlight dipswitch was now foot-operated to the left of the clutch pedal.

The chassis was of similar design to the Victor chassis, but included a number of cost-savers in its manufacture. Pressed cross members were used, some channel and some ½ ellipses welded or rivetted together to make tubular members. Rubber bushings were used for springs and shackles and self-lubricating rubber bushes were used in the brake mechanism—which was still Girling as before.

The engine compartment showed a number of changes too. The valve rocker covers were no longer bolted at their edges to the cylinder head—instead they had just four studs along the centre-line of each cover to hold them in place. The cover on the exhaust side of the engine had a spring-loaded filler cap for oil and a breather pipe bridged the two rocker covers from the air filter. No longer was the dynamo driven directly from the front end of the crankshaft: it was now mounted on brackets on the exhaust side of the engine and was belt driven. The fan was a pressed-steel one mounted on the front of the water pump spindle and the engine was no longer mounted on the traditional cross-shaft. Instead, its front mounting brackets, which were pressed steel, were attached to the lower bolts of the timing case and then, via rubber blocks, to the other halves of the brackets which were bolted to the inner web of the box-section chassis frame.

The Sixteen models followed much the same lines as the Twelves. With both models, some changes had been made to the cooling of the cylinder heads and both had cross water flow—that is, water fed into the exhaust side of the cylinder head and out of the inlet side. The general appearance of the Sixteen Saloon and Drophead models was similar to the smaller versions and the interior trim and appointments followed the same pattern. The floor-

*1939 Twelve Drophead during World War 2.*

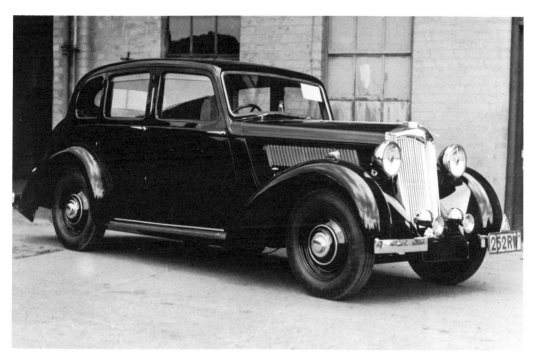

*1939 Twelve (1½ Litre) Saloon*

*A 1939 Saloon Body ready for mounting.*

*1939 Sixteen Saloon ( 2½ Litre)*

mounted dipswitch, the umbrella-handle handbrake, the instrumentation and switches were all the same—even in the re-introduced Big Four Kestrel. Perhaps the one saving grace (to the Riley purist of pre-1938 persuasion) was that four speed gearbox, because many people encountered problems with the 3 speed overdrive unit from a handling point of view and the four was easier to use. The final drive ratio was very similar being 4 : 1 instead of the earlier 3.97 : 1.

These seven Riley models continued into production until 1940, when, like most engineering plants, the factory was turned over to war work and the manufacture of munitions—again. However, during the second World War, enthusiasm was maintained if production of Rileys was not and, just as after the Great War, the Company was ready to launch a new range of cars as soon as it was permitted to do so.

The Company had maintained a modest flow of advertising during the War and by November 1944, we were told that the new Riley would be 'new'—a new chassis and new body, but the Riley engine, to give 'Magnificent Motoring' (a phrase which was to remain in use for some years). By the summer of 1945, that new car was released to an unsuspecting Public. Unsuspecting, because the pre-war Riley enthusiast had been rather disappointed with the 1939 models and did not expect the attractive lines of this new model—neither did

*1939 Sixteen Drophead Coupé*

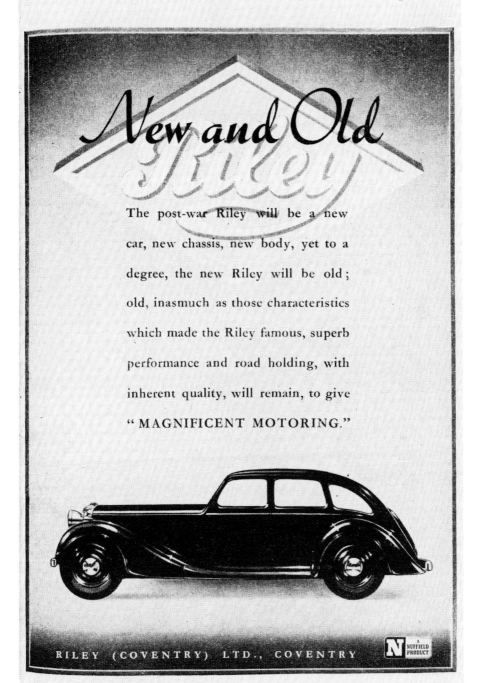

# New and Old

The post-war Riley will be a new car, new chassis, new body, yet to a degree, the new Riley will be old; old, inasmuch as those characteristics which made the Riley famous, superb performance and road holding, with inherent quality, will remain, to give

## "MAGNIFICENT MOTORING."

RILEY (COVENTRY) LTD., COVENTRY

A NUFFIELD PRODUCT

A9

*The re-introduced 1939 Kestrel 16 h.p., now with louvred bonnet sides.*

they expect the innovations it brought with it: for it truly was a credit to the people who designed it.

The new 1½ litre Saloon was long and low—and very sleek for 1945, having been based on the Close-Coupled Touring Saloon design but streamlined for a new motoring age. The car had a fabric-covered roof, recalling the early Thirties and Rileys of a bygone age, pleasantly rounded coach lines and mudwings which, whilst a little bulbous, blended well into the overall design. The headlamps were faired into the inner wing valances and the overall effect of the design was extremely pleasing.

The interior of the car followed the same concept as the 1939 models, with walnut capped doors and fascia, and a walnut instrument board. The same handbrake was used as on the pre-war Nuffield Rileys and by and large, the mechanics were much the same too. The same four-speed gearbox was used and the engine was mounted in much the same was as before.

The engine now used a duplex chain for camshaft drive, which was thought by many to be an improvement on the gear drive of the earlier models. Whether or not it was depends upon one's point of view—and whether one has driven a car with exceptionally noisy worn timing gears or not!

New features of this new model included a superb independent front suspension—not unlike the front suspension of the contemporary Citroen—and a vastly improved steering which employed a rack and pinion. This really was a great improvement over the cam and roller type of earlier models and restored the precision steering which had been the characteristic of the Riley worm and wheel design. Brakes were now Girling 10¼ in. hydro-mechanical and Dunlop 16 in. wheels were shod with Dunlop (naturally) 5.75 × 16 in. tyres.

The new car was tremendously successful and won much acclaim by Public and Press alike. It was soon joined by a 2½ Litre version, using the same body design and features. What a great shame, though, that a post-war Two-Seater in the mould of the Sprite did not materialise—it almost did, but not quite.

Rileys were never used in competition after the takeover in the way that they had been before, though they achieved quite respectable successes in a number of major rallies—and as saloon car racing gained in popularity, so Rileys were seen to acquit themselves well in that sphere too.

As the 1½ and 2½ Litre cars established themselves, it was decided to expand the range from just two models, though still using only the two basic chassis types. In February 1948, the 2½

*The 1940 Kestrel 16 h.p., now devoid of trim on the bonnet sides.*

Litre Two/Three Seat Roadster was launched in an attempt to secure a share of the potentially lucrative American market. A Two Seat version was produced for a while, following the home market preference for two seats and a floor gear-change. However, its production life was rather short-lived, the model being discontinued in 1951 after just three years.

The new Roadster was on the same chassis as the 2½ Litre Saloon, so was of rather long wheelbase for a Two/Three Seater. It was a bit of a squeeze to accommodate three people in comfort, but it did so, together with an enormous amount of luggage. It had a foldaway hood (quite like the 1933 Two-Door Lynx) and had a steering column mounted gearchange to keep the floor area clear for that third passenger, who in any case would have had to put a foot either side of the transmission tunnel. The Two/Three Seat Roadster was certainly not the most elegant carriage for the centre passenger, especially if that passenger happened to be a lady wearing a then-fashionable pencil skirt, but it was undeniably an interesting car and one to be much sought-after in later years.

In the same year, another interesting variation on the 2½ Litre chassis was introduced. This was the 2½ Litre Drophead Coupé—quite a worthy successor to the still-born Big Four Lynx of 1938. The Drophead was a Two-Door Four/Five Seater—literally a Two Door Drophead version of the 2½ Litre Saloon. The Drophead design was also built on the 1½ Litre chassis as early as 1946 and speculation over how many of this version were built varies between just two and a dozen. Anyway, the 2½ Drophead was deleted from production in 1951, having seemingly failed to capture enough of the Riley-owning Public's imagination to justify more being built.

Also during 1948, Riley was to sever an important link with its past by vacating the Coventry factory to move to Abingdon, joining MG—the idea being that the two specialist and sporting names of the Nuffield empire should be together under the same roof. At the time of the move, the 1½ Litre Saloon, the 2½ Litre Saloon, Drophead and Roadster were all in

**The RILEY 1½ litre Saloon**

Riley 'Torsionic' Independent front suspension, finger-light steering, Girling hydro-mechanical brakes, an entirely new body with a 51" rear seat and dust-proof luggage accommodation of unique dimensions are outstanding features of the post-war Riley car.

The famous 1½ litre Riley engine with hemispherical head, inter-axle seating, four-speed gearbox, torque tube transmission—characteristics responsible for Riley individuality — are retained and, with many new refinements, blend to give MAGNIFICENT MOTORING.

RILEY (COVENTRY) LTD. COVENTRY

production, so the move itself must have been a marathon task. It was at this time, of course, that much of the remaining pre-war Riley material was disposed of, because many of the records were incomplete due to war damage. So there didn't seem much point in keeping a pile of old material that wasn't then seen to be of much importance—archives didn't mean as much then as now.

Over this transition period, a number of interesting projects were being played with, including one most interesting $2\frac{1}{2}$ Litre Six-Light Limousine, built at Coventry in 1946/7, which rather resembled the very elegant Van Den Plas Princess limousine of the period. However, like many projects which had gone before, it was to be still-born. Another, which did achieve limited production, was a Bonallack-built exercise on the $1\frac{1}{2}$ Litre chassis of 1947/9 known as the Rapid Coupé—a two door design with a flat windscreen which was quite similar in profile to the factory built $2\frac{1}{2}$ Litre Drophead.

With the demise of the $2\frac{1}{2}$ Litre Drophead and Roadster from the Riley range, only the two basic models remained—the $1\frac{1}{2}$ Litre Saloon and the $2\frac{1}{2}$ Litre Saloon. In 1953, the $2\frac{1}{2}$ Litre model was discontinued, to be replaced by the Pathfinder Saloon.

The Pathfinder was still a coachbuilt saloon body and employed the familiar $2\frac{1}{2}$ Litre engine, but it broke with tradition because it didn't look a Riley any more, according to many, and it had a body very similar in design to another car in the now BMC Group range— the Wolseley 6-90. In fact, on close examination, it can be seen that the Pathfinder had quite a number of feature differences from the Wolseley.

The Pathfinder was a big car, with bench seats and a right hand gearchange. It had an all-steel body and was the interim between the demise of the Riley as many had known it and the new, last phase in the seventy-year history of the breed. That interim was short-lived, and with the passage of the $1\frac{1}{2}$ Litre Saloon in 1955 and the Pathfinder in 1957, the final break with the past had come. From now on, cars bearing the Riley badge were to share bodies and power plants with other cars in the BMC range of products. Some called it rationalisation, some called it badge-engineering. Whatever else it was, it was certainly a fact—and people still bought Riley-badged cars, so that was justification enough.

The next car in the Riley line was the Two-Point-Six, the first car to share everything but detail trim and its badge with another. Now it was a Wolseley with a Riley badge—and the next phase in Riley's long history was to be its last. The BMC re-organisation would succumb to another, more final re-organisation, the Leyland/BMC merger.

*1946 $1\frac{1}{2}$ Litre Saloon*

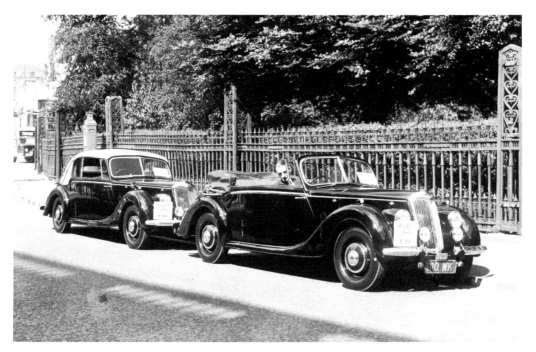

*A pair of 1946 1½ Litre Drophead Coupés*

*1945 2½ Litre Saloon*

## SPECIFICATIONS

| | |
|---|---|
| MODEL | **1½ Litre Twelve**                               *Year:* 1939–40 |

**CHASSIS**

Box section mainframe with fabricated tubular crossmember.
*Wheelbase:* 9 ft. 0 in.
*Track:* Front 4 ft. 0 in. Rear 4 ft. 0 in.
*Type of Wheels:* Dunlop pressed-steel disc 4.0 × 16 in. bolt-on.
*Tyres:* Front 5.75 × 16 in. Rear 5.75 × 16 in.
*Braking System:* Girling mechanical rod operating wedge brakes in 13 in. drums.

**TRANSMISSION**

*Clutch Type:* Borg & Beck Single dry 8 in. plate.
*Gearbox Type:* 4 speed synchromesh.
*Gear Selecting Mechanism:* Central floor-mounted.
*Gear Ratios:* 1st—19.4:1, 2nd—11.2:1, 3rd—7.25:1, 4th—4.88:1, Reverse—19.4:1
*Gearbox Oil Capacity:* 2 pints.
*Rear Axle Oil Capacity:* 2¾ pints.
*Rear Axle Type:* Semi-floating banjo, torque tube drive to spiral bevel gears.
*Rear Axle Ratio:* 4.88:1

**ENGINE**

*Engine Type:* Riley 1½ litre.
*RAC H.P. Rating:* 11.9
*Cubic Capacity:* 1496 cc.
*Number of Cylinders:* 4
*Firing Order:* 1, 2, 4, 3
*Bore:* 69 mm.
*Stroke:* 100 mm.
*Cylinder Head:* P.R. detachable, hemispherical combustion chambers.
*Valve Gear:* 45° overhead operated by high camshafts via tappets and short pushrods.
*Tappet Clearances (Hot):* Inlet 0.003 in. Exhaust 0.004 in.
*Valve Timing:* Inlet opens 0° before TDC, closes 55° after BDC
      Exhaust opens 50° before BDC, closes 20° after TDC.
      *Sprite Series:* Inlet opens 20° before TDC, closes 50° after BDC.
      Exhaust opens 50° before BDC, closes 20° after TDC.
*Number of Main Bearings:* 3
*Diameter of Main Bearings:* F—1¾ in. C—2¼ in. R—1¾ in.
*Diameter of Big End Bearings:* 1⅞ in.
*Sump Capacity:* 8 pints.
*Type of Oil Pump:* Gear Driven.
*Normal Oil Pressure (Hot):* 30—50 p.s.i.
*Cooling System:* Pump and Fan.
*Type of Ignition:* Coil & Distributor.
*Method of Advance/Retard:* Automatic centrifugal.
*Contact Breaker Gap:* 0.012—0.016 in.
*Plug Gap:* 0.030 in.
*Make and Type of Plug:* Lodge C14, HNP.
*Number, Make and Type of Carburetters:* Single SU H2 standard series.
      Twin SU HV3 Sprite series.
*Type of Inlet Manifold:* Cast alloy bolt-on with hot spots.
*Type of Exhaust Manifold:* Cast iron bolt-on.
*Location of Fuel Tank:* Rear
*Capacity of Fuel Tank:* 10 gallons.
*Method of Fuel Feed:* AC mechanical pump.

**MODELS AVAILABLE**

      Chassis only £235 (1940—£266)
1939–40 Twelve Saloon £310 (1940—£341)
      Twelve Sprite Saloon £335 (1940—£368.10. 0)
      Twelve Drophead £335 (1940—£368.10.0)
      Twelve Sprite Drophead £360 (1940—£396)

| | |
|---|---|
| MODEL | **Sixteen**                                     *Year* 1939–40 |

**CHASSIS**

Box-section mainframe with tubular crossmembers.
*Wheelbase:* 9 ft. 8 in.
*Track:* Front 4 ft. 3 in. Rear 4 ft. 3 in.

*The Torsionic front suspension of the post-war models.*

*A very interesting drophead on the 1½ Litre chassis, this is a Rapid Coupé body by Bonallack, from 1947–49. Not the kind of thing one normally associates with this company, since their principal field was truck bodies and trailers. Clearly, however, they saw a market potential for a 1½ Litre drophead after the Factory decision not to offer their version in volume. Some survive, but only a few were built.*

*Type of Wheels:* 4.5 × 16 in. Dunlop pressed steel bolt-on.
    3.50 × 18 in. on Kestrel 16.
*Tyres:* Front 6.25 × 16 in. Kestrel 5.50 × 18 in.
    Rear 6.25 × 16 in. Kestrel 5.50 × 18 in.
*Braking System:* Girling mechanical rod with wedge-operated shoes in 14 in. drums.

**TRANSMISSION**

*Clutch Type:* Borg & Beck single dry 10 in. plate.
*Gearbox Type:* 4 speed synchromesh.
*Gear Selecting Mechanism:* Central floor-mounted lever.
*Gear Ratios:* 1st—14.60:1, 2nd—8.60:1, 3rd—5.67:1, 4th—4:1, Reverse—14.60:1
*Gearbox Oil Capacity:* 2 Pints.
*Rear Axle Oil Capacity:* 4 pints.
*Rear Axle Type:* Semi-floating banjo type with enclosed drive to spiral bevel gears.
*Final Drive Ratio:* 4:1

**ENGINE**

*Engine Type:* Riley Big Four.
*RAC H.P. Rating:* 16.07
*Cubic Capacity:* 2443 cc.
*Number of Cylinders:* 4
*Firing Order:* 1, 2, 4, 3
*Bore:* 80.5 mm.
*Stroke:* 120 mm.
*Cylinder Head:* P.R. 12 stud detachable with hemispherical combustion chambers.
*Valve Gear:* 45° inclined overhead operated from high twin camshafts through tappets
    & short pushrods.
*Tappet Clearances Hot:* Inlet 0.003 in. Exhaust 0.004 in.
*Valve Timing:* Inlet opens 7° before TDC, closes 50° after BDC.
    Exhaust opens 50° before BDC, closes 17° after TDC.
*Number of Main Bearings:* 3
*Diameter of Main Bearings:* All 2.559 in.
*Diameter of Big End Bearings:* 2.359 in.
*Sump Capacity:* 12 pints.
*Type of Oil Pump:* Gear driven from camshaft.
*Normal Oil Pressure (Hot):* 30—50 p.s.i.
*Cooling System:* Pump thermostat and fan.
*Type of Ignition:* Coil and distributor.
*Method of Advance/Retard:* Automatic centrifugal.
*Contact Breaker Gap:* 0.016 in.
*Plug Gap:* 0.032 in.
*Make of Type of Plug:* Champion L10 or Lodge C14.
*Number, Make and Type of Carburetters:* Single downdraught SU.
*Type of Inlet Manifold:* Cast alloy bolt-on with hot-spots.
*Type of Exhaust Manifold:* Cast iron bolt-on.
*Location of Fuel Tank:* Rear.
*Fuel Capacity:* 10 gallons.
*Method of Fuel Feed:* AC mechanical pump.

**MODELS AVAILABLE**

| 1939: | Sixteen Saloon | £385 | —Sixteen Drophead | £410 |
| | Kestrel Saloon | £410 | —Chassis only | £310 |
| 1940: | Sixteen Saloon | £423.10 | —Sixteen Drophead | £451 |
| | Kestrel Saloon | £451 | —Chassis only | £358.10 |

**MODEL**

**1½ Litre**                                                   *Year:* 1945–55

**CHASSIS**

Box section mainframe with tubular and box section cross-members.
*Wheelbase:* 9 ft. 4½ in.
*Track:* Front 4 ft. 4¼ in. Rear 4 ft. 4¼ in.
*Type of Wheels:* Dunlop Steel disc 4.0 × 16 in.
*Tyres:* Front 5.75 × 16 in. Rear 5.75 × 16 in.
*Braking System:* Girling hydromechanical with 10 in. drums.

**TRANSMISSION**

*Clutch Type:* Borg & Beck single dry 8 in. plate.
*Gearbox Type:* 4 speed synchromesh.
*Gear Selecting Mechanism:* Central floor-mounted.
*Gear Ratios:* 1945/52 1st—19.8, 2nd—11.2, 3rd—7.2, 4th—4.88, Reverse As first.
    1952/55 1st—20.37:1, 2nd—11.74:1, 3rd—7.58:1, 4th—5.25:1, Reverse As
    first.

*A 1948 2½ Litre Drophead Coupé (note the shallow windscreen header).*

*The 1950 2½ Litre Drophead—now with a deeper windscreen header.*

*The 1949 2½ Litre 2/3 Seat Roadster chassis*

*A very early 2½ Litre Drophead Coupé, built in 1946/47.*

*Gearbox Oil Capacity:* 2 pints.
*Rear Axle Oil Capacity:* 2¾ pints.
*Rear Axle Type:* Semi-floating banjo, spiral bevel to 1952—hypoid to 1955.
*Rear Axle Ratio:* 4.88/5.25 :1

ENGINE

*Engine Type:* Riley 1½ litre.
*RAC H.P. Rating:* 11.9
*Cubic Capacity:* 1496 cc.
*Number of Cylinders:* 4
*Firing Order:* 1, 2, 4, 3
*Bore:* 69 mm.
*Stroke:* 100 mm.
*Cylinder Head:* Detachable with hemispherical combustion chambers.
*Valve Gear:* 45° overhead operated from high camshafts via tappets and short pushrods.
*Tappet Clearances (Hot):* Inlet 0.003 in. Exhaust 0.004 in.
*Valve Timing:* Inlet opens (9°) 7° before TDC, closes (45°) 48° after BDC
    Exhaust opens (56°) 48° before BDC, closes (20°) 20° after TDC
    1948–52 in brackets.
*Number of Main Bearings:* 3
*Diameter of Main Bearings:* F&R—1.75 in. C—2.75 in.
*Diameter of Big End Bearings:* 1.875 in.
*Sump Capacity:* 10 pints.
*Type of Oil Pump:* Gear Driven.
*Normal Oil Pressure (Hot):* 40 p.s.i.
*Cooling System:* Pump and fan.
*Type of Ignition:* Coil and distributor.
*Method of Advance/Retard:* Automatic centrifugal.
*Contact Breaker Gap:* 0.016 in.
*Plug Gap:* 0.025 in.
*Make and Type of Plug:* Champion L10S.
*Number, Make and Type of Carburetters:* Single SU H2.
*Type of Inlet Manifold:* Cast alloy bolt-on with hot-spots.
*Type of Exhaust Manifold:* Cast iron bolt-on.
*Location of Fuel Tank:* Rear.
*Capacity of Fuel Tank:* 12½ gallons.
*Method of Fuel Feed:* AC mechanical pump.

MODELS AVAILABLE

1945–55 : 1½ Litre Saloon
Prices (Not including Tax) : 1945 £555          1951 £714
                             1946 £555—£675     1952 £714—£860
                             1947 £675          1953 £860—£850
                             1948 £675          1954 £850—£800
                             1949 £675—£714     1955 £800
                             1950 £714
1946-Drophead Coupé–£675

MODEL                          **2½ Litre**                                   *Year:* 1946–53

CHASSIS

Box section mainframe with box and tubular cross members.
*Track:* Front 4 ft. 4¼ in. Rear 4 ft. 4¼ in.
*Type of Wheels:* Dunlop steel disc bolt-on.
*Tyres:* Front 6.00 × 16 in. Rear 6.00 × 16 in.
*Braking System:* Girling Hydro-mechanical with drums.

TRANSMISSION

*Clutch Type:* Borg & Beck single plate 10 A6G.
*Gearbox Type:* 4 speed synchromesh.
*Gear Selecting Mechanism:* Central remote floor mounted lever.
*Gearbox Oil Capacity:* 2 pints.
*Rear Axle Oil Capacity:* 4 pints.
*Rear Axle Type:* Semi-floating banjo, spiral bevel to 1952—Hypoid thereafter.
*Rear Axle Ratio:* 4.11 :1

ENGINE

*Engine Type:* Riley 2½ litre
*RAC H.P. Rating:* 16.07

*A very interesting prototype—a 1946/47 2½ Litre Six-Light Saloon.*

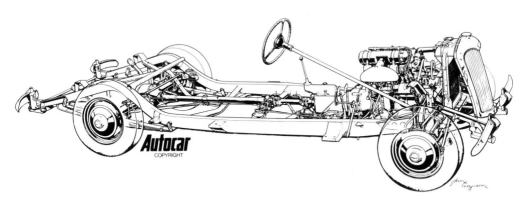

*Riley 2½ litre chassis*

*1953 2½ Litre RMF Saloon*

*Last of the RM Series, a 1955 1½ Litre RME Saloon*

*Cubic Capacity:* 2443 cc.
*Number of Cylinders:* 4
*Firing Order:* 1, 2, 4, 3
*Bore:* 80.5 mm.
*Stroke:* 120 mm.
*Cylinder Head:* P.R. detachable 12 stud with hemispherical combustion chambers.
*Valve Gear:* 45° overhead from high camshafts via tappets and short pushrods.
*Diameter of Valve Heads:* Inlet 1.856 in. Exhaust 1.604 in.
*Tappet Clearances (Hot):* Inlet 0.003 in. Exhaust 0.004 in.
*Valve Timing:* Inlet opens 17° before TDC, closes 43° after BDC.
     Exhaust opens 45° before BDC, closes 20° after TDC.
*Number of Main Bearings:* 3
*Diameter of Main Bearings:* 2.559 in.
*Diameter of Big End Bearings:* 2.362 in.
*Sump Capacity:* 14 pints.
*Type of Oil Pump:* Gear driven vertical.
*Normal Oil Pressure (Hot):* 30—40 p.s.i.
*Cooling System:* Pump, thermostat and fan.
*Type of Ignition:* Coil and distributor.
*Method of Advance/Retard:* Automatic centrifugal.
*Contact Breaker Gap.* 0.010—0.012 in. (Later 0.014—0.016 in.)
*Plug Gap:* 0.030 in.
*Make and Type of Plug:* Champion NA8.
*Number, Make and Type of Carburetters:* Twin SU Type H4.
*Type of Inlet Manifold:* Cast alloy bolt-on.
*Type of Exhaust Manifold:* Cast iron bolt-on.
*Location of Fuel Tank:* Rear mounted.
*Method of Fuel Feed:* Electric Pump.

MODELS AVAILABLE

| | 1946 | 1947 | 1948 | 1949 | 1950 | 1951 | 1952 | 1953 |
|---|---|---|---|---|---|---|---|---|
| 1946–53 : 2½ Litre Saloon | £880 | £880 | £880 | £958 | £958 | £958 | £1055 | £1055 |
| 2½ Litre Drophead | | | £950 | £995 | £970 | £958 | | |
| 2½ Litre 2/3 Seater | | | £880 | £958 | £958 | £958 | | |

MODEL         **Pathfinder 2½ Litre**                                      *Year:* 1953–57

CHASSIS        Box-section chassis with welded steel 4 door saloon body.
*Wheelbase:* 9 ft. 5½ in.
*Track:* Front 4 ft. 6 in. Rear 4 ft. 6½ in.
*Type of Wheels:* 5.0 × 16 in. Dunlop steel disc 5-stud bolt-on.
*Tyres:* Front 6.50 × 16 in. Rear 6.50 × 16 in.
*Braking System:* Girling hydraulic drum brakes with wedge operated shoes. Mechanical handbrake.

TRANSMISSION    *Clutch Type:* Borg & Beck single dry 10 in. plate.
*Gearbox Type:* 4 speed synchromesh.
*Gear Selecting Mechanism:* Right hand floor mounted lever.
*Gear Ratios:* 1st—13.59:1, 2nd—8.446:1, 3rd—5.88:1, 4th—4.11:1, Reverse—18.42:1 Overdrive ratiosʙ 3rd—4.11:1, 4th—2.87:1.
*Gearbox Oil Capacity:* 4¼ pints, extra 1⅓ pints for O/D box.
*Rear Axle Oil Capacity:* 3¾ pints.
*Rear Axle Type:* Semi-floating banjo type with hypoid gears and open propeller shaft.
*Final Drive Ratio:* 4.11:1

ENGINE         *Engine Type:* Riley 2½ Litre.
*RAC H.P. Rating:* 16.07
*Cubic Capacity:* 2443 cc.
*Number of Cylinders:* 4
*Firing Order:* 1, 2, 4, 3
*Bore:* 80.5 mm.
*Stroke:* 120 mm.
*Cylinder Head:* P.R. 12 stud detachable with hemispherical combustion chambers.
*Valve Gear:* 45° inclined overhead operated from high twin camshafts through tappets
  & short pushrods.
*Tappet Clearances Hot:* Inlet 0.011 in. Exhaust 0.011 in.

*Valve Timing:* Inlet opens 12° before TDC, closes 53° after BDC.
Exhaust opens 55° before BDC, closes 20° after TDC
*Number of Main Bearings:* 3
*Diameter of Valve Heads:* Inlet 1.830 in. Exhaust 1.604 in.
*Diameter of Main Bearings:* F—2.625 in. C—2.625 in. R—2.625 in.
*Diameter of Big End Bearings:* 2.3625 in.
*Sump Capacity:* 13 pints.
*Type of Oil Pump:* Gear driven from camshaft.
*Normal Oil Pressure (Hot):* 30—40 p.s.i.
*Cooling System:* Pump thermostat and fan.
*Type of Ignition:* Coil and distributor.
*Method of Advance/Retard:* Automatic vacuum/centrifugal.
*Contact Breaker Gap:* 0.014—0.016 in.
*Plug Gap:* 0.025 in.
*Make of Type of Plug:* Champion NA8.
*Number, Make and Type of Carburetters:* Twin SU Type H4.
*Type of Inlet Manifold:* Cast alloy bolt-on.
*Type of Exhaust Manifold:* Cast iron bolt-on.
*Location of Fuel Tank:* Rear.
*Fuel Capacity:* 13 gallons.
*Method of Fuel Feed:* SU electric pump.

MODELS AVAILABLE    1953–54: Pathfinder Saloon  £975
1954–56: Pathfinder Saloon  £875
Overdrive available at extra cost from Chassis Number RMH–3436.
1956–57: Pathfinder Saloon  £940
The prices quoted above do not include tax.
Last Chassis Number—MA. . . /6652.

*The 2½ Litre 2/3 Seater prototype*

*1948 2½ Litre 2/3 Seat Roadster*

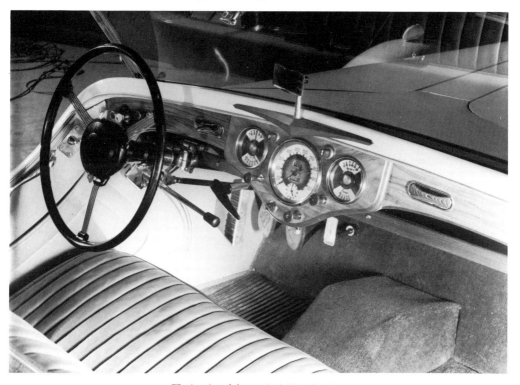

*The interior of the 1948 2½ Litre Roadster*

*First of a new line—the full-scale Pathfinder mock-up.*

*The Pathfinder prototype body*

*The 1953 Pathfinder running prototype*

*Front quarter view of 1954 Pathfinder Saloon*

*Rear quarter view of 1954 Pathfinder Saloon*

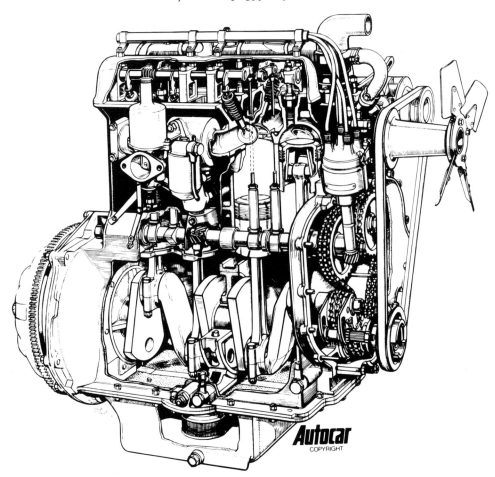

*The Post-war 1½ Litre engine*

The characteristic Riley radiator is retained, but the head lamps are built into the inner wing valances to reduce wind resistance and simplify cleaning.

## SPECIFICATION

**Engine.**—12 h.p., four cylinders, 69×100 mm. (1,496 c.c.). Overhead valves at 90 degrees in hemispherical combustion chambers. Three-bearing crankshaft. Aluminium alloy pistons. S.U. carburettor Lucas coil ignition. Mechanical fuel pump. Full-flow oil filter. Cross-flow pump cooling.

**Transmission.**—Borg and Beck clutch. Four-speed gear box Synchromesh on second, third and top. Overall ratios: First 19.8, second 11.2, third 7.2, top 4.88 to 1 Enclosed propeller-shaft to spiral bevel rear axle

**Brakes.**—Girling Hydro-mechanical in 10in. drums.

**Suspension.**—Independent front and half-elliptic rear springs.

**Steering.**—Special Riley, with 17in. adjustable steering wheel.

**Fuel Tank Capacity.**—12½ gallons.

**Leading Dimensions.**—Wheelbase 9ft. 4½in. Track 4ft. 3in. Overall length 14ft. 10in., width 5ft. 2½in., height 4ft. 9in. Ground clearance 7in.

**Tyres.**—Dunlop 5.75×16 on wide-base rims. Disc wheels.

**Weight.**—24½ cwt.

# THE BEST RILEY YET

### New 1½-litre Saloon Exhibits Remarkable Characteristics on the Road

AS most keen drivers well know, and all Riley enthusiasts are firmly convinced, the history of motoring has been enriched by many a good Riley model. These cars have always had a character of their own, upon which a definite tradition has become founded. The design has been original, and essentially progressive. The cars have always had potentialities well beyond the average of the day, and features different from the usual and especially attractive.

Witness, for example, the original Riley Nine Monaco saloon. It was the first small car which held the road like a large one; the first small car to give ample room for four people with luggage under cover in a compact and yet comfortable saloon body; the first to have a four-speed gear box with a really quiet and useful third speed, and the only car of its time sold with an engine so well designed that although it was *par excellence* a normal car engine it was also ready to be tuned for racing purposes, and did, indeed, distinguish itself in the racing field. This was because the crankshaft was sturdy, the valve gear light, the overhead valves were inclined in a hemispherical head, and the valve ports free, and, in common with the inlet manifold, machined to smooth regular surfaces.

The Nine was the first of a remarkable series of cars. Space precludes the Riley history up to date, but many other fine models, including the pre-war 1½-litre and the Sixteen-Four, will jump to the memory. These cars had complete individuality of design. Future cars will maintain that individuality, and the first of them to be announced, the post-war 1½-litre, has an even more strikingly individual character than any previous Riley model.

No doubt the reader will have already studied the illustrations, so there is scarcely need to tell him that the appearance of the car, long, broad, and yet low, is most attractive. What may be concealed within this graceful exterior will most engender curiosity. Riley recipes

A more graceful tail than that of the new Riley is difficult to imagine. From the practical viewpoint it has the merit of providing a luggage boot of considerable capacity.

608

Although compact and low built, the entirely new post-war 1½-litre Riley saloon provides plenty of room for five p
attraction of looking graceful from any angle, as seen in other views on the

are simplicity, in conjunction with making the best possible use of what experience has already proved to be good ;
plenty of power and not too much weight ; concentration
upon those features of rigidity, weight distribution, suspension and steering which can so vitally affect the " feel "
and the absolute safety of the car on the road.

Except for the engine, which is the well-known and well-
tried 1½-litre, the car is a new production. There are a
great many details of special interest in the construction,
but it is desired by the makers to withhold them until
such time as cars are actually coming off the production
line, which should be towards the end of September. *The
Autocar* has been offered the somewhat unusual course of
trying out the car on the road first, and presenting impressions of its behaviour some time in advance of describing
its mechanical construction.

On all counts the performance is truly remarkable. By
some means best known to themselves the Riley " back-
room" boys have achieved a suspension combining a really
comfortable "level" ride, with a sureness of road holding
which is quite outstanding.

## Superb Roadholding in Comfort

The way this car can be taken round curves is astonishing. Not many racing cars would do better. It can be
" placed " to an inch to negotiate a curve at high speed,
and it proceeds with a certainty that suggests running on
rails which have been banked. There is no skidding, tail
wagging, outward roll, or sawing at the steering wheel.
What is so surprising is that this road holding has been
achieved in conjunction with a suspension which is not in
the least hard, but is in fact well above the average for
comfort. One estimates that this car can quite safely be
taken round a sharp curve at a speed 20 per cent. faster
than the average good driver would essay on a normally
good car. Lest this appreciation of a supremely good
cornering ability should in any way be misunderstood it is
necessary to explain that a car which can be cornered
exceedingly fast without risk is incomparably more safe
at customary speeds than one which is verging on the
uncontrollable at customary speeds. Moreover the good
cornering car can be relied upon to help out the staid
driver in an emergency from causes outside his control.

Some further remarks about this suspension are called
for. It is of the type which deals faithfully with bad sur-

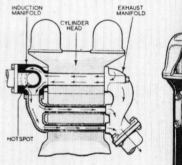

Although the ex-
haust and induction
manifolds are on
opposite sides of
the cylinder head,
heating of the
mixture is achieved
by by-passing some
of the exhaust gases
in the direction in-
dicated

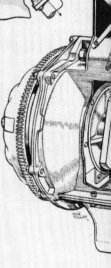

High - efficiency
Riley engine
features include
overhead valves se
at 90 deg. in spheri
cal combustion
chambers, central
sparking plugs
valve operation by
rockers with short
light push rods from
twin camshafts,
counterbalanced
crankshaft, and ful
pressure lubrication.
In this partly cut-
away view colour
is used to emphasise
moving parts

**609**    The 90-degree overhead valves are operated through short push rods and rockers from camshafts located in the crankcase.

faces as well as good ones. As an example the car can be driven quite comfortably with the near-side wheels on the grass verge of a country road. Another point is that the riding is pretty well as good in the rear seats as it is in the front; it is quite possible to write legibly on a paper resting on one's knee while the car is cruising at 50 m.p.h.

To give a more definite impression of the feelings of the driver when handling this new Riley for the first time: The engine is mounted on rubber so effectively that it is as smooth running as anyone would wish, from the highest r.p.m.—somewhere about 4,500—down to a low-speed crawl on top gear. The maximum speed, by the way, we should estimate at about 80 m.p.h., lacking the opportunity to test it against the stop-watch. The engine is also flexible, and has plenty of power at low r.p.m., hence there is no need to perform a lot of gear changing in normal

ar has the

driving. As applies to all Rileys, but more so than to the best ones of the past, this is a dual-purpose car. Either one can drive it peaceably and comfortably, and make a good average speed without effort, or one can take advantage of the latent possibilities afforded by its good power-to-weight ratio, use the gear box to advantage, and make play with the road holding and cornering ability, and so put up an average speed over a long run which is quite surprisingly high. The 1½-litre is a fine engine, and will stand up to hard driving.

When a fresh driver takes over control of the car his impressions are these: First that the driving position is "typically Riley"; one sits up rather than lolls back, and the adjustable steering wheel tucks nicely in. Then the tapering bonnet and fairly narrow radiator afford excellent visibility. Carried on a tunnel, the gear lever is short, and close to the left hand. There is no need to use first gear to start. One eases in the clutch and gives a touch on the accelerator, and the car moves sweetly away. As there is synchromesh on second, third, and top, gear changing is perfectly easy—it asks for no skill, but only for deliberate movement. In a short distance one is in top gear, cruising quietly along and ready to take notice.

### Excellent Steering

At first, to one coming off a faithful pre-war car, the steering feels a shade stiff, or perhaps firm. It is a special form of steering gear, is quick in response, and has next to no backlash. Within a mile you have acquired the feel of it, and in five miles you think it is a superb sort of steering; which indeed it is. We gather that it can be set lighter if desired, but the firmness is there purposely in order to damp sudden movements on the part of the driver. There is no kick-back from the front wheels. The car follows the steering with complete accuracy, and immediately. As a result it can be steered with a notable exactness. If you decide to go round a curve one foot from the verge, the car obeys exactly, without two bites at the cherry, so to speak. It is the same at all speeds which you care to attempt, and one that has to be tried to be fully appreciated.

Before going far one naturally tries out the brakes

The engine and four-speed gear box unit from the near side. Engine design has not been materially altered; 54 b.h.p. is developed. The gear box has synchromesh on second, third and top

610

*Autocar*

AUGUST 24, 1945

These also are something special, the Girling hydro-mechanical. They are a revelation in braking. The pedal requires scarcely more pressure than is normally applied to an accelerator. At the very instant you touch the pedal you feel that the brakes begin to take hold. There is no lost motion, and the quickness with which you slow down the car is exactly proportional to the pressure you put on the pedal. The braking is exceptionally smooth, and as powerful as you like to make it, and one more asset to this quite remarkable car.

It might perhaps be thought that, denied as one has been for so long the experience of freely trying out a new car, there may be a tendency to be over-enthusiastic, but we feel that a similar verdict will come from every other experienced driver who handles this car in the future. Some characteristics have been built into the new Riley that have not been evident before.

As regards the ability to climb hills, the car was tried on the old Cotswold favourites, Willersey, Saintbury, and Fish. So long is it since we used them that the curves and corners have become unfamiliar. With this car it seems that it is no longer a question of how easily or otherwise the hills can be climbed, but of how fast the driver feels inclined to take them. Fish can be a top gear climb, or very fast with the use of third. Third is good enough for the steepest part of Willersey.

There is ample room for three people in the rear seat of the new Riley and deep wells provide plenty of leg room. The interior trimming is notably neat. Experience shows that the "ride" in the rear seats is as comfortable as in front. Left : The instruments and minor controls are neatly arranged in a central panel. Steering wheel "reach" is adjustable by the telescopic steering column.

Some description of the saloon coachwork, which later will be followed by a drop-head coupé, will be of interest. The body is set low on the chassis, but it has plenty of head room. The seats also are low and wide, and con-siderable leg room is given to the rear seat, which will take three people in comfort, by the use of fairly deep footwells. This body follows customary Riley practice in having wide doors, with four lights, and the rear doors extend to the depth of the rear seat cushion. The front seats are of the adjustable chair type. The interior trim is in excellent style and of simple good taste. At the front is a V windscreen, and the section in front of the driver is arranged to open with a winding handle. The roof is fabric covered on a perforated metal panelling, so as to save weight and avoid drumming.

The 1½-litre engine has not been altered in any material points. The construction is essentially rigid, the four cylinders being formed in one casting integral with the greater part of the crankcase, forming a solid support for a massive counterbalanced crankshaft carried in three main bearings. At the front is an enclosed distribution gear which drives a pair of camshafts, one on each side of the cylinder block. The valves are operated through overhead rockers and light short push rods. The valve ports have a through flow, on the one side to the exhaust and on the other to an inlet manifold having an S.U. carburettor.

The connecting rods are steel forgings of H section, and the pistons are of aluminium alloy with four rings. Particular care has been devoted to the lubrication system. A pump of high capacity draws oil from the crankcase and passes it under pressure through a large filter, whence it passes to the crankshaft, big-end, and camshaft bearings and to the rocker gear and timing. The cooling system also is interesting. A water pump actuated in conjunction with a fan by a triangular belt drive delivers cool water to the cylinder head, where there is a cross flow from the exhaust to the inlet side, ensuring that the regions of greatest heat receive adequate cooling. Circulation is arranged to be greater in the cylinder head than in the block.

Later there will be a 16 h.p. four-cylinder Riley engine, of 80.5 × 120 mm. (2,443 c.c.). This will be put into a car similar to the 1½-litre, and should give a phenomenal performance.                                                                M. T.

# CHAPTER TWO

# Three Score Years and Ten— the Last Rileys

In 1957 the Pathfinder ceased production, to be replaced by the Two-Point-Six, bringing to an end the last link with the Rileys of the past. The Riley engine was no longer to be used— a basic design which had been developed, enlarged and improved over three decades from the first Nine in 1926.

Now, Riley was to be a B.M.C. Group product, resulting from what came to be a practice credited to the British Motor Corporation—badge engineering. That was a very unfair accusation to lay at B.M.C.'s door, however, because that practice first came into use in 1931 and of all companies to embark upon the policy, it was the maker of the 'Best Car in the World'—yes, Rolls Royce! So, in terms of industry precedents, B.M.C. had nothing at all to be ashamed of as a result of using this marketing ploy. Whilst the product now had no resemblance to the 'real' Rileys of the past—except for the radiator shell—the Company was offering the relative quality of appointments which had always set Riley apart from the run-of-the-mill, thereby satisfying a continuing demand.

So, the Two-Point-Six was launched to replace the Pathfinder. This new model had a body shape similar to its predecessor, a shape it now shared with the Wolseley 6/90. It also shared the big six-cylinder engine—the 'C' Series B.M.C. unit—and a common gearbox. 16 in. pressed steel wheels were used and these were fitted with 6.00 × 16 in. tyres.

Shortly after the announcement of the Two-Point-Six came another $1\frac{1}{2}$ Litre car under the Riley badge—the One-Point-Five. This model also shared its body, engine, gearbox and running gear with a Wolseley model—the 1500. It was a further sign of B.M.C.'s rationalisation of the product ranges—and, of course, a logical way of offsetting tooling costs for more than one model. In production terms, it was the sensible thing to do, but to the dyed-in-the-wool Riley enthusiast it was far from ideal. Nonetheless, the Riley One-Point-Five sold quite well for a few years and, at least, it helped keep the Riley flag flying.

In 1959, the British Motor Corporation introduced a range of cars which were to herald even further rationalisation of their product range—the $1\frac{1}{2}$ Litre Farina—styled models. Originally the new styling was introduced just for the Austin Cambridge and Morris Oxford models, but these were soon joined by others under the Wolseley, MG and Riley badges.

The Riley version of this new range was known as the 4/68 and was perhaps the least adventurous car to carry the badge. It was a 1500 cc. car which showed signs of slightly better attention to finish than its less expensive sister cars. It featured the usual array of better instrumentation set in a walnut fascia, walnut door cappings and leather upholstery.

The Riley car now appealed to a rather different cross-section of the market. Riley buyers now were people who wanted a car which was a cut above the average, but not necessarily

*The One-Point-Five prototype, using the body originally
intended for the Morris Minor.*

of sporting inclination—many people who bought the 4/68 were perfectly content with the past traditions of the name to set them apart from the mundane. The 4/68's only two claims to anything even resembling sporting tendencies were a pair of carburetters instead of just one and the badge on the front of the car.

Later the 4/68 was updated a little and renamed the 4/72 to accompany its enlarged, 1622 cc., engine. It was also joined by a small relative in a Riley version of the very successful Austin Mini. The newcomer was called the Elf and was basically a Mini with a small boot at the back and a Riley-shaped radiator shell at the front. Again, the new car had a Wolseley sister—the Wolseley Hornet. The name Elf was used because the former Riley small—sports name—Imp—had been 'stolen' by Rootes for their mini car.

There was a general feeling of disappointment in Riley circles about the Elf, because it didn't look quite right with its boot extension and many felt that the Mini-Cooper might well have carried a Riley badge. That really would have been a latter-day attempt at reviving some of Riley's former glory.

Anyway, the Elf it was and, like most of its sister cars of the period, it sold on the strength of past glories. It was a little better appointed than the ordinary Mini but it was a Mini with a Riley badge.

The next stage—and really the last—in Riley's development was with the introduction of the Austin and Morris 1100s. Again, badge-engineering prevailed and soon there were Wolseley, MG, Riley and even Van den Plas versions. The first Riley of this last generation

*1957 One-Point-Five Saloon Mark I*

was to be named 'Kestrel' to the mild annoyance again of the purists and again it was an upmarket, two carburetter, version of the Austin/Morris car with a Riley badge.

When the 1300 engine was introduced, so the Kestrel II became a 1275 briefly, then a 1300 and when the revised body styling of the 1300 range came in 1967 so the Riley version became known simply as the 1300. This then was the Riley, still upmarket but appealing largely to a rather different market from the Coventry Rileys, in that one-upmanship in cars was now a common feature of the motoring world—because Everyman had a car, his neighbour had to have a better one! And the Riley 1300 served that market quite well, although it was also quite a tuneable machine and with a well tuned, and slightly modified, engine it was capable of some quite sporting performance as this author knows from experience. However, that was not with a perfectly standard factory-built car.

The 1300 represented the ultimate development of the Riley named product and it is interesting now to compare it with the earliest production four-wheeled Riley car. Both had transverse engines and drive and both were fitted with engines of a little over one litre capacity. The earlier car had mid-engine and rear drive configuration (a feature regaining popularity in the late 60s) whereas the later car had front engine and front drive. For those who were prepared to try it, the later car was able to give quite Riley-like performance in fact, with its rack and pinion steering (albeit slightly heavy because of the front-wheel drive) and, when improved, positive engine and predictable suspension.

During this period of B.M.C. Rileys, production had moved away from Abingdon and

many Rileys were produced at Cowley in the Morris plant—all part of the rationalisation process. Ultimately they were produced at Longbridge in the Austin factory and that was where the name was laid to rest.

In 1968, in an attempt to confirm the survival of an all-British motor manufacturer, the British Motor Corporation and the Leyland Motor Corporation were encouraged to merge to form the British Leyland Motor Corporation. There were some common features of interest— both produced cars and both produced trucks, but there were conflicts of management style in the two companies which were clearly beyond reconciliation and the result was an ill-matched marriage which faced enormous problems.

However, whatever the politics of the situation, the decision was made in late 1969 to discontinue the production of cars under the Riley name. It seems that B.L.M.C. could not justify low-volume production and sales (8,000–10,000 per year) in their overall plan and so, almost exactly the God-given lifespan of Man after the birth of Riley's entry into the Motor Industry, the Riley badge was laid to rest and the flag lowered for the last time.

There were to be no more Riley cars. The three-score-years-and-ten of the car which was 'As Old as the Industry—As Modern as the Hour' had come and gone. Rest in Peace.

*Slightly different styling from the Pathfinder, the 1957
Two-Point-Six shared its body, and engine, with a Wolseley.*

SPECIFICATIONS

| | |
|---|---|
| MODEL | **Two-Point-Six Saloon** *Year:* 1957–59 |

CHASSIS

Box-section chassis with welded steel 4 door saloon body.
*Wheelbase:* 9 ft. 5½ in.
*Track:* Front 4 ft. 6⅜ in. Rear 4 ft. 6⅜ in.
*Type of Wheels:* 5.0 × 16 in. Dunlop steel disc 5-stud bolt-on.
*Tyres:* Front 6.70 × 16 in. Rear 6.70 × 16 in.
*Braking System:* Girling hydraulic drum brakes with wedge operated shoes. Mechanical handbrake.

TRANSMISSION

*Clutch Type:* Borg & Beck single dry 10 in. plate.
*Gearbox Type:* 4 speed synchromesh.
*Gear Selecting Mechanism:* Right hand floor mounted lever for manual gearbox & column mounted lever for automatic transmission.
*Gear Ratios:* Manual 1st—12.93:1, 2nd—8.03:1, 3rd—5.60:1, 4th—3.90:1, O/D 3rd—4.11:1, O/D 4th—2.87:1, Reverse—17.52:1
*Gearbox Oil Capacity:* Manual 4½ pints, extra 1⅓ pints OD. Automatic 15 pints.
*Rear Axle Oil Capacity:* 3¾ pints.
*Rear Axle Type:* Semi-floating banjo type with hypoid gears and open propeller shaft.
*Final Drive Ratio:* Manual (without O/D) & Automatic 3.90:1. Manual with overdrive 4.11:1

ENGINE

*Engine Type:* B.M.C. 'C' Series.
*Cubic Capacity:* 2639.4 cc.
*Number of Cylinders:* 6
*Firing Order:* 1, 5, 3, 6, 2, 4
*Bore:* 79.375 mm.
*Stroke:* 88.9 mm.
*Cylinder Head:* Cast iron water-cooled bolt-on.
*Valve Gear:* Vertical overhead valves operated by single camshaft via tappets and push-rods.
*Tappet Clearances Hot:* Early Inlet 0.012 in. Exhaust 0.012 in.
          Late Inlet 0.023 in. Exhaust 0.023 in.
*Number of Main Bearings:* 4
*Main Bearing Dia:* 2.3745 in.
*Sump Capacity:* 11½ pints.
*Type of Oil Pump:* Gear driven from camshaft.
*Normal Oil Pressure (Hot):* 50 p.s.i.
*Cooling System:* Pump, thermostat and fan.
*Type of Ignition:* Coil and distributor.
*Method of Advance/Retard:* Automatic vacuum/centrifugal.
*Contact Breaker Gap:* 0.014—0.016 in.
*Plug Gap:* 0.025 in.
*Make and Type of Plug:* Champion N5 or NA8.
*Number, Make and Type of Carburetters:* Twin SU Type H4.
*Type of Inlet Manifold:* Cast alloy, bolt-on.
*Type of Exhaust Manifold:* Cast iron, bolt-on.
*Location of Fuel Tank:* Rear
*Fuel Capacity:* 13 gallons.
*Method of Fuel Feed:* SU electric pump.

MODELS AVAILABLE

1957–59: Two-Point-Six Saloon (Manual): £940.
1957–59: Two-Point-Six Saloon (Auto): £1055.
Chassis numbers from UA./. .401—2500, see text Appendix 1 of Volume 11 for identification codes.

*1959 One-Point-Five Saloon Mark II*

*Last of the One-Point-Fives, the 1963 Mark III*

| | | |
|---|---|---|
| MODEL | **One-Point-Five Saloon** | *Year:* 1957–65 |

CHASSIS Integral construction chassis/body unit—Four Door Saloon.
*Wheelbase:* 7 ft. 2 in.
*Track:* Front 4 ft. $2\frac{7}{8}$ in. Rear 4 ft. $2\frac{5}{16}$ in.
*Type of Wheels:* $3.0 \times 14$ in. Dunlop steel disc 4-stud bolt-on.
*Tyres:* Front $5.00 \times 14$ in. Rear $5.00 \times 14$ in.
　　From HSR1/10701 $5.60 \times 14$ in. $5.60 \times 14$ in. (1959 on)
*Braking System:* Girling hydraulic drum brakes with wedge operated shoes in 9 in.
　　front and 8 in. rear drums. Mechanical handbrake.

TRANSMISSION *Clutch Type:* Borg & Beck single dry 8 in. plate.
*Gearbox Type:* 4 speed synchromesh.
*Gear Selecting Mechanism:* Central floor mounted lever on remote extension from
　　gearbox.
*Gear Ratios:* 1st—13.56:1, 2nd—8.25:1, 3rd—5.12:1, 4th—3.73:1, Reverse—17.73:1
*Gearbox Oil Capacity:* $4\frac{1}{2}$ pints.
*Rear Axle Oil Capacity:* $1\frac{3}{4}$ pints.
*Rear Axle Type:* Semi-floating banjo type with hypoid gears and open propeller shaft.
*Final Drive Ratio:* 3.73:1

ENGINE *Engine Type:* B.M.C. 'B' Series.
*Cubic Capacity:* 1489 cc.
*Number of Cylinders:* 4
*Firing Order:* 1, 3, 4, 2
*Bore:* 73.025 mm.
*Stroke:* 88.9 mm.
*Cylinder Head:* Cast iron water-cooled bolt-on.
*Valve Gear:* Vertical overhead valves operated by single camshaft via tappets and
　　pushrods.
*Tappet Clearances Hot:* Inlet 0.015 in. Exhaust 0.015 in.
*Number of Main Bearings:* 3
*Sump Capacity:* $7\frac{1}{2}$ pints.
*Type of Oil Pump:* Gear driven from camshaft.
*Normal Oil Pressure (Hot):* 50 p.s.i.
*Cooling System:* Pump, thermostat and fan.
*Type of Ignition:* Coil and distributor.
*Method of Advance/Retard:* Automatic vacuum/centrifugal.
*Contact Breaker Gap:* 0.014—0.016 in.
*Plug Gap:* 0.025 in.
*Make of Type of Plug:* Champion N5.
*Number, Make and Type of Carburetters:* Twin SU Type H4.
*Type of Inlet Manifold:* Cast alloy bolt-on.
*Type of Exhaust Manifold:* Cast iron bolt-on.
*Location of Fuel Tank:* Rear.
*Fuel Capacity:* 7 gallons.
*Method of Fuel Feed:* SU electric pump.

MODELS AVAILABLE 1957–60 : One-Point-Five 　　　: £575—C/n HSR1/101–18121.
1960–61 : One-Point-Five Mk 2 : £575—C/n HSR1/18122–27897.
1961–65 : One-Point-Five Mk3 : £580—C/n R/HS2/101–12184.
The prices quoted above do not include tax.

| | | |
|---|---|---|
| MODEL | **4/68 and 4/72 Saloons** | *Year:* 1959–69 |

CHASSIS Integral construction chassis/body unit— 4 Door Saloon.
*Wheelbase:* 4/68 8 ft. $3\frac{5}{16}$ in. 4/72 8 ft. $4\frac{3}{16}$ in.
*Track* Front 4 ft. $2\frac{9}{16}$ in. Rear 4 ft. $2\frac{3}{8}$ in.
*Type of Wheels:* $4.0 \times 14$ in. Dunlop steel disc 4-stud bolt-on.
*Tyres:* Front $5.90 \times 14$ in. Rear $5.90 \times 14$ in.
*Braking System:* Girling hydraulic drum brakes with wedge operated shoes in 9 in.
　　drums front and rear. Mechanical handbrake.

TRANSMISSION *Clutch Type:* Borg & Beck single dry 8 in. plate.
*Gearbox Type:* 4 speed synchromesh.
*Gear Selecting Mechanism:* Central floor mounted lever on remote extension from gear-
　　box.

One of the new Farina-styled BMC saloons in
1959 was the 4/Sixty Eight Saloon

The first Mini-based Riley, the 1961 Elf Mk. I 848 cc. Saloon

*Gear Ratios:* 1st—15.64:1, 2nd—9.52:1, 3rd—5.91:1, 4th—4.33:1, Reverse 20.45:1
*Gearbox Oil Capacity:* 4½ pints.
*Rear Axle Oil Capacity:* 1¾ pints.
*Rear Axle Type:* Semi-floating banjo type with hypoid gears and open propeller shaft.
*Final Drive Ratio:* 4.33:1

ENGINE

*Engine Type:* B.M.C. 'B' Series.
*Cubic Capacities:* 4/68 1489 cc. 4/72 1622 cc.
*Number of Cylinders:* 4
*Firing Order:* 1, 3, 4, 2
*Bore:* 4/68 73.025 mm. 4/72 76.2 mm.
*Stroke:* 88.9 mm.
*Cylinder Head:* Cast iron water-cooled bolt-on.
*Valve Gear:* Vertical overhead valves operated by single camshaft via tappets and
     pushrods.
*Tappet Clearances (Cold):* Inlet 0.015 in. Exhaust 0.015 in.
*Number of Main Bearings:* 3
*Sump Capacity:* 7½ pints.
*Type of Oil Pump:* Gear driven from camshaft.
*Normal Oil Pressure (Hot):* 30—50 p.s.i.
*Cooling System:* Pump, thermostat and fan.
*Type of Ignition:* Coil and distributor.
*Method of Advance/Retard:* Automatic vacuum/centrifugal.
*Contact Breaker Gap:* 0.014—0.016 in.
*Plug Gap:* 0.024—0.026 in.
*Make of Type of Plug:* 4/68 Champion N5, 4/72 Champion N9Y.
*Number, Make and Type of Carburetters:* Twin SU Type HD4.
*Type of Inlet Manifold:* Cast alloy bolt-on.
*Type of Exhaust Manifold:* Cast iron bolt-on.
*Location of Fuel Tank:* Rear.
*Fuel Capacity:* 10 gallons.
*Method of Fuel Feed:* SU electric pump.

MODELS AVAILABLE

1959–61 : 4/68 Saloon : £725. C/no.R/HS1/101–R/HS1/11084.
1961–63 : 4/72 Saloon : £745.
1963–65 : 4/72 Saloon : £758. | C/no.R/HS3/11101
1965–68 : 4/72 Saloon : £761. } to R/HS3/25291
1968–69 : 4/72 Saloon : £791. |
1969    : 4/72 Saloon : £803. |
Automatic transmission listed at £68 extra for 4/72 model. The prices quoted above
do not include tax.

MODEL

**Elf Saloon**                                              *Year:* 1961–69

CHASSIS

Integral construction chassis/body unit—2 Door Saloon.
*Wheelbase:* 6 ft. 8 1/32 in.
*Track:* Front 3 ft. 11⅞ in. Rear 3 ft. 9⅞ in.
*Type of Wheels:* 4.0×10 in. Dunlop steel disc 4-stud bolt-on.
*Tyres:* Front 5.20×10 in. Rear 5.20×10 in. or 145×10 in. radial. or 145×10 in.
     radial.
*Braking System:* Lockheed hydraulic drum brakes with wedge operated shoes in 7 in.
drums front and rear. Mechanical handbrake.

TRANSMISSION

*Clutch Type:* Borg & Beck single dry 7¼ in. plate.
*Gearbox Type:* 4 speed synchromesh.
*Gear Selecting Mechanism:* Central floor mounted lever. Remote extension from gearbox
     on Mk3.
*Gear Ratios:* 1st—13.657:1, 2nd—8.177:1, 3rd—5.317:1, 4th—3.765:1, Reverse—
     13.657:1
*Gearbox Oil Capacity:* Gearbox integral with transverse engine.
*Final Drive Type:* Gearbox connected to engine through intermediate gear from crank-
     shaft. Transverse driveline to front wheels.
*Final Drive Ratio:* 3.765:1

ENGINE

*Engine Type:* B.M.C. 'A' Series.
*Cubic Capacities:* Mk 1 848 cc. Mks 2 & 3 998 cc.
*Number of Cylinders:* 4

*1963 Elf Mark II Saloon*

*1965 Kestrel 1100 Saloon Mark I*

*Firing Order:* 1, 3, 4, 2
*Bore:* Mk 1 62.9 mm. Mks 2 & 3 64.58 mm.
*Stroke:* Mk 1 68.26 mm. Mks 2 & 3 76.2 mm.
*Cylinder Head:* Cast iron water-cooled bolt-on.
*Valve Gear:* Vertical overhead valves operated by single camshaft via tappets and
  pushrods.
*Tappet Clearances (Cold):* Inlet 0.012 in. Exhaust 0.012 in.
*Number of Main Bearings:* 3
*Sump Capacity:* 8½ pints.
*Type of Oil Pump:* Gear driven from camshaft.
*Normal Oil Pressure (Hot):* 50 p.s.i.
*Cooling System:* Pressurised, pump, thermostat & fan.
*Type of Ignition:* Coil and distributor.
*Method of Advance/Retard:* Automatic vacuum/centrifugal.
*Contact Breaker Gap:* 0.014—0.016 in.
*Plug Gap:* 0.025 in.
*Make of Type of Plug:* Champion N5 or N9Y.
*Number, Make and Type of Carburetters:* Single SU Type HS2.
*Type of Inlet Manifold:* Cast alloy bolt-on.
*Type of Exhaust Manifold:* Cast iron bolt-on.
*Location of Fuel Tank:* Rear.
*Fuel Capacity:* 5½ gallons.
*Method of Fuel Feed:* SU electric pump.

MODELS AVAILABLE  1961–62: Elf Mk 1 Saloon: £475: C/no R/A2S1/156851—310706.
1962–65: Elf Mk 2 Saloon: £475: C/no from R/A2S2/369601.
1965–66: Elf Mk 2 Saloon: £493:
1966–68: Elf Mk 3 Saloon: £525: ⎫ from R/A2S3/930221
1968–69: Elf Mk 3 Saloon: £550: ⎭ to R/A2S3/1337993.
Automatic transmission: £75, 4 speed, available Mk 3 only. Total Elf production
1961–69 estimated 30.912. The prices quoted above do not include tax.

*The final Elf, the Mark III Saloon*

*1966 4/Seventy Two Saloon*

*An interesting diversion from the Farina-styled saloon was this
1966 Siam-di-Tella Pickup built in Argentina. So nothing is
new, Riley having built their first truck in 1908!*

| | | |
|---|---|---|
| MODEL | **Kestrel 1100 & 1275 Saloons** | *Year:* 1965–68 |

CHASSIS      Integral construction chassis/body unit—4 Door Saloon.
*Wheelbase:* 7 ft. 9½ in.
*Track:* Front 4 ft. 3½ in. Rear 4 ft. 2⅞ in.
*Type of Wheels:* 4.0 × 12 in. Dunlop steel disc 4-stud bolt-on.
*Tyres:* Front 145 mm × 12 in. Rear 145 mm. × 12 in.
*Braking System:* Lockheed hydraulic 8.39 in. front disc and 8 in. rear drums with
    wedge operated shoes and mechanical handbrake.

TRANSMISSION      *Clutch Type:* Borg & Beck single dry 7⅛ in. plate.
*Gearbox Type:* 4 speed synchromesh.
*Gear Selecting Mechanism:* Central floor mounted lever with remote extension from
    gearbox.
*Gear Ratios:* Manual 1st—14.99, 2nd—8.98, 3rd—5.83, 4th—3.76, Reverse—14.99 :1.
    Auto 1st—10.11, 2nd—6.94, 3rd—5.49, 4th—3.76, Reverse 10.11 :1.
*Gearbox Oil Capacity:* Gearbox integral with transverse engine.
*Final Drive Type:* Gearbox connected to engine through intermediate gear from crank-
    shaft. Transverse driveline to front wheels.
*Final Drive Ratio:* 3.76 :1

ENGINE      *Engine Type:* B.M.C. 'A' Series.
*Cubic Capacities:* 110 1098 cc. 1275 MkII 1275 cc.
*Number of Cylinders:* 4
*Firing Order:* 1, 3, 4, 2
*Bore:* 1100: 64.58 mm, 1275 Mk II: 70.61 mm.
*Stroke:* 1100: 83.72 mm, 1275 Mk II: 81.28 mm.
*Cylinder Head:* Cast iron water-cooled bolt-on.
*Valve Gear:* Vertical overhead valves operated by single camshaft via tappets and
    pushrods.
*Tappet Clearances (Cold):* Inlet 0.012 in. Exhaust 0.012 in.
*Number of Main Bearings:* 3
*Sump Capacity:* 8½ pints.
*Type of Oil Pump:* Gear driven from camshaft.
*Normal Oil Pressure (Hot):* 30—60 p.s.i.
*Cooling System:* Pressurised, pump, thermostat & fan.
*Type of Ignition:* Coil and distributor.
*Method of Advance/Retard:* Automatic vacuum/centrifugal.
*Contact Breaker Gap:* 0.014—0.016 in.
*Plug Gap:* 0.028 in.
*Make of Type of Plug:* Champion N5 or N9Y.
*Number, Make and Type of Carburetters:* Twin SU Type HS2.
*Type of Inlet Manifold:* Cast alloy bolt-on.
*Type of Exhaust Manifold:* Cast iron bolt-on.
*Location of Fuel Tank:* Rear.
*Fuel Capacity:* 8 gallons.
*Method of Fuel Feed:* SU electric pump.

MODELS AVAILABLE      1965–66 : Kestrel Mk 1 1100 Saloon : £645 : From C/no.R/AS1/ 101.
1966–67 : Kestrel Mk 1 1100 Saloon : £672 : Last C/no.R/AS1/12223.
1967–68 : Kestrel Mk 2 1275 Saloon : £692 : From C/no.R/AS4/12224.
1968     : Kestrel Mk 2 1100 Saloon : £692 : Last C/no.R/AS4/16714.
4 speed automatic transmission : £75 : Optional extra Mk 2 only. The prices quoted
    above do not include tax.

| | | |
|---|---|---|
| MODEL | **1300 Saloon** | *Year:* 1968–69 |

CHASSIS      Integral construction chassis/body unit—Four Door Saloon.
*Wheelbase:* 7 ft. 9½ in.
*Track:* Front 4 ft. 3½ in. Rear 4 ft. 2⅞ in.
*Type of Wheels:* 4J × 12 in. Dunlop steel disc 4-stud bolt-on on early 12G cars,
    4C × 12 in. on later cars.
*Tyres:* Front 145 mm. × 12 in. Rear 145 mm. × 12 in.
*Braking System:* Lockheed hydraulic 8.39 in. front disc and 8 in. rear drums with
    wedge operated shoes and mechanical handbrake.

*As Old as the Industry*

*Another view of the Siam-di-Tella pickup.*

*Last car to carry the Riley badge—the 1968 1300 Saloon*

TRANSMISSION

*Clutch Type:* Borg & Beck single dry 7⅛ in. plate.
*Gearbox Type:* 4 speed synchromesh.
*Gear Selecting Mechanism:* Central floor mounted lever with remote extension from gearbox.
*Gear Ratios:* Early 12G : 1st—13.16, 2nd—8.3, 3rd—4.91, 4th—3.44, Reverse 13.16 :1
Late 12G: 1st—13.21, 2nd—7.92, 3rd—5.61, 4th—3.65, Reverse 13.21 :1
12H Type : 1st—12.85, 2nd—8.3, 3rd—5.22, 4th—3.65, Reverse—12.85 :1
Auto Tran : 1st—10.11, 2nd—6.94, 3rd—5.49, 4th—3.76, Reverse 10.11 :1
*Gearbox Oil Capacity:* Gearbox integral with transverse engine.
*Final Drive Type:* Gearbox connected to engine through intermediate gear from crankshaft. Transverse driveline to front wheels.
*Final Drive Ratio:* Early 12G: 3.44:1, Late 12G : 3.65:1, 12H : 3.65:1, Automatic: 3.76:1

ENGINE

*Engine Type:* B.M.C. 'A' Series.
*Cubic Capacity:* 1275 cc.
*Number of Cylinders:* 4
*Firing Order:* 1, 3, 4, 2
*Bore:* 70.61 mm.
*Stroke:* 81.28 mm.
*Cylinder Head:* Cast iron water-cooled bolt-on.
*Valve Gear:* Vertical overhead valves operated by single camshaft via tappets and pushrods.
*Tappet Clearances (Cold):* Inlet 0.012 in. Exhaust 0.012 in.
*Number of Main Bearings:* 3
*Sump Capacity:* 8½ pints.
*Type of Oil Pump:* Gear driven from camshaft.
*Normal Oil Pressure (Hot):* 30—50 p.s.i.
*Cooling System:* Pressurised, pump, thermostat & fan.
*Type of Ignition:* Coil and distributor.
*Method of Advance/Retard:* Automatic vacuum/centrifugal.
*Contact Breaker Gap:* 0.014—0.016 in.
*Plug Gap:* 0.028 in.
*Make and Type of Plug:* Champion N5 or N9Y.
*Number, Make and Type of Carburetters:* Twin SU Type HS2.
*Type of Inlet Manifold:* Cast alloy bolt-on.
*Type of Exhaust Manifold:* Cast iron bolt-on.
*Location of Fuel Tank:* Rear.
*Fuel Capacity:* 8 gallons.
*Method of Fuel Feed:* SU electric pump.

MODELS AVAILABLE

9/1968–11/1968 : 1300 Saloon : £712 : From C/No. R/A4S5/16175.
11/1968–10/1969: 1300 Saloon : £730 : Last C/No. R/A4S5/21629.
4 Speed Automatic Transmission available as optional extra : £75.
The prices quoted above do not include tax.

# CHAPTER THREE

# Post War Riley Colours

As Rileys became available again in 1945/6, black seemed to be the most common colour, in line with the austerity imposed by necessity after the second World War, though some time later more colours were added. In any case, all the finishes offered on the $1\frac{1}{2}$ and $2\frac{1}{2}$ Litre Saloon models were almost always with black, since that was normally the colour of the roof covering, although a few cars are known to have been produced with coloured fabric roofs to special order.

Soon maroon, green and ivory were added to the lonely Black, with matching upholstery of course, and by the end of 1946, two-tone colour schemes began to appear. One of particular note was the special finish applied to the late Earl Mountbatten of Burma's car—this, like all of his cars, was painted pale blue below the window line, including the top panels of the bonnet, and black above the window line with black wings. Many public personalities used Rileys after the war and the Company demonstrated its willingness to provide special finishes —at a price. And there is no doubt that the special Mountbatten finish inspired many more.

By the end of 1948, the Saloon models were offered in Black with red, green, brown or beige upholstery; in maroon with red upholstery; in green with green or beige upholstery; finally in ivory with red, green or brown upholstery. In addition to this, the $2\frac{1}{2}$ Litre Drophead Coupé was also available in Scarlet, Light Green or Ming Blue with beige upholstery. The $2\frac{1}{2}$ Litre Roadster was offered in Ivory with red upholstery, Black with red upholstery, or with beige upholstery and Scarlet, Light Green or Ming Blue paintwork. The upholstery colour of the open models determined the colour of the hood and all coloured cars were available with Black wings.

Not surprisingly, Riley's move to Abingdon brought with it a similarity in colour schemes to that other member of the Nuffield family with which the Company shared accommodation, MG. So, from July 1949, the Saloon and Coupé models were offered in Black with beige, maroon, green or brown upholstery; in Autumn Red with beige or maroon trim; in Almond Green with beige or green interior; or in Sun Bronze with maroon. The $2\frac{1}{2}$ Litre Roadster was now available in Black, with beige, red or green trim; in Clipper Blue or Almond Green with beige trim; in Red with beige or red trim; or in Ivory with red or green upholstery.

Metallic finishes appeared in September 1951, under the description of 'Metallichrome', and the Saloon models were offered in metallic Almond Green or Grey finishes. Almond Green cars had either beige or green upholstery and Grey cars came with only maroon trim. Beige or maroon interiors came with Autumn Red or Black paintwork and Black cars were also available with green or brown upholstery.

For the 1953 Season's cars, Woodland Green replaced Almond Green and Silver Streak Grey replaced what was previously listed as just Grey. The interior colour of the Silver Streak Grey cars was now red instead of maroon, but in all other respects the colour schemes were as for the previous Season.

By January 1954, the two models in the Riley catalogue were quite different from each other in styling, but not in colours. The RME 1½ Litre Saloon and the Pathfinder were both available in Black with maroon, green or biscuit upholstery; in Green with green or biscuit; in Maroon with maroon or biscuit; in Blue with grey interiors—and both were offered in Grey, though the RME was available with rust, maroon or green trim, whereas the Pathfinder interior choices were grey or maroon. The RME was also available in Ivory, originally with either rust or maroon trim, but by December 1954 this—and the interior colour of the Grey cars—had been limited to maroon only.

Only minor changes were introduced for the 1956 Season, in September 1955, and these included Connaught Green becoming the green for that Season and the interior colours for the Grey finish being changed to grey or biscuit.

A veritable splash of colours came in December 1956, when Duotone was the new fashion, and carpet colours were now a separate feature of the interior trim scheme. These new colours were:

| *Above the waist* | *Below the waist* | *Upholstery* | *Carpet* |
| --- | --- | --- | --- |
| Swiss Grey | Charcoal Grey | Grey or Maroon | Maroon |
| Rose Taupe | Kashmir Beige | Maroon or Biscuit | Maroon or Brown |
| Blue | Steel Grey-blue | Grey | Blue |
| Black | Black | Green, Biscuit, Maroon | Green, Brown, Maroon |
| Charcoal Grey | Charcoal Grey | Grey or Maroon | Maroon |
| Kashmir Beige | Kashmir Beige | Maroon or Biscuit | Maroon or Brown |
| Cedar Green | Cedar Green | Biscuit | Green |
| Maroon | Maroon | Maroon or Biscuit | Maroon or Brown |

From this point, it is much easier to deal with the colour schemes applicable to the various models, rather than on a year-by-year basis, because the choices of colours became so wide after the introduction of the One-Point-Five and Two-Point-Six models and there are relatively few models.

To begin with the One-Point-Five, it was offered in no less than thirteen colour choices on its introduction, which included:

| *Above the waist* | *Below the waist* | *Upholstery* | *Carpet* |
| --- | --- | --- | --- |
| Birch Grey | Black | Red & Pale Beige | Red |
|  |  | Green & Pale Beige | Green |
|  |  | Blue & Pale Beige | Grey |
| Kashmir Beige | Damask Red | Red & Pale Beige | Red |
| Birch Grey | Yukon Grey | Red & Pale Beige | Red |
|  |  | Green & Pale Beige | Green |
| Chartreuse Yellow | Black | Green & Pale Beige | Green |
| Leaf Green | Old English White | Green & Pale Beige | Green |
|  |  | Biscuit & Cream | Brown |
| Damask Red | Old English White | Red & Pale Beige | Red |
|  |  | Biscuit & Cream | Brown |
| Florentine Blue | Old English White | Blue & Pale Beige | Blue |
| Black | Black | Red & Pale Beige | Red |
|  |  | Green & Pale Beige | Green |
|  |  | Biscuit & Cream | Brown |
| Yukon Grey | Yukon Grey | Red & Pale Beige | Red |
|  |  | Green & Pale Beige | Green |
| Leaf Green | Leaf Green | Green & Pale Beige | Green |
|  |  | Biscuit & Cream | Brown |
| Florentine Blue | Florentine Blue | Blue & Pale Beige | Blue |
| Damask Red | Damask Red | Red & Pale Beige | Red |
|  |  | Biscuit & Cream | Brown |
| Birch Grey | Birch Grey | Red & Pale Beige | Red |
|  |  | Green & Pale Beige | Green |
|  |  | Blue & Pale Beige | Blue |

The second colour shown under the heading of upholstery was the colour used in the centre panels of the seating and was edged with the primary colour, which also was used on the side and rear panels. Clearly, this colour range was popular, because it continued without change until the 1961 model year. Even then, only one minor change was made and that was to replace Leaf Green with a new shade, Cumberland Green, in both single and duotone colour choices.

The Mark 3 One-Point-Five brought with it in the 1962 Season a rationalised and new range of colours—only three colour options offering more than one choice of upholstery colour. There were eleven paint choices now and only three duotones. The monotone paint and their respective upholstery colours were: Dove Grey or Black paintwork with Cardinal Red interior; Damask Red with Dove Grey; Arianca Beige with a choice of Golden Beige or Powder Blue trim; Old English White with a choice of Cardinal Red or Powder Blue; Island Green with a choice of Golden Beige or Chinese Green and finally Florentine Blue or Bermuda Blue paint with Powder Blue trim. The Duotones were: Florentine Blue and Bermuda Blue bodywork with powder blue; Island Green and Old English White with Chinese Green inside; finally Arianca Beige and Pale Ivory with Golden Beige. In all cases, the carpeting was matched in colour to the upholstery, except that Golden Beige trim was matched to Arianca Beige carpets. These colours remained the range until 1964, when one addition was made—that was Aquamarine monotone with Chinese Green upholstery.

Even in the 1965 model year, the basic colours available remained the same as in the previous three Seasons, but they were shuffled around a little. For example, Golden Beige upholstery was now deleted, as was Dove Grey. Cardinal Red was the only colour trim available now with Old English White, Damask Red and Arianca Beige/Pale Ivory exteriors. Chinese Green was the only trim available with Island Green bodywork and the duotone Island Green/Old English White was replaced by Aquamarine/Old English White. The monotone Arianca Beige was deleted from the range. By the end of that Season, of course, the model itself was deleted.

The Two-Point-Six, when it was introduced in 1957, was available in only one monotone finish—Black (shades of Henry Ford!)—and six duotone schemes. Upholstery was two-tone as well and where a single colour was named, such as maroon, the interior was finished in two tones of that colour, with the dark tone on the outer panels of the seats and the upper panel of the door trims and the lighter shade in the centre seat panels and lower door panels.

The original range of duotones offered on the Two-Point-Six consisted of:

| Above the waist | Below the waist | Upholstery | Carpet |
|---|---|---|---|
| Shannon Green | Leaf Green | Duotone Green | Green |
| | | Brown & Biscuit | Green |
| Basilica Blue | Teal Blue | Duotone Grey | Blue |
| Charcoal Grey | Frilford Grey | Duotone Grey | Blue |
| | | Duotone Maroon | Blue |
| Maroon | Kashmir Beige | Duotone Maroon | Maroon |
| | | Brown & Biscuit | Maroon |
| Black | Frilford Grey | Duotone Maroon | Blue |
| | | Duotone Grey | Maroon |
| Black | Chartreuse Yellow | Duotone Green | Green |
| | | Brown & Biscuit | Green |

Before the end of the first Season, the blue carpets options with Charcoal Grey/Frilford Grey and Black/Frilford Grey had been deleted and replaced with all maroon (perhaps someone realised that blue and maroon just don't go together).

The single tone Black was added to by early 1958 and so the monotone range now consisted of five colour choices, with a variety of upholsteries:

| Bodywork Colour | Upholstery Colours | Carpet Colour |
|---|---|---|
| Black | Duotone Maroon | Maroon |
| | Duotone Green | Green |
| | Brown & Biscuit | Maroon |
| Shannon Green | Duotone Green | Green |
| | Brown & Biscuit | Green |
| Basilica Blue | Duotone Grey | Blue |
| Yukon Grey | Duotone Grey | Maroon |
| | Duotone Maroon | Maroon |
| Maroon | Duotone Maroon | Maroon |
| | Brown & Biscuit | Maroon |

By April 1958, the duotone Black/Chartreuse Yellow was discontinued, but all the others remained available until the end of the 1958 Season, when, in October, three duotones were changed as part of a rationalisation of Nuffield paint colours. No changes were to the available trim colours, but Basilica Blue/Teal Blue was replaced by Basilica Blue/Florentine Blue; Charcoal Grey/Frilford Grey was replaced by Yukon Grey/Birch Grey and Black/Frilford Grey was replaced by Black/Birch Grey. All the rest of the colour schemes continued until the Two-Point-Six model was deleted from the range in favour of the new Farina-styled 4/Sixty Eight.

The 4/Sixty Eight was originally offered, in April 1959, with six colour choices:

| Above the waist | Below the waist | Upholstery | Carpet |
|---|---|---|---|
| Leaf Green | Leaf Green | Green | Green |
| Birch Grey | Birch Grey | Crimson or Blue | Crimson or Grey |
| Damask Red | Damask Red | Crimson | Crimson |
| Yukon Grey | Birch Grey | Crimson | Crimson |
| Damask Red | Old English White | Crimson | Crimson |
| Connaught Green | Leaf Green | Green | Green |

No Black was offered initially, but this was to change as the 1960 Season approached and the colour choice was doubled in scope, with a further six colours being added to the range:

| Above the waist | Below the waist | Upholstery | Carpet |
|---|---|---|---|
| Black | Black | Crimson, Green or Blue | Crimson, Green or Grey |
| Old English White | Old English White | Crimson | Crimson |
| Black | Birch Grey | Crimson | Crimson |
| Leaf Green | Old English White | Green | Green |
| Florentine Blue | Florentine Blue | Blue | Grey |
| Florentine Blue | Old English White | Blue | Grey |

For the 1961 Season, the last for the 4/Sixty Eight, the colour range was completely revised and there were eleven colour options for this model, consisting of:

| Above the waist | Below the waist | Upholstery | Carpet |
|---|---|---|---|
| Black | Black | Beige or Maroon | Green or Mushroom |
| Maroon | Maroon | Beige | Mushroom |
| Whitehall Beige | Whitehall Beige | Maroon | Mushroom |
| Old English White | Old English White | Blue | Blue |
| Porcelain Green | Porcelain Green | Beige | Green |
| Clipper Blue | Clipper Blue | Beige | Blue |
| Smoke Grey | Smoke Grey | Blue | Blue |
| Maroon | Whitehall Beige | Maroon | Mushroom |

| *Above the waist* | *Below the waist* | *Upholstery* | *Carpet* |
|---|---|---|---|
| Clipper Blue | Smoke Grey | Beige | Blue |
| Smoke Grey | Old English White | Blue | Blue |
| Black | Old English White | Maroon | Mushroom |

It will be noted that there were no colour variations available for upholstery in the 1961 Season—it was considered that there were sufficient choices with the exterior colour range and there was an end to it. But views clearly softened with the introduction of the 4/Seventy Two, which heralded the 1962 Season, since options of upholstery were then made available to special order and these are shown below in brackets behind the basic colour. Paint finishes were re-vamped too, so the new colour range looked like this:

| *Above the waist* | *Below the waist* | *Upholstery, with carpet to blend* |
|---|---|---|
| Dove Grey | Dove Grey | Crimson (Green or Reef Blue) |
| Arianca Beige | Arianca Beige | Crimson (Mushroom) |
| Maroon | Maroon | Mushroom (Crimson) |
| Black | Black | Crimson (Reef Blue) |
| Iris Blue | Iris Blue | Reef Blue |
| Almond Green | Almond Green | Green |
| Sandy Beige | Arianca Beige | Crimson (Mushroom) |
| Old English White | Dove Grey | Crimson (Green or Reef Blue) |
| Porcelain Green | Almond Green | Green |
| Old English White | Iris Blue | Reef Blue |

Ten colour choices in all, which remained stable through to the 1965 Season, when a couple of minor changes were made, otherwise leaving the range substantially the same until 1967. The 1965 Season saw the end of special order interior colours and the two changes which were made were to upholstery colours for two of the duotone paint finishes. Old English White/Dove Grey now came with Reef Blue trim and Sandy Beige/Arianca Beige exterior featured Mushroom as the standard interior.

The 1967 model year saw a few new colours in and a few old ones out, leaving the range like this:

| *Above the waist* | *Below the waist* | *Upholstery, with carpet to blend* |
|---|---|---|
| Black | Black | Cardinal Red |
| Cumulus grey | Cumulus Grey | Cardinal Red |
| Arianca Beige | Arianca Beige | Cardinal Red |
| Almond Green | Almond Green | Green |
| Maroon | Maroon | Mushroom |
| Arianca Beige | Sandy Beige | Mushroom |
| Cumulus Grey | Old English White | Reef Blue |
| Almond Green | Porcelain Green | Green |
| Trafalgar Blue | Smoke Grey | Reef Blue |

Yet a few more old colours out and a few new ones in for 1968 resulted in the range being still ten colour choices:

| *Above the waist* | *Below the waist* | *Upholstery, with carpet to blend* |
|---|---|---|
| Black | Black | Cardinal Red |
| Dominican Blue | Dominican Blue | Reef Blue |
| Faun Brown | Faun Brown | Cardinal Red |
| Almond Green | Almond Green | Green |
| Paladin Red | Paladin Red | Mushroom |
| Snowbery Whiter | Snowberry White | Black |
| Faun Brown | Sandy Beige | Mushroom |

| Above the waist | Below the waist | Upholstery, with carpet to blend |
|---|---|---|
| Dominican Blue | Snowberry White | Reef Blue |
| Almond Green | Porcelain Green | Green |
| Trafalgar Blue | Smoke Grey | Reef Blue |

Finally, the 1969 Season brought with it an air of austerity—the cold wind of demise was beginning to blow. There were now to be only eight monotones available around four interior colour schemes. These were Black or Damask Red with Icon Red interior; Cumulus Grey or Blue Royale with Galleon Blue inside; Snowberry White, Connaught Green or Persian Blue all with Black trim; then Albatross Beige with Mushroom upholstery. That was the 4/72.

When the Elf was introduced in 1961, as an offshoot of the tremendously successful B.M.C. Mini, it was available in a range of six duotones with only Grey upholstery, regardless of the colour of paintwork chosen and no monotones. However, by mid-year this situation had changed and there were colour co-ordinated interiors to give the following choices:

| Roof Colour | Below the roof | Upholstery, with carpet to blend |
|---|---|---|
| Florentine Blue | Chartreuse Yellow | Powder Blue |
| Old English White | Cumberland Green | Porcelain Green |
| Whitehall Beige | Damask Red | Cardinal Red |
| Old English White | Florentine Blue | Powder Blue |
| Old English White | Birch Grey | Powder Blue, Porcelain Green or Cardinal Red |
| Birch Grey | Yukon Grey | Powder Blue, Cardinal Red or Dove Grey |

This remained the colour range for the Elf through to the end of the 1967 Season with only two changes; the first, in 1964, was the addition of Arianca Beige/Pale Ivory duotone with Cardinal Red upholstery. In 1965, the new colour became Pale Ivory/Arianca Beige, with the beige tone below the waist. Also in 1965, Old English White/Birch Grey and Birch Grey/Grey/Yukon Grey both lost the interior colour options and were available only with cardinal Red trim.

In 1968, when colours were changed across the range, a single monotone became available for the Elf, in company with six duotones:

| Roof colour | Below the roof | Upholstery, with carpet to blend |
|---|---|---|
| Snowberry White | Snowberry White | Black |
| Pale Ivory | Faun Brown | Cardinal Red |
| Snowberry White | Cumberland Green | Porcelain Green |
| Whitehall Beige | Damask Red | Cardinal Red |
| Snowberry White | Persian Blue | Powder Blue |
| Snowberry White | Birch Grey | Cardinal Red |
| Snowberry White | Yukon Grey | Cardinal Red |

In common with the 4/Seventy Two and the 1300 models, the Elf was only available in 1969 in monotone colours. Snowberry White and Mineral Blue paint came with Black trim; Connaught Green and Porcelain Green with Porcelain Green interior; Damask Red had Icon Red and Faun Brown came with Mushroom upholstery.

The Kestrel, which caused controversy among the purists because of the revival of the name (the Riley version of the Mini would almost certainly have been the Imp if Rootes had not been using it by then), was introduced to expand the sales potential of the Austin/Morris 1100 in 1965 and was available in six monotones and four duotones:

| Above the waist | Below the waist | Upholstery, with carpet to blend |
|---|---|---|
| Snowberry White | Snowberry White | Cherokee Red |
| Sandy Beige | Sandy Beige | Mushroom |
| Aquamaraine | Aquamarine | Horizon Blue |
| Agate Red | Agate Red | Cherokee Red |
| Cumberland Green | Cumberland Green | Green |
| Black | Black | Cherokee Red |
| Snowberry White | Sandy Beige | Mushroom |
| Snowberry White | Cumberland Green | Green |
| Sandy Beige | Arianca Beige | Mushroom |
| Aquamarine | Snowberry White | Horizon Blue |

1967 saw no change in the colour schemes for the Kestrel, but as it became the Mark 2 version in 1968, and with the change of paint colours throughout the BMC range of cars, the colours for the 1968 Season became:

| Above the waist | Below the waist | Upholstery, with carpet to blend |
|---|---|---|
| Snowberry White | Snowberry White | Black |
| Faun Brown | Faun Brown | Mushroom |
| Aquamarine | Aquamarine | Horizon Blue |
| Maroon B | Maroon B | Cherokee Red |
| Almond Green | Almond Green | Green |
| Black | Black | Cherokee Red |
| Snowberry White | Sandy Beige | Mushroom |
| Snowberry White | Almond Green | Green |
| Faun Brown | Sandy Beige | Mushroom |
| Snowberry White | Aquamarine | Horizon Blue |

Maroon B was a very strange name for a colour, but distinguished the shade of the slightly lighter Maroon used on the 1100/1300 models from that used on the other models. By 1969, the 1300, like its companions in the Riley stable, was available in only monotones, eight in all.

Snowberry White, Connaught Green and Bermuda Blue came with Black trim. Faun Brown and Sandy Beige had Mushroom inside: Trafalgar Blue and Cumulus Grey had Galleon Blue interiors and Damask Red came with Icon Red.

So, the post-war age of Riley was ended, having made up for what it lacked in choice of models with a very wide range of colours. Some were considered perhaps a little gaudy—such as the Black and Chartreuse Yellow of the Two-Point-Six model, with its duotone green interior (though the Brown and Biscuit option did soften it a little)—but at least it can fairly be said that the post-war Riley Company made an honest effort to keep pace with market trends. Now, before the end of the 1969 Season, Riley was the first casualty of the new BLMC's self-examination.

One final colour feature worthy of mention here is the colour of post-1938 Riley badges. The pre-war 12 h.p. and 16 h.p. cars were fitted with dark blue vitreous enamelled badges, but when the 2½ Litre was introduced in 1946, it came with the identifying feature of a pale blue badge—almost a Cambridge Blue. This colour identification of radiator badges continued to the Pathfinder—and even the Two-Point-Six had a light blue badge. All of the later cars were fitted with a dark blue, still vitreous enamelled, badge and the last cars—those of the 1969 season, had a small Leyland motif, the wheeled 'L', fitted just above the sill in front of the front doors.

CHAPTER FOUR

# Riley Ramblings

It is interesting to note now, at the beginning of the 1980s, how respect for the post-1938 Riley cars has grown—how they have become accepted (even respectable) as historic vehicles with the growth of interest in vintage and classic cars and the inevitably diminishing opportunity for people to own such cars. This is largely due to the reducing stock of available vehicles, coupled with the resultant increase in prices through a combination of market forces and higher restoration costs, plus the greater number of investors in vintage or classic car stock for investment rather than enthusiasm. Compare that with the rejection they suffered not too many years ago—partly from those who would accept nothing beyond 1938 as Rileys.

With the passage of time, we now look back and see just how many characteristics of the 'Riley' Riley were inherited by the 'RM' Riley. The car had a chassis (many cars were beginning to be built without), it had an ash body-frame skinned with aluminium alloy and steel together with steel mudwings. It had one feature which has been much-imitated and become very fashionable in more recent times—the fabric covered roof. The coachwork was undoubtedly Riley and bore a marked resemblance to the 1937/8 Close-Coupled Touring Saloons, though it was a little longer. Whatever else, it was certainly elegant—and it *was* a Riley.

It has been said that the front suspension was developed along the lines of the contemporary Citroen Light 12 and Light 15 models. Whether that was true or not, the "Torsionic" front suspension was very successful and, in the words of *The Autocar*: 'The way this car can be taken round curves is astonishing. Not many racing cars would do better'. The press generally thought very highly of this new heir to the Riley legend and considered it a worthy bearer of the name.

In hindsight, it seems that they were right. Its growth in popularity is well exemplified by the growth in membership of the Riley RM Club, which was founded in 1969 and had a strength of some 1500 by the end of 1980.

Riley did not produce a post-war successor to the tremendously successful line of pre-war two seaters which had culminated in the Sprite, so the admittedly small, but very enthusiastic, band of 2 seat sports car buyers were forced to look elsewhere.

One company which sought to fill that need was the Donald Healey Motor Company Limited of Warwick. Donald Healey had a very healthy respect for Rileys, having used them in competition in their heyday. He finished well up in the 1933 International Alpine Trial with a Brooklands Nine (KV5392—the same car which, two months earlier, had been driven in the Le Mans 24hrs and was to secure the Rudge-Whitworth Biennial Cup the next year for Riley). So Mr. Healey knew what went to make a good sports car. And he set about giving the sporting fraternity the benefit of his knowledge in the shape of the Healey Silverstone Sports Two Seater.

This new car was unashamedly an out-and-out sports car. It enjoyed power from the $2\frac{1}{2}$ Litre Riley engine (which qualifies it for mention in these pages, as a Riley spin-off). It was not a particularly elegant sports car, but it was sporting—spartan too—and it established quite a reputation for itself. However, tastes in sports cars were changing and it eventually proved a little too spartan for the modern age of the Fifties: the New Elizabethan Era demanded something a little more sophisticated—which meant a softer ride and more creature comforts such as wind-up windows in the doors. Hitherto, British sports cars still used detachable side-screens.

Today, there is a very healthy respect for the Healey Silverstone—named after the then recently-established new home of British Motor Racing. But it was not always so—it is not too many years ago that a sound example could be bought for around £75 and driven away. However, some things have a habit of going full circle, thankfully, and the Association of Healey Owners is testament to that, providing a focal point for these fine cars now.

Riley's own Two/Three Seater Roadster did offer better creature comforts than the Healey, but was not really a sports car. It does not seem to have sold particularly well partly, probably, due to its rather long wheelbase—which did not endow it with the best of handling characteristics—and its slightly curious looking long, flat rear deck. Nonetheless, it was used with some success in competition, especially in rallies and driving tests. Furthermore, one Two/Three Seater was put very much to a test of reliability and durability, being entered by its owner, Geoff Beetson, for the Le Mans 24 hrs Race in 1950. It was driven by Beetson and Robert Lawrie to complete the 24 hours, in a creditable 17th place overall, at an average speed of 74.519 miles per hour. The distance covered was 1788.5 miles. Admittedly, the car was prepared by Riley Motors Limited and lightened extensively, as well as being fitted with an extra petrol tank to give it 30 gallons capacity but it was still quite an achievement—especially for a private entrant.

There was still a lot of life left in pre-war Rileys too, many proving the point by winning races, rallies and driving tests in competition with all kinds and sizes of other makes of cars—vintage and sometimes much more modern. Indeed, over the last thirty years or so, the reliability of Rileys in competition has renewed the legend and many new (to Vintage and Classic events, that is) cars—originals and specials—have come on to the scene to keep the Riley name among the catalogue of winners.

Quite a number of Riley $1\frac{1}{2}$ and $2\frac{1}{2}$ Litre RM cars were used in rallies in the post-war years with no mean success and, in the mid to late Fifties, could be seen 'mixing it' with the best of competitors such as contemporary Jaguars and Ford Zephyrs in saloon car racing—and they certainly did not disgrace themselves in the results tables. With the advent of the Pathfinder's 110 b.h.p. engine, many an early $2\frac{1}{2}$ Litre was given a new lease of life with a part-transplant to make it go a little quicker even than its already-respectable performance. Even the odd pre-war Big Four has enjoyed a little 'tweaking' to improve its acceleration.

The One-Point-Five appears to have been built at Longbridge and Abingdon and once it had become accepted as the model-of-the-day, it, too, was 'breathed upon' and made to go quite quickly for both rallying and saloon car racing—at a time when production saloons for racing still looked like production saloons. Apparently though, the One-Point-Five front suspension was capable of producing some quite exciting experiences for its occupants and a way to reduce the excitement level was found by fitting Morris Minor front torsion bars—which was one way of making sure that the car did not disgrace itself when faced with competition.

During the currency of the One-Point-Five's production, a small and quite attractive fibreglass coupe was launched on to the market, utilising mechanical components of the Riley—another Riley spin-off. That car was the Rochdale Olympic GT, which was produced in small numbers and now has a following which is provided for by the Rochdale Register.

By the mid-1960s, nothing exciting was happening to Rileys, except that there were a few Cooper-engined Elves being raced in the then-popular Mini-versus-Ford Anglia battles which took place in modified saloon car club events. The great pity was that BMC did not choose the Riley badge for the Mini-Cooper and return the name to some form of factory-sponsored motor sport. Somehow, it would have been rather nice to see Paddy Hopkirk win the Monte Carlo Rally in a Riley!

By the time the Kestrels had arrived, BMC had approved certain tuning extras for 'A' Series engine and the Downton-produced camshafts which were available were a tremendous advance in the attempt to make cars such as the last 1300 model quite Riley-like in the degree of excitement they were capable of giving. As it was, that late engine gave 70 b.h.p. in production form, but with the Downton camshaft performance was considerably improved without any appreciable loss of tractability.

So, as the axe fell, Rileys had moved away from the original Riley ideal, but had managed to continue making cars which remained a cut above the average. Whether it was still 'As Modern as the Hour' or even 'Magnificent Motoring' was a matter for individual opinion. That opinion, though, seemed strong enough still, for it persuaded as many people to buy cars with Riley badges on their fronts as bought such cars as Lotus. Indeed, those companies such as Lotus would no doubt have been delighted to achieve the production figures of the contemporary Riley.

In the light of much later events, who can say what was the right marketing decision in British Leyland's first major model re-organisation? The fact is that just 17 models were produced after the second World War under the Riley banner and, to the end, they were produced in sufficient numbers to justify a small manufacturing unit continuing production, but it was felt that BL's production overheads were so great that rationalisation was inevitable.

Those last seventeen models were:

| | |
|---|---|
| Twelve Saloon (Standard & Sprite Series engines) | : 1939–40. |
| Twelve Drophead (Standard & Sprite engines) | : 1939–40. |
| Sixteen Saloon | : 1939–40. |
| Sixteen Drophead | : 1939–40. |
| Sixteen Kestrel Saloon | : 1939–40. |
| 1½ Litre Saloon | : 1945–55. |
| 2½ Litre Saloon | : 1946–53. |
| 2½ Litre 4/5 Seat Drophead | : 1948–51. |
| 2½ Litre 2/3 Seat Roadster | : 1948–51. |
| Pathfinder 2½ Litre Saloon | : 1953–57. |
| Two-Point-Six Saloon | : 1957–59. |
| One-Point-Five Saloon | : 1957–65. |
| 4/Sixty Eight Saloon | : 1959–61. |
| 4/ Seventy Two Saloon | : 1961–69. |
| Elf Saloon | : 1961–69. |
| Kestrel Saloon | : 1965–68. |
| 1300 Saloon | : 1968–69. |

It should be noted that all of the prices quoted on the data sheets for the post-war Rileys are exclusive of purchase tax. This was a deliberate decision, taken so as to give a true comparison of ex-factory prices throughout—and it is interesting in that context to compare the ex-factory price of the first side-valve saloon produced after the Great War (in 1921)—£850—with that of the last family saloon—the 4/72 at £803.

Purchase tax however, did affect prices pretty drastically and its sometimes wild fluctuations certainly had an adverse effect on the stability of the British home car market. For example, in the period covered by this book, the rate of purchase tax varied no less than twelve times between 25% and 66.66%!

In 1940, purchase tax was 33.33% to support a war effort. In 1947, cars costing more than £1,000 ex-works went to a tax rate of 66.66% to support the peacetime recovery of Britain. In April 1950, it was unified at 33.33% again and in the following year, all rates were doubled to 66.66%. In April 1953, as the economy was stabilising, the rate was lowered again, this time to 50%: then in October 1955 it was unceremoniously jacked up again to 60%, with a magnanimous reduction to 50% following in April 1959. 5% was added in July 1961 and another generous reduction in April 1962 brought it back down, now to 45%. In November 1962 tax was reduced again, to 25%, and things really did remain stable for a few years then, until the umpteenth budget of 1966 put it up to 27.5%, followed (as seemed characteristic of the government of the day) by another increase in March 1968 to 33.33%. Finally, just to rub salt into the industry's wounds, the rate went up again in November 1968 to 36.66%, at which rate it remained until the demise of the Riley name.

Such instability in Britain's taxation policy was, regrettably, reflected in the performance of what was then the Nations' biggest industry—the motor industry. Riley suffered in 1969—we have witnessed many more sufferings since then.

# Riley Model Identification from 1939

Identification of the cars built after the Nuffield take-over of Riley in 1939 is not so complex as for the previous ranges, because in the immediate pre-war period, there were only four models, later five with the re-introduction of the 16 h.p. Kestrel.

The $1\frac{1}{2}$ litre cars were identified with the number prefix '29' and a letter 'D' denoted Drophead, 'S' denoted Saloon: in both cases, the letter followed the number as with earlier models. The only additional identifying feature related to the Sprite engine which again was signified by a prefix 'S' before everything. Thus, a standard drophead would be identified as '29D 8001' for example, whereas a Sprite Drophead (as it was known) would be 'S29D 8001'. $1\frac{1}{2}$ litre chassis numbers commenced for the 1939 Season with 8001.

The Sixteen also continued with a numbering system following the original Riley method, though now the number prefix was '49' and the letter prefix 'D', 'S' or 'K', denoting Drophead, Saloon or Kestrel. So a 1939 Kestrel might have been Chassis number '49K 1501', the Sixteens commencing with that number (1501) for the new Season.

When the manufacture of cars began again in 1945, the new $1\frac{1}{2}$ Litre was the herald of what was to come from Riley and it began production from Chassis number 35 (continuing the pattern of year identification as before) S (denoting Saloon) 10001 (being the first chassis in the Series)—35S10001. The old numbering system continued until 1952, when RME became the prefix to Chassis number 20505. The re-styled RME commenced production at Chassis number 21855 and ceased production in 1955 at Chassis number 23950.

Whilst 'S' denoted Saloon in the post-war numbering sequence, 'D' denoted Drophead Coupé, of which models were built on $1\frac{1}{2}$ and $2\frac{1}{2}$ Litre chassis, 'SS' denoted Two/Three Seat Roadster on the $2\frac{1}{2}$ Litre chassis and '2S' denoted the Two Seat Roadster.

The post-war $2\frac{1}{2}$ Litre models also followed the pre-war system, so the first new $2\frac{1}{2}$ Litre Saloon was 56 (year code) S (Saloon) 2001—56S2001—production commencing late in 1946. The Roadster went into production at Chassis number 2802 and the $2\frac{1}{2}$ Litre Drophead at Chassis number 5006. As with the $1\frac{1}{2}$ Litre, the chassis prefix changed for the $2\frac{1}{2}$ Litre in 1952, starting with Chassis number RMF/9911, production of this model ceasing at Chassis number 10960 in 1953.

The new system adopted in 1954 used a three-letter prefix, followed by two digits, then the Chassis number itself in four digits. The letters in the prefix denoted the model—'M' for the $2\frac{1}{2}$ Litre engined Pathfinder and 'U' for the Two-Point-Six. This was followed by a letter to denote whether the vehicle was sold as a Saloon 'A', or a Chassis 'K'. The last letter identified the paint colour—'A'=Black, 'B'=Grey, 'C'=Red, 'D'=Blue, 'E'=Green, 'F'=Beige, 'G'=Brown and 'H' was for the CKD (completely knocked down) condition in which cars to be assembled overseas were finished. The first digit of the prefix denoted the

drive position and market type of car. So that a figure '1' would indicate Right Hand Drive for Home Market sale, '2' would indicate Right Hand Drive for Export, '3' was for Left Hand Drive, '4' was specifically for the North American market and '5' was for CKD kits of either Left or Right Hand Drive types. The last digit in the code was to signify the type of paint finish, because it was now important to know what kind of material had been used if a car needed repair after an accident, since certain paint types are totally incompatible. Therefore '1' indicated Synthetic paint finish, '2' represented Synobel (a particular finish brandname), '3' told us that Cellulose finish had been applied, '4' indicated Metallic finish and '5' was for Primer finish (used on CKD kits).

From all this, we would conclude that a Blue Metallic Right-Hand-Drive Pathfinder Saloon built after 1954 would have a Chassis number which would read thus: MAD14/2500. The Chassis number of a Left-Hand-Drive Two-Point-Six in Grey Synthetic finish sold to the United States would therefore read like this: UAB41/1500.

The Pathfinder was the last of the old generation, passing with Chassis number 5652 in 1957. The new Two-Point-Six came along with Chassis number 501 in August 1957, disappearing in May 1959 with Chassis number 2500.

The One-Point-Five Saloon began production in 1957 with Chassis number HSR1/501, the Mark 1 version finishing production at Chassis number HSR1/18121 in May 1960. The Mark 2 followed in direct sequence of numbers at HSR1/18122 and ran on to HSR1/27897, ceasing production in October 1961. The Mark 3 had a different prefix, in that the digit was changed to indicate a new model. This new version of the One-Point-Five ran from Chassis number R/HS2/101 in October 1961, finishing with Chassis number R/HS2/12184 in 1965.

The next new model was the 4/68 Saloon, introduced in April 1959 with Chassis number R/HS1/101. It was discontinued in October 1961 at Chassis number R/HS1/11084, with the introduction of the 4/72 model. The 4/72 started production with Chassis number R/HS3/11101 in September 1961 and continued until October 1969, ending with number R/HS3/25291.

With the success of the Mini, BMC decided that it would be good marketing strategy to offer a couple of up-market versions of that car, the Riley Elf (they could not now use Imp, because it was now in use by another car manufacturer, having been adopted without protest) was the more expensive version. The Elf Mark 1 was introduced in October 1961 at Chassis number R/A2S1/156851, the number sequence running in with other versions of the Mini cars (Austin, Morris and Wolseley). The Mark 1 ceased production with Chassis number R/A2S1/310706 in November 1962. In January 1963, the Elf Mark 2 arrived with the number R/A2S2/369601 and continued in production until September 1966. The Mark 3, introduced in October 1966, started production with Chassis number R/A2S3/930221 and was discontinued in October 1969 at Chassis number R/A2S3/1337993. It is estimated that some 30,912 Elf models were built in total over the eight years of production.

The final stage in the development of Riley models was the introduction of a Riley version of the Austin/Morris 1100 series of cars. Many unkind things have been said about BMC policy at that time, accusing them of 'introducing badge-engineering' and 'pioneering decline'. If the second comment was meant as a consequence of the first—and in most cases it was— then that accusation cannot fairly be levelled at the British Motor Corporation, as it then still was. We must look further back in history for the 'pioneer of badge-engineering' in Britain— to 1931 in fact—when Rolls-Royce set the 'new standard for motorists of sporting taste', by introducing the Bentley 3½ Litre: a Rolls-Royce by any other name. It is probably true to say, in fact, that the differences between the BMC 'badge-engineered' cars were greater than

those between Rolls-Royce and Bentley models. But, it is all academic now anyway; the cars have been built and history has been made for good or ill.

The Riley version of the 1100 was introduced as the Kestrel in September 1965 and continued in production until October 1967, beginning with Chassis number R/AS1/101 and ending with Chassis number R/AS1/12223. The 1275 cc. engine was available as an optional extra between June 1967 and October 1967, the Kestrel 1300 being introduced at the same time as the Mark 2 1100, now as a definitive model. The Mark 2 1100 was discontinued at Chassis number 13421 and the Kestrel 1300 ran from number R/AS4/12224 ending with R/AS4/16714.

The last new model to carry the Riley badge was the 1300 Saloon, being introduced in September 1968 at Chassis number R/A4S5/16715 and ending, with the Marque itself, at Chassis Number R/A4S5/21629. One of the proudest names in the history of motoring was gone.

# Road Tests—1939–69

In the thirty years after the takeover of the original Riley Company, a great deal happened to the world of motoring. It is against this background of turbulence that the reader is asked to consider the merits of the cars built under the Riley name in that period.

The first thing which happened was a general election in Britain in 1945, bringing to power a new government which set itself the task of changing the face of British Industry in such a way that it would never again be the same. It certainly achieved that, but perhaps not really in the way it intended. The first problem the recovering motor industry had to face was the actual re-building of many of its factories—especially in Coventry, which was so badly savaged by wartime bombing. Its next task was to re-settle and renew the industry's workforce —and if that was not enough, it had to come to terms with a nationalised steel industry which was poorly equipped to meet its needs; indeed it never did.

The most important task for all British industry was to export all it could and perhaps here is a key to the reason that the motor industry did not re-invest as perhaps it should have done. For one thing, it was simply too busy trying to keep pace with production demand and for another, it didn't have the capital. So it staggered from crisis to crisis, with government doing its worst by crippling taxation of the home market and heavy taxation of industry when, instead of pouring aid overseas, it might well have been giving tax concessions to recovering industry. Rather than do that, the record shows that industry was treated as a naughty capitalist instead of the whole key to the nation's survival in a bitterly competitive post-war world market place.

One has to realise that, in this environment, the good old days of hand crafted cars simply had to go—even Rolls Royce realised that, with volume-produced chassis and body components taking over from the individually-built cars of past years. Therefore, the RM Riley was to be the last Riley with real craftsmanship built into it. Even so, Riley badged cars were a cut above the average—and the press was not unkind. . . . . . . .

# The
# New 12 h.p. Riley
### SALOON

**DKV 433**

## An Attractive Car in which Lively Performance is Coupled with Good Accommodation and Appearance

A MORE than passing acquaintance with the 1½-litre Riley of a year ago, made a road test of the new 12 h.p. saloon of considerable interest. The general impression gained is that, judged by contemporary standards, this model is one of the finest cars to emanate from the Riley factory. It possesses all the desirable attributes of its popular forbear, plus many more which give it a far wider appeal.

The characteristic four-cylinder Riley engine with inclined o.h.v. has a high power output throughout the speed range and produces it with commendable smoothness. The new system of engine mounting at the pivotal axis of the unit is undoubtedly largely responsible for this feature, and although capable of a high rate of r.p.m., it is possible also to crawl along in top gear (4.88 to 1) without any noticeable engine flutter.

On the other hand, at speeds in the region of 70 m.p.h., there is a marked absence of fuss, and a main-road cruising speed of 55-60 m.p.h. can be maintained for long periods with no sign of tiredness on the part of the engine, driver or passengers.

Fuel economy is another good feature, 28 m.p.g. being obtained in the course of 250 miles, which included a considerable proportion of town running.

The four-speed gearbox has synchromesh on second, third and top, and a neat remote control brings the short gear lever within easy reach of the driver's hand. A somewhat definite movement was necessary on the car tested when making a gear change; this model, however, was not long out of its running-in period, and the slight stiffness would no doubt disappear with use.

Steering is of the Bishop cam type with a column adjustable for length and height. A thin-rimmed spring-spoked wheel provides a good grip and damps out any vibration which may be transmitted from the road wheels. Being somewhat high-geared —2¼ turns from lock to lock—the steering gives a pleasant feeling of accuracy and control, this being particularly noticeable when negotiating corners at speeds rather higher than normal. The castor action is also good. Yet, except when turning at low speeds on full lock, when a little effort is necessary to get "the last inch," the steering is in no wise heavy.

Suspension is a point to which, nowadays, the purchaser pays considerable attention, and, in this respect, what is

## "The Motor" Data Panel (Riley 12 h.p. Saloon)

Price, £310; 28.3 m.p.g.; tax, £9; weight (unladen), 24¼ cwt.; turning circle, 32 ft. (2¼ turns lock to lock).

OVERALL WIDTH · 5'·3"
FRONT SEAT WIDTH · 44"
REAR SEAT WIDTH · 43"
TRACK, FRONT · 4'·0", REAR · 4'·3½"
5'·3½"
SEAT ADJUSTMENT · 3½"
GROUND CLEARANCE · 7"
9'·0"
14'·3"

| ENGINE | | | CHASSIS | |
|---|---|---|---|---|
| No. of cyls. | .. | 4 | Frame | .. Down-swept box-section |
| Bore and stroke | .. | 69 x 100 mm. | Springs | .. Semi-elliptic |
| Capacity | .. | 1,496 c.c. | Brakes | .. Girling |
| Valves | .. | O.h.v. | Tyres | .. 5.75 x 16 |
| Rating | .. | 11.9 h.p. | Tank | .. 10 galls. (rear) |
| B.H.P. | .. | 52 at 4,750 r.p.m. | Glass | .. Triplex |

### PERFORMANCE

| | Top | 3rd |
|---|---|---|
| | m.p.h. secs. | secs. |
| 10-30 | 10.7 | 6.75 |
| 20-40 | 12.7 | 8.8 |
| 30-50 | 16.6 | 13 |
| 40-60 | 20.25 | — |
| | m.p.h. | |
| Max. | 73.61 | 57 |

| 0.30 m.p.h. | .. | 7 secs. |
| 0.50 m.p.h. | .. | 19.2 secs. |
| 0.60 m.p.h. | .. | 29.7 secs. |
| Standing ¼-mile | .. | 24.5 secs. |

### GEARS            HILLS

| Top | .. 4.88 to 1 | Max. grdnt. 1 in 11.0 |
| 3rd | .. 7.25 to 1 | Max. grdnt. 1 in 6.8 |
| 2nd | .. 11.2 to 1 | Max. grdnt. 1 in 4.4 |
| 1st | .. 19.4 to 1 | Max. grdnt. 1 in 2.6 |

Engine speed 3,000 r.p.m. at 50 m.p.h.
PULL, Tapley Q figure, 195

### BRAKES

| 30 m.p.h. to stop | | lb. on pedal |
|---|---|---|
| 120 | ft. | .. 31 |
| 60 | ft. | .. 60 |
| Best  32.5 ft. (93%) | | .. 132 |

**SEATING.**—Black figure portrays woman 5 ft. 5 ins. high, 26 ins. from hips. White figure shows 6-ft. man, 30 ins. from hips. Scale of drawing ⅟₁₆ actual size.
**HILL-CLIMBING.**—Maximum gradients for each gear are shown. Where 1 in 6.5 is recorded the car will climb Edge, South Harting, Kirkstone and Rest and Be Thankful Hills.
**BRAKES.**—Scale gives distance in feet from 30 m.p.h. as determined by a Ferodo-Tapley meter. Pressures needed to stop in shortest distance, in 60 ft. (normal short stop) and in 120 ft. or "slow up" are also shown. Average figures are 50 lb. for 60 ft., and about double for shortest: 100 lb. is the maximum pressure for average woman. If the 60-ft. and shortest-stop pressures are close together (e.g., 60 ft., 50 lb.—shortest, 72 lb.), the brake tends to fierceness.

April 4, 1939

ᵀʰᵉMotor      350      *April 4, 1939.*

## NEW 12 H.P. RILEY . . Contd.

**COMMODIOUS.** Practically the whole of the rear portion of the car is devoted to luggage carrying. The large boot lid lifts upward to obviate unnecessary lifting of heavy suitcases.

probably the greatest improvement in the whole car, has been made. Without in any way sacrificing the road holding for which Rileys have long been noted, a more resilient form of suspension has been devised which flattens out the bumps in a truly commendable manner. Even quite rough by-roads in the Cotswolds area were negotiated smoothly at speeds which, in earlier models, would have called forth protest from the rear-seat passengers.

Brakes are of the Girling two-leading-shoe pattern and, needless to say, are well up to their work, being light and smooth in operation and providing a thoroughly adequate " crash brake " efficiency should occasion arise. The handbrake, which operates on the rear wheels only, is of the pistol-grip variety, and is situated at the centre underneath the facia.

### Improved Body Styling

Apart from mechanical efficiency, considerable improvements have been made as regards passenger comfort and accommodation.

The new body style, which possesses really attractive lines, provides good acommodation both at front and rear, and, despite the low overall height of the car, adequate headroom. The individual front seats have a wide range of adjustment for legroom and are well upholstered with leather. We should

WINDOW CONTROL

**DRAUGHTPROOF.** The rear quarter windows slide to provide draughtless ventilation and are controlled by the small wing-nut shown.

have preferred the backs to have been a little more upright, but this cannot be construed as criticism, because, in our case, a rather more upright driving position than normal is generally adopted.

Rear-seat accommodation is well planned, deep elbow recesses and a centre-folding armrest permitting three

passengers to be accommodated if desired. A further point worthy of comment in this regard is the elimination of deep footwells.

The saloon is of the six-light variety and these, together with the deep windscreen and narrow pillars, give good all-round visibility. The rear quarter windows slide to provide draughtless ventilation and are regulated by a neat wing-nut device.

Wide doors give easy entrance and exit, and the fact that the rear doors are hung from the rear quarters and open backwards reduces the likelihood of getting dirt and wet from the rear wings on trousers and stockings.

The facia is of neat design and is equipped with two sets of grouped instruments. Underneath, and extending the full width of the scuttle, there is a deep shelf capable of accommodating maps and small parcels in addition to the usual impedimenta which usually accumulates in such places.

### Lots of Luggage Room.

A point of considerable moment to those whose motoring with a full complement of passengers includes other than day trips, is luggage accommodation, and in this regard the Riley scores highly. Practically the whole of the commodious tail is devoted to luggage carrying, and an experiment to see just how much could be packed in and the lid still shut, produced quite astonishing results. Another point— the lid shifts upwards, thus obviating the necessity for unnecessary lifting of heavy suitcases. Furthermore, a light is provided inside the boot, connected with the saloon interior light to ensure that it will not be inadvertently used.

Also accommodated in the tail is the spare wheel, which has its own compartment and is readily accessible.

Underneath all this is the 10-gallon petrol tank, which is very thoughtfully provided with a filler on each side.

The price of the Riley Twelve is £310, as tested. For those who require even higher performance, a similar model is available with a " Sprite " engine at an extra cost of £25.

SIX-LIGHT. The new saloon possesses well-balanced lines and plenty of window space ensures good all-round visibility.

B14

November 17th, 1939.

*The Autocar*

# "THE AUTOCAR" ROAD TESTS

## No. 1,311.—16 h.p. Riley Saloon

EVER since it was first produced, rather more than two years ago, the Riley Sixteen has been a star car, one of those exceptional British machines that feels "right" from all angles. It is unusual in being given four cylinders with an engine capacity of almost 2½ litres, making it one of the biggest fours in existence ; but then Riley's as a firm have always shone in the production of fours, and from its inception the planning of the car was seen to be highly satisfactory. It is an outstandingly smooth four-cylinder, and the power produced gives this Riley a performance of an exceptional order.

With reconstruction of the company some time ago, the Sixteen came in for various modifications, much of the nature already applied to the Twelve, but the general character of the car was fully retained. In place of the three-speed gear box with overdrive ratio originally fitted, a four-speed box with synchromesh on second, third and top is now used.

### High Performance with Economy

This car, tried under wartime conditions, presents an interesting illustration of the compromise that can be afforded between high performance and economy. A setting had been adopted for the S.U. carburettor which was capable of giving good m.p.g. results, yet the acceleration and maximum speed were not sacrificed to any unreasonable extent, as the figures indicate, including a timed maximum exceeding 81 m.p.h. Something, however, must be lost if better petrol consumption figures than were formerly obtained are to be secured, and, as applies generally to-day, the results cannot fairly be compared with those previously recorded for a similar car.

This fairly big-engined machine, capable of putting the miles behind it very rapidly indeed, can also show well over 30 m.p.g. A test which did not exceed 30 m.p.h. or involve

any appreciable use of the gears gave 35.8 m.p.g., and it was also discovered that 32 m.p.g. was obtained when using the car on a main road in a manner which justified the possession of so lively and powerful a machine, running up to 60-65 m.p.h., employing the gears to restore the speed rapidly after checks, and generally treating it as a high-performance machine, though coasting in neutral where opportunity of doing so usefully was afforded. The coasting allowed in the section concerned undoubtedly contributed materially to this particular highly creditable figure, but it is a car which by virtue of its weight and mechanical freeness coasts very readily, so that when neutral is engaged at, say, 60-65, a considerable distance can be covered before the speed falls below 50 m.p.h., and thus the general impression of continuity of progress is not irritatingly disturbed.

On the carburettor setting employed it was still possible to pull down to about 6 m.p.h. on top gear and to get away readily from this pace. Compared with its behaviour when set to the best possible advantage in normal times the engine was inclined to be hard at the lower end of the scale, and it took a little while to get it running really properly from cold.

### Striking Averages Obtained

If 75s and 80s are to be used to-day an appreciable consumption of petrol must be accepted, but even if this car is kept within the 70 mark for greater economy there is a very fine impression of its sweeping along irresistibly, and in the clearer driving conditions of the moment striking average speeds can be obtained. Its performance is of a calibre having very great value to-day to someone who is legitimately in possession of perhaps a greater quantity of petrol than the average, and who has to cover big distances, bearing in mind the obvious advantage if the greater part of a long journey can be completed in daylight.

It flies over the normal sort of main-road hill on top gear, and is a joy, too, up steeper gradients involving third or second, which are capital ratios, well spaced, quiet, and giving a fine surge of power without fuss or effort. Second was put in up the usual 1 in 6½ hill, taken after dark, but with a faster approach in daylight third would probably have served. On Pool petrol there was some pinking when accelerating and pulling fairly hard.

Apart from the performance available, the charm of this car lies in the evident solidity of it, the way in which it sits on the road and takes corners. The driver feels that he is in exactly the right position in relation to the big spring-spoked wheel, and that he has power over the car—

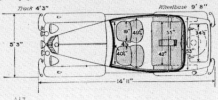

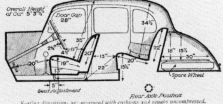

Seating dimensions are measured with cushions and squabs uncompressed.

A17

092  *The Autocar*  November 17th, 1939.

## "The Autocar" Road Tests

**DATA FOR THE DRIVER.** 17-11-39

### 16 H.P. RILEY SALOON.

PRICE, with four-door six-light saloon body, £385. Tax, £12.

RATING: 16 h.p., four cylinders, o.h.v., 80.5 × 120 mm., 2,443 c.c.

WEIGHT, without passengers, 29 cwt. 0 qr. 14 lb. LB. PER C.C.: 1.34.

TYRE SIZE: 6.25 × 16in. on bolt-on steel disc wheels.

LIGHTING SET: 12-volt. Automatic voltage control.

TANK CAPACITY: 10 gallons; approx. normal fuel consumption, 25-34 m.p.g.

TURNING CIRCLE: (R.): 38ft.; (L.): 41ft. GROUND CLEARANCE: 8in.

### ACCELERATION

| Overall gear ratios. | From steady m.p.h. of | | |
|---|---|---|---|
| | 10 to 30 | 20 to 40 | 30 to 50 |
| 4.25 to 1 | 13.3 sec. | 13.3 sec. | 14.6 sec. |
| 6.06 to 1 | 8.9 sec. | 8.9 sec. | 10.0 sec. |
| 10.04 to 1 | 5.9 sec. | 6.6 sec. | |
| 17.00 to 1 | — | — | |

From rest to 30 m.p.h. through gears ... ... 5.9 sec.
To 50 m.p.h. through gears 14.9 sec.
To 60 m.p.h. through gears 22.2 sec.

### SPEED

m.p.h.

Mean maximum timed speed over ¼ mile ... ... ...

Best timed speed over ¼ mile ... 81.08

Speeds attainable on indirect gears (normal and maximum):—

1st ... ... ... ... 20—25
2nd ... ... ... ... 34—42
3rd ... ... ... ... 55—66

WEATHER: Showers, cold; Wind fresh, N.W. Barometer 29.60 in.

Performance figures for acceleration are the means of several runs in opposite directions, with two up.

*(Latest model described in "The Autocar" of July 7th, 1939.)*

not that it is difficult or heavy to control, but in the sense of being able to direct precisely the position on the road of a machine which feels alive and which has the power to send the speed soaring. It is an absolutely safe-feeling car. The steering is quite high geared, has strong caster action, and gives the impression of direct connection with the front wheels, that is, it is not in any sense vague. For low-speed turning it is a little on the heavy side, in which connection particularly big-section tyres, of 6.25in., probably have an influence.

As regards general comfort, the half-elliptic suspension achieves a high level. Practically never is any considerable reaction from the road wheels noticeable. The general progress is smooth and untroubled, with at times a very slight front-end pitching tendency, which never builds up into any appreciable movement.

The gear change is excellent. A vertical remote-control lever is in a very good position, and the synchromesh engages smoothly for both leisurely and fairly quick changing. A rapid and most effective drop to third can readily be made at considerable road speed.

The "going" abilities are matched by the stopping abilities of the Girling brakes, and a sure, straight-line retarding effect is given with moderate pedal pressure. They are the kind of brakes that enable a driver to run up fast to a difficult situation in the knowledge that he can command the position, though, of course, fierce braking from speed is one way of wasting petrol. The hand-brake lever is of the pull-and-push type, set under the instrument board.

Really good, firm support is afforded by the front seats, and driving position is variable over a considerable range by means of a telescopically adjustable steering wheel, in addition to the fore-and-aft adjustment seat.

The instruments are clear, and they include an engine thermometer. A pleasing effect is given to the interior by the use of a polished wood instrument board and door cappings. Ventilating louvres are placed over the door windows. In the back seats plenty of leg room is afforded without foot wells being used, and there is a central folding arm rest.

An exceptionally large luggage compartment is provided, and the lid gives really good access to it, lifting up and being secured automatically in the raised position. The spare wheel and wheel tools are reached through the same lid, being placed under a shelf, and the Riley has the valuable fitting of Jackall hydraulic four-wheel jacks, for which the operating mechanism is under the bonnet.

There is a large unobstructed engine oil filler, the dipstick is convenient, and the sparking plugs are accessible, placed centrally in the V between the two valve rocker gear shafts, as is usual in Riley design.

**RILEY**

A broad and deep windscreen is noticeable and the pillars are not by any means obstructively wide. Near-side vision is good and the left-hand wing lamp can just be seen; the right-hand wing is well within view.

A18

OCTOBER 10, 1947    *Autocar*                                    899

No. 1338

1½-LITRE

RILEY

SALOON

# *The Autocar* ROAD TESTS

## DATA FOR THE DRIVER

### 1½-LITRE RILEY

**PRICE,** with four-door four-light saloon body, £675, plus £188 5s purchase tax. Total £863 5s.

**RATING** : 11.9 h.p., 4 cylinders, o.h.v., 69 × 100 mm, 1,496 c.c. TAX (1947), £15.

**BRAKE HORSE-POWER** : 55 at 4,500 r.p.m.   **COMPRESSION RATIO** : 6.75 to 1.

**WEIGHT,** without passengers, 24 cwt 1 qr.   LB. PER C.C. : 1.82.

**TYRE SIZE** : 5.75 × 16in on bolt-on steel disc wheels.

**LIGHTING SET** : 12-volt. Automatic voltage control.

**TANK CAPACITY** : 12½ gallons ; approx. fuel consumption range, 25-29 m.p.g.

**TURNING CIRCLE** : 30ft (L and R).   **MINIMUM GROUND CLEARANCE** : 7½in.

**MAIN DIMENSIONS** : Wheelbase, 9ft 4½in. Track, 4ft 4½in (front and rear).
Overall length, 14ft 11in ; width, 5ft 3½in ; height, 4ft 11in.

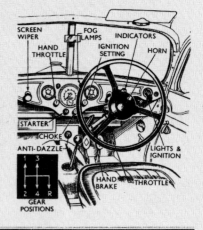

| ACCELERATION | | | | | Steering wheel movement from lock |
|---|---|---|---|---|---|

| Overall gear ratios | *From steady m.p.h. of* | | | | to lock : 2½ turns. |
|---|---|---|---|---|---|
| | 10 to 30 | 20 to 40 | 30 to 50 | | Speedometer correction by Electrical |
| 4.89 to 1 | 12.7 sec. | 13.3 sec. | 15.3 sec. | | Speedometer : 10 (car speedometer) |
| 7.23 to 1 | 8.6 sec. | 9.5 sec. | 12.0 sec. | | = 8 ;   20 = 18.5 ;   30 = 28.5 ; |
| 11.20 to 1 | 6.4 sec. | — | — | | 40 = 37.5 ;   50 = 47 ;   60 = 54.5. |
| 19.42 to 1 | — | — | — | | Speeds attainable on indirect   M.p.h. |

From rest through gears to:—
gears (by electrical speedo-   (normal
meter)   ..   ..   ..   and max.)

| | | | | |
|---|---|---|---|---|
| 30 m.p.h. | .. | .. | 7.8 sec. | 1st   ..   ..   ..   14–21 |
| 50 m.p.h. | .. | .. | 19.0 sec. | 2nd   ..   ..   ..   30–36 |
| 60 m.p.h. | .. | .. | 31.2 sec. | 3rd   ..   ..   ..   48–54 |

**WEATHER** : Dry, warm ; wind negligible.

Acceleration figures are the means of several runs in opposite directions.

*Current model described in " The Autocar " of February 22, 1946.*

---

IT is possible to take a national pride in the fact that so very good a car in the overall sense as the 1½-litre Riley is produced in this country. This, indeed, is a first-rate example of a type of car which can be said to be peculiar to the British motor industry and which is made better here than anywhere else in the world. The qualities that make it so desirable in an experienced British motorist's eyes are exactly those to appeal to owners in other countries, among them economy of running, comfort of the suspension, and a remarkable accuracy of control which, allied with other features such as a really rigid frame, gives the car an extremely high safety factor.

By no means least, the Riley is modern, with its torsion bar independent front suspension and an external appearance which takes the eye and yet is not gaudy. The frontal treatment in particular shows a concession towards present tendencies, in the building-in of the head lamps, yet the characteristics of a " real car " are retained.

The present occasion is not the first on which *The Autocar* has had road experience of the 1½-litre Riley, but it has afforded a more long-distance opportunity than hitherto of judging the car and of forming opinions which can come only from living with a car in everyday conditions for a time. A very high opinion indeed has been formed of this car, and not for a few features or for its spirited performance alone, but because of a combination of points of appeal in the design and general arrangement

and in its behaviour on the road. The result is to make one feel strongly that here is a car well designed and honestly and soundly built, which should give an owner excellent service, and which has such qualities as to lift motoring far above the plane of transport alone.

There is performance in plenty for most requirements as regards the top end of the speed range and decided life in the acceleration ; the figures coldly measured by stop-watch come as something of a favourable surprise when one remembers that an engine of only 1½ litres is pulling a saloon body of generous size for four people and not a feather-weight, cramped for space. Further, it possesses a suspension of exceptional merit in both the comfort afforded and the stability provided for cornering and holding the car four-square to the road at speed. It feels completely safe, and passengers, as well as the driver, have the impression of travelling in a train as regards the better features of railway travel. In addition it is a suspension remarkably effective in taking the sting out of really bad surfaces such as are found away from the big towns in overseas territories. Passengers with experience of many cars describe the rear seat riding as altogether exceptional for the absence of shock and for the fact that they are not thrown sideways during fast cornering, even though a central arm rest is not fitted.

From the first moment of starting the engine in the garage in the morning, throughout a day's run with all

900 *Autocar* OCTOBER 10, 1947

# *Autocar* ROAD TESTS
## —continued—

its variety of conditions—traffic, speed on the clear stretches, and climbing—this Riley conveys the suggestion as strongly as it is possible for it to be conveyed of robustness and efficiency. Also one senses quality not only in things that can be seen, but beneath the surface, too.

The Riley firm are second to none in length of experience of building a high-output 1½-litre four-cylinder engine, and a remarkably good unit they produce. This engine will rev freely and still remain smooth, and even at its limit of performance on top gear it still makes no fuss, and consequently no sense of strain is induced in the driver or passengers. On level ground, with no help from the wind, a speed of 74 m.p.h. was recorded on *The Autocar's* master speedometer; perhaps 3 or 4 m.p.h. beyond that creditable figure could be gained under more helpful conditions. The car quickly gets up into the 60s and holds the speed well, but such is the engine's behaviour that within the limit available, the road conditions and the driver's ideas of the moment are alone the factors governing the speed which shall be used.

## An All-round Appeal

It is not a function of this Road Test to make comparison with the 1½-litre's more powerful and longer-wheelbase companion, the 2½-litre, a Road Test of which *The Autocar* has already published. It may, however, be remarked by one who has sampled the two cars under similar conditions, with a lapse of time between the tests, that the 1½-litre comes as no disappointment for, as already indicated, it has enough sheer performance to make it interesting to drive and, in conjunction with its qualities of road holding, to give it 40 m.p.h. averaging capabilities without tiring the occupants or making the driver work hard. It is a capital all-rounder, by which is meant that besides being able to travel fast it is tractable and flexible, and in fact shows these qualities to a remarkable extent. It can be handled largely on top and third gears in traffic, yet be started smoothly from rest on second gear, and climb all but the more unusual kind of hill on third gear. Second gear sufficed to take it comfortably up a 1 in 6½ gradient on which baulking by other traffic occurred and a fast approach was prevented. An ignition setting control is provided, and with this moved towards the retarded position pinking on the present petrol is virtually eliminated without noticeable loss of performance.

The steering is quite high geared, but is not heavy, and gives the driver an exceptional accuracy of control which, coupled with the fact that the riding is about as stable and

Full use of the available width is made in the rear seat by the absence of elbow rests, and good leg room is provided by means of wells, which incorporate comfortably sloped foot rests. The wallet-type pockets are practical.

even-keel as that of a saloon car is ever likely to be, leaves him unconcerned at what other people on the road may do, for gaps can be shot with complete certainty. Little indication is given by the car's behaviour of what is the ideal speed at which a driver strange to it should take fast bends. It can be cornered with minimum movement of the wheel with a feeling of complete balance, and the safety margin in this as in other connections is wide. The Girling hydro-mechanical brakes do their full share in maintaining this margin, and throughout the test never at any time left the driver with the uneasy suggestion of being near the point of "running out of brake."

The gear change is among the excellent features, with synchromesh on second, third and top of an effectiveness which seldom lets the driver over-ride it and grate teeth. On the infrequent occasions when he does do this, he usually realizes that his clutch technique has been at fault. The lever itself is vertical and all its movements are silkily smooth yet positive. The hand-brake control, of pull-out type under the instrument board, is handy enough to reach and out of the way as regards forming an obstruction, but a pull-up lever between the front seats would be preferred. That remark, plus the fact that a perfect off-the-clutch position is not found for the left foot, and the personal point that it is regarded as a pity that the car is not fitted with a sliding roof, are, indeed, the only adverse comments to be offered, other than on points of detail which arise on every car, and on which opinion is to some extent a matter of individual inclinations. As regards a sliding roof, it is realized, of course, that overseas this fitting is apt to be more a disadvantage than an asset, whilst even in this country by no means every motorist is partial to it.

The driving position brings the driver close up to the spring-spoked wheel, which is telescopically adjustable, and he has extremely satisfactory vision through the deep V windscreen. An average-height driver can see enough of the near-side wing to be useful, and does not notice the central strip of the screen frame as an obstruction to vision. The section of the screen in front of the driver can be opened out. A very good rearward view is given by the mirror, though on a much reduced scale. The horn note is strong but not raucous. The off-side head lamp beam was set too close to the car, reducing the range more than was ideal for fast night driving, but in spite of the built-in principle the beam is readily adjustable.

A luggage boot of very considerable carrying capacity rounds off a body of excellent lines and practical features. The engine is neat and well finished, with its main auxiliaries accessible. It started and warmed up from cold with less use of the mixture control than is general; a hand throttle is fitted for the benefit of those who still like to warm up before moving off. Among the instruments is that now rare but valuable provision, an engine water thermometer. Twin petrol tank fillers make filling up easy from either side and the tank is of a generous size as regards range without replenishing.

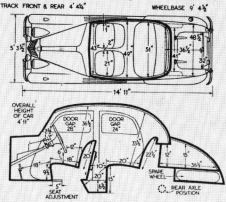

TRACK FRONT & REAR 4' 4½"   WHEELBASE 9' 4½"

5' 3½"   2"   48½   43   49   51   36½   41   32½   21"

14' 11"

OVERALL HEIGHT OF CAR 4' 11"

DOOR GAP 28"   DOOR GAP 24"

2½   6"   33½   22½   12"   15"   36½

18"   9½   18"   10"   20"   15"   SPARE WHEEL

5"   6½   REAR AXLE POSITION

SEAT ADJUSTMENT

Measurements are taken with the driving seat at the central position of fore and aft adjustment. These body diagrams are to scale.

922                      THE AUTOCAR,

No. 1361

2½-litre

RILEY SPORTS

THREE-SEATER

# The *Autocar* ROAD TESTS

## DATA FOR THE DRIVER

### 2½-LITRE RILEY SPORTS THREE-SEATER

**PRICE**, with open three-seater body, not quoted in Great Britain. Export only at present.

**RATING** : 16 h.p., four cylinders, overhead valves, 80.5 × 120 mm, 2443 c.c.

**BRAKE HORSE-POWER**: 100 at 4,500 r.p.m. **COMPRESSION RATIO**: 6.85 to 1.

**WEIGHT**, without passengers : 27 cwt 2 qr. LB per C.C. : 1.26.

**TYRE SIZE** : 6.00 × 16in on bolt-on steel disc wheels.

**LIGHTING SET** : 12-volt. Automatic voltage control.

**TANK CAPACITY** : 20 gallons : approximate fuel consumption range, 20-24 m.p.g.

**TURNING CIRCLE**: (R) 36ft; (L) 37ft. **MINIMUM GROUND CLEARANCE**: 7in.

**MAIN DIMENSIONS** : Wheelbase, 9ft 11in. Track, 4ft 4½in (front and rear).
     Overall length, 15ft 6in ; width, 5ft 6in ; height, 4ft 7in.

**ACCELERATION**

| Overall gear ratios | From steady m.p.h. of | | | |
|---|---|---|---|---|
| | 10 to 30 | 20 to 40 | 30 to 50 | |
| 4.11 to 1 | 10.2 sec | 10.2 sec | 10.8 sec | |
| 5.83 to 1 | 7.0 sec | 7.4 sec | 8.0 sec | |
| 8.86 to 1 | 5.0 sec | 5.3 sec | — | |
| 15.00 to 1 | — | — | — | |

| From rest through gears to :— | | | | sec. |
|---|---|---|---|---|
| 30 m.p.h. | .. | .. | .. | 5.9 |
| 50 m.p.h. | .. | .. | .. | 14.0 |
| 60 m.p.h. | .. | .. | .. | 19.0 |
| 70 m.p.h. | .. | .. | .. | 28.0 |
| 80 m.p.h. | .. | .. | .. | 38.3 |

Steering wheel movement from lock to lock : 3 turns.

Speedometer correction by Electric Speedometer :—

| Car Speedometer | Electric Speedometer | Car Speedometer | Electric Speedometer |
|---|---|---|---|
| 10 | = 10 | 60 | = 58 |
| 20 | = 20 | 70 | = 66.25 |
| 30 | = 29.75 | 80 | = 76 |
| 40 | = 39 | 90 | = 85.75 |
| 50 | = 48 | | |

| Speeds attainable on gears (by Electric Speedometer) | | | M.p.h. (normal and max.) |
|---|---|---|---|
| 1st | .. | .. | 21–26 |
| 2nd | .. | .. | 40–44 |
| 3rd | .. | .. | 60–65 |
| Top | .. | .. | 98 |

**WEATHER** : Dry, warm ; fresh wind.

Acceleration figures are the means of several runs in opposite directions.

LIGHTS & IGNITION    SCREEN WIPER    PANEL LIGHT    FOG LAMPS

INDICATORS            SCREEN WIPER

HAND THROTTLE   CHOKE

HAND BRAKE    STARTER

BONNET LOCK   GEAR LEVER   IGNITION SETTING

ANTI-DAZZLE         PUSH IN FOR R

*Current model described in " The Autocar "*
*of March 19, 1948.*

THIS open model on the 2½-litre Riley chassis represents a return to an open car in the modern style by a firm which through the years has usually offered open sports cars in addition to closed models. The current three-seater was designed with a view particularly to the American market and under present conditions it is unfortunately purely an export model, to the extent that no home market price is quoted for it. The price overseas varies, of course, on different markets, but it is understood that it is closely comparable with that of the 2½-litre saloon.

No attempt has been made to provide a car with a very much higher maximum speed than that of the fleet saloon, and the same gear ratios are used. Characteristically, the body is solidly built and there is thus no very great saving of weight over the saloon. With the latest engine, developing 100 brake horse power, the test results show that the acceleration performance is in some respects better than that of the saloon previously tested by *The Autocar*. An impression is certainly gained of the all-round performance being brisker than the saloon's.

It is intended purely as a two-three-seater of sporting character and additional seats are not provided in the tail of the body, which is devoted to a luggage locker of truly vast capacity. By the use for the first time on a Riley of a steering-column gear change the full benefit of a one-piece type of seat is gained as regards useful width avail-

able and ease of getting in and out by either door. This open model feels every bit as " solid " on the road as the closed car in spite of the absence of the stiffening effect of a steel roof, a fact which emphasizes the rigidity of the box-section frame which forms its foundation. The export nature of this model was stressed by the fact of the car undergoing test being fitted with left-hand drive.

So well-known is the behaviour of the 2½-litre Riley saloon, which has proved so successful in the post-war period, that it was no surprise to find that the natural cruising speed is in the region of 75 m.p.h., and this is a thoroughly comfortable rate on a top gear of 4.11 to 1. The genuine maximum available closely approaches 100 m.p.h., with a fine surge of acceleration available on second and third gears. But it can be treated a good deal as a top gear car, for the engine proves decidedly more flexible at low speed than earlier examples, and picks up strongly ; the pinking that occurs under such conditions on the petrol at present available in Great Britain would probably be absent on fuels of higher octane value obtainable elsewhere.

This car's averaging capabilities on a journey are altogether exceptional, and it puts its 45 miles or so into an hour with consummate ease even over the usual English roads that constantly provide handicaps in the shape of bends and speed limits. One can readily visualize the car

SEPTEMBER 24, 1948   923

This view shows the three-seater in the enclosed state. The side screens are efficient draught and rain excluders. When the hood is down the wide windscreen can be folded flat on the scuttle, a position which may appeal in hot climates and in which condition the car was tested for maximum speed.

flying across France, for example, at a 50-plus average, or again between cities in South Africa or Australia, where 500-mile hops are a commonplace, and at the same time taking in its stride the deteriorations of road surface by virtue of the excellent qualities of its torsion bar front suspension and long half-elliptic rear springs.

### Unhurried Speed

At 50 to 60 m.p.h. this car seems hardly to be moving, and on occasions when the driver may not be specially trying to hurry he is apt to receive a surprise on glancing at the speedometer to find that the needle is sitting between 70 and 75 when he had not been consciously thinking of speed and had supposed that he was doing around 65 m.p.h. Speeds up to about 85 m.p.h. are obtained really readily on stretches of road such as are found fairly frequently in England, and from the performance table it will be observed that the Riley reached a genuine 80 m.p.h. in a mean time substantially below two-thirds of a minute, from a standing start. For the ultimate speed to be seen it needs appreciable space in which to build up the revs, and the occasion offered as part of this test to time the car over the Belgian road where Lt. Col. Goldie Gardner recently broke class records. A total run of approximately six miles was available and the speedometer reached a reading of just over 100 m.p.h. during two electrically timed kilometre runs, the average of which gave 97.98 m.p.h. This was with the hood down and screen flat. The fuel used would be somewhat superior in octane value to un-alloyed Pool.

Above all is the factor of safety always associated with Rileys and seen in very high measure in this model. The car sits firm and square on the road, takes corners on an even keel even when high speeds are being held, and gives the driver every possible impression that he is closely in touch with its control through the steering and is able to

put it just where he wants on the road. The steering is firm and not in the least spongy and has good castor action. A degree of heaviness for low-speed turning can be excused in the light of this steering's admirable qualities for fast driving with the utmost confidence. Such is the feeling of complete safety afforded that even in darkness nearly 100 miles can be put into a little more than two hours over typical English roads.

The brakes, too, are in keeping; they are of the Girling hydro-mechanical type with two leading shoes in the front drums. Without being at all fierce at any time they deal faithfully with the high speeds of this car and do not require heavy pressure on the pedal. As regards both power available and the way in which the braking efficiency is maintained under continued hard use, the latest brakes are a decided improvement upon the braking experienced on the earlier 2½-litre Riley.

### Driving Position

The new gear change works well of its kind and has the important point that there is a positive stop against the unintentional engagement of reverse. A knob on the end of the lever has to be pushed in before reverse gear can be selected. In all respects, both in the driving compartment and under the bonnet, the left-hand drive fits in well, and as the steering wheel is placed as far as possible over to the left the full width of the wide front seat is made available. Naturally the car will be supplied with right-hand drive for countries with the same rule of the road as in Great Britain. The driver's foot positions are comfortable and he has an excellent view outwards over the handsomely long bonnet—which is lower than on the saloon—and also he has a proper view of both front wings. At speed there was some flapping from the hood against its frame, but a lined version in future production will overcome this point, and an improved arrangement of the

Left : Deep bumpers with massive overriders somewhat alter the front appearance of the three-seater in comparison with the saloon. At both front and rear the bumpers curve round to protect the sides of the wings. The bonnet line is lower than on the saloon. Right : The hood, in an attractive plastic material, is neat and goes entirely out of sight when down.

"THE AUTOCAR" ROAD TESTS . . . continued

driving mirror will give a better view behind with the hood up.

It is easy to raise and lower the hood, and with it down a beautifully quiet, swift form of travel is experienced, a sensation in motoring which, indeed, could hardly be bettered in fine weather. As has already been indicated, there is nothing at all flimsy about the open body and one has the feeling of sitting well down in it. Nor, curiously enough, does the driver experience any. disadvantage through not having a separate seat with a rounded back rest to support the shoulders, this no doubt being largely because the lateral stability of the car is such that there is extremely little tendency for the occupants to be thrown sideways during fast cornering. Good protection against draught and rain is given by the side screens, which attach to the doors by quick-action fastenings.

The concession which the current Rileys make to present-day fashion in the enclosing of the head lamps in faired tunnels, though they are not built into the wings, strikes one as being ample, and one has a feeling of pleasure and relief that the front-end appearance remains typically British and yet not old-fashioned by current standards. The bonnet remains of the type opening in two sections, but is now released by means of a remote-control knob at each side of the driving compartment.

### Over 400 Miles Without Refuelling

A petrol tank of 20-gallon capacity gives a cruising range of around 450 miles without refilling, according to the speeds that are used, and there are twin fillers concealed by the lid of the luggage compartment, which can be locked. To obtain the total fuel reading a switch on the instrument panel is pressed, the reading given by the gauge being, as it were, in two sections, of which twelve gallons are indicated in the usual way when the ignition is switched on, and the remaining quantity, which is consumed first, upon depression of the switch mentioned.

Starting from cold was immediate with very brief use of the choke for the twin carburettors, and the engine quickly attained working temperature. The subsequent reading of the thermometer fitted on the instrument board seldom exceeded 70 deg C.

Mention of the average speeds obtained under night conditions suggests sufficiently the kind of beam given by the head lamps ; both have double-filament bulbs, the beams being deflected downwards for anti-dazzle purposes—a

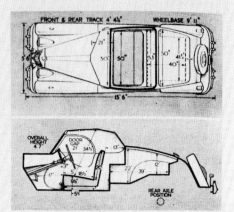

Measurements are taken with the driving seat at the central position of fore and aft adjustment. These body diagrams are to scale.

system which seems to worry some oncoming drivers in this country. Jacking is conveniently carried out at two points in front, where sockets are provided, and at a point on each side just ahead of the rear wings. The bumpers which this model carries have been designed particularly to cope with American conditions. The way in which they are wrapped round to protect the vulnerable wing corners low down is very practical, and these bumpers are noticeably more solid than is often the case.

As a whole this car gives the strongest possible impression, always associated with the Riley *marque*, of efficient design in the first instance, and honest workmanship and construction. With its high performance, its useful seating capacity and its quite exceptional luggage space, it should have an especial appeal to those overseas who want a car of character capable of covering big distances fast and tirelessly to the driver and passengers, more particularly, of course, in countries where the weather remains settled for long periods. It would have a considerable appeal, too, at home among connoisseurs if economic conditions permitted this model to be sold here.

Left : The tail is used entirely for luggage and fuel tank space. A truly enormous luggage-carrying capacity is provided, it will be observed. The twin fillers for the 20-gallon tank are inside the boot lid. A fishtail on the end of the exhaust pipe gives the engine a subtly " sports " note. Right : The bonnet opens in two sections, as on the Riley saloon models, and is released by means of a control at each side of the driving compartment.

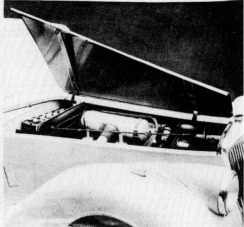

# The Motor Continental Road Test No. 8C/50—

**Make** : Riley            **Type** : 2½-litre Saloon

**Makers** : Riley Ltd., Abingdon-on-Thames, Berks.

## Dimensions and Seating

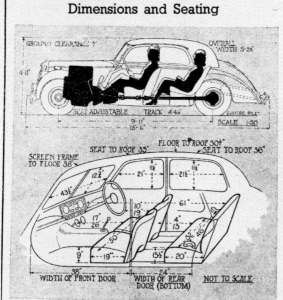

## In Brief

Price £958, plus purchase tax £266 17 2
   equals £1,224 17 2.

| | |
|---|---|
| Capacity .. .. .. | 2,443 c.c. |
| Unladen kerb weight .. | 29½ cwt. |
| Fuel consumption .. | 19.6 m.p.g. |
| Maximum speed .. | 90.1 m.p.h. |
| Maximum speed on 1 in 20 gradient .. .. | 75 m.p.h. |
| Maximum top gear gradient | 1 in 11.2 |

Acceleration,
| | |
|---|---|
| 10-30 m.p.h. in top. .. | 9.7 secs. |
| 0-50 m.p.h. through gears | 11.9 secs |

Gearing,
19.5 m.p.h. in top at 1,000 r.p.m.
62.1 m.p.h. at 2,500 ft. per min. piston
   speed.

## Specification

**Engine**
| | |
|---|---|
| Cylinders .. .. .. | 4 |
| Bore .. .. .. | 80.5 mm. |
| Stroke .. .. .. | 120 mm. |
| Cubic capacity .. .. | 2,443 c.c. |
| Piston area .. .. | 31.6 sq. ins. |
| Valves .. .. .. | O.H. (at 90°) |
| Compression ratio .. | 6.8 : 1 |
| Max. power .. .. | 100 b.h.p. |
| at .. .. | 4,500 r.p.m. |
| Piston speed at max. b.h.p. | 3,500 ft. per min. |
| Carburetter .. | Two S.U. (H4 type) |
| Ignition .. .. | 12-volt Lucas coil |
| Sparking plugs .. | Champion NA8 |
| Fuel pump .. .. | S.U. electric |
| Oil filter .. .. | Full-flow Tecalemit |

**Transmission**
| | |
|---|---|
| Clutch .. .. | Borg and Beck |
| Top gear (S.) .. .. | 4.11 |
| 3rd gear (S.) .. .. | 5.83 |
| 2nd gear (S.) .. .. | 8.86 |
| 1st gear .. .. | 15.0 |
| Propeller shaft .. | Enclosed |
| Final drive .. .. | Spiral bevel |

**Chassis**
| | |
|---|---|
| Brakes | Girling hydro-mech (2LS on front) |
| Brake drum diameter .. | 12 ins. |
| Friction lining area .. | 136.5 sq. ins. |

Suspension :
| | |
|---|---|
| Front .. | Independent (torsion bar) |
| Rear .. .. | Semi-elliptic |
| Shock absorbers .. .. | Girling |
| Tyres .. .. .. | 6.00 × 16 |

**Steering**
| | |
|---|---|
| Steering gear .. | Riley rack and pinion |
| Turning circle .. .. | 36 ft. |
| Turns of steering wheel, lock to lock .. | 2½ |

**Performance factors** (at laden weight as tested)
| | |
|---|---|
| Piston area, sq. ins. per ton .. | 19.15 |
| Brake lining area, sq. ins. per ton | 83 |
| Specific displacement, litres per ton-mile | 2,270 |

*Fully described in " The Motor," September 22, 1948.*

## Test Conditions

Dry, moderate winds ; Belgian Premium petrol.

## Test Data

### ACCELERATION TIMES on Two Upper Ratios

| | Top | 3rd |
|---|---|---|
| 10-30 m.p.h. .. .. .. | 9.7 secs. | 7.3 secs. |
| 20-40 m.p.h. .. .. .. | 10.6 secs. | 7.6 secs. |
| 30-50 m.p.h. .. .. .. | 11.85 secs. | 8.3 secs. |
| 40-60 m.p.h. .. .. .. | 13.45 secs. | 10.05 secs. |
| 50-70 m.p.h. .. .. .. | 15.95 secs. | |
| 60-80 m.p.h. .. .. .. | 21.75 secs. | — |

### ACCELERATION TIMES Through Gears

| | |
|---|---|
| 0-30 m.p.h. .. .. | 4.65 secs. |
| 0-40 m.p.h. .. .. | 7.55 secs. |
| 0-50 m.p.h. .. .. | 11.9 secs. |
| 0-60 m.p.h. .. .. | 16.85 secs. |
| 0-70 m.p.h. .. .. | 24.3 secs. |
| 0-80 m.p.h. .. .. | 36.75 secs. |
| Standing quarter-mile .. | 21.1 secs. |

### FUEL CONSUMPTION

| | |
|---|---|
| 31.5 m.p.g. at constant 30 m.p.h. |
| 26.25 m.p.g. at constant 40 m.p.h. |
| 24.5 m.p.g. at constant 50 m.p.h. |
| 21.5 m.p.g. at constant 60 m.p.h. |
| 18.75 m.p.g. at constant 70 m.p.h. |
| 15.5 m.p.g. at constant 80 m.p.h. |
| Overall consumption for 178 miles, 9.08 gallons = 19.6 m.p.g. |

### MAXIMUM SPEEDS
**Flying Quarter-mile**
| | |
|---|---|
| Mean of four opposite runs .. | 90.1 m.p.h. |
| Best time equals .. | 90.9 m.p.h. |

**Speed in Gears**
| | |
|---|---|
| Max. speed in 3rd gear .. | 73 m.p.h. |
| Max. speed in 2nd gear .. | 50 m.p.h. |
| Max. speed in 1st gear .. | 27 m.p.h. |

### WEIGHT
| | |
|---|---|
| Unladen kerb weight .. .. | 29½ cwt. |
| Front/rear weight distribution | 51/49 |
| Weight laden as tested .. | 33 cwt. |

### INSTRUMENTS
| | |
|---|---|
| Speedometer at 30 m.p.h. .. | Accurate |
| Speedometer at 60 m.p.h. .. | 11½% fast |
| Speedometer at 90 m.p.h. .. | 6 % fast |
| Distance recorder .. .. | 3 % fast |

### HILL CLIMBING (at steady speeds)
| | |
|---|---|
| Max. top-gear speed on 1 in 20 .. | 75 m.p.h. |
| Max. top-gear speed on 1 in 15 .. | 65 m.p.h. |
| Max. gradient on top gear .. | 1 in 11.2 (Tapley 200 lb./ton) |
| Max. gradient on 3rd gear .. | 1 in 8.4 (Tapley 265 lb./ton) |
| Max. gradient on 2nd gear .. | 1 in 5.7 (Tapley 395 lb./ton) |

### BRAKES at 30 m.p.h.
| | |
|---|---|
| 0.31 g. retardation (=97 ft. stopping distance) with 30 lb. pedal pressure. |
| 0.43 g. retardation (=70 ft. stopping distance) with 50 lb. pedal pressure. |
| 0.72 g. retardation (=42 ft. stopping distance) with 100 lb. pedal pressure. |
| 0.78 g. retardation (=38.5 ft. stopping distance) with 140 lb. pedal pressure. |

## Maintenance

**Fuel tank** : 12½ gallons. **Sump** : 14 pints, S.A.E. 30 (to 0°C.), S.A.E. 20 (to −18°C.), S.A.E. 10 (below −18°C.). **Gearbox** : 2 pints, S.A.E. 140 (to −12°C.), S.A.E. 80 (below −12°C.). **Rear axle** : 4 pints (as gearbox S.A.E.). **Steering gear** : Pack with grease. **Radiator** : 21 pints (1 drain tap), at base R.H.S. **Chassis lubrication** : By grease gun every 1,000 miles to front suspension (8 points), intermediate shaft (2 points), prop. shaft trunnion (1 point), water pump (1 point). Each 5,000 miles to wheel bearings. **Ignition timing** : 4° to 8° B.T.D.C., full advance. **Spark plug gap** : .025 in. to .030 in. **Contact-breaker gap** : .012 in. to .015 in. **Valve timing** : I.O. 17° B.T.D.C., I.C. 43° A.B.D.C. ; E.O. 45° B.B.D.C., E.C. 20° A.T.D.C. **Tappet clearances** (hot) : Inlet .003 in., exhaust .004 in. **Front-wheel toe-in** : Nil. **Camber angle** : 1°. **Castor angle** : 3°. **Swivel-pin inclination** : 11°. **Tyre pressures** : Front 24 lb., rear 24 lb. **Brake fluid** : Girling. **Lamp bulbs** : All single-pole. Head lamps, nearside double filament, 36/35 watts ; offside, 36 watts ; side, tail, roof and stop lamps, 6 watts ; ignition, panel and petrol-gauge lamps, 2 watts ; reversing lamp, 24 watts ; trafficators, 3 watts ; dash lamp, 2.4 watts ; fog lamp 48 watts ; pass lamp, 48 watts.      Ref. B/25/50

B4

July 5, 1950.                                         The Motor

# —The RILEY 2½-litre Saloon

### A high-performance car of marked character and unusual stability

feel that he had complete control of the vehicle but this confidence was also imparted to the passengers. The low centre of gravity and absence of roll contribute in part to this freedom from worry, but the steering gear itself, with rack and pinion mechanism almost entirely free from backlash and with very strong self-centring action, also plays its part. Even on the roughest roads there was only slight reaction on the steering wheel, but it must be conceded that a good deal of muscular effort is needed on the rim particularly at low speeds in the traffic, whilst parking the car can be very heavy work indeed. At over, say, 40 m.p.h., however, the steering appears to be markedly lighter and there is no doubt it is in the speed ranges of 40/80 m.p.h. that this

GRAND TOURIST.—A test extending across five European countries allowed the 2½-litre Riley to reveal its speed and stamina. It is seen above at Aix-les-Bains.

THE testing of high performance cars on Continental roads can be justified not only by the requirements of safety during time trials at upwards of 80 m.p.h., but also because the longer distances and higher average speeds possible abroad are of great assistance in bringing out the good and, let it be admitted, some of the bad points of any given type.

The four-cylinder 2½-litre Riley was the second British car to be the subject of a run of this kind, upon which report was made in "The Motor" of December 18, 1946. On that occasion a total distance of some 4,000 miles was covered and on the recent test of the current, basically unchanged model the distance was over 2,000 miles. These embraced almost every condition likely to be encountered by the car user in Europe or the U.S.A. For some days the car was driven in London, many miles were covered on special motor roads at high average speeds, mountainous country was experienced in Switzerland and Italy, and very fast main road motoring was indulged in not only on the straight sections of the French roads but also on the more twisting sections at the base of the French Alps and the narrow, poorly surfaced roads of Southern Germany. The car was driven in every condition from one-up to more than fully loaded with four persons and a great weight of luggage. The predominant conclusion from these trials is that the 2½-litre Riley is a car of exceptional character, having a number of unusually meritorious features coupled with a few points which may be legitimately the target of criticism. Overriding everything else is the feeling of astonishment that so much usable road performance can be offered for so relatively low a price. Not only is the maximum speed on the right side of 90 m.p.h., but the usable road speed may be reckoned at anything

between 70/80 m.p.h. Although the piston speed is admittedly high in these circumstances the engine is so stiff in construction that it runs smoothly, coolly and with every air of enjoyment. The performance did not vary a hair's breadth during the entire course of our test, and figures quoted in the data table were taken at the end of 2,000 miles of hard driving and with cross wind which gave no assistance to speed in one direction. The fact that the four times taken for a quarter-mile stretch showed a maximum variation of one per cent. is significant of the car's character as a whole, and in this connection it must be put on record that the steering of the car gives the driver a complete feeling of confidence in all circumstances.

### Widely Varying Roads

Road surfaces in Europe vary far more than they do in this country; to give some examples, there is the flat, smooth, concrete of the German Autobahn, the rough and sometimes highly cambered pavé of France, the relatively smooth, but highly polished, roads of Italy which can be exceedingly slippery in the wet, and the very potholed surfaces of some of the frontier roads where war damage has not yet been made good. The Riley was taken over all of these both in dry and wet conditions, and not only did the driver

car makes its greatest appeal. The suspension by torsion bar at the front and leaf springs at the rear is firm but sufficiently flexible to absorb the shocks of motoring at high speeds over rough roads without inconvenience to the driver and front-seat passenger, although conditions in the rear seat are definitely not so favourable and a marked motion of the radiator shell and front wing shows that whilst the fore part of the frame is adequately

UNOBSTRUCTED.—The deep locker accommodates a large quantity of luggage and is not obstructed by the separately mounted spare wheel. The dual filler caps are a great advantage.

The **Motor** *July 5, 1950.*

FOR THE DRIVER.
—An adjustable steering column, remote gear control, and facia panel carrying accurate and clearly calibrated instruments are points of appeal to the keen driver.

## Riley Road Test - - Contd.

stiff for English conditions it permits a degree of torsional flexibility under the more severe conditions of Continental travel.

This fact, coupled with the fairly high muscular effort called for in driving, brings to mind the fact that the Riley embodies many of the characteristics typical of the vintage type of car including very marked ability to cover many miles in the hour without effort. On the road south from Avallon to Challon an average of rather over a mile a minute was sustained for an hour and distances of between 50/54 miles in the hour could readily be attained on the Continent and approached under favourable conditions in this country. It is unfortunate that on the car tested the braking system developed a minor but baffling defect, and it is possible that the figures quoted in the data panel taken before many miles had been run are less satisfactory than the best of which the design is capable.

### Minor Modifications

Turning from the mechanical aspects of the car to those of the body, there have been few changes since the car was last road tested, but amongst them have been the abolition of the opening window for the driver, a new instrument panel which bears both tachometer and speedometer dials, and a unit supplying hot or cold air to the interior of the body and the back of the windscreen. All the hot air can, if necessary, be diverted to the screen slots, and although the installation would scarcely be adequate for overcoat-free motoring in a really cold climate it supplies a ready method of supplying fresh air to the interior with a useful degree of

warmth in ordinary mild weather motoring.

Although now well-known, the lines of the car continue to command admiration. Many competent judges think the 2½-litre Riley with its relatively long bonnet one of the best combinations of the modern trend with British tradition, but a penalty for the low roofline has to be paid in limited visibility. Although the Riley is one of the rare modern cars in which both sides of the front end are in plain view, the depth of the windows is circumscribed, and the rear seat occupants in particular see but little of the surrounding country. Similarly, the slope of the tail severely limits the volume of luggage which can be put under lock and key, but if the owner is willing to run with the lid raised but a few inches, and secured to the bumper by an elastic cord, the carrying capacity is practically doubled.

### Drivers' Details

The instruments can clearly be read both by night and by day, and there are warning lights which tell the driver when the heater fan motor is running and when the headlamps are in the high beam position. The latter indicator was a good deal too bright on the car tested, but it is believed that this matter has had attention on current production cars. Two foglights are supplied, operated by a separate switch, and in this connection it should be mentioned that there are now eight similar switches placed in a row below the instruments. Although neat, this arrangement can be confusing at times, and with an engine that is octane-sensitive one would enjoy a more refined advance and retard mechanism than a push-pull control on that side of the panel which is remote from the driving position with a right hand steering column. This control is, of course, supplementary to the automatic advance and retard, even so it can be used with advantage.

A wide parcels tray is placed beneath the instrument panel, and this is most useful for carrying guide books and similar items; smaller objects such as matchboxes and film containers, on the other hand, can sometimes get trapped behind the conduits leading air to the base of the windscreen.

There is a reasonably bright interior light on each side of the car, and further items for the convenience of the owner are pockets in all doors and ashtrays adjacent to each side window. From a practical standpoint one is glad to see that the sides of the bonnet are quickly detachable so that ordinary routine attention such as changing oil filters, adjusting valve gear, etc., is carried out in reasonable conditions, whilst both the battery and the tool kit come immediately into view by being placed on each side of the scuttle. For the greater part of the Continental journey the oil consumption of the car was virtually nil, and it was unnecessary to add water. The car is, on the other hand, somewhat sensitive to tyre pressures, low figures markedly increasing the effort needed for steering and promoting considerable squeal on the corners.

### Average Consumption

The fuel consumption may be considered normal in relation to the power of the engine, and the average speeds attained, but especially on a car of this kind a range of little over 200 miles on one filling is insufficient, and it should also be noted that for quick replenishment it is imperative to remove the caps on both fillers. These minor criticisms do not seriously detract from the merit of the Riley, and it is legitimate to take into account the extraordinarily trouble-free running which has been characteristic of the model since its introduction. Engines which have covered between 40/50,000 miles with nothing more than routine attention are common amongst Riley owners and this is all the more remarkable in that the top gear ratio is sufficiently low to provide top gear acceleration between 10/30 m.p.h. in under 10 seconds, whilst the exceptional briskness of the car when full use is made of the gear-box is well exemplified by the 0/50 acceleration time of just under 12 seconds.

For the long-distance, hard-driving motorist who wishes to travel fast with complete confidence and safety and to be free from expensive maintenance bills, the Riley 2½-litre is a car which can be very thoroughly recommended.

FOR THE PASSENGERS.—Comfortable bucket seats hold the driver and front passenger steady during fast driving, and the rear seats have ample footroom in deep floor wells.

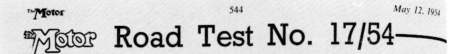

# The Motor Road Test No. 17/54

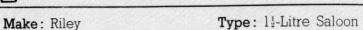

**Make:** Riley      **Type:** 1½-Litre Saloon

**Makers:** Riley Motors Ltd., Cowley, Oxford

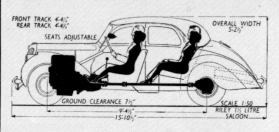

FRONT TRACK 4·4½"
REAR TRACK 4·4½"
OVERALL WIDTH 5·2½"
SEATS ADJUSTABLE
GROUND CLEARANCE 7½"
SCALE 1:50
RILEY 1½ LITRE SALOON
9·4½"
15·10½"

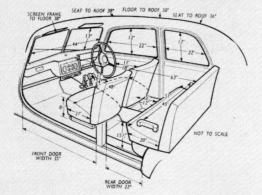

SCREEN FRAME TO FLOOR 38"
SEAT TO ROOF 38"
FLOOR TO ROOF 50"
SEAT TO ROOF 36"
FRONT DOOR WIDTH 33"
REAR DOOR WIDTH 32"
NOT TO SCALE

## Test Data

**CONDITIONS.** Weather: Fine, warm, little wind. Surface: Dry tar macadam. Fuel: Premium grade.

**INSTRUMENTS**

| | | |
|---|---|---|
| Speedometer at 30 m.p.h. | .. .. | 2" fast |
| Speedometer at 60 m.p.h. | .. .. | 6% fast |
| Distance recorder | .. .. | Accurate |

**MAXIMUM SPEEDS**

**Flying Quarter Mile**

| | |
|---|---|
| Mean of Four Opposite Runs | .. 74.7 m.p.h. |
| Best Time equals | .. .. 76.3 m.p.h. |

**Speed in Gears**

| | |
|---|---|
| Max. speed in 3rd gear | .. .. 53 m.p.h. |
| Max. speed in 2nd gear | .. .. 36 m.p.h. |

**FUEL CONSUMPTION**

39.5 m.p.g. at constant 30 m.p.h.
36.5 m.p.g. at constant 40 m.p.h.
33.0 m.p.g. at constant 50 m.p.h.
26.0 m.p.g. at constant 60 m.p.h.
Overall consumption for 1186.5 miles, 46.6 gallons, equals 25.4 m.p.g.
Fuel tank capacity 12½ gallons.

**ACCELERATION TIMES Through Gears**

| | | |
|---|---|---|
| 0-30 m.p.h. | .. .. .. | 7.2 sec. |
| 0-40 m.p.h. | .. .. | 11.7 sec. |
| 0-50 m.p.h. | .. .. | 18.6 sec. |
| 0-60 m.p.h. | .. .. | 31.8 sec. |
| 0-70 m.p.h. | .. .. | 59.5 sec. |
| Standing Quarter Mile | .. .. | 24.3 sec. |

**ACCELERATION TIMES on Two Upper Ratios**

| | Top | 3rd |
|---|---|---|
| 10-30 m.p.h. | 11.8 sec. | 8.1 sec. |
| 20-40 m.p.h. | 12.2 sec. | 9.3 sec. |
| 30-50 m.p.h. | 14.7 sec. | 12.0 sec. |
| 40-60 m.p.h. | 21.6 sec. | — |
| 50-70 m.p.h. | 40.9 sec. | — |

**WEIGHT**

| | | |
|---|---|---|
| Unladen kerb weight | .. .. | 26 cwt. |
| Front/rear weight distribution | .. | 49/51 |
| Weight laden as tested | .. | 29½ cwt. |

**HILL CLIMBING (At steady speeds)**

| | |
|---|---|
| Max. top gear speed on 1 in 20 .. .. .. .. | 55 m.p.h. |
| Max. top gear speed on 1 in 15 .. .. .. | 47 m.p.h. |
| Max. gradient on top gear .. .. | 1 in 11.1 (Tapley 200 lb./ton) |
| Max. gradient on 3rd gear .. .. | 1 in 7.6 (Tapley 290 lb./ton) |
| Max. gradient on 2nd gear .. .. | 1 in 5.5 (Tapley 400 lb./ton) |

**BRAKES at 30 m.p.h.**

0.94 g retardation (= 32 ft. stopping distance) with 140 lb. pedal pressure
0.82 g retardation (= 37 ft. stopping distance) with 100 lb. pedal pressure
0.63 g retardation (= 48 ft. stopping distance) with 75 lb. pedal pressure
0.42 g retardation (= 72 ft. stopping distance) with 50 lb. pedal pressure
0.26 g retardation (= 116 ft. stopping distance) with 25 lb. pedal pressure

SCALE A
17/54
POWER AVAILABLE
FUEL CONSUMPTION
POWER REQUIRED
APPROX. H.P. AT REAR WHEELS
FUEL CONSUMPTION AT STEADY SPEED-GALLONS PER 1,000 MILES
M.P.H.

Drag at 10 m.p.h. .. .. 40 lb.
Drag at 60 m.p.h. .. .. 170 lb.
**Specific fuel consumption** when cruising at 83% of maximum speed (i.e., 59.8 m.p.h.) on level road, based on power delivered to rear wheels .. .. .. 0.68 pints/b.h.p./hr

SCALE A
MAX. SPEED
17/54
M.P.H.
TOP GEAR
THROUGH GEARS
¼ MILE
TIME IN SECONDS

## Maintenance

**Sump:** 10 pints, S.A.E. 30. **Gearbox:** 2 pints, S.A.E. 90 (hypoid). **Rear Axle:** 2½ pints, S.A.E. 90 (hypoid). **Steering gear:** Grease. **Radiator:** 13 pints (2 drain taps). **Chassis Lubrication:** By grease gun every 1,000 miles to 13 points. **Ignition timing:** 8° B.T.D.C. (with hand-control at full advance). **Spark plug gap:** 0.025 in. **Contact breaker gap:** 0.014-0.016 in. **Valve timing:** Inlet opens 7° B.T.D.C. and closes 48° A.B.D.C. Exhaust opens 48° B.B.D.C. and closes 20° A.T.D.C. **Tappet clearances:** (Hot) Inlet 0.015 in. Exhaust 0.015 in. **Front wheel toe-in:** Nil. **Camber angle:** 1°. **Castor angle:** 3°. **Tyre pressures:** Front 22 lb. Rear 24 lb. **Brake fluid:** Girling. **Battery:** Lucas 12-volt, 51 amp./hr. **Lamp bulbs:** Head lamps, 42/36 watt (Lucas No. 354); side, tail, stop and roof lamps, 6 watt (Lucas No. 207); reversing lamp, 36 watt (Lucas No. 57); fog lamps, 48 watt (Lucas No. 162); ignition, panel and fuel gauge lamps, 2.2 watt (Lucas No. 987); trafficators, 3 watt (Lucas No. 256).

Ref. B/15/54.

c 16

May 12, 1954   THE MOTOR

# .The RILEY 1½-litre Saloon

A Well-built and
Excellently-finished
1½-litre Car with
Notably Good
Handling Qualities

## In Brief

| | | | |
|---|---|---|---|
| ice: £850 plus purchase tax £355 5s. 10d. equals £1,205 5s. 10d. | | | |
| apacity | ... | ... | 1,496 c.c. |
| nladen kerb weight | ... | 26 cwt. |
| el consumption... | ... | 25.4 m.p.g. |
| aximum speed | ... | 74.7 m.p.h. |
| aximum speed on 1 in 20 gradient | ... | 55 m.p.h. |
| aximum top gear gradient | ... | 1 in 11.1 |
| cceleration: | | |
| 10-30 m.p.h. in top | ... | 11.8 sec. |
| 0-50 m.p.h. through gears | 18.6 sec. |
| earing: 15.4 m.p.h. in top at 1,000 r.p.m.: 58.3 m.p.h. at 2,500 ft. per min. piston speed. | | | |

MODERNIZED by the removal of running boards and the fitting of new front wings and spatted rear wheels the Riley 1½-litre nevertheless retains its classic outline.

WHILST the latest 1½-litre Riley was recently in our hands for an extended road test, we were approached by a stranger who pointed to his own identical model standing a few yards away and informed us that it was his sixteenth Riley. This fact (which we were subsequently able to check from another source) seems singularly apposite as an introduction to this road test report, because it epitomizes the user-enthusiasm and affection that has for so long been inspired by the marque Riley.

There are 1½-litre cars that are livelier, or roomier, or more economical, but the Riley couples a happy mean in these respects with such a sterling blend of all that is in the best British traditions of good engineering, excellent finish, good looks and notably roadworthy behaviour that its appeal is not hard to understand.

The 1954 model represents the latest example of a type which was one of the first completely new post-war designs to be launched in this country. Subsequent experience in the hands of the public has suggested the need for no major changes, although various detail improvements have been incorporated from year to year. The

latest of such changes (incorporated for the London Motor Show last year) took the form of new wings and the elimination of running boards to provide a more modern appearance without disturbing the good lines of the car as a whole; these changes also enabled the twin fog lamps to be built in at the front and wheel spats to be introduced at the rear.

The full mechanical specification is reproduced in a data panel, but one or two characteristically Riley features should be mentioned here. The engine, for example, is notable for the use of hemispherical combustion chambers with inclined valves operating from a pair of highly placed camshafts, one on each side of the block, to give many of the advantages of twin overhead camshafts without any timing complications during top overhauls. This car was also one of the first British makes to employ independent front suspension embodying torsion bars and the now-widely-used wishbones of unequal length. Also notable in this age of quantity-produced pressed-steel bodies, is the retention of coachbuilt construction.

As one would expect, the performance of this latest Riley is closely on a par with that of the 1953 type tested (on Pool petrol) a little over a year ago, the maximum

speed of 74.7 m.p.h., in fact, differing by a mere 0.1 m.p.h. The latest model did, however, show distinct gains in constant-speed fuel consumption recordings, confirmed by an improvement of 5% in the overall figure, despite the fact that the latest test was taken over a high mileage which included not only the performance tests but also a considerable distance over hilly West Country roads.

In the main, it is true to describe the 1½-litre Riley performance as lively rather than startling, but the combination of its response to the accelerator and its essential roadworthiness makes it a car in which good averages can be put up over long distances with a pleasing absence of strain.

More will be said of handling qualities later. So far as the engine is concerned, the Riley unit has always been a willing performer and the current example proved no exception. A genuine 60 m.p.h. seems to suit the car particularly well and the engine is, in fact, quieter at this speed than at 50-55 m.p.h., at which the noise level —never high—is at its maximum. At low speeds there is a very reasonable degree of flexibility for a four-cylinder unit and it is notable that there is no trace whatever of pinking or running-on when premium fuel is used; it was never found necessary, in fact, to use the ignition control, but this now-rare feature should be a useful adjunct where, through choice or necessity, low-grade fuels are used.

Reference has already been made to the improvement in fuel consumption and, in the light of the points just mentioned, the engine obviously takes well to the present economical setting; for those who place more importance on performance than economy, however, alternative settings giving more emphasis on the top end of the range might prove an advantage as shown by the fact that, on the model tried, the acceleration tailed off noticeably above 65 m.p.h. in top gear, whilst 53 m.p.h. was maximum

DISTINCTIVE lines are allied with such practical features as twin fuel fillers, widely spaced bumper bars and a large rear window.

HIGH-GRADE leather is used for the seats and this combined with the real wood used for facia and fillets gives the interior an air of quality and refinement. Notable points are the centre and side arm-rests at the rear, the very adequate roof lights and a telescopic-ally adjustable steering column.

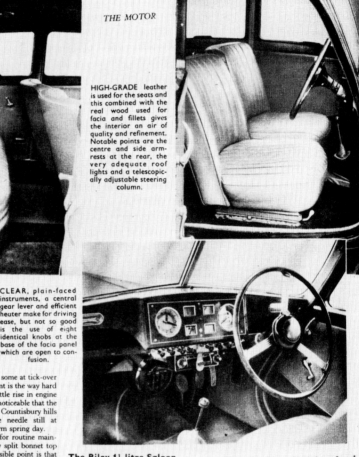

in third, with 40 m.p.h. as a natural changing-up speed. For those who use their cars in competitions, a twin-carburetter induction system is available.

Starting at all times proved easy, but the engine is not so sweet as some at tick-over speeds. A very good point is the way hard driving produced very little rise in engine temperature, and it was noticeable that the tops of both Porlock and Countisbury hills were reached with the needle still at 175 degrees F., on a warm spring day.

Access to the engine for routine maintenance via the centrally split bonnet top is quite good, and a sensible point is that both hinged portions can be opened together and retained in the open position by convenient catches.

CLEAR, plain-faced instruments, a central gear lever and efficient heater make for driving ease, but not so good is the use of eight identical knobs at the base of the facia panel which are open to confusion.

### Central Gear Lever

There is a very positive action about the clutch but it is, nevertheless, sufficiently smooth for easy starts to be made in second gear on the level. The pedal travel is comparatively long and, on the car tried, it was necessary to depress it fully to free the drive completely. Provided this was done, the gear change proved both easy and straightforward, and the neat central control lever is of the type which so many enthusiasts prefer. Competition-minded drivers will find snatch changes comparatively easy between first and second and between third and top; the through-the-gate movement between second and third makes this technique a little more difficult in this instance, but still quite possible. Upward changes are, however, pleasantly rapid in any case without resort to trick tactics. Gear noise is commendably low.

Owing to the transmission tunnel, there is no room for the driver's clutch foot at the side of the pedal, but this difficulty has been partially overcome by shaping the casing of the tunnel to form a rest which

The Riley 1½-litre Saloon - - - - - - - - -

takes the weight of the driver's foot off the pedal. There could, however, be more room for the pedal itself with advantage, the present spacing being barely adequate for those wearing wide-fitting shoes.

As will be seen from the accompanying data, the brakes provide good stopping power with moderate pedal pressures, and to this comment may be added the information that Porlock hill was deliberately descended in top gear in order to throw all the work of this two-mile descent on to the brakes; no signs of fade were apparent when the car was brought to a standstill on the still-steep gradient below the bottom corner.

The hand-brake is of the pistol-grip type to the right of the steering column and, whilst it is quite satisfactory, a pull-up lever between the seats and close to the gear lever would obviously offer greater convenience.

Suspension on the current models is rather softer than on the original 1½-litre type with a corresponding improvement in general riding comfort. There is very little roll on corners and damping is normally very satisfactory, but fast drivers might

prefer slightly more restraint for fast cornering on bad surfaces. The Riley remains, however, a car which inspires very notable confidence on give-and-take roads, the steering being accurate and the general cornering qualities above average. The effort required on the wheel is moderate rather than light and there is some road reaction through the wheel. A much-appreciated refinement is an extensible steering column.

From the driver's angle, the general layout of the controls and seating gives instant confidence, but the array of identically shaped knobs beneath the facia requires learning before one's hand automatically finds the right knob at the right moment—especially at night when the instrument lighting provides no help. The instruments themselves are comprehensive and clear-faced, with black markings on a gold background. At night they are illuminated by rheostat-controlled indirect lighting which, even when dimmed to the maximum, is rather bright for some tastes, the more so as the illumination of the central group is augmented by escaped light from the warning lamps for

the heater and the headlight main beam.

The confidence which the 1½-litre Riley inspires is undoubtedly augmented by the excellent view of both front wings obtained from the driving seat and a useful detail is the provision of transparent ruby "pips" on the tops of the side lamps. All-round visibility is also good, although the top of the screen causes some restriction of upward view for a very tall driver and the tapered upper portions of the screen pillars are also slightly obtrusive in such cases. In wet weather, larger areas of wiped screen would be welcome.

Rearward, the back window gives a good view and the anti-dazzle mirror is appreciated at night. Those who like to drive with an elbow on the door sill or to put their heads out of the window for reversing will note with approval that the windows disappear completely into the doors. A neat detail is the provision of a pair of flush-fitting vizors which give protection from a head-on sun.

An adequate heater and demister of the recirculating type is provided as standard in countries where it is considered necessary, but the provision of draughtless ventilation in cold weather calls for a rather careful adjustment of windows because hinged ventilating panels are not part of the normal equipment. In hot weather, side ventilators in the scuttle are a distinct aid to a cool interior. The Riley is, incidentally, commendably free from excessive wind noise.

The front bucket seats are well shaped to give support on corners and their high squabs provide a restful but fairly alert position. At the rear, the seat cushion might be shaped to give a little more sup-

TWIN fog lamps are built into the revised front of the latest 1½-litre car

the seats is in keeping with the whole. Both interior and exterior, in fact, have that distinct air of quality which is so satisfying to motorists who want more from a car than mere transport.

On the electrical side, the headlamps provide a very good range and are supplemented by a pair of built-in fog lamps, whilst a good interior detail is the provision of roof lamps which are really adequate for map reading. An unusual detail is a push-button dipper on the facia, which is quick, although not particularly comfortable, to use and gives no indication of whether the lamps have been left dipped or otherwise. The radio equipment, when provided, is notable for the use of two speakers.

Stowage space for luggage and oddments is well planned, with useful parcel shelves

- - - Contd.

A FLAT FLOOR and plenty of unobstructed room make the stowage of luggage an easy task in the Riley, the spare wheel being housed separately beneath and being extracted between the bumper bars.

port to the thighs with advantage, but, even so, the general standard of comfort is very good and is aided considerably by fixed arm rests on the doors as well as the usual central folding arm rest.

In general finish and appointments, the Riley reaches a high standard, and the provision of what the Americans have been known to call "genuine tree wood" for the main portion of the facia board and the window mouldings and door cappings, is a most pleasing feature, whilst the use of beautifully trimmed high-grade leather for

under the facia and behind the rear squab, map pockets in the front doors and a really excellent boot offering a clear floor for luggage, with tool receptacles in the wing recesses and a separate compartment for the spare wheel below.

With its many traditional British features, its good road manners and its excellent build and finish, this latest 1½-litre Riley will continue to appeal to discerning drivers whose tastes run to an individual car of very pleasing up-to-date, but not ultra-modern, line.

## Mechanical Specification

**Engine**

| | |
|---|---|
| Cylinders | 4 |
| Bore | 69 mm. |
| Stroke | 100 mm. |
| Cubic capacity | 1,496 c.c. |
| Piston area | 23.2 sq. in. |
| Valves | Pushrod o.h.v. (2 camshafts) |
| Compression ratio | 6.8/1 |
| Max. power | 55 b.h.p. |
| at | 4,500 r.p.m. |
| Piston speed at max. b.h.p. | 2,960 ft. per min. |
| Carburetter | S.U. horizontal |
| Ignition | Coil |
| Sparking plugs | Champion L10S |
| Fuel Pump | AC mechanical |
| Oil filter | Vokes external full-flow (throw-away element) |

**Transmission**

| | |
|---|---|
| Clutch | 8-in. Borg and Beck |
| Top gear (s/m) | 5.125 |
| 3rd gear (s/m) | 7.585 |
| 2nd gear (s/m) | 11.736 |
| 1st gear | 20.372 |
| Propeller shaft | Divided Hardy Spicer, open |
| Final drive | Hypoid bevel |
| Top gear m.p.h. at 1,000 r.p.m. | 15.4 |
| Top gear m.p.h. at 1,000 ft./min. piston speed | 23.3 |

**Chassis**

| | |
|---|---|
| Brakes | Girling hydraulic (2LS on front) |
| Brake drum diameter | 10 in. |
| Friction lining area | 131 sq. in. |
| Suspension: Front | Torsion bar |
| Rear | Semi-elliptic |
| Shock absorbers: Front and rear | Telescopic hydraulic |
| Tyres | 5.75-16 |

**Steering**

| | |
|---|---|
| Steering gear | Rack and pinion |
| Turning circle: Left | 30 ft. |
| Right | 30 ft. |
| Turns of steering wheel, lock to lock | 2¼ |

**Performance factors** (at laden weight as tested):

| | |
|---|---|
| Piston area, sq. in. per ton | 15.7 |
| Brake lining area, sq. in. per ton | 88.8 |
| Specific displacement, litres per ton mile | 2,000 |

Fully described in *The Motor*, October 14, 1953, and October 15, 1952.

## Coachwork and Equipment

| | |
|---|---|
| Bumper height with car unladen: | |
| Front (max.) 20 in., (min.) 12 in. | |
| Rear (max.) 23½ in., (min.) 11½ in. | |
| Starting handle | Yes |
| Battery mounting | On scuttle |
| Jack | Bevelift |
| Jacking points | Four (below bumper over-riders) |
| Standard tool kit: Pump, grease gun, 3 double-ended set spanners, 3 double-ended box spanners, tommy bar, brake bleeding tube, adjustable spanner, hammer, screwdriver, 2 tyre levers, pliers, type valve spanner, distributor screwdriver, and gauge. | |
| Exterior lights: Two headlamps (double dipping), two built-in fog lamps, two side lamps, two combined tail, number plate, reversing and stop lamps. | |
| Direction indicators | Semaphore type, self-cancelling |
| Windscreen wipers | Electric, two blades |
| Sun vizors | Two, flush fitting |
| Instruments: Speedometer (with total trip mileage), clock, ammeter, water thermometer, fuel gauge and pressure gauge. | |
| Warning lights | Ignition, headlamp main beam, heater fan |
| Locks: | |
| With ignition key | Driver's door and boot |
| With other keys | None |
| Glove lockers | None |
| Map pockets | In front doors |
| Parcel shelves | Below facia and behind rear squab |
| Ashtrays | Four (two in facia and two in rear doors) |
| Cigar lighters | None |
| Interior lights | Two (above rear doors) |
| Interior heater: Re-circulating type with screen demisting, fitted as standard in territories where required. | |
| Car radio | Optional extra |
| Extras available: Rev. counter, ventilating air scoops to front windows, badge bar, H.M.V. radio. | |
| Upholstery material | Leather |
| Floor covering | Carpet |
| Exterior colours standardized: Black, maroon, green, blue, grey and ivory. | |
| Alternative body styles | None |

THE AUTOCAR, 10 AUGUST 1956       183

*Autocar*
# ROAD TESTS

No. 1606

# RILEY PATHFINDER
### WITH OVERDRIVE

*A contemporary style of background suits the graceful curves of the Pathfinder. It has a dignified appearance, without being severe*

THE Riley Pathfinder, latest in a long line of favourites of the connoisseur, attracts those who know cars well and, having weighed the pros and cons, accept its shortcomings in the light of its advantages. It has a big, long-stroke, four-cylinder engine at a time when most cars of similar capacity have near-square sixes, but it is a well-developed, dependable and powerful unit. It is unusually well equipped in terms of instruments, controls and lighting, and the lavish nature of the furnishings and fittings is evident. It is indeed a large car.

For these qualities a small penalty in weight must be paid, and the Pathfinder proves to be substantial, both to control and to manœuvre. But it is a willing car, with performance to spare and viceless handling qualities, of a type which cover up the occasional misjudgment.

It was first announced at the London Show of 1953, and the only legacy from the car it then superseded was the four-cylinder, overhead-valve 2½-litre engine. The basic design of this engine may well go down in motoring history as one of the most famous ever produced. The two camshafts are mounted high on each side of the cylinder block, and the inclined valves open on a hemispherical combustion chamber, which makes for high efficiency. This engine, which has a stroke-bore ratio of 1.49 to 1—gives of its best to the driver who has a natural feeling for the car and does not regard it just as a means of getting from point A to point B. It will accelerate in normal top gear from 12 m.p.h., but to enjoy its performance to the full the gear box should be used, when the car's response is a matter for real enthusiasm.

Starting operation would be easier if the switches for starter motor and ignition were closer. Both hands are needed for this simple operation, for the ignition switch is on the right of the steering column and the choke and starter button are on the left—both the latter screened to some extent by the wheel. A much appreciated fitting is the hand throttle, by which the driver can set the engine at a speed faster than the normal tick-over when warming up or manœuvring under difficulties. A rev-counter and oil pressure and water temperature gauges are amenities the knowledgeable owner will appreciate. There is also a hand control over-riding the automatic advance and retard of the ignition.

The engine produces its power smoothly in most road conditions, the slight roughness of a four-cylinder unit being noticed only when pulling at low speeds in top gear. It responds very well to snap throttle openings, and acceleration times recorded are good when the weight of the car—31¼ cwt—is borne in mind. The time taken for the standing quarter-mile—21sec—is particularly good for a car of its weight. The slightly less favourable times of acceleration for this model, compared with those secured in the previous Road Test of a Pathfinder (*The Autocar*, 25 February, 1955), are attributable possibly to the hydraulic actuation of the clutch now used. This is one of the more important modifications which have been made since the model was introduced.

The overdrive is intended as a cruising and economy gear, and nothing is gained in performance by using overdrive ratios for acceleration. The figures in the accompanying data panel tell their own story, and when taking standing start figures only normal ratios were used. It is possible to engage overdrive in second gear, and accelerate to over 70 m.p.h. in this ratio, but this is an academic

*The gear lever does not interfere with seat adjustment. Standard equipment includes a heating and demisting unit and a vacuum operated screen washer; its button is under the right corner of the facia*

## RILEY PATHFINDER . . . .

exercise rather than a practice which one would normally adopt.

With the overdrive push-pull control in the engaged position, the car will hold normal gear up to maximum speed in that ratio unless the accelerator pedal is released momentarily above 32 m.p.h., when overdrive will come into operation. At speeds below 28 m.p.h. the overdrive is disengaged automatically, and a free wheel is available in direct drive below this drop-out speed down to stall point.

If, in overdrive, the driver wishes to revert to the normal ratio suddenly for overtaking or in emergency, depression of the accelerator pedal beyond its usual arc of travel operates a kick-down switch which puts overdrive out of action, but he must be careful not to do this when the road speed is in excess of that attainable in the normal gear concerned. This accounts for the slightly inferior acceleration and maximum speed figures listed for overdrive third as compared with normal top.

By careful use of the throttle it was possible to obtain acceleration figures in overdrive for the 30-50 m.p.h. range, but in normal driving, when overdrive is brought into use at speeds of 50 m.p.h. or above, such a "fairy foot" technique is not commonly employed, and the operation of the overdrive unit is quite straightforward.

The normal gear ratios suit the car very well indeed and enable the driver to get the best performance from the

184 THE AUTOCAR,

*A well-sprung cushion, and a seat back set at a comfortable angle, permit the maximum amount of relaxation in the rear compartment. There is an armrest on each door, and an ashtray in the centre of the front seat back*

engine; the overdrive ratios encourage a less enterprising approach and a more relaxed method. Overdrive third is so close to normal top in ratio that the difference is hardly discernible, though in fact both acceleration and maximum speeds are superior in normal drive top. The high overdrive top—2.87 to 1—is very much a Continental cruising gear. It gives on suitable English roads a feeling of being wafted along in comparative silence with the speedometer on the 90 m.p.h. mark and the rev counter needle recording 3,000 r.p.m.

Maximum speeds on the indirect normal ratios were reached at 5,500 r.p.m., which is unusually fast for this size of long-stroke engine. Most drivers would appreciate a revolution limit being marked on the tachometer, and a car with a genuine maximum of 100 m.p.h. is worthy of a speedometer that gives a margin above that figure.

For fast touring the Pathfinder is excellent—it covers the ground effortlessly. There is a self-centring action about the steering which gives a good feel when cornering. The driver can choose his line with complete confidence, knowing that the car will follow it precisely. There is no tendency to wander at any speed, and the steering is pleasantly light except at low speeds.

The combination of long torsion bars at the front and coil springs at the rear gives the car a suspension that is suitably firm for high-speed driving and yet quite comfortable when the car is taken slowly over indifferent surfaces. Passengers found it possible to sleep in the back seat when the car was being driven quite briskly.

In contrast with the performance side of the Pathfinder, it is also very likeable when used for domestic errands or the kind of sight-seeing journey that might take place during a holiday or a weekend. The engine is very versatile, and it pulls strongly at low speeds.

Constant use of the overdrive shows up when fuel consumption is considered; the present car's figure of 23.7 m.p.g. compares very favourably with that of the previous Pathfinder Road Test when 21 m.p.g. was recorded. The lowest figure with the present car was the result of a morning start in a suburban area through rush-hour traffic—in fact, the most unfavourable conditions in which a test of consumption can take place; 25.9 m.p.g. was obtained by maximum use of the overdrive and minimum speed in the indirect gears with three persons aboard.

Hydraulic operation of the clutch has cut out the slight judder that was apparent with the previous model, and a smooth take-off can be made at all times. No slip was evident, even when full power was being used during the testing. The action is light and progressive, and the pedal is set at a convenient angle. In contrast with other B.M.C.

*A bright plated rubbing strip protects the bottom panels and rear wing quarters. There is a very good view to the rear*

cars, the Riley still retains vertical clutch and brake pedals pivoting on a shaft beneath the floor, and there is no doubt that they are more pleasant to operate than the pendant type. There was no draught from the lever apertures in the floor.

The fallacy that it is necessary to have a steering column mounted gear lever to permit three people to be accommodated on the front seat is dispelled by the positioning of the Pathfinder's neat gear change on the driver's right. It is out of the way when entering the car, the movements between gears are precise, and the synchromesh on second, third and top works satisfactorily. When the lever is put into third gear, a driver may find that a particular position of window winder and door handle catches his knuckles. Some drivers may find the central arm rest inconveniently high.

A vacuum servo assists the hydraulic operation of the brakes. The effect is praiseworthy, although the assistance, in terms of pedal pressure, is not readily noticed. Persistent stops from 80 and 90 m.p.h. had no ill effect on the linings, and even when they were very hot there was no fade or unevenness. The hand brake is effective, but it is of the umbrella type, under the facia, and does not come readily to hand. It is not in keeping with the character of the car.

The driving position with the seat adjustment range available is good, and the driver has ample forward visibility

*In this illustration the bonnet is opened wider than the supporting strut will allow. Prominent are the battery, away from the exhaust heat; screen wash bottle, screen wiper motor and heater unit. The cast alloy rocker covers, with their interconnecting oil breather pipe, give a fine appearance to the engine*

veneer facia are the driving light and windscreen wiper switches.

The twin Windtone horns are operated by the half-ring mounted on the steering wheel, and a short radial movement of this half-ring to left or right actuates the trafficators. The head light dipswitch is a short, flexible lever mounted on the right side of the steering column; some drivers found that it tended to obstruct the right knee when in the dipped position.

The interior of the Pathfinder is very well finished, and the deeply upholstered, leather-covered seats give an air of luxury. The rear compartment is especially comfortable. There is a wide central folding armrest, the back of the front seat is recessed to provide extra knee room, and there are twin roof lights which act as courtesy lights when the doors are opened, and are also controlled by an independent switch. All the doors close easily and firmly, and little draught was noticed. Because of the shape of the car, wind noise is at a low level and the coachwork keeps very clean even on a " dirty weather " day.

By housing the spare wheel in a hinged tray beneath the luggage locker floor, the manufacturers have made available the maximum amount of room in the locker. There is accommodation for large suitcases, the floor is covered with

*The head lights, which have a beam suiting the performance of the car, are supplemented by twin built-in fog lamps*

with plenty of headroom, owed in part to the fact that the chassis frame members sweep out within the wheelbase and permit a sunken floor. The windscreen pillars are apt to form an obstruction to driving vision because of their comparative thickness. The driving mirror, which can be dipped, gives a good field of view through the wide rear window.

The generous seat width gives good support to the thighs, and the steering wheel is positioned so that the driver can adopt a comfortable but alert position. The steering column is adjustable for length, but the adjustment is not quite so simple as the instruction book would have it. There is sufficient foot room around the pedals, and a small pad is provided at the side of the gear box cover for the driver to rest the left foot, though not with the left leg at full stretch.

The instruments and the majority of the control switches are well laid out in front of the driver and one either side of the steering column. Three large circular dials—inset in a black panel to avoid reflection—can be read easily through the top half of the steering wheel. An attractive form of " black " lighting is used for illuminating the panel at night, and a two-position switch permits the driver, if he wishes, to light the speedometer only. In the centre of the polished

*The locker lid is reinforced for rigidity and to prevent vibration. Lifting jack and tools are housed within the wing on the right. A reversing light is fitted in each rear lamp cluster*

THE AUTOCAR, 10 AUGUST 1956

# RILEY PATHFINDER . . . .

matting, and the lid is supported by hinged struts in the open position. The electrically operated petrol pump is housed in the right side of the locker where it is out of the way of luggage and also remote from underbonnet heat which might cause vapour locks in a hot climate or during prolonged storming of mountain passes.

A strut supports the bonnet in the open position, and this allows sufficient room for routine replenishing of oil and water and similar maintenance. The majority of the auxiliaries are accessible, but the twin S.U. carburettors, their adjustments, and the fuel pipe unions are tucked away and hidden by the air cleaner.

The Pathfinder is one of the cars which are still provided with a starting handle; it is housed with other tools in the luggage locker. There are 12 lubrication points which require attention every 1,000 miles, the majority of these are on the steering and front suspension joints.

## RILEY PATHFINDER WITH OVERDRIVE

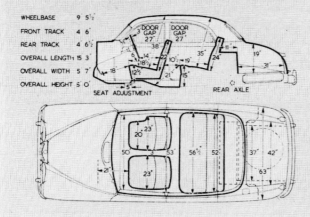

| | |
|---|---|
| WHEELBASE | 9 5½ |
| FRONT TRACK | 4 6 |
| REAR TRACK | 4 6½ |
| OVERALL LENGTH | 15 3 |
| OVERALL WIDTH | 5 7 |
| OVERALL HEIGHT | 5 0 |

Measurements in these ⅛in to 1ft scale body diagrams are taken with the driving seat in the central position of fore and aft adjustment and with the seat cushions uncompressed

## PERFORMANCE

**ACCELERATION:** from constant speeds.
Speed Range, Gear Ratios and Time in sec.

| M.P.H. | *2.87 to 1 | 4.1 to 1 | *4.11 to 1 | 5.88 to 1 | *5.91 to 1 | 8.45 to 1 | 13.59 to 1 |
|---|---|---|---|---|---|---|---|
| 10—30 | — | — | — | 7.8 | — | 5.6 | 4.5 |
| 20—40 | — | 11.2 | — | 7.5 | — | 5.7 | — |
| 30—50 | 18.8 | 11.6 | 11.5 | 8.2 | 8.2 | 7.2 | — |
| 40—60 | 20.3 | 12.5 | 12.6 | 9.4 | 9.4 | — | — |
| 50—70 | 24.5 | 13.8 | 14.5 | 11.3 | 11.5 | — | — |
| 60—80 | 33.0 | 17.0 | 18.0 | — | — | — | — |

* Overdrive ratios.

From rest through gears to:

| M.P.H. | | | | sec. |
|---|---|---|---|---|
| 30 | .. | .. | .. | 5.5 |
| 50 | .. | .. | .. | 13.1 |
| 60 | .. | .. | .. | 18.8 |
| 70 | .. | .. | .. | 24.7 |
| 80 | .. | .. | .. | 35.0 |
| 90 | .. | .. | .. | 51.8 |

Standing quarter mile, 21.0 sec.

**SPEEDS ON GEARS:**

| Gear | | | M.P.H. (normal and max.) | K.P.H. (normal and max.) |
|---|---|---|---|---|
| Top | (mean) | | 97.1 | 156.2 |
| | (best) | | 100.2 | 161.3 |
| 3rd | .. | .. | 58—75 | 93—121 |
| 2nd | .. | .. | 35—52 | 56—84 |
| 1st | .. | .. | 22—32 | 35—51 |
| **OVERDRIVE** | | | | |
| Top | (mean) | | 82.5 | 132.8 |
| | (best) | | 88.0 | 141.6 |
| 3rd | .. | .. | 80—91 | 128.7—146.5 |
| 2nd | .. | .. | 68—74 | 109.4—119.1 |

**TRACTIVE RESISTANCE:** 16.2 lb per ton at 10 M.P.H.

**TRACTIVE EFFORT:**

| | Pull (lb per ton) | Equivalent Gradient |
|---|---|---|
| Top | 189 | 1 in 11.7 |
| Third | 292 | 1 in 7.6 |
| Second | 406 | 1 in 5.6 |

**BRAKES:**

| | Efficiency | Pedal Pressure (lb) |
|---|---|---|
| | 84 per cent | 100 |
| | 74 per cent | 75 |
| | 61 per cent | 50 |

**FUEL CONSUMPTION:**
23.7 m.p.g. overall for 320 miles (11.9 litres per 100 km.).
Approximate normal range 17—26 m.p.g. (16.6–10.8 litres per 100 km.).
Fuel, first grade.

**WEATHER:** Sunny, slight breeze; dry concrete surface.
Air temperature 72 deg. F.
Acceleration figures are the means of several runs in opposite directions.
Tractive effort and resistance obtained by Tapley meter.
Model described in *The Autocar* of 25th February, 1955.

**SPEEDOMETER CORRECTION: M.P.H.**

| Car speedometer | .. | 10 | 20 | 30 | 40 | 50 | 60 | 70 | 80 | 90 | 95 | 100 |
|---|---|---|---|---|---|---|---|---|---|---|---|---|
| True speed | .. | 11 | 19 | 28 | 37 | 47 | 57 | 66 | 77 | 86 | 90 | 95 |

## DATA

**PRICE** (basic), with saloon body, £940.
British purchase tax, £471 7s.
Total (in Great Britain), £1,411 7s.
Extras: Radio £46 10s.
Overdrive £63 15s.

**ENGINE:** Capacity: 2,443 c.c. (149 cu in).
Number of cylinders: 4.
Bore and stroke: 80.5 × 120 mm (3.169 × 4.725 in).
Valve gear: overhead valves, pushrods.
Compression ratio: 7.25 to 1.
B.H.P. 110 at 4,400 r.p.m. (B.H.P. per ton laden 63.9).
Torque: 134 lb ft at 3,000 r.p.m.
M.P.H. per 1,000 r.p.m. on top gear, 20.1
M.P.H. per 1,000 r.p.m. on overdrive, 28.71.

**WEIGHT** (with 5 gals fuel), 31¼ cwt (3,506 lb).
Weight distribution (per cent): F, 52.7; R, 47.3.
Laden as tested: 34½ cwt (3,856 lb).
Lb per c.c. (laden): 1.57.

**BRAKES:** Type: F, two trailing shoe; R, leading and trailing shoe.
Method of operation: F, hydraulic, servo-assisted; R, hydraulic servo-assisted.
Drum dimensions: F, 12in diameter; 2¼in wide. R, 12in. diameter; 2¼in wide.
Lining area: F, 70.6 sq in. R, 89.5 sq in (92.9 sq in per ton laden).

**TYRES:** 6.00—16 in.
Pressures (lb per sq in): F, 27; R, 27 (normal).

**TANK CAPACITY:** 13 Imperial gallons.
Oil sump, 13 pints.
Cooling system, 17¾ pints (including heater).

**TURNING CIRCLE:** 35ft 6in (L and R).
Steering wheel turns (lock to lock): 3½.

**DIMENSIONS:** Wheelbase: 9ft 5½in.
Track: F, 4ft 6in; R, 4ft 6½in.
Length (overall): 15ft 3in.
Height: 5ft 0in.
Width: 5ft 7in.
Ground clearance: 7in.
Frontal area: 21.8 sq ft (approximately).

**ELECTRICAL SYSTEM:** 12-volt; 63 ampère-hour battery.
Head lights: double dip; 42—36 watt bulbs.

**SUSPENSION:** Front, independent, torsion bars and wishbones. Rear, coil springs and radius arms. Anti-roll bar position behind rear axle.

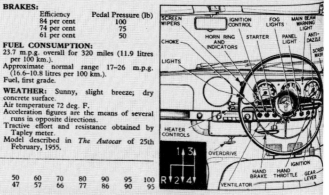

*Distinguishing    the Two-Point-Six    from its predecessors are a more upright radiator grille, a bright metal waistline, larger auxiliary lamps (no longer recessed in the front apron) and head lamp hoods*

## *Autocar* ROAD TESTS 1665        Riley Two-Point-Six

A MINOR change of face and a major change of power unit have transformed the rather rugged Riley Pathfinder into a quieter and more refined successor—the Two-Point-Six—which has thereby lost a little of both its individuality and of its performance in terms of maximum speed. In place of the twin-camshaft four-cylinder engine of 2,442 c.c. is the familiar 2.6-litre power unit common to other B.M.C. products. To those who would compare this model directly with the current Wolseley Six-Ninety, which it resembles closely, the differences in mechanical specification are of interest.

Under the bonnet there is increased power (101 b.h.p. against 97) and greater torque at a faster crankshaft speed; higher final drive gearing plus tyres of larger section give 20.4 m.p.h. per 1,000 r.p.m. as compared with 18.93 m.p.h. in top gear.

Thus equipped, the new Riley goes 4 m.p.h. faster than the Wolseley (tested on 15 March of this year), and takes 10 seconds less to reach 80 m.p.h. from a standstill. The last Pathfinder tested (10 August, 1956) went 4 m.p.h. faster than the Two-Point-Six, but was 2½ seconds slower to 80.

Exceptionally smooth operation of the six-cylinder engine is, however, deceptive in that one is now less conscious of the work being done than was the case with the rather fruity four-cylinder, and it only *seems* less lively. Nevertheless, the intermediate acceleration figures show that full use must be made of the gear box when in haste, for the power supply at low crankshaft speeds does not make light of a weight (two up) of almost 1¼ tons. Yet the engine remains sweet down to even 12 m.p.h. in top gear, and is willing to pull away smoothly from this speed.

Thereafter it remains completely period-free until some 5,000 r.p.m. are reached, and shows no distress until valve bounce becomes evident at about 5,500 r.p.m.—beyond its useful limit. It starts instantly on a cold morning with little use of the manual enrichment control, and warms quickly.

Undoubtedly this Riley is best suited to such fast, straight highways as abound on the European continent. Even without the optional overdrive (not fitted to the car tested) it will cruise with commendably little noise and effort at speeds up to 80 m.p.h., and the third ratio can be usefully employed to more than 70 m.p.h. To move a vehicle of this bulk and mass at high speeds requires considerable energy in the form of fuel, but a sensitive foot on the throttle and a limit of about 2,500 r.p.m. (50-55 m.p.h.) reap their reward in consumption figures better than 25 m.p.g.

Hard driving reduces the safe range between refuelling stops to less than 200 miles. The filler cap, high on the left rear wing, is concealed beneath a hinged panel. It is sometimes difficult to open, especially if screwed up tightly, and there is blow-back at full delivery from a garage electric pump. Premium, as opposed to 100-octane fuel, was used throughout the test, and pinking could be detected at times.

Fortunately the spacings of the four forward ratios are matched admirably to the engine characteristics, and the great majority of drivers are likely to approve of the gear change mechanism, via a short side lever between the door and seat cushion. A slightly longer lever might be preferable, but this would impede entry and exit. There is very effective synchromesh baulking between the upper three ratios and the movement is reasonably light, but it would be easier to "slice" from second to third if the gate were narrower and the lateral movement lighter.

Not always could first speed be engaged silently from rest when the oil was hot. Take-offs in second can be accomplished with little clutch judder, but first is clearly intended to be used for this. At first acquaintance there is a danger, when changing from third to second, of overcoming the reverse gear protection spring when bringing the lever across the gate. The indirect gears are distinctly audible on drive

*Behind the traditional Riley radiator shell is now a conventional B.M.C. six-cylinder engine. The driver cannot see his left front wing*

984

# Riley
# Two-Point-
# Six . . .

*Clean lines like these make for silent travel at speed. Polished discs cover the wheels. A lid over the fuel filler must be opened with the ignition key*

and over-run, but not objectionally so. The clutch is fully up to its work, however hardly used; there was some lost motion in the transmission of the car tested.

Adding greatly to one's pleasure and confidence at the Riley's wheel is one of the most effective braking systems which we have experienced. This is the latest self-adjusting Lockheed H.S. design, which incorporates hydraulic cylinders of unequal diameters in each front drum, the larger pistons actuating the trailing shoes, as featured on some American models 20 years ago. Additionally, the front drums have a larger swept area than the rear. A vacuum-servo motor provides lag-free assistance which never induces any kick of the pedal. Although the braking figures recorded were not exceptional, because of a tendency for the rear wheels to lock with only two people aboard, the stopping power and consistent behaviour from high speeds were well above average and the resistance to fade excellent.

A peculiarity of the system—at any rate, on the car tested—is that a second consecutive jab on the pedal decreases its travel by an inch or so, the effect being more pronounced than a conventional system's behaviour when in need of adjustment. Weak shoe return springs are inherent in the design, and there is thus some time lag while the larger, trailing shoe piston in each front drum discharges fluid back to the master cylinder. Thus, on the second application appreciably less fluid has to be moved to bring the shoes into contact with the drums.

The pistol-grip hand-brake is powerful, but awkwardly placed beneath the steering column, so that the driver must crook his arm around the wheel to reach it.

In unhappy contrast to the brakes is the steering, which has the unforgivable combination of low gearing (four turns of the wheel from lock to lock for a mean turning circle of about 37 feet) and heaviness. Low-speed manoeuvring calls for excessive effort and arm movement, and the mechanism

feels very dead at "town" speeds. Despite this, some reactions reach the driver's hands while the car is passing over rough surfaces. As tested, the Riley would quickly exhaust any motorist who elected to take it on an Alpine tour. The gentle driver in particular will experience a marked reluctance of the car to deviate from a straight line, and a slow response to minor corrections.

More forceful progress is qualified by increased feel, and within its limitations the handling is never dangerous or vicious—although an excess of tyre squeal sometimes gives pedestrians and other road users the converse impression. Initial expectations of understeer at high speed are not fulfilled, and near the limit of adhesion it is the tail which tends to unstick first. Very wisely, a range of tyre pressures to cover variations in load and cruising speed is listed by the makers. For the high speed test figures only the tyres were inflated to a recommended 30 lb sq in.

The dished steering-wheel is of large diameter, and a full horn-ring is recessed within it. This rattled annoyingly, and was indefinite in operation. The wheel is mounted telescopically with a spanner-operated pinch bolt for adjustment; but even in its long-reach position—which could comfortably be longer—the finger-tips can only just reach the flexible lever of the head-lamp dipping switch.

Road-holding inevitably is related to steering, and the Two-Point-Six is too ponderous to be driven very fast on tortuous roads by the average owner. When pressed, however, it rolls very little, and, once into the corner with roll established, it remains stable and keeps all four wheels on *terra firma*. The suspension system gives a satisfactory compromise between security in extreme conditions and passenger comfort—particularly for those in the front seats. The spring damping seems just right; but the retention of a separate boxed chassis frame has not resulted in thorough insulation from road noises, and cat's-eye reflectors can be heard and felt with emphasis.

Well-arranged and spaced pedals are complemented by a recess in the bell-housing cover for the driver's left foot, but it does not allow enough stretch for full relaxation. Layout of the minor controls on the facia is generally sensible—in a vertical group to the driver's right (wipers, panel and road lamps, plus the vacuum-type screen-wash button), and a horizontal group to his left (ignition, starter and mixture). At either side of the central radio speaker cavity are switches for the standard fog- and long-range supplementary lamps—both extremely effective fittings. The head lamps have 60-watt elements on full beam, and are well up to the car's performance. The long-range lamp circuit is cut off when the head lamps are dipped. There is no provision for signal-flashing with the head lamps. Incidentally, *The Autocar* staff generally prefers a more distinctive (to the touch) and positive lamp switch than the pull-and-twist type.

Before the driver are large matched speedometer and tachometer dials, of which the needles are well damped and steady. Four other dials are scattered around the radio

*The weighty bonnet is not counterbalanced. Beneath it finish and layout of the accessories is fine, but deep mudguards obstruct the mechanic*

985

speaker (fuel level, dynamo charge, oil pressure and coolant temperature), and below it is a clock. To read these the driver must deflect his gaze through a wide angle and, particularly at night, this entails a dangerous "blind" of perhaps three seconds. At night the main dial needles and indices are lit with "black light," and the others by a second movement of the panel switch.

This facia layout scheme leaves somewhat limited space for a glove compartment in front of the passenger. It is inexcusable that a vehicle of this quality, and with such pretensions for long-distance travel, should have no further provisions for maps and other impedimenta of the seasoned voyager than a shallow shelf behind the rear squab. When fitted, the radio controls are remote from the driver, above the passenger's knees—where there is a dangerous edge.

Flashing direction signals are operated by a lever above the steering wheel boss; the only indication of their functioning is a minute illuminated button in the facia, out of the driver's sight behind the steering column. On the car tried the self-cancelling gear was not consistently reliable —nor was the warning button. Two screen wipers (single-speed) park horizontally to the right; their operating arc is not sufficient to reach within several inches of the passenger's door pillar. The driving-mirror is well placed, and has a dipping reflector. There are two sun vizors.

A conventional heating and ventilation system, incorporating a controlled three-position air intake flap ahead of the screen, is installed. This would be more versatile if the booster motor were fitted with a rheostat switch, and there is too much concentration of heat on the driver's left ankle. There is no provision for warming the feet of the

*Above: Instruments are scattered. A small locker in the facia provides the only stowage space for front seat occupants. Quality of material and finish is first class. Recesses in the front seat squab add a little knee room to the rear compartment*

*Right: A right-hand gear lever aids—and a wide transmission tunnel impedes— three-abreast seating— There is a short-reach rest for the driver's left foot*

rear-seat passengers, but the body joints generally proved free from all but minor draughts.

Of the four large doors, the driver's only may be locked from outside, but the other three each has a most considerate and welcome innovation for the protection of very young passengers; a small lever below the door catch, which can be reached only when the door is ajar, can be set to lock only the interior handles. Good quality leather for the wearing surfaces of the seat trim and a liberal area of polished wood for facia and door cappings convey an air of quality and luxury to the interior.

Either individual front seats or a one-piece bench may be specified by Riley customers, the latter type being fitted to the example under review. The squabs would suit most human frames better with more support for the small of the back, and the cutaway in the driver's side of the cushion to accommodate the gear lever interferes with the symmetry of the cushion springing. A wide, folding centre arm-rest is too high in its lowered position, and obstructs the driver's left elbow. The seat on our car was a little slack on its runners.

Although the driver sits fairly high relative to the deep, curved screen, the high scuttle and wide bonnet pressing do not allow him a sight of his near-side wing. His view

*Capacious, conveniently shaped and nicely trimmed, the luggage locker also is loaded easily. The spare wheel tray is lowered by the wheelbrace*

986

THE AUTOCAR, 20 DECEMBER 1957

## Riley Two-Point-Six . . .

when reversing is more restricted than is usual these days, the bottom sill of the rear window being rather high relative to his eye level. Also, with only one or two aboard the car rides tail-high.

Rear seat passenger space has been sacrificed somewhat to luggage capacity, and with the front seat well back (to suit a 5ft 9in driver) there is little leg room to spare in the aft compartment. The back-rest is too vertical for most tastes, and insufficiently resilient. It was felt that a reduction in its thickness need not prejudice comfort, and would allow another two or three inches of longitudinal space.

Above each rear door is a courtesy lamp, switched on when the door is opened; opening of either front door

switches on a map-reading lamp beneath the facia. Rear passengers would appreciate better sound insulation from the ticking of the electric fuel pump in the boot, especially at low speeds when other noises are at a minimum.

Regular servicing of the Riley is best attended to according to the excellent fixed-price voucher system applicable to all B.M.C. cars. Motorists who service their own cars may be interested in the makers' advice to lubricate, every 1,000 miles, nine points on the front suspension linkage, five nipples on the universal joints of the two-piece propeller shaft, two on the handbrake linkage and one on the gear lever linkage.

Although the large and robust Riley Two-Point-Six falls a little short of expectations in some of the essentials for effortless and comfortable travel, it can cover long mileage journeys at high speeds without mechanical fuss.

## RILEY TWO-POINT-SIX

| | |
|---|---|
| WHEELBASE | 9' 5½' |
| FRONT TRACK | 4' 6¾' |
| REAR TRACK | 4' 6¼' |
| OVERALL LENGTH | 15' 5½' |
| OVERALL WIDTH | 5' 7' |
| OVERALL HEIGHT | 5' 1' |

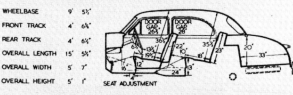

SEAT ADJUSTMENT

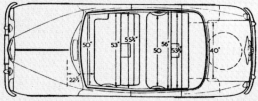

*Measurements in these ½in to 1ft scale body diagrams are taken with the driving seat in the central position of fore and aft adjustment and with the seat cushions uncompressed*

## DATA

PRICE (basic), with 4-door saloon body, £940.
British purchase tax, £471 7s.
Total (in Great Britain), £1,411 7s.

ENGINE: Capacity: 2,639.4 c.c. (161.07 cu in).
Number of cylinders: 6.
Bore and stroke: 79.4 × 88.9 mm (3.12 × 3.5in).
Valve gear: o.h.v., pushrods.
Compression ratio: 8.3 to 1.
B.H.P. (gross): 101 at 4,500 r.p.m. (B.H.P. per ton laden 60).
Torque: 141.5 lb ft at 2,500 r.p.m.
M.P.H. per 1,000 r.p.m. on top gear, 20.4.

WEIGHT: (with 5 gals fuel), 31 cwt (3,470 lb).
Weight distribution (per cent): F, 53.7; R, 46.3.
Laden as tested: 34 cwt (3,806 lb).
Lb per c.c. (laden): 1.44.

BRAKES: Type: Lockheed H.S.
Method of operation: Hydraulic.
Drum dimensions: F, 11⅛in diameter; 2⅛in wide. R, 11in diameter; 2⅛in wide.
Lining area: F, 93.5 sq in. R, 76.5 sq in (100 sq in per ton laden).

TYRES: 6.70—15in.
Pressures (lb sq in): F, 24; R, 24 (normal). F, 24; R, 26 (laden). F, 30; R, 30 (for fast driving).

TANK CAPACITY: 13 Imperial gallons.
Oil sump, 11½ pints.
Cooling system, 24 pints.

TURNING CIRCLE: 36ft 9in (L). 37ft 6½in (R).
Steering wheel turns (lock to lock): 4.

DIMENSIONS: Wheelbase: 9ft 5½in.
Track: F, 4ft 6¾in; R, 4ft 6¼in.
Length (overall): 15ft 5½in.
Height (unladen): 5ft 1in.
Width: 5ft 7in.
Ground clearance: 6½in.
Frontal area: 21.8 sq ft (approximately).

ELECTRICAL SYSTEM: 12-volt; 57 ampère-hour battery.
Head lights: Double dip; 60–36 watt bulbs.

SUSPENSION: Front, torsion bars and wishbones. Rear, half-elliptic springs with live axle.

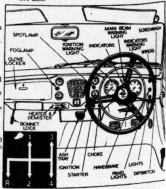

## PERFORMANCE

ACCELERATION: from constant speeds.
Speed Range, Gear Ratios and Time in sec.

| | 3.9 to 1 | 5.6 to 1 | 8.0 to 1 | 12.9 to 1 |
|---|---|---|---|---|
| M.P.H. | | | | |
| 10—30 .. | — | 7.9 | 5.1 | 4.1 |
| 20—40 .. | 11.4 | 7.4 | 5.4 | — |
| 30—50 .. | 11.6 | 8.3 | 6.6 | — |
| 40—60 .. | 13.1 | 8.9 | — | — |
| 50—70 .. | 15.1 | 11.0 | — | — |
| 60—80 .. | 18.6 | — | — | — |

From rest through gears to:

| M.P.H. | | sec. |
|---|---|---|
| 30 | .. | 5.2 |
| 50 | .. | 11.8 |
| 60 | .. | 17.4 |
| 70 | .. | 23.8 |
| 80 | .. | 32.5 |
| 90 | .. | 49.8 |

Standing quarter mile, 20.6 sec.

SPEEDS ON GEARS:

| Gear | | M.P.H. (normal and max.) | K.P.H. (normal and max.) |
|---|---|---|---|
| Top .. | (mean) | 93 | 149.7 |
| | (best) | 96.5 | 155.3 |
| 3rd .. | .. | 60—78 | 97—125 |
| 2nd .. | .. | 40—53 | 64—85 |
| 1st .. | .. | 24—32 | 39—51 |

SPEEDOMETER CORRECTION: M.P.H.

| Car speedometer | .. | .. | .. | 10 | 20 | 30 | 40 | 50 | 60 | 70 | 80 | 90 |
|---|---|---|---|---|---|---|---|---|---|---|---|---|
| True speed | .. | .. | .. | 10 | 19.5 | 29 | 38.5 | 48 | 57 | 67 | 76 | 86 |

TRACTIVE RESISTANCE: 30 lb per ton at 10 M.P.H.

TRACTIVE EFFORT:

| | | Pull (lb per ton) | Equivalent Gradient |
|---|---|---|---|
| Top | .. .. | 197 | 1 in 11.3 |
| Third | .. .. | 288 | 1 in 7.7 |
| Second | .. .. | 405 | 1 in 5.4 |

BRAKES: (in neutral at 30 m.p.h.):

| Efficiency | Pedal Pressure (lb) |
|---|---|
| 43 per cent | 25 |
| 72 per cent | 50 |
| 85 per cent | 75 |
| 89 per cent | 100 |

FUEL CONSUMPTION:
19 m.p.g. overall for 1,220 miles (14.9 litres per 100 km).
Approximate normal range 15.5—25.2 m.p.g. (18.2—11.2 litres per 100 km).
Fuel, Premium.

WEATHER: Dry, no wind.
Air temperature 54 deg F.
Acceleration figures are the means of several runs in opposite directions.
Tractive effort and resistance obtained by Tapley meter.
Model described in *The Autocar* of 23 August, 1957.

The Motor      892      *January 11, 1961*

# The Motor Road Test No. 2/61

**Make:** Riley              **Type:** One-Point-Five

**Makers:** Riley Motor Co., Ltd., Abingdon-on-Thames, Oxford

## Test Data

*World copyright reserved ; no unauthorized reproduction in whole or in part.*

**CONDITIONS:** Weather : Cool and dry ; gusty wind, 10-20 m.p.h. (Temperature 51°F., Barometer 29.2 in. Hg.) Surface : Dry tar macadam. Fuel : Premium grade pump petrol (approx. 96 Octane Rating by Research Method).

### INSTRUMENTS
Speedometer at 30 m.p.h. .. .. 5% fast
Speedometer at 60 m.p.h. .. .. 2% fast
Speedometer at 80 m.p.h. .. .. 3% fast
Distance recorder .. .. .. accurate

### WEIGHT
Kerb weight (unladen, but with oil, water and fuel for approx. 50 miles) .. .. 18½ cwt.
Front/rear distribution of kerb weight .. 59/41
Weight laden as tested .. .. 22½ cwt.

### MAXIMUM SPEEDS
**Flying Quarter Mile**
Mean lap of banked track .. .. 82.4 m.p.h.
Best one-way quarter mile time equals 87.4 m.p.h.

**"Maximile" Speed** (Timed quarter mile after one mile accelerating from rest.)
Mean of opposite runs .. .. 80.2 m.p.h.
Best one-way time equals .. .. 84.1 m.p.h.

**Speed in gears**
Max. speed in 3rd gear .. .. 78 m.p.h.
Max. speed in 2nd gear .. .. 50 m.p.h.
Max. speed in 1st gear .. .. 30 m.p.h.

### FUEL CONSUMPTION
41.0 m.p.g. at constant 30 m.p.h. on level.
37.5 m.p.g. at constant 40 m.p.h. on level.
33.5 m.p.g. at constant 50 m.p.h. on level.
30.0 m.p.g. at constant 60 m.p.h. on level.
25.5 m.p.g. at constant 70 m.p.h. on level.

**Overall Fuel Consumption** for 1,273 miles, 49.5 gallons, equals 25.7 m.p.g. (11.0 litres/100 km.)

**Touring Fuel Consumption** (m.p.g. at steady speed midway between 30 m.p.h. and maximum less 5% allowance for acceleration) 29.8. m.p.g.
Fuel tank capacity (maker's figure) .. 7 gallons.

### STEERING
Turning circle between kerbs:
Left .. .. .. .. .. 31 ft.
Right .. .. .. .. .. 32½ ft.
Turns of steering wheel from lock to lock 2½.

### BRAKES from 30 m.p.h.
0.93 g retardation (equivalent to 32½ ft. stopping distance) with 100 lb. pedal pressure.
0.82 g retardation (equivalent to 36½ ft. stopping distance) with 75 lb. pedal pressure.
0.66 g retardation (equivalent to 45 ft. stopping distance) with 50 lb. pedal pressure.
0.36 g retardation (equivalent to 83 ft. stopping distance) with 25 lb. pedal pressure.

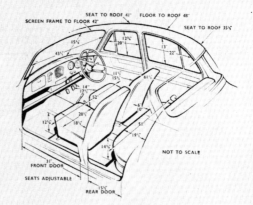

TRACK :- FRONT 4'-3"  REAR 4'-2½"
OVERALL WIDTH 5'-1"
5'-0" UNLADEN
GROUND CLEARANCE 6¾"
SCALE 1 : 50 — 7'-2" — 12'-9¼"
**RILEY ONE-POINT-FIVE**

SCREEN FRAME TO FLOOR 42"  SEAT TO ROOF 41"  FLOOR TO ROOF 48"  SEAT TO ROOF 35¾"
NOT TO SCALE
FRONT DOOR
SEATS ADJUSTABLE
REAR DOOR

### ACCELERATION TIMES from Standstill
0-30 m.p.h. .. .. .. .. 5.2 sec.
0-40 m.p.h. .. .. .. .. 8.2 sec.
0-50 m.p.h. .. .. .. .. 12.5 sec.
0-60 m.p.h. .. .. .. .. 18.9 sec.
0-70 m.p.h. .. .. .. .. 28.5 sec.
Standing quarter mile .. .. 20.9 sec.

### ACCELERATION TIMES on Upper Ratios

| | Top gear | 3rd gear |
|---|---|---|
| 10-30 m.p.h. | 11.8 sec. | 8.2 sec. |
| 20-40 m.p.h. | 13.1 sec. | 8.4 sec. |
| 30-50 m.p.h. | 14.8 sec. | 8.8 sec. |
| 40-60 m.p.h. | 18.4 sec. | 11.4 sec. |
| 50-70 m.p.h. | 22.1 sec. | 16.5 sec. |

### HILL CLIMBING at sustained steady speeds
Max. gradient on top gear .. .. 1 in 12.7 (Tapley 175 lb./ton)
Max. gradient on 3rd gear .. .. 1 in 8.9 (Tapley 250 lb./ton)
Max. gradient on 2nd gear .. .. 1 in 5.2 (Tapley 420 lb./ton)

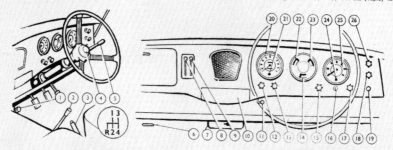

1. Dip switch. 2. Gear lever. 3. Handbrake. 4. Horn button. 5. Direction indicator switch and warning light. 6. Bonnet release. 7. Heater, demister control. 8. Air control. 9. Temperature control. 10. Radio Panel. 11. Trip reset. 12. Choke. 13. Starter. 14. Fuel gauge. 15. Fog lamp switch. 16. Ignition switch. 17. Panel light switch. 18. Wipers switch. 19. Screen washer control. 20. Speedometer. 21. High beam warning light. 22. Oil pressure gauge. 23. Water temperature gauge. 24. Dynamo charge warning light. 25. Rev. counter. 26. Lights switch.

January 11, 1961     893     The **Motor**

# The Riley One-Point-Five

## In Brief

Price (as tested) £575 plus purchase tax £240 14s. 2d. equals £815 14s. 2d.

| | | |
|---|---|---|
| Capacity | .. .. .. | 1,489 c.c. |
| Unladen kerb weight | .. | 18½ cwt. |

Acceleration :

| | |
|---|---|
| 20-40 m.p.h. in top gear | 13.1 sec. |
| 0-50 m.p.h. through gears | 12.5 sec. |

| | | |
|---|---|---|
| Maximum direct top gear gradient | .. .. | 1 in 12.7 |
| Maximum speed .. | .. | 82.4 m.p.h. |
| "Maximile" speed | .. | 80.2 m.p.h. |
| Touring fuel consumption | | 29.8 m.p.g. |

Gearing : 18.6 m.p.h. in top gear at 1,000 r.p.m.; 31.8 m.p.h. at 1,000 ft./min. piston speed.

## A Compact, High-performance Four-seater Saloon

IN trying to select a car, many motorists encounter this difficulty: if they want a bigger engine and more performance, they usually have to accept a larger body to go with it. A lot of owners never need any more interior accommodation than is provided by economy cars in the 850-1,000 c.c. class, comfortable for two people and adequate for four, but would like a bigger engine giving more performance and more effortless travel. The Riley complies exactly with this specification with a tuned version of the 1½-litre B.M.C. " B " type engine fitted to a car which has light controls and the ability to fit into small spaces.

Since our last test of the One-Point-Five, three years ago, very few changes have been made in either the mechanical specification or the bodywork. A change which might seem almost insignificant is that the tyre size has been increased from 5.00-14 to 5.60-14. The difference in effective gearing, only about 1½%, passes unnoticed, but the handling has improved appreciably. With nearly 60% of the

unladen weight at the front of the car the front tyres support very nearly 11 cwt., and previously they felt and sounded rather overloaded in fast cornering. The increased tyre size together with improvements in design and tread compounds have eliminated a good deal of tyre scrub and squeal, although the car still has considerable basic understeer. This balance is much affected, particularly in wet conditions, by the amount of power transmitted and on corners it is very easy to spin the lightly laden inside rear wheel by careless use of the throttle. There is a fair amount of roll and a tendency for the back axle to hop on bumps, but although this is not one of the fastest cornering cars on the market it is certainly unusually stable and controllable and can be driven right to the limit without exhibiting any vicious habits at all.

The rack and pinion steering gives the lightness and precision of control that one expects from this kind of mechanism and the car needs practically no conscious attention on the straight, except in very heavy cross-winds, but high speed cruising was spoiled by an unpleasant vibration of the wheel and steering column at speeds over 65 m.p.h. Balance weights were fitted to the front wheels but presumably the tyres had worn out of balance again since they were last checked.

In conjunction with the " big engine, small car " formula, the final drive has been selected to make top gear effectively

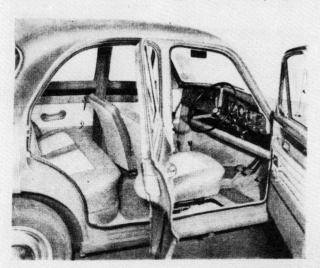

INDIVIDUAL front seats and a rear compartment with room for two adults can be seen in this view through the front-hinged doors.

c5

EASY to load, the luggage locker now has internal hinges and torsion-bar balancing springs for its lift-up lid.

SENSIBLE refinement recently added to the Riley is a full-width parcel shelf beneath the polished wood facia panel. Instruments include an r.p.m. indicator.

## The Riley One-point-Five

an overdrive ratio providing entirely effortless cruising rather than the best top gear performance. Top and third gears fall on each side of the optimum value for maximum speed with the result that the car is only 4 m.p.h. slower in third gear than it is in top, but there are compensations that many people will feel outweigh any loss of speed. In the course of hurried journeys to the Midlands, the car was cruised at full throttle for the entire length of M1 without any indication that the engine was being worked unduly hard and, indeed, the tachometer showed only 4,000-4,500 r.p.m. At these speeds the engine noise is below the threshold of wind roar which is rather prominent around the square lines of the body even with all the windows shut.

Not unnaturally, this overdrive cruising effect is bought at the expense of low speed pulling power in top gear; although the engine is very flexible and able to pull right down to under 10 m.p.h. in the highest ratio, the Riley is essentially the sort of car that demands continual use of the gears in order to get the best out of it. It is unlikely that Riley buyers will object to this aspect since the gearbox is an extremely good one combining very powerful synchromesh with a light movement of the rigid lever. With high maxima in the reasonably quiet intermediate gears, keen drivers will derive considerable pleasure from its use,

although, in traffic, the difficulty of selecting first gear at rest can be tiresome. Apart from a period in the region of 4,000 r.p.m. and another slight one at 5,000, the engine is fairly smooth. It will run to 6,000 r.p.m., to the accompaniment of some mechanical fuss, but most people will prefer to limit the speed to a less obtrusive 5,000 r.p.m. giving about 40 m.p.h. in second gear and 65 in third.

From the point of view of octane rating, Mixture grade fuel proved entirely adequate but premium was necessary to suppress a tendency to run-on after hard use on the cheaper petrol. It was a quick starter but rather slow to warm up.

Most people of average height will adjust the driving seat back as far as it will go to achieve a comfortable distance from the pedals; this gives a fairly straight arm position relative to the steering wheel which is set at an unusually flat angle.

*(Continued on page 895)*

TWIN CARBURETTERS on a 1½-litre o.h.v. engine give this compact four-door, four-seat saloon brisk performance in the gears and effortless fast cruising.

c4

January 11, 1961                                895                                The Motor

# The Riley One-point-Five—Contd.

Whilst the high-mounted seats will accommodate a variety of sizes, tall drivers usually want to move their seat back farther than it will go without alteration of the anchorage position and tall passengers are restricted by an even more limited range of adjustment. No doubt the amount of rearward movement is intentionally reduced to leave just adequate room for rear-seat passengers, but this seems a mistaken policy when a car is so often driven with the back unoccupied.

### Comfortable Ride

The ride is comfortable in most circumstances with a notable freedom from pitch and is sufficiently well damped for travelling fast on bumpy and wavy roads without anxiety. Very rough roads, however, throw the back axle about and produce some working of the body and doors. These are the only circumstances in which the integral structure does not feel quite as rigid as it might be.

Visibility is good in most directions and a short falling bonnet which allows the road to be seen quite close ahead is particularly useful in fog. The windscreen pillars, on the other hand, are rather thicker than is fashionable on cars of more recent design, and at night the long-range headlamps give a beam of adequate range but quite inadequate spread in either the dipped or main beam positions.

The instrument layout is of traditional design with a polished dashboard and large, clearly marked dials. The rev. counter on the right of the panel is matched by a speedometer on the left which proved more accurate than usual

EXTERIOR details of the Riley include an automatic reversing lamp, bumper over-riders and hinged ventilators on the front doors to assist a standardized fresh air heating system.

with an optimism of less than 3% over the upper half of the speed range. On the left of the facia two knobs sliding in vertical slots control the quantity of incoming air and the heat supply, whilst an air distribution control less accessibly placed lower down and nearer to the bulkhead enables a quantity of air to be diverted to the windscreen.

There is no doubt that this 18½-cwt.

60 b.h.p. saloon offers an unusual combination of qualities not obtainable elsewhere at a price of approximately £815. The standard equipment, which includes heater, screen washers and reversing light, and the excellent brakes, add to the comfort and safety with which the rapid acceleration and cruising speeds up to 80 m.p.h. can be enjoyed.

© Temple Press Limited, 1961.

---

## Specification

**Engine**

| | |
|---|---|
| Cylinders | 4 |
| Bore | 73.025 mm. |
| Stroke | 88.9 mm. |
| Cubic capacity | 1,489 c.c. |
| Piston area | 26.0 sq. in. |
| Valves | Overhead (pushrods) |
| Compression ratio | 8.3/1 |
| Carburetters | 2 S.U. (type H. 4) |
| Fuel pump | S.U. electric |
| Ignition timing control | Centrifugal and vacuum |
| Oil filter | Tecalemit or Purolator full flow |
| Max. power (gross) | 66.5 b.h.p. at 5,200 r.p.m. |
| | (60 b.h.p. net at 4,800 r.p.m.) |
| Piston speed at max. b.h.p. | 3,030 ft./min. |

**Transmission**

| | |
|---|---|
| Clutch | Borg and Beck 8 in. s.d.p. |
| Top gear (s/m) 3.73; 3rd gear (s/m) 5.12; 2nd gear (s/m) 8.25; 1st gear 13.56; Reverse 17.73. | |
| Propeller shaft | Hardy Spicer, open |
| Final drive | Hypoid bevel |
| Top gear m.p.h. at 1,000 r.p.m. | 18.6 |
| Top gear m.p.h. at 1,000 ft./min. piston speed | 31.8. |

**Chassis**

| | |
|---|---|
| Brakes | Girling hydraulic (2 l.s. front) |
| Brake diameters | Front 9 in., rear 8 in. |
| Friction area | 124 sq. in. total lining area |
| Suspension: | |
| Front: Independent by transverse wishbones and torsion bars. | |
| Rear: Live axle and semi-elliptic springs. | |
| Shock Absorbers: | |
| Front and rear: Armstrong lever type. | |
| Steering gear | Rack and pinion |
| Tyres | 5.60 — 14 Dunlop tubeless |

## Coachwork and Equipment

| | |
|---|---|
| Starting handle | Yes |
| Battery mounting. In engine compartment on l.h. side of seuttle. | |
| Jack | Bipod pillar type |
| Jacking points One each side of car (external) | |
| Standard Tool kit: Plug spanner, tommy bar, hub-plate remover, combined wheel brace and starting handle, jack, tool bag. | |
| Exterior lights: 2 headlamps, 2 sidelamps, 2 stop/tail lamps, number plate/reversing lamp. | |
| Number of electrical fuses | Two |
| Direction indicators | Self-cancelling amber flashers |
| Windscreen wipers | Twin blade, self-parking Lucas |
| Windscreen washers | Trico, vacuum operated |
| Sun visors | Two |
| Instruments: Speedometer (with decimal trip recorder), rev. counter, oil pressure gauge, water temp. gauge, fuel contents gauge. | |
| Warning lights: Generator, main beam and direction indicators. | |
| Locks: with ignition key. Front door and luggage boot | |
| with other keys. | None. |
| Glove lockers | One in facia with lid |
| Map pockets | None |
| Parcel shelves: Full width shelf below facia and shelf behind rear seat. | |
| Ashtrays: One in each front door and one above propeller shaft. | |
| Cigar lighters | None |
| Interior lights: On door pillar with courtesy switches on front doors. | |
| Interior heater: Smiths 3½ kW. fresh air heater (standard). | |
| Car radio | Radiomobile (optional extra) |
| Extras available | Radio |
| Upholstery material: Leather and leathercloth (Duotone) | |
| Floor covering | Carpets |
| Exterior colours standardized | 6 |
| Alternative body styles | None |

## Maintenance

| | |
|---|---|
| Sump | 7½ pints, S.A.E. 30 (Summer) |
| | S.A.E. 20 W (Winter) |
| Gearbox | 4½ pints, S.A.E 30 |
| Rear Axle | 1½ pints, S.A.E. 90 |
| Steering gear lubricant | S.A.E. 90 |
| Cooling system capacity | 13 pints (2 drain taps) |
| Chassis lubrication: By grease gun every 1,000 miles to 9 points, and every 12,000 miles to 1 point. | |
| Ignition timing | 6° b.t.d.c. |
| Contact-breaker gap | .014 to .016 in. |
| Sparking plug type | Champion N.5 |
| Sparking plug gap | .024 to .026 in. |
| Valve timing: | |
| Inlet opens at t.d.c. and closes 50° a.b.d.c. | |
| Exhaust opens 35° b.b.d.c. and closes 15 a.t.d.c. | |
| Tappet clearances (Hot): | Inlet .015 in. |
| | Exhaust .015 in. |
| Front wheel toe-in | Nil |
| Camber Angle | ½° |
| Castor angle | 3° |
| Steering swivel pin inclination | 9° |
| Tyre pressures: Front 24 lb. | Rear 24 lb. |
| Brake fluid | Girling |
| Battery type and capacity: Lucas 12v., 58 amp. hr. | |

c7

# The Riley 4/72 (with Automatic Transmission)

## TRUE TO FORM

EPICYCLIC gearing and an automatic clutch were first offered to Riley car buyers in September 1933, so the 1962-model Riley which we have been testing recently has a long tradition behind its optional fully-automatic transmission. Whereas the original "Preselectagear" Rileys had manual gear selection without any form of automatic control, however, this latest model can be left to change its own gears automatically yet provides the driver with a large measure of manual control over gear selection should he so desire. Although the twin-camshaft engine which was a Riley speciality between October 1926 and August 1957, and which in various forms was conspicuous in racing, is now extinct, the latest 4/72—a sturdy and rather heavy saloon—obtains fairly brisk performance from an efficient twin-carburetter engine, and the car is truer than some people realize to the pattern set by most of its predecessors.

Enlarged to 1,622 c.c. as compared with the 1,489 c.c. of a similar-looking 4/68 model which it replaces, this Riley 4/72 is a very-well-equipped saloon with comfortable room for up to five people and a considerable volume of luggage. A top speed comfortably in excess of 80 m.p.h. is not spectacular, synchromesh-geared cars probably being faster by about 3 m.p.h., but the effortlessness of a fully-automatic transmission makes this a more lively car in traffic than such figures as rest-to-60 m.p.h. acceleration in 20.6 sec. might suggest—an expert doing his utmost with an old-style gear lever might pull about 2 sec. off this time, but on many occasions in traffic would almost certainly let the two-pedal car get away from him.

### In Brief

Price (including automatic trans-
mission as tested) £813 plus purchase
tax £373 17s. 3d. equals £1,186 17s. 3d.
Price with synchromesh gearbox (in-
cluding purchase tax) £1,087 13s. 11d.
Capacity ... ... ... 1,622 c.c.
Unladen kerb weight ... 22¼ cwt.
Acceleration:
20-40 m.p.h. in kick-down range
         5.5 sec.
0-50 m.p.h. through gears 13.5 sec.
Maximum top-gear gradient
         approx. 1 in 9.3
Maximum speed ... ... 81.3 m.p.h.
"Maximile" speed ... 79.1 m.p.h.
Touring fuel consumption 26.5 m.p.g.
Gearing: 16.6 m.p.h. in top gear at
1,000 r.p.m.; 28.4 m.p.h. at 1,000 ft./
min. piston speed.

## A La Carte

OUR Riley 4/72 test model was, it must be emphasized, *fully* automatic in respect of its transmission. It was quite normal to "take the Table d'Hôte menu" and leave gear selection entirely to the automatic devices, which made a very good job of picking gears to suit most speeds and throttle openings. This Riley is, however, the costliest of five B.M.C. cars which use substantially the same body shell, and one of the most powerful of the quintet, so we felt that selecting gears "à la carte" with

the manual over-ride control was an appropriate driving technique on many occasions.

Apart from the usual selector lever positions, which provide reverse gear, neutral, and a parking lock setting, this transmission has two selector positions marked "D" and "L". Fully automatic selection of the three forward gears in accordance with speed and load takes place when the lever is put at "D" for Drive, and in the lower half of the speed range in each gear the hydraulic torque converter provides extra tractive effort. Once top gear has engaged, it remains in use until the car speed drops appreciably below 20 m.p.h. or until extra "kick down" pressure is applied to the accelerator pedal—this kick-down action (it requires considerable foot pressure) produces 2nd gear at any speed below about 45 m.p.h., and 1st gear below about 15 m.p.h.

Moving the selector lever from "D" (for

Drive) to "L" (for Low) is a natural enough action, the sturdy lever which moves over a quadrant behind the steering wheel having to be eased out (to let it pass a "gate" which guards against accidental movement into any position save "D" and Neutral) and moved down one notch to the end of its quadrant. There is no over-ride to make this control ineffective if a downward gear-shift would over-rev. the engine, the driver being trusted not to change down at speeds above about 60 m.p.h. If the car is in top gear when the lever is moved from "D" to "L" middle gear will engage, promptly but with very reasonable smoothness even if the throttle be completely closed at the time. If the car is in 2nd or 1st gear when the change from "D" to "L" is made, nothing happens immediately but upward changes of gear are completely prevented.

During acceleration from rest there is little point in playing with the selector lever, for although automatic upward changes occur at just under 5,000 r.p.m. during

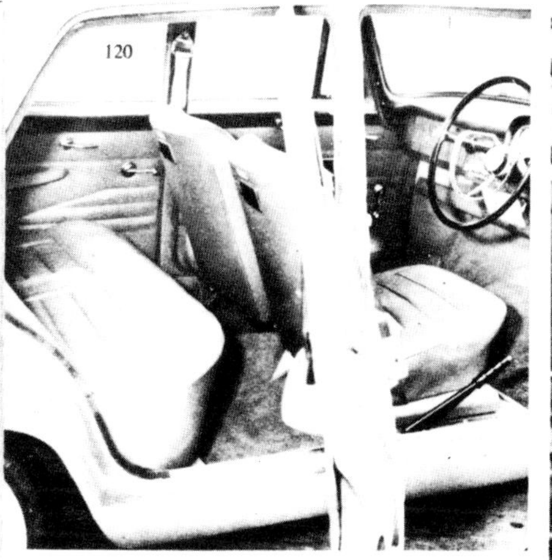

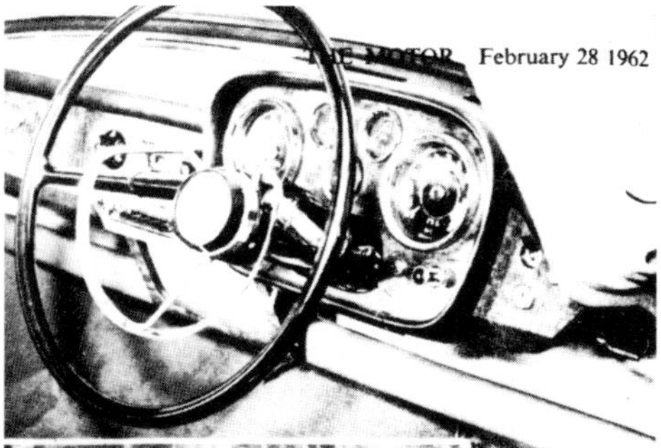

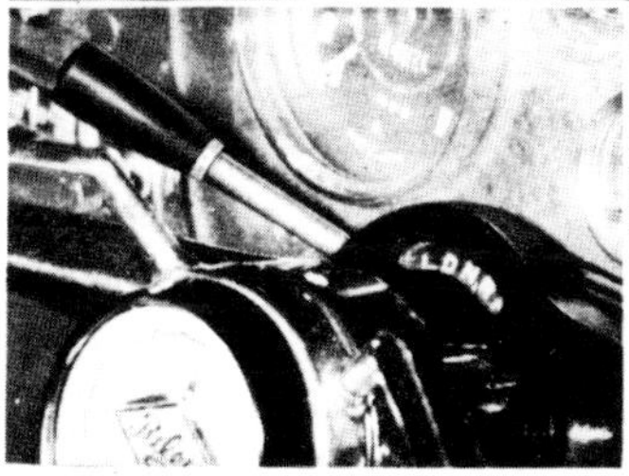

**Polished wood on the doors and facia, a carpeted floor and leather upholstery make this Riley luxurious in the traditional British manner. The instrument panel is neat and readable. *Inset:* The stubby selector lever for the fully automatic transmission.**

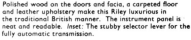

## The Riley 4/72

full-throttle driving, using manual selection to delay changes until 5,500 r.p.m. only reduces the rest-to-60 m.p.h. time by 1.3 sec., at the cost of considerable extra fuss and strain. If traffic is liable to enforce the sort of hesitation which would invite the automatic devices to make a premature upward gearchange however, one can start in "L", move the lever to "D" momentarily when ready to let middle gear engage and then almost immediately back to the "L" position which will hold middle gear in use, and finally move the lever to "D" again (leaving it there) when the time comes for letting top gear engage.

More frequently by far, one uses the selector lever to engage middle gear whilst slowing down before a corner or a traffic check, to gain engine braking or to have the best accelerating gear in use sooner than by a "kick down" change. Keen drivers will use this smooth clutchless change, into a ratio which at moderately high road speeds gives 45% more engine r.p.m. than would top gear, with considerable frequency. On hills climbed at moderate speeds, selecting middle gear manually is often slightly preferable to letting the hydraulic torque converter provide the requisite extra engine r.p.m. and tractive effort automatically.

A full set of instruments is provided on this Riley, with clearly calibrated circular black dials. An engine r.p.m. indicator is even more interesting on a car with fully-automatic transmission than it would be in conjunction with the alternative four-speed synchromesh gearbox.

## On and Off Duty

WE have thought fit to emphasize in this test report that the easy traffic driving which any automatic transmission provides, is, in this instance, fully compatible with keen and skilful driving. The 20-25% extra cost of the Riley 4/72 in

## Specification

**Engine**

| | |
|---|---|
| Cylinders | Four |
| Bore | 76.2 mm. |
| Stroke | 88.9 mm. |
| Cubic capacity | 1,622 c.c. |
| Piston area | 28.3 sq. in. |
| Valves | o.h.v. (pushrods) |
| Compression ratio | 8.3/1 |
| Carburetter | Two S.U. type H.D.4 |
| Fuel pump | S.U. electrical |
| Ignition timing control | Centrifugal and vacuum |
| Oil filter | Full flow |
| Max. power (net) | 68 b.h.p. (71 b.h.p. gross) |
| at | 5,000 r.p.m. |
| Piston speed at max. b.h.p. | 2,910 ft./min. |

**Transmission**

(Borg-Warner automatic)

Clutch: Hydraulic torque converter with 2:1 maximum ratio.

| | |
|---|---|
| Top gear | 4.3 |
| 2nd gear | 6.23 |
| 1st gear | 10.28 |
| Reverse | 8.99 |
| Propeller shaft | Single-piece open |
| Final drive | Hypoid bevel |
| Top gear m.p.h. at 1,000 r.p.m. | 16.6 |
| Top gear m.p.h. at 1,000 ft./min. piston speed | 28.4 |

**Chassis**

Brakes ... Girling hydraulic drum type (two l.s. at front)

Brake dimensions ... 9 in. dia.; widths 2¼ in. at front and 1¾ in. at rear

Friction areas: 146.6 sq. in. of lining area working on 240 sq. in. rubbed area of drums.

Suspension:
Front: Independent by transverse wishbones, coil springs and anti-roll torsion bar.
Rear: Rigid axle, half-elliptic leaf springs and anti-roll torsion bar.

Shock absorbers: Armstrong lever-arm hydraulic (front units form upper wishbone pivots).

Steering gear ... Cam Gears cam-and-peg type

Tyres ... Dunlop 5.90—14

## Coachwork and Equipment

Starting handle ... Yes

Battery mounting ... To right of engine

Jack ... Bevel-geared bipod type

Jacking points ... One external socket under each side of body

Standard tool kit: Jack, wheelbrace, hub cap lever, starting handle, spark-plug spanner and tommy bar, grease gun.

Exterior lights: Two headlamps, 2 sidelamps, 2 stop/tail lamps, rear number-plate lamp, reversing lamp.

Number of electrical fuses ... Two

Direction indicators ... Amber flashers, self-cancelling

Windscreen wipers ... Self-parking electrical twin-blade

Windscreen washers ... Trico suction-operated

Sun visors ... Two, hinge mounted

Instruments: Speedometer with total and decimal trip distance recorders, r.p.m. indicator, clock, coolant thermometer, oil pressure gauge, ammeter, fuel contents gauge.

Warning lights: Dynamo charge, headlamp main beam, turn indicators.

Locks:
With ignition key: Ignition/starter switch, either front door, petrol filler cap.
With other keys: Luggage boot and glove box.

Glove lockers ... One on facia, with lockable lid

Map pockets ... None

Parcel shelves ... Under each side of facia and behind rear seat

Ashtrays ... Two in front doors and 2 behind front seats

Cigar lighters ... None

Interior lights: Two on centre body pillars, with courtesy switches on doors.

Interior heater ... Fresh-air type, with screen de-misters

Car radio ... Optional extra, H.M.V. type 600T or 620T

Extras available: Automatic transmission, radio, rimbellishers or wheel discs.

Upholstery material: Leather on wearing surfaces, matching leathercloth elsewhere.

Floor covering ... Pile carpets

Exterior colours standardized: Six single colours (4 duotone combinations at extra cost).

Alternative body styles ... None

## Maintenance

Sump (including filter): 7½ pints, S.A.E. 30 above freezing or S.A.E. 20 below freezing.

Synchromesh gearbox: 4½ pints, S.A.E. 30 oil; Fully automatic transmission to be topped-up every 3,000 miles with Shell S-6051 or Regent 4571 Texamatic.

Rear axle ... 2½ pints, S.A.E. 90 hypoid oil

Steering-gear lubricant ... S.A.E. 90 hypoid oil

Cooling system capacity ... 9½ pints (2 drain taps)

Chassis lubrication ... By grease gun every 1,000 miles to 9 points

Ignition timing ... 4° before t.d.c. static

Contact-breaker gap ... 0.014-0.016 in.

Sparking-plug type ... Champion N5

Sparking-plug gap ... 0.024-0.026 in.

Valve timing: Inlet opens at t.d.c. and closes 50° after b.d.c.; exhaust opens 35° before b.d.c. and closes 15° after t.d.c.

Tappet clearances (cold):
Inlet and exhaust ... 0.015 in.

Front wheel toe-in ... 1/16-1/8 in.

Camber angle ... ¾-1°

Castor angle ... 1½°

Steering swivel-pin inclination ... 6½°

Tyre pressures:
Front ... 23 lb.
Rear ... 25 lb.

Brake fluid ... Girling heavy-duty (S.A.E. Spec. 70-R-3)

Battery type and capacity ... Lucas BT9A, 12 volt 58 amp. hr.

THE MOTOR   February 28 1962                                                                121

comparison with a similarly roomy Austin A60 will only be paid by somebody keen enough on motoring to want the extra power, fuller equipment or better furnishing. Possibly it requires mentioning that the Riley is just as roomy as the slower cars of similar outline, and at any given speed it is just as economical of fuel although full use of twin-carburetter performance will inevitably raise running costs slightly. We sampled fuels cheaper than the premium grades which most motorists buy, and are satisfied that the 4/72 Riley owner is unlikely to be annoyed by pinking when touring in countries where fuel is below premium quality.

As a business car, this model has a good appearance and travels briskly. As a family model, it has individual front seats for two people, and three adults are not unreasonably crowded together in the rear compartment where wheel arches do little

## Road Manners

SUSPENSION must be a compromise, and on this car the compromise is acceptable. Anti-roll bars at both ends of the chassis prevent the body leaning over very much on corners, but some rattles on rough going suggest that they put a strain on the integral body's torsional rigidity. The ride seems, on the whole, to be more satisfactory at open road speeds than it is during slower driving.

Tested with the car at rest, the steering mechanism produces visible movement of the front wheels in response to even the smallest movement of the steering wheel, yet on the road it does not feel especially positive. Flexibility, as distinct from backlash, is made apparent by the need to steer against powerful self-centring action, and before the limit of adhesion is approached

*Below left:* A familiar B.M.C. shape despite the wider track. Heavily chromed bumpers sweep round to the wheel arches protecting the corners of the body.

*Below right:* The boot, which has a low floor for easy loading, will swallow large and awkwardly shaped loads.

*Bottom:* Twin S.U. carburetters distinguish the Riley "B" series engine from less powerful versions in the B.M.C. range.

more than round off the ends of the cushion.

Useful and acceptable though it is, we felt that this car could readily have been improved in detail. The front seats provide very slight lateral support, but their backrest shaping is far from ideal and the adjustment range was not sufficient for all drivers over 6 ft., although some were quite comfortable. Roominess in the rear compartment is perfectly satisfactory, and there are side armrests plus a folding central armrest, but once again the seat shaping leaves something to be desired. Our test model had optional B.M.C. safety harness for the front seats, but mountings angled out from central body pillars very close to the passengers' heads seem themselves to constitute unacceptably dangerous projections. Facia panel layout can be praised for legibility of instruments and for keeping the lighting switch distinct from other controls, though to place the wiper switch and the washer control on opposite sides of the steering wheel seems ergonomically bad.

During our test, a safety switch on the gearbox which is intended to prevent the starter being used when the car is in gear gave some trouble, rendering the starter inoperative until two wires behind the ignition switch were coupled as a get-you-home measure. Two things which this unlucky fault (quickly cured once a replacement switch was obtained) brought into prominence were, that this car has a starting handle, and that this design unlike some automatic transmissions also permits the engine to be started by towing at about 20 m.p.h. Although this was never necessary, the car proved to be a reluctant starter after frosty nights in the open, with a low cranking speed which may have been caused by gearbox drag.

the driver is using quite appreciable effort at quite large steering angles. As cornering speeds rise the car's understeer diminishes, but there are no sudden or vicious changes of behaviour. In normal driving, however, one wonders whether quite so much effort and concentration should be required by a car of this size and speed.

So rapidly have disc brakes become popular that one looks with caution at drum brakes on this sort of car, but in fact such caution seems totally unnecessary. These brakes are not self-adjusting for wear, but repeated stops from speeds above 60 m.p.h. do not seem to worry them, and when carrying weight in the rear compartment retardations better than the 0.89 g. recorded with our standard two-and-equipment load are attainable. Pedal pressures are satisfactory rather than especially light, and the pull-up handbrake copes easily with 1-in-4 slopes and will even hold the car on 1-in-3.

At moderate speeds this is not an especially quiet car, and in relation to its price it must be described as fussy at 50 m.p.h. or so. This effect is less evident during fast driving, and although at maximum speed the r.p.m. needle is near the start of an amber sector on the tachometer (from 5,000 to 5,500, where a red sector starts) there is no audible reason for not treating this as a motorway cruising speed. Unusually and rather conveniently, wind noise (never very pronounced) seems

to be slightly less when the ventilator panels are hinged open. When they are closed, some audible air leaks occur assisting a controllable fresh-air heater of no more than moderate potency in its task of keeping passengers comfortable.

# The **Motor** Road Test No. 8/62

**Make:** Riley     **Type:** 4/72 (With automatic transmission)

**Makers:** Riley Motor Co., Ltd., Abingdon on Thames, Oxford.

## Test Data

*World copyright reserved ; no unauthorized reproduction in whole or in part.*

**CONDITIONS:** *Weather : Fine and dry with 20 m.p.h. wind. (Temperature 40°-45°F., Barometer 29.7-29.8 in. Hg.) Surface : Dry tarred macadam and concrete. Fuel : Premium-grade pump petrol (Approx. 97 octane rating by Research Method)*

### INSTRUMENTS

| | |
|---|---|
| Speedometer at 30 m.p.h. | 5% fast |
| Speedometer at 60 m.p.h. | 3% fast |
| Speedometer at 80 m.p.h. | 4% fast |
| Distance recorder | 1% fast |

### WEIGHT

| | |
|---|---|
| Kerb weight (unladen, but with oil coolant and fuel for approx. 50 miles) | 22¼ cwt. |
| Front, rear distribution of kerb weight | 56, 44 |
| Weight laden as tested | 26 cwt. |

### MAXIMUM SPEEDS

| | |
|---|---|
| Mean lap speed around banked circuit | 81.3 m.p.h. |
| Best one-way ¼-mile time equals | 85.7 m.p.h. |

**"Maximile" Speed.** (Timed quarter mile after one mile accelerating from rest.)

| | |
|---|---|
| Mean of opposite runs | 79.1 m.p.h. |
| Best one-way time equals | 82.6 m.p.h. |

**Speed in gears** (automatic upward changes at full throttle)

| | |
|---|---|
| Max. speed in 2nd gear | 52 m.p.h. |
| Max. speed in 1st gear | 34 m.p.h. |

### FUEL CONSUMPTION

38.5 m.p.g. at constant 30 m.p.h. on level.
34.5 m.p.g. at constant 40 m.p.h. on level.
30.5 m.p.g. at constant 50 m.p.h. on level.
26.0 m.p.g. at constant 60 m.p.h. on level.
22.5 m.p.g. at constant 70 m.p.h. on level.
18.5 m.p.g. at constant 80 m.p.h. on level.

**Overall Fuel Consumption** for 1,578 miles, 66.9 gallons, equals 23.6 m.p.g. (11.97 litres/100 km.)

**Touring Fuel Consumption** (m.p.g. at steady speed midway between 30 m.p.h. and maximum, less 5% allowance for acceleration) .. 26.5 m.p.g.

Fuel tank capacity (maker's figure) .. 10 gallons.

### STEERING

Turning circle between kerbs:

| | |
|---|---|
| Left | 35½ ft. |
| Right | 34½ ft. |
| Turns of steering wheel from lock to lock, 3. | |

### BRAKES from 30 m.p.h.

0.89 g retardation (equivalent to 33⅓ ft. stopping distance) with 85 lb. pedal pressure.
0.81 g retardation (equivalent to 37 ft. stopping distance) with 75 lb. pedal pressure.
0.51 g retardation (equivalent to 59 ft. stopping distance) with 50 lb. pedal pressure.
0.29 g retardation (equivalent to 104 ft. stopping distance) with 25 lb. pedal pressure.

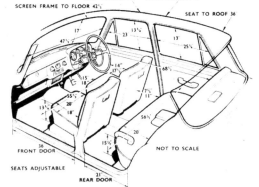

OVERALL WIDTH 5'- 3½"

TRACK — FRONT 4 - 2½"
     REAR 4 - 3½"

4 - 10¼" UNLADEN

18"    12½"    GROUND CLEARANCE 6½"    20½"   15

SCALE 1:50    8 - 4¼"    RILEY 4/72 AUTOMATIC

14 - 10¾"

SCREEN FRAME TO FLOOR 42½"    SEAT TO ROOF 41"   FLOOR TO ROOF 47"    SEAT TO ROOF 36

FRONT DOOR 36    REAR DOOR 21    SEATS ADJUSTABLE 22½

NOT TO SCALE

### ACCELERATION TIMES from standstill

| | With automatic changes | Using manual changes of gear at 5,500 r.p.m. |
|---|---|---|
| 0-30 m.p.h. | 5.6 sec. | 5.6 sec. |
| 0-40 m.p.h. | 8.8 sec. | 8.8 sec. |
| 0-50 m.p.h. | 13.5 sec. | 13.2 sec. |
| 0-60 m.p.h. | 20.6 sec. | 19.3 sec. |
| 0-70 m.p.h. | 31.4 sec. | 30.6 sec. |
| Standing quarter mile | 22.1 sec. | not recorded |

### ACCELERATION TIMES On Upper Ratios

| | "Kick down" range | Top gear |
|---|---|---|
| 0-20 m.p.h. | 3.3 sec. | |
| 10-30 m.p.h. | 4.1 sec. | |
| 20-40 m.p.h. | 5.5 sec. | 9.6 sec |
| 30-50 m.p.h. | 7.9 sec. | 12.1 sec |
| 40-60 m.p.h. | 11.8 sec. | 16.8 sec |
| 50-70 m.p.h. | 17.9 sec. | 20.2 sec |

### HILL CLIMBING at sustained steady speeds

Max. gradient on top gear approx. 1 in 9.3 (Tapley 240 lb. ton.)

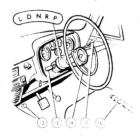

L D N R P

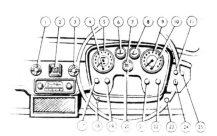

1. Temperature control. 2. Clock. 3. Heater-air control. 4. High beam warning light. 5. Speedometer. 6. Ammeter. 7. Oil pressure gauge. 8. Fuel gauge. 9. Rev. counter. 10. Ignition warning light. 11. Main light switch. 12. Dip switch. 13. Gear lever. 14. Horn ring. 15. Direction indicator and warning light control. 16. Handbrake. 17. Windscreen wipers control. 18. Trip reset. 19. Heater-fan control. 20. Water temperature gauge. 21. Panel light switch. 22. Choke. 23. Bonnet release. 24. Ignition. 25. Screen washer button.

# RILEY ELF Mk 2

RILEYS of old combined a sporting performance with luxury and elegance a cut above the average. The modern Elf does the same—the average in this case being the B.M.C. Mini on which it is based. Certainly the latest version, the Mark 2, with bigger 998 c.c. engine giving 4 b.h.p. extra over the former 848 c.c. unit and a much improved torque range, has that zest in performance so often associated with Rileys in the past. The extra power becomes apparent, not so much by an increased maximum speed (which is improved by about 4 m.p.h.) but in greater flexibility, making the Elf an excellent top and third gear small car demanding less frequent resort to the gear lever than the earlier model.

At £127 more than the basic Morris or Austin Mini, the Riley is more fully equipped, with heater, screen washers, leather-faced seats, polished wood facia, extended luggage boot, better trimming and carpeting, duotone finish and wheel embellishers. Whether these items, the performance and the prestige of owning a Riley are worth the extra outlay in these days of hardening economy, depends on your approach to motoring; if you want Mini virtues coupled with superior comfort, trim, equipment and finish, you should consider the Elf seriously.

## More power, less effort

WHATEVER the radiator, nameplate and fittings, the Riley Elf remains a Mini, with all that means in joyful motoring in today's conditions. It has the same upright driving position, the same wide doors and easy entry, small pedals, ample leg space in front, and large window area. Instead of the capacious open parcel shelf below the central instrument panel, however, there is a polished wood facia with lidded glove boxes to left and right, while the seating, trim and carpeting are more luxurious.

The changes, with the separate extended luggage boot, sound insulation and other de luxe fitments, add about ¾ cwt. to the car's weight and made themselves felt in the performance of the Mk. 1 Elf. The larger engine of the Mk. 2 cancels out this crticism, bringing a welcome improvement in acceleration and maximum speed. An enlarged bore (from 63 to 64.58 mm. as on the Morris 1100) and stroke (from 68.26 to 76.2 mm. by using a new crankshaft) produce 38 b.h.p. at 5,250 r.p.m. instead of

34 at 5,500 and an 18 per cent increase in maximum torque at 200 r.p.m. less engine speed—in short, more power with extra flexibility.

With this unit, and using The Motor's road test of the Mk. 1 Elf's counterpart, the Wolseley Hornet Mk. 1, as a yardstick, the 0 to 30 m.p.h. figures are improved from 5.9 to 5.6 secs., 0 to 40 m.p.h. from 10.6 to 9.4 secs., and 0 to 50 m.p.h. from 16.9 to 15.2 secs. The maximum speed is increased from 71.8 to 75.7 m.p.h., but the most noticeable advantage lies in the improved flexibility of the car; one can come down to speeds well below 30 m.p.h. in top gear, yet retain the ability to pass slower cars without the need for changing down.

Acceleration in top gear from 10 to 30 m.p.h. on the Hornet took 12.9 secs., whereas the Mk. 2 Elf needs 9.8 secs., and 20 to 40 m.p.h. in top took 14 secs. by the Hornet and 9.3 secs. by the Elf. The third gear performance is equally good. Fuel consumption naturally proved higher, at 35.75 m.p.g. to 39.7 m.p.g. by the Hornet 1 in a test of over 1,400 miles; the Mk. 2 Elf's touring consumption of 39.33 m.p.g. is some 4½ m.p.g. higher than before.

## Mini cornering magic

THE unique ADO 15 layout—transverse engine and gearbox, front-wheel drive, all-independent rubber cone suspension and rack and pinion steering—combines to give cornering

---

### In Brief

| | |
|---|---|
| Price £475 plus purchase tax £99 10s. 5d. equals £574 10s. 5d. | |
| Capacity ..  ..  ..  ..  .. | 998 c.c. |
| Unladen kerb weight  ..  ..  .. | 12¼ cwt. |
| Acceleration: | |
| 20-40 m.p.h. in top gear  ..  .. | 9.3 sec. |
| 0-50 m.p.h. through gears  ..  .. | 15.2 sec. |
| Maximum top gear gradient  ..  .. | 1 in 11 |
| Maximum speed  ..  ..  ..  .. | 75.7 m.p.h. |
| Overall fuel consumption ..  ..  .. | 35¾ m.p.g. |
| Touring fuel consumption  ..  .. | 39.3 m.p.g. |
| Gearing: 14.85 m.p.h. in top gear at 1,000 r.p.m. | |

## Riley Elf

The flat floor makes entry to the two-door Riley Elf an easy matter, and gives more legroom at front and rear. The seats are trimmed in leather and leathercloth.

powers which have drawn forth many eulogies in print. A marked understeerer, the car can be flung into corners at seemingly excessive speeds, yet with the throttle firmly open it would maintain an unflinching line. Lifting-off in the corner not only slows the car but also reduces the understeer and tightens the radius without instability, a fortunate combination if a corner has been entered too fast, and the car's steering action is so pleasingly light, and so predictable at all times and in all weathers, that the Elf, like its brother Minis, rates amongst the safest and easiest of cars to drive in average give-and-take conditions.

### The ride

FIRM, well-damped suspension means very little body roll, but the ride on rough roads is marred by the periodic bouncing motion peculiar to Minis. Despite the use of much sound-deadening material on various parts of the body shell, including the wheel arches, there remains a good deal of mechanical buzz inside the Elf, coupled with considerable road rumble. The Dunlop C41 tyres can be heard at work, and in wet weather change to a shrill note.

The delights of that willing engine and the excellent road-holding are offset by a mediocre gearchange. The central lever is too whippy for precise changing, and placed slightly too forward for comfortable reach by a driver of average height, especially when wearing the diagonal safety belt, while the change forward in the gate from second to third tires the wrist when driving in heavy traffic. In compensation, the ratios are excellently chosen, and the change from third to top, with abundant power still available, is excellent. But the indirect gears on the test car were noisy, while as usual with B.M.C. gearboxes, immediate and silent engagement of bottom gear with the car at rest meant "nursing" it in through second. Lady drivers may find the clutch pressure rather heavy. Starting from cold required little choke, and the engine quickly warmed to its work. Idling on the test car was rather rough when the engine was thoroughly warm, with a tendency to stall.

The stopping powers of the Elf have been brought up to its Mk. 2 performance. The brakes are drums all round, but the lining area has been increased at the front by using broader

shoes; changes have also been made to the master cylinder and the linings. Braking is more efficient, but considerable pedal pressure is still required for sudden stops, while some fade is apparent under hard braking from high speed. The handbrake, located between the two front seats, is sensibly strong and effective, and held the car on a 1 in 3 gradient.

Following the usual Mini layout, the instruments are set centrally; they comprise a 90 m.p.h. speedometer (embodying mileage recorder, fuel gauge, and ignition/high beam warning lights), a temperature gauge, with a facia light switch below the speedometer. All are set in the polished wood facia, which will appeal to those who like the traditional treatment, although the veneer of the glove box lids clashed with that of the facia, while the practical and commodious open parcel shelves are much missed. Large companion boxes on the doors are some com-

Looking the same as the old 848 c.c. transverse-mounted unit, the Mk. 2 Elf engine (*below*) has a bore and stroke of 64.58 mm. × 76.2 mm. (998 c.c.) and adds considerably to the liveliness of the car.

pensation, being invaluable for stowing books, maps and shopping, while there are similar boxes at the rear, flanking the seat. There is no crash padding of any kind in the front, the black trimming on the upper and lower edges of the wood facia being uncompromisingly hard.

Below the facia, in a row, are the pull-out heater knob, wiper switch, central ignition-starter switch, the simple, sensible light switch (up for off, down for side lights and fully down for headlights) and the choke control. Below these is the screen washer button, and the fresh air heater, a most effective device, again with simple one-lever control, in conjunction with a booster for warm or cold air. All these controls are rather too far from the driver to be reached comfortably, especially if the safety belt is worn.

The instruments on a car of this class and price might well have included a hand-set mileage trip recorder, while surprisingly the screen wipers are non self-parking. Those on the test car did not work at first, owing to the slackening of a vital nut holding the drive-cable in place. The steering column is clear of controls save on the right where the self-cancelling direction indicator stalk is located, with green telltale light at the tip. There is an interior bonnet lock handle below the dash. The 15¾ in. steering wheel with central horn push has only two spokes, but the driver's left hand on the rim obstructs his view of the speedometer. Pedals are small and widely spaced, but heel-and-toe use of brake and accelerator is just possible. A foot headlight dipper is located left of the clutch pedal.

## Drawing room treatment

COMFORTABLE foam rubber seats are upholstered with leather cloth faced with real leather. The front seats are still very upright but have generous fore and aft adjustment, and tilt well forward for access to the rear seats in this two-door saloon. The general standard of trimming is pleasing, with kick

plates on the doors, good carpets, sun visors and safety belt anchorages set in the floor as standard. Driving with one of the sliding front windows open produces an unpleasant flutter to the ears, which can be alleviated by opening the hinged rear windows slightly; these are also useful for draughtless ventilation. The standard Mini's simple wire-pull door handles are replaced by small plated levers, less easy to work and rather close to the back of the doors, so that one can trap the fingers between them.

Three can be taken at a pinch in the rear seat, which is quite comfortable unless those at the front are pushed back when legroom hardly exists; a tall passenger can easily touch the roof with his head. A switch-operated rooflight is set above the nearside door. All round visibility is good, save for taller drivers whose eye level is close to the roof.

The Elf has a dummy radiator grille similar to that of the Riley 1.5; it is integral with the hinged bonnet, which makes this component rather heavy to open, and also restricts access to the engine. The tail, like that of the Hornet, is distinguished by the projecting luggage boot, which diminishes the Mini's pertness of appearance, but is extremely useful for keeping larger luggage under cover. It has a carpeted interior, and is just over 2 feet deep and 3 feet wide. There is further space for flatter articles in another compartment under the rear seat, and on the parcel shelf behind the rear seat squab. The spare wheel and battery are carried beneath the boot floor, where they discourage attention.

Wrap-round chromed bumpers with over-riders, two-tone finish and bright-plated wheel embellishers fortify the de luxe character which is the essence of the Riley Elf. It is a pleasant and well-furnished Mini variant for the owner who doesn't mind paying over £100 more for trimmings, and who now gets the added urge of the bigger engine for his money.

Out of sight below the boot floor (*below left*) are the spare wheel and the battery. The separate boot adds 2½ cubic feet to the luggage carrying capacity. With the lid closed (*right*) the Elf has a distinctive rear view, shared only by that other luxury Mini, the Wolseley Hornet.

## Coachwork and Equipment

| | | | | |
|---|---|---|---|---|
| Starting handle | None | Sun visors | 2 | Ashtrays .. 3 |
| Battery mounting | In luggage boot | Instruments: Speedometer with distance recorder, | | Cigar lighters .. None |
| Jack | Side lift | fuel gauge, oil pressure gauge, engine temperature | | Interior lights .. Roof light |
| Jacking points | Beneath sills | gauge. | | Interior heater: Fresh air, 3½kw heater/demister unit. |
| Standard tool kit: Jack, wheelbrace, tommy bar, | | Warning lights .. Main beam, flasher, ignition | | Car radio .. Radiomobile (as extra) |
| box spanner, toolbag. | | Locks: | | Extras available: Radio, whitewall or Weather- |
| Exterior lights: Headlamps, sidelamps, rear lamps, | | With ignition key: Ignition/starter. | | master tyres, seat belts. |
| number-plate lamp. | | With other keys: Door, boot. | | Upholstery material: Leather and leather cloth. |
| Number of electrical fuses | 2 | Glove lockers | 2 | Floor covering .. Pile carpet with underfelt |
| Direction indicators | Flasher | Map pockets: Companion boxes on doors, and | | Exterior colours standardized .. 7 duotones |
| Windscreen wipers | Lucas DR3a non-parking | each side of rear seat. | | Alternative body styles .. None |
| Windscreen washers | Wingard | Parcel shelves .. Behind rear squab | | |

## Maintenance

| | | | |
|---|---|---|---|
| Sump, gearbox and final drive (integral unit): | Sparking plug type | N5 | Camber angle .. 1°-3° positive |
| 8½ pints, S.A.E. 30 (32°F-10°F, SAE 20; below | Sparking plug gap .024 to .026 in. | | Castor angle .. 3° |
| 10°F, SAE 10). | Valve timing: Inlet opens 5° b.t.d.c. and closes | | Steering swivel pin inclination .. 9½° |
| Steering gear lubricant .. SAE 140 | 45° a.b.d.c.; exhaust opens 40° b.b.d.c. and | | Tyre pressures: |
| Cooling system capacity: 6½ pints (2 drain taps). | closes 10° a.t.d.c. | | Front .. 24 lb. |
| Chassis lubrication: By grease gun every 3,000 | Tappet clearances (cold): | | Rear 22 lb. |
| miles to 8 points. | Inlet .012 in. | | Brake fluid .. S.A.E. 70 R3 |
| Ignition timing .. 5° b.t.d.c. | Exhaust .012 in. | | Battery type and capacity: Lucas 12-volt, 34 |
| Contact breaker gap .. .014 to .016 in. | Front wheel toe-out ⅛ in. | | amp.-hour at 20-hour rate. |

AUTOCAR, 8 June 1967

13

# Autocar ROAD TEST
## NUMBER 2135

JOC 503E

# Riley Kestrel 1275 1,275 c.c.

**AT A GLANCE:** Familiar B.M.C. model with latest engine option. Only 3 more peak b.h.p. but much improved torque characteristics. Increased performance throughout range. Higher overall gearing gives more restful cruising, less mechanical noise and much improved fuel consumption. Ride and handling as excellent as ever.

**MANUFACTURER**
Riley Motors Ltd., Cowley, Oxford.

**PRICES**

| | | |
|---|---|---|
| Basic .. .. | .. | £692 0s 0d |
| Purchase Tax .. | .. | £160 6s 1d |
| Total (in G.B.) .. | .. | £852 6s 1d |

**EXTRAS (inc. P.T.)**

| | | |
|---|---|---|
| Seat belts (each) .. | .. | £3 0s 0d |
| Radio (and aerial) .. | .. | £34 8s 4d |

**PERFORMANCE SUMMARY**

| | | |
|---|---|---|
| Mean maximum speed | .. | 88 m.p.h. |
| Standing start ¼-mile | .. | 20·7 sec |
| 0-60 m.p.h. .. | .. | 17·3 sec |
| 30-70 m.p.h. (through gears) .. .. | .. | 20·3 sec |
| Fuel consumption .. | .. | 33·0 m.p.g. |
| Miles per tankful .. | .. | 264 |

SOON after the Morris 1100 appeared in August 1962, B.M.C. standardized its long stroke 1,098 c.c. engine in all their small-medium size cars, and in the small B.M.C. sports cars. This unit

was the final stretch possible, within the fixed cylinder bore centres, of the A-series engine introduced so long ago and gave little scope for further development. For the M.G., Riley, Princess and Wolseley 1100s, twin carburettors and expensive manifolding were added to give a power boost for more performance. Last week's announcement of a 1,275 c.c. option for the twin-carburettor 1100s is therefore important, because it includes much of the ruggedness of the Cooper S engine with the docility of a carefully developed single-carburettor tune.

By juggling with components already in production, B.M.C. engine designers have mated the 1275S cylinder block with an 1100 transmission which is unchanged except for a much higher-geared final drive. The Sprite 1275 cylinder head, with its 8.8-to-1 compression ratio and smaller valves than the Cooper S, is used with the single 1·5in. S.U. carburettor and cast manifolding already on the automatic 1100s. The 1275S cylinder block is inherently much stronger than the 1100 block which it replaces, as the cylinder spacing has been revised, and there is evidence of three years racing experience in the detail improvements. For example the pushrod-tappet cover is now cast integral with the block, replacing the original pressed steel cover. The nitrided Cooper S crankshaft is not fitted.

The result is a docile, sturdy little unit, deliberately de-tuned to 58 b.h.p. (only 3 b.h.p. more than the twin-carburettor 1100), but with signifi-

cantly higher torque throughout the range. Perhaps the 1967 horses are stronger than ever before; despite the much higher gearing, the new car was even livelier than one expected, and is now as quick as anything in its class. Not even a discreet little 1275 badge is attached to show off the latest improvement for the Jones's benefit, and the rest of the coachwork and chassis is unchanged. The 1,275 c.c. engine is optional for the M.G., Riley, Wolseley and Vanden Plas 1100s, costing an extra £24 11s 8d, the new total Kestrel price being £852 6s 1d.

The brand new 3·65 to 1 final drive ratio has raised overall gearing by 13 per cent, though internal gearbox ratios themselves remain the same; there is still no synchromesh on first gear.

### Improved Performance

Performance comparison with the Wolseley 1100 we tried in 1965, and the MG 1100 we tested way back in 1962 are interesting. On hindsight the Wolseley 1100 appears to have been a little below top form, possibly because it was new and its engine "tight" at the time of test, whereas the MG 1100 was in typical condition. Acceleration in any particular gear was almost the same as before, because the extra torque just about nullified the higher gearing. Because this higher gearing allowed us to hold intermediate gears a little longer, standing start sprints were a little livelier than before. We could stay in third for a snap change above 70 m.p.h. in the 1275 car, whereas 65 m.p.g. felt quite enough in the original 1100s. ▶

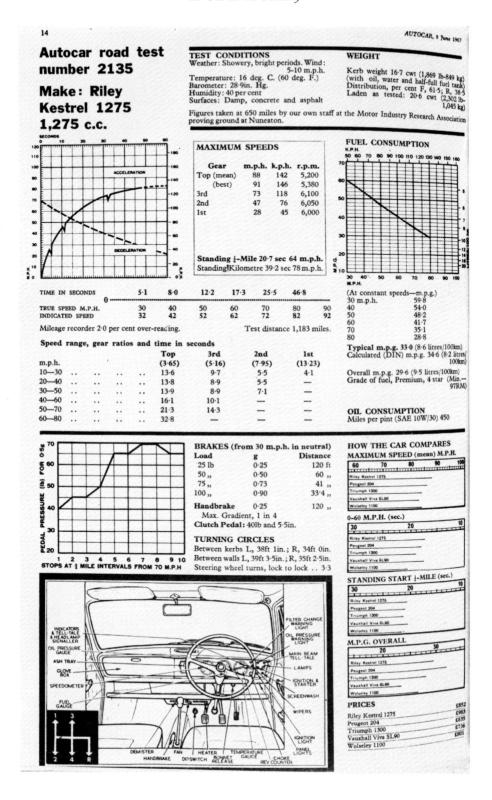

14

AUTOCAR, 8 June 1967

# Autocar road test number 2135

## Make: Riley Kestrel 1275
## 1,275 c.c.

**TEST CONDITIONS**
Weather: Showery, bright periods. Wind: 5–10 m.p.h.
Temperature: 16 deg. C. (60 deg. F.)
Barometer: 28·9in. Hg.
Humidity: 40 per cent
Surfaces: Damp, concrete and asphalt

Figures taken at 650 miles by our own staff at the Motor Industry Research Association proving ground at Nuneaton.

**WEIGHT**
Kerb weight 16·7 cwt (1,869 lb–849 kg) (with oil, water and half-full fuel tank)
Distribution, per cent F, 61·5; R, 38·5
Laden as tested: 20·6 cwt (2,302 lb–1,045 kg)

### MAXIMUM SPEEDS

| Gear | m.p.h. | k.p.h. | r.p.m. |
|---|---|---|---|
| Top (mean) | 88 | 142 | 5,200 |
| (best) | 91 | 146 | 5,380 |
| 3rd | 73 | 118 | 6,100 |
| 2nd | 47 | 76 | 6,050 |
| 1st | 28 | 45 | 6,000 |

Standing ¼-Mile 20·7 sec 64 m.p.h.
Standing Kilometre 39·2 sec 78 m.p.h.

| TIME IN SECONDS | 5·1 | 8·0 | 12·2 | 17·3 | 25·5 | 46·8 | |
|---|---|---|---|---|---|---|---|
| TRUE SPEED M.P.H. | 30 | 40 | 50 | 60 | 70 | 80 | 90 |
| INDICATED SPEED | 32 | 42 | 52 | 62 | 72 | 82 | 92 |

Mileage recorder 2·0 per cent over-reading.   Test distance 1,183 miles.

**Speed range, gear ratios and time in seconds**

| m.p.h. | Top (3·65) | 3rd (5·16) | 2nd (7·95) | 1st (13·23) |
|---|---|---|---|---|
| 10—30 | 13·6 | 9·7 | 5·5 | 4·1 |
| 20—40 | 13·8 | 8·9 | 5·5 | — |
| 30—50 | 13·9 | 8·9 | 7·1 | — |
| 40—60 | 16·1 | 10·1 | — | — |
| 50—70 | 21·3 | 14·3 | — | — |
| 60—80 | 32·8 | — | — | — |

**FUEL CONSUMPTION**

(At constant speeds—m.p.g.)
| | |
|---|---|
| 30 m.p.h. | 59·8 |
| 40 | 54·0 |
| 50 | 48·2 |
| 60 | 41·7 |
| 70 | 35·1 |
| 80 | 28·8 |

Typical m.p.g. 33·0 (8·6 litres/100km)
Calculated (DIN) m.p.g. 34·6 (8·2 litres/100km)

Overall m.p.g. 29·6 (9·5 litres/100km)
Grade of fuel, Premium, 4 star (Min.—97RM)

**OIL CONSUMPTION**
Miles per pint (SAE 10W/30) 450

**BRAKES** (from 30 m.p.h. in neutral)

| Load | g | Distance |
|---|---|---|
| 25 lb | 0·25 | 120 ft |
| 50 „ | 0·50 | 60 „ |
| 75 „ | 0·73 | 41 „ |
| 100 „ | 0·90 | 33·4 „ |

Handbrake 0·25 120 „
Max. Gradient, 1 in 4
Clutch Pedal: 40lb and 5·5in.

**TURNING CIRCLES**
Between kerbs L, 38ft 1in.; R, 34ft 0in.
Between walls L, 39ft 3·5in.; R, 35ft 2·5in.
Steering wheel turns, lock to lock .. 3·3

STOPS AT ¼ MILE INTERVALS FROM 70 M.P.H

**HOW THE CAR COMPARES**

MAXIMUM SPEED (mean) M.P.H.
Riley Kestrel 1275 / Peugeot 204 / Triumph 1300 / Vauxhall Viva SL90 / Wolseley 1100

0-60 M.P.H. (sec.)
Riley Kestrel 1275 / Peugeot 204 / Triumph 1300 / Vauxhall Viva SL90 / Wolseley 1100

STANDING START ¼-MILE (sec.)
Riley Kestrel 1275 / Peugeot 204 / Triumph 1300 / Vauxhall Viva SL90 / Wolseley 1100

M.P.G. OVERALL
Riley Kestrel 1275 / Peugeot 204 / Triumph 1300 / Vauxhall Viva SL90 / Wolseley 1100

**PRICES**

| | |
|---|---|
| Riley Kestrel 1275 | £852 |
| Peugeot 204 | £983 |
| Triumph 1300 | £835 |
| Vauxhall Viva SL90 | £736 |
| Wolseley 1100 | £801 |

INDICATORS & TELL-TALE & HEADLAMP SIGNALLER
OIL PRESSURE GAUGE
ASH TRAY
GLOVE BOX
SPEEDOMETER
FUEL GAUGE
FILTER CHANGE WARNING LIGHT
OIL PRESSURE WARNING LIGHT
MAIN BEAM TELL-TALE
LAMPS
IGNITION & STARTER
SCREENWASH
WIPERS
IGNITION LIGHT
PANEL LIGHTS
DEMISTER   FAN   HEATER   TEMPERATURE GAUGE
HANDBRAKE   DIPSWITCH   BONNET RELEASE   CHOKE   REV COUNTER

AUTOCAR, 8 June 1967 15

*Leather upholstery and a handsome, neatly laid-out wooden dashboard give the Kestrel interior a quality look*

Now an owner could either use his 1275 Kestrel (or M.G., Wolseley or Princess) as a relaxed high-geared tourer, or could stir the gear lever about for that slightly improved acceleration.

In bald figures, a standing start quarter-mile took 20·7sec, against 21·3 for the M.G. 1100, while 70 m.p.h. was reached in 25·5sec instead of a previous 28·6sec. Because we limited r.p.m. to the 6,000 red marking on the rev-counter (whereas the M.G. 1100 does not have a rev-counter), speeds in the indirect gears were no better than before; the 1275 recorded 28, 47 and 73 m.p.h., compared with the M.G. 1100s 28, 49 and 75 m.p.h.

### Reduced Noise

However, the most significant improvements were in the 1275's obvious ruggedness, and relaxed "feel," rather than in actual acceleration. The 1275 engined 1100 is now the highest geared of all the small transverse engined B.M.C. cars, and felt much more relaxed at any road speed. There was a useful reduction in the tiresome transmission whines that have afflicted Minis and 1100s for years. At a speed-limited 70 m.p.h., top gear r.p.m. has been cut from a busy 4,700 r.p.m. to 4,100 r.p.m. The cast exhaust manifold must also absorb more vibration than the fabricated unit it replaces. There is virtually no change in exhaust note, though experts might just detect a suggestion of that deep-throated burble for which the 1275S unit is famous.

Predictably, fuel consumption of this bigger mildly tuned engine was slightly better than previously. Whereas the M.G. 1100 gave an over-

all 29·1 m.p.g., and the Wolseley 1100 26·5 m.p.g., the Kestrel recorded 29·6 m.p.g. without any attempt at driving economically. Steady speed fuel consumptions were also much better than before. The 1275 Kestrel's 59·8 m.p.g. at a steady 30 m.p.h. (M.G.; 51·0 m.p.g.) would be exceptionally good for any car, while its 48·2 m.p.g. at 50 m.p.h. compares well with 43 m.p.g. for the M.G. 1100.

Apart from the new engine-transmission power pack, the Kestrel 1275 is virtually unchanged, and behaves very similarly to all the other 1100 variants. The ride comfort and road-holding of the now world-famous Hydrolastic suspension is still remarkable by any standards, though there is still room for improvement in the insulation of the main passenger compartment from the road noise ▶

*The only obvious external difference between the 1,275 c.c. and the standard 1,098 c.c. engines is the single carburettor. The oil filter and fan belt are awkward to reach*

that finds its way into the car from the front suspension on certain surfaces.

The Kestrel could also benefit from improved brakes. The pedal "feel" itself is poor, as the system feels characteristically spongy and lacks precision. When used hard the brakes fade much earlier than expected; they became uncertain and smoked well before the end of our rigorous fade test, when many other cars would not have faltered.

In the 1100 family tree, the Kestrel is more expensive than any except the prestige-conscious Princess 1100 and has a well fitted out interior to

suit; this is the only other 1100 to have a rev-counter. Like the other instruments, it is very clearly calibrated and steady reading. The seats are leather-covered, and have two-position floor brackets. When fixed in their rearward bolts every driver on our staff could make himself comfortable, though the steering wheel position is too flat for complete comfort.

With the optional Radiomobile in the recommended B.M.C. position, it was all too easy to bark one's knuckles on the radio controls when making a snappy change into first or third; the springy gear-lever linkage

aggravated this a little. Heater controls, set low down in the middle of the facia, are very difficult to reach with seat belts on, while other minor controls are grouped indiscriminately to the right of the rev-counter.

Though not a new model in itself, the 1275 Riley Kestrel is one of the best combinations to be released by B.M.C. for some time. Its main attractions will be the relaxed docility of the new engine and the improved fuel consumption, but enthusiasts will probably have noticed already that the engine could be converted very quickly to Cooper S trim and beyond.

## SPECIFICATION: RILEY KESTREL 1275 (FRONT ENGINE, FRONT-WHEEL DRIVE)

**ENGINE**
Cylinders .. 4, in line
Cooling system .. Water; pump, fan and thermostat
Bore .. 70.6mm (2.78in.)
Stroke .. 81.3mm (3.20in)
Displacement .. 1,275 c.c. (77.9 cu. in.)
Valve gear .. Overhead, pushrods and rockers
Compression ratio 8.8-to-1
Carburettor .. S.U. H54
Fuel pump .. S.U. electric
Oil filter .. Full flow, renewable element
Max. power .. 58 b.h.p. (net) at 5,250 r.p.m.
Max. torque .. 69 lb. ft. (net) at 3,500 r.p.m.

**TRANSMISSION**
Clutch .. Borg and Beck, diaphragm spring, 7.13in. dia.
Gearbox .. 4-speed, synchromesh on 2nd, 3rd and Top, central control
Gear ratios .. Top 1.00, Third 1.41, Second 2.178, First 3.625, Reverse 3.625.
Final drive .. Helical spur gears, 3.65 to 1

**CHASSIS AND BODY**
Construction .. Integral with all-steel body

**SUSPENSION**
Front .. Independent, wishbones and interconnected Hydrolastic suspension units

Rear .. Independent, trailing arms with interconnected Hydrolastic suspension units, anti-pitch and anti-roll bars

**STEERING**
Type .. Rack and pinion Wheel dia. 16.25in.

**BRAKES**
Make and type .. Lockheed disc front, drum rear
Servo .. None
Dimensions .. F, 8.0in. dia. R, 8.0in. dia., 1.25in. wide shoes
Swept area .. F, 133.2 sq. in.; R, 63 sq. in. Total 196.2 sq. in. (190 sq. in.) per ton laden

**WHEELS**
Type .. Pressed steel disc, four studs 4.0in. wide rim
Tyres—make .. Dunlop
—type .. C41 cross-ply tubeless
—size .. 5.50—12in.

**EQUIPMENT**
Battery .. 12-volt 43-amp.hr.
Generator .. Lucas d.c.
Headlamps .. Lucas sealed beam 120–90 watt (total)
Reversing lamp .. No provision
Electric fuses .. 2

Screen wipers .. Single speed, self-parking
Screen washer .. Standard, manual plunger
Interior heater .. Standard, fresh-air type
Safety belts .. Extra, anchorages built in
Interior trim .. Leather seats, pvc headlining
Floor covering .. Carpet
Starting handle .. No provision
Jack .. Screw pillar, ratchet handle
Jacking points .. Central, one each side
Windscreen .. Zone toughened
Underbody protection .. Phosphate treatment prior to painting
Other bodies .. None

**MAINTENANCE**
Fuel tank .. 8 Imp. gallons (no reserve) (36.4 litres)
Cooling system .. 6.75 pints (including heater) (3.8 litres)
Engine sump .. 8.5 pints (4.8 litres) SAE 10W/30
Gearbox and final drive .. Change oil every 3,000 miles; Change filter element every 3,000 miles
Grease .. 4 points every 3,000 miles
Tyre pressures .. F, 28; R, 24 p.s.i. (all conditions)

**PERFORMANCE DATA**
Top gear m.p.h. per 1,000 r.p.m. 16.9
Mean piston speed at max. power 2,795 ft./min.
B.h.p. per ton laden 56.4

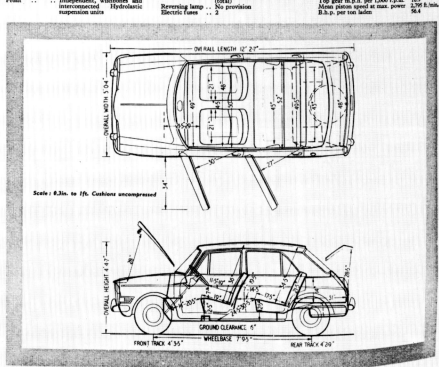

OVERALL LENGTH 12' 2.7"
OVERALL WIDTH 5' 0.4"
Scale: 0.3in. to 1ft. Cushions uncompressed
OVERALL HEIGHT 4' 4.7"
GROUND CLEARANCE 6"
FRONT TRACK 4' 3.5"    WHEELBASE 7' 9.5"    REAR TRACK 4' 2.9"

# Bibliography

The following is a list of references many of which were used in the preparation of this book:

*Catalogue of Riley Engines* 1904.
*Catalogue of Riley Motor Bicycles (& Fore-Cars)* 1904.
*Catalogue of Riley Tricars* 1907.
*Book of the 9 h.p. Riley Car* 1907.
*The Book of the 12—18 Riley* 1908.
*Catalogue of 10 h.p. and 12—18 h.p. Cars* 1911.
*Catalogue of 10 h.p. and 12—18 h.p. Cars* 1913.
*Catalogue of Riley Four-Cylinder Cars* 1914.
*The Riley Eleven General Catalogue* 1923.
*The Eleven Riley Sports* Leaflet, 1923.
*General Catalogue of Riley Bodywork and Models* 1924.
*The Catalogue of the Car that is As Old as the Industry* 1925.
*The Riley Redwingers* Brochure, 1925.
*Owner's Handbook for the 1925 Riley Twelve.*
*Riley Book of Sales Information 1925/26* Season.
*1926 Riley Twelve Owner's Handbook.*
*General Catalogue of the Riley Twelve 1927* Season: August 1926.
*General Catalogue of the Riley Range of Cars* May 1927.
*Introductory Leaflet for the Riley 11/50/65 Supercharged Sports* 1927.
*General Catalogue of the New Riley Models for 1928* October 1927.
*Riley Book of Sales Information 1927/28* Season.
*Handbook of the Riley Nine* 1928.
*Riley Nine Catalogue for 1929* November 1928.
*Catalogue of the Riley Sixes for 1929* November 1928.
*Handbook of the New Riley Six* 1929.
*The Riley Romance* Reprint of book, 1930.
*The 'Plus' Series Riley Nine Handbook* 1930.
*Riley Nine 'Plus' Series Brooklands Speed Model* Leaflet, 1931.
*The Riley Six Owner's Handbook* 1931.
*Handbook of the Plus Ultra Series Riley Nine.*
*1932 Season Riley Nine & Six-Fourteen Marine Engines* October 1931.
*The Riley Alpine Handbook* 1932.
*Handbook of the Riley Stelvio* 1932.
*1933 Season Riley Nine, Six-Twelve & Six-Fourteen Cars* October 1932.
*Introductory Leaflet for Riley 'Grebe' 6/12 Sports Model* 1933.

*1933 Riley Nine Owner's Handbook.*
*The Most Successful Car in the World: 1934 Cars,* October 1933.
*1934 Riley Nine Handbook.*
*The Riley Six Owner's Handbook* 1934.
*The Riley Imp* Leaflet 1934.
*The Riley Ulster Imp* Leaflet, 1934.
*1935 Riley Nine Handbook.*
*Handbook of the Riley Six-Fifteen* 1935.
*1½ Litre Leaflet for Falcon & Kestrel Models* 1935.
*The 1½ Litre Riley Handbook* 1935.
*Introductory Leaflet for 1936 1½ Litre 'Sprite' Model* October 1935.
*Salesman's Data Book of Riley Cars* 1935/36 Season.
*General Catalogue of Riley Cars* 1936 Season.
*The Riley Falcons, 1½ Litre & Six-Cylinder Models* Brochure 1936.
*Riley 'Lynx-Sprite' and 'Kestrel-Sprite' Models* Leaflet, 1936.
*Riley Cars* General Leaflet, 1936.
*1936 Riley Nine Handbook.*
*The Riley 1½ Litre Owner's Handbook* 1936.
*Salesman's Data Book of Riley Cars* 1936/37 Season.
*The Riley Fifteen-Six Handbook* 1936/7.
*General Catalogue of Riley Cars* 1937 Season.
*Riley 1½ Litre Sprite Series* Leaflet, 1937.
*The Riley 1½ Litre Owner's Handbook* 1937.
*The Riley Eight-Ninety* Brochure, 1937.
*The New Riley Range 1937–38 Season* Leaflet, September 1937.
*Salesman's Data Book of Riley Cars* 1937–38 Season.
*For Enthusiasts Only, Sprite Series* Leaflet, 1938.
*Riley Fifteen-Six* Brochure, 1938.
*Handbook of the 1½ Litre Riley* 1938.
*The Riley 1½ Litre Models* Brochure, 1938.
*The Riley Victor Saloon* Brochure, 1938.
*The Riley Blue Streak 2½ Litre Models* Leaflet, 1938.
*Handbook of the 16 h.p. Riley* 1938.
*Riley Motors Limited Chassis Numbering Sequence List 1930–48,* 1948.
*Owner's Handbook of the 1½ Litre Riley* 1948.
*Riley General Catalogue* 1948.
*Owner's Handbook of the 2½ Litre Riley* 1951.
*Workshop Manual for the 2½ Litre Riley* 1953.
*The Riley Pathfinder Owner's Handbook* 1955.
*Riley Maintenance Manual 1930–1956,* HADDLETON, S. V., 1956.
*The Riley Pathfinder* Brochure, 1956.
*The Riley Two-Point-Six* Brochure, 1957.
*The Riley Two-Point-Six Owner's Handbook* 1957.
*The New Riley One-Point-Five* Brochure, 1958.
*The Riley 4-Sixty Eight* Brochure, 1961.
*Riley 4-Sixty Eight Owner's Handbook* 1961.

*Owner's Handbook for the Riley One-Point-Five* 1962.
*The Riley Elf* Brochure, 1963.
*The Production and Competition History of the pre-1939 Riley Motor Cars,* BIRMINGHAM, DR. A. T. 1965.
*Riley 4-Seventy Two Owner's Handbook* 1965.
*The Riley One-Point-Five* Brochure, 1965.
*Riley Models* Brochure, 1965.
*The Riley Kestrel* Dealer Introduction Package, 1965.
*The Riley Kestrel* Brochure, 1966.
*Riley Kestrel Handbook* 1966.
*Riley 1300 Mk II Handbook* 1968.
*The Riley 4-Seventy Two* Brochure, 1968.
*The Riley 1300 Mk II* Brochure, 1969.
*The Story of Brooklands Motor Course,* BODDY, W.
*The Motor Sport Book of Donington,* BODDY, W.
*The Automobile Engineer Magazine.*
*The Autocar Magazine.*
*Light Car and Cyclecar Magazine.*
*The Motor Magazine.*
*Motor Sport Magazine.*
*Practical Motorist Magazine.*
*The Riley Record Magazine.*
*Speed Magazine.*

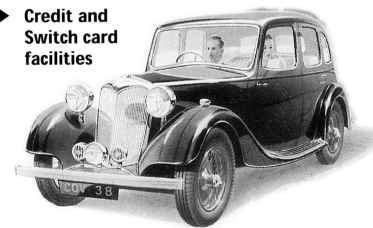

# Index

Illustrations are indicated by page numbers in bold type. Headings consisting of figures (e.g. 1½ litres) are arranged as if the figures were spelt out. The letters 'ff' after a page number indicate that the information will be found on that page and following pages.